"This book is the most ambitious attempt yet to reconstruct Peter's own theology from the various sources in the New Testament. Many have said that this cannot be done. They should not continue to say that without reading this book."

—**Richard Bauckham**
University of Cambridge

"Studies on the theology of Paul abound. But what about Simon Peter? Can a 'theology of Peter' even be written? In his impressive *Vox Petri*, Gene Green outlines striking and often-overlooked points of convergence between the testimony of Peter as preserved in the Gospel of Mark, the Acts of the Apostles, and 1 Peter. The end result is a major contribution to Petrine studies and a must-read for anyone interested in whether the voice of Peter can still be heard in the pages of the New Testament."

—**Brant Pitre**
author of *Jesus and the Last Supper*

"Recent scholarship has sought to revisit Simon Peter's long-neglected and frequently caricatured profile as the leading disciple of Jesus in Scripture and early Christian memory. But what might happen if one were to take one logical step further, drawing out and synthesizing such glimpses of a remembered Peter into a more coherent picture of this first among the apostles? Gene Green offers his answer in a composite theology of Peter as a New Testament teacher and writer: one who 'got by with a little help from his friends,' yet can rightly be pictured at the wellspring and 'head of the table' of Christian theology. Warmly recommended as a book with which to think about the shape of the apostolic church, its leadership, and its beliefs."

—**Markus Bockmuehl**
University of Oxford

"The New Testament is often thought to be comprised of strong Pauline and Johannine voices, along with the Synoptics and Acts. Gene Green calls us to hear the Petrine voice. The historical Peter, he argues, stands especially behind the Gospel of Mark, the Petrine speeches of Acts, and 1 Peter. Building upon recent scholarship on the status of testimony and upon his own work on the Petrine letters, Green shows that Peter's voice sounds the central notes of Christian faith, from the suffering and exalted Messiah, to the New Exodus and the Passover Lamb, to the Spirit-filled people of God in the last days. A rich invitation to recovering the centrality of the Petrine witness!"

—**Matthew Levering**
Mundelein Seminary

"In a time where Pauline theologies are ubiquitous, Gene Green rightfully asks: What about a Petrine theology? Constructing a Petrine theology is difficult because the sources have been judged as ill-suited to give access to Peter's life and thought. In *Vox Petri*, Green carefully assesses the reliability of our sources for Peter's voice arguing that the Gospel of Mark, Peter's speeches in Acts, and 1 Peter provide authentic testimony. From these building blocks, Green constructs a vivid account of Peter's theology. He traces themes such as the Isaianic New Exodus, the coming of the Kingdom of God, Christology in the key of the rejected stone, and many more. A meticulous and careful reader, Green avoids the dichotomy between the Peter of faith and the Simon of history and gives a successful account of Peter's theological voice for the good of the church."

—Darian R. Lockett
Talbot School of Theology, Biola University

"Gene Green puts hard-nosed historical inquiry in the service of the church's faith and life as he excavates Peter's contribution to Christian theology. His robust study identifies the apostle as the church's theologian, mediating and contextualizing Jesus's message for communities of Christ-followers after Jesus's resurrection. This maximal reading of the New Testament witness is a noble contribution to contemporary study of Peter."

—Joel B. Green
Fuller Theological Seminary

"Peter, the Galilean fisherman, the rock, the denier of Jesus, the first among the apostles, is described on many occasions in the New Testament, but his own voice appears silent. In this landmark study, Gene Green argues that is not the case. Rather, he suggests that we have not listened attentively enough in order to hear the voice of Peter in the New Testament. Instead, Green argues that the voice of Peter can still be heard behind the Gospel of Mark, in the speeches attributed to him in Acts, and in the letter that bears his name—1 Peter. With meticulous attentive listening, Green seeks to hear the genuine voice of Peter and to present an integrated understanding of the theology of Peter. In this manner, this book challenges long-held assumptions about New Testament documents, the recoverability of the authentic Peter, and the history of earliest Christianity. As such, it will occasion rich debate and stimulate further study in the quest to hear again the voice of the real Peter, the first among the disciples of the Lord."

—Paul Foster
School of Divinity, University of Edinburgh

"Gene Green has capped his long-time interest in the Petrine literature with this work that first tries to establish the sources for Petrine thought and then tries to draw out their theology. While he brackets discussing 2 Peter (a book in itself) the rest is here: Mark, Peter in Acts, Pauline reference to Peter, and, of course, 1 Peter. This is not a naive gathering of all possible source material, but a critical defense of the nature and analysis of the content of the various sources. It will be controversial, and Professor Green knows that, but it is scholarly, aware, and passionately reasoned. I recommend this work to anyone interested in the teaching and theology of the apostle Peter, and the controversies surrounding it."

—Peter Davids
author of *2 Peter and Jude: A Handbook on the Greek Text*

"Gene Green's book, *Vox Petri*, fills a lacuna in Petrine scholarship. Drawing from testimony theory and its importance in antiquity, Green unites Peter's sayings in Mark, Acts, and 1 Peter into one cohesive voice, presenting the utterances of the apostle as foundational to early Christian theology. This book will be of interest for scholars and pastors and could be fruitfully employed as a class text."

—Sean A. Adams
University of Glasgow

"Green asserts that the Peter that we meet in the Gospels and follow in Acts is directly responsible for 1 Peter. As he searches for the apostle Peter's voice, particularly in 1 Peter, Green takes the reader on a helpful and thorough journey through the New Testament and beyond. Green makes a compelling case for a unique Petrine theology, and not merely a reworking of Pauline theology."

—Dennis R. Edwards
North Park Theological Seminary

VOX PETRI

VOX PETRI

A Theology of Peter

GENE L. GREEN

Foreword by Michael J. Gorman

CASCADE *Books* • Eugene, Oregon

VOX PETRI
A Theology of Peter

Copyright © 2020 Gene L. Green. All rights reserved. Except for brief quotations in critical publications or reviews, no part of this book may be reproduced in any manner without prior written permission from the publisher. Write: Permissions, Wipf and Stock Publishers, 199 W. 8th Ave., Suite 3, Eugene, OR 97401.

Cascade Books
An Imprint of Wipf and Stock Publishers
199 W. 8th Ave., Suite 3
Eugene, OR 97401

www.wipfandstock.com

PAPERBACK ISBN: 978-1-5326-8309-1
HARDCOVER ISBN: 978-1-5326-8310-7
EBOOK ISBN: 978-1-5326-8311-4

Cataloguing-in-Publication data:

Names: Green, Gene L. Gorman, Michael J.

Title: Vox Petri : a theology of Peter / by Gene L. Green. Foreword by Michael J. Gorman.

Description: Eugene, OR: Cascade Books, 2020. | Includes bibliographical references and index.

Identifiers: ISBN 978-1-5326-8309-1 (paperback) | ISBN 978-1-5326-8310-7 (hardcover) | ISBN 978-1-5326-8311-4 (ebook)

Subjects: LCSH: Peter, the Apostle, Saint. | Bible. Peter—Criticism, interpretation, etc. | Bible. Peter—Theology.

Classification: BS2515 G74 2019 (print) | BS2515 (ebook)

Manufactured in the U.S.A.   JANUARY 7, 2020

For Deborah
Coheir of the gracious gift of life

Contents

Foreword by Michael J. Gorman | xiii
Preface | xv
Abbreviations | xviii

Introduction: Peter—The "Lost Boy" of Christian Theology | 1

Chapter 1   Sources for a Petrine Theology | 7

    Critical Assessment of the Sources | 9

    Looking Back and Looking Ahead | 17

Chapter 2   The Testimony of Peter | 19

    Testimony | 20

        Contemporary Discussion on Testimony | 21

        Ancient Discussion on Testimony | 29

    The Testimony of Peter | 31

        The Testimony of Peter and the Gospel of Mark | 32

        The Testimony of Peter and the Acts of the Apostles | 46

        The Testimony of Peter and 1 Peter | 71

        The Problem of Petrine Testimony in 2 Peter | 96

    The Testimony of Peter and the Possiblity of a Petrine Theology | 98

CONTENTS

Chapter 3   The Gospel of Mark and the Testimony of Peter | 101

   Mark's Audience | 108

      Early Church Testimony on Mark's Audience | 108

      Internal Testimony for Mark's Audience | 110

      The Location of Mark's Audience | 112

   Mark's Audience and Peter's Message | 118

Chapter 4   The Theology of Peter in the Gospel of Mark | 126

   Mark's Theological Framework | 128

      God's New Exodus | 128

      The Gospel Epic | 131

      The Development of the New Exodus Theology | 142

   The Kingdom Is Coming | 148

      The Proclamation of the Kingdom | 148

      Jesus' Authority and the Kingdom | 151

   Christology in Mark | 160

      "Your God Reigns!" Jesus the King | 161

      "You Are the Christ" | 162

      The Son of God | 169

      The Son of Man | 174

      Jesus the Lord | 180

      The Shepherd of Israel | 183

      Jesus the Teacher | 184

      The Rejected Stone | 186

      Jesus the Priest | 189

      The Messiah's Revelation and Concealment | 190

      Peter's Christology in Mark | 193

   Soteriology in Mark | 194

      Jesus' Rule and Salvation | 194

      Jesus' Sufferings and Salvation | 195

      Jesus' Resurrection | 205

   Discipleship in Mark | 209

      Discipleship and Christology | 209

      Discipleship and Suffering | 214

      The Disciples' Incomprehension | 217

The Community of Disciples | 219
    A Household | 221
    A Temple | 222
    A Flock | 224
    A Ship | 224
    A Community of Learners | 225
    Followers of the Jesus Way | 226

The Ethics of Discipleship | 226
    Ethics and the Kingdom of God | 227
    The Ethics of Following Jesus | 228
    Ethics and Eschatology | 229
    An Ethic of Obedience | 230

Peter's Testimony in Mark | 231

Chapter 5   The Acts of the Apostles and the Testimony of Peter | 234

Peter and the Beginnings of Christian Theology | 236

Petrine Speeches in Acts and Early Christian Theology | 242

Chapter 6   The Theology of Peter in the Acts of the Apostles | 245

The Framework of Peter's Theology in Acts | 247
    The New Exodus in Acts and the Petrine Speeches | 248
    Acts and Epic | 252
    The New Age Has Come—The Gospel of the Kingdom | 254
    The Plan of God | 259

The Jesus Story | 262
    Petrine Christology in Acts | 264

Proclamation and Response | 278
    Salvation and Inclusion | 279
    The Human Condition | 284
    God's Salvation | 285

The Coming of the Spirit | 289

The Community | 293

Petrine Ethics | 295

Petrine Eschatology | 297

Peter's Testimony in the Acts of the Apostles | 299

Chapter 7 First Peter and the Testimony Peter | 301

Peter's Testimony | 302

Peter and the Authorial Community | 304

The Recipients of 1 Peter | 305

    The Recipients' Ethnicity | 306

    Strangers and Resident Aliens | 309

    The Social Orders and the Recipients' Situation | 312

Chapter 8 The Theology of Peter in 1 Peter | 315

The Plan of God | 316

    Future and Present | 316

    Past and Present | 319

    The New Exodus | 322

The God Who Plans | 327

    God's Transcendence and Immanence | 327

    Creator, Father, and Judge | 328

The Character of God | 333

    The Holy One | 333

    The God of Grace and Glory | 334

    The Power of God | 337

    God and the Resurrection of Christ | 337

The Person and Work of Jesus Christ | 338

    Christ's Role in God's Plan | 339

    The Person of Christ | 340

    The Work of Christ—Sufferings and Glories | 349

    The Glories of Christ | 357

The Holy Spirit in 1 Peter | 367

    Sanctified by the Spirit (1:2) | 368

    The Testimony of the Spirit of Christ (1:11) | 369

    The Gospel Proclamation through the Holy Spirit (1:12) | 370

    The Spiritual House (2:5) | 371

    The Spirit of Glory and God (4:14) | 372

    The Holy Spirit in Peter's Theology | 373

Christian Community in 1 Peter | 373
    The People of God | 376
    The Household and Temple of God | 379
    The Flock of God | 382
    Christians | 382
    God's Elect and Holy People | 383
  The Holy Way of Life | 384
    The Former Life | 384
    Turning from Darkness to Light | 385
    The New Life in the Will of God | 387
    The Imitatio Dei and the Imitatio Christi | 388
    The Christian Way of Life | 390
    Living Under the Orders of Society | 393
    Peter on the Christian Way of Life | 398
  Peter's Testimony 1 Peter | 399

Chapter 9 Vox Petri—Peter's Theological Contribution to the Church | 401

  A Theology of Peter | 403
    The Plan of God | 405
    The New Exodus | 406
    The Person and Work of Christ | 407
    The Agency of the Holy Spirit | 411
    The Salvation of God | 412
    The Christian Community | 413
    The Last Things | 414
    The Honorable Way of Life | 415
  Peter and the Foundations of Christian Theology | 417

Bibliography | 419
Author Index | 447
Index of Ancient Sources | 455

Foreword

When I was a graduate student, I took an intriguing seminar on 1 Peter taught by the late Paul Meyer. One of the scholars of 1 Peter whose work we considered was John Elliott. Some years earlier, Elliott had published an important essay entitled "The Rehabilitation of an Exegetical Step-Child: 1 Peter in Recent Research."[1]

The present book might be subtitled "The Rehabilitation of an Historical and Theological Stepchild"—not 1 Peter, but simply Peter. This provocative volume builds substantively on what a few others have hinted at. It will almost certainly challenge many perspectives on two significant, interrelated subjects: the nature of the New Testament's witness to Peter, and Peter's historical and theological significance. The author, Gene Green, is himself an established authority on 1 Peter. He now turns his attention from the letter to the person, the one Jesus calls "the rock."

Green's basic thesis is clear: we find the true *vox Petri*—the voice, if not the precise words, of Peter—in various parts of the New Testament, and that voice is testimony to a Peter who "stands at the very beginning of Christian theology," as an ecclesial leader and theological innovator of the first order. Thus, Green will not permit us to think of Peter as playing second theological fiddle to Paul. Rather, he contends, at points Paul *echoes* Peter. In a very real sense, Green argues, we must speak of "Petrine primacy."

It is important to stress that this assertion about Petrine primacy is a theologically polyvalent, robust, and nuanced one, but it is not fundamentally about ecclesial authority or succession. Accordingly, Green's understanding of Petrine primacy might well expand the horizons of at least some Roman Catholic readers to encompass a more ecumenical vision of Peter and his office. At the same time, those of us who call ourselves "Protestant" in one way or another may be especially challenged. For Green's

---

1. John H. Elliott, "The Rehabilitation of an Exegetical Step-Child: 1 Peter in Recent Research," *Journal of Biblical Literature* 95 (1976) 243–54. Subsequently, Elliott published books and commentaries on 1 Peter.

bold thesis, if correct, means that we can no longer think (even if we would never say it publicly) that Peter is the Catholics' apostle while Paul is ours. Already at the end of chapter one, Green makes the following claim:

> Peter is, indeed, *the church's* theologian, the Rock to whom we are *all* indebted for our understanding of the gospel of Christ. Others will do their own riff on his theology, but he lays down the theme. *Jesus* handed off to *Peter*, and Peter took the *lead* as the rest joined in. *We owe him a debt greater than we dared imagine.*[2]

The nature of that debt depends on how Green's thesis is received by various reading communities, both academic and ecclesial. Going against the grain of much historical-critical scholarship (but developing the hints mentioned briefly above), he argues that the Gospel of Mark, the Acts of the Apostles, and 1 Peter preserve reliable testimony to the voice, and the theology, of Peter. Along the way, Green offers us a veritable feast of interpretative insight into Mark, Acts, and 1 Peter so that even those who are undecided about the overall thesis will benefit from Green's exposition of these New Testament texts. New exodus and new age, atonement and resurrection, Jesus' suffering messiahship and exalted lordship, discipleship and suffering, God's Spirit and God's salvation: these are some of the common elements of Petrine theology found in the writings Green examines. While Green rightly argues that these elements are essentially the common motifs of early Christianity, he also shows the common Petrine flavor they possess in the texts examined.

This, then, is a richly learned tome that both questions the status quo and offers new perspectives, with arguments to support them. Of course, such a bold rereading will not fully convince everyone. After all, the mark of good scholarship is sometimes as much in challenging assumptions as it is in providing definitive alternatives (as if anything in scholarship were "definitive"). Yet even the most historically and/or theologically cautious cannot ignore Green's important work. In fact, to do so would be irresponsible.

Christian unity depends, at least to some degree, on a shared evaluation of Peter. There will no doubt always be some degree of diversity in this (hoped-for) unity of appreciation for Peter. None of us can forecast where the historical and theological conversations might go. At the end of the day, however, and at the end of this book, one thing is certain: if we are in Simon Peter's debt, it is in no small measure because we are also in Gene Green's debt.

—Michael J. Gorman

Raymond E. Brown Chair of Biblical Studies and Theology, St. Mary's Seminary & University

Former Dean, St. Mary's Ecumenical Institute

2. Emphasis added but, I feel quite certain, in a way that captures Green's claim. Later, Green asserts that Peter "was the apostle who, after Jesus, gave the church its theological direction."

Preface

Peter and I have been walking together for a long time. Our journey began not long after arriving at the University of Aberdeen, where I was accepted into the PhD program in New Testament. In the first meeting at the Faculty of Divinity, Prof. Robin Barbour asked me, "What would you like to work on?" As a freshly-minted MA student, still a babe wet behind the exegetical ears, I had no idea what direction my studies might take. After inquiring about my abilities in Greek, Hebrew, and German, Prof. Barbour handed over a skeleton key, pointed me to an office, and said, "When you have something, come on back." That's the way things happened there in those days.

One of the books in the sparse collection I carted from Chicago to Scotland was Stephen Neill's familiar volume *The Interpretation of the New Testament, 1861–1961*. The pages were already well-underlined and worn since it served as a class text in a course on New Testament Criticism taught by Dr. Walter Elwell. Neill pointed up the divergent opinions of E. G. Selwyn and F. W. Beare regarding the date, circle, and setting of 1 Peter saying, "It may be that definite solutions of this Petrine problem will forever evade us; we must pursue the matter in hope, and not lie down too easily under the frustration of mutually contradictory solutions."[1] Soon thereafter I read Jack Elliott's seminal essay in the *Journal of Biblical Literature* entitled "1 Peter: The Rehabilitation of an Exegetical Stepchild."[2] The journey with 1 Peter began with Neill and Elliott at my side, along with a bottle of British cider that possessed surprising properties. Oscar Cullmann, E. G. Selwyn, F. W. Baere, J. N. D. Kelley, Karl Herman Schelkle, Leonhard Goppelt, Ernest Best, and an array of hard-bound and photocopied friends joined the journey. A few years later Professors I. Howard Marshall and Ernest Best

---

1. Stephen Neill, *The Interpretation of the New Testament, 1861–1961* (Oxford: Oxford University Press, 1964), 344.

2. John H. Elliott, "The Rehabilitation of an Exegetical Step-Child: 1 Peter in Recent Research," *JBL* 95 (1976) 243–54.

approved the dissertation entitled "Theology and Ethics in 1 Peter." Joy and relief filled heart and home.

After many years teaching 1 Peter in seminary, university, and church classes in the United States and Latin America, an invitation arrived to write a commentary in Spanish on *1 Pedro y 2 Pedro*[3] for the Comentario Bíblico Hispanoamericano, one of the first series to come out of Latin America. The library and staff at Tyndale House in Cambridge afforded the bibliographic and community support needed for the project and Dr. Justo González provided editorial assistance by correcting the infelicities in my Spanish composition and asking all the right interpretive questions. The commentary on the Petrine letters became the last volume to be published in this strong and significant series. A new marketing director made the unfortunate and unwarranted proclamation that "commentaries don't sell."

First Peter was a constant companion through decades of teaching and research. Its interplay with the Old Testament, Jewish, and early Christian thought continued to hold my attention. The way the epistle interacted with cultural trends in the Roman world revealed an author who was not only embedded in his own community but also interacted wisely with the environment in which early Christianity developed. He, as Paul, was attempting a deep contextualization of the gospel within the world of Roman Asia Minor. And he wrote well. Whether the product of the author's own pen or a production aided by a skilled amanuensis, the epistle was intended to be read aloud in public assembly. Every Greek reader should put voice to its marvelous cadences. First Peter draws us into the intricately woven tapestry of first-century Christianity in the Roman Empire.

Although I had come to know the author through this letter, I did not think much about him, about Peter. If this was indeed a genuine epistle of the apostle, what did it reveal about his theology? Were there other witnesses to his thought that could be drawn together to help us understand not only the portrayal of Peter in the Gospels, Acts, and Galatians but the fuller frame of his understanding of the gospel? While books on the theology of Paul fill shelf after shelf at eye level, the collection on Peter's theology is small and tucked way down below, out of sight, dusty. I received an invitation to write a book on Peter's theology for a new series, but the email remained in my inbox for nearly a year. Could such an endeavor really be accomplished? It seemed quixotic given the critical landscape that surrounded the witnesses to Peter's thought. After much hesitation and consultation, I accepted. The project, however, quickly grew beyond bounds given the imperative to address the myriad of critical issues that wanted attention. Through this long leg of the journey, Peter the apostle came more and more into focus. His knowledge of the good news of Jesus Christ is deep, his commitment to the church is passionate, and his theological creativity is surprisingly underestimated in the academy and the church, as Martin Hengel rightly

---

3. Eugenio Green, *1 Pedro y 2 Pedro* (Miami: Editorial Caribe, 1993).

noted.[4] Peter steps over boundaries, as did Jesus, and brings together factions in ways that sorely need to be emulated in our day. Peter stands at the very beginning of Christian theology. We are all indebted to him, whether we recognize it or not. He has been a constant companion who sowed the gospel of Christ into our hearts and minds.

The book quickly spilled over the confines of the series, so the editor and I agreed that it would be best to find another home for *Vox Petri: A Theology of Peter*. Cascade, an imprint of Wipf and Stock, picked up the book for publication. Many thanks are due to Michael Thomson, editor and friend, for his help in assuring that *Vox Petri* has a good home. I also thank Wheaton College and Graduate School for the sabbatical time granted to complete this journey and to the Wheaton College Alumni Association for some of the financial support that helped underwrite seasons of research in England. The staff at Tyndale House in Cambridge opened the doors wide at 36 Selwyn Gardens, showing tremendous support for this research. Anyone who has studied there knows the joys of that blessed library and the community that gathers there. A fellowship of assistants, fondly known collectively as TAs, helped with many aspects of this book. They developed bibliography, copied chapters and articles, and did hard and precise editorial work. They appear on every page. Those who reviewed the manuscript and wrote endorsements have provided great encouragement as this project came to its close. My heart-felt thanks goes out to Dr. Michael Gorman who wrote the foreword to *Vox Petri*. I treasure his careful reading along with his kind and judicious comments. The love and support of my family has helped sustain this project. I thank my daughters, Gillian and Christiana, for their unflagging enthusiasm and my wife, Deborah, who joyfully accompanied me though all the decades of working and walking with Peter. We are coheirs of the gracious gift of life, as Peter says, and I am profoundly grateful for her encouragement, wisdom, and willingness to travel countless roads in the United States, Scotland, England, the Dominican Republic, and Costa Rica.

This one's for you, Deborah. "Here's looking at you, kid."

---

4. Martin Hengel, *Saint Peter: The Underestimated Apostle* (Grand Rapids: Eerdmans, 2010).

Abbreviations

AB	Anchor Bible
AGJU	Arbeiten zur Geschichte des antiken Judentums und des Urchristentums
AnBib	Analecta biblica
AThR	Anglican Theological Review
ATJ	Ashland Theological Journal
BA	Biblical Archaeologist
BBR	Bulletin for Biblical Research
BDAG	Bauer, W., et al. *Greek-English Lexicon of the New Testament and Other Early Christian Literature.* 3rd ed. Chicago: University of Chicago Press, 1999.
BDF	Blass, F., et al. *A Greek Grammar of the New Testament and Other Early Christian Literature.* Chicago: University of Chicago Press, 1961.
BECNT	Baker Exegetical Commentary on the New Testament
BHT	Beiträge zur historischen Theologie
Bib	Biblica
BJRL	Bulletin of the John Rylands Library
BNTC	Black's New Testament Commentaries
BSac	Bibliotheca sacra
BSNTS	Bulletin of the Studiorum Novi Testamenti Societas
BT	The Bible Translator
BZNW	Beihefte zur Zeitschrift für die neutestamentliche Wissenschaft

CBQ	Catholic Biblical Quarterly
CJ	Classical Journal
CSB	Christian Standard Bible
CTR	Criswell Theological Review
EKKNT	Evangelisch-katholischer Kommentar zum Neuen Testament
EQ	Evangelical Quarterly
ESV	English Standard Version
ExpTim	Expository Times
FB	Forschung zur Bibel
FRLANT	Forschungen zur Religion und Literatur des Alten und Neuen Testaments
HThKNT	Herders theologischer Kommentar zum Neuen Testament
HTR	Harvard Theological Review
ICC	International Critical Commentary
IEJ	Israel Exploration Journal
Int	Interpretation
JBL	Journal of Biblical Literature
JETS	Journal of the Evangelical Theological Society
JFA	Journal of Field Archaeology
JR	Journal of Religion
JSNT	Journal for the Study of the New Testament
JSNTSup	Journal for the Study of the New Testament: Supplement Series
JSOT	Journal for the Study of the Old Testament
JTS	Journal of Theological Studies
LAE	Deissman, A. *Light from the Ancient East*. Grand Rapids: Baker, 1965.
LCL	Loeb Classic Library
LD	Lectio divina
LEC	Library of Early Christianity
LNTS	Library of New Testament Studies
LSJ	Liddell, H. G., R. Scott, and H. S. Jones, *A Greek-English Lexicon*. 9th ed. with revised supplement. Oxford: Clarendon, 1996.
LTQ	Lexington Theological Quarterly
LXX	Septuagint

MM	Moulton, J. H., and G. Milligan. *The Vocabulary of the Greek Testament.* Grand Rapids: Eerdmans, 1949.
NAC	New American Commentary
NASB	New American Standard Bible
NCB	New Century Bible
Neot	Neotestamentica
NICNT	New International Commentary on the New Testament
NIDNTT	Brown, C., ed. *New International Dictionary of New Testament Theology.* 4 vols. Grand Rapids: Zondervan, 1975–1985.
NIGTC	New International Greek Testament Commentary
NIV	New International Version
NovT	Novum Testamentum
NovTSup	Novum Testamentum Supplements
NRSV	New Revised Standard Version
NSBT	New Studies in Biblical Theology
NTAbh	Neutestamentliche Abhandlungen
NTM	New Testament Message
NTOA	Novum Testamentum et Orbis Antiquus
NTS	New Testament Studies
NTTS	New Testament Tools and Studies
OCD	Hornblower, S., and A. Spawforth, eds. *Oxford Classical Dictionary.* 3rd ed. Oxford: Oxford University Press, 1996.
PNTC	Pillar New Testament Commentary
SANT	Studien zum Alten und Neuen Testaments
SBB	Stuttgarter biblische Beiträge
SBLDS	Society of Biblical Literature Dissertation Series
SBLMS	Society of Biblical Literature Monograph Series
SBT	Studies in Biblical Theology
SE	Studia evangelica
SNTSMS	Society for New Testament Studies Monograph Series
StBibLit	Studies in Biblical Literature
TBC	Torch Bible Commentaries

TDNT	Kittel, G., and G. Friedrich, eds. *Theological Dictionary of the New Testament*. Translated by G. W. Bromiley. 10 vols. Grand Rapids: Eerdmans, 1964–1976.
TGST	Tesi Gregoriana, Serie Teologia
THNTC	Two Horizons New Testament Commentary
TLNT	Spicq, C. *Theological Lexicon of the New Testament*. Translated and edited by J. D. Ernest. 3 vols. Peabody, MA:Hendrickson, 1994.
TNTC	Tyndale New Testament Commentaries
TSAJ	Texte und Studien zum antiken Judentum
TynBul	Tyndale Bulletin
WBC	Word Bible Commentary
WUNT	Wissenschaftliche Untersuchungen zum Neuen Testament
ZNW	Zeitschrift für die neutestamentliche Wissenschaft und die Kunde der älteren Kirche

INTRODUCTION

Peter—The "Lost Boy" of Christian Theology

Peter is one of the "lost boys" of Christian theology. Indeed, he could be regarded as their captain.[1] While Peter is a beloved disciple given his impetuous nature and his restoration after failure, he rarely comes to mind as a theological leader in the early or contemporary church. He has become a trope in the pulpit and popular Bible studies as the bold, yet failed and restored, disciple. Protestants have felt alienated from him since the time of the Reformation because the Roman Catholic Church claimed him and the keys of the Kingdom. For them Peter was the one who had authority and his successors continue to maintain it. On the other hand, Luther and all those who followed him and his Reformation compatriots ended up with Paul as their patron. Critical scholarship has further alienated us from Peter since it relegated him to the Neverland of theology. Is it possible to hear his voice within the pages of the New Testament? Are not all the Petrine materials in the New Testament critically suspect? Some believe we can only recover fragments of the true tradition regarding Peter and his theology. While we may recognize the contours of his life as a fisherman, a disciple, and a leader, the details elude us since the evidence regarding his true voice has come under scholarship's glaring gaze. A large cadre of scholars hold that, at best, we can only find the "Peter of faith" and not the "Simon of history." Peter is hidden behind layers of early ecclesial tradition. Therefore, the way Peter is remembered in the pages of the New Testament shapes the

---

1. In J. M. Barrie's novel *Peter Pan*, the "lost boys" are "the children who fall out of their perambulators when the nurse is looking the other way. If they are not claimed in seven days they are sent far away to the Neverland to defray expenses. I'm captain." Peter, the apostle, is indeed their captain.

theological structures associated with him. Many reject the historicity of the assertion that Peter's testimony is foundational for Mark, dismiss the idea that Peter's true voice can be found in the speeches of Acts, and hold grave suspicions about his participation in the composition of the epistles that go by his name.

The argument of this study, however, is that Peter stands behind the first telling of the Jesus story in Mark. We can also identify the shape of his theology through his speeches in Acts. Moreover, 1 Peter contains reliable testimony regarding his instruction to early believers in Asia Minor. Second Peter, on the other hand, presents a unique set of critical problems that make discussion of its contribution to Petrine theology very difficult indeed. Early in the history of the church questions arose regarding its authenticity, and these have risen to a crescendo in contemporary scholarship. Just a few commentaries argue that the epistle is authentic. While being among those who have attempted to make a case for Petrine authorship of that letter, I hold the conclusions lightly as did those in the first centuries of the church. The voice in that letter is decidedly different, as any second-year Greek student or a careful reader of the English text will recognize. Untangling the critical debate and then sorting through the commonalities and differences between 2 Peter and the rest of the Petrine witnesses lays beyond the scope of this book. That project must wait for another day and another person. Any such attempt may be a quixotic exercise, a bridge too far for anyone who wishes to respond to all the critical and theological issues at the heart of the question. I beg my readers' forbearance as I sidestep the issue. While we may build a case for Paul's theology without engaging the "deutero-Paulines," in the same way, it is possible to leave 2 Peter aside for the moment as we follow the contours of what we actually do know about the *vox Petri*.

Even in this more chastened enterprise, many would regard unpacking Peter's theology as a journey that may not end well. Upon telling the late Prof. I. Howard Marshall about this project, he became quiet and thoughtful, then responded in his inimical way: "Can't be done!" Some readers will likely echo his statement and, at times, I have been among them. Is it really possible to ferret out Peter's voice from all these materials that have come down to us in redacted form?

Through the course of this study the conviction has grown that the church has preserved for us the music of Peter's theology and that, far from being barely audible strains, they constitute the symphonic melody that runs through all Christian theology. Peter was the Rock, but not only with respect to his leadership in the early church. His insights were truly foundational for Christian theology as a whole. He stands as the first to tell the Jesus story and give it its particular shape. Our fundamental understanding of the meaning of the cross comes through him. Jesus' crucifixion was not a perverse tragedy but salvific since he came "to give his life a ransom for many" (Mark 10:45). He was a theological innovator who, though nowhere near as erudite as the apostle Paul, made such significant contributions that even Paul is indebted to him. Opening the door of salvation to the Gentiles was his doing. Barnett even suggests that the "traditions" Paul received regarding the Lord's Supper and the death and resurrection of Christ (1 Cor 11:23–25; 15:3–7) may be traced back to Peter himself.[2] Paul echoes Peter.

Often scholars regard Peter, or rather the author of 1 Peter, as a warmed-over Paulinist since fragments of Paul's thought appear to be within. But the New Testament story looks different when we view it from a Petrine perspective and allow Peter his own voice, albeit one that speaks less profoundly than Paul. Some hold Peter to be the archetype of Jewish Christianity that stood in conflict with the Gentile-oriented Paul. The old Tübingen school still holds classes.[3] But the New Testament witness runs in the other direction. Peter was not an agonistic but a conciliatory figure who understood the inclusive nature of the gospel and the unity of the Christian community amidst its diversity. We are indebted to him for our understanding of the scope of God's salvation and Christian mission.

Towards the end of his life, the late Martin Hengel declared that Peter was truly the *Underestimated Apostle*.[4] This study stands within that newer Petrine school. Peter was an eyewitness and leader, but also the one who mediated the theology of Jesus and contextualized it for the Jewish and Gentile communities after the resurrection and ascension of Christ. Peter is the theological Rock who leads us to the true Rock, who is Christ. Peter was the first apostle chosen, the first to confess that Jesus was truly the Christ, the first among the inner circle of three to speak out at the time of the transfiguration, and the one remembered as the first witness of the resurrection of Christ. He failed in his initial understanding of Jesus' declaration of the crucifixion and denied the Lord at the time of his passion. But he was also the first to be restored ("But go, tell his disciples and Peter"). Subsequently Christ charged him to feed his sheep and lambs, and he did so as the first leader of the early church. He also innovated through his understanding, divinely inspired, that Christ's hope was for the Gentiles, those who had been excluded and othered by his fellow Israelites. Before the Jerusalem leaders he testified as the key witness for Gentile inclusion without cultural conversion. The early church later remembered Peter as the decisive theologian who stood against heresy and who was conciliatory, bringing the whole church together.[5]

---

2. Paul W. Barnett, *Paul in Syria: The Background to Galatians* (Milton Keynes: Paternoster, 2014), 71–75. Barnett compares Paul's teaching in 1 Cor 15:3–5 with Peter's in Acts 10:40–41, 43, as well as comparing Peter and Paul's rendition of the *kerygma* in Acts 10 and 13.

3. Michael Goulder, *St. Paul Versus St. Peter: A Tale of Two Missions* (Louisville: Westminster John Knox, 1994).

4. Martin Hengel, *Saint Peter: The Underestimated Apostle* (Grand Rapids: Eerdmans, 2010).

5. Pheme Perkins says, "Peter is the universal 'foundation' for all the churches. . . . There is no figure who compasses more of that diversity than Peter" (*Peter: Apostle for the Whole Church* [Edinburgh: T. & T. Clark, 2000], 184). Markus Bockmuehl runs a similar line, saying, "Peter is the rock, an eyewitness to the passion and resurrection of Jesus, and he is a witness, healer, miracle worker, and martyr. Beginning as a fisherman from Capernaum, the apostle became a centrist, bridge-building, and uniting figure in the early church, often pictured with Paul as the twin pillars of the Roman church. A sincere, if flawed, disciple of Jesus" (*Simon Peter in Scripture and Memory: The New Testament Apostle*

His words orient the church to this very day, regardless of whether we recognize his theological leadership or not. The "lost boy" is the one charged by Jesus to be the Captain.

Affirming the likelihood of excavating Peter's contribution to Christian theology is easy enough. Demonstrating it is another story. Can we trust our sources? Do they offer reliable witness to Peter's testimony about Christ? The burden of the first chapters of this book is to examine that very question. At the start of the journey, the question of methodology comes to the fore. As argued in chapter 2, there are those who write on Peter's theology and place the historical critical questions to one side, completely ignoring that there are any problematic issues with our sources. They believe that all the Petrine materials can be taken *prima facie* as having come directly from the apostle. On the other end of the spectrum stands the vast array of scholars who believe that all we can do is examine the church's constructed memory of Peter. Between those poles are the scholars who have attempted to use the best of the historical critical method in their examination of the sources, whether the sources are the NT documents or those in the second and third centuries which hold the living memory of Peter. Their conclusion is that we can say some things about Peter but believe the witness to be so redacted that a considerable gap exists between the Simon of history and the Peter of faith. Accordingly, we do not hold enough substance to construct a theology of Peter.

The very vivid memory of Peter in the early church, however, nudges us towards a more positive assessment of the materials at hand. As Pheme Perkins has ably argued, Peter was regarded in the second century as a theological, and not simply an ecclesiastical, leader. If you wanted to support or negate a theological position, you would appeal to Peter.[6] Indeed, throughout the New Testament there is a "Petrine primacy" that shows Peter as the principal during the moments of great theological foment in church.[7] These early positive assessments alert us to the ancient view that Peter was the theological Rock.

The suggestion made in the second chapter of this volume is that the historical critical method, with its commitment of multiple attestation for verification and sometimes overwrought historical skepticism, needs to be replaced with the epistemological category of testimony. In ancient and in contemporary epistemology—from Aristotle to Jennifer Lackey—testimony holds center stage as a principal means of human knowing. Testimony is concerned with sources and reliability, both with regard to what occurred and what was said. It does not accept that every witness is

---

in the Early Church [Grand Rapids: Baker Academic, 2012], 180).

6. Perkins, *Peter*, 131–81; Markus Bockmuehl, *The Remembered Peter in Ancient Reception and Modern Debate* (Tübingen: Mohr Siebeck, 2010), 101.

7. John Meyendorff, ed., *The Primacy of Peter* (Crestwood, NY: St. Vladimir's Seminary Press, 1992); William Thomas Kessler, *Peter as the First Witness of the Risen Lord: An Historical and Theological Investigation* (Rome: Editrice Pontificia Università Gregoriana, 1998).

valid but rather affirms that we may receive a testimony as faithful if we can posit that the source is credible and that any defeaters that arise are defeated, to use Lackey's terminology.[8] Within the domain of ancient historiography, written and oral testimonies were evaluated. Speeches were expected to conform to the general gist of what was actually spoken. Ancient witnesses were not simply "making it up as they go along," Indiana Jones style. Responsible historians skewered those who played loose with the evidence. On the other hand, those who reflected on historiography understood deeply that testimony must adapt itself to the audience and not only hold to what occurred in deed and word. Ancient historians placed rhetorical concerns alongside historical questions. They recognized that testimony would, and indeed should, always be shaped with reference to the audience and not be presented simply as a flat narrative dislocated from contemporary audience concerns. In the realm of our New Testament authors, this meant that an author, like Luke, for example, was both a historian and theologian.[9]

With regard to the testimony of Peter, both that which comes from him and is about him, we should expect a degree of rhetorical framing within the witnesses. Mark, for example, shaped the oral witness of Peter regarding Jesus to a certain extent, just as Peter related and interpreted the deeds and words of Jesus. Luke held theological concerns when he offered his rendering of Peter's speeches. He summarized them and ferreted out the essentials while, at the same time, holding to his overall purposes in writing to Theophilus and other first readers of Luke-Acts. First Peter was not simply the composition of the apostle; rather, Peter joined together with an authorial community when he composed that missive.

Given the rhetorical concerns bound up with testimony, we may be tempted to attempt to strip away the redaction from the received witnesses. But the argument here is that the interpretation inherent in testimony does not draw us away from the witnesses but rather takes us closer to the sources. It is history and interpretation, received witness and rhetoric, all the way down. We have in hand the testimonies which offer us Peter's understanding of the gospel along with interpretation. This is the *vox Petri*. Within a Gadamerean framework, we may say that the meaning emerges in the fusion of horizons.[10] The ancient and contemporary epistemological category of testimony makes place for witness and interpretation, welcoming both. While we may indeed isolate Petrine themes that run through the materials associated with the apostle, we should not embark on the quixotic task of seeking the pure, unsullied Peter. While we hear the *ipsissima vox Petri*, the true voice of Peter, we do not have the *ipsissima verba Petri*. We know the apostle and his theology through those who worked with his witness, whether they be Mark, Luke, or the amanuensis and community who

---

8. See the discussion in chapter 2.
9. I. Howard Marshall, *Luke: Historian and Theologian* (Downers Grove, IL: InterVarsity, 1988).
10. Hans-Georg Gadamer, *Truth and Method* (New York: Continuum, 2004).

aided the apostle in writing 1 Peter. As Cicero remarked to his amanuensis Tiro, Peter could say to those who handled his testimony, "Without you I am completely mute."[11]

When offering testimony, some modification of what is received always occurs. But this does not reduce testimony down to vacuous rhetoric and no more. When it comes to the testimony of Peter, both that about him and from him, we must ask whether the apostle truly stands behind the testimony that has been handed down to us. This survey of Petrine theology is limited to three major witnesses—the Gospel of Mark, the Petrine speeches in Acts, and 1 Peter. While the New Testament contains other evidences of Peter's thought, including the encounter with Paul in Galatians 2 and 2 Peter, this examination is limited to the core materials that are attributable to Peter. The question that the second chapter of this book focuses upon is whether Peter's preaching is the source for Mark's presentation of the gospel, whether Peter stands behind the speeches attributed to him in the Book of Acts, and whether the apostle is the author of 1 Peter. Second Peter has been left to the side for the moment, as intriguing as that epistle is.

The study which follows examines the various witnesses to Peter's theology one by one. How do these books present Peter's theology? The task is problematized by the various genres through which Peter's testimony comes down to us—bios, embedded speeches, and an epistle. Yet throughout each are woven the patterns of Peter's theology as well as notable differences in thought. But the end goal is to ferret out from the various witnesses the contours of Peter's theology. The surprise at the end is that Peter's theology is strikingly familiar, a musical score we have heard over and again. If the assessment of Peter's role in the development of Christian theology is correct, then this is as it should be. Peter's theology is *foundational* for the church and its themes are taken up over and again within the pages of the New Testament and beyond. Peter is, indeed, the church's theologian, the Rock to whom we are all indebted for our understanding of the gospel of Christ. Others will do their own riff on his theology, but he lays down the theme. Jesus handed off to Peter, and Peter took the lead as the rest joined in. We owe him a debt greater than we dared imagine.

---

11. Cicero, *Fam.* 16.10.2.

CHAPTER 1

Sources for a Petrine Theology

The available sources that bear witness to Peter's theology number fewer than for Paul. This does not mean, however, that the New Testament offers us little Petrine material. The question which we must immediately confront is whether to include all the evidence from these writings as we attempt to outline Peter's thought. Concerns abound regarding whether we can truly hear the apostle's voice in these witnesses. All the Gospels recount Peter's words and deeds. Early Christian tradition identified one of these, Mark, as representing Peter's very teaching. Eusebius, the church historian (AD 260/65–339/40), quoted a tradition from Papias (early second century AD), traceable back to John, which stated, "And the Presbyter used to say this, 'Mark became Peter's interpreter and wrote accurately all that he remembered, not, indeed, in order, of the things said or done by the Lord. . . . Mark did nothing wrong in thus writing down single points as he remembered them.'"[1] Scholars have often questioned the credibility of this tradition, but if it holds, it would point us back to Mark as a principal source for Peter's perspective on the story of Jesus. Indeed, if the two-document hypothesis regarding the origins of the Synoptics holds true, then the Gospels of Matthew and Luke would be rooted in Mark and, by extension, in the preaching of Peter. The Gospel of John offers its own unique portrait of Peter, although John likely knew the Gospel of Mark.[2]

---

1. Eusebius, *HE* 3.39.15.
2. Richard Bauckham, ed., *The Gospels for All Christians: Rethinking the Gospel Audiences* (Grand Rapids: Eerdmans, 1998), 147–71.

The second major source for the life and teaching of Peter is the Book of Acts, in which Peter appears as the principal protagonist in the first twelve chapters. We hear his voice again during the Jerusalem Council where James based the Council's decision on the testimony of Peter and the prophet Amos (15:6–11, 13). Whether the speeches in Acts present a faithful record of Peter's teaching or simply reflect Luke's theological aims is a question that has long occupied scholars. The common opinion is that "the speeches in Acts represent the portions of the book where Luke exercised his literary license most freely. He composed the speeches and inserted them at key points in order to present his own understanding of how the events he reports should be interpreted."[3] The speeches, on this view, represent neither the *ipsissima verba* (the very words) nor the *ipsissima vox* (the very voice) of Peter.[4] But not all are this skeptical of Luke's historiography, affirming that the author indeed preserves a credible account of Peter's voice and views.

The two epistles composed under Peter's name constitute a third source, but even these do not present an unambiguous witness regarding Peter's thought. Numerous commentators call into question the authenticity of 1 Peter, despite the early testimony in 2 Peter 3:1 and that of the Fathers, who unanimously affirmed Petrine authorship of the letter. A number of contemporary scholars, however, are hesitant to dismiss 1 Peter as a pseudepigraphic work. On the other hand, the authenticity of 2 Peter has been disputed from ancient times. Current scholarly consensus identifies 2 Peter as pseudepigraphic too, though even here there are dissenters. The book was not used extensively in the early centuries, and Eusebius classifies 2 Peter as one of the "disputed" books.[5] The style and themes are quite different from 1 Peter, leading many to conclude that Petrine authorship of the second is unlikely. Can we, then, recover Peter's teaching from the whole or part of these letters?

The final New Testament source for Peter's life and teaching is the letters of Paul. Paul met with Peter in Jerusalem for two weeks (Gal 1:18), and fourteen years later, he returned to the city to lay out his gospel before Peter, James, and John (Gal 2:1–10). Sometime later, he publicly confronted Peter in Antioch (Gal 2:11–14). Many regard these passages as the most reliable eyewitness accounts about Peter. In 1 Corinthians 15:15 Paul repeats the earliest testimony regarding Peter as being the first witness of the resurrected Christ. In 9:5 he mentions Peter's itinerate ministry, which may have taken him through Corinth (see 1:10–12; 3:21–23). The early church also preserved

---

3. Mark Allan Powell, *What Are They Saying About Acts?* (Mahwah, NJ: Paulist, 1991), 30–31.

4. The argument of this book, laid out in chapter 2, is that testimony is an essential epistemological category for understanding the NT witness regarding Peter. Testimony is interpreted history, and, as noted below, it includes belief while being appropriately linked with the facts to which it bears witness. All the witnesses to Peter's words and work come down to us via testimony which shapes the received tradition. In the end, therefore, we possess the faithfully interpreted structures of Peter's perspectives, his *ipsissima vox*, though we do not necessarily have his exact words or his *ipsissima verba*. The next chapter thoroughly discusses testimony and its implications for hearing Peter's theology.

5. Eusebius, *HE* 3.25.3; 3.3.1, 4.

the memory of Peter. The sources include the Apostolic Fathers and the various writings ascribed to Peter, such as the Apocalypse of Peter, the Gospel of Peter, and the Acts of Peter.[6] However, this study will not work with the Pauline testimony regarding Peter nor the memory of Peter preserved in the early church but rather those sources in which we hear the *vox Petri* from the apostle himself.

The available sources are more numerous than they might appear at first glance,[7] but they are hardly unambiguous. May we extract information regarding Peter's life and teaching from some of these works, or do they represent no more than early Petrine traditions? Amidst the considerable testimony regarding Peter handed down to us, may we hear the *vox Petri*?

CRITICAL ASSESSMENT OF THE SOURCES

Critical questions regarding the reliability of the extant sources for Peter's theology have hindered attempts to outline his thought and contribution to the development of Christian theology. The impression left is that we can do little more than know the "Peter of faith" since the "Simon of history" remains shrouded in mystery.[8] Indeed, research on the life and teaching of Peter follows a path which parallels Jesus studies, yet without the same level of scholarly debate regarding the reliability of the New Testament witnesses regarding Peter. Consequently, few studies on the life of Peter appear on the shelves in comparison to the number on Jesus or Paul. The bibliography on his theology is even smaller. While multiple tomes discuss Pauline theology and acknowledge that it is foundational for Christian thought, Peter's theological

---

6. See, for example, F. Lapham, *Peter: The Myth, the Man, and the Writings* (London: T. & T. Clark, 2003). This study will not deal with the second century and later evidence regarding Peter's theology.

7. F. J. Foakes-Jackson comments, "St. Peter presents a very difficult problem. As to the greatness of his character, the impression he has left—not only on the New Testament, but on posterity as well—no room is left for doubt. As to the actual facts regarding him, no one can deny that they are few and indefinite. The author has been repeatedly asked whether it is possible to construct an account of the Apostle with the materials at our disposal. His answer to this question is that his chief difficulty is to compress what should be said into a small volume" (*Peter: Prince of Apostles* [London: Hodder & Stoughton, 1927], v). The tension between Peter's large presence and the preservation of the "few and indefinite" facts about Peter merits closer attention.

8. As noted by Timothy Wiarda, *Peter in the Gospels: Pattern, Personality, and Relationship* (Tübingen: Mohr Siebeck, 2000), 15–16; Rudolf Pesch, *Simon-Petrus: Geschichte und geschichtliche Bedeutung des ersten Jüngers Jesu Christi* (Stuttgart: Anton Hiersemann, 1980). Lapham concurs: "Yet of his life and work little is definitively known; and from traditional sources alone it would be a difficult task indeed to explicate a distinctive Petrine theology" (Lapham, *Peter*, 1). For a survey of various approaches to the portrait of Peter, see Wiarda, *Peter*, 9–33.

contribution goes unrecognized.[9] As F. F. Bruce once said, "A Paulinist (and I myself must be so described) is under constant temptation to underestimate Peter."[10]

Given the state of the evidence, can we construct a theology of Peter? Some would say that if the goal is to hear the authentic *vox Petri* using the New Testament, we cannot arrive at our destination. Lapham, for example, holds that the witness of the New Testament is too unreliable, but, by taking the writings of the second-century church, we can recover "a common and distinctive tradition" surrounding Peter.[11] Lapham maps out how we may understand the "Peter of faith" but rejects the possibility that this figure is somehow connected to the "Simon of history."[12] Others, however, hold a maximalist position that affirms all the New Testament sources *prima facie* and holds that they paint a fulsome and accurate picture of the apostle and his thought. Indeed, from some of these writings, one would hardly be aware that questions regarding the reliability of the sources for Peter's teaching even existed. They synthesize the witnesses regarding Peter's life and teaching without paying much attention to the question of how the early church may have filtered and modified the witness about him. For example, in his discussion of the "Sources and Methods" for constructing Peter's life and thought, David Gill states, "The sources that we shall work with are the books of the New Testament. Peter is prominently mentioned in all four Gospels, the Acts, his two letters, and also in 1 Corinthians and Galatians."[13] Even his discussion of 2 Peter fails to mention the critical storm which has surrounded this letter since the early centuries of the Church.[14]

Carsten Thiede likewise holds a maximalist position regarding the Petrine materials, although he acknowledges the critical problems. He affirms that the witnesses

---

9. For a survey of key Protestant scholarship on Peter see Larry W. Hurtado, "The Apostle Peter in Protestant Scholarship: Cullman, Hengel, and Bockmuehl," in *Peter in Early Christianity*, ed. Helen K. Bond and Larry W. Hurtado (Grand Rapids: Eerdmans, 2015), 1–15. See also the summary of scholarship on Peter vs. Paul in Bockmuehl, *The Remembered Peter*, 31–60.

10. F. F. Bruce, *Peter, Stephen, James, and John: Studies in Early Non-Pauline Christianity* (Grand Rapids: Eerdmans, 1980), 42. See Hengel, *Saint Peter*. Foakes-Jackson's assessment is not quite as charitable: "A most distinguished scholar once told the writer that his opinion was that St. Peter was a very second-rate personage as compared with St. Paul, and that he owed his prestige solely to the fact that he had known Jesus" (*Peter*, xii).

11. Lapham, *Peter*, 1.

12. "It is important to recognize that the purpose of this survey of Petrine writings is not to attempt to discover the 'real' historical Peter behind the myth, were such an enterprise possible. As is the case with every renowned figure of the past, Peter is as much the product of the myth, as the myth is of him, and any attempt to demythologize must result in failure. For our purposes, it is of small moment whether or not Peter, for instance, actually took deliberate steps towards Jesus on the waters of Galilee (Matt 14:29). What *is* important is that tradition has it that he did; and we need to ask why this is so, and what might be the textual, theological and sociological ramifications of such a tradition" (Lapham, *Peter*, 2–3).

13. David W. Gill, *Peter the Rock: Extraordinary Insights from an Ordinary Man* (Downers Grove, IL: InterVarsity, 1986), 25.

14. Gene L. Green, *Jude and 2 Peter* (Grand Rapids: Baker Academic, 2008), 140–50.

for Peter's life and teaching are: "The four Gospels, Acts, 1 Corinthians, Galatians, and 1 and 2 Peter." But, while noting the historical skepticism surrounding the gospels and Papias's testimony concerning Peter's contribution to Mark, he does not unpack the critical problems.[15] With regard to the testimony about Peter in Acts, he concludes, "It is, however, worth remembering that if there have to be presuppositions in historical—and by all means critical—analysis, they must always be in favor of the text, rather than the analyst. In other words, Peter's portrait in Acts, even if based on this solitary witness for the first twelve-and-a-half chapters, is *a priori* not questionable, but reliable."[16] His approach to the Petrine letters is similar, accepting the witness of both while mentioning the critical problems: "Throughout this book, we have treated both letters as Peter's in accordance with the (literary) historian's approach of taking a literary source *a priori* seriously on its own claim *until* the contrary can be or has been proved conclusively."[17] Similarly, F. F. Bruce's small study on non-Pauline Christianity includes a section on Peter that does not trace the critical discussion regarding the Petrine witness.[18]

Between the minimalist and maximalist approaches, a number of scholars raise questions about the reliability of the New Testament witnesses regarding Peter yet still find enough historical threads to weave a picture—sometimes robust, sometimes skeletal—of the life and teaching of the apostle. In one of the principal studies on Peter penned during the last century, Oscar Cullmann stated, "In view of the nature of the sources it would be a rash undertaking to try to present a 'theology' of the apostle Peter. Even if one holds that the First Epistle of Peter was written by the apostle himself, the basis for this undertaking is too small."[19] Yet Cullmann traces some principle themes based upon the available evidence and even comes to the conclusion that Peter should be granted "a place of honor at the beginning of all Christian theology."[20] He concludes that Peter "certainly possesses a much greater significance in the foundation of Christian theology than we are accustomed to assume."[21] Cullman's appraisal of the Petrine material is moderate: we can know something about some main streams in Peter's theology, but we cannot hope to construct a comprehensive outline of his thought. Cullmann also holds the conviction that Peter's contribution to Christian theology was foundational and that we can outline a few of its principle points.[22] Based

---

15. Carsten Thiede, *Simon Peter: From Galilee to Rome* (Grand Rapids: Zondervan, 1988), 17–18; *Geheimakte Petrus: Auf den Spuren des Apostels* (Stuttgart: Kreuz, 2000), 14.

16. Thiede, *Simon Peter*, 103; *Geheimakte Petrus*, 147–49.

17. Thiede, *Simon Peter*, 173; *Geheimakte Petrus*, 257–68.

18. Bruce, *Peter, Stephen, James, and John*, 15–48. Similarly John Meyendorff, ed., *The Primacy of Peter* (Crestwood, NY: St. Vladimir's Seminary Press, 1992); Stephen K. Ray, *Upon This Rock: St. Peter and the Primacy of Rome in Scripture and the Early Church* (San Francisco: Ignatius, 1999).

19. Oscar Cullmann, *Peter: Disciple-Apostle-Martyr* (London: SCM, 1962), 66.

20. Cullmann, *Peter*, 67.

21. Cullmann, *Peter*, 69.

22. Cullmann, *Peter*, 66–70.

on a much more positive assessment of the credibility of the Petrine witnesses, Hengel concurs that Peter is a competent theological thinker who laid out the christological and soteriological foundations of the *kerygma*.[23]

Foakes-Jackson constructs his work on the life of Peter with full confidence in the witness of the Gospels, Acts, and the Pauline epistles. His assessment of the Petrine literature is, however, more cautious. While acknowledging the strong and early testimony regarding the authenticity of 1 Peter, the situation of persecution which the letter envisions places it outside the supposed author's lifetime. Also, Foakes-Jackson cannot square this letter with the portrait of Peter found elsewhere: "That Peter could have written the letter is hard to believe. The author is not the Peter of the Gospels and hardly the Peter of Acts."[24] Yet he is struck by the early reception of the letter and concludes that it at least represents his doctrine. In the end, he believes that "whether Peter was actually the author of the Epistle is here comparatively unimportant."[25] Foakes-Jackson declares his solidarity with critics "in every age" who reject 2 Peter as a genuine work of the apostle. He sees the letter as a supplement to the first missive. The second letter showed that Peter was not only a pastor but also the "great opponent of the antinomian gnosticism" in the second century.[26] His study does not utilize the letters to any significant extent, although he explores second century and later traditions regarding the apostle. Following a similar line, Gaechter's exploration of *Petrus und seine Zeit*[27] extensively mines the Petrine material found in the Gospels and Acts but leaves to one side any discussion of the letters ascribed to Peter.

The ecumenical study on *Peter in the New Testament*,[28] edited by Brown, Donfried, and Reumann, begins its analysis with the references to Peter in the Pauline letters before moving to Acts, which the study-group members and editors do not treat as "straight history." Acts is a composition from the 80s which made use of earlier sources and tends to dramatize and theologize early Christian history.[29] This stance, however, does not prevent them from tracing some outlines of Peter's role in the early church as they critically examine the witness in Acts and tease out aspects of Petrine history. The discussion on Acts 10–11 exemplifies the tensions and tentativeness which characterize the study. While "one possible explanation of the picture in Acts 10–11 is that Luke is giving us *history*, even though it be dramatized history. . . . Another possibility . . . is that we have here a creation of Lucan *theology*."[30] The editors examine

23. Hengel, *Saint Peter*, 86–89.
24. Foakes-Jackson, *Peter*, 119.
25. Foakes-Jackson, *Peter*, 116.
26. Foakes-Jackson, *Peter*, 122.
27. Paul Gaechter, *Petrus und seine Zeit* (Innsbruch; München: Tyrolia, 1958).
28. Raymond E. Brown, et al., eds., *Peter in the New Testament: A Collaborative Assessment by Protestant and Roman Catholic Scholars* (Minneapolis: Augsburg, 1973).
29. Brown, et al., *Peter in the New Testament*, 44.
30. Brown, et al., *Peter in the New Testament*, 44.

the Petrine witness in each of the Gospels, outlining and comparing the portrait of Peter in each, while keeping a close eye on the three levels of witness: the history in the Gospels, the pre-Gospel sources or tradition, and the redaction of each evangelist.[31] While acknowledging that 1 Peter is likely pseudonymous, the importance of the work is that it preserves a tradition which honors Peter in the very regions where Paul had considerable influence. In a similar way, the tradition about Peter as one who was connected to Jesus and who could arrest misinterpretations about Paul gives the pseudonymous 2 Peter its value.[32] In summary, the study collects a good deal on the historical Peter and gathers together the images of Peter in the New Testament, but it does not put forward anything like a Petrine theology.

Pesch's work, published seven years after *Peter in the New Testament*, goes through the exercise of seeking the historical aspects of the Petrine story told in the New Testament.[33] Some material developed due to rhetorical concerns, but Pesch identifies a number of historical reflections of Peter's life and thought, such as the Gospels' record of his preeminence among the apostles, his confession of Jesus, and his witness to the resurrection.[34] Pesch does not take the Petrine letters as witness for anything more than the "Peter of faith."[35] His treatment of Acts is similar to the Gospels while he places considerable weight on the Pauline testimony regarding the apostle.[36] Pesch's study exhibits a cautious yet somewhat hopeful approach to the Petrine material in the New Testament while also going beyond to the Petrine traditions in the early church. His study concludes with an examination of the "Petrine image" in all this literature and a final reflection on the primacy of Peter, even over Paul, in the canonical witness and in the later church.[37]

Gnilka traces a line similar to Pesch as he works through the historical materials in order to ferret out the basic data regarding the "Simon of history."[38] We can locate him in Bethsaida and later in Capernaum, where he labored as a fisherman. After his call to be a disciple, his house became a base for Jesus. Jesus named him Cephas and yet he denied the Lord. Afterwards, however, he saw the risen Christ in a vision. Alongside the historical discussion, Gnilka draws out the image of Peter as portrayed in each of the Gospels and Acts. This image is developed further in the two pseudonymous epistles attributed to the apostle, although Gnilka rejects the idea that the letters are the product of a Petrine school.

---

31. Brown, et al., *Peter in the New Testament*, 11.
32. Brown, et al., *Peter in the New Testament*, 16–17, 149–56.
33. Pesch discusses the question of the sources for such study in Pesch, *Simon-Petrus*, 5–7.
34. Pesch, *Simon-Petrus*, 23, 38, 43–44.
35. Pesch, *Simon-Petrus*, 150–52.
36. Pesch, *Simon-Petrus*, 59–71.
37. Pesch, *Simon-Petrus*, 160–70.
38. Joachim Gnilka, *Petrus und Rom: Das Petrusbild in den ersten zwei Jahrhunderten* (Freiburg; Basil; Wien: Herder, 2002).

Pheme Perkins launches her study of Peter by noting that the early church was not a unified movement which later fell into division and decline but was rather an amalgam of disparate voices,[39] and in this she finds richness. "Understood from an aesthetic viewpoint," she says, "divergence and even clashes of perspective enhance the fascination, the beauty, and even the credibility of an artistic vision. Such visions are not trivial. Unlike 'objective facts,' they have the power to move the human heart and mind beyond the narrow limits of a particular personal or even social experience."[40] Perkins argues that the "figure of Peter played very different roles for diverse communities," yet in the end, "the apostle might serve as a unifying figure for diverse forms of Christianity."[41] For Perkins, the image of Peter is not polarizing or the source of controversy; rather, he becomes a centrist and the focus of Christian unity. In this assertion, she is not concerned with the "Simon of history" but rather with how Peter was received and perceived in the church. It is the "image of Peter" which "has played a crucial role in shaping Christian communities,"[42] and the multiple New Testament witnesses hone the image in various ways. Yet Perkins affirms that although we cannot recover a clear picture of the apostle's life from the New Testament, we may apply critical methodology's criterion of multiple attestation to establish a particular fact from the life of Jesus and, indeed, that of Peter.

As *Peter in the New Testament*, Perkins is able to find some historical strands in the New Testament accounts. She does not, however, accept the historicity of the Petrine speeches in Acts[43] nor admit the stories regarding trials and imprisonments in Acts as reliable witnesses regarding Peter. Instead, she states only that "the tradition that Peter suffered such persecution in Jerusalem is highly probable."[44] Perkins relegates the struggle with the historicity of the accounts to a secondary position since

---

39. So Michael Goulder, *St. Paul Versus St. Peter: A Tale of Two Missions* (Louisville: Westminster John Knox, 1994), ix.

40. Perkins, *Peter*, 2. So Bart Ehrman, who, while accepting some of the New Testament history about Peter, relegates it to a place of secondary importance. The Gospels make statements "not in order to provide us with history lessons about life in first-century Roman Palestine, but in order to advance important Christian points of view" (*Peter, Paul, and Mary Magdalene: The Followers of Jesus in History and Legend* [Oxford: Oxford University Press, 2006], 10). Michael Grant adopts this familiar stance: "For historical documents are by no means what they set out to be. Actual events, as such, are not what they are primarily interested in. Certainly, such facts can be found in these books, if one looks carefully enough. However, they do not appear for their own sake, but rather for reasons that are *religious*. The books of the New Testament are religious, not historical, documents.... As some like to put it, therefore, the Gospels cannot be described as history at all, but rather as *salvation-history*" (*Saint Peter: A Biography* [New York: Scribner, 1994], 26–27). According to Grant, the portrait of Peter in Acts is similarly shaped and we cannot rely on 1 and 2 Peter as credible witnesses for the apostle's life and teaching. Goulder concurs: "The Gospels almost always give us the theology of their authors, and sometimes true tradition about Jesus" (*St. Paul Versus St. Peter*, xi).

41. Perkins, *Peter*, 3, 5.

42. Perkins, *Peter*, 13.

43. Perkins, *Peter*, 34–35.

44. Perkins, *Peter*, 37.

the "Peter of faith" found in the Gospels, Acts, the Petrine epistles, and later Christian literature takes preeminence. The Petrine traditions are far from being weak. Peter becomes "the universal 'foundation' for all the churches. The canon itself might be viewed from this Petrine perspective."[45]

Wiarda's research on *Peter in the Gospels*[46] attempts to work within the tensions between the "Peter of faith" and the "Simon of history" by adopting a narrative approach to the Gospels—at least with respect to the pericopes that show the pattern of Peter's well-intentioned actions and the subsequent corrections he endures. The bulk of Wiarda's study seeks to identify the common narrative threads in the Gospels without fully losing sight of the bedrock historical question. Wiarda concludes that the Gospel writers did indeed shape the narrative about Peter, but in recognizing this shaping, he does not dodge the historical question. He acknowledges the issue: "A fundamental question in current scholarship concerns the degree to which the evangelists were either conservative redactors or creative composers."[47] He offers his study as a piece of evidence in the debate, having identified multiple attestation for one characteristic of Peter: "Both the reversal pattern and a distinctively characterized Peter are present in several streams of gospel material."[48] Wiarda thinks that we can at least locate the historical Peter's person and experiences. Wiarda plays on the same field as Brown, Donfried, Reumann, and Perkins, yet with a more positive assessment of the level of history that can be extracted from the sources.[49]

A most interesting line of research on Peter comes from the pen of Markus Bockmuehl. In his books, *The Remembered Peter in Ancient Reception and Modern Debate* and *Simon Peter in Scripture and Memory*, Bockmuehl does not attempt an historical reconstruction of the life and theology of Peter from the NT witnesses. He states, "Any conventional quest of the 'historical Peter' runs into the ground rather swiftly."[50] He acknowledges the questions surrounding the authenticity of the two epistles which bear the apostle's name and echoes the skepticism of many regarding Peter's connection with the Gospel of Mark. Bockmuehl opts for a methodological approach to Peter which sidesteps the "archaeological" approach which seeks to find Peter in the extant NT texts. He asks, "But can we really say anything historically meaningful about Peter if we have no significant written sources extant from his lifetime?"[51]

---

45. Perkins, *Peter*, 184.
46. Wiarda, *Peter*.
47. Wiarda, *Peter*, 207.
48. Wiarda, *Peter*, 213.
49. In the same way, William Thomas Kessler comes to positive conclusions after assessing the Gospel evidence. See Kessler, *Peter as the First Witness of the Risen Lord: An Historical and Theological Investigation* (Rome: Editrice Pontificia Università Gregoriana, 1998).
50. Bockmuehl, *Simon Peter in Scripture and Memory*, 3.
51. Bockmuehl, *Simon Peter in Scripture and Memory*, 5.

Bockmuehl affirms that we can locate Peter by going downstream, as he says, from the original events of Peter's life and seeking to construct a vision of Peter's person and work through the memory of him left within both the Eastern and Western churches. He recognizes that memory is malleable and far from objective, but argues that we can indeed locate the "living memory" of the apostle within the early church. This is the stream from which Bockmuehl draws his water. He attempts to show that Peter's "enormous profile in subsequent tradition of early Christian faith and thought can be harnessed as a significant asset for historical study rather than being discarded as an inconvenient liability."[52] Bockmuehl has switched up the game by focusing on reception history as a means to work back to Peter.

Although unique, Bockmuehl's approach is similar to Lapham's in its emphasis on the received traditions about Peter. But he comes to a more positive assessment of what we can truly recover about Peter from the early non-canonical witnesses. Bockmuehl keeps the historical question in mind while pushing it down the road, leaving us wondering why the same attempt to recover the "memory" of Peter cannot be carried out more fruitfully with those witnesses which are historically closer to the apostle.[53] Ferreting out Peter from the memory of the apostle is a challenging task, no matter where along the historical stream one wishes to enter. Bockmuehl's argument is also somewhat similar to Perkins's. She examines the post-apostolic traditions as well but connects them more closely to the NT witnesses than does Bockmuehl. "Based on the surviving evidence," she says, "narrative traditions concerning Peter undergo a major development in the last third of the second century. Earlier writings, such as the *Apocalypse of Peter* (Eth./Gk.) or the *Gospel of Peter*, remain close to the first-century material. Expansions may be added from other traditions, such as the Jewish apocalyptic found in 2 Peter or in the *Apocalypse of Peter* (Eth./Gk.). Such additions do not alter the basic versions of the Peter traditions found in the first century. Where the early tradition is largely silent, the early second-century material remains silent as well."[54] As Perkins, Bockmuehl keeps the historical question in mind while staking his claim in the post-apostolic period. But he does not tie a tight knot between later Christian "memory" of Peter and the NT witnesses.

Perkins's *Peter* and Brown, Donfried, and Reumann's *Peter in the New Testament* make modest attempts to locate the "Simon of history" from the NT, and Bockmuehl does the same using the post-apostolic materials. On the other hand, Terence Smith's

---

52. Bockmuehl, *The Remembered Peter*, 11. On the memory of Peter in early church, also see Todd D. Still, "Images of Peter in the Apostolic Fathers"; Paul Foster, "Peter in Noncanonical Traditions," in *Peter in Early Christianity*, ed. Helen K. Bond and Larry W. Hurtado (Grand Rapids: Eerdmans, 2015), 161–67, 222–62.

53. Hurtado expresses reserve as well regarding Bockmuehl's approach, saying, "These sources *may* also, to some degree, reflect something of an earlier impact of the historical figure, but one needs cogen criteria by which to determine this" ("The Apostle Peter in Protestant Scholarship: Cullman, Hengel, and Bockmuehl," 13).

54. Perkins, *Peter*, 146.

work remains focused upon an examination of the various New Testament portrayals of the "Peter-figure." While Smith questions the historical foundations of the New Testament and later witness about Peter,[55] he nevertheless remarks, "It remains true that early Christian writings contain a wide variety of material about him." The nature of the witness defines his objective: "This diverse material is of great significance for understanding and evaluating the image of Peter during the first two centuries, since it reflects what various Christian writers believed about the apostle."[56] Smith's quest for the "Peter-figure" stops well short of the historical affirmations which characterize *Peter in the New Testament* and Perkins's *Peter*. It does, however, allow Smith to explore the images of Peter to the fullest extent without dismissing the testimony of any witness. Dschulnigg[57] and Grappe[58] likewise only focus upon the image of Peter within the New Testament and later Christian literature, explaining how the "Peter of faith" developed in various Christian communities. Grappe and Smith contend that the images of Peter bring us to the heart of early Christian controversies.[59] As mentioned above, Lapham follows the same line of identifying Petrine traditions rather than Petrine history,[60] while Bockmuehl works back to front by examining the traditions to find Petrine history.[61]

LOOKING BACK AND LOOKING AHEAD

These authors present a varied assessment of the portrayals of Peter preserved for us within the New Testament and early Christian literature. While some receive the New Testament witnesses at face value, others find within these pages nothing more than portraits of the apostle painted to support a particular perspective in the church via the name and authority of Peter. Still others attempt to steer a middle ground by critically examining the historical evidence and arrive at a positive or negative assessment of each historical element. They assess evidence which might contribute to our understanding of the "Simon of history," all the while noting how the New Testament

---

55. Smith comments at the outset, "However, not only is there widespread scholarly disagreement concerning the historical accuracy of both the Gospel record and the traditions embedded within the Acts of the Apostles, but there is also a good deal of room for doubt whether the Markan Gospel or Acts' Petrine speeches enshrine ideas which derive directly from the historical Peter, far less whether 1 or 2 Peter may be accepted as having been composed by him" (*Petrine Controversies in Early Christianity: Attitudes Towards Peter in Christian Writings of the First Two Centuries* [Tübingen: Mohr Siebeck, 1985], 2).

56. Smith, *Petrine Controversies in Early Christianity*, 4–5.

57. Peter Dschulnigg, *Petrus im Neuen Testament* (Stuttgart: Katholisches Bibelwerk, 1996).

58. Christian Grappe, *Images de Pierre aux deux premiers siècles* (Paris: Presses Universitaires de France, 1995).

59. Grappe, *Images de Pierre aux deux premiers siècles*, 291–93; Smith, *Petrine Controversies in Early Christianity*, 6–7.

60. Lapham, *Peter*.

61. Bockmuehl, *The Remembered Peter*; *Simon Peter in Scripture and Memory*.

authors or later traditions shaped the material. Both those who wish to speak about the "Peter of faith" and those who understand this figure in relation to the "Simon of history" look to the common pieces of evidence within the portraits as they attempt to outline the image of Peter. The Petrine pictures which emerge are strikingly disparate. Some view Peter's image as a rallying point for one wing of early Christianity against Paul or against heresy, while others regard him as the unifying figure within the early church and its factions.[62] While most of the studies focus primarily on Peter's life and role of leadership within the early church, a few take the additional step of associating the apostle with certain theological themes, some of which became foundational for the whole of Christian theology. These studies do not arrive at consensus regarding the person of Peter, his role in the early church, or his teaching. Is the Rock a myth and construct of the early church or can we locate his life and thought? Can we identify a historically grounded image of Peter while recognizing the active role the church played in preserving his story and teaching?

The position marked out in this study is that within the pages of the New Testament, we hear faithful witnesses who allow us to recover the *ipsissima vox* of Peter, although not necessarily the apostle's *ipsissima verba*. Ancient Christian historians both received and shaped the story of Peter in the historical narratives. These are not contrary assertions. We and the church through the centuries possess a witness regarding Peter which is epistemologically credible when evaluated by the norms of ancient historiography. Indeed, the witness is robust enough to allow us to construct an outline of Peter's teaching which became foundational for Christian theology. Moreover, Peter's role as the Rock speaks of his place as a witness of the resurrection and the leader of the early church and his centrality in the development of Christian theology.

---

62. The discussion about his role has clear overtones of and implications for Roman Catholic and Protestant dialogue, the one tagged as the "Church of Peter" and the other identified as the "Church of Paul." See Franz Mussner, *Petrus und Paulus—Pole der Einheit: Eine Hilfe für die Kirchen* (Freiburg: Herder, 1976).

CHAPTER 2

The Testimony of Peter

Any conclusion regarding whether the New Testament and later Christian literature provide us with a picture of the "Simon of history," the "Peter of faith," or some combination of the two, revolves around the question of methodology. Every author who examines the life and teachings of the apostle begins with a methodological framework that guides their study and helps determine its outcomes. The nature of the materials studied, however, calls for appropriate methodological approaches, whether the investigator's purpose is to discover the specific gravity of a particular substance or to reveal the social impact of a certain piece or body of literature. If the methodology is not suited to the investigative task, the results may be clear but their usefulness questionable. Interpreting poetry as if it were a scientific text or reading physics as if the language were nothing but metaphor could deaden our aesthetic sense or bring disastrous results in bridge construction. What critical methodology is appropriate for studying the materials preserved for us regarding the life and teaching of Peter?

A number of studies adopt the Petrine material garrisoned in the New Testament without any critical reflection on the sources and their manipulation, claiming that the historical witness is *prima facie* that of Peter. We should read these texts as they stand with no further questions asked. This approach will hardly do in an era which has learned to deconstruct historical narratives, looking for the social power structures to which they bear oblique or more direct witness. We have learned that historical concerns can be overrun by broader theological, rhetorical, or narrative interests. Therefore, we are not surprised that the bulk of the scholarly discussion about Peter leans towards approaches which require some additional support from the evidence before accepting the affirmations made about him and his teaching. The end result of this approach, however, is a spotty picture of who Peter was and what he taught. The evidence presented through a methodology which values multiple-attestation yields semi-solid conclusions and a less than robust final portrait of the apostle.

Given the unsatisfactory nature of the portraits that stem from a historical-critical methodology, we are not surprised that quite a few studies remain content with examining the various sources attached to Peter that testify to the early church's beliefs concerning him. The "Peter of faith" becomes the sole concern since, in the end, he is the only one whom we can know. The object of the study has here shifted from Peter to his champions. Them we can hear; him we cannot.[1] We can outline their belief structures, and this is sufficient since the image of Peter is what really counted for them (and, supposedly, for us). The historical thicket encourages us to walk this alternate path.

TESTIMONY

Those who claim that the witnesses present only an image of Peter have, perhaps unknowingly, embarked on an epistemological journey that may swing us around to a more positive assessment regarding what can be known about the "Simon of history." They have taken the testimonies about Peter and assembled what they see as their witness to the apostle without troubling with the question of historical reliability. All that matters in the end is the belief. But while testimonial knowledge, by its very nature, includes belief, it is at the same time appropriately linked with the facts to which it bears witness. Testimony demands belief, both on the part of the speaker and hearer (or writer and reader), but it does not divorce itself from the events and protagonists about which it bears witness. Testimony is an essential epistemological category and serves as the source of much human knowledge, although it has not been granted a significant place in the historical and critical study of the New Testament.[2]

1. Kevin Vanhoozer comments on the way literary-critical approaches have taken center-stage, eclipsing historical study: "While agreeing that the 'how' and the 'what' of discourse are legitimate objects of textual study, one may nevertheless wonder what has happened to the 'about what' of discourse, that is, the question of reference to historical reality" (*First Theology: God, Scripture and Hermeneutics* [Downers Grove, IL: InterVarsity, 2002], 258). Similarly, Pope Benedict XVI calls into question the facile dismissal of history as an essential element of Christian faith: "For it is of the very essence of biblical faith to be about real historical events. It does not tell stories symbolizing suprahistorical truths, but is based on history, history that took place here on this earth." And so, "If we push this history aside, Christian faith as such disappears and is recast as some other religion" (*Jesus of Nazareth: From the Baptism in the Jordan to the Transfiguration* [New York: Doubleday, 2007], xv).

2. C. Stephen Evans remarks on the reflex of negatively assessing testimony: "Some historical scholars argue quite explicitly that testimony is of little or no historical value. Thus, for them the fact that Luke or Matthew witness to some historical incident provides little or no evidential support for the historicity of the incident. On the contrary, the degree of suspicion and skepticism attached to ancient witnesses sometimes appears to be so great that testimony is weighted negatively, so that an assertion that an incident occurred is prima facie evidence that something else probably happened. The burden of proof is always on the Gospel accounts, and they are judged worthless or nearly so until

Contemporary Discussion on Testimony

In his study on testimony and epistemology, Coady observes that "testimony is very important in the formation of much that we normally regard as reasonable belief and that our reliance upon it is extensive."[3] He shows it is not limited to "the everyday or the merely practical." Many theoretical domains, such as the social sciences, history, and even the physical sciences, rely on the testimony of individuals or groups. Coady forwards testimony as a significant epistemological category that is often undervalued yet functions as a principal means of knowing the world and its history. Indeed, "we are greatly indebted to testimony at the level of both common sense and theory for much of what we usually regard as knowledge."[4] Coady notes how this category has enjoyed little or no epistemological importance in the West since the time of the Renaissance. "Modern epistemologists," he observes, "tirelessly pursue the nature and role of memory, perception, inductive and deductive reasoning but devote no analysis and argument to testimony although prima facie it belongs on this list."[5] Yet Coady and numerous other contemporary epistemologists are now exploring the nature of testimony and argue for its central role in epistemology.[6] Moreover, the orientation

---

we have independent confirmation or evidence of their veracity.... The New Testament records are regarded as reflecting the needs and situation of the Early Church, and as embodying little concern for historical accuracy" (*The Historical Christ and the Jesus of Faith: The Incarnational Narrative as History* [Oxford: Clarendon, 1996], 334).

3. C. A. J. Coady, *Testimony: A Philosophical Study* (Oxford: Clarendon, 1992), 7–8. Jennifer Lackey, an epistemologist, whose specialization is the study of testimony, likewise states: "Our dependence on testimony is as deep as it is ubiquitous. We rely on the reports of others for our beliefs about the food we eat, the medicine we ingest, the products we buy, the geography of the world, discoveries in science, historical information, and many other areas that play crucial roles in both our practical and intellectual lives.... Were we to refrain from accepting the testimony of others, our lives would be impoverished in startling and debilitating ways" ("Introduction," in *The Epistemology of Testimony*, ed. Jennifer Lackey and Ernest Sosa [Oxford: Clarendon, 2006], 1).

4. Coady, *Testimony*, 13.

5. Coady, *Testimony*, 6. So Lackey, "Introduction," 1.

6. See, for example, Elizabeth Fricker, "The Epistemology of Testimony," *Proceedings of the Aristotelian Society* 61 (1987) 57–83; Ernest Sosa, *Knowledge in Perspective: Selected Essays in Epistemology* (Cambridge: Cambridge University Press, 1991); Elizabeth Fricker, "Telling and Trusting: Reductionism and Anti-Reductionism in the Epistemology of Testimony," *Mind* 104 (1995) 393–411; Robert Audi, "The Place of Testimony in the Fabric of Knowledge and Justification," *American Philosophical Quarterly* 34 (1997) 405–22; Peter J. Graham, "What Is Testimony?," *Philosophical Quarterly* 47 (1997) 227–32; Peter Lipton, "The Epistemology of Testimony," *Studies in History and Philosophy of Science* 21 (1998) 1–31; Jennifer Lackey, "Testimonial Knowledge and Transmission," *Philosophical Quarterly* 49 (1999) 471–90; Catherine Z. Elgin, "Take It From Me: The Epistemological Status of Testimony," *Philosophy and Phenomenological Research* 65 (2002) 291–308; Stephen L. Reynolds, "Testimony, Knowledge, and Epistemic Goals," *Philosophical Studies* 110 (2002) 139–61; Martin Kusch, *Knowledge by Agreement: The Programme of Communitarian Epistemology* (Oxford: Oxford University Press, 2002); Martin Kusch and Peter Lipton, "Testimony: A Primer," *Studies in History and Philosophy of Science Part A* 33.2 (2002) 209–17; Matthew Weiner, "Accepting Testimony," *Philosophical Quarterly* 53 (2003) 256–64; Lackey, "Introduction"; Jennifer Lackey and Ernest Sosa, eds., *The Epistemology of Testimony* (Oxford: Clarendon, 2006); Jennifer Lackey, "The Nature of Testimony," *Pacific Philosophical Quarterly* 87 (2006) 177–97; Jennifer Lackey, "It Takes Two to Tango: Beyond

away from testimony as a reliable category comes into conflict with both ancient and global epistemologies which regard testimony as essential and central for human understanding.

Testimony is a source of knowledge which, unsurprisingly, marked the Mediterranean world of the first century and which appears repeatedly within the pages of the New Testament as the biblical authors sought to bear witness to Christ in their world. Epistemology was at the heart of Christian mission, and testimony was the category the apostles and others employed vigorously. Augustine likewise held that testimony occupies a significant place in the human quest for knowledge:

> Far be it also from us to deny that we have learned from the testimony of others; otherwise, we would not know that there is an ocean; we would not know that there are lands and cities which the most celebrated fame commends; we would not know of the men and their works which we have learned in the reading of history; we would not know the news that is daily brought to us from everywhere, and is confirmed by evidence that is consistent and convincing; finally, we would not know in what places and from what persons we were born; because we have believed these things on the testimonies of others. But it is most absurd to deny this, and we must confess that, not only the senses of our own bodies, but also those of other persons have added very much to our knowledge.[7]

As Augustine notes, testimony resides at the heart of the domain of history. And it is here where the study of Peter's life and teaching must begin.

In this current era, when the quest for certain knowledge appears quixotic, we should not be surprised at the reemergence of testimony as an important epistemological framework. Questions about foundationalist approaches to knowledge abound and the quest for certainty through empirical evidence seems wrong-headed. We have come to understand better the nature of perception and social location in the process of communication and interpretation. It is this very realization which opens the door for a rediscovery of testimony which binds historical affirmation and belief together.

How might we define testimony? The most common domain where testimony holds a respected place is within legal proceedings, though not all testimony is received as valid. According to Coady, contemporary formal legal testimony has the following characteristics:

Reductionism and Non-Reductionism in the Epistemology of Testimony," in *The Epistemology of Testimony*, ed. Jennifer Lackey and Ernest Sosa (Oxford: Clarendon, 2006), 160–89; Jennifer Lackey, "Knowing from Testimony," *Philosophy Compass* 1.5 (2006) 432–88; Robert C. Roberts and W. Jay Wood, *Intellectual Virtues: An Essay in Regulative Epistemology* (Oxford: Oxford University Press, 2007), 104–8; Jennifer Lackey, *Learning from Words: Testimony as a Source of Knowledge* (Oxford: Oxford University Press, 2008).

7. Augustine, *On the Trinity* 15.12.21 (Augustine, *On the Trinity: Books 8–15*, ed. Gareth B. Matthews [Cambridge: Cambridge University Press, 2002], 192–93).

(*a*) It is a form of evidence.

(*b*) It is constituted by persons A offering their remarks *as* evidence so that we are invited to accept *p* because A says that *p*.

(*c*) The person offering the remarks is in a position to do so, i.e., he has the relevant authority, competence, or credentials.

(*d*) The testifier has been given a certain status in the inquiry by being formally acknowledged as a witness and by giving his evidence with due ceremony.

(*e*) As a specification of (*c*), within English law and proceedings influenced by it, the testimony is normally required to be firsthand (i.e., not hearsay).

(*f*) As a corollary of (*a*), the testifier's remarks should be relevant to a disputed or unresolved question and should be directed to those who are in need of evidence on the matter.[8]

Coady argues that not all these conditions apply to natural or informal testimony since, for example, we may accept hearsay (*e*) and not direct witness as testimony in common discourse. We accept, for example, reporters' accounts of events at which they were not present. We do not require formal swearing-in ceremonies, required in the courtroom, if we are to receive informal testimony (*d*), yet we will make judgments regarding the competence or credibility of a witness's testimony. Coady, then, enumerates the conventions that he believes govern natural testimony:

A speaker S testifies by making some statement *p* if and only if:

(1) His stating that *p* is evidence that *p* and is offered as evidence that *p*.
(2) S has the relevant competence, authority, or credentials to state truly that *p*.
(3) S's statement that *p* is relevant to some disputed or unresolved question (which may or may not be *p*?) and is directed to those who are in need of evidence in the matter.[9]

In his discussion of the "rationality of testimony," Vanhoozer presents his own definition, which omits Coady's consideration of the relevance of the testimony to a question posed (3): "We are invited to accept *p* because A says that *p*, and because A is in a position to say so; in other words, A's stating *p* is offered as grounds for accepting *p*."[10]

But not everyone who discusses testimony would combine the metaphysics of testimony (the question of "What is testimony?") with the epistemology of testimony (the question of "What distinguishes good from bad testimony?") as have Coady and

---

8. Coady, *Testimony*, 32–33.
9. Coady, *Testimony*, 42.
10. Vanhoozer, *First Theology*, 359.

Vanhoozer.[11] We need to recognize that the question of truth-conditions in testimony can and should be distinguished from the question of the nature of testimony. Indeed, failure to do this may result in a frustrated discussion regarding testimony and what it can deliver. One will define it with the truth-conditional question at the center while another may understand it as independent of truth-conditions.[12] Fricker, in contrast to Coady's narrow view of testimony, forwards a broad view which lays to one side the epistemological component. Fricker understands testimony as a "broader category of tellings generally." She states, "A hearer generally knows that she has been told that P just in virtue of observing an appropriate such performance." This, for her, is testimony and, as such, places "no restrictions either on subject matter, or on the speaker's epistemic relation to it."[13] This broad view of testimony may be stated in the following way:

> S testifies that p if and only if S's statement that p is an expression of S's thought that p.[14]

This definition of testimony does not carry the clutter of Coady's view since it only addresses the metaphysical and not the epistemological question. But in our discussion we cannot leave to one side the epistemological question regarding what constitutes testimonial knowledge. Also, Fricker's definition is much too broad since, as Lackey observes, "then *any* expression of thought, from conversation fillers and polite responses to encouraging cheers and the reciting of acting lines, turns out to be an instance of testimony."[15]

Lackey presents a useful definition of testimony which focuses not only on the metaphysics of the act of testifying but also on the respective role of the speaker and hearer. On the part of the speaker or writer, there is intention to offer testimony to the hearer or reader, something that could be called "*ostensible testimony*."[16] However, a hearer or reader may receive as testimony some communication from a speaker or writer which may not be intended as testimony, such as the private journal of Sylvia Plath. Lackey combines both speaker and hearer testimony in her general definition of testimony:

---

11. A point discussed in Lackey, "The Nature of Testimony," 179–80.

12. So notes Lackey: "One of the main questions in the epistemology of testimony is how we successfully acquire justified belief or knowledge on the basis of what other people tell us. This, rather than what testimony *is*, is often taken to be the issue of central import from an epistemological point of view. Because of this, those who are interested in the epistemic status of testimonial beliefs often embrace a very broad notion of what it is to testify, one that properly leaves the distinction between reliable and unreliable (or, otherwise epistemically good and bad) testimony for epistemology to delineate" ("Introduction," 2).

13. Fricker, "Telling and Trusting," 396–97.

14. Lackey, "The Nature of Testimony," 182.

15. Lackey, "The Nature of Testimony," 184.

16. Lackey, "The Nature of Testimony," 188.

> S testifies that *p* by making an act of communication *a* if and only if (in part) in virtue of *a*'s communicable content, (1) S reasonably intends to convey the information that *p*, or (2) *a* is reasonably taken as conveying the information that *p*.

This definition does not take into account whether the testimony is either good or bad. Indeed, testimony may be either—it is not *inherently* good or bad epistemologically. The presumption that testimony is *de facto* bad is without warrant.

The question of justified belief through testimony is the second question on the table and the one that fixes our attention in historical inquiry. What conditions must exist for testimonial justification? There are two principal views regarding testimonial justification.[17] The non-reductivist view, according to Lackey, states that "hearers may be justified in accepting the reports of speakers, albeit defeasibly, merely on the basis of a speaker's testimony."[18] If there is no relevant information which would defeat the testimony, it should be accepted simply on the basis of having been spoken. Or, as Lackey puts it: "So long as there is no available evidence *against* accepting a speaker's report, the hearer has no positive epistemic work to do in order to justifiedly accept the testimony in question."[19] The reductivist view, on the other hand, argues that "in order to be justified in accepting the reports of speakers, hearers must have reasons for trusting certain speakers and reports, and in particular that these reasons cannot themselves be ineliminably based on the testimony of others."[20] In other words, there must be some independent positive reason to accept the testimony's truth-conditions. The absence of evidence to the contrary is insufficient warrant for accepting the testimony.[21] So while the non-reductivist view may be accused of fostering gullibility, the reductivist view reduces testimony down to that which can be verified through other sources. Indeed, those additional epistemological resources are often out of reach or otherwise unavailable.

Lackey has been working on a third way beyond reductionism and non-reductionism which also addresses the need for testimonial knowledge to account for the role of both the speaker and the hearer. Lackey's 1999 definition of testimonial knowledge addressed both the connection of the speaker with the facts about which she gives testimony and the criterion that the hearer must not have any undefeated defeaters (evidence to the contrary which has not been knocked-down) which would negate the testimony. Testimonial knowledge may therefore be understood in the following way:

---

17. See Fricker, "Telling and Trusting"; Lackey, "Testimonial Knowledge and Transmission"; Elgin, "Take It From Me"; Lackey, "It Takes Two to Tango." For a brief summary of the following point, see Lackey, "Introduction," 4–6.
18. Lackey, "Testimonial Knowledge and Transmission," 474.
19. Lackey, "Introduction," 4.
20. Lackey, "Testimonial Knowledge and Transmission," 474.
21. Lackey, "Introduction," 5.

> For every speaker S and hearer H, H comes to know that p via S's statement that p only if (i) S's statement that p is appropriately connected with the fact that p; and (ii) H has no defeaters indicating the contrary.[22]

Lackey has modified this view somewhat in her attempt to show how the work of justification is distributed between the speaker and the hearer. More recently she proposed what she calls Dualism:

> For every speaker A and hearer B, B justifiedly believes that p on the basis of A's testimony that p only if: (1) B believes that p on the basis of the content of A's testimony that p, (2) A's testimony that p is reliable or otherwise truth conductive, and (3) B has appropriate positive reasons for accepting A's testimony that p.[23]

Point (3) in Lackey's revised statement may seem to put her strongly in the reductivist camp. However, she responds:

> Dualism has the justificatory work being *shared* between the speaker and the hearer, leaving the work for the positive-reasons condition far less burdensome. Specifically, since condition (2) of dualism takes care of the reliability of the testimony in question, (3) merely has to ensure that the hearer's acceptance of the testimony is rationally acceptable. More precisely, on my view, the positive reasons possessed by a hearer need to be such that they render it, at the very least, *not irrational* for her to accept the testimony in question. This is a substantially weaker condition than that required by reductionists.[24]

What is called for in (3) may be no more than a general conformity with information available from other sources rather than an independent verification of every point within the testimony. Lackey's Dualism steers between gullibility and the need for auxiliary confirmation before any testimony may be accepted.

To believe someone's testimony is not the same as suspending critical faculties and becoming gullible, taking every statement of testimony as necessarily true. Nor do we divorce the testimony from the facts about which a speaker testifies. Testimony suggests that we assess the credibility of a witness by the witness's connection to the facts and whether there are "undefeated defeaters" which would negate the truth condition of the testimony, though we may not be in a position to verify independently all the "facts of the matter." It asks questions about whether there are adequate positive reasons for accepting the testimony. However, we do not look for collateral verification of every statement through other means of knowledge ("sense-perception, memory,

---

22. Lackey, "Testimonial Knowledge and Transmission," 490.
23. Lackey, "It Takes Two to Tango," 169.
24. Lackey, "It Takes Two to Tango," 172.

and inference"²⁵). We receive the witness's testimony on these conditions. Coady edged close to Lackey's notion of "defeaters" and rational acceptability in his statement:

> We may have 'no reason to doubt' another's communication even where there is no question of our being gullible; we may simply recognize that the standard warning signs of deceit, confusion, or mistake are not present. This recognition incorporates our knowledge of the witness's competence, of the circumstances surrounding his utterance, of his honesty, of the consistency of the parts of his testimony, and its relation to what others have said, or not said, on the matter. It may also incorporate some reference to the inherent likelihood of what is reported.[26]

If we admit testimony as a means of historical knowledge, we may rightly ask questions about the intent, coherence, and competence of the one who bears witness.[27] At the same time, knowing through testimony does not demand that all available evidence be produced before accepting each and every statement made in the testimony. Knowledge gained by testimony is not the same as absolute knowledge, and it therefore confronts us with the choice of whether to accept or reject it. Ricoeur discusses the "Hermeneutics of Testimony" and concludes: "We must choose between philosophy of absolute knowledge and the hermeneutics of testimony."[28] Testimony is not the same as scientific knowledge, with its multiple guarantees, yet it holds out a claim of reliability, not relativity. Vanhoozer acknowledges the risk of "acquiring false beliefs" here but also reminds us that it makes one "open to receiving a greater number of true beliefs and an interpretive framework for understanding the life and fate of Jesus."[29]

---

25. Lackey, "Testimonial Knowledge and Transmission," 473–74. C. Stephen Evans critiques the historian's attempt to find "self-transcendence" and "autonomy," saying, "Classical foundationalism says I should not believe a proposition unless I have objectively certain evidence for that proposition. The problem immediately arises, of course, as to whether I have evidence for my evidence. To stop a regress, it appears that I must have some evidence that either requires no evidence or that I am willing to accept without evidence. If I don't have enough evidence of the former sort, then it appears I am stuck with the latter" ("Critical Historical Judgment and Biblical Faith," in *History and the Christian Historian*, ed. Ronald A. Wells [Grand Rapids: Eerdmans, 1998], 50). Testimony moves beyond the quixotic quest for transcendence.

26. Coady, *Testimony*, 47.

27. Vanhoozer remarks, "Authorship is a hermeneutical as well as historical category insofar as it relates to the ethos of the work, particularly a work of 'I-witness' testimony. In testimony the questions 'Who?' and 'What' converge, for if the text is 'I-witness' testimony then the integrity of the 'I' makes all the difference. For the authority of testimony depends not only on the correctness of the reports but on the competence or ethos of the witness" (*First Theology*, 263). Lackey's condition (3) above would require a bit more.

28. Paul Ricoeur, *Essays on Biblical Interpretation*, ed. Lewis S. Mudge (Philadelphia: Fortress, 1980), 153.

29. Vanhoozer, *First Theology*, 270. Richard Bauckham puts the matter this way: "To repeat, trusting testimony is indispensable to historiography. This trust need not be blind faith. In the 'critical realist' historian's reception and use of testimony there is a dialectic of trust and critical assessment. But the assessment is precisely an assessment of the testimony as trustworthy or not. What is not possible is independent verification or falsification of everything the testimony relates such that reliance on

Through testimony, a witness of events makes faith possible for the one who hears the testimony. The statement is offered, the connection of the witness to the facts is assessed, and potential defeaters are evaluated. The one who receives testimony indeed makes judgments. But, if we refuse to accept any historical testimony unless it can be verified by some criterion such as multiple attestation, our knowledge of history will look like a poorly assembled collection of museum artifacts presented without context or interpretation to show their significance.[30] Testimony, a principal source of human knowledge, would be left no epistemological space if we were to demand independent verification for each proposition it presents. It would serve us little, both in the realm of historical knowledge and in other domains of human knowing.

As noted above, the uniqueness of testimony lies in the way it combines not only a witness to significant events but also some interpretation of those events. The person who offers testimony is not merely an objective observer but an involved participant who bears witness to the events and their meaning. The witness is not disengaged or distant since testimony is "a genre that attempts to convey the fact and meaning of singular events of absolute significance."[31] The witness cannot reproduce what was seen or heard but can only report on that event, and with the report comes the interpretation or story of what was witnessed. As such, it is much more than a record of the facts of the matter—as if they could be divulged without undergoing any interpretive processes. *This act of interpretation is a theological movement.* Bauckham remarks, "Eyewitness testimony offers us insider knowledge from involved participants. It also offers us engaged interpretation, for in testimony, fact and meaning coinhere, and witnesses who give testimony do so with the conviction of significance that requires to be told."[32] Testimony, therefore, has a confessional dimension, and this "'confessional' kernel of testimony is certainly the center around which the rest gravitates."[33] All history based upon testimony is interpreted history, including the history of Jesus

---

testimony would no longer be needed. Testimony shares the fragility of memory, which is testimony's sole access to the past, while also, when it predates living memory, existing only as archived memory, cut off from the dialogical context of contemporary testimony" (*Jesus and the Eyewitnesses: The Gospels as Eyewitness Testimony* [Grand Rapids: Eerdmans, 2017], 490).

30. So Bauckham: "Gospels scholarship must free itself from the grip of the skeptical paradigm that presumes the Gospels to be unreliable unless, in every particular case of story or saying, the historian succeeds in providing independent verification. For such a suspicious approach the Gospels are not believable until and unless the historian can verify each claim that they make to recount history. But this approach is seriously faulty precisely as a historical method. It can only result in a misleadingly minimal collection of uninteresting facts about a historical figure stripped of any real significance. Neither in this nor in countless other cases of historical testimony can the historian verify everything. Testimony asks to be trusted" (*Jesus and the Eyewitnesses*, 506).

31. Ricoeur, *Essays on Biblical Interpretation*, 123.

32. Bauckham, *Jesus and the Eyewitnesses*, 505. Bauckham concludes, "It is in the Jesus of testimony that history and theology meet" (*Jesus and the Eyewitnesses*, 508). Or, as Markus Bockmuehl remarks, "Events do not, after all, subsist in splendid isolation from their interpretation" (*Seeing the Word: Refocusing New Testament Study* [Grand Rapids: Baker Academic, 2006], 162).

33. Ricoeur, *Essays on Biblical Interpretation*, 134.

and his disciples.³⁴ Such is its nature. The combination of participation and witness found in the prologue of Luke may at first strike us as compromising the credibility of the witnesses ("Just as they were handed on to us by those who from the beginning were eyewitnesses and servants of the word" [Luke 1:2]), but the witnesses' proximity to and their participation in gospel events would have been regarded as a marker of credibility.

Ancient Discussion on Testimony

The discussion about testimony is relevant for interpreting New Testament history since, as mentioned previously, it was a category well understood in the ancient world and the New Testament authors made use of it. Aristotle discussed the nature of testimony in his *Ars Rhetorica*, in which he defines rhetoric "as the faculty of discovering the possible means of persuasion in reference to any subject whatever" (1.2.1). Aristotle identifies two categories of proofs which are used in persuasion: "As for proofs [πίστευων],³⁵ some are inartificial, others artificial. By the former, I understand all those which have not been furnished by ourselves but were already in existence, such as witnesses [μάρτυρες], tortures, contracts, and the like; by the latter, all that can be constructed by system and by our own efforts. Thus we have only to make use of the former, whereas we must invent the latter" (1.2.2). Persuasion via the testimony of a witness, which is one of the inartificial (atechnic or nonartistic) proofs, is especially dependent upon the character of the witness. One cannot verify every detail within a testimony, so the viability of the witness becomes all important, much beyond the persuasion of argument or the disposition of the hearer. This is Aristotle's first kind of proof: "Now the proofs furnished by the speech are of three kinds. The first depends upon the moral character of the speaker, the second upon putting the hearer into a certain frame of mind, the third upon the speech itself, in so far as it proves or seems to prove" (1.2.4). Indeed, Aristotle says, "moral character, so to say, constitutes the most effective means of proof" (1.2.4), and such proof is at the heart of testimony.³⁶ So the witness does more than simply narrate events but rather is in the place of a moral authority, as one who gives credible witness, which serves as the basis for understanding and faith. The witnesses who give testimony regarding the past may be "ancient or recent" (1.15.13, 15–16), but witnesses can also be "interpreters of oracles

---

34. "But the interpretive act of writing a Gospel intended continuity with the testimony of the eyewitnesses who, of course, had already interpreted, who could not but have combined in their accounts the empirically observable with the perceived significance of the events" (Bauckham, *Jesus and the Eyewitnesses*, 472).

35. Cf. Acts 17:31. Such demonstrative proofs provide conviction according to Aristotle (*Rhet.* 2.20.9).

36. "The orator persuades by moral character when his speech is delivered in such a manner as to render him worthy of confidence; for we feel confidence in a greater degree and more readily in persons of worth in regard to everything in general, but where there is not certainty and there is room for doubt, our confidence is absolute" (Aristotle, *Rhet.* 1.2.4).

for the future" (1.15.14).³⁷ This may account, in part, for the frequency with which New Testament authors appeal to fulfilled prophecy as part of Christian witness, their correct interpretation providing testimony. Aristotle did, however, put considerable stock in witnesses from the past since they cannot be bribed ("Ancient witnesses are the most trustworthy of all, for they cannot be corrupted" [1.15.16]), while by no means dismissing living witnesses.

In an earlier generation, Thucydides discussed testimony in relationship to writing history. He admitted that writing history entailed judgments regarding received testimony. In his methodological discussion, he states, "Now the state of affairs in early times I have found to have been such as I have described, although it is difficult in such matters to credit [πιστεῦσαι] any and every piece of testimony [τεκμηρίῳ]" (1.20.1).³⁸ Yet the difficulties in sorting through the testimony did not incapacitate Thucydides. "Still," he states, "from the evidence [τεκμηρίων] that has been given, any one would not err who should hold the view that the state of affairs in antiquity was pretty nearly such as I have described it.... He should regard the facts as having been made out with sufficient accuracy, on the basis of the clearest indications, considering that they have to do with early times" (1.21.1). Testimony was important, and Thucydides sought informed testimony from those who were witnesses of the events while not being reluctant to record his own observations about the events he personally witnessed. His overarching concern was to seek reliable testimony: "But as to the facts of the occurrences of the war, I have thought it my duty to give them, not as ascertained from any chance informant nor as seemed to me probable, but only after investigating with the greatest possible accuracy each detail, in the case both of the events in which I myself participated and of those regarding which I got my information from others" (1.22.2). Thucydides did not receive every testimony since not every witness could be considered trustworthy. He also recognized that the testimony of others would indeed favor one side or another, that is, the perspective of the one who gave witness was included in the report. Testimony was dependent upon memory as well, and these factors yielded multiplex reports.

---

37. Aristotle gives an example: "Thus, for instance, Themistocles interpreted the wooden wall to mean that they must fight at sea." He refers here to Heroditus 7.141, which recounts how enquiry was made to the oracle at Delphi. The oracular response given by the priestess at Delphi included the statement, "Yet shall a wood-built wall by Zeus all-seeing be granted unto the Trito-born, a stronghold for thee and thy children." Interpreting the oracle as difficult (7.142), Themistocles son of Neocles nevertheless rightly interpreted it (7.143) and thus saved the day: "Themistocles thus declaring, the Athenians judged him to be a better counselor than the readers of oracles." To interpret the oracle other than he did would have meant ruin.

38. τεκμηρίῳ also appears in Acts 1:3. It is "that which causes someth. to be known in a convincing and decisive manner; *proof* (demonstrative proof)" (*BDAG* 994). Thucydides noted that testimony could be distorted and this demanded that the historian take special care: "So averse to taking pains are most men in the search for the truth, and so prone are they to turn to what lies ready at hand" (1.20.3).

These difficulties did not deter Thucydides from using testimony as his principal source, despite the labor this involved: "And the endeavour to ascertain these facts was a laborious task, because those who were eye-witnesses of the several events did not give the same reports about the same things, but reports varying according to their championship of one side or the other, or according to their recollection" (1.22.3). He attempted to avoid myths in order to present a history which would profit those in his day and in the years to come since, he notes, his prime concern was not to entertain: "And it may well be that the absence of the fabulous [μυθῶδες] from my narrative will seem less pleasing to the ear, but whoever shall wish to have a clear view both of the events which have happened and of those which will some day, in all human probability, happen again in the same or a similar way—for these to adjudge my history profitable will be enough for me" (1.22.4). With all the attendant difficulties of working with testimony, Thucydides was able to piece together a history which combined informed perspective with critical historical investigation (cf. Luke 1:1–4). This is the nature of testimony.

THE TESTIMONY OF PETER

How may we know anything about the life and theology of Peter? The New Testament preserves for us both the testimony of Peter himself and testimony about Peter. Indeed, the appeal to testimonial knowledge runs through ancient discussion regarding Peter and the sources associated with him. The witnesses which have come down from him and about him are all marked by the claims we would expect regarding the eyewitness nature of the testimony and the reliability of the witnesses. These are the primary concerns when testimony becomes the foundation for historical knowledge. The testimony is not a fabricated history, purely the creation of the ones who testify. Nor is the testimony of Peter distanced and objective but rather an involved and interpretive witness which joins together the elements of history and theology. This testimony, as all testimony, has both objective and subjective dimensions. It is much more than "just the facts," which Sgt. Joe Friday frequently requested in the old TV drama *Dragnet*. The theological message of the history comes to us as part of the cloth woven from testimony. The theology cannot nor should not be teased out in an attempt to present a supposed objective and verifiable-at-every-point historical profile of the apostle and his teaching.

Our knowledge of Peter's theology arrives via testimony. As such, it comes to us as an interpreted history, tied to Peter yet modified with reference to the audience. It does not come as "pure Peter," untouched as a transcript of the apostle's thoughts or even deeds. Rather, testimonial knowledge about Peter connects communities to Peter through this interpreted history. We have, therefore, the *vox Petri*, the faithfully interpreted voice of the apostle, instead of the *verba Petri*, a mere transcript of his teaching. Bock takes up the discussion regarding the *impsissima vox* of Jesus, saying,

"We do not have 'his very words' in the strictest sense of the term. . . . It is clear that the writers give us a reduced and summarized presentation of what Jesus said and did." Bock recognizes that "written history involves perspective."[39] The same holds for our knowledge regarding Peter. The ancient and contemporary category of testimony offers a framework within which we can understand how received story and interpretation hold together. The *vox Petri* is nothing other than the testimonial knowledge we have of the apostle's teaching.

The Testimony of Peter and the Gospel of Mark
Ancient Perspectives on Petrine Testimony in Mark

The Petrine testimony begins with the Gospel of Mark. From antiquity, the church associated this gospel with the testimony of Peter that Mark both heard and recorded. Two independent sources, Papias and Justin Martyr, acknowledge that Mark's Gospel derives from Peter.[40] Other ancient sources reference the association of Mark with Peter's preaching (including the Muratorian Canon, Irenaeus, Clement of Alexandria, Tertullian, the Anti-Marcionite Prologue to Mark, Origen, and Jerome), but these may be dependent upon earlier tradition.[41] France, however, questions whether these are all based upon Papias's account "since none of the writers before Eusebius mentions Papias as a source for their information. The fact that they agree with the essence (though not the wording) of Papias's account by no means requires that they derived their information from him."[42]

Moreover, no ancient source suggests that Mark cobbled his Gospel together from independent pericopae, as a form-critical approach would suggest. Rather, at the center of ancient testimony is the principal role Peter's witness played in the composition of this Gospel. Mark's Gospel was based on Peter's testimony regarding Jesus' life and labor.

The most well-known reference to Mark's dependence upon Peter's preaching comes from Papias, Bishop of Hierapolis, who wrote five books entitled *Interpretation of Our Lord's Declarations* at the start of the second century. These volumes have not survived, save for the quotations found in Eusebius's *Ecclesiastical History*.[43] Eusebius

---

39. Darrell L. Bock, "The Words of Jesus in the Gospels: Live, Jive, or Memorex?," in *Jesus Under Fire. Modern Scholarship Reinvents the Historical Jesus,* ed. Michael J. Wilkins and J. Moreland (Grand Rapids: Zondervan, 1995), 77–78, 81.

40. Bauckham (*Jesus and the Eyewitnesses*, 237–38) would add to these two a reference from Clement of Alexandria (*Stromata* 7.17 [7.106.4]) to Basilides, a second-century Egyptian gnostic, who bolstered his claims by appeal to his master Glaucias, "the interpreter of Peter," an assertion which parallels the claim found in Papias (*HE* 3.19.15) that Mark was Peter's interpreter. This mimicry shows the early acknowledgment of Mark's role in relation to Peter.

41. Bauckham, *Jesus and the Eyewitnesses*, 235.

42. R. T. France, *The Gospel of Mark: A Commentary on the Greek Text* (Grand Rapids: Eerdmans, 2002), 37n72.

43. "There are said to be five books of Papias, which bear the title *Interpretation of Our Lord's*

does not hold Papias in high regard due to his millennial views (3.39.11–13) and even derides him for being "very limited in his comprehension, as is evident from his discourses" (3.39.13). Yet Eusebius acknowledges Papias as a valid source of historical testimony due to his association with those who had heard the apostles. He quotes Papias's comments on method: "But if I met with anyone who had been a follower of the elders anywhere, I made it a point to inquire what were the declarations of the elders. What was said by Andrew, Peter, or Philip. What by Thomas, James, John, Matthew, or any other of the disciples of our Lord. What was said by Aristion, and the presbyter John,[44] disciples of the Lord; for I do not think that I derived so much benefit from books as from the living voice of those that are still surviving" (3.39.4). Papias places a premium upon the testimony of the disciples of the Lord as mediated by those who heard them. Eusebius comments on Papias's account and especially values that which Papias received from these first-hand witnesses (3.39.7), while also acknowledging that there were some things Papias "received by tradition" (3.39.8).

Papias wrote an account of the origins of Mark's Gospel, quoted by Eusebius:

> And the Presbyter used to say this, "Mark became Peter's interpreter and wrote accurately all that he remembered [ἐμνημόνευσεν], not, indeed, in order, of the things said or done by the Lord. For he had not heard the Lord, nor had he followed him, but later on, as I said, followed Peter, who used to give teaching as necessity demanded but not making, as it were an arrangement of the Lord's oracles, so that Mark did nothing wrong in thus writing down single points as he remembered [ἀπεμνημόνευσεν] them. For to one thing he gave attention, to leave out nothing of what he had heard and to make no false statements in them." (3.39.15)

Both the credibility and the interpretation of this declaration have generated considerable discussion. A number of authors discount Papias's account altogether, regarding it as nothing more than unreliable fabrication. Brown, Donfried, and Reumann ask, "Did Mark get his tradition from Peter?" Their response is far from positive: "Here the probability of invention increases."[45] They hold to the view that the Gospels do not represent eyewitness testimony but rather the material they contain

---

Declarations. Irenæus also made mention of these as the only works written by him, in the following terms: 'These things are attested by Papias, who was John's hearer and the associate of Polycarp, an ancient writer, who mentions them in the fourth book of his works. For he has written a work in five books'" (3.39.1, Eusebius, *Eusebius's Ecclesiastical History* [Peabody, MA: Hendrickson, 1998], 103). The Eusebius quotations are from, Eusebius, *Eusebius's Ecclesiastical History* unless otherwise indicated.

44. Eusebius differentiates between John the apostle and John the Presbyter (*HE* 3.39.5–7). See B. W. Bacon, "The Elder John, Papias, Irenæus, Eusebius, and the Syriac Translator," *JBL* 1 (1908) 1–23; Johannes Munck, "Presbyters and Disciples of the Lord in Papias: Exegetic Comments on Eusebius, Ecclesiastical History, III, 39," *HTR* 52 (1959) 223–43.

45. Brown, et al., *Peter in the New Testament*, 195. For a summary of the objections to the credibility of Papias's witness, see Kurt Niederwimmer, "Johannes Markus und die Frage nach dem Verfasser des zweiten Evangeliums," *ZNW* 58 (1967) 172–88.

is "derivative from earlier sources that were once or several times removed from oral, eyewitness presentation."[46] Perkins concurs, noting that the Gospel of Mark lacks understanding of Jewish customs and Palestinian geography. It also presents a negative portrait of Peter, an unlikely occurrence had Peter been the author's source. So, "scholars today recognize that Mark is not based upon memories of the apostle Peter."[47] Indeed, Brown and Meier note that major Petrine scenes found in Matthew are absent from Mark (Matt 14:28–31; 16:17–19; 17:24–27).[48] Goulder likewise puts no stock in the Papias testimony, regarding it as a piece of "wishful thinking designed to defend the Gospels against those who pointed out contradictions between them."[49] Lapham, while doubting that Papias is correct about the direct lineage from Peter, admits that at least "some kind of Petrine source lies, indirectly at least, behind Mark."[50] But his acknowledgment of some "Petrine source" is only an affirmation regarding a Petrine tradition, a far cry from asserting that Peter himself stands behind this Gospel.

Not everyone is ready to dismiss Papias. Hooker states that "Papias may well be right, therefore, in claiming that the gospel was written by someone who had known Peter."[51] France questions whether the early traditions of the Fathers regarding the Gospels should be summarily rejected,[52] while both Hengel and Bauckham vigorously defend the credibility of Papias's account.[53] Bond cautiously argues that "a Petrine link to Mark's Gospel is not as self-evidently impossible as many critical scholars suppose."[54]

---

46. Brown, et al., *Peter in the New Testament*, 195. So Pheme Perkins, *Peter: Apostle for the Whole Church* (Edinburgh: T. & T. Clark, 2000), 53.

47. Perkins, *Peter*, 53. So Michael Grant does not admit to a close association of Mark with Peter "since the author of *Mark* is very ignorant of Palestinian geography" (*Saint Peter: A Biography* [New York: Scribner, 1994], 31).

48. Raymond E. Brown and John Meier, *Antioch and Rome: New Testament Cradles of Catholic Christianity* (Mahwah, NJ: Paulist, 1983), 196.

49. Michael Goulder, *St. Paul Versus St. Peter: A Tale of Two Missions* (Louisville: Westminster John Knox, 1994), 16.

50. Lapham, *Peter*, 10.

51. Morna D. Hooker, *The Gospel According to Mark* (Peabody, MA: Hendrickson, 1991), 6. So, for example, C. E. B. Cranfield, *The Gospel According to Saint Mark* (Cambridge: Cambridge University Press, 1959), 3–5; Vincent Taylor, *The Gospel According to Mark* (Grand Rapids: Baker, 1966), 1–8; Robert H. Gundry, *Mark: A Commentary on His Apology for the Cross* (Grand Rapids: Eerdmans, 1993), 1026–49; James R. Edwards, *The Gospel According to Mark* (Grand Rapids: Eerdmans, 2002), 4; France, *The Gospel of Mark*, 35–41; Bauckham, *Jesus and the Eyewitnesses*, 155–82.

52. France, *The Gospel of Mark*, 38–39.

53. Martin Hengel, *Studies in the Gospel of Mark* (Philadelphia: Fortress, 1985), 47–53; Bauckham, *Jesus and the Eyewitnesses*, 202–39.

54. Helen K. Bond, "Was Peter behind Mark's Gospel?," in *Peter in Early Christianity*, ed. Helen K. Bond and Larry W. Hurtado (Grand Rapids: Eerdmans, 2015), 60. Bond's cautious affirmation is evident in her conclusion: "On a very general level, we have access to the kind of things Jesus said and did, but there is still a great deal of scope for the distortion of memory (both Peter's and Mark's) and perhaps more importantly the present needs of the Christian group to which they belonged as it sought to explain itself following the cataclysmic events of persecution, revolt, and the fall of the temple."

Papias's historic witness concurs with other affirmations regarding Peter's contribution to the Gospel of Mark. These offer us adequate positive reasons for embracing Papias's testimony. In his *Dialogue with Trypho*, written somewhere between AD 155 and 161, Justin Martyr makes an oblique reference to Peter's contribution to the Gospel. He states, "It is said that he changed the name of Peter, one of the apostles," recounting that "it has been written in his memoirs that this happened" (καὶ γεγράφθαι ἐν τοῖς ἀπομνημονεύμασιν αὐτοῦ γεγενημένου καὶ τοῦτο, 106.3).[55] Justin goes on to state that Jesus likewise changed the names of the brothers James and John "to Boanerges, which interpreted means 'Sons of Thunder'" (τοῦ Βοανεργὲς, ὅ ἐστιν υἱοὶ βροντῆς). The only place where the Gospels mention this change to "Boanerges... Sons of Thunder" is Mark 3:17 (3:16 speaks of Peter's name change). Justin's source is "his memoirs," the antecedent to "his" being Peter, who is highlighted in the previous clause in the Greek. The classification of this Gospel as Peter's "memoirs" or "that which was remembered" (τοῖς ἀπομνημονεύμασιν) from Peter is similar to Papias's description of how Mark wrote down what he "remembered" (ἀπεμνημόνευσεν) from Peter. Yet Justin is not dependent upon Papias. Both Justin and Papias place Mark as one who is a credible witness to what Peter preached, and they accept his testimony about Peter. Bauckham[56] argues that in Papias's quotation, the one who was doing the remembering is Peter rather than Mark. However, Papias's topic is what Mark was doing. He "became Peter's interpreter" and "wrote" all that "he remembered." Mark wrote down points "as he remembered them."[57] Nothing here indicates that Papias changed the subject from Mark to Peter in these affirmations. Moreover, Clement of Alexandria records a similar observation that Mark wrote down what he remembered from Peter.[58] Mark remembered—and recorded—Peter's memoirs.

Mark essentially wrote the "memoirs" of Peter, similar to Xenophon's "Memoirs" of Socrates (*Memorabilia* 1.3.1).[59] He recorded[60] what Peter said about Jesus. While contemporary Western culture is dominated by paper and computers at the expense of memory, ancient authors made much use of their powers of memory. While we would freely associate the word "memory" with "untrustworthy" and "weak," they would associate it with words such as "reliable" and "powerful." Seneca the Elder laments the decline in his memory with the advent of old age, yet recalls its once prodigious powers:

> I do not deny that my own memory was at one time so powerful as to be positively prodigious, quite apart from its efficiency in ordinary use.... My

---

55. Original translation.
56. Bauckham, *Jesus and the Eyewitnesses*, 211.
57. Cf. Cicero, *Topica* 1.5.
58. Eusebius, *HE* 6.14.6–7.
59. Bauckham, *Jesus and the Eyewitnesses*, 212. Bauckham, however, argues that the Papias quote indicates that Mark is Peter's "Memoirs" of Jesus.
60. As ἀπομνημονεύω in Xenophon, *Agesilaus* 1.2; cf. *Cyrophaedia* 8.2.14.

memory used to be swift to pick up what I wanted it to; but it was also reliable in retaining what it had taken in. . . . But I must ask you not to insist on any strict order in the assembling of my memories; I must stray at large through all my studies, and grab at random whatever comes my way. (*Controversies* 1, Preface 3–4)[61]

Unsurprisingly then, memory and composition merge in Mark's account of Peter's proclamation. Papias notes this.

The Anti-Marcionite Prologue, from the second half of the second century, points to Mark's role as Peter's interpreter and as the one who wrote down the Gospel: "He was the interpreter of Peter. After the death of Peter himself, he wrote down this same gospel in the regions of Italy."[62] The Prologue implies that the source for Mark's Gospel was Peter. The dating of Mark's composition concurs with Irenaeus who, writing in the first half of the second century, likewise indicates that Mark interpreted for Peter and recorded his preaching: "Mark, the disciple and interpreter of Peter, did also hand down to us in writing what had been preached by Peter" (*Against Heresies* 3.1.1). Sometime later in the second century, or perhaps in the first decade of the third, Clement of Alexandria asserts the same regarding the relationship between Peter and Mark. Eusebius quotes him as saying, "When Peter had proclaimed the word publicly at Rome, and declared the gospel under the influence of the spirit; as there was [*sic*] a great number present, they requested Mark, who had followed him from afar, and remembered [μεμνημένον] well what he had said, to reduce these things to writing, and that after composing the gospel he gave it to those who requested it of him. Which, when Peter understood, he directly neither hindered nor encouraged it" (*HE* 6.14.6–7). Unlike previous references in the Anti-Marcionite Prologue and Irenaeus, Clement dates the composition of Mark during Peter's lifetime. This discrepancy points to an independent tradition that preserves the key points of the story: Mark was Peter's interpreter; he wrote down what Peter proclaimed. As Papias, Clement emphasizes the role of Mark's memory of this preaching. But Justin Martyr sounds this note as well and therefore we need not infer that Clement was dependent upon Papias. Also, both Clement and Papias comment on the way Mark followed Peter, but the language Clement uses is different, suggesting that he is not drawing directly from Papias.[63] On the other hand, the role of Mark as Peter's interpreter and the comment that Mark wrote what Peter proclaimed are persistent themes through

---

61. See the discussion and caveats in Jocelyn Penny Small, *Wax Tablets of the Mind: Cognitive Studies of Memory and Literacy in Classical Antiquity* (London: Routledge, 1997), 188–201.

62. Taylor, *Gospel According to Mark*, 3.

63. Papias says that Mark neither heard the Lord οὔτε παρηκολούθησεν αὐτῷ, ὕστερον δέ, ὡς ἔφην, Πέτρῳ while Clement simply says that Mark ἀκολουθήσαντα αὐτῷ.

these texts. These notes are sustained through the third[64] and the fourth century.[65] All this has the ring of reliable testimony.

Various witnesses testify about the relationship between Mark and Peter and the fact that Mark wrote what he remembered of Peter's teaching. While we cannot entirely discount the dependence of later accounts upon Papias, we can at least acknowledge the independent attestation of this relationship found in Justin Martyr. But the persistence of this tradition, even in the face of other variations in the accounts—such as whether Mark wrote before or after Peter's death—suggests that we are dealing with more than two independent witnesses. Papias's account is especially important since he names his sources, those being the ones who were in a position to serve as witnesses to the history he records. While he did not talk to Mark, he heard from John the Presbyter, a disciple of the Lord, who served as witness regarding Mark's role as one who bears witness about Peter's preaching.[66] The language of testimony, with its emphasis upon memory and eyewitness information, dominates this and other accounts.[67] The way Papias relates the process of writing is designed to show that he used the best practices in recording history by going directly to those who were in a position to bear witness. His message is that his account was based upon credible testimony.

Papias and others record that Mark served as Peter's interpreter.[68] Papias adds an additional comment that Mark was careful in his task since he gave attention "to leave out nothing of what he had heard and to make no false statements in them."[69] As Bauckham observes, while such language was common stock in ancient historiography,[70] it was also a claim sometimes made by translators who wished to affirm their faithfulness to an original.[71] This may suggest a translation philosophy which keeps the original sense in mind but makes it accessible through paraphrase, which would preserve the *ipsissima vox* of the original. On the other hand, Mark's role, according to Papias, may have tended toward the more literal side of the spectrum since he identifies Mark

---

64. Origen, as noted in *HE* 6.25.5; Hippolytus on 1 Peter 5:13.

65. Jerome, *Comm. in Matt. Prooemium* 6; Epiphanius, *Panarion* 51.6.10 (Epiphanius, *The Panarion of Epiphanius of Salamis* [Leiden: Brill, 1994], 2.31).

66. Eusebius, *HE* 3.39.4, 15.

67. So Bauckham: "So we may see Papias's Prologue as claiming that he followed the best practice of historians: he made careful inquiries, collected the testimonies of eyewitnesses, set them down in a series of notes, and finally arranged his material artistically to form a work of literature. His preference for the testimony of eyewitnesses, obtained at second or third hand, is therefore that of the historian, for whom, if direct autopsy was not available (i.e., the historian himself was not present at the events), indirect autopsy was more or less essential" (*Jesus and the Eyewitnesses*, 27).

68. *HE* 3.39.15; Anti-Marcionite Prologue; Irenaeus, *Adv. Haer.* 3.1.2; Jerome, *Comm. in Matt., Prooemium* 6.

69. *HE* 3.39.15.

70. Cf. Lucian, *How to Write History* 47; Dionysus of Halicarnassus, *De Veterum Censura* 5.

71. Philo, *Mos.* 2.31–34; Josephus, *Ant.* 10.218; 1.17. So, too, Cornelius Nepos (Bauckham, *Jesus and the Eyewitnesses*, 208–9).

as Peter's "interpreter." Contrast Cicero's description of his role as translator of great orators:

> I translated the most famous orations of the two most eloquent Attic orators, Aeschines and Demosthenes, orations which they delivered against each other. And I did not translate them as an interpreter [*interpres*], but as an orator, keeping the same ideas and forms, or as one might say, the 'figures' of thought, but in language which conforms to our usage. And in so doing, I did not hold it necessary to render word for word, but I preserved the general style and force of the language. (*On the Best Kind of Orators* 5.14)

An interpreter sticks closer to the source than does an orator. The interpreter's primary concern is faithfulness to the source, though adaptation to the receptor is necessary for understanding. On the other hand, the orator always holds in mind the particular turns of the audience. Cicero remarks that his translations, while remaining faithful to ideas, do not hold to each word. His concern is to reproduce a rhetorical effect. We need not assume, however, that Mark was simply a slavish translator. The point made in Papias's quotation is that, in this process, he was faithful as an interpreter. His approach was like that of one dealing with a sacred text (Philo, *Mos.* 2.31, 34).[72] He did not play loose with his source. Once again, the Papias account brings us to the heart of ancient discussions about historiography and its connection to the events reported.

Papias includes a curious note that Mark "wrote accurately all that he remembered [ὅσα ἐμνημόνευσεν; so Justin Martyr, *Dialogue with Trypho* 106.3], not, indeed, in order [οὐ μέντοι τάξει], of the things said or done by the Lord" (*HE* 3.39.15). As mentioned previously, the antecedent of "he" in this case is Mark, who recalled and recorded that which Peter once preached. The observation that Mark lacked "order" is odd, considering that this was a trait which characterized notes or drafts instead of final compositions. Compare Papias's comment to Aulus Gellius's reflection on his own compositional practices:

> But in the arrangement of my material I have adopted the same haphazard order that I had previously followed in collecting it. For whenever I had taken in hand any Greek or Latin book, or had heard anything worth remembering, I used to jot down whatever took my fancy, of any and every kind, without any definite plan or order; and such notes I would lay away as an aid to my memory, like a kind of literary storehouse, so that when the need arose of a word or a subject which I chanced for the moment to have forgotten, and the

---

72. "Reflecting how great an undertaking it was to make a full version of the laws given by the Voice of God, where they could not add or take away or transfer anything, but must keep the original form and shape, they proceeded to look for the most open and unoccupied spot in the neighbourhood outside the city." (2.34)

books from which I had taken it were not at hand, I could readily find and produce it. (*Attic Nights*, Preface 2)⁷³

The piece composed by Gellius was not a final composition but rather notes which, in this case, aided memory when the sources were not at hand. Plutarch likewise commented on his method in composing *Table Talk*, stating, "The conversations which follow have been written in a haphazard manner, not systematically but as each came to mind" (*Moralia* 629D). Plutarch wrote these conversations down as pieces of them "came to mind" (εἰς μνήμην ἦλθεν), but the written product was hardly an orderly account. So, too, Pliny the Younger relates how Septicius Clarus urged him to publish his letters.⁷⁴ Pliny responded to the request and explained, "I have now made a collection, not keeping to the original order as I was not writing history, but taking them as they came to my hand" (*Letters* 1.1).

"Order," on the other hand, marked the final stage of a history. Lucian said that in writing history one would gather memoranda (ὑπομνημά), then impose order in the final production: "When he has collected all or most of the facts let him first make them into a series of notes [ὑπομνημά], a body of material as yet with no beauty or continuity. Then, after arranging them into order [τάξιν], let him give it beauty and enhance it with the charms of expression, figure, and rhythm."⁷⁵ Mark, then, appears to have composed something short of a full history. Instead, he collected the *chreia* of Peter, which were the sayings and doings of the Lord. Eusebius records this observation saying: ὅς πρὸς τὰς χρείας ἐποιεῖτο τὰς διδασκαλίας (*HE* 3.39.15). Instead of translating the passage "who [Peter] used to give teaching as necessity demanded" we best understand *chreia* in the rhetorical sense of an anecdote. Aelius Theon says, "A chreia (*khreia*) is a brief saying or action making a point, attributed to some specified person or something corresponding to a person, a maxim (*gnômê*) and reminiscence (*apomnêmoneuma*) are connected with it. Every brief maxim attributed to a person creates a chreia" (*Progymnasmata* 3 [96]).⁷⁶ A *chreia* could be either a saying, a recorded action,

---

73. He goes on to say, "It therefore follows, that in these notes there is the same variety of subject that there was in those former brief jottings which I had made without order or arrangement, as the fruit of instruction or reading in various lines" (2). See Small's comment on these texts (*Wax Tablets of the Mind*, 179–80).

74. Cf. Clement of Alexandria, *HE* 6.14.6-7, regarding the way Mark was urged to write what he recalled from Peter's preaching.

75. Lucian, *How to Write History* 48; cf. Quintilian 10.6.1–2; Porphyry, *Life of Plotinus* 8; Luke 1:3.

76. George A. Kennedy, ed., *Progymnasmata: Greek Textbooks of Prose Composition and Rhetoric* (Atlanta: SBL, 2003), 15. Or, "a saying or act that is well-aimed or apt, expressed concisely, attributed to a person, and regarded as useful for living" (Ronald F. Hock and Edward N. O'Neil, eds., *The Chreia in Ancient Rhetoric: The Progymnasmata* [Atlanta: Scholars, 1986], 26). See also Ronald F. Hock and Edward N. O'Neil, eds., *The Chreia in Ancient Rhetoric: Classroom Exercises* (Atlanta: SBL, 2002); Vernon K. Robbins, "The Chreia," in *Greco-Roman Literature and the New Testament: Selected Forms and Genres*, ed. David E. Aune (Atlanta: Scholars, 1988), 1–23; Mary Ann Beavis, *Mark's Audience: The Literary and Social Setting of Mark 4:11–12* (Sheffield: Sheffield Academic, 1989), 25–31. For a full discussion of this point in relation to Mark, see Bauckham, *Jesus and the Eyewitnesses*, 214–17.

or a combination of the two. Working with them was part of the elementary education for children who read, copied, memorized, and manipulated them.[77]

The Papias quotation says that Peter "gave teaching in *chreia*" and that Mark remembered (ἀπεμνημόνευσεν) and recorded these. Mark's composition reflects the anecdotal nature of Peter's preaching and accounts for the somewhat staccato effect of Mark's Gospel. The *chreia* which Peter related were not themselves placed in formal order ("But not making, as it were, an arrangement [σύνταξιν] of the Lord's oracles") and Mark, when writing what he remembered, did not impose upon them the type of formal order one would normally expect in a history or biography. Papias contrasts Mark's final composition with that of Matthew which did indeed reflect the type of order expected of a final composition.[78]

The external evidence we possess from Papias, Justin Martyr, and other ancient authors all points in the same direction: Mark preserved Peter's preaching in his Gospel. The way Papias refers to the process of composition includes the historiographic marks which signal that his account, derived from John the Presbyter, is indeed credible. The contact with eyewitnesses, the emphasis on memory or memoirs, the question of order, and the concern for not making false statements all point to a history related by a reliable witness. There are no undefeated defeaters in Papias's account which call into question the veracity of this testimony. Moreover, what we hear from Papias finds confirmation in Justin Martyr and in other sources, although we cannot have complete certainty regarding the way earlier testimony may have influenced later identification of Mark's Gospel with Peter. There are sufficient differences between the later accounts and Papias to suggest that Papias's and Justin Martyr's records were not the only accounts of this association which circulated in the church. The *vox Petri*, therefore, lay behind Mark's composition. Peter's theology dominates this Gospel. Although the one who bears witness shapes the testimony, the quotation from Papias indicates that Mark took care to stay as close as possible to what Peter said, even given the process of translation. He acted as an interpreter, not a rhetor. We cannot affirm categorically that no other sources made their contribution to Mark's composition. At best we can state that the bulk of Mark's account comes from Peter, although we have no means of teasing-out what or where other influences might appear.

In Mark, we have, first, the testimony of Peter about Jesus, which Papias's account refers to as the *chreia* (τὰς χρείας) and the "Lord's oracles" (τῶν κυριακῶν ... λογίων). Second, according to Papias and the other accounts, Mark bears witness to that which Peter taught. His testimony regarding Peter is credible as one who has followed Peter and who acted as his interpreter and the person who, at the behest of others, wrote the memoirs of Peter, though not in order. The lack of final order is part of the claim

---

77. Beavis, *Mark's Audience*, 26. See also Hock and O'Neil, *The Chreia in Ancient Rhetoric: Classroom Exercises*.

78. *HE* 3.39.16: Ματθαῖος μὲν οὖν Ἑβραΐδι διαλέκτῳ τὰ λόγια συνετάξατο; "Matthew arranged his oracles in the Hebrew dialect" (my translation).

that Mark was a careful translator and witness in that he did not alter what came to him since Peter's message itself exhibited a similar lack of order. Mark was careful "to leave out nothing of what he had heard and to make no false statements in them." Mark allowed the *vox Petri* to be heard. We may not be able to verify every piece of the testimony preserved in Mark, but such is the nature of testimony. The witness has the necessary competence and credibility, whether we are talking about Peter's witness regarding Jesus or Mark's testimony regarding Peter. In sum, there are no undefeated defeaters. There is a reliable connection to the events, and there are adequate positive epistemic reasons to accept this testimonial knowledge.

Contemporary Perspectives on Petrine Testimony in Mark

The internal evidence supports the conclusion that Peter indeed stands behind the Gospel of Mark. C. H. Turner has argued that the Gospel of Mark appears to have been originally a story told from the point-of-view of an eyewitness. But, upon recording the story, the narrative was altered from "we" to "they" in those passages which focus upon the movements of Jesus with his disciples and in those which move from a generic plural to a reference to Jesus in the singular. This feature is characteristic of Mark but not the other Synoptics. Turner presents the evidences such as: "1:21 'they enter Capernaum; and at once he taught on the sabbath in the synagogue'; 5:38 'they come to Jairus's house; and he sees the tumult'; 9:33 'and they came to Capernaum: and when he was in the house, he asked them'"[79] (also, for example, 10:32; 11:12, 27; 14:32).[80] Turner observes that we can even 'back-translate' to the original in one case and smooth out a curiously awkward part of the narrative:

> [In] 1:29, 'they left the synagogue and came into the house of Simon and Andrew with James and John,' the hypothesis that the third person plural of Mark represents a first person plural of Peter makes what as it stands is a curiously awkward phrase into a phrase which is quite easy and coherent. 'We left the synagogue and came into our house with our fellow-disciples James and John. My mother-in-law was in bed with fever, and he is told about her.' . . . So, too, 1:16, 'He saw me and Andrew my brother.'[81]

Turner concludes that "Mark's story is told as from a disciple and companion, while Matthew and Luke are less directly interested in that particular point of view."[82]

---

79. C. H. Turner, "The Gospel According to St. Mark," in *A New Commentary on Holy Scripture*, ed. Charles Gore, et al. (London: SPCK, 1937), 48.

80. For the complete details, see C. H. Turner, "Marcan Usage: Notes, Critical and Exegetical, on the Second Gospel," *JTS* 26 (1925) 225–40; Bauckham, *Jesus and the Eyewitnesses*, 181–82.

81. Turner, "Marcan Usage," 226; Turner, "The Gospel According to St. Mark," 48.

82. Turner, "Marcan Usage," 226. See also Turner, "The Gospel According to St. Mark." Taylor follows Turner but concludes, "In very many of these cases the suggestion is attractive and cogent, but in each case it is the content of the story rather than the construction itself which supports it. . . . But it would be fair to claim that these usages suggest that Mark stands nearer to primitive testimony

However, Bauckham sails a different tack here, stating that "what Turner actually observed was a subtlety of Mark's narrative skill that makes Peter the focalizing character for much of the Gospel story. It does not mean that we virtually hear Peter's words in these passages, as Turner tended to think, but it is part of the evidence that Mark has carefully and deliberately written a Petrine Gospel."[83] Mark indeed focalizes Peter, but since testimony includes both text and interpretation, the phenomenon that both Turner and Bauckham observe is likely about Mark's source as well as his unique presentation from his source. Bauckham sails hard by this conclusion, saying, "Mark's Gospel is no mere transcript of Peter's teaching, nor is the Petrine perspective merely an undersigned survival of the way Peter told his stories. While it does correspond to features of Peter's oral narration, Mark has deliberately designed the Gospel in such a way that it incorporates and conveys this Petrine perspective."[84] To state this another way, in Mark's Gospel we hear the *vox Petri*.

Bauckham sets his main heading to the way Mark opens and closes his Gospel with a story about Peter that forms an *inclusio* around the whole narrative (1:16–18; 16:7) and suggests that "Peter is the witness whose testimony includes the whole."[85] Indeed, the prominent position Peter has at the beginning and end of the narrative is complemented by the greater frequency with which his name appears in Mark than the other Synoptics.[86] This kind of *inclusio* is a characteristic of eyewitness testimony, such as that found in *Alexander* by Lucian, which appears to be composed with reference to Rutilianus's eyewitness account. Rutilianus enters at the beginning and end of this account (4, 60), and he is mentioned throughout with more frequency than any other character, save Alexander.[87] Similarly, in Porphyry's *Life of Plotinus*, Amelius appears as the dominant character besides Plotinus. The narratives which include him stand at the start and finish of the work, forming an *inclusio* (1, 21–22).[88] Traces of Peter's eyewitness testimony—such as the first- to third-person plural shifts, the *inclusio* of the narratives which highlight Peter, and the prominence of Peter's name—all suggest that Mark was composed as an account drawn from Peter's proclamation, just as Papias, Justin Martyr, and other ancient authors state. Mark appears to be founded

---

than Matthew or Luke" (*Gospel According to Mark*, 47–48). T. W. Manson runs Turner's evidence and comes to a similar, yet somewhat more cautious conclusion regarding the role of Peter in the composition of Mark: "Petrine reminiscence is part of the foundation, perhaps the main part; but other sources have made their contribution" (*Studies in the Gospels and Epistles*, ed. Matthew Black [Manchester: Manchester University Press, 1962], 45). Bauckham uses Turner's argument as a foundation for his argument that Mark reflects a Petrine perspective (*Jesus and the Eyewitnesses*, 155–82).

83. Bauckham, *Jesus and the Eyewitnesses,* 546; cf. 164–66, 546–47. Some, including the present author, have erroneously concluded that Bauckham endorsed Turner's conclusion.

84. Bauckham, *Jesus and the Eyewitnesses*, 179, 547 (repeated for emphasis).

85. Bauckham, *Jesus and the Eyewitnesses*, 125.

86. Taylor, *Gospel According to Mark*, 168; Robert A. Guelich, *Mark 1–8:26* (Dallas: Word, 1989), 50; Bauckham, *Jesus and the Eyewitnesses*, 125, 148–49.

87. Bauckham, *Jesus and the Eyewitnesses*, 150.

88. Bauckham, *Jesus and the Eyewitnesses*, 151–54, 512.

upon Peter's testimony and we would therefore expect that Peter's point of view takes precedence in this Gospel.

In the second edition of *Jesus and the Eyewitnesses*, Bauckham strengthens his argument that "Peter was the principle eyewitness source of Mark's Gospel"[89] by observing that "Peter is the most frequently named character in Gospel" and that he is "both the first disciple of Jesus to be named in Mark's Gospel and also the last."[90] He underscores his contention by an appeal to the Gospel's literary genre, a *bios* "written within living memory of the subject" that attaches great importance to eyewitness testimony.[91] In addition to the *inclusio* mentioned above, Bauckham stresses the importance of seeing the principle eyewitness at the very beginning of the *bios*, as is the case in Mark.[92]

After responding to critics regarding the importance of the Petrine *inclusio* in Mark, Bauckham adds that implicit eyewitness testimony is characteristic of ancient *bioi*, citing examples from Plutarch's *Life of Caesar* and *Life of Pompey* as well as Josephus's *Jewish War*. Using implicit eyewitnesses "was a way of indicating the eyewitness sources of important events that the authors themselves could not claim to have witnessed, in a manner that did not disrupt the narrative flow of their stories."[93] In the case of Mark, the female disciples Mary Magdalene and Mary the mother of James the Little, Joses, and Salome play such a role (Mark 15:40–41, 47; 16:1, 4–7). "That Mark portrays the women as eyewitnesses is not only significant in its own right," Bauckham argues. "It is also an important confirmation of my claim that he portrays Peter as his principal eyewitness. It is precisely because Peter drops out of the narrative after chapter 14 that the women are needed as eyewitnesses in the rest of Mark's narrative."[94] Bauckham's contribution is double-edged as it points not only to Peter as the principle eyewitness behind this Gospel but also elevates the way women take principle roles in gospel history and testimony.

The validity of a witness may be undermined if the person proves to be unreliable when it comes to those points within the testimony which can be verified. While we have warrant to accept the ancient testimony that Mark is Peter's testimony about Jesus, if we can show that Mark's record is unreliable, we may question whether we are dealing with valid testimony. This is not to retreat to a minimalist approach, which argues that we can only accept that which can be independently verified. Rather, what is at question is the general credibility of the one who gives testimony. As Catherine Elgin states:

---

89. Bauckham, *Jesus and the Eyewitnesses*, 509. See chapter 19, "Eyewitnesses in Mark (Revisited)."
90. Bauckham, *Jesus and the Eyewitnesses*, 510.
91. Bauckham, *Jesus and the Eyewitnesses*, 510.
92. Bauckham, *Jesus and the Eyewitnesses*, 512.
93. Bauckham, *Jesus and the Eyewitnesses*, 534.
94. Bauckham, *Jesus and the Eyewitnesses*, 524, 520–23.

We assess testimony in light of a variety of factors that bear on its warrant.... To make effective use of testimony requires that we be neither too gullible nor too skeptical. We should neither accept nor reject every offering. Rather, we need to consider whether the information attested to meshes with our other cognitive commitments to yield a system that, as a whole, is reasonable in light of what we already had reason to believe. This requires that we attune ourselves not just to the bald statement of fact but also to the speaker, the context, and the institutions that underwrite it.[95]

Is Mark a Credible Witness?

A further question is whether Mark is truly the author of the Gospel. Niederwimmer, for example, argues that the author, far from being of Palestinian origin, was really a Gentile Christian since, for example, he is not familiar with Palestinian geography.[96] Niederwimmer states that a Palestinian would not need to call the Gentile woman in Mark 7:26 a "Syrophoenician" but simply a "Phoenician." However, Mark was writing from Rome, for a Roman audience presumably, and they would indeed need the differentiation of this region from the more well-known Libophoenicia in North Africa.[97] Niederwimmer also argues that Mark's explanations of Jewish customs (as in 7:3) betrays the hand of an author who is not Jewish,[98] but such explanatory notes should also be read in light of the audience's lack of familiarity with Jewish customs—a position wholly in accord with the assumption that the original readers were located in Rome.

On the positive side of the ledger, Mark is replete with Semitic words which points strongly in the direction of an author familiar with Aramaic and who has indeed engaged in translation. As Hengel has observed, "I do not know any other work in Greek which has as many Aramaic or Hebrew words and formulae in so narrow a space as does the second Gospel. They are too numerous and too exact to be explained as the conventional barbarisms... of the miracle worker and magician."[99] The attempts to discredit the Markan testimony have not been wholly successful.[100] Mark stands as a credible witness to Peter's proclamation as one who both heard and translated his proclamation, and who was his disciple.[101] Whatever "image" Mark gives of Peter

95. Elgin, "Take It From Me," 307.

96. Niederwimmer, "Johannes Markus und die Frage nach dem Verfasser des zweiten Evangeliums," 178–83.

97. See Hengel, *Studies in the Gospel of Mark*, 29, 137–38n164.

98. Niederwimmer, "Johannes Markus und die Frage nach dem Verfasser des zweiten Evangeliums," 183–85.

99. Hengel, *Studies in the Gospel of Mark*, 46 (see esp. 1–58). More recently, Maurice Casey has argued that the Gospel is a translation from Aramaic (*Aramaic Sources of Mark's Gospel* [Cambridge University Press, 1998]).

100. For a good review of the arguments regarding authorship, see Gundry, *Mark*, 1026–45.

101. Hengel, *Saint Peter*, 36–48.

comes from one who was on the inside and stood in a position to interpret and present the teaching of the apostle. Testimony is always an interpreted account of events which conveys "the fact and meaning of singular events of absolute significance."[102]

Mark's Gospel, according to ancient witness, represents the testimony of Peter regarding Christ. This Gospel may have been the foundation for the Synoptic tradition along with Q, although this is hardly a settled matter. If Mark was one of the sources used by Matthew and Luke, and at least known by John,[103] then the gospel story handed down to us finds its roots in the preaching of Peter as translated by Mark. The other Gospel honored Mark's composition by using it, although it was not a finished literary composition but rather a collection of Peter's *chreia* regarding Christ. They engaged in *imitatio*, the type of literary borrowing which was done with great pieces of literature such as the works of Homer and which showed honor to the source as it adopted and adapted the material to a new end.[104] Why Matthew and Luke would have used a document which was not a finished piece and hardly deemed a high literary masterpiece may be answered with reference to Peter's role in Mark's composition. The borrowing may have more to do with Peter as Mark's source than Mark as a fine and finished piece of literature. Hengel explores this issue from the angle of the church's preservation of Mark even when it had the other Synoptics at hand: "The best explanation of the fact that the Second Gospel lived on in the church, although Matthew had taken over about 90 percent of the material in it, is that the work of Mark was from the beginning bound up with the authority of the name of Peter."[105] For now, however, our interest is the way Mark preserves the core of Peter's teaching and is therefore a source that may be used in the exploration of Peter's theology.[106] The role Peter and the Gospel of Mark played in the development of the Christian story and theology is a matter we will examine later.[107]

---

102. Vanhoozer, *First Theology*, 269.

103. See Bauckham, *The Gospels for All Christians*, 147–71. For the history of the question, see D. Moody Smith, *John Among the Gospels: The Relationship in Twentieth-Century Research* (Columbia, SC: University of South Carolina Press, 2001).

104. See, for example, Dionysius of Halicarnassus, *Pompey* 3.1–14; R. A. Derrenbacker Jr., *Ancient Compositional Practices and the Synoptic Problem* (Leuven: Leuven University Press; Dudley, MA: Peeters, 2005).

105. Hengel, *Studies in the Gospel of Mark*, 52. As I write this, the sad news has just come that Martin Hengel, our beloved professor from Tübingen, passed away on July 2, 2009, at the age of 82. We will greatly miss his voice and wisdom.

106. While being more cautious in her assessment of Peter's role in Mark's composition, Bond states, "If there is a connection between Mark and Peter, as I have argued, it is tempting to speculate whether some of Mark's theology also goes back to Peter. Quite possibly it does" (Bond, "Was Peter behind Mark's Gospel," 61). Tempting, indeed.

107. See chapters 3 and 4.

VOX PETRI
The Testimony of Peter and the Acts of the Apostles
Speeches in Ancient Historiography

A considerable portion of Acts of the Apostles consists of speeches. This second volume of Luke/Acts contains twenty-four or more speeches,[108] depending on what forms of direct address we classify as a speech.[109] These occupy close to three hundred of the one thousand verses in this book. The first twelve chapters of Acts dedicate a large portion of the narrative to the addresses and acts of Peter. Peter also makes an appearance at the Jerusalem Council (15:7–11). His presentation at that meeting is the final of eight speeches in Acts ascribed to Peter (1:15–22; 2:14–36 [with the Eleven], 38–40; 3:11–26; 4:8–12, 19–20 [with John]; 5:29–32 [with the other apostles]; 10:27–29, 34–43, 47; 11:4–17; 15:7–11). The history of the early church as recorded by Luke, whom the Fathers named as the author of Luke/Acts, is distinct from contemporary histories that tend not to include speeches as part of the historical narrative. Luke embraced the historiographic conventions of his day. Ancient historians commonly inserted lengthy speeches into their histories since these served to explicate the events which were selected and arranged in the history. Indeed, as Gempf notes, "Conventional Greek historiography regarded history as a matter of both πράξεις καὶ λόγοι [deeds and words]."[110] Polybius comments that the public speeches and discourses "sum up events and hold the whole history together" (12.25a.3). The speeches were part of the history and one of the means by which history itself moved forward.[111]

---

108. While Martin Dibelius would count twenty-four (*Studies in the Acts of the Apostles* [London: SCM, 1956], 138), as does Joseph Fitzmyer (*The Acts of the Apostles* [New York: Doubleday, 1998], 104), Marion Soards puts the number at twenty-seven or twenty-eight, also noting that there are seven or more "partial speeches" and three dialogues (*The Speeches in Acts: Their Content, Context, and Concerns* [Louisville: Westminster John Knox, 1994], 1).

109. Scholars are not fully agreed regarding what should count as a speech and, consequently, how many speeches appear in Acts (Soards, *The Speeches in Acts*, 18–22). The words spoken to the lame man (3:4, 6), the deliberations in the Sanhedrin (4:16–17), or Peter's dialogue with Ananias and Sapphira (5:3–4, 8–9) should not be considered speeches. Soards provides a useful definition: "A speech is a deliberately formulated address made to a group of listeners" (*The Speeches in Acts*, 20). This is not unlike the definition proposed by Fitzmyer, who would include addresses to individuals ("an address directed to a group or an individual in a nonprivate setting, usually involving the attention of a number of people" [*The Acts of the Apostles*, 103]). The list here provided includes the verses which identify the speaker and also names those whom the author indicates were with Peter when he spoke. I have not included the apostolic prayer (4:23–30) or the address of the Twelve which guided the choice of the seven who were in charge of food distribution (6:2–4), even though these were public pronouncements where Peter was present and may have been the protagonist.

110. Gempf, "Public Speaking and Published Accounts," in *The Book of Acts in Its Ancient Literary Setting*, ed. Bruce W. Winter and Andrew D. Clarke (Grand Rapids: Eerdmans; Carlisle: Paternoster, 1993), 264.

111. Gempf even argues that the speeches are "events in their own right" ("Public Speaking and Published Accounts," 261). While Gempf underscores the essential nature of speeches with this comment, his remark blurs the distinctive role of speeches and events in ancient historiography.

Writers of history sought not only to display the facts but also the causes of events and the reasons for either the failure or success of the recorded acts and words. Polybius regards interpretation as an essential function of the historian—the one who writes history but does not move on to interpret it is someone who betrays the craft. In his extended assault on the practices of the historian Timaeus, Polybius advocates for interpretation:

> The peculiar function of history is to discover, in the first place, the words actually spoken, whatever they were, and next, to ascertain the reason why what was done or spoken led to failure or success. For the mere statement of a fact may interest us but is of no benefit to us: but when we add the cause of it, study of history becomes fruitful.... But a writer who passes over in silence the speeches made and the causes of events and in their place introduces false rhetorical exercises and discursive speeches, destroys the peculiar virtue of history (12.25b.1–4).

The speeches are a principal vehicle within the text for interpreting the historical narrative and, therefore, become particularly important for studying the theology of Acts. Cadbury underscores this point, saying, "Like the choral passages in the Greek drama, they explain to the reader the meaning of the events. It is the speeches which specially interest the theologically inclined, as the majority of attentive readers of Acts have usually been."[112] While we must unpack the speeches to reveal the theology preserved in Acts, opening this box requires going through layers of packaging.

While the speeches are replete with theology, the question is whether the theology reflected in them is that of Peter or the author of Acts. Are these addresses free inventions of the author, or do they, in some way, reflect what was actually spoken by the apostle on these or perhaps other occasions?[113] What principles of ancient historiography guided the author in his use of sources (if indeed he used any) and the presentation of the content of speeches?

---

112. Cadbury, "The Speeches in Acts," in *The Beginnings of Christianity*, ed. F. J. Foakes Jackson and Kirsopp Lake (Grand Rapids: Baker, 1979), 402. Cogan remarks that "Thucydides believed that an understanding of the Peloponnesian War required the exhibition of the public statements of policy or of the rationales for policy" and "that political addresses can provide for the perception of motivations behind and meanings attributed to the events as they occurred" (*The Human Thing: The Speeches and Principles of Thucydides's History* [Chicago: University of Chicago Press, 1981], 3). See Henry R. Immerwahr, "Pathology of Power and the Speeches in Thucydides," in *The Speeches in Thucydides*, ed. Philip A. Stadter (Chapel Hill: University of North Carolina Press, 1972), 16; Hans-Peter Stahl, "Speeches and Course of Events in Books Six and Seven of Thucydides," in *The Speeches in Thucydides*, ed. Philip A. Stadter (Chapel Hill: University of North Carolina Press, 1972), 61–62; Colin W. Macleod, *Collected Essays* (Oxford: Clarendon, 1983), 69.

113. For a summary of research on the speeches in Acts, see Osvaldo Padilla, *The Speeches of Outsiders in Acts: Poetics, Theology and Historiography* (Cambridge: Cambridge University Press, 2008), 16–41.

Martin Dibelius's well-known 1949 essay on "The Speeches in Acts and Ancient Historiography"[114] argues the case that "in the last analysis, however, he [the author of Acts] is not an historian but a preacher; we must not allow our attempts to prove the authenticity of the speeches to cloud our perception of their kerygmatic nature."[115] The content of the speeches, according to Dibelius, is testimony to the creative artifice of the book's author, and we should not seek the treasure of a historical core which served as their foundation. Schweizer remarks on the general acceptance of this view saying, "Ever since Martin Dibelius's essay about this subject, it has been more and more widely recognized that the speeches are basically *compositions by the author of Acts* who, to be sure, utilized different kinds of material for particular passages."[116] The vigorous debate which ensued over whether the speeches are in any way historically authentic has led some, like Soards, to avoid the historical question altogether. His study on *The Speeches in Acts* eschews "questions of sources, methods of composition, and the issue of historicity" since it is his "firm *opinion* that such questions have been raised (correctly) without ever having been clearly answered, because given our resources it is finally impossible to produce definitive answers."[117] There is no way to know whether Luke is summarizing speeches or simply inventing them *ex nihilo*. Cadbury arrives at a similar conclusion: "Without more knowledge of the sources than is available to us in the case of Acts, it is impossible to know just how far this or any other ancient writer is writing his speeches 'out of his own head.'"[118]

The reasons for the skepticism of some and the agnosticism of others regarding the historicity of the speeches in Acts are rooted in the arguments forwarded by Dibelius and elaborated by others. The first question is whether ancient historians sought to discover and record what was actually spoken or their own rhetorical concerns guided their composition. Dibelius's position is that ancient historians did not feel compelled to reproduce speeches as they had been delivered. We may compare, for example, the versions of a speech Claudius delivered before the Roman Senate regarding the Gauls. One edition comes down to us in an inscription, while another was recorded by Tacitus.[119] Tacitus's rendition of the speech was highly modified due to stylistic considerations. Also, when Josephus reports speeches found in the Bible, he sees no need to follow the text before him. Moreover, speeches inserted more than once take

---

114. Dibelius, *Studies in the Acts of the Apostles*, 138–91.

115. Dibelius, *Studies in the Acts of the Apostles*, 183.

116. Eduard Schweizer, "Concerning the Speeches in Acts," in *Studies in Luke-Acts*, ed. Leander E. Keck and J. Louis Martyn (Nashville: Abingdon, 1966), 208. So Ernst Haenchen, *The Acts of the Apostles: A Commentary* (Philadelphia: Westminster, 1971), 35–37, 39–41, 104n1; Ulrich Wilckens, *Die Missionsreden der Apostelgeschichte: Form-und traditionsgeschichtliche Untersuchungen* (Neukirchen-Vluyn: Neukirchener, 1974).

117. Soards, *The Speeches in Acts*, 16n53.

118. Cadbury, "The Speeches in Acts," 405.

119. See William Stearns Davis, ed., *Rome and the West*, (Boston: Allyn and Bacon, 1913), 186–88; Tacitus, *Annals*, 10.24.

on a different character with each telling, such as the address by Herod regarding war against the Arabs (cf. *BJ* 1.373–79; *Ant.* 15.127–46).[120] Dibelius concludes that this "shows how little he feels bound by respect for the text."[121] The author's aims, and not those of the speaker, dominate in the historian's rendition of the speeches.

Thucydides provides another well-known talking point in this discussion. In his *History of the Peloponnesian War*, he remarks on the methodology employed in recording speeches:

> As to the speeches that were made by different men, either when they were about to begin the war or when they were already engaged therein, it has been difficult to recall with strict accuracy the words actually spoken, both for me as regards that which I myself heard, and for those who from various other sources have brought me reports. Therefore, the speeches are given in the language in which, as it seemed to me, the several speakers would express, on the subjects under consideration, the sentiments most befitting the occasion, though at the same time I have adhered as closely as possible to the general sense of what was actually said. (1.22.1)

According to Dibelius, Thucydides was the historian who "raised the speech to an artistic device of the highest order."[122] Dibelius takes note of Thucydides's admission that it was difficult to retain accurately (ἀκρίβεια) what was actually spoken, and therefore, he "allowed the speakers to express themselves in the way he thought individuals would have found it necessary to speak on the subject to be discussed."[123] At the same time, Thucydides claimed to have adhered to the "general sense" (ξύμπασα γνώμη) of what had been said, thus generating questions in his interpreters "concerning the relationship of subjective judgment and objective reproduction in the speeches."[124] Dibelius observes that since Thucydides is writing a contemporary history, he is indeed in a position to know something of the "objective basis" of the speeches, and "on this foundation he can now build up and elaborate the speeches as he considers necessary."[125] But even given this kernel, Dibelius questions whether Thucydides's speeches were faithful to the situation rather than the person to whom they were ascribed. Despite this pondering, he concludes that Thucydides's "chief concern is what is characteristic of the situation rather than what is characteristic of the persons."[126]

---

120. Cadbury likewise observes Josephus's habit, saying, "Where we can confront his *Antiquities* with their Old Testament source, [he] sometimes merely transforms into his own prosy platitudes the substance of the original passage, sometimes inserts in inappropriate scenes long diatribes of his own composing" ("The Speeches in Acts," 405).

121. Dibelius, *Studies in the Acts of the Apostles*, 139.
122. Dibelius, *Studies in the Acts of the Apostles*, 140.
123. Dibelius, *Studies in the Acts of the Apostles*, 141.
124. Dibelius, *Studies in the Acts of the Apostles*, 141.
125. Dibelius, *Studies in the Acts of the Apostles*, 142.
126. Dibelius, *Studies in the Acts of the Apostles*, 142.

While admitting that Thucydides's speeches may reflect some historical core, Dibelius also notes that subsequent historians departed from his expressed concern for the sources and placed more emphasis upon the "rhetorical arts." He remarks on the way Dionysius of Halicarnassus critiques Thucydides (*Pompeius* 3) and how Sallust interprets the events of his history through the speeches he inserts. For these, the crudeness of Thucydides's style was the trouble. In the end, Dibelius concludes, an ancient historian did not hold that his chief obligation was "that of establishing what speech was actually made; to him, it is rather that of introducing speeches into the structure in a way which will be relevant to his purpose."[127] Even if the content of a speech lay at hand, the historian was not obliged to use it since such historical scraps "will serve as an artistic device to help to achieve the author's aims."[128]

Does this historiographic tradition inform the work of the author of Acts? According to Dibelius, the speeches Luke records are not intended to present the various sides of a debate—the author has a point of view which he wishes to promote. "The author does not wish to be impartial," Dibelius remarks, "indeed he wants to plead his cause."[129] Luke is preaching and does not allow each side to present its position, unlike the way Sallust presented Caesar and Cato. In speeches such as that in Athens (Acts 17), Luke "is not concerned with portraying an event which happened once in history; . . . he is concerned with a typical exposition, which is in that sense historical, and perhaps was more real in his own day than in the apostle's time. He follows the great tradition of historical writing in antiquity in that he freely fixes the occasion of the speech and fashions its content himself."[130] The author's interest is in interpreting the events of the history according to his own perceptions, and given his purpose, we should not expect the speeches to be "authentic" in a contemporary sense. The main theme of the speeches is that of the book as a whole and not that of a particular historical situation portrayed in the narrative.[131] Therefore, we are not surprised to find common elements appearing in speeches of different actors on Luke's stage[132] as

127. Dibelius, *Studies in the Acts of the Apostles*, 144.
128. Dibelius, *Studies in the Acts of the Apostles*, 145.
129. Dibelius, *Studies in the Acts of the Apostles*, 151.
130. Dibelius, *Studies in the Acts of the Apostles*, 155.

131. Dibelius, *Studies in the Acts of the Apostles*, 174–75. So John T. Townsend, "The Speeches in Acts," AThR 42 (1960) 157–58; Cadbury, "The Speeches in Acts," 407; Hans Conzelmann, *Acts of the Apostles* (Philadelphia: Fortress, 1987), xliii.

132. Schweizer speaks of "*a far-reaching identity of structure*" in the speeches. He examines the speeches and identifies this general scheme: "(a) Direct address . . . (b) Appeal for attention . . . (c) Pointing out a misunderstanding among the audience . . . (d) Frequently the speech starts out with a quotation of Scripture . . . (e) The christological kerygma . . . (f) Scriptural proof proper . . . (g) For (g) the same holds as was said about (c), with the sole addition that this point is frequently treated in conjunction with the Christ-kerygma . . . (h) The proclamation of salvation appears everywhere, and . . . is connected with the call to repentance . . . (i) The focusing of the message upon the specific audience." He concludes that "*one and the same author* is decisively involved in the composition of all the speeches here investigated" and so "basically the Paul of Acts speaks exactly like Peter" ("Concerning the Speeches in Acts," 210–12). Conzelmann calls these "persistent elements" in the speeches (*Acts of*

well as a common style throughout.[133] Indeed, given the overarching concern of the author, some of the speeches simply do not fit with the historical narrative where they are located. Dibelius reiterates his point down to the very end: the author of Acts "is not an historian but a preacher."[134]

Dibelius moves a step further by disassociating Luke's practice in Acts from that in the Gospel. In the Gospel he needed to fit into an extant tradition and therefore did not take a creative hand to his sources. Cadbury reflects on the same question:

> Perhaps the strongest argument in favor of a genuine element in the speeches of Acts is the parallel case of the words of Jesus in Luke. In Acts we are dealing with a writer who, as the verbal likenesses to the gospels of Mark and Matthew make plain, in his former volume carried over short sayings of his actors and dialogue, if not long formal addresses, with very slight change from his written sources. May we not infer that he did the same thing with the words of Peter and Paul?[135]

As Dibelius, he notes that Luke may have used a different method in the Gospel than in Acts since he was "dealing with different kinds of material" which goes back to the early tradition.[136] Therefore Luke did not have the same creative freedom that he had in writing Acts. In Acts he is a historian writing literature, and since he was the first to attempt a Christian history, he was free to play the evangelist.[137]

Since the speeches in Acts include eight attributed to Peter, these might be a significant source for constructing a Petrine theology. However, the objections which Dibelius and others raise regarding their authenticity have turned many away from hearing them as a witness of Peter's thought. How could we discern whether the speeches reflect any historical core which may be attributed to Peter? Given the ancient historiographic practices regarding the way speeches were recorded, should we not expect the viewpoint expressed within them to be that of Luke rather than the speakers represented in the narrative? Indeed, the common elements in the speeches suggest that the voice is that of the author of Acts and not the actors in the narrative.

Not everyone, however, would agree that ancient historians played loose with their sources for their history and submersed them completely under their own rhetorical concerns. Witherington, for example, objects to the perspectives of Dibelius, Cadbury, and others by emphatically stating that "there was no *convention* that

---

the Apostles, xliii).

133. Conzelmann states, "Nevertheless, the speeches do not attempt to reflect the individual style of the speaker, but rather the substantial unity of early Christian (i.e., normative) preaching" (*Acts of the Apostles*, xliii).

134. Dibelius, *Studies in the Acts of the Apostles*, 184.

135. Cadbury, "The Speeches in Acts," 416.

136. Cadbury, "The Speeches in Acts," 416.

137. Dibelius, *Studies in the Acts of the Apostles*, 185.

ancient historians were free to create speeches."¹³⁸ Some, of course, did precisely this, and the practice was widespread or conventional enough to invite comment by those who chose to avoid this approach to writing history. Polybius, for example, rails on Timaeus and others whose creative powers eclipsed the historian's task: "But a writer who passes over in silence the speeches made and the causes of events and in their place introduces false rhetorical exercises and discursive speeches, destroys the peculiar virtue of history. And of this Timaeus especially is guilty, and we know that his work is full of blemishes of the kind" (12.25b.4). The audacity of Timaeus is that he "gives no report of what was actually spoken" (12.25a.5). Yet Timaeus was well-known and approved by many who put confidence in him (12.25c.1).¹³⁹ Josephus likewise invented speeches—this no one doubts since his rhetorical compositions placed in patriarchal mouths are not rooted in the soil of their supposed scriptural source. In the speeches recorded by Dionysius of Halicarnassus rhetorical concerns eclipsed the attention to historical fact. Hemer observes, "In Dionysius literary and rhetorical criteria are elevated above the historical conscience."¹⁴⁰ Creating speeches was a convention embraced by a number of ancient historians. But even if it were not a *conventional* or common practice, it was a practice. There can be no doubt that historians at times invented speeches. The questions are what kind of historical reporting was deemed appropriate and what model did Luke follow when he penned the speeches in Acts? Did Luke let his rhetorical and theological concerns eclipse any interest in historical faithfulness?

Deeds and Words in Ancient Historiography

As noted previously, history writing in the ancient world was a matter of recording both πράξεις καὶ λόγοι (deeds and words).¹⁴¹ Speeches were a part of the history, so discussion about the use of sources for speeches often parallels the reflection on how the historian recorded the events of history. All the utterances in a history, as Polybius noted, "sum up events and hold the whole history together" (12.25a.3). While the reflections on ancient historiography singled out the peculiar issues surrounding recording deeds and words, common principles applied to both. For example, Lucian

---

138. Ben Witherington, *The Acts of the Apostles: A Socio-Rhetorical Commentary* (Grand Rapids: Eerdmans, 1998), 40.

139. "Perhaps, therefore, some might wonder how, being such as I have proved him to be, he meets with such acceptance and credit from certain people. The reason of this is that, as throughout his whole work he is so lavish of fault-finding and abuse, they do not form their estimate of him from his own treatment of history and his own statements, but from the accusations he brings against others, for which kind of thing he seems to me to have possessed remarkable industry and a particular talent." Timaeus would make a stellar contemporary politician.

140. Colin J. Hemer, *The Book of Acts in the Setting of Hellenistic History* (Winona Lake, IN: Eisenbrauns, 1990), 77; George A. Kennedy, *New Testament Interpretation Through Rhetorical Criticism* (Chapel Hill: University of North Carolina Press, 1984), 114.

141. Gempf, "Public Speaking and Published Accounts," 264.

(*How to Write History*) will not abide those who cannot get the geographical details correct (26) or who have no knowledge of their subject matter (29). Such people "invent and manufacture whatever 'comes to the tip of an unlucky tongue'" (32). A true historian, however, will maintain a single loyalty: "This, as I have said, is the one thing peculiar to history, and only to Truth must sacrifice be made. When a man is going to write history, everything else he must ignore" (40). The historian should pay critical attention to sources as he ferrets out the reliable ones: "He should for preference be an eyewitness, but, if not, listen to those who tell the more impartial story, those whom one would suppose least likely to subtract from the facts or add to them out of favour or malice" (47). Involvement in the history, credible sources, and judicious evaluation of testimony are the bedrock of historiography for Lucian.

The historian should also attend to questions of arrangement and style, a consideration which Lucian places alongside his concern for faithful reporting of events (48) which will hand down "a true account of what happened" to posterity (42). In the same way, the historian should pay due attention to style in recording speeches while, at the same time, remaining faithful to the historical setting and persons: "If a person has to be introduced to make a speech, above all let his language suit his person and his subject [ἐοικότα τῷ προσώπῳ καὶ τῷ πράγματι], and next let these also be as clear [σαφέστατα] as possible. It is then, however, that you can play the orator and show your eloquence" (58). The requisite that speeches be "clear" [σαφέστατα] is not a statement about the need for eloquence or clarity of expression but rather that speeches should be certain or true.[142] Lucian's concern for truth in reporting the deeds of history here attaches to the speeches as well. He is also concerned for suitability (ἐοικότα) to the "person" and "subject," but what is suitable or likely for a speaker to say is not detached from what was spoken. Lucian's final note regarding speeches embraces rhetoric ("Then, however, you can play the orator and show your eloquence"), a concern for historians when chronicling the deeds of history as well (47).[143] According to Lucian, the historian should let the speech image the speaker—both in language and subject matter—and there should be historical certainty. But the historian should exhibit a rhetorical concern, letting his eloquence come through. These two emphases are not antithetical for Lucian any more than his concern for accurate recording of deeds, on the one hand, and arrangement and style, on the other, are in conflict. Quintilian likewise applauded the use of fine rhetoric in his comments on Livy's method while underscoring his faithfulness to both the setting of the speeches and their speakers (10.1.101).[144] Due to his own literary concerns, Quintilian does not explore this relationship between history and rhetoric in any depth.

---

142. See Homer, *Odyssey* 2.31; *Iliad* 4.440; *LSJ* 1586.

143. "When he has collected all or most of the facts let him first make them into a series of notes, a body of material as yet with not beauty or continuity. Then, after arranging them into order, let him give it beauty and enhance it with the charms of expression, figure, and rhythm." See also 51.

144. "Livy has wonderful charm and brilliant transparency in narrative, while in his set speeches

The double foci of historical faithfulness and rhetorical adaptation evolved from the well-discussed statement Thucydides made about speeches. In his *History of the Peloponnesian War*, he begins the methodological declaration by noting how he deals with the testimony which has come to him. He muses on the difficulty of accrediting every piece of testimony, yet his concern for faithfulness is the bedrock of his history: "Now the state of affairs in early times I have found to have been such as I have described, although it is difficult in such matters to credit any and every piece of testimony [τεκμηρίῳ]" (1.20.1). He reiterates this affirmation (1.21.1), elaborating that he has not given "greater credence to the accounts, on the one hand, which the poets have put into song, adorning and amplifying their theme, and, on the other, which the chroniclers have composed with a view rather of pleasing the ear than of telling the truth." His concern for the truth leads him to avoid those accounts in which rhetorical concerns overtake the history, whether the sources are poets or chroniclers occupied with the effect of their public recitations. Thucydides values accuracy and evidence (1.21.1). His reflection on recording speeches parallels his norms for recording the deeds of history. He states:

> As to the speeches that were made by different men, either when they were about to begin the war or when they were already engaged therein, it has been difficult to recall with strict accuracy the words actually spoken, both for me as regards that which I myself heard, and for those who from various other sources have brought me reports. Therefore the speeches are given in the language in which, as it seemed to me, the several speakers would express, on the subjects under consideration, the sentiments most befitting the occasion, though at the same time I have adhered as closely as possible to the general sense [τὰ δέοντα]¹¹⁶ of what was actually said [τῶν ἀληθῶς λεχθέντων] (1.22.1)

---

he is eloquent beyond description, so beautifully is everything adapted to the circumstances and the speakers. As for emotions, particularly the softer ones, the least I can say is that no historian has ever presented them more attractively."

145. Hornblower rejects the notion that τὰ δέοντα means simply that which seems appropriate (*A Commentary on Thucydides* [Oxford: Clarendon, 1991], 1:60); rather, Thucydides is trying to be accurate in reporting and not merely to present what was probably the case (see Thucydides 1.22.2). Macleod makes the case that τὰ δέοντα (as in Aristotle, *Poetics* 1450b5; *Rhetoric* 1355b10), are "those elements that a speech needs in order to present its case effectively." They are "in clear contrast to τῶν ἀληθῶς λεχθέντων. In fact, Thucydides has created rhetorically ideal equivalents to the actual wording while, as he says, sticking as closely as possible to the gist of it." But there is more to the "general sense" than simply the gist of the content, at least as Polybius understood Thucydides. Macleod, however, does have an important point: "This is not an idle game of the intellect. In the speeches Thucydides does what any artist and any historian must do: he refashions his subject in order to draw out its significance" (*Collected Essays*, 68–69). History is always text and interpretation. See also the careful discussions in John Wilson, "What Does Thucydides Claim for His Speeches?," *Phoenix* 36 (1982) 95–103; F. E. Adcock, *Thucydides and History* (Cambridge: Cambridge University Press, 1963), 27–34.

While impediments keep him from recording the *ipsissima verba*, he seeks to preserve the *ipsissima vox*. Immediately following his statement about the speeches, he lays out his approach to the deeds which he records:

> But as to the facts [ἔργα] of the occurrences of the war, I have thought it my duty to give them, not as ascertained from any chance informant nor as seemed to me probable, but only after investigating with the greatest possible accuracy each detail, in the case both of the events in which I myself participated and of those regarding which I got my information from others. And the endeavour to ascertain these facts was a laborious task, because those who were eye-witnesses of the several events did not give the same reports about the same things, but reports varying according to their championship of one side or the other, or according to their recollection. And it may well be that the absence of the fabulous [μυθῶδες] from my narrative will seem less pleasing to the ear, but whoever shall wish to have a clear view both of the events which have happened and of those which will some day, in all human probability, happen again in the same or a similar way—for these to adjudge my history profitable will be enough for me. And, indeed, it has been composed, not as a prize-essay to be heard for the moment, but as a possession for all time. (1.22.2–4)

As with the speeches, Thucydides claims to take care with his sources which report the deeds of history. He notes that he was able to witness some events, as he had heard some speeches, yet other events were reported to him, as was the case with the speeches. He knows there was inaccurate reporting, so he avoids recording the fabulous and will not allow the pleasure of hearing the narrative overshadow his historical concern. He is writing for posterity and not just for the moment. His critical capacity is fully engaged, and he will not allow either the rhetorical concerns of his sources or his audience to override his reporting.

So in reporting deeds (1.22.2–4) and in recording speeches (1.22.1) Thucydides demonstrates a deep commitment to what actually happened ("Only after investigating with the greatest possible accuracy each detail") and what was actually spoken ("I have adhered as closely as possible to the general sense of what was actually said [τῶν ἀληθῶς λεχθέντων]"). This was a difficult task given the problems of evaluating the sources, on the one hand, and of recording and memory, on the other. Yet he claims faithfulness to the deeds of the history just as he affirms his faithfulness to the speakers, the subject, and the occasion of the speeches as he adheres to the "general sense" (τὰ δέοντα) of what was "actually said." What he says of the deeds he says of the speeches. With the speeches, however, he must admit his creative hand ("Therefore the speeches are given in the language in which, as it seemed to me, the several speakers would express, on the subjects under consideration, the sentiments most befitting the occasion"), but even here he admits to faithfulness both to the person and the setting of the speech (as Lucian after him, who said, "Above all let his language suit his person and his subject"). He has testimony from his own memory and the reports of others regarding what was "actually said," and he is unwilling to betray this in order to give full vent to his own rhetorical artistry.

As noted above, Polybius follows a similar track. His standards for recording the deeds of history correspond to those applied in reporting speeches. He presents these two together within the same frame:

> A historical author should not try to thrill his readers by such exaggerated pictures, nor should he, like a tragic poet, try to imagine the probable utterances of his characters or reckon up all the consequences probably incidental to the occurrences with which he deals, but simply record what really happened and what really was said [τῶν δὲ πραχθέντων καὶ ῥηθέντων κατ' ἀλήθειαν], however commonplace. For the object of tragedy is not the same as that of history but quite the opposite. The tragic poet should thrill and charm his audience for the moment by the verisimilitude of the words he puts into his characters' mouths, but it is the task of the historian to instruct and convince for all time serious students by the truth of the facts and the speeches he narrates [διὰ τῶν ἀληθινῶν ἔργων καὶ λόγων], since in the one case it is the probable that takes precedence, even if it be untrue, the purpose being to create illusion in spectators, in the other it is the truth, the purpose being to confer benefit on learners. (2.56.10–12)

The same norms apply for recording both the deeds and the speeches of the history since both are essential to the historian's purpose of conferring "benefit on learners." Rhetorical concerns should not overtake the historian's task nor should mere imagination be his tool. Polybius appears to keep Thucydides's words in mind and is cautious about allowing probability to rule. Thucydides admitted to using "the language in which, as it seemed to me, the several speakers would express . . . the sentiments most befitting the occasion" (1.22.1), but Polybius throws in the cautionary note which will not permit the historian to run with the point without Thucydides's strong tether to "the general sense of what was actually said [τῶν ἀληθῶς λεχθέντων]."[146] We hear another loud echo from Thucydides in Polybius's history: "Nor is it the proper part of a historian to practice on his readers and make a display of his ability to them, but rather to find out by the most diligent inquiry and report to them what was actually said [<τὰ> κατ' ἀλήθειαν ῥηθέντα], and even of this only what was most vital and effectual" (36.1.7).

Polybius expresses special caution regarding the way the historian should not let his own rhetoric carry him away from the historical event. He critiques Timaeus for

---

146. Walbank interprets Polybius as saying that "in reporting a speech a historian must restrict himself to what was actually said, and indeed the most important part of that, but he may cast it in his own words, which may in fact be identical for different occasions. In short τὰ κατ' ἀλήθειαν ῥηθέντα does not mean 'the actual words spoken'; it means 'the sense of what was said,' indeed something very close to Thucydides's ἡ ξυμπᾶσα γνώμη τῶν ἀληθῶς λεχθέντων" (*Speeches in the Greek Historians* [Oxford: Blackwell, 1965], 8).

not writing "the words spoken nor the sense of what was really said" (12.25a.5). In this critique he allows for recording either the *ipsissima verba* or the *ipsissima vox*, but will give no place to mere rhetorical flourish. Timaeus has "made up his mind as to what ought to have been said, he recounts all these speeches and all else that follows upon events like a man in school of rhetoric attempting to speak on a given subject, and shows off his oratorical power, but gives no report of what was actually spoken [τῶν κατ' ἀλήθειαν εἰρημένους]" (12.25a.5). Whether the historian records events or speeches which interpret them, diligent inquiry is required. This, Polybius details, includes "the industrious study of memoirs and other documents and a comparison of their contents" (12.25e.1). He is diligent in working with sources and critical as he compares their content. The history will also cover certain terrain so the historian engages in "the survey of cities, places, rivers, lakes, and in general all the peculiar features of land and sea" (12.25e.1). Finally, Polybius remarks, the historian must take account of "political events" (12.25e.1). This is not enough, however, since one must obtain an understanding of the meaning of events and movements of history (12.25e.2–12.25g.4). The speeches, in particular, are part of the historian's arsenal to describe the movements and meaning within the history (12.25b.4). Polybius also makes a strong case for the historian's personal involvement in the history.

In his *On Thucydides*, Dionysius of Halicarnassus reflects on Thucydides's speeches, judging them from the standpoint of their rhetorical effect and suitability (e.g., 42, 44–46, 49, 51). While he quotes and acknowledges Thucydides's claim to adhere "as closely as possible to the general sense of what was actually said" (41), he questions whether Thucydides accomplished his mission. On the other hand, Dionysius observes his technique: "Thucydides assigns to both sides speeches such as each might naturally have made. They are suited to the characters of the speakers and relevant to the situation, and neither inadequate nor overdone" (36). Dionysius regards Thucydides's speeches as appropriate yet as creative compositions, representing what the various speakers "might naturally have made." While Dionysius does not discuss the question of the sources Thucydides employed, he makes critical historical judgments in his extensive evaluation of the speeches in the history.

In summary, the discussion regarding writing speeches in histories parallels ancient reflection on recording deeds. Sources should be consulted and used critically and, indeed, it is preferable for the historian to have been an eyewitness and earwitness of some aspects of the history he is writing. The historian must always keep in mind that he is writing for posterity and should not attempt to flatter those of his own time. The concern for posterity will also keep him from sacrificing truth upon the altar of rhetorical flourish. What the various speakers said in the history cannot be reported exactly according to Thucydides, although Polybius raises this as a possibility more so than his predecessor. In any case, the historian should adhere "as closely as possible to the general sense [τὰ δέοντα] of what was actually said [τῶν ἀληθῶς λεχθέντων]" (Thucydides, *History of the Peloponnesian War* 1.22.1). Historians remembered and echoed Thucydides's interest in being faithful to the speaker's sense. Even Dionysius of Halicarnassus took careful note of his concern (*On Thucydides* 41), although he questioned whether Thucydides had indeed remained true to this affirmation. Polybius makes the strongest case against those, such as Timaeus, who would invent speeches. Such practice was out of line with the very nature of historical writing. On the other hand, the sources repeatedly sound the note from Thucydides that the speech should be suitable to the person making it and the setting in which it was given. Herein we observe a concession to the difficulty of recording the exact words voiced by the speaker on a particular occasion. The speech had to "fit" well given all the historian knew about the times and persons, preserving also the *ipsissima vox*. But we hear caution even here: suitability to both the person and setting are not fully adequate. As in the case of deeds, there must be some tether to what actually occurred, whether the event was spoken or acted out on the stage of history.

But at the same time, rhetorical concerns were very much in play. Even for Dionysius of Halicarnassus, the historical question he puts to Thucydides is whether the rhetoric of the speakers in the history was suited to the times when they spoke. The historian must also take into account his own audience; hence he must keep the form of his expression in mind. Given these concerns, we are not surprised to find a common voice throughout the various speeches. Indeed, this is precisely what we would expect of authors who are holding in tension historical faithfulness and the need for their history to speak to those of their day.[147] The historian must not only present facts but must also interpret them, and, in the first instance, this comes through his selection and arrangement of the material. The speeches play an important role here in that they are the vehicle that most particularly offers perspective on the deeds. The recognition that speeches had an essential place in the interpretation of history assists us in getting to the heart of the apparent tension between historical and rhetorical concerns. Walsh's comments on Livy and other historians are instructive and worth citing at length:

> But it is vital to remember here that Livy is an exponent of Isocratean theories of "rhetorical" history, in which historiography is regarded as "opus oratorium maxime." Further, the insertion of composed speeches, a convention as old as Herodotus, is ingrained in Roman history-writing. Just as Sallust composed the speeches of Caesar and Cato in his *Catiline* although the original versions were accessible for reproduction, just as Tacitus redrafted a speech of the emperor Claudius in a style markedly more elegant than the original, so Livy's speeches differ invariably in presentation (and occasionally in content) from the versions he read in his sources. But the purpose of these composed

---

147. So Gempf, who says, "In fact, the write-up of a speech in an ancient history *does call* for rhetorical skill simply because the author must, while being faithful to the main lines of the historical 'speech-event,' adapt the speech to make it 'speak to' a new audience in a different situation." He adds, "A recorded speech is not a transcript, but woe betide the historian if the speech is not *faithful* to the alleged situation and speaker" ("Public Speaking and Published Accounts," 264).

speeches is not an empty demonstration of rhetorical virtuosity; Livy attempts to "get inside" the speaker, and to present, through the words attributed to him, a psychological portrait of his qualities.[148]

In other words, instead of taking us *away* from a historical speaker and his concerns, the rhetorical art of the historian is intended to bring the reader *toward* the speaker by getting inside his perspectives. There is more to recording any aspect of history than chronicling events and citing words. The historian's task is one of interpretation; hence the rhetorical art is to bring the reader closer to the history. While a historian may take unwarranted liberties with this, as did Timaeus in Polybius's estimation, we should not assume that evidences of the author's rhetorical craft constitute proof of his unfaithfulness to the deeds or speeches of history. All history is interpreted history and thus will contain a subjective element.[149]

Petrine Speeches in Acts of the Apostles

The history Luke presents in Acts of the Apostles includes, as did all ancient histories, both πράξεις καὶ λόγοι (deeds and words). The question that occupies us here is whether Luke adhered to the conventions laid down by Thucydides, Polybius, and Lucian, who would not allow the rhetorical interests of the historian to eclipse the concern for what was "actually spoken." Or was Luke like Timaeus, who invented his speeches with little concern for investigation and sources and therefore, in the end, provided "no report of what was actually spoken"? As noted above, ancient historians tended to treat the question of πράξεις καὶ λόγοι (deeds and words) in similar ways.

---

148. Patrick G. Walsh, *Livy: His Historical Aims and Methods* (Cambridge: Cambridge University Press, 1961), 219–20. See Cogan, *The Human Thing*, 3–4, 121, 233–34; Macleod, *Collected Essays*, 68. Commenting on Herodotus's use of speeches in his histories, Paavo Hohti says, "According to Herodotus history consists of the actions of men. Speeches illustrate the influence of the individual and, by the same time, his responsibility." Herodotus was the first to integrate speeches into historiography. Hohti does not, however, discuss the question of authenticity: "Authentic or not, the speeches convey motivation for action—words and deeds have a natural relation" (*The Interrelation of Speeches and Action in the Histories of Herodotus* [Helsinki: Societas Scientiarum Fennica, 1976], 142).

149. So Stahl: "But we have learned that mere narration of any set of historical facts already implies a subjective element (because presentation includes judgment, evaluation, selection, arrangement, in short: interpretation)—to recognize, I say, the inherent subjective character of any historical narration at the same time allows us, in this field too, to rediscover and appreciate more fully the categories which Thucydides applied for selecting and presenting events" ("Speeches and Course of Events in Books Six and Seven of Thucydides," 61). The combined concern for history and rhetoric surfaces in Baker's use of a "narrative-identity model" for interpreting Acts. The focus is on social identity, memory, and narrative. Baker notes, "Group identity is grounded [in] its social memory and may include shared formative narratives, beliefs, and practices, and are often embodied in a prototypical ingroup member from the past.... As new situations emerge, the group may remember/reinterpret the prototypical ingroup member in a new light in order to address the new context" (Coleman A. Baker, *Identity, Memory, and Narrative in Early Christianity: Peter, Paul, and Recategorization in the Book of Acts* [Eugene, OR: Pickwick, 2011], 25). Baker's narrative-identity model drives toward the combination of the historical and rhetorical concerns evident in ancient historiography and the Book of Acts.

Speeches presented particular problems for the historian since there were no transcripts of what was actually said, although shorthand was not unknown (Quintilian 11.2.25). Moreover, the peculiar function of the speeches was to interpret the events of history. Nonetheless, reflection on the historian's task regarding recording speeches paralleled that of recording the deeds. Sources were sought and the historian evaluated the testimony handed down regarding both deeds and words before including it in the history. Eyewitnesses were valued as were earwitnesses, and the historian's own involvement as a witness to both the deeds and words was considered virtuous. According to best practices, the fabulous was to be shunned as the historian sought to avoid simply providing entertainment for his present audience but to write a work that would hold value for posterity. We may, therefore, rightly ask how Luke dealt with the πράξεις of this history as a key to understanding his approach to the λόγοι. What we discover about the former will provide insight into the latter.

Luke's own declarations in the prologues to Luke and Acts provide the first keys to his approach to historical writing. Luke summarizes the content of his first volume in his prologue to Acts: "In the first book, Theophilus, I wrote about all that Jesus did and taught [ποιεῖν τε καὶ διδάσκειν]" (1:1). In focusing upon the deeds and words of Jesus, the author recognized, as did other ancient historians, that historical writing must include both events and speeches. As his βίος of Jesus, Luke's second volume brought together both the events and speeches of early Christian history.[150] Luke also locates himself squarely within ancient historiographic traditions in his prologue to the first volume (Luke 1:1–4). As was common among ancient historians, he acknowledges that others have gone about the task of writing a similar history to the "historical account" (διήγησιν)[151] he is about to pen ("Many have undertaken to set down an orderly account [διήγησιν] of the events [πραγμάτων] that have been fulfilled among us"). By mentioning these other histories, Luke may imply that he referenced or used them as sources when constructing his own history. As Luke, Dionysius of Halicarnassus (*Roman Antiquities* 1.7.1–3) reveals the historical narratives he used, juxtaposing them

---

150. The declaration that the first volume was about what "Jesus began [ἤρξατο] to do and to teach" (NIV) may imply that the second volume contains the continuing deeds and speeches of Jesus (C. K. Barrett, *The Acts of the Apostles* (Edinburgh: T. & T. Clark, 1994), 1:66; Darrell L. Bock, *Acts* (Grand Rapids: Baker Academic, 2007), 52). While Jesus remains an active figure in Acts (e.g., Acts 9), he is not the principal actor or speaker in the narrative. Luke's expression may only mean that the narrative in these two volumes starts from the very beginning ("All that Jesus did and taught from the beginning," NRSV; so Conzelmann, *Acts of the Apostles*, 3; F. J. Foakes-Jackson and Kirsopp Lake, *The Acts of the Apostles: English Translation and Commentary* [Grand Rapids: Baker, 1920–33], 3; cf. Luke 1:3, ἄνωθεν, "from the beginning").

151. Lucian, *How to Write History* 55; Polybius 3.4.1; 3.38.4; 3.39.1; Diodorus Siculus 11.20.1; Dionysius of Halicarnassus, *Roman Antiquities* 1.7.4; 2 Macc 2:32; 6:17; François Bovon, *Luke 1: A Commentary on The Gospel of Luke 1:1–9:50* (Minneapolis: Fortress, 2002), 19; Joel B. Green, *The Gospel of Luke* (Grand Rapids: Eerdmans, 1997), 5, 38; Darrell L. Bock, *Luke: 1:1–9:50* (Grand Rapids: Baker, 1994), 56; Joseph A. Fitzmyer, *The Gospel According to Luke (I–IX)* (Garden City, NY: Doubleday, 1981), 292; *BDAG* 245.

with the oral testimony he also received (cf. Luke 1:2).[152] Dionysius carefully acknowledges his sources to make sure that no one can accuse him of inventing the events he records. By noting that there were others who wrote historical accounts regarding the same subject, Luke is not critiquing them but only pointing to their role with respect to his own composition, thereby affirming the credibility of his own history.[153] Indeed, by referencing the other writings, he elevates their status as works worthy of imitation (μίμησις/*imitatio*).[154] Dionysius of Halicarnassus even names those authors whom he considers worthy of *imitatio* when writing history (*Letter to Gnaeus Pompeius* 3).[155] The author of Acts also attends to "the events" (πραγμάτων) of the history. While Alexander correctly observes that ancient historians most commonly spoke of the πράξεις (deeds) of history,[156] ancient historians also referred to the subject or the events of history using the cognate πράγματα.[157] The "events" or subject of the history may include not only the deeds but also the words spoken in the history.[158]

Luke also places himself within ancient historiographic traditions by mentioning what the eyewitnesses of these events had handed down ("Just as [καθὼς] they were

152. "For it is possible that those who have already read Hieronymus, Timaeus, Polybius, or any of the other historians whom I just now mentioned as having slurred over their work, since they will not have found in those authors many things mentioned by me, will suspect me of inventing them and will demand to know how I came by the knowledge of these particulars. Lest anyone, therefore should entertain such an opinion of me, it is best that I should state in advance what narratives and records I have used as sources. I arrived in Italy at the very time that Augustus Caesar put an end to the civil war ... and having from that time to this present day ... lived at Rome, learned the language of the Romans and acquainted myself with their writings, I have devoted myself during all that time to matters bearing upon my subject. Some information I received orally from men of the greatest learning, with whom I associated; and the rest I gathered from histories written by the approved Roman authors—Porcius Cato, Fabius Maximus, Valerius Antias, Licinius Macer, the Aelii Gellii and Calpurnii, and many others of note; with these works, which are like the Greek annalistic accounts, as a basis, I set about the writing of my history."

153. Contra Bovon, *Luke 1*, 19.

154. See Derrenbacker Jr., *Ancient Compositional Practices and the Synoptic Problem*; Octavian Baban, *On the Road Encounters in Luke-Acts: Hellenistic Mimesis and Luke's Theology of the Way* (Milton Keynes, UK: Paternoster, 2006).

155. "You wished to learn my opinion of Herodotus and Xenophon, and expressed the desire that I should write about them. I have done this in the essays which I addressed to Demetrius on the subject of imitation. The first of these contains an enquiry into the nature of imitation itself. The second discusses the question of which particular poets and philosophers, historians and orators, should be imitated. The third, in which the question of how imitation should be done, is as yet incomplete. In the second book I write as follows concerning Herodotus, Thucydides, Xenophon, Philistus and Theopompus (these being the writers whom I judged to be most suitable for imitation)."

156. Loveday Alexander, *The Preface to Luke's Gospel: Literary Convention and Social Context in Luke 1:1–4 and Acts 1:1* (Cambridge: Cambridge University Press, 1993), 112.

157. "The history of the events" (τὴν ἱστορίαν τῶν πραγμάτων) (Josephus, *Life* 40). As Luke, Dionysius speaks about the historical narrative of the events which have occurred: "But it remains for me to say something also concerning the history itself—to what periods I limit it, what subjects I describe [περὶ τίνων ποιοῦμαι πραγμάτων τὴν διήγησιν], and what form I give to the work" (Dionysius of Halicarnassus, *Roman Antiquities* 1.7.4).

158. See Lucian, *How to Write History*, 58.

handed on to us by those who from the beginning were eyewitnesses [αὐτόπται] and servants of the word" [1:2]). The meaning of Luke's affirmation in 1:2 is not entirely clear. The clause which begins with καθὼς may refer to the way the previous historical accounts (1:1, διήγησιν) of the events (πραγμάτων) that occurred were based upon eyewitness testimony.[159] In that case, Luke would be making a statement regarding the credibility of his sources referred to in 1:1. On the other hand, Nolland observes that "the καθὼς clause can be located either before or after the clause with which it is compared."[160] He argues that the clause parallels the previous affirmation about Luke's written sources (1:1) and looks forward to v. 3. In other words, this reading understands that Luke claims to have used two types of sources: those written and the testimony of those who were "eyewitnesses." This reading is preferable since Luke's point in v. 2 is about what was handed on "to us" (ἡμῖν) rather than what the "eyewitnesses" handed on to "many" (v. 1, πολλοί) who previously drew up historical accounts. The content of what the "eyewitnesses and servants of the word" had "handed on" (παρέδοσαν)[161] must be supplied from the preceding context. In this case the content would be "the events" (v. 1, πράγματα).[162] Luke, therefore, notes that he has two sources—the historical accounts and the eyewitness testimony—both of which had to do with the πράγματα of the life of Jesus. As other authors of his day, Luke affirms that he used both written sources and eyewitness testimony (most likely oral) in composing his history (cf. Lucian, *How to Write History* 47). His reference to the eyewitnesses was, as van Unnik notes, "a safeguard against fallacies and opened the way to the truth."[163] Such testimony was a hedge against "mere hearsay evidence" (Polybius 4.2.3). Luke once again displays a knowledge of best historiographic practices which have come down to him and claims to have adhered to them.

Luke's methodological assertions in the prologues to Luke and Acts place him squarely within the discussion regarding history writing which can be traced through Thucydides, Polybius, and Lucian. We expect him to avoid the specious practices of Timaeus that Polybius critiqued so severely. The question is whether he adhered to these "best practices" or took a maverick approach to writing history, allowing rhetorical concerns to eclipse the record of the events or seeking to flatter rather than write for posterity. In answering this question we should first consider how Luke dealt with the πράξεις ("deeds") of the history since these serve as an indicator of how he handled the λόγοι ("words"). It is most likely that, as with Thucydides, Polybius, and

---

159. So I. Howard Marshall, *The Gospel of Luke: A Commentary on the Greek Text* (Grand Rapids: Eerdmans, 1978), 41; Fitzmyer, *The Gospel According to Luke (I–IX)*, 294; Alexander, *The Preface to Luke's Gospel*, 118; Bock, *Luke*, 57; Bovon, *Luke 1*, 20–21.

160. John Nolland, *Luke 1–9:20* (Dallas: Word, 1989), 8.

161. The verb is active and not passive voice as the NRSV implies. The subject of the clause in v. 2 is: "The eyewitnesses and servants of the word" (οἱ ... αὐτόπται καὶ ὑπηρέται γενόμενοι τοῦ λόγου).

162. So Josephus, *Contra Apion* 1.50, 53; Polybius 9.2.2; Diodorus Siculus 1.3.6; 2.1.4.

163. W. C. van Unnik, "Once More St. Luke's Prologue," *Neot* 7 (1973) 14. See Polybius 4.2.2–3; Dionysius of Halicarnassus, *Roman Antiquities* 1.6.1.

Lucian, the principles which guided how he chronicled events were also in play when he recorded speeches, with due consideration to the particular challenges facing historians when recording the spoken word. As demonstrated above, those authors held to common principles for investigating, evaluating, and telling both the deeds and words of history. Therefore, the way Luke records deeds will supply some clues regarding how he handled speeches.

Colin Hemer's work on *The Book of Acts in the Setting of Hellenistic History*[164] offers us the most detailed and documented study of Luke's historiographic practices in Acts. In this underutilized study, Hemer looks at the text of Acts "as we have it to see how it stands up historically."[165] In opening the question, Hemer states, "I am merely asking whether Acts is essentially unreliable in what it narrates of Paul and the primitive church and insisting that we should not make the judgment based on easy extrapolation from the corroborations or difficulties of a few debated passages, unless they are shown to be central to the veracity of the book."[166] Hemer nuances the definition of "historicity," asking whether Luke is "in general a trustworthy source by the standards of his day, whether he exhibits accuracy or inaccuracy of mind, a general conscience for, or a general disregard of, historical fact."[167] He discusses the canons of ancient historiography (chapter 3)[168] at some length before launching into a detailed analysis of the narrative in Acts in light of ancient literature and archaeology. Hemer sifts through Acts in light of the independent historical record which has come down to us (chapters 4–5), including discussion on the relationship of Acts to the Epistles and the sources the author utilized (chapters 6–8) as well as his own participation in that history.[169] His conclusion begins with a comment on the "pronounced lack of discussion about the relation of the Acts of the Apostles . . . to the world and history around it," especially in light of the "wealth of new data from inscriptions and papyri

---

164. Hemer, *The Book of Acts in the Setting of Hellenistic History*. See also Colin J. Hemer, "Luke the Historian," *BJRL* 60 (1977–1978) 28–51.

165. I. Howard Marshall, foreword to *The Book of Acts in the Setting of Hellenistic History*, by Colin J. Hemer (Winona Lake, IN: Eisenbrauns, 1990), viii.

166. Hemer, *The Book of Acts in the Setting of Hellenistic History*, 29.

167. Hemer, *The Book of Acts in the Setting of Hellenistic History*, 47. See the discussion on 49.

168. Hemer, *The Book of Acts in the Setting of Hellenistic History*, 63–100. He notes that "historiography is a relevant part of the context" (*The Book of Acts in the Setting of Hellenistic History*, 99), examining the points of view which run through the ancient discussion on the topic: "(1) the existence of a distinctive and rigorous theory of historiography; (2) the stress on eyewitness participation; (3) the importance of interviewing eyewitnesses; (4) the limitation of coverage to material where the writer has privileged access to evidence of guaranteed quality; (5) the stress on travel to the scene of events; (6) the prospect then (and for us) of checking details with contemporary documents; (7) the occasional insistence on the use of sources for speeches; and (8) the vigour of the concept of 'truth' in history 'as it actually happened'" (*The Book of Acts in the Setting of Hellenistic History*, 100).

169. Hemer argues that the "we" sections of Acts are evidence of the author's own involvement in the history, this interpretation giving "the most reasonable explanation" (*The Book of Acts in the Setting of Hellenistic History*, 312–34).

from the Graeco-Roman world."¹⁷⁰ Hemer rises to this task and, after careful examination of the extant evidence, concludes, "By and large, these perspectives all converged to support the general reliability of the narrative, through the details so intricately yet often unintentionally woven into the narrative."¹⁷¹ In other words, Luke was no Timaeus.

Hemer affirms the credibility of the narrative, given the extant data, yet acknowledges the historical difficulty presented by the reference to Theudas (Acts 5:36–37). The Acts account in the recorded speech of Gamaliel locates him chronologically before Judas, although his revolt occurred some forty years later than Judas during the time when Fadus was procurator, at least according to Josephus (*Ant.* 20.5.1.97–98).¹⁷² This may constitute a historical inaccuracy, although we cannot assume *a priori* that Luke was wrong and not Josephus. On the other hand, even if this is "a genuine historical error," Hemer remarks, it "would not be of sufficient magnitude to call into question the basic credibility of the author."¹⁷³ The reliability of the historical record in Acts is in harmony with the author's own claims in the prologues about having used best practices in the composition of his narrative. Given Luke's reliability as a historian, where we have the opportunity to verify his references against the historical record, we should assume that he exercised the same type of care with the speeches as he did with the deeds of the history. It is highly unlikely that he, as Timaeus, departed from his sources in order to invent speeches. To put the matter another way, Luke roots his history in written and eyewitness testimony connected to the events and words reported. His account demonstrates a high degree of reliability which inclines us to accept this testimony. Moreover, we do not have adequate undefeated defeaters to discredit the testimony provided.¹⁷⁴ It is not irrational to accept the testimony he presents.¹⁷⁵

Luke Timothy Johnson admits that the author of Acts "is impressively precise in matters of local color and detail. Places are where he says they are; things seemed to have worked pretty much the way he describes them; he accurately records the titles, functions, and time of tenure of various local officials. He captures the peculiarities of different regions. All of these suggest an author close to the scene."¹⁷⁶ Johnson even admits that even when we compare Acts with Paul's letters, it appears that Acts "provides a reliable if partial framework for reconstructing that portion of Paul's career."¹⁷⁷

170. Hemer, *The Book of Acts in the Setting of Hellenistic History*, 411.

171. Hemer, *The Book of Acts in the Setting of Hellenistic History*, 412. In addition to Hemer's study, see also Martin Hengel, *Acts and the History of Earliest Christianity* (Philadelphia: Fortress, 1979), 1–68; Fitzmyer, *The Acts of the Apostles*, 126–27.

172. Hemer, *The Book of Acts in the Setting of Hellenistic History*, 162–63.

173. Hemer, *The Book of Acts in the Setting of Hellenistic History*, 412n5.

174. Lackey, "It Takes Two to Tango," 169.

175. Lackey, "It Takes Two to Tango," 172.

176. Luke Timothy Johnson, *The Acts of the Apostles* (Collegeville, MN: Liturgical, 1992), 5.

177. Johnson, *The Acts of the Apostles*, 5.

His conclusion accords with Hemer's findings: "Where we can check him on details, Luke's factual accuracy in the latter part of Acts is impressive."[178] However, Johnson urges caution since such careful attention to detail "is also characteristic of good fiction!" While the author may have faithfully portrayed the world of the early church, this does not mean that we can have full confidence "that he got exactly right the sequence or meaning or character of events that form the substance of his narrative."[179] Luke's presentation appears to appropriate "Hellenistic literary and social tropes" and his treatment of Paul places his hero "in settings and scenes evocative of Hellenistic models."[180] We may say that Luke has interpreted Christian history in light of extant narratives within his social world. After pointing up the tensions between Paul's letters and Acts, he concludes that we should avoid extreme positions: "It is true that we cannot, because of Luke's artistry, determine the extent or even the existence of written sources. But this does not imply that Luke did not make use of tradition or that he made up events solely from his imagination. Likewise, because Luke selected and shaped his story does not mean that it is simply fiction."[181]

Johnson's caution is well taken since we cannot verify every event of the history nor can we resolve every historical conundrum. Yet Luke makes a claim to participate in a particular genre, that of history writing, and he also points the reader to his methodology, which accords with the best practices of the era. These included the use of written as well as eyewitness sources, in addition to his own participation in some aspects of the history about which he writes.[182] Such practices included the avoidance of hearsay and myth. As Hengel notes, "Luke is no less trustworthy than other historians of antiquity. People have done him a great injustice in comparing him too closely with the edifying, largely fictitious, romance-like writings in the style of the later acts of apostles, which freely invent facts as they like and when they need them."[183] Polybius's critique of Timaeus shows that simply fabricating history was not an accepted practice although it was an approach employed by Timaeus and others. In other words, while some invented events in their history, Luke's prologues and his practices, as far as we can verify them, show that he did not embrace that approach to history. He demonstrated the type of rhetorical concern which was part of ancient historiography, as we will see below, but he did not submerge historical concerns under these rhetorical interests. His history is interpreted, as we would expect from a work

---

178. Johnson, *The Acts of the Apostles*, 5.

179. Johnson, *The Acts of the Apostles*, 5.

180. Johnson, *The Acts of the Apostles*, 5. For example, Paul and Barnabas are identified by the citizens of Lystra as Hermes and Zeus, evoking Ovid's story of Philemon and Baucis (*Metamorphosis* 8.613–738), and Paul's speech in Athens remind the reader of the type of philosophic debates described by Lucian (*The Eunuch*).

181. Johnson, *The Acts of the Apostles*, 7.

182. See the discussion on the "we" sections in Acts in Hemer, *The Book of Acts in the Setting of Hellenistic History*, 312–34.

183. Hengel, *Acts and the History of Earliest Christianity*, 60.

of history based on testimony, but this acknowledgment does not push Acts into the category of historical fiction.

We possess compelling evidence of the way that the author of Acts used his sources when we compare the Gospel of Luke with Mark and Q.[184] Luke's handling of these sources in composing his gospel offers a vivid illustration of his method for appropriating the material, especially the speeches, which were part of those documents he refers to in the prologue of the Gospel ("Since many have undertaken to set down an orderly account of the events that have been fulfilled among us" [Luke 1:1]).[185] Those who bring into question Luke's handling of the deeds and speeches in Acts must seek some way to differentiate the author's practice here from that employed in writing the first volume. Dibelius first raised the question whether the methodology in recording speeches in Luke and Acts was the same, concluding that it was not:

> The difference from the method followed in Acts is clear. When he wrote the Gospel, Luke had to fit in with a tradition which already had its own stamp upon it, so that he had not the same literary freedom as when he composed the Acts of the Apostles. On the other hand, unless we are completely deceived, he was the first to employ the material available for the Acts of the Apostles, and so was able to develop the book according to the point of view of an historian writing literature."[186]

Dibelius argues from the position that Luke was faithful to his sources when composing his Gospel, these being Mark and Q, but the reason for this was that there was already an extant tradition, one written and known, to which he needed to conform. However, Dibelius failed to recognize that most ancient historians made their appeal, at least in part, to traditions which were *already known* at their time. The language of received tradition permeates ancient discussion on historiography.[187] Yet even in the face of well-known tradition, some authors chose to depart from it. Josephus, for example, claims to have written according to what was handed down to him (*Against Apion* 1.50, 53), yet he could embellish the narrative and speeches from his

---

184. I assume the four source theory of Streeter (*The Four Gospels: A Study of the Origins, Treating of the Manuscript Tradition, Sources, Authorship, and Dates* [London: Macmillan, 1924]) and others, e.g., Marshall, *The Gospel of Luke*; Fitzmyer, *The Gospel According to Luke (I–IX)*; Christopher M. Tuckett, *The Revival of the Griesbach Hypothesis: An Analysis and Appraisal* (Cambridge: Cambridge University Press, 1983); Bock, *Luke*; Nolland, *Luke 1–9:20*; Bovon, *Luke 1*. See the discussions in James D. G. Dunn, *Jesus Remembered* (Grand Rapids: Eerdmans, 2003); Delbert Royce Burkett, *Rethinking the Gospel Sources: From Proto-Mark to Mark* (New York: T. & T. Clark, 2004); John S. Kloppenborg, *Q, The Earliest Gospel: An Introduction to the Original Stories and Sayings of Jesus* (Philadelphia: Westminster John Knox, 2008).

185. As Hengel says, "Going by ancient standards, the relative reliability of his account can be tested in the gospels by a synoptic comparison with Matthew and Mark. We have no reason to assume that he acted completely differently in Acts from the way in which he composed his first work, and that he made up his narrative largely out of his head" (*Acts and the History of Earliest Christianity*, 61).

186. Dibelius, *Studies in the Acts of the Apostles*, 185.

187. van Unnik, "Once More St. Luke's Prologue," 14.

own store even when his readers had at hand the Scriptures, the very text from which he allegedly drew.[188] The mere existence of an established tradition did not provide sufficient restraint to keep Josephus from taking considerable liberty with his source. Dibelius's assertion that Luke would have used caution in composition given the existing tradition is not an adequate explanation for why the author would have followed his sources more closely in the Gospel than in Acts. In the face of existing traditions, Luke could have taken considerable liberty with his sources or he could have hugged them closely. Unlike Josephus, Luke does the latter.[189] He is selective in his use of his source material in the Gospel and adapts it to his own purposes, as one would expect from an author engaged in *imitatio*,[190] without swamping his source beneath the sea of his own rhetoric.

Over and again we are impressed with Luke's close reading and careful handling of Mark and Q, as a reading of a gospel synopsis illustrates.[191] We have no reason to suspect that his method was any different in writing Acts.[192] Since he adhered closely to his source material in composing the Gospel, we should expect that he did the same in Acts. Luke and Acts are one book in two volumes, the two being unified on various levels. They are stitched together as one continuous narrative by the prologues, the theological themes, and the structure of the books.[193] Their respective length, which

---

188. The examples are legion. Compare Exodus 17:8 and Josephus, *Antiquities* 3.39–42 (3.2.1); Exodus 19:16–25 and Josephus, *Antiquities* 3.79–88 (3.5.2–3).

189. Comparing the speeches in Josephus and Acts, Hemer concludes, "Those of Josephus are in the full rhetorical tradition. Whatever we say of those in Acts, we must acknowledge that they are quite different in kind" ("Luke the Historian," 50).

190. Derrenbacker Jr., *Ancient Compositional Practices and the Synoptic Problem*.

191. Compare Jesus' last day discourse in Mark 13:1–3 and Luke 21:5–33, or the way Luke handles Q (Matt 11:7–19 and Luke 7:24–35; Matt 11:20–42 and Luke 10:13–15; Matt 12:43–45 and Luke 11:24–26).

192. So also Jonathan W. Lo, who argues that "Luke's use of the Gospel of Mark in his Gospel proves to be remarkably instructive for understanding how the evangelist adapts a known source. Luke contains about half of the Gospel of Mark, but when he uses Mark as a source he follows it closely and rarely expands Mark's texts. . . . Luke's usage of Mark may show that Luke can be a reasonably faithful redactor of existing traditions" ("Did Peter Really Say That? Revisiting the Petrine Speeches in Acts," in *Peter in Early Christianity*, ed. Helen K. Bond and Larry W. Hurtado [Grand Rapids; Eerdmans, 2015], 74). See also Osvaldo Padilla's, "The Speeches in Acts: Historicity, Theology, and Genre," in *Issues in Luke-Acts: Selected Essays*, ed. Sean A. Adams and Michael Pahl (Piscataway, NJ: Gorgias, 2012), 171–93; *The Acts of the Apostles: Interpretation, History, and Theology* (Downers Grove, IL: IVP Academic, 2016), 139.

193. Green, *The Gospel of Luke*, 6–10. The debate regarding the unity of Luke-Acts is larger than can be discussed here. See the excellent survey of the matter in Joseph Verheyden, "The Unity of Luke-Acts: What Are We Up To?," in *The Unity of Luke-Acts*, ed. Joseph Verheyden (Leuven: Peeters, 1999), 3–56. Parsons and Pervo ("Rethinking the Unity of Luke and Acts," in *Rethinking the Unity of Luke and Acts* [Minneapolis: Fortress, 1993]) speak of five levels of unity discussed in the literature (summarized by Verheyden, "The Unity of Luke-Acts," 6–7): "The author and the canon . . . the genre, the narrative, and the theology of the work." While Parsons and Pervo wish to emphasize the distinct nature of the two books, Tannehill and Marshall stress their essential unity (Tannehill, *The Narrative Unity of Luke-Acts: A Literary Interpretation* [Philadelphia: Fortress, 1991–94]; Marshall, "Acts and

is nearly the same, was determined by the standard size of papyrus scrolls.[194] Compositionally it becomes quite difficult to distinguish between Luke and Acts. Cadbury's assertion that in the Gospel and Acts we are "dealing with different kinds of material" cannot be sustained.[195] We are therefore inclined to expect a consistency in method in the use of sources in both volumes, even with regard to recording speeches. These two volumes were composed as a single unit, and we should not think that the author changed his method for including source material in this second volume. Put simply, we hear a faithful reporting of the testimony handed down to him regarding the speeches of Paul, and Stephen, and Peter in the speeches in Acts. Luke carefully handled his sources whether they reported the events or the speeches that he wrote down in his history.

Luke's assertions about his historical method and the evidence we have as we compare him with his known sources lead us to believe that he, like Thucydides, held a deep commitment to what actually happened ("Only after investigating with the greatest possible accuracy each detail" [1.22.1]) and what was actually spoken ("I have adhered as closely as possible to the general sense of what was actually said" [1.22.1]). Like Thucydides, and unlike Livy or even Josephus, Luke writes of the events happening during his own time.[196] He carefully investigated (Luke 1:3; cf. Lucian, *How to Write History* 47) and used reliable sources, both written and oral, but at the same time he paid particular attention to rhetorical concerns. While he was the preacher, as Dibelius and others have noted, his theological concerns did not supplant his interest in the deeds and words of history as handed down to him. To do that would, in the

---

the 'Former Treatise,'" in *The Book of Acts in Its Ancient Literary Setting*, ed. Bruce W. Winter and Andrew D. Clarke [Grand Rapids: Eerdmans, 1993]). Marshall concludes that "Acts is to be seen in close literary association with the Gospel. They form two parts of one work, conceived in its final form as a unity, whether or not the original composition of the Gospel took place independently of the plan to produce a two-part work"("Acts and the 'Former Treatise,'" 182).

194. The standard scroll was no longer than twenty sheets of papyrus stitched together (Pliny, *Natural History* 13.23 §77), although Pliny may be speaking about how much papyrus may be manufactured from a stalk of the plant (Harry Y. Gamble, *Books and Readers in the Early Church: A History of Early Christian Texts* [New Haven, CT: Yale University Press, 1995], 265n10). Standard scroll length, according to Aune, was between 35 and 40 feet (*The New Testament in Its Literary Environment* [Philadelphia: Westminster, 1987], 117–18). Authors attempted to keep the size of books roughly the same, with Luke and Acts being roughly 35 and 32 feet respectively. Gamble, however, estimates average scroll size to be about 3.5 meters (11.5 feet) (*Books and Readers in the Early Church*, 45). When a book was too long for one scroll, it was divided into two volumes (for example, Diodorus Siculus 1.41.10). See Jack Finegan, *Encountering New Testament Manuscripts: A Working Introduction to Textual Criticism* (London: SPCK, 1975), 20–21.

195. Cadbury, "The Speeches in Acts," 416.

196. T. Francis Glasson, "The Speeches in Acts and Thucydides," *Expository Times* 76 (1965) 165. Glasson draws the author of Acts within the historiographic tradition of Thucydides, noting that the speeches were not verbatim reports: "It is not surprising that the final result betrays traces of the author's style." We should not forget that the speeches in Thucydides, as those in Acts, were no more than a précis. Luke even indicates, as Horsley observes ("Speeches and Dialogue in Acts," *NTS* 32 (1986) 609–11), that more was spoken than the author recorded (see 2:40; 4:1–3; 7:54; 10:44; 13:42; 17:32; 20:36; 22:22; 24:22; 26:24).

words of Polybius, destroy "the peculiar virtue of history" (12.25b.4). Ancient historians held rhetoric and historical investigation in tension with each other, attending to their sources, the meaning of events, and their audience. While Polybius critiqued Timaeus since he "shows off his oratorical power, but gives no report of what was actually spoken" (12.25a.5), he ascribed to the idea that historians should interpret events (12.25b.1–4). Moreover, the historian was expected to attend to rhetorical style after historical considerations were satisfied. The space given to rhetoric included more than assuring that the speeches suited the "person and his subject." Once grounded in his sources, the person, and circumstances, "it is then, however, that you can play the orator and show your eloquence" (Lucian, *How to Write History* 58). The historian needed to present his subject faithfully *and* hold in mind the concerns of his audience. Interpretation of the sources was encouraged, and eloquence was not shunned in writing speeches.

At this intersection we begin to understand how Luke has been viewed as no more than the "preacher." While Dibelius and others have identified common themes and a consistent rhetorical style laced through the speeches in Acts as evidence that the author paid scant attention to his sources, this weave of history and rhetoric is exactly what we would expect from an ancient historian.[197] Gempf elaborates on the need for this mixture, saying, "In fact, the write-up of a speech in an ancient history *does call* for rhetorical skill simply because the author must, while being faithful to the main lines of the historical 'speech-event,' adapt the speech to make it 'speak to' a new audience in a different situation."[198] Ancient discussion on rhetoric and history critiqued the eclipse of history by rhetoric, yet celebrated rhetoric as a proper

---

197. The starting point in this analysis is often the common theological themes strung throughout the letter, with little attention given to either the distinctives in each speech or to the way history and rhetoric (and here theology) were joined in ancient historiography. For example, Shubert says, "In short, the first cycle of speeches of Acts is chs. 1–5. Here the main features of the Lukan theology are set forth. Peter is the spokesman for the Twelve. In the second cycle (chs. 6–20) the Lukan theology is fully developed in its various aspects (20:27, 'I did not shrink [a typically Lukan litotes] from declaring to you the *whole* counsel of God')" ("The Final Cycle of Speeches in the Book of Acts," *JBL* 87 [1968] 2). Similarly, Townsend comments, "The speeches in Acts are not entirely independent of each other. In addition to containing various similarities of style, they also reveal an interdependence of thought" ("The Speeches in Acts," 151). Townsend does not view the similarities as evidence of a common Christian *kerygma*: "In content and outline the speeches of Paul resemble more closely the speeches of Peter than they do the *kerygma* found in the Pauline epistles" ("The Speeches in Acts," 157–58). He concludes that "there is no evidence of more than one theology in Luke's speeches" ("The Speeches in Acts," 159).

198. Gempf, "Public Speaking and Published Accounts," 264. Witherington, commenting on Soards's (*The Speeches in Acts*) conclusions, adds, "Whatever sources Luke may have used for these speeches, he has made them his own in terms of style, vocabulary, syntax, and the like, it is safe to say that they *at least* reflect Luke's rhetorical skill, since what we have in almost every case is a précis or edited summary of a speech, and not an entire speech" (*The Acts of the Apostles*, 46). Walbank's cultural explanation for the mix of history with rhetoric may be a stretch, however: "Greek's 'quick response to language' made them more disposed to react to rhetorical passages" (*Speeches in the Greek Historians*, 2).

Peter's Testimony in Acts of the Apostles

The combination of history and rhetoric swings us back round to the essential nature of testimony. Luke's history provides the marks of presenting testimony which is reliable or "truth conductive," and we, as the first readers, have "appropriate positive reasons" for accepting this testimony.[200] Critical examination of testimony received was part of "best practices" in ancient historiography based upon testimony, and Luke displays this critical capacity. Moreover, as argued above, testimony combines both the witness regarding significant events and the interpretation of those events. The one who offers testimony is not a mythic objective observer but rather an involved participant who bears witness to the events and their meaning. The witness does not stand apart, disengaged from events, since testimony presents both what occurred and the event's significance. The witness cannot reproduce what was seen or heard but can only report on that event, and with the report comes the interpretation or story of what was witnessed. Polybius commented on his sources for writing history, saying, "I have been present at some of the events and have the testimony of eyewitnesses for others"[201] (4.2.1; cf. Luke 1:3). Thucydides noted that history is built upon testimony: "Now the state of affairs in early times I have found to have been such as I have described, although it is difficult in such matters to credit any and every piece of testimony [τεκμηρίῳ]" (1.20.1; cf. Acts 1:3).[202] Luke has likewise used sources, both written and oral, which themselves interpret the history which they hand down. Our author, therefore, has both inherited and shaped the testimony in this history. This observation should not lead us to conclude that the deeds and speeches of this history have become so far removed from the events that occurred that we cannot hope to read what transpired. Event and interpretation define the nature of history as based upon testimony. The historian was expected to interpret the events, getting inside their nature to make the meaning clear. It's history and interpretation all the way down.

The speeches in Acts, therefore, should not be dismissed as mere Lukan inventions which evidence no higher concern on the author's part than the display of his own rhetorical skill and the preservation of his own perspective. He holds to his sources, which provided testimony, yet he shapes that which was handed down to him

---

199. Macleod makes this point with regard to Thucydides (*Collected Essays*, 52–53, 68).

200. Lackey, "It Takes Two to Tango," 169.

201. The concept of testimony is present here, although the word does not appear in the Greek: τὰ δὲ παρὰ τῶν ἑωρακότων ἀκηκοέναι.

202. Although τεκμηρίοις is rightly translated "proofs" (see Barrett, *The Acts of the Apostles*, 69; Bock, *Acts*, 54; *BDAG* 994), such proofs give evidence, being signs of some reality. In this respect they are part of testimony.

in order to present his theological understanding of the events and speeches that have transpired. The speeches, as we would expect, taste of the author's viewpoint and are accented with his rhetorical voice. We should not expect to hear the *ipsissima verba* of any of the actors on this stage. But if Luke is indeed a credible historian of his age, as his own methodological reflections and the evidence we can verify confirm, then we may indeed hope to hear within these pages the *ipsissima vox* of the ones who speak as he, too, "adhered as closely as possible to the general sense of what was actually said" (Thucydides 1.22.1). Luke is not like Timaeus, who "shows off his oratorical power, but gives no report of what was actually spoken" (Polybius 12.25a.5). We may not be able to fully tease out what interpretive elements Luke wove together with the Petrine speeches in Acts. On the one hand, every speech summarizes Peter's words. We can expect that Luke remained faithful to the "gist" of the apostle's ideas, staying faithful to both the person and the setting to which he bears witness.[203] We should also not forget that the author of Acts wrote one history with one approach to his sources. His careful handling of his sources when composing the Gospel was most likely his method when composing the second volume of his work. With these qualifications in mind, we may affirm that we hear the particular perspectives of Paul, Stephen, and also Peter in the speeches recorded in Acts.

The Testimony of Peter and 1 Peter

Peter in 1 Peter

Two letters in the New Testament bear Peter's name. Depending on whether they are connected in some way to the apostle himself, these may or may not be sources for understanding the structure of Peter's theology. The author of 1 Peter identifies himself as "Peter, an apostle of Jesus Christ" (1:1a). He is known by name to the churches located north and west of the Taurus mountains in Anatolia. The author calls the believers in this region "the exiles of the Dispersion of Pontus, Galatia, Cappadocia, Asia, and Bithynia" (1:1b). Elliott notes that these Roman provinces cover 129,000 square miles,[204] an area populated by native Celts who lived under Roman rule.[205] Although well-known through this vast region, the author does not include himself amongst those responsible for the evangelization of the letter's recipients. He speaks about their evangelists in the third person. They are "those who brought you the good news by the Holy Spirit sent from heaven" (1:12). Although Peter was an itinerant (Gal 2:11; 1 Cor 9:5), we possess no evidence from elsewhere in the New Testament that he traveled to

---

203. Perkins at least acknowledges this latter point: "These variations are evidence that Luke has adapted each speech to fit the narrative context in which it was set" (*Peter*, 34).

204. John H. Elliott, *1 Peter: A New Translation with Introduction and Commentary* (New York: Doubleday, 2000), 84.

205. Stephen Mitchell, *The Celts in Anatolia and the Impact of Roman Rule* (Oxford: Clarendon, 1993).

Anatolia.²⁰⁶ While Peter may have traveled through Anatolia at some period, we have no reliable evidence that he did journey there.

Although he was not their evangelist, the author stands with his readers. In solidarity with the "elders" of these congregations, he calls himself "a fellow elder" (NIV; συμπρεσβύτερος).²⁰⁷ He says that he was "a witness of the sufferings of Christ" and "one who shares in the glory to be revealed" (5:1), descriptors that place him in solidarity both with Christ who suffered and is glorified (1:11) and with the recipients who are suffering and will likewise partake in Christ's glory (4:13–14; 5:5, 10). Moreover, in 5:1 and throughout the letter the author assumes that the readers knew the gospel story about Jesus (1:12) as well as Peter's particular role in that history. He does not have to explain how he was a "witness of the sufferings of Christ," whether we understand this as a reference to being an "eyewitness" of Christ's sufferings or "one who bears witness" about them.²⁰⁸ The author's reference to his participation "in the glory to be revealed" may, as Selwyn suggests, allude to Peter's presence at the transfiguration, which prefigured the final revelation of the Lord's glory (1 Pet 4:13).²⁰⁹ Selwyn's position has not been widely embraced because the focus of the claim is about the future revelation of Christ's glory (τῆς μελλούσης ἀποκαλύπτεσθαι δόξης).²¹⁰ However, 2 Peter 1:16–18 links the transfiguration with the "coming" of Christ since the first

---

206. There is, however, some later testimony that he traveled there, though these witnesses are late and derived from 1 Peter 1:1. Eusebius says that "Peter appears to have preached through Pontus, Galatia, Bithynia, Cappadocia, and Asia to the Jews who were scattered abroad" (*HE* 3.1.2). This statement appears to be based solely on Eusebius's recall of 1 Peter 1:1, which he loosely quotes from memory (so also Jerome, *De vir. ill.* 1). Sometime between AD 374 and 376, Epiphanius noted that Peter traveled frequently in Pontus and Bithynia (*The Panarion of Epiphanius of Salamis*, 1,104.27.6.6) but this testimony also depends on 1 Peter. While Peter may have traveled through Anatolia at some period, we have no reliable evidence that he did journey there. Elliott mentions Peter's absence from Anatolia as an argument against Petrine authorship of the letter. But Peter, as Paul, could communicate with churches which were not known to him personally. Wisely, Elliott states that the lack of Peter's missional activity in Asia Minor is not a knock-down argument against authenticity: "The weight of this as an argument against Petrine authorship, however, is uncertain" (*1 Peter*, 121).

207. This self-description is not an argument against Petrine authorship (see Francis Wright Beare, *The First Epistle of Peter* [Oxford: Basil Blackwell, 1970], 198; Elliott, *1 Peter*, 121, 816–18). This is hardly the "slip" of the real author who mistakenly unmasks himself. The passage clearly identifies the author as a witness of Christ's sufferings and not only a fellow elder. Sometime later, Eusebius could speak of the apostles as elders (*HE* 3.39.4; see also R. A. Campbell, "The Elders of the Jerusalem Church," *JTS* 44 [1993] 511–28), and Paul the apostle could call himself an "elder" (Phlm 9), although he may refer here simply to his age. It is unlikely that a post-apostolic author would have attributed this title of humility to Peter (Karen H. Jobes, *1 Peter* [Grand Rapids: Baker Academic, 2005], 300–301).

208. Elliott, *1 Peter*, 819; Aristotle, *Rhetoric* 1375b–1376a; and see below.

209. Edwin Gordon Selwyn, *The First Epistle of Peter: The Greek Text with Introduction, Notes, and Essays* (London: Macmillan, 1947), 228–29.

210. Paul J. Achtemeier, *1 Peter: A Commentary on First Peter* (Minneapolis: Fortress, 1996), 324; Elliott, *1 Peter*, 820–21; Thomas R. Schreiner, *1, 2 Peter, Jude* (Nashville: Broadman & Holman, 2003), 232–33; Jobes, *1 Peter*, 302; Ben Witherington, *A Socio-Rhetorical Commentary on 1-2 Peter* (Downers Grove, IL: IVP Academic, 2007), 227.

event anticipates and guarantees the second.[211] In the same way, 1 Peter 5:1 makes a claim about Peter's role as a witness and present participant (κοινωνός)[212] of that which is to come—a position Selwyn takes which most have ignored. As Peter is already "a fellow elder and witness" so also, at present, he is "one who shares." Indeed, 2 Peter 1:16–18 may look back not only to the gospel account of the transfiguration (Mark 8:38–9:1 and plls.) but also to 1 Peter 5:1 since the author knows the first letter (2 Pet 3:1). However we understand the details of 5:1, the point remains that the way the author refers to himself presupposes that the first readers/hearers of this letter knew about Peter's life and role in the church. In the same way, Paul could refer to Peter with little introduction in his circular letter to the Galatians (Gal 2:1–14), which some of the recipients of 1 Peter had likely read/heard. Peter's story circulated where he had not traveled.

The author locates himself in "Babylon" along with believers there who convey their greeting ("She who is in Babylon, chosen together with you, sends you her greetings" [1 Pet 5:13, NIV]). "Babylon" probably refers to Rome since it was a common metaphorical name for the imperial city in Jewish and rabbinic literature[213] as well as the Book of Revelation (14:8; 16:19; 17:5, 9, 18; 18:2, 10, 21). Eusebius comments that Clement of Alexandria and Papias locate Peter at Rome with Mark (*HE* 2.15).[214] Eusebius confirms the identification, saying, "Peter made mention of Mark in the first epistle, which he is also said to have composed at the same city of Rome, and that he showed this fact by calling the city by an unusual figure of speech, Babylon." Elsewhere he relates that Peter was crucified and buried at Rome, basing his assertion on the testimonies of Gaius and the bishop of Corinth, Dionysius (*HE* 2.25.5–8). Ignatius likewise locates Peter at Rome (*Rom.* 4.3), as do Irenaeus (*Adv. Haer.* 3.1, 3) and Tertullian (*De praescriptione haereticorum* 36; *Adv. Marcionem.* 4.5).[215] In addition to 1 Peter 5:13, the Pauline prison epistles, written from Rome (Col 4:11; Phlm 24), and 2 Timothy 4:11, which locates Paul at Rome, place Mark in the city. Among his other references to Mark's association with Peter, Eusebius cites Origen's commentary on Matthew in which he said that Mark composed a Gospel as Peter explained it to him (*HE* 6.25.3–6; 3.39.14–15).[216] Eusebius also records that Papias had received

---

211. Richard Bauckham, *Jude, 2 Peter* (Waco, TX: Word, 1983), 216–17; Green, *Jude and 2 Peter*, 219–21.

212. Beare, *The First Epistle of Peter*, 199; Peter H. Davids, *The First Epistle of Peter* (Grand Rapids: Eerdmans, 1990), 177.

213. Elliott, *1 Peter*, 882–84, assembles the evidence well.

214. According to Eusebius, Peter had arrived in the imperial city after Simon the Sorcerer (*HE* 2.14).

215. See Foakes-Jackson, *Peter*, 151–63; Cullmann, *Peter*, 71–157; Daniel William O'Connor, *Peter in Rome: The Literary, Liturgical, and Archeological Evidence* (New York: Columbia University Press, 1969); Thiede, *Simon Peter*, 171–84; Richard Bauckham, "The Martyrdom of Peter in Early Christian Literature," *Aufsteig und Niedergang der römischen Welt* 2.26.1 (1992) 539–95; Grant, *Saint Peter*, 147–58; Perkins, *Peter*, 168–71; Thiede, *Geheimakte Petrus*, 249–56.

216. Ulrich H. J. Körtner, "Markus der Mitarbeiter des Petrus," *ZNW* 71 (1980) 160–73; Hengel,

information from John the Presbyter that Mark was "the interpreter of Peter" (*HE* 3.39.14–15). Although some of the testimony in the early church derives from this passage (as *HE* 6.25.5), the bulk of the testimony goes beyond what ancient authors could deduce from 1 Peter 5:13 and therefore serves as independent confirmation of 5:13. The evidence from the New Testament and the early church points to Peter's presence in Rome along with Mark, precisely as indicated in 1 Peter 5:13.

The author of 1 Peter is also in the company of Silvanus when he wrote (5:12).[217] The brief commendation he receives ("Whom I consider a faithful brother") suggests that the first readers of this letter knew him or at least knew about him.[218] Silvanus (transliterated from Latin as Σιλουανός) was also one of Paul's companions (1 Thess 1:1; 2 Thess 1:1; 2 Cor 1:19) and may be identified with Silas, who appears with Paul in Acts (15:22, 27, 32, 40; 16:19, 25, 29; 17:4, 10, 14, 15; 18:5).[219] His participation in the Pauline mission through Asia Minor during the so-called second missionary journey would explain why the author of 1 Peter need merely mention him in his commendation. The readers knew who he was. Apart from 1 Peter 5:12, no early tradition locates Silvanus at Rome. He was, however, a Roman citizen (Acts 16:37–38) and someone Peter knew since both were present at the Jerusalem Council (Acts 15:22, 27).

Elliott assumes that Silvanus in 1 Peter 5:12 is the very person we know from the Pauline mission, yet he does not accept that 1 Peter is authentic.[220] Achtemeier likewise suggests that though the letter is pseudonymous, Silvanus could be the bearer. But he demurs since "it is likely that by the time this letter was written he was, if still alive, too old to undertake such a rigorous journey."[221] So, he muses that an otherwise unknown Silvanus is the person mentioned. Alternately, Silvanus may be part of the fiction of pseudepigraphy as Brox suggests.[222] Elliott's position strains credulity since it assumes that Silvanus would be a willing party to the pseudepigraphy of an otherwise unknown author (Elliott argues that Silvanus was the messenger who circulated the letter, not Peter's amanuensis). Achtemeier's argument, as he admits, "remains . . . nothing more than conjecture."[223] Brox's position is perhaps the most

---

Saint Peter, 36–48.

217. See the discussion below regarding whether Silvanus served as Peter's amanuensis or messenger who carried the letter.

218. Elliott, *1 Peter*, 871.

219. BDAG, 923; MM, 574; ABD 6.22; Hemer, *The Book of Acts in the Setting of Hellenistic History*, 230; Elliott, *1 Peter*, 871. Achtemeier is more cautious on this point: "Although such an identity of Silas/Silvanus is possible, perhaps even probable, it is finally no more than an assumption, since the name was not uncommon and is also known in Hellenistic culture, appearing in Greek literature, inscriptions, and papyri" (*1 Peter*, 351).

220. Elliott, *1 Peter*, 871.

221. Achtemeier, *1 Peter*, 351.

222. Norbert Brox, *Der erste Petrusbrief* (Zürich: Benzinger; Neukirchen-Vluyn: Neukirchener, 1986), 241–42.

223. Achtemeier, *1 Peter*, 351.

consistent, but its force depends on assuming that the letter was not written to the believers mentioned in 1 Peter 1:1 or that it was presented to the churches of Asia Minor as a long-lost missive of the apostle Peter. In either case, we cannot identify any good reason why an anonymous author would include Silvanus's name since he was not associated with Peter apart from his brief mention at the Jerusalem Council, where, moreover, he was called by his Greek name, Silas.[224] Mentioning him would not strengthen a pseudepigrapher's aim of presenting the letter as an authoritative writing of the apostle Peter. The least problematic of all solutions is that Silvanus was with Peter in Rome and served as either the messenger, the amanuensis who penned the letter, or both (see below).

Ancient Perspectives on 1 Peter

The early church unanimously accepted 1 Peter as an authentic letter of the apostle Peter. The earliest note on the book's authenticity is 2 Peter 3:1, "This is now, beloved, the second letter I am writing to you." The first letter was undoubtedly 1 Peter, with the second letter presented as confirmation of the first's message.[225] During the fourth century Eusebius classified 1 Peter as one of the "recognized books" that were neither disputed nor spurious (*HE* 3.25.2-3; so Origen, *Com. Matt.* 1). In this classification he summarizes the historic and universal testimony of the church regarding the letter's authenticity. The "ancient presbyters" used it and admitted it (3.3.1, 4), yet other books bearing Peter's name—such as the Acts, Gospel, preaching, and Revelation—were not so received (3.4.2). Between 2 Peter 3 and *HE* 3, the church spoke with one voice about the book's authenticity. The book was known and used extensively by numerous authors, with vocabulary, allusions, or citations from the book appearing as early as 1 Clement (ca. AD 96).[226] Modern commentators are not alone in recognizing that early authors used 1 Peter. Eusebius remarked how Polycarp (*HE* 4.14.9; died ca. AD 155/56) and Papias (3.39.16; ca. AD 140) employed it. The book is even attributed to Peter by numerous early authors, the first being Irenaeus (*Adv. Haer.* 4.9.2; 5.7.2; 4.16.5; 4.32.2; ca. AD 180), followed by Tertullian (*Scorp.* 12; ca. AD 160-220), Origen (*HE* 6.25.8; ca. 185-254), and Eusebius.[227]

The book appears in all early canonical lists save for the Muratorian Fragment, which, as often noted, is partially mutilated. This may account for its absence in this list or its omission may be due to scribal carelessness.[228] The canonical lists from the

---

224. See Jobes, *1 Peter*, 321.

225. See the discussion on these points in Green, *Jude and 2 Peter*, 309-11.

226. See the assembled evidence and assessment in Charles Bigg, *A Critical and Exegetical Commentary on the Epistles of St. Peter and St. Jude* (Edinburgh: T. & T. Clark, 1901), 7-15; Achtemeier, *1 Peter*, 44-46; Elliott, *1 Peter*, 138-48; Donald A. Hagner, *The Use of the Old and New Testaments in Clement of Rome* (Leiden: Brill, 1973), 238-46.

227. Again, see Bigg, *Peter and Jude*, 11-15; Elliott, *1 Peter*, 146-48.

228. See Bruce M. Metzger, *The Canon of the New Testament: Its Origin, Development, and*

Eastern Church from the third through fifth centuries place 1 Peter at the head of the catholic letters immediately after James, while in the second century Clement of Alexandria begins his list with 1 Peter (he does not include James). In the Western Church, 1 Peter leads in the lists of catholic letters in the second up to the beginning of the fourth century (save for the Muratorian Fragment, however we might date it). From the late fourth century onward, James comes before 1 Peter as in the Eastern lists.[229] After examining the evidence, Elliott remarks, "With the single exception of 1 John, 1 Peter is the only one of the Catholic Epistles whose authority was never questioned."[230] Indeed, the attestation is as strong as the acknowledged Pauline Epistles. Not only did the church accept the letter but located it in a position of prominence in the canonical lists.[231]

Achtemeier, however, points out that Ignatius of Antioch does not refer to 1 Peter, a surprise since Ignatius traveled through the regions addressed in 1 Peter. He doubts that the early allusions to the letter in 1 Clement show dependence on the letter and observes that Peter is not named as the book's author until the latter part of the second century. He therefore dates the letter in the early second century.[232] However, Elliott's detailed work on the early allusions to 1 Peter swamp Achtemeier's suggestions.[233] Moreover, Achtemeier fails to recognize Eusebius's comments that early authors, such as Papias and Polycarp, knew and used the letter and that the "ancient presbyters" employed and admitted it (see above). In fact, early authors often quoted or alluded to books they accepted without naming their source. Save for the odd omission of 1 Peter from the Muratorian Fragment, there is an absence of any evidence from the early church that 1 Peter was anything other than what it appears to be—a letter from Peter. The testimony regarding its authenticity is ancient, universal, and uniform.

Taken all together, the early evidence for the authenticity of the letter is strong. Everything is as we would expect it to be, with the direct and indirect testimonies aligned and consistent. Peter was associated with Mark according to the letter and the witness of the early church. He and Mark were in Rome, and Peter wrote from there according to early testimony and 1 Peter. According to Galatians and 1 Peter, churches in Anatolia knew Peter despite the fact that he was not their evangelist. The author's association with Silvanus does not surprise since we know from Acts 15 that

---

Significance (Oxford: Clarendon, 1987), 200; Lee Martin McDonald, *The Formation of the Christian Biblical Canon* (Peabody, MA: Hendrickson, 1995), 217. On the Muratorian Fragment, see Geoffrey Mark Hahneman, *The Muratorian Fragment and the Development of the Canon* (Oxford: Clarendon, 1992), 181; David R. Nienhuis, *Not By Paul Alone: The Formation of the Catholic Epistle Collection and the Christian Canon* (Waco: Baylor, 2007), 46.

229. Nienhuis, *Not by Paul Alone*, 92–97.

230. Elliott, *1 Peter*, 148.

231. On the shape of the canon in relationship to the Catholic Epistles, see Neinhuis, *Not by Paul Alone*, and also his discussion of the order of the Catholic Epistles (*Not by Paul Alone*, 85–86).

232. Achtemeier, *1 Peter*, 45–46.

233. Elliott, *1 Peter*, 138–46.

Peter knew him. Indeed, whatever Pauline flavor the letter has may be due not only to Peter's association with Paul but also Silvanus and perhaps Mark (see below). No piece of the puzzle is out of place. The testimonies regarding the authenticity of the letter harmonize completely and are corroborated by the ancient and universal voice of the early church. We must still ask whether there are "undefeated defeaters" to this testimony such as the presence of the *verba Pauli*, the absence of the *verba Christi*, the nature and date of the persecutions, and the stylistic abilities of the author. But that discussion should only begin after acknowledging the strong and consistent early testimonies to the letter's authenticity, which could not be engineered nor accounted for simply on the basis of the information contained in the letter. The early testimony leads to one conclusion: that the letter was produced by the apostle Peter.

Contemporary Perspectives on 1 Peter

For many years scholars regarded the author of 1 Peter as a Paulinist and argued that the presence of the *verba Pauli* show that the author was dependent upon Pauline literature and thought. In his refutation of Petrine authorship, Beare states that "the book is strongly marked by the impress of Pauline theological ideas, and in language the dependence upon St. Paul is undeniably great. All through the Epistle, we have the impression that we are reading the work of a man who is steeped in the Pauline letters, who is so imbued with them that he uses St. Paul's words and phrases without conscious search, as his own thoroughly-assimilated vocabulary of religion."[234] Beare argued that the author used Ephesians, written by a later Paulinist. Some decades earlier, Foster concluded that some 50 percent of 1 Peter showed connections with the Pauline epistles.[235] Schrage went further than either Foster or Beare, stating that the letter is more Pauline than Paul himself.[236] The letter, therefore, comes from a time later than Paul, and even late enough for Paul's letters to have been at least partially collected and circulated.[237]

First Peter does contain some similarities with Pauline thought, such as the expression "in Christ" (3:16; 5:10, 14) and Peter's understanding of the use of the gifts

---

234. Beare, *The First Epistle of Peter*, 44. This view, from Beare's original edition in 1958, remained unchanged in the third edition published in 1970. See the Supplement (*The First Epistle of Peter*, 216–20).

235. Ora Delmer Foster, "The Literary Relations of 'The First Epistle of Peter,'" *Transactions of the Connecticut Accademy of Arts and Sciences* 13 (1913) 376.

236. Wolfgang Schrage, *Die "Katholischen" Briefe: Die Briefe Des Jakobus, Petrus, Johannes, und Judas* (Gottingen: Vandenhoeck and Ruprecht, 1973), 60.

237. On the Pauline influence in 1 Peter, see, for example, A. E. Barnett, *Paul Becomes a Literary Influence* (Chicago: University of Chicago Press, 1941), 61–68; Andrew F. Walls, introduction to *The First Epistle General of Peter*, by Alan M. Stibbs (Grand Rapids: Eerdmans, 1959), 39–42; Bo Reicke, *The Epistles of James, Peter and Jude* (Garden City, NY: Doubleday, 1964), 70; Karl-Martin Fischer, *Tendenz und Absicht des Epheserbriefes* (Göttingen: Vandenhoeck & Ruprecht, 1973), 15; Gene L. Green, "Theology and Ethics in 1 Peter" (PhD diss., The University of Aberdeen, 1979), 77–87.

in Christian service (4:10; 1:12). Goppelt adds to this list the idea of Christ's "revelation" (1:7, 13; 4:13), God's calling (1:15; 2:9, 21; 3:9; 5:10), and Christian "conscience" (2:19). He concludes, "The letter undoubtedly arose in a Church tradition influenced by the terminology and concepts of Paul."[238] Moreover, the domestic code in 1 Peter, which includes teaching on the Christian responsibility to the State (2:13–3:7), has clear parallels with the Pauline instruction found in Romans (13:1–7), Ephesians (5:21–6:8), and Colossians (3:18–22). Horrell discusses the Pauline traditions in 1 Peter, including in his survey the epistolary frame, 1 Peter's use of "in Christ," the term *charisma* in 4:10, the parallel paraenetic tradition of non-retaliation (1 Thess 5:15; Rom 12:17; 1 Pet 3:9), the teaching on obligations to the state (Rom 13:1–7; 1 Pet 2:13–17) and household (Col 3:18–4:1; Eph 5:21–6:9; 1 Pet 2:18–3:7), along with other parallels, such as the call to non-conformity (Rom 12:2; 1 Pet 1:14). Yet Horrell stops short of calling 1 Peter the work of a Paulinist. "Taken together," he says, "the above observations lead to the conclusion that 1 Peter shows clear signs of awareness of and dependence upon Pauline language and tradition." While he concludes that clear Pauline influence is evident in 1 Peter, the letter falls short of being Pauline in theology.[239]

Horrell is correct that 1 Peter is not thoroughly Pauline. Elements of Paul's teaching are strikingly absent, such as justification, the question of gospel and law, the church as the body of Christ, the relationship between Jews and Gentiles in God's plan, and the role of the Spirit in the Christian life.[240] But Horrell does not fully acknowledge the commonly held position that not all the supposed Pauline teaching needs be traced directly to Paul since such elements were simply part of common Christian instruction.[241] We can account for the commonalities between the domestic code in 1 Peter and the Pauline epistles, plus other catechetical and liturgical elements, by recognizing that both authors drew from the church's *didache,* a point argued some time ago by Carrington and Selwyn.[242] Achtemeier judiciously concludes, "It is apparent that while there are some developments of Pauline ideas in 1 Peter, along with certain Pauline turns of phrase, 1 Peter is not a deliberate attempt to theologize in the Pauline mode, or to defend Paulinism as a way of carrying on theological reflection."[243]

---

238. Leonhard Goppelt, *A Commentary on 1 Peter* (Grand Rapids: Eerdmans, 1993), 30.

239. David G. Horrell, *Becoming Christian: Essays on 1 Peter and the Making of Christian Identity* (London: T. & T. Clark, 2013), 12–20.

240. Alan Hugh McNeile, *New Testament Teaching in Light of St. Paul's* (Cambridge: Cambridge University Press, 1923), 135–60; James Moffatt, *The General Epistles: James, Peter, and Judas* (London: Hodder & Stoughton, 1928), 85; Selwyn, *The First Epistle of Peter,* 20; Brox, *Der erste Petrusbrief,* 46–51. Achtemeier (*1 Peter,* 15–19) and Elliott (*1 Peter,* 37–40) present good summaries and evaluations of the relationship between 1 Peter and the Pauline literature.

241. J. Ramsey Michaels, *1 Peter* (Waco: Word, 1988), xliii–xlv; Achtemeier, *1 Peter,* 18–19.

242. Philip Carrington, *The Primitive Christian Catechism* (Cambridge: Cambridge University Press, 1940); Selwyn, *The First Epistle of Peter,* 363–466; Elliott, *1 Peter,* 40.

243. Achtemeier, *1 Peter,* 19. So Elliott, who says, "Consequently, it can no longer be claimed that the Petrine author was dependent on Paul for his thoughts and formulations, that he was a

Elliott has been especially effective in helping us understand 1 Peter on its own terms and not simply as a letter from a warmed-over Paulinist. Reading 1 Peter with new eyes means bringing the letter out from under the shadow of Paul. "It is high time," Elliott asserts, "for 1 Peter to be liberated from its 'Pauline captivity' and read as a distinctive voice of the early Church."[244]

Unsurprisingly, most contemporary commentators do not evoke the *verba Pauli* in 1 Peter to refute Petrine authorship of 1 Peter. The "Paulinisms" in the letter do not defeat the testimony of the early church regarding the authenticity of the letter. If there are Pauline influences in the letter, such as the expression "in Christ," we can account for these on the basis of the pervasive influence of Paul and his thought in the early church. Moreover, Peter knew Paul and spent time with him on more than one occasion (Gal 1:18–20; 2:1–14; Acts 15). Indeed, Paul publicly confronted Peter in Antioch since he did not live according to the gospel which he and Paul had agreed upon (Gal 2:1–10, 11–21). Peter's associates, Mark and Silvanus, had also participated in the Pauline mission, and their presence with Peter may have been another means by which Paul's teaching could have come to and influenced Peter (see above). Given this complex of relationships, we would expect to hear at least some echo of Paul in 1 Peter. A total absence of Paul's influence would be the real surprise.

The supposed absence of the *verba Christi* in 1 Peter is another argument sometimes raised against the authenticity of the letter. Since Peter was one of the twelve, a member of the inner circle of three, first witness of the resurrection, and the leader of the early church, we would anticipate some quotations from Jesus' teaching in 1 Peter. As Best says, "If the author of 1 Peter had heard Jesus teach on as many occasions as Peter did, we would expect to find strong reminiscences of Jesus' words in the letter."[245] Robert Gundry and Ernest Best entered into a celebrated debate over the *verba Christi* in 1 Peter.[246] Gundry argued that the presence of the *verba Christi* constituted evidence

---

representative of exclusively Pauline theology, that he was a member of a Pauline or post-Pauline circle, or that he was in dialogue or dispute with Pauline theology or its distortions" (*1 Peter*, 40).

244. Elliott, *1 Peter*, 40. Elliott's conclusion is worth quoting in full: "The differences between 1 Peter and the Pauline writings are numerous and striking. They constitute incontestable evidence that, while one or more of the Pauline letters may have been known to the author of 1 Peter, the Petrine author constructed, on the basis of the same tradition known to Paul, a distinctive pastoral message and spoke with a distinctive voice. Proponents of this more nuanced assessment of the relationship between 1 Peter and Paul and the Pauline letters, stressing a mutual reliance on preexistent tradition, have increased in number and now represent the majority view."

245. Ernest Best, *1 Peter* (Grand Rapids: Eerdmans, 1971), 52.

246. Robert H. Gundry, "*Verba Christi* in 1 Peter: Their Implications Concerning the Authorship of 1 Peter and the Authenticity of the Gospel Tradition," *NTS* 13 (1967) 336–50; Ernest Best, "1 Peter and the Gospel Tradition," *NTS* 16 (1970) 95–113; Robert H. Gundry, "Further *Verba* on *Verba Christi* in First Peter," *Bib* 55 (1974) 211–32. For different assessments of their work, see Gerhard Maier, "Jesustradition im 1. Petrusbrief?," in *The Jesus Tradition Outside the Gospels*, ed. David Wenham (Sheffield: JSOT, 1984), 85–128; Achtemeier, *1 Peter*, 10–12; Elliott, *1 Peter*, 24–25; Jobes, *1 Peter*, 17–18. Most give Best the crown for his more cautious assessment of the evidence. While Best acknowledges that the author of 1 Peter knows a few blocks of material from the gospel tradition

that Peter had written the letter since the bulk of the allusions to his teaching come from limited parts of the gospel narrative where Peter was a participant. Best, on the other hand, countered that the affinities between 1 Peter and the Gospels are due to the common use of the gospel traditions.

The author of 1 Peter knew this tradition[247] and draws from certain gospel text plots.[248] For example, the dominical teaching recorded in Matthew 5:16b appears in 1 Peter 2:12b, while 1 Peter 3:14 echoes Matthew 5:10. The author also weaves Jesus' concept found in Matthew 5:16a into 1 Peter 2:12a. Peter appears to have in mind the whole teaching gathered in Matthew 5:10-16. That passage "has to do with the witness of a good life and the conversion to God which is brought through it, as well as the steadfastness of the saints under persecution, their joy through persecution, and the maintenance of a righteous life. All these are key themes in 1 Peter."[249] Similarly, the author mines the teaching recorded in Mark 10:42-45. First Peter 1:18 and Mark 10:45 preserve a common tradition. There is also a parallel, unduly rejected by Best, between Mark 10:42 and 1 Peter 5:3. The use of κατακυριεύω (katakurieuō, "lord it over") demonstrates the relationship as does the concept of being an example. In Mark 10:45 Jesus is the example for the disciples, while in 1 Peter 5:3 the elders are examples for the flock of God. The theme of service is common to this section in Mark 10 and 1 Peter. The teaching of Jesus was not unknown to the author since he integrates sections from it into his discourse. We cannot say, however, that these are personal reminiscences of the Lord's sayings.

The author of 1 Peter is aware of the gospel traditions, although, like most NT authors, he does not signal that he is quoting the words of Jesus. A few direct quotations

---

found in Luke, Rainer Metzner (*Die Rezeption des Matthäusevangeliums im 1. Petrusbrief: Studien zum traditionsgeschichtlichen und theologischen Einfluß des 1. Evangeliums aud fen 1. Petrusbrief* [Tübingen: Mohr Siebeck, 1995]) argues for the letter's dependency upon the Gospel of Matthew.

247. Achtmeier (*1 Peter*, 10-11) sees the clearest affinities between 1 Pet 3:14/Matt 5:10; 1 Pet 2:12b/Matt 5:11-12; 1 Pet 1:4/Matt 25:34; 1 Pet 1:11/Luke 24:26-27. Elliott acknowledges quite a few more: "1 Pet 1:10-12 (Matt 13:17; Luke 24:26); 1:13 (Luke 12:35); 1:17 (Matt 6:9; Luke 11:2); 2:12 (Matt 5:16); 2:19-20 (Luke 6:27-36); 3:9 (Matt 5:38-42/Luke 6:29-30); 3:14 (Matt 5:10); 4:5 (Matt 12:36); 4:13-14 (Matt 5:10-11/Luke 6:22-23, 28); 5:6 (Luke 14:11); 5:7 (Matt 6:25-34)" (*1 Peter*, 24). Elliott questions Metzner's (*Die Rezeption des Matthäusevangeliums im 1. Petrusbrief*) conclusion that the author was dependent on 1 Peter since he "underestimates the differences among the affinities, fails to adequately consider the mutual use of common tradition, and begs the question as to the relative dating of these letters" (*1 Peter*, 25).

248. Dale C. Allison ("The Pauline Epistles and the Synoptic Gospels: The Pattern of the Parallels," *NTS* 28 [1982] 1-32) argues that Paul likewise draws from limited text plots in the gospel tradition. On the adoption of the Jesus tradition in Paul's teaching, see David Michael Stanley, "Pauline Allusions to the Sayings of Jesus," *CBQ* 23 (1961) 26-39; David L. Dungan, *The Sayings of Jesus in the Churches of Paul: The Use of the Synoptic Tradition in the Regulation of Early Church Life* (Philadelphia: Fortress, 1971); David Wenham, ed., *The Jesus Tradition Outside the Gospels* (Sheffield: JSOT, 1985); Victor Paul Furnish, *Jesus According to Paul* (Cambridge: Cambridge University Press, 1993); Harm W. Hollander, "The Words of Jesus: From Oral Traditions to Written Record in Paul and Q," *NovT* 42 (2000) 340-57.

249. Green, "Theology and Ethics in 1 Peter," 76.

from Jesus surface in Acts 20:35 and 1 Corinthians 11:24-25, but these are the exceptions. First Corinthians 7:10-11 refers to but does not quote Jesus' teaching, and 9:14 alludes to Jesus' command regarding payment for gospel labor.[250] Peter, as Paul, adopts Jesus' sayings according to the ancient literary practice of *imitatio* by adapting authoritative sources material to his own ends.[251] Commenting on the process of *imitatio*, Horace noted how difficult it was to adapt sources as one sought to make the material one's own: "It is hard to treat in your own way what is common: . . . . In ground open to all [*publica materiaes*, material part of the public domain] you will win private rights [*privati iuris*] if you do not linger along the easy and open pathway, if you do not seek to render word for word as a slavish translator, and if in your copying [*desilies imitator*] you do not leap into the narrow well" (*Ars Poetica* 131-34). Here Horace remarks on the creative way the poet uses tradition, adapting it to their own purposes. Dionysius of Halicarnassus says that authors who use the work of others should "judge whether any modification is required in the [source] material used—I mean subtraction, addition, or alteration—and to carry out such changes with a proper view of their future purposes" (*On Literary Composition* 6; see Seneca, *Epistulae* 79.6). One should rework and not merely reproduce the ideas of another. In doing *imitatio*, "the *imitator* must always penetrate below the superficial, verbal features of his exemplar to its spirit and significance."[252] The imitated text becomes a recreated text. Behind *imitatio* stands material which serves as the "tradition," which, in poetry and other literature, "both conditions the later poet's work and helps him to formulate its distinctive qualities."[253] Those models one would draw from were regarded as "the books" and due honor is given to their authors through the practice of *imitatio* or μίμησις (*mimēsis*).[254] In the same way, Peter creatively adapts and integrates sections of Jesus' teaching relevant to his purpose of giving ethical instruction to those who are enduring the pressures of persecution, creatively adapting them to his ends. Peter's concern is to use his sources, whatever they may be, to further his support of the persecuted recipients of this letter.[255]

But the allusions to the dominical teaching hardly constitute an argument in favor of Petrine authorship of 1 Peter as Gundry attempted to show. Achtemeier observes, "If Gundry demonstrates anything, it is that 1 Peter is dependent on the present

---

250. Dungan, *The Sayings of Jesus in the Churches of Paul*, 146-47.

251. On the practice, see Green, *Jude and 2 Peter*, 159-62; Gene L. Green, "Intertextuality and Sociology in Early Christianity: A Study of 2 Peter and Jude," in *Reading Jude with New Eyes: Methodological Reassessments of the Letter of Jude*, ed. Robert L. Webb and Peter H. Davids (London: T. & T. Clark, 2009), 1-25.

252. D. A. Russell, "*De Imitatione*," in *Creative Imitation and Latin Literature*, ed. David Alexander West and Tony Woodman (Cambridge: Cambridge University Press, 1979), 5.

253. Gian Biagio Conte, *The Rhetoric of Imitation: Genre and Poetic Memory in Virgil and Other Latin Poets*, ed. Charles Segal (Ithaca: Cornell University Press, 1986), 37.

254. Russell, "*De Imitatione*," 3.

255. Green, "Theology and Ethics in 1 Peter," 122-23.

shape of the Jesus tradition as preserved in the canonical Gospels."[256] Achtemeier's observation, while correct, does not address the additional question of the relationship between the tradition and Peter. The assumption is that the gospel tradition and the "Peter of history" are not related. It is likely, however, that Peter stood behind the tradition, especially given his strong contribution to the Gospel of Mark (see above). That the author of 1 Peter knows the gospel tradition is certain, but he may have also helped shape it and preserve it.[257]

However we understand the relationship between the Jesus tradition and the author of 1 Peter, the evidence certainly does not lead to the conclusion that Peter was not the author of 1 Peter. As noted above, New Testament authors tend not to quote the *verba Christi*, so the letter's lack of direct quotations comes as no surprise.[258] The gospel tradition was quite large (John 21:25) and was preserved and circulated in the early church, so the absence of the *verba Christi* in the NT epistles becomes a problem in general and not simply an argument against the traditional authorship of this letter. Wenham suggests that the Jesus traditions were already well-known in the Pauline churches and when Paul writes "he simply assumes familiarity with the Jesus-tradition and draws on it or reacts with it in a way that his well-taught readers will have understood and appreciated."[259] The author of 1 Peter appears to make the same assumption. The echoes of Jesus would have had a familiar ring to the readers (1:12). Also, we recognize that our author integrates the teaching of Jesus in accordance with ancient literary practices regarding the adoption of authoritative source material (*imitatio*, see above). Given the practice, we would expect allusions to and not direct quotations of Jesus' teaching. Unsurprisingly, recent commentators mention but do not argue strongly that the paucity of reminiscences of the life and teaching of Jesus in the letter is a significant argument against the letter's authenticity.[260] We do not have here a defeater which would undo the testimony of the early church regarding the letter's authenticity.

---

256. Achtemeier, *1 Peter*, 10.

257. This is precisely the point Bauckham argues. The Gospel informants, including the apostles and others, "did not merely start the traditions going and then withdraw from view but remained for many years the known sources and guarantors of traditions of the deeds and words of Jesus" (*Jesus and the Eyewitnesses*, 30).

258. In addition to Allison, "The Pauline Epistles and the Synoptic Gospels," see Stanley, "Pauline Allusions to the Sayings of Jesus"; Nikolaus Walter, "Paulus und die urchristliche Jesustradition," *NTS* 31 (1985) 498–522; Hollander, "The Words of Jesus."

259. David Wenham, "Paul's Use of the Jesus Tradition: Three Samples," in *The Jesus Tradition Outside the Gospels*, ed. David Wenham (Sheffield: JSOT, 1984), 29.

260. Senior simply echoes this argument against authenticity but does not examine it (*1 and 2 Peter* [Wilmington, DE: Glazier, 1980], 4). Achtemeier argues that the presence of the *verba Christi* in 1 Peter does not demonstrate that Peter was the author of the letter. But he simply mentions that the lack of personal reminiscences about Jesus is "an argument often cited against the authenticity of 1 Peter" (*1 Peter*, 9–12). He does not lay out his this case. Elliott likewise mentions it but does not develop the point (*1 Peter*, 120).

Horrell's discussion of 1 Peter takes the question of influences upon the author of the letter a step further. As noted above, Horrell recognizes the Pauline imprint on 1 Peter but wisely stops short of regarding the epistle as the product of a Paulinist. He traces the Gospel traditions in the letter, as have others.[261] But he also points up other traditional elements which made their way into the fabric of the letter, such as the author's vision of his readers as diaspora exiles (e.g., 1 Pet 1:1; Jas 1:1; Heb 11:13), the christological interpretation of Isaiah 53 (1 Pet 1:19; 2:21–25; Acts 8:28–35), the common paraenesis with James (1 Pet 5:5b–9; Jas 4:6–10), and the christological creeds which focus on "Christ's saving work and subsequent exaltation" (1 Pet 1:18–21; 2:21–25; 3:18–22; 1 Cor 15:3–4; 1 Tim 3:16; 2 Tim 1:9–10; Titus 2:14).[262] Horrell concludes that the letter is an "'epistle of tradition,' both Pauline and non-Pauline." Yet the author is not merely a compiler of traditions but rather pens "a creative and distinctive letter into which a wide range of Christian traditions are incorporated."[263] The letter is a masterpiece of intertextuality, a "mosaic of other texts," creatively brought together by an otherwise unknown author.[264] Horrell does not see this letter as a product of a Petrine circle but instead an early Christian synthesis ascribed to the one who was remembered as the leader of the early church. Peter was, a Perkins notes, "a leader of the whole church."[265] Horrell concludes that "the content of the letter displays not particularly 'Petrine' character."[266] The name "Peter" became attached to it only because of the apostle's prominence in the early church.

Horrell underscores that 1 Peter incorporates a broad range of early traditions, but then so do Paul and James. These early Christian authors, while each unique in their contributions, were members of larger mobile and highly communicative community. Within their pages we witness common uses of the OT texts and common catechetical material such as the domestic codes, hymnic elements, creedal formulas, and dominical sayings. Indeed, for decades we have recognized that Peter and others surface for us the substructures of early Christian *didache*. We are hard-pressed to find an exception. What makes 1 Peter outstanding is not the use of common stock teaching in the church but rather the intensity of the intertextuality. This is not, however, evidence against Petrine authorship any more than the use of common teaching material becomes grounds for doubting Pauline authorship of Romans or 1 Corinthians. Early Christians engaged deeply in *imitatio*, adopting and adapting traditional material for their own ends. And given the central role Peter played within the life of the early church, we would *expect* a letter by him to be the place to find a locus of traditional materials.

261. Horrell, *Becoming Christian*, 21–22.
262. Horrell, *Becoming Christian*, 20–25.
263. Horrell, *Becoming Christian*, 26.
264. Horrell, *Becoming Christian*, 28.
265. Horrell, *Becoming Christian*, 42, citing Perkins, *Peter*, 120.
266. Horrell, *Becoming Christian*, 42.

Horrell states that the content of 1 Peter does not display a "particularly 'Petrine' character." At no point does Horrell show how the letter is not Petrine but merely asserts that it is not because of the integration of varied traditions from the early church. His claim that the letter does not have a Petrine character also does not jibe with his observation that 1 Peter is "a creative and distinctive letter."[267] Moreover, Horrell fails to show what Petrine theology might look like. This would be a necessary step to support the claim that the character of the letter is not Petrine. First Peter is the composition of a leader in the early church who is in touch with a vast array of traditions and who provides a centrist theology for the church, as we might expect from one who is a principle ecclesial and theological leader.[268] We would expect him to sound like others and not a voice dissimilar to the rest. Applying the criterion of dissimilarity in order to evaluate authenticity is not sound methodology.

For a number of years, many regarded the nature of the persecutions described in 1 Peter as evidence that the letter comes down to us from the post-apostolic era. The persecuted churches in Asia Minor faced governmental repression of the type meted out during the administration of Pliny the Younger, the governor of Bithynia, early in the second decade of the second century. The letter, therefore, comes from a period well after Peter's death. Beare became a strong advocate of this view.[269] He recalled the persecution that broke out during the reign of Trajan and the correspondences the emperor had with Pliny about the Christian problem. Pliny, who became governor around AD 110–11, asked Trajan whether merely being a Christian constituted a crime or whether one had to be associated with offenses attached to the name (*Letters* 10.96.2).[270] Beare recognizes the injunction in 1 Peter 4:16 as a direct response to this situation: "Yet if any of you suffers as a Christian, do not consider it a disgrace." As he says, "Pliny's description of his experience and methods could not conceivably correspond more closely to the words of 1 Peter 4:12–16; and there is certainly nothing resembling it to be found elsewhere in ancient literature or in official documents."[271] First Peter must therefore come from the same time as Pliny's letter.

Goppelt, however, effectively countered Beare by asserting that 1 Peter nowhere reflects Pliny's policy of demanding that those accused of being Christians offer wine and incense to the image of the emperor (*Letters* 10.96.5).[272] Goppelt notes that the persecutions the recipients endured were not those under Nero or Domitian either. From Selwyn onward, commentators have recognized that the persecutions reflected in the letter are "sporadic, personal, and unorganized social ostracism of Christians,

---

267. Horrell, *Becoming Christian*, 26.

268. See chapter 5 for a discussion of Peter's theology in the epistle.

269. Beare, *The First Epistle of Peter*, 32–34.

270. Pliny inquires, "Whether it is the mere name of Christian which is punishable, even if innocent of crime, or rather the crimes associated with the name."

271. Beare, *The First Epistle of Peter*, 33.

272. Goppelt, *A Commentary on 1 Peter*, 43.

probably reinforced at the local level by the increasing suspicions of Roman officials at all levels."[273] We cannot identify the persecutions in the letter with any set period in the early church. Rather, they reflect the type of hostility directed at this seeming aberrant movement that was the church's lot since the earliest days of the proclamation of the gospel. Achtemeier rightly concludes, "As a result, we cannot fix a specific date to the persecutions reflected in 1 Peter, and such references to persecution are therefore of no value in seeking to determine whether Simon Peter could still have been alive when they occurred, and hence could have been the author of the letter."[274] He and other contemporary commentators do not appeal to the nature of the persecutions as an argument against Petrine authorship of the letter either. This is not an argument which defeats the testimony of the early church regarding the letter's authenticity.

The most powerful argument against the authenticity of 1 Peter is the Greek style of the letter. Could a Galilean fishermen have produced a letter written in such polished Greek? Beare contended:

> In the third place, and most decisively, the Epistle is quite obviously the work of a man of letters, skilled in all the devices of rhetoric, and able to draw upon an extensive and even learned vocabulary. He was a stylist of no ordinary capacity, and he writes some of the best Greek in the whole New Testament, far smoother and more literary than that of the highly-trained Paul. This is a feat plainly far beyond the powers of a Galilean fisherman, who at the time of the Crucifixion could neither read nor write even his own native tongue (Aramaic). For the word ἀγράμματος in Acts 4:13 means exactly that—not merely 'unlearned,' but actually 'illiterate.' It is quite probable that there was some bilingualism in Galilee, and that a fisherman would be able to manage enough of the Greek of the marketplace to bargain for a good price for his fish, but that he should ever become a master of Greek prose is simply unthinkable.[275]

The Greek style of the letter is elevated, although not all agree on the level of linguistic refinement. Kelly cautions about praising the style too highly since it is "unimaginative, monotonous, and at times clumsy," even though the author had "a technical training which we could not plausibly attribute to Peter."[276] Kelly's assessment is perhaps a bit too low since the letter contains some of the best Greek of the

---

273. Jobes, *1 Peter*, 9. So Selwyn, *The First Epistle of Peter*, 52–55; Best, *1 Peter*, 39–42; Michaels, *1 Peter*, lxiii–lxvii; Achtemeier, *1 Peter*, 28–36; Elliott, *1 Peter*, 97–103; Schreiner, *1, 2 Peter, Jude*, 28–31. Elliott (*1 Peter*, 103) summarizes his survey of the evidence, saying, "In sum, the manner in which Christian suffering is mentioned, described, and addressed in this letter points not to organized Roman persecution as its cause but to local social tensions deriving from the social, cultural, and religious differences demarcating believers from their neighbors."

274. Achtemeier, *1 Peter*, 36.

275. Beare, *The First Epistle of Peter*, 46–47.

276. J. N. D. Kelly, *A Commentary on the Epistles of Peter and Jude* (Grand Rapids: Baker, 1969), 31. So Achtemeier, *1 Peter*, 2.

New Testament and its author displays a high degree of rhetorical ability.[277] The style, Achtemeier notes, is neither Grand nor Simple but Middle.[278] According to *Rhetorica ad Herennium*, "The Grand type consists of a smooth and ornate arrangement of impressive words. The Middle type consists of words of a lower, yet not of the lowest and most colloquial, class of words. The Simple type is brought down even to the most current idiom of standard speech" (4.8.11). First Peter's Greek, while not displaying the highest stylistic features, was "probably beyond" that which could be produced by a Palestinian fisherman "who lacked formal education."[279] Elliott concurs that the style of 1 Peter is "polished Attic" (which may be identified with the "Middle" style) and represents the work of "an author of some education."[280] This is not the Greek of a tradesman whose mother tongue was Aramaic.

Jobes nuances the assessment 1 Peter's Greek by showing that "the Greek of 1 Peter arguably exhibits bilingual interference that is consistent with a Semitic author for whom Greek is a second language."[281] In examining the Greek of the letter, Jobes utilizes the concept of linguistic or dynamic interference, which analyzes the way linguistic structures of one language are imposed upon another. She lays out the criteria whereby we may identify linguistic interference and concludes that the author was indeed bilingual and that his Greek shows Semitic influence.[282] Although the author was Semitic, Jobes does not see this as conclusive evidence for determining the authorship of the letter. Whether or not Greek was prevalent enough in Galilee for Peter to have learned it up to the level of this letter and whether a fisherman could have acquired such rhetorical skill remain unanswered questions in Jobes's analysis. She is, however, willing to say, "The issue of whether Peter wrote the letter cannot be so

---

277. So Achtemeier, *1 Peter*, 2; Elliott, *1 Peter*, 64; Lauri Thurén, *The Rhetorical Strategy of 1 Peter* (Åbo: Åbo Akademi University, 1990); Lauri Thurén, *Argument and Theology in 1 Peter: The Origins of Christian Paraenesis* (Sheffield: Sheffield Academic, 1995).

278. Achtemeier, *1 Peter*, 2n8. Achtemeier mistakenly attributes the following quotation to Quintilian.

279. Achtemeier, *1 Peter*, 2–3.

280. Elliott, *1 Peter*, 64, 120.

281. Jobes, *1 Peter*, 7, and the excursus (325–38). The Semitic influence on the author's diction has not gone unnoticed by others (William L. Schutter, *Hermeneutic and Composition in 1 Peter* [Tübingen: Mohr, 1989], 83; Elliott, *1 Peter*, 64), although Achtemeier cautions, "The absence of influence of the language of the Hebrew Bible or the Targumim on the one hand, and the clear influence of the LXX on the other, show that the author was at home in Greek rather than Semitic culture, and such is likely not to have been the case with Simon Peter" (*1 Peter*, 7).

282. She concludes that "Semitic interference is indicated by (a) the use of prepositions . . . (b) the use of the genitive personal pronoun . . . (c) the position of the attributive adjectives, and (d) the use of the dative case with ἐν. . . . A comparison of the syntactical profile of 1 Peter with Josephus and Polybius clearly shows that its syntax, at least as measured by these fourteen syntactical criteria, is not nearly as 'good' as Polybius, or even as good as Josephus, if 'good' is defined as the Greek style and syntax of a natively proficient speaker" (Jobes, *1 Peter*, 334).

summarily dismissed by appeals to the quality of the epistle's Greek without further critical investigation of several key questions."[283]

How well did people know Greek in Galilee of the first century, and could a tradesman like Peter have learned to write Greek at the "middle" level? Schreiner[284] evokes Hengel's work[285] to show the penetration of Greek into Galilee. He also observes that Galilee was near the Decapolis and so "linguistic contact and overlap between the two areas was inevitable." Sepphoris in Galilee was a Hellenistic city and, he adds, as a businessman, Peter "would almost certainly have known Greek." Schreiner also appeals to Sevenster's volume on the topic,[286] which makes a case that ordinary people in Galilee would have known Greek. He also reminds us of the ossuaries inscribed in Greek and documents such as letters written during the rebellion under bar Kochba that used the language. Greek was even found at Qumran, and Josephus indicated that motivated Jews could write Greek well (*Ant.* 20.262–65). Greek inscriptions also point to a more widespread knowledge and use of the language. Schreiner therefore concludes, "Greek certainly was known and commonly used in Palestine." Peter, he adds, "almost certainly knew Greek and used it well." His praise does not end there: "Peter may have had the capacity to write excellent Greek."[287]

Not everyone assesses the linguistic skills of the Galileans the same way. In his study of the Hellenization of Galilee, Horsley concludes that "literacy in Judea and Galilee was concentrated among the political-cultural elite. . . . It seems highly unlikely that many villagers were literate."[288] He cautions against concluding that the situation in the Gentile city of Sepphoris was indicative of the rest of Galilee, stating that "there is much less of an indication that Greek was an everyday language in the rest of Lower Galilee. Pidgin Greek may have been common, but a bilingual situation seems unlikely given evidence now available."[289] Social status and linguistic ability were bound together. Those adept at Greek were the social elite. Josephus gives us another window into the extent to which his people learned Greek. For his own part, he studied the language diligently but could not rid himself of his accent (*Ant.* 20.263). Learning other tongues, however, was not encouraged among the Jews of his era: "For our people do not favor those persons who have mastered the speech of many nations" (20.264). Learning the law and interpreting the meaning of Scripture were

---

283. Jobes, *1 Peter*, 8.

284. Schreiner, *1, 2 Peter, Jude*, 33.

285. Martin Hengel, *Judaism and Hellenism: Studies in Their Encounter in Palestine During the Early Hellenistic Period* (Philadelphia: Fortress, 1974).

286. J. N. Sevenster, *Do You Know Greek? How Much Greek Could the First Jewish Christians Have Known?* (Leiden: Brill, 1968).

287. Schreiner, *1, 2 Peter, Jude*, 34–35.

288. Richard A. Horsley, *Archaeology, History, and Society in Galilee: The Social Context of Jesus and the Rabbis* (Valley Forge, PA: Trinity, 1996), 158.

289. Richard A. Horsley, *Archaeology, History, and Society in Galilee*, 171; Richard A. Horsley, *Galilee: History, Politics, People* (Valley Forge, PA: Trinity, 1995), 247.

valued more highly than learning other languages. The apostle Philip, from Bethsaida, was adept enough at Greek for Greeks to seek him out from among the apostolic band (John 12:20–21),[290] but we cannot assess his level of linguistic proficiency nor can we start from this statement and generalize about the extent to which Galileans knew Greek. Chancey draws together the rather disparate evidence regarding Greek in Galilee and shows the weakness of the evidence for widespread use of the language there. The "epigraphic corpus is quite small," and what evidence we do possess "[tells] us little about the everyday language of the common people."[291] There are loan-words and names borrowed from Greek. Moreover, "those involved in trade with the coastal cities, and educated civic elites" may have known the language. But the evidence "by no means makes clear . . . that Greek was widely used among the Galilean masses."[292] Chancy draws together the available epigraphic evidence from Galilee during this period, something Hengel failed to do, and concludes that "enthusiastic claims about the high number of Galileans proficient in Greek are difficult to support."[293] Officials and elites would have known the language, but outside the sphere of government, it becomes difficult to affirm the widespread knowledge of Greek. Chancy notes that there was an up-tick in the use of Greek in inscriptions during Antipas's reign, but the real increase occurred with the arrival of more Romans to Galilee during the second century. Before this, the Greek inscriptions are scant. Aramaic appeared to remain the common tongue.[294] All told, we lack the evidence to support the idea that Peter, as a Galilean fisherman, would have known Greek well enough to write 1 Peter. Given the evidence from Galilee during this period, it is unlikely that he would have acquired Greek proficiency.

Waltner, however, argues that given Peter's travels over twenty-five years, he would have had sufficient contact with Greeks to have learned the language well.[295]

---

290. On Bethsaida, see Rami Arav and Richard A. Freund, eds., *Bethsaida: A City By the North Shore of the Sea of Galilee*, vol. 1 (Kirksville, MO: Thomas Jefferson University Press, 1995); Ravi Arav, "New Testament Archaeology and the Case of Bethsaida," in *Das Ende der Tage und die Gegenwart des Heils: Begegnungen mit dem Neuen Testament und seiner Umwelt*, ed. Michael Becker and Wolfgang Fenske (Leiden: Brill, 1999), 75–99; Ravi Arav, "Bethsaida," *IEJ* 51 (2001) 239–46. For a survey of the positions on the use of Greek in Galilee, see Stanley E. Porter, "Jesus and the Use of Greek in Galilee," in *Studying the Historical Jesus: Evaluations of the State of Current Research*, ed. Bruce Chilton and Craig A. Evans (Leiden: Brill, 1994), 123–54.

291. Mark A. Chancey, *The Myth of a Gentile Galilee* (Cambridge: Cambridge University Press, 2002), 180.

292. Chancey, *The Myth of a Gentile Galilee*, 180. And see the fuller discussion in Mark A. Chancey, *Greco-Roman Culture and the Galilee of Jesus* (Cambridge: Cambridge University Press, 2005), 122–65.

293. Chancey, *Greco-Roman Culture and the Galilee of Jesus*, 161–65.

294. Chancey, *Greco-Roman Culture and the Galilee of Jesus*, 165. The situation in Galilee was analogous to Egypt where the rural population lacked knowledge of the language of those who occupied their land (Thomas J. Kraus, "'Uneducated,' 'Ignorant,' or Even 'Illiterate'? Aspects and Background for an Understanding of ΑΓΡΑΜΜΑΤΟΙ [and ΙΔΙΩΤΑΙ] in Acts 4:13," *NTS* 45 [1999] 441).

295. Erland Waltner and J. Daryl Charles, *First-Second Peter, Jude* (Scottdale, PA: Herald, 1999), 177.

Having lived in Latin America for thirteen years and written two books in Spanish, I am sympathetic to his argument. People who live on foreign soil sometimes become adept in the language of their host community, even attaining professional-level proficiency. Peter had a surprising rhetorical presence, given the testimony in Acts 4:12 regarding his παρρησίαν, or rhetorical boldness.[296] However, the Sanhedrin regarded Peter and John as "uneducated and ordinary" men (ἀγράμματοί ... καὶ ἰδιῶται). This could mean that they were illiterate and ignorant, but, in this context, it more likely focuses on their lack of professional training in the law (cf. John 7:15, πῶς οὗτος γράμματα οἶδεν μὴ μεμαθηκώς;).[297] In this passage we see Peter and John through the eyes of their critics. The apostles did not appear to have been trained in Torah and could even be regarded as illiterate. In the end, however, the comments recorded in Acts are germane to the Jewish context in which the events took place and do not speak directly to whether or not Peter could have known Greek. The recognition, however, that Peter lacked formal Torah training suggests that he was not versed in Greek either. Indeed, Joshua ben Gamala established compulsory education in the synagogue sometime before the destruction of the Second Temple (Talmud, *Baba Bathra* 21a), but the primary concern was instruction in the Law. First students were obliged to begin studies at sixteen or seventeen, but later he instituted education starting at age six or seven. Given when such education was established, most likely Peter did not have the benefit of any formal training.

The consistent testimony from the early church is that Peter found Greek to be a linguistic challenge. He worked with translators. Two of them, Mark (see above) and Glaucias (Clement of Alexandria, *Stromata* 7.17), are mentioned in the Fathers. We would expect, therefore, that if Peter wrote 1 Peter, then he would have employed someone who could translate what he spoke, not simply an amanuensis. Translation was a common art that facilitated the cultural growth of the Romans as they translated Greek texts into Latin. The translator stood *inter pares*, that is, "between the two sides."[298] This cultural move appears again as the gospel, first communicated in Aramaic, now spread through the Mediterranean basin in Greek.[299] Some could speak fluent Greek as Paul (Acts 21:37), while others, like Peter, utilized translators. The fact that someone used a translator did not necessarily mean that the person was ignorant of the receptor language. Cato the Elder chose not to speak to the Athenians in Greek

---

296. Johnson, *The Acts of the Apostles*, 78; Barrett, *The Acts of the Apostles*, 233; Witherington, *The Acts of the Apostles*, 195; Bock, *Acts*, 195.

297. See the discussions in Johnson, *The Acts of the Apostles*, 78; Barrett, *The Acts of the Apostles*, 233-34; Witherington, *The Acts of the Apostles*, 195-96; Bock, *Acts*, 195-96; *BDAG* 15, 468.

298. *OCD* 1545.

299. The fact that Greek was the chosen language for the Gospel of Mark and Romans, written to Latins in Rome, or 1-2 Corinthians and Philippians, written to Latin provincials, is a curious feature of early Christianity. Did the early church ride the wave of the popularity of all things Greek? Or, since Latins were the social elite who held power and money, is the Greek of the NT evidence of the lower class of the early adherents to the gospel?

but used a translator, even though he knew Greek well. He refused to be swept up with the popularity of all things Greek (Plutarch, *Cato Maior* 12.4). Peter's case, however, was different. He apparently needed help with the language, and people like Mark and Glaucias assisted him. Translation word for word could be done, but translation of the sense was regarded more highly.[300] In such translation, the translator's stamp on the original becomes quite evident as rhetorical concerns take precedence over literalism. Faithfulness to content, not form, was the ideal. So we would expect that the Greek of 1 Peter to represent Peter's thought but not be a slavish representation of the original.

Some years ago, Selwyn suggested that Silvanus, a Hellenistic Jew, served as Peter's amanuensis (1 Pet 5:12; also known as Silas, see above) and would therefore be the person responsible for the fine diction of 1 Peter.[301] According to Selwyn, Silvanus would not only have contributed to the style of the letter but also would have contributed to its content. Selwyn believed Silvanus was responsible for the affinities between 1 Peter and the Thessalonian correspondence. First Peter 5:12 appears to signal that Silvanus served as an amanuensis since Peter says that he wrote the letter "through Silvanus" (Διὰ Σιλουανοῦ . . . δι' ὀλίγων ἔγραψα). However, recent studies have shown that the expression γράφω διά commonly designated the messenger who carried a letter and not the scribe who wrote it.[302] Richards admirably presents a wide range of

---

300. "And I did not translate them as an interpreter, but as an orator, keeping the same ideas and the forms, or as one might say, the 'figures' of thought, but in language which conforms to our usage. And in so doing, I did not hold it necessary to render word for word, but I preserved the general style and force of the language. For I did not think I ought to count them out to the reader like coins, but to pay them by weight, as it were" (Cicero, *De optimo genere oratorum* 14); "Though all the same it need not be a hard and fast rule that every word shall be represented by its exact counterpart, when there is a more familiar word conveying the same meaning. That is the way of a clumsy translator. Indeed my own practice is to use several words to give what is expressed in Greek by one, if I cannot convey the sense other" (Cicero, *De finibus* 3.4.15); "Nor must you be so faithful a translator, as to take the pains of rendering [the original] word for word; nor by imitating throw yourself into straits, whence either shame or the rules of your work may forbid you to retreat" (Horace, *Ars poetica* 133–34); "For I myself not only admit but freely proclaim that in translating from the Greek (except in the case of the holy scriptures where even the order of the words is a mystery) I render sense for sense and not word for word. For this course I have the authority of Tully who has so translated the Protagoras of Plato, the Œconomicus of Xenophon, and the two beautiful orations which Æschines and Demosthenes delivered one against the other. What omissions, additions, and alterations he has made substituting the idioms of his own for those of another tongue, this is not the time to say. I am satisfied to quote the authority of the translator who has spoken as follows in a prologue prefixed to the orations. I have thought it right to embrace a labour which though not necessary for myself will prove useful to those who study. I have translated the noblest speeches of the two most eloquent of the Attic orators, the speeches which Æschines and Demosthenes delivered one against the other; but I have rendered them not as a translator but as an orator, keeping the sense but altering the form by adapting both the metaphors and the words to suit our own idiom. I have not deemed it necessary to render word for word but I have reproduced the general style and emphasis. I have not supposed myself bound to pay the words out one by one to the reader but only to give him an equivalent in value" (Jerome, *Letters* 57.5).

301. Selwyn, *The First Epistle of Peter*, 9–17, 241–42.

302. Michaels, *1 Peter*, 306–7; Achtemeier, *1 Peter*, 8–9, 350; Elliott, *1 Peter*, 123–24, 872–74; E. Randolph Richards, "Silvanus Was Not Peter's Secretary: Theological Bias in Interpreting διὰ Σιλουανοῦ . . . ἔγραψα in 1 Peter 5:12," *JETS* 43 (2000) 417–32; Jobes, *1 Peter*, 320. Goppelt presents

epigraphic evidence that shows how this idiomatic phrase identified and, indeed, accredited the messenger since that person would be charged not only with the delivery of the document but also would provide additional commentary.[303] The sole exception to this rule is found in Eusebius (*HE* 4.23.11), who cites Dionysius of Corinth, saying that the Romans wrote 1 Clement through Clement (διὰ Κλήμεντος γραφεῖσαν). Clement was not the scribe but rather the commissioned author of the letter written on behalf of the Roman church. Contextual considerations here demand that we understand γράφω διά as something other than a designation of the letter's messenger. Richards and others recognize this as an alternate use of the phrase but, rightly, insist that this is not an example that shows that the phrase was used to identify a secretary.[304] The way Dionysius of Corinth (and Eusebius) understand the phrase, however, shows that exceptions to the general rule can be made. Such is the dynamic nature of language. *Ad hoc* concept formation occurs all the time, both in oral and written communication. All concepts bend by broadening or narrowing in use, although their lexical entry remains the same. Communication entails more than encoding and decoding concepts using the sign system (language) but depends heavily on contextual information to be successful. Such concept broadening from "messenger" to "responsible party" occurs in the way Dionysius uses γράφω διά (*HE* 4.23.11).[305] Contextual considerations lead us to this conclusion and not simply the lexical entries. Determining the meaning of the phrase does not merely depend on counting the number of times it communicates "to send via." In the same way, contextual information should be part of the interpretive strategy for understanding 1 Peter 5:12.

While we may say that the author could well have meant that Silvanus was the messenger (Διὰ Σιλουανοῦ ... ἔγραψα), the author modifies the concept in use by adding the phrase δι' ὀλίγων. "Briefly" turns the reader's attention to the process of composition and not to the agent who carried the letter.[306] Therefore, as in *HE* 4.23.11, Διὰ Σιλουανοῦ ... δι' ὀλίγων ἔγραψα focuses upon the one commissioned with writing the letter identified as a brief communication. We cannot separate off δι' ὀλίγων from Διὰ Σιλουανοῦ ... ἔγραψα as Richards attempts to do. He argues that Διὰ Σιλουανοῦ is the phrase which signals the messenger while, he admits, ἔγραψα talks of composition. At this point, Richards's case breaks since only with some clarifying verb could

---

the evidence yet opts for the view that Silvanus was the secretary (*A Commentary on 1 Peter*, 368-69).

303. Richards, "Silvanus Was Not Peter's Secretary"; E. Randolph Richards, *The Secretary in the Letters of Paul* (Tübingen: Mohr Siebeck, 1991), 14-67; E. Randolph Richards, *Paul and First-Century Letter Writing: Secretaries, Composition, and Collection* (Downers Grove, IL: InterVarsity, 2004), 183-84.

304. Richards, "Silvanus Was Not Peter's Secretary," 423-24. See also Michaels, *1 Peter*, 306; Achtemeier, *1 Peter*, 350n26; Elliott, *1 Peter*, 872-73.

305. Gene L. Green, "Lexical Pragmatics and Biblical Interpretation," *JETS* 50 (2007) 799-812.

306. Witherington, *Letters and Homilies for Hellenized Christians*, 244-47. The focus is upon the shortness of the composition. In fact, P72 has διὰ βραχέων ("briefly," as in Heb 13:22), which communicates the same idea. Compare Plato, *Philebus* 31d; 2 Macc 6:17, which use δι' ὀλίγων to refer to a brief oral address.

Διὰ Σιλουανοῦ ever become an idiom which designated a messenger. Although Διὰ Σιλουανοῦ . . . ἔγραψα is not a common way to name an amanuensis, here the author uses it to designate the person he commissioned to write this document. The author, then, would have approved the content of the letter before dispatching it, thus assuring that the content was truly his own.[307] Scribes sometimes served as messengers as well, and Silvanus could have done double duty.[308]

In the end, however, it matters little whether or not Silvanus was the amanuensis or messenger who carried the letter. Using secretaries was common practice, and these agents would, in some cases, take dictation and, in others, be given greater compositional responsibilities.[309] We expect that Peter, as someone working outside his mother tongue, would have utilized the services of an amanuensis in composition. This person was most likely Silvanus, but even if it was not, someone would need to fill this role. Moreover, the testimony from the early church indicates that Peter needed a translator. Given his linguistic skill, an epistle from him would most likely be a translated document and not a composition spoken in Greek and transcribed by his amanuensis. He needed greater help than merely putting his words to papyrus. Therefore, we would anticipate 1 Peter to exhibit some Semitic linguistic interference, as Jobes indicates, given that Peter's secretary would have been bilingual. We may also account for the fine stylistic features of the letter to be the product of this secretary and not Peter himself. The secretary, whoever he was, would also be the person responsible for citing the LXX instead of quoting and translating from the Hebrew Bible. No matter who wrote the book, we may rightly expect that he would have utilized this translation, which became the authoritative Scriptures of the Greek speaking church.[310] Finally, while the *verba* of the letter were certainly those of the author's amanuensis/translator, the *vox* would be that of the author himself, who, according to common practice, would have approved the content (Cicero, *Ad Fam.* 5.20 [128]) and added the final greeting in his own hand. In other words, the Greek of a document attributed to Peter should be better than what a Galilean fisherman of this period could have

---

307. Richards, *The Secretary in the Letters of Paul*, 53–56; Richards, *Paul and First-Century Letter Writing*, 171–77. By sealing the letter or by summarizing of the contents or incuding a farewell in their own hand, authors demonstrated they were responsible for the contents of the whole letter, even those freely composed by an amanuensis.

308. John L. White, *Light from Ancient Letters* (Philadelphia: Fortress, 1986), 216.

309. On the range of scribal practices from transcription to contribution and even composition, see Richards, *The Secretary in the Letters of Paul*; Richards, "Silvanus Was Not Peter's Secretary."

310. See Karen H. Jobes and Moises Silva, *Invitation to the Septuagint* (Grand Rapids: Baker Academic, 2000), 183–205 and bibliography; R. Timothy McLay, *The Use of the Septuagint in New Testament Research* (Grand Rapids: Eerdmans, 2003), 137–70; Jennifer M. Dines, *The Septuagint* (London; New York: T. & T. Clark, 2004), 142–49. The use of the LXX in 1 Peter is no more an issue than its use in Hebrews or even the Pauline letters. Why would the pervasive presence of the LXX be an argument against the author being Semitic? Indeed, the LXX "was read and exegeted even in the synagogues of the Hellenists in Jerusalem" (Martin Hengel, *The Septuagint as Christian Scripture: Its Prehistory and the Problem of Its Canon* [Edinburgh: T. & T. Clark, 2002], 108).

produced. First Peter's fine Greek is not a defeater which can undo the testimony of the early church regarding the Petrine authorship of the letter. Rather, the Greek style serves as an oblique support of the letter's authenticity. What we would anticipate from him as he gives testimony is precisely what we see.

We therefore have no cogent reason to reject the early, widespread, and consistent testimony of the early church that 1 Peter is an authentic letter of the apostle Peter. Rejecting the authenticity of the letter has become the settled conclusion among many scholars, but a reexamination of the evidence does not warrant the easy rejection exhibited in some commentaries. The traditional reasons for rejecting Petrine authorship are, at times, arguments to the contrary. The early testimony regarding the letter's authenticity is consistent with the historical evidence regarding authenticity. All the details from within and outside the letter are consistent and cohere together, including the presence of Mark with the author, the Roman origin of the letter, and even the fine Greek of the epistle. No detail is out of place, and no piece of the testimony has undefeated defeaters. We may therefore accept 1 Peter as a representative of Peter's theology.

This is not to say that the theology presented in the letter comes to us without other influences impinging upon it. If the letter is a translation of Peter's thought, then the apostle's translator and amanuensis left his stamp upon the document. Every translation, as every testimony, is an interpretation and commentary. The letter represents the *vox Petri* but not the exact *verba Petri*. As with the other works which provide testimony to Peter's thought, 1 Peter comes to us as a document which shows the influence of an authorial community. While we cannot expect to hear "pure Peter" as we read these pages aloud, we can expect that the content was approved by the apostle. The testimony in Mark, the Petrine speeches in Acts, and 1 Peter all present us with Peter as interpreted by those who sought to communicate his preaching and thought for the church. He stands behind each witness, but we must recognize that his voice is mediated and, therefore, colored by those who wrote on his behalf. These witnesses faithfully record his testimony and, in the case of 1 Peter, the apostle would have given the final approval of what his translator/amanuensis wrote in his name. If there is a "Petrine School"[311] which stands behind this letter, it consists of those who participate as members of Peter's authorial community,[312] such as Mark and Silvanus, as well as Peter himself. Indeed, the common threads found in the literature associated

---

311. John H. Elliott, *A Home for the Homeless: A Social Exegesis of 1 Peter, Its Situation and Strategy* (Philadelphia: Fortress, 1981), 267-95; Marion L. Soards, "1 Peter, 2 Peter, and Jude as Evidence for a Petrine School," *Aufstieg und Niedergang der römishen Welt* 2.25.5 (1988) 3827-49; David Horrell, *The Epistles of Peter and Jude* (London: Epworth, 1998); Chatelion Counet, "Pseudepigraphy and the Petrine School: Spirit and Tradition in 1 and 2 Peter and Jude," *HvTSt* 62 (2006) 403-24. Elliott says the letter reflects the voice of a Petrine group in the Roman church "of which Silvanus and Mark were members" (*1 Peter*, 130; *A Home for the Homeless*, 272).

312. For this concept, see Johannes A. Loubser, "Media Criticism and the Myth of Paul, the Creative Genius, and His Forgotten Co-Workers," *Neot* 34 (2000) 329-45 and Richards's comments on letters as community compositions (*Paul and First-Century Letter Writing*, 32-36).

with Peter, such as 1 and 2 Peter and Mark, are not merely evidences of a "Petrine School" in Rome but rather the raw materials of a genuine Petrine theology mediated to the church through those who assisted Peter in his ministry and compositions.

First Peter itself frames its message to the believers in Asia Minor as testimony which comes not only from Peter but also the prophets and the Christian messengers who bore witness to the Gospel in the provinces enumerated in 1:1. At the end of the opening thanksgiving of the letter (1:3–12), Peter focuses on the salvation of God which the prophets predicted and which Christ realized through his sufferings and glories (1:10–11). Christian messengers announced this good news, being empowered by the Holy Spirit (1:12). This section takes up the concept of testimony in its attempt to strengthen these believers who experienced suffering through social ostracism, verbal abuse, and even physical attack (5:10–11). In his exposition regarding God's salvation, announced in the previous verses as a present reality and a future hope (1:5, 9), Peter shows how the prophets announced its coming. They bore witness to the sufferings and glories of Christ, the center of God's saving plan, before the events occurred: "the Spirit of Christ within them . . . testified in advance to the sufferings destined for Christ and the subsequent glory" (or "glories," τὰς . . . δόξας). These were unable to interpret their oracles: "The prophets who prophesied of the grace that was to be yours made careful search and inquiry, inquiring about the person or time that the Spirit of Christ within them indicated when he testified in advance" regarding Christ's sufferings and subsequent glorification. To these "it was revealed that they were not serving themselves but you." In other words, the oracles are now rightly interpreted in light of Jesus Christ's death, resurrection, and ascension, and heralds proclaim this message (1:12). In *Ars Rhetorica*, Aristotle discussed testimony, commenting that those who offer testimony about events could be from the past or present, "ancient or recent" (1.15.13, 15–16). Moreover, "interpreters of oracles for the future" (1.15.14) could also serve as witnesses who offer reliable testimony. Correct interpretation of oracles provides testimony. While the prophets gave testimony, only in the present are their words understood and interpreted properly. Peter reminds his readers of the ancient prophetic testimony by which the Spirit of Christ "testified in advance" (προμαρτυρόμενον, 1:11). The implication is that this prior witness was written.[313] Peter underscores the reliability of this witness since it came from the "Spirit of Christ," which was in the prophets, and this serves as proof that inspires confidence. Aristotle remarked that "moral character, so to say, constitutes the most effective means of proof" (1.2.4), and such proof is at the heart of testimony.[314] Peter

---

313. The word appears only here in extant ancient literature at least until the beginning of the eighth century AD when it is used in two papyri to refer to issues that letters had previously borne witness (PLond IV 1343, 27; 1356, 32; *BDAG* 872).

314. "The orator persuades by moral character when his speech is delivered in such a manner as to render him worthy of confidence; for we feel confidence in a greater degree and more readily in persons of worth in regard to everything in general, but where there is not certainty and there is room for doubt, our confidence is absolute" (1.2.4).

adds that the same Spirit accredits those who now bear witness regarding the sufferings and glory of Christ (1:12). Their witness comes with divine sanction as also that of the prophets (cf. Acts 5:32; 1 John 5:6; John 15:26–27) as they announce the events which constitute the gospel. The report which was communicated (ἀνηγγέλη)[315] to their hearers in Asia Minor was the testimony of the gospel events, both predicted and fulfilled.

Peter's Testimony in 1 Peter

Peter adds his own testimony (5:1, 12) to the oracular witness of the prophets, now rightly interpreted. He stands as one who was a witness of Christ's sufferings (5:1, μάρτυς) and who now gives testimony (5:12, ἐπιμαρτυρῶν) regarding God's grace. In 5:1 he identifies himself as "a witness of the sufferings of Christ," which may mean either that he regards himself as an eyewitness of Christ's sufferings or as someone who now bears witness to his sufferings.[316] Within reflection on testimony, the distinction is artificial since the one who bears witness is precisely the one who has seen something and is therefore capable of bearing witness to those events.[317] Peter's witness regards the whole of Christ's passion, which, while centered on the cross, is not limited to it. His focus is upon Christ's "sufferings." The NT regards Peter, with the apostles, as an eyewitness who then proclaimed what he saw (Luke 24:48; Acts 1:8, 22; 2:32; 3:15; 5:32).[318] In Acts 10:39–43 Peter sees himself as a witness of the life, death, and resurrection of Jesus of Nazareth as well as one who gives testimony ("We are witness to all that he did. . . . They put him to death . . . but God raised him . . . and allowed him to appear . . . to us who were chosen by God as witnesses"). The NT always portrays him as someone who does more than preach the story handed down to him from others. He saw what his readers did not (1 Pet 1:8). In this sermon at the house of Cornelius, Peter juxtaposes this apostolic witness with that of the prophets (10:43) as he does here in 1 Peter (5:1; 1:10–12). The combination of the apostolic and

---

315. BDAG, 59.

316. Elliott, *1 Peter*, 819.

317. As Antiphon, *Against the Stepmother for Poisoning* 1.28; *Hymn 4 to Hermes* 372; Xenophon, *Cyropaedia* 1.6.16; Plato, *Symposium* 175e.

318. Contra Kelly, *A Commentary on the Epistles of Peter and Jude*, 198; Michaels, *1 Peter*, 280–81; Davids, *The First Epistle of Peter*, 176–77; Elliott, *1 Peter*, 818–20. Achtemeier hits wide of the mark in his insistence that Peter did not see the crucifixion and could not therefore claim to be an eyewitness (*1 Peter*, 323). Goppelt rightly links Peter's position as eyewitness with his testimony (Goppelt, *A Commentary on 1 Peter*, 342; Eugenio Green, *1 Pedro y 2 Pedro* [Miami: Editorial Caribe, 1993], 275–76; Bigg, *Peter and Jude*, 186–87; Selwyn, *The First Epistle of Peter*, 228; Karl H. Schelkle, *Die Petrusbriefe, Der Judasbrief* [Freiburg: Herder, 1961], 128; Wayne Grudem, *1 Peter* [Grand Rapids: Eerdmans, 1988], 186; Schreiner, *1, 2 Peter, Jude*, 232; Jobes, *1 Peter*, 301). As Bede says, "For it is clear that the same Peter, together with his fellow apostles James and John, heard the aforesaid voice above the Lord when he was glorified on the mountain, according to the faith of the Gospels" (*The Commentary on the Seven Catholic Epistles of Bede the Venerable* [Kalamazoo, MI: Cistercian, 1985], 131). Μάρτυς (1 Pet 5:1) does not mean "martyr." We should interpret it within the letter's reflection regarding testimony.

prophetic witnesses appears again in 2 Peter 1:16–21. As an eyewitness, Peter was in position to offer the kind of proofs which were the mark of valid testimony (Aristotle, *Ars Rhetorica* 1.2.2). Moreover, the content of his testimony was identical with that of the prophets, which centered on Christ's sufferings and glories (1:10–12). Multiple witnesses were deemed to have great value (Plato, *Gorgias* 471e).

Peter takes a further step by summarizing the content of this letter as testimony regarding God's grace ("This is the true grace of God" [5:12]) that centers on Christ's sufferings and glories as predicted through the prophets' testimony ("Who prophesied of the grace that was to be yours" [1:10]). This letter, then, stands as the final bracket of an *inclusio* that surrounds the gospel message that the letter's recipients had received (1:12). The message preached to them was, in the first instance, witnessed by the prophets, and now Peter, the one who is qualified to give testimony as an eyewitness, confirms it. Peter evokes the apostolic and prophetic witness as he develops his theology to address the different situations of his readers (again, cf. Acts 10:39–43). Testimony stands at the very center of Petrine theology. But the testimony of this letter should be framed within the wider story of Peter's role as the principle witness regarding Christ's sufferings and glorification. As Elliott notes, "The identification of Peter as the preeminent witness in nascent Christianity to Jesus' suffering, death, and resurrection was an element of early Petrine tradition."[319] 1 Peter, then, serves as an essential source for understanding the theology of the prime witness of the Christ's sufferings and glorification. Moreover, the testimony of Peter regarding Christ, along with that of the prophets, serves as the foundation for the faith of the church.[320]

The Problem of Petrine Testimony in 2 Peter

The most problematic piece of Petrine testimony comes from 2 Peter. The author introduces himself in 1:1 as Peter, an apostle of Jesus Christ ("Simeon Peter, slave and apostle of Jesus Christ"). At various points within this letter, he supplements this identification by alluding to incidents in Peter's life, some of which the letter's first readers knew as anyone who read the gospel narrative. In 1:17–18 he recalls his experience with the Lord Jesus in the Mount of Transfiguration (Matt 17:1–5; Mark 9:2–7; Luke 9:28–35). The author also betrays a consciousness of his imminent demise due to the prophecy given him by the Lord (1:14), this being most likely a reference to the prophecy recorded in the Gospel of John (21:18–19). The identification of the

---

319. Elliott, *1 Peter*, 818–19; Cullmann, *Peter*, 70–157; Kessler, *Peter as the First Witness of the Risen Lord*.

320. Erich Seeberg, "Wer war Petrus? Bemerkungen zu J. Haller, Das Papsttum, Idee und Wirklichkeit," *ZKG* 53 (1934) 581; Kessler, *Peter as the First Witness of the Risen Lord*, 109–10. Cullmann opens the space for regarding Peter as standing at the beginning of Christian theology: "Although he was anything but a theologian, I think that here too he should be given the place of honor at the beginning of Christian theology." Further, he asserts that "He certainly possesses a much greater significance in the foundation of Christian theology than we are accustomed to assume" (*Peter*, 67, 69).

letter with Peter is underscored in 2 Peter 3:1, where the author declares this to be the "second letter" he is writing to these recipients, the first most likely being 1 Peter. Finally, the author presents himself as a companion in ministry with Paul, and he places his own teachings on a par with those of the apostle to the Gentiles (3:15–16). The author intends that his readers recognize this letter as an authentic work of the principle apostle, Peter.

However, not a few in both ancient and modern times have questioned the authenticity of the letter. They declare that it is a pseudonymous writing, possibly penned during the second century, which placed the name of Peter in the opening greeting and added the personal notes enumerated above as part of the mechanism of pseudepigraphy. In 1988 Bauckham stated, "The Petrine authorship of 2 Peter has long been disputed, but only since the beginning of this century has the pseudepigraphical character of the work come to be almost universally recognized."[321] Bauckham's assessment holds true to this day despite the attempts by a number of scholars to defend the traditional view of Petrine authorship.[322] The arguments forwarded to affirm the authenticity of the letter have not received a favorable hearing, and the failure to convince cannot be fully ascribed to entrenched skepticism. The unevenness of the letter's reception in the early church and the ancient concerns voiced about its origin are mirrored in current literature. The contemporary reader must decide, on the one hand, whether the arguments against the book's authenticity are cogent and, on the other, whether there is sufficient warrant to affirm that the letter came from Peter and represents his testimony.

Although my assessment of the authenticity of 2 Peter leans towards the acceptance of the letter as a work traceable to the apostle, this study will leave the book to one side given the depth of the controversy surrounding its authenticity. The purpose here is to ferret out a reasonable outline of Peter's theology from three witnesses, a

---

321. Richard Bauckham, "The Letter of Jude: An Account of Research," *Aufsteig und Niedergang der Römischen Welt* 2.25.5 (1988) 3719.

322. Bigg, *Peter and Jude*; Edward Michael Bankes Green, *2 Peter Reconsidered* (London: Tyndale, 1959); J. A. T. Robinson, *Redating the New Testament* (Philadelphia: Westminster, 1976); Michael Green, *The Second Epistle General of Peter and the General Epistle of Jude* (Grand Rapids: Eerdmans, 1987); Donald Guthrie, *New Testament Introduction* (Downers Grove, IL: InterVarsity, 1990); Green, *1 Pedro y 2 Pedro*; Douglas J. Moo, *2 Peter and Jude* (Grand Rapids: Zondervan, 1996); J. Daryl Charles, *Virtue Amidst Vice: The Catalogue of Virtues in 2 Peter 1* (Sheffield: Sheffield Academic, 1997); Waltner Charles, *1 and 2 Peter, Jude*; Michael J. Kruger, "The Authenticity of 2 Peter," *JETS* 42 (1999) 645–71; Schreiner, *1, 2 Peter, Jude*; Green, *Jude and 2 Peter*, 139–50. Witherington argues that the book preserves Petrine material along with traditions drawn from Jude and Paul (*Letters and Homilies for Hellenized Christians*, 260–72). Davids ponders the question of authenticity as he listens to Michael Green's defense and Richard Bauckham's rejection, concluding himself that we "cannot have a conclusive answer" (*The Letters of 2 Peter and Jude* [Grand Rapids: Eerdmans, 2006], 130). After a further examination of Bauckham's claim that 2 Peter is a pseudepigraphical testament, Davids remarks on the ascription of the letter to Peter "that we by the nature of the case cannot know *from historical investigation* whether this is in some sense actual or is a pseudepigraphical attribution" (*The Letters of 2 Peter and Jude*, 149).

large enough task as it stands. The witnesses regarding Peter's thought from Paul, the Gospels besides Mark, and the early church must be left for other laborers in this field.[323] The present volume seeks to make a small contribution to that larger study by arguing that Peter was foundational for Christian theology and that his voice is indeed recoverable, although we cannot fully ferret out his *verba* from the testimony. Peter is present at the beginning of the church and its the theology. Peter's foundational work was carried out in the company of others and never in isolation. He is among the other disciples, both in his leadership and in his theological testimony. Yet his voice remains for the church through the centuries.

THE TESTIMONY OF PETER AND THE POSSIBLITY OF A PETRINE THEOLOGY

Can we recover Peter's theology? If indeed we can, what was the shape of his theology? The New Testament offers us a variety of sources for understanding the theology of Peter. Peter's preaching stands behind the Gospel of Mark, the Book of Acts records a number of Peter's speeches, and 1 Peter provide witness to the apostle's teaching and ministry. The testimony within 2 Peter may be linked with Peter, but given the extent of the questions about the book's authenticity and the divergences from the thought in the first epistle ascribed to the apostle, this work will not be considered in this study. Both Galatians and 1 Corinthians Paul makes special mention of Peter, but these are Paul's portrayal of Peter and do not offer us sufficient access to the *vox Petri*. The focus of this study is on those documents which find their source in the ministry of Peter. The resources we have for understanding Peter's thought extend beyond the first century as Peter became a principle figure in the early church's reflection—as Lapham has helped us understand. The church received and adapted the story and theology of Peter in documents such as *The Apocalypse of Peter*, *The Gospel of Peter*, and *The Acts of Peter*, which Lapham examines alongside the canonical Petrine epistles. These documents may yield "a distinctive Petrine theology" and "might reflect the Apostle's essentially moderating influence" in the early church.[324] Lapham believes that the available evidence only provides us with an image of Peter, the "Peter of faith," and no more. But, again, our primary interest lies with those texts which can be traced back to the "Simon of history," who is the real figure behind the "Peter of faith."

While acknowledging that the New Testament presents us with the *vox Petri*, all the documents we have bear the marks of others who were involved in their

---

323. The edited volume by Helen Bond and Larry Hurtado (*Peter in Early Christianity* [Grand Rapids: Eerdmans, 2015]), works by Hengel (*Saint Peter*) and Bockmuehl (*The Remembered Peter*; *Simon Peter in Scripture and Memory*), and the earlier edited collection by Bruce Chilton and Craig Evans (*The Missions of James, Peter, and Paul: Tensions in Early Christianity* [Leiden: Brill, 2005]) are hopeful signs of renewed interest in the foundational apostle for the church.

324. Lapham, preface to *Peter*, ix. Also see Terence V. Smith, *Petrine Controversies in Early Christianity*.

composition. Mark translated Peter's proclamation, and Luke adapted Peter's speeches in accordance with his rhetorical concerns. First Peter bears the stamp of an amanuensis whose role in their composition was considerable. Every portrait we have of Peter and every account we hear from Peter bear the marks of interpretation. While we hear the *vox Petri*, we do not have in hand the untouched *verba Petri*. This observation could lead us back to Lapham's suggestion that all we may ever see of the apostle is the church's image of him. As he says, "Peter is as much the product of the myth, as the myth is of him, and any attempt to demythologize must result in failure."[325]

However, testimony is the overarching category that helps us understand the history and purpose of each of these documents. Mark remembered and translated the memoirs of Peter, his testimony. The Gospel records Peter's eyewitness and earwitness account, and Mark received this testimony and translated Peter's *chreiai*. In this he acted as an interpreter and not a rhetor. Luke investigated and received eyewitness as well as documentary witness to the speeches of Peter, and he incorporated these also with a view to his own rhetorical concerns in accordance with the canons of ancient historiography. We can ascribe 1 Peter to the apostle himself, according to the testimony of the early church, yet it bears the stamp of an amanuensis who likely did more than record word for word what Peter dictated. Rather, the person worked with his witness and improved the document's rhetorical effect. Indeed, the amanuensis likely served as his translator as well. Yet in accordance with ancient compositional practices, Peter as the author would have given final approval to the document before its dispatch. Peter claims to be presenting his testimony, which he buttresses with that of the prophets.

Understanding how testimony functions as an epistemological category helps us receive the history that undergirds these documents. The witnesses are credible, and there are no undefeated defeaters that undermine the testimony. We do not have collateral confirmation for every testimonial claim made along the way, but we do have epistemic reason for accepting the testimony presented, as noted in the preceding discussions on these books. Embracing history that comes through testimony is not the same as claiming that we have absolute knowledge of every piece of the testimony. Moreover, testimony is not just about history reported but also the interpretation of events. Testimony comes from witnesses who are engaged, not disengaged, and we expect it to include interpretation of those events reported and recorded. It is, as Ricoeur stated, "a genre that attempts to convey the fact and meaning of singular events of absolute significance."[326] We would expect, therefore, that the testimony received from Peter would be interpreted by the various authors who recorded his witness or who helped him in the process of composition. We should not view these interpretations as somehow separating us from the apostle but rather as the contribution of those who help us get inside the witness of the apostle himself. Moreover, Peter himself was a

---

325. Lapham, *Peter*, 2.
326. Ricoeur, *Essays on Biblical Interpretation*, 123.

participant not only in giving the testimony but also in the final stage of redaction. He would have been the one to approve the final draft of the letter sent to the churches of Anatolia. He was also present with Mark and most likely would have seen the record of his *chreiai* which Mark composed (if, that is, Mark wrote before his death). We do not know, however, what kind of contact he had with the author of Acts. Testimony provides us with both history and interpretation, so we should expect to hear in our sources the *vox Petri* but also the particular nuances of the various members of these authorial communities in which he participated. Testimonial knowledge, which includes interpretation, should not make us reticent about collapsing the distance between the "Peter of faith" and the "Simon of history."

In approaching the subject of Peter's theology, we expect to discover some notable differences between Mark's presentation, Peter's speeches in Acts, and 1 Peter. Yet at the same time, we may expect to find common threads running through the literature associated with Peter, which will allow us to hear the particular theological contribution of the apostle. Therefore, an examination of Peter's theology should, on the one hand, seek to preserve the particular interpretive nuances regarding Peter and, on the other hand, draw together the foundational themes of Peter's thought. Any attempt, however, to ferret out the "real Peter" from the interpretive notes would be a quixotic exercise that would outstrip the available evidence and break apart an essential element in the Petrine testimony. Interpretation belongs to the witness. The following chapters, therefore, will examine the theology of each witness and wrap together those themes that appear to be the particular contribution of the apostle to the theology of the church. Peter was an important theological voice in the early church, and his contribution is part of the bedrock of Christian theology. We have not recognized his contribution, yet the *vox Petri* courses though our most basic understanding of the Christian faith.

CHAPTER 3

The Gospel of Mark and the Testimony of Peter

From early in the second century onward, the written testimony of the church pointed to the preaching of Peter as the source of the story presented in the Gospel according to Mark. Papias, whose words are preserved for us by Eusebius, was the first but not only church father to record this connection.[1] The link between Peter and the Gospel of Mark was not, however, Papias's creation but rather predated him. Papias commented on the sources of the testimony he received, noting his preference for verbal testimony, or the "living voice," over books. So he made it a point to listen to those who had been followers of the "elders," that is, the players at the beginning of the gospel story, such as "Andrew, Peter, or Philip." He wanted to make his inquiries from those who could relate what they had heard from the first-hand witnesses of Jesus' life and teaching. According to Eusebius, however, Papias did not eschew tradition completely. Speaking about the Gospel of Mark, Papias noted that "the Presbyter"[2] was the source for his statement that "Mark became Peter's interpreter and wrote accurately all that he remembered" (*Hist. eccl.* 3.39.4, 7, 8, 15). In other words, according to Papias, we may trace back the content of the Gospel of Mark primarily to the apostle Peter's preaching. If

---

1. For the full discussion on this and other points in this paragraph, see "Peter and the Gospel of Mark" in chapter 1, "Sources for the Theology of Peter."

2. This Presbyter is John, who may be John the apostle or another called John (Eusebius, *Hist. eccl.* 3.39.5–7). Gundry argues that the Presbyter is this other John (*Mark*, 1030), whereas Bauckham concludes that "John the Elder was the Beloved Disciple and the author of the Gospel of John" (*Jesus and the Eyewitnesses*, 422–23).

we may rely on this testimony, Mark then becomes the principle witness for Peter's rendition of the Jesus story and, as such, must be our first port of call if we wish to embark on a journey through the apostle's theology.

As noted previously, Papias's record of the statements from the Presbyter regarding Mark's compositional process leads to the conclusion that Mark's rendition of Peter's preaching adheres faithfully to its source.[3] Mark recorded Peter's *chreiai*,[4] a *chreia* being, according Aelius Theon, "a brief saying or action making a point, attributed to some specified person or something corresponding to a person, a maxim and reminiscence are connected with it. Every brief maxim attributed to a person creates a *chreia*" (*Progymnasmata* 3 [96]). Mark handled the *chreia* with care, being as comprehensive as possible in recording them and following the original as closely as he could.[5] He was Peter's interpreter and, as such, did not act as an orator who would take greater liberties with his source material. Mark wrote down Peter's *chreiai* but did not attempt to give his writing the polish one would expect in a final composition. The way Papias expresses this is that Mark lacked the "order" (οὐ μέντοι τάξει) of a final composition. His description marks the Gospel as a draft document or working notes instead of a final polished literary product. The image Papias draws of Mark is that of a scribe who restrained his rhetorical license in order to represent his source as faithfully as possible, and, according to Papias, the composition itself bears witness to this restraint. This does not mean that he rendered Peter's preaching "word for word" in his role as an interpreter or translator,[6] but he penned a close representation of Peter's ideas. In fact, the Greek of the Gospel at times presents a very literal translation from Aramaic,[7] which provides further confirmation from within the book that Mark was a translator who did not stray far from his source. His handling of Peter's *chreiai* was like that of a person who works with a sacred text (Philo, *Mos.* 2.31, 34).[8] Mark's

---

3. See the full discussion on this and other points in this paragraph in chapter 1, "Sources for the Theology of Peter."

4. ὅς πρὸς τάς χρείας ἐποιεῖτο τάς διδασκαλίας (*HE* 3.39.15).

5. "For to one thing he gave attention, to leave out nothing of what he had heard and to make no false statements in them" (*HE* 3.39.15).

6. Cicero, *On the Best Kind of Orators* 5.14.

7. Maurice Casey, *Aramaic Sources of Mark's Gospel* (Cambridge: Cambridge University Press, 1998), 254–55. See Casey's discussion on linguistic interference among bilingual people (*Aramaic Sources of Mark's Gospel*, 93–110). See also Bruce Chilton, et al., *A Comparative Handbook to the Gospel of Mark: Comparisons with Pseudepigrapha, the Qumran Scrolls, and Rabbinic Literature* (Leiden: Brill, 2010).

8. "So when they had won his approval, they immediately began to fulfill the objects for which that honorable embassy had been sent; and considering among themselves how important the affair was, to translate laws which had been divinely given by direct inspiration, since they were not able either to take away anything, or to add anything, or to alter anything, but were bound to preserve the original form and character of the whole composition, they looked out for the most completely purified place of all the spots on the outside of the city." Clement of Alexandria classified Mark's Gospel as "Scripture" (*HE* 2.15.1–2).

composition falls short of a polished *bios* of Jesus since it had the character of working notes taken from memory (Lucian, *How to Write History* 48).⁹

Clement of Alexandria notes that Peter came to Rome and confronted Simon the Magician, "the first author of all heresy" (*Hist. eccl.* 2.13.5). The community there listened to Peter's "teaching of the divine proclamation" yet was not satisfied with hearing it once. So,

> with every kind of exhortation [they] besought Mark, whose Gospel is extant, seeing that he was Peter's follower, to leave them a written statement of the teaching given them verbally, nor did they cease until they had persuaded him, and so became the cause of the Scripture called the Gospel according to Mawrk. And they say that the Apostle, knowing by the revelation of the spirit to him what had been done, was pleased at their zeal, and ratified the scripture for study in the churches (*Hist. eccl.* 2.15.1–2).

The church at Rome "exhorted Mark . . . to make a record of what was said" (*Hist. eccl.* 6.14.6), which he did. He then distributed the Gospel among those who asked him for it (τὸ εὐαγγέλιον μεταδοῦναι τοῖς δεομένοις αὐτοῦ).¹⁰ Clement remarks that Mark was qualified to write this Gospel since he was Peter's follower or attendant who served him (ἀκόλουθον ὄντα Πέτρου).¹¹ So, in response to their entreaty, Mark took the teaching Peter had delivered and left a written memoir (λιπαρῆσαι ὡς ἄν καὶ διὰ γραφῆς ὑπόμνημα τῆς διὰ λόγου παραδοθείσης αὐτοῖς καταλείψοι διδασκαλίας). In other words, the teaching contained in Mark is that of Peter, not Mark. Mark's part was to write the historical memoir (ὑπόμνημα; see Polybius 1.1.1), which was a record of the testimony handed down verbally by Peter (διὰ λόγου παραδοθείσης αὐτοῖς). Clement uses the language of testimony in describing Mark's composition and goes on to

---

9. My purpose here is not to enter into the discussion regarding the genre of this or other gospels. Although we could argue that Mark is similar to an ancient *bios*, the way the church fathers frame the character of his composition shows their awareness that this book is not a well-crafted literary composition. The current categories in the discussion regarding gospel genre do not open space for a document which is more like a draft than a final and complete piece of literature. See, for example, Charles H. Talbert, *What Is a Gospel? The Genre of the Canonical Gospels* (Macon, GA: Mercer University Press, 1986); David E. Aune, *The New Testament in Its Literary Environment* (Philadelphia: Westminster, 1987); Robert M. Price, *Deconstructing Jesus* (Amherst, NY: Prometheus, 2000); Richard A. Burridge, *What Are the Gospels? A Comparison with Graeco-Roman Biography* (Grand Rapids: Eerdmans, 2004).

10. Clement does not take up the issue of how the Gospel was copied and distributed. The emphasis on the agency of the church at Rome in this process may imply that they became the literary patron who underwrote the publication of the Gospel. Such financial matters were commonly not spoken about directly. The way Clement frames the relationship between Mark and the Roman church points to Mark's control and Peter's approval of the process of composition and distribution, although the church had named the theme they petitioned Mark to write. Though Mark would have been a client of the Roman church, he maintained literary freedom. The Roman church oriented Mark towards others and, as patron, helped assure immortality for the Gospel as told by Peter. See Barbara K. Gold, *Literary Patronage in Greece and Rome* (Chapel Hill: University of North Carolina Press, 1987), 173–76.

11. *LSJ*, 52; Plato, *Sym* 203c; Antiphon 2.1.4; Thucydides 6.28; Plutarch, *Caes.* 10.3.

affirm the apostle Peter's assent or validation of the final composition (κυρῶσαί τε τὴ γραφὴν εἰς ἔντευξιν ταῖς ἐκκλησίαις; "ratified the scripture for study in the churches"). Whatever redactional role Mark had in coloring the narrative, Clement sees Mark as one who remembered and wrote in a way that met with the apostle's final approval. Similarly, the liberties an amanuensis may have taken in composing a letter did not make the final composition that of the scribe since the author would have read and approved the final product.[12]

Eusebius also refers to Origen's commentary on Matthew in which he stated that Mark had composed a gospel as Peter explained it to him (*Hist. eccl.* 6.25.5).[13] Origen comments that Mark "wrote it in accordance with Peter's instructions (ὑφηγήσατο αὐτῷ), whom also Peter acknowledged as his son in the catholic epistle, speaking in these terms: 'She that is in Babylon, elect together with you, saluteth you; and so doth Mark my son.'" Origen suggests that Peter did not simply consent to the writing of Mark's Gospel but also guided him in the process (ὑφηγήσατο αὐτῷ).[14] According to Origen, Peter played an active role when Mark composed the Gospel, a point which supports Clement's observation regarding Peter's approval of the document. Origen's view was that the compositional process was more complex than Mark merely recording Peter's *chreia*.

The skepticism regarding the testimony of the Fathers about the origins of Mark is rather surprising given their singular voice and the way that this testimony accounts for the phenomena in the book itself. Hengel remarks on the many scholars who have dismissed their witness, stating:

> The systematic rejection of these varied historical notes about the origin of the gospels, which are dated to the second and third centuries, is the typical result of a dogmatic criticism that does not bother with history. Even apart from the types of historical evidence concerning the personal relationship between Peter and the evangelist Mark, the very fact that the person of Peter is so absolutely important in the earliest gospel deserves a historical explanation that makes sufficient sense.

Hengel goes on to ask the critical question that, in the end, motivates this study about Peter's role as the foundational theologian in the church: "*How can Peter have maintained such an overarching importance in the Synoptic Gospels—beginning with Mark and still applicable (in spite of the time difference) in John—but also in Acts and*

---

12. E. Randolph Richards, *The Secretary in the Letters of Paul* (Tübingen: Mohr Siebeck, 1991), 53–56; E. Randolph Richards, *Paul and First-Century Letter Writing: Secretaries, Composition, and Collection* (Downers Grove, IL: InterVarsity, 2004), 74–80.

13. Ulrich H. J. Körtner, "Markus der Mitarbeiter des Petrus" (1980) 160–73; Martin Hengel, *Der unterschätzte Petrus: Zwei Studien* (Tübingen: Mohr Siebeck, 2006), 58–78.

14. *LSJ*, 1908; Lysius, *Olympic Oration* 33.3; Plato, *Res* 403E; Aristotle, *Eth. nic.* 1108a; Diodorus Siculus 17.90.1.

already in select Pauline letters, such as Galatians and 1 Corinthians?"[15] The composite picture that we receive from the early church and the canon is that Peter played a central role in the composition of Mark and, indeed, a central role in the mission and theological development of the church.

Peter's central role in the composition of Mark left footprints in the Gospel itself. Not so many years ago, Hengel commented on the Petrine *inclusio* in this Gospel.[16] Peter is the first disciple called in the narrative, along with Andrew, his brother (1:16-17). Peter again appears as the last disciple mentioned in the narrative and, here in Mark, Jesus singles him out from the rest: "But go, tell his disciples and Peter that he is going ahead of you to Galilee; there you will see him, just as he told you" (16:7). The parallel passages in Matthew and Luke do not retain the focus on Peter (Matt 28:7, 10; Luke 24:5-9). Bauckham correctly observes that "the two references form an *inclusio* around the whole story, suggesting that Peter is the witness whose testimony includes the whole."[17] The narrative itself emphasizes Peter's role more prominently than the other Synoptics, with the apostle being mentioned proportionally more often in Mark than in Matthew and Luke.[18] At various points in the story, Mark makes special mention of Peter in relation to the other disciples (1:29-31, 36), and, indeed, "Peter is actually present through a large proportion of the narrative from 1:16 to 14:72."[19] The structure and coloring of the narrative bear the marks of Peter's prominence in Mark's Gospel. The *vox Petri* heard here retains its personal character. We are close to the apostle and his story here, not separated from him and his views by layered tradition or redaction. We hear him and not simply an echo of his voice which the church remembered.

The consensus of the church fathers is that Mark was not produced by an author who worked up multiple sources or simply crafted his unique telling of the story according to his own or his readers' interests. Rather, the book is a redaction of Peter's gospel story. But we cannot say that Mark added nothing to the shape or character of the narrative. Mark was Peter's translator and every translation is, in the end,

---

15. Martin Hengel, *Saint Peter: The Underestimated Apostle* (Grand Rapids: Eerdmans, 2010), 48 (his emphasis). France likewise comments, "Modern scholarship has had a remarkable propensity to regard early church traditions of this nature as automatically suspect. Actual arguments against taking the traditions seriously are not so common" (France, *The Gospel of Mark*, 38). See the discussion of the early tradition in chapter 1, "Sources for a Petrine Theology"; Gundry, *Mark*, 1026-38.

16. Martin Hengel, *The Four Gospels and the One Gospel of Jesus Christ: An Investigation of the Collection and Origin of the Canonical Gospels* (Harrisburg, PA: Trinity, 2000), 81-83; Bauckham, *Jesus and the Eyewitnesses*, 124-27, 170; Hengel, *Saint Peter*, 41-42. Hengel did not fully move to this conclusion in Hengel, *Studies in the Gospel of Mark*, 61-62.

17. Bauckham, *Jesus and the Eyewitnesses*, 125.

18. See the discussion in Reinhard Feldmeier, "Die Darstellung des Petrus in den synoptischen Evangelien," in *Das Evangelium und die Evangelien: Vorträge vom Tübinger Symposium 1982*, ed. Peter Stuhlmacher (Tübingen: Mohr Siebeck, 1983), 267-71; Bauckham, *Jesus and the Eyewitnesses*, 125-26; Hengel, *Saint Peter*, 28-29.

19. Bauckham, *Jesus and the Eyewitnesses*, 126.

an interpretation that responds to the particular linguistic and cultural turns of the audience. Indeed, there are points within the Gospel where Mark demonstrates his awareness of his audience's cultural limitations. He adds explanatory glosses when cognizant that the readers did not have the necessary contextual information available to interpret the events or words in Peter's account (as Mark 7:3–4, 11). He also draws out a theological conclusion based upon Jesus' teaching reading defilement ("Thus he declared all foods clean" [7:19]), although this gloss may be attributed to his source. The many explanatory γάρ clauses in the Gospel are additional editorial elements from the author, although these likewise may not have been Mark's own clarifications.[20] In his comment that underscores the importance of Jesus' teaching on the desolating sacrilege, Mark directly addresses those who received the Gospel, saying, "Let the reader understand" (ὁ ἀναγινώσκων νοείτω [Mark 13:14]). Mark mentions the reader who, according the ancient practice, read the Gospel aloud. The "reader" is the one who read a text to others (Luke 4:16; Acts 15:21; Col 4:16; 1 Thess 5:27) or may be anyone who read a text out loud to themselves (Acts 8:28).[21] In the former case, Mark's words imply the presence of a community that hears the story read to them. This may be the same community that solicited the document's composition according to Clement of Alexandria (*Hist. eccl.* 6.14.6–7). The line between the written text and the spoken word is smudged. We become aware that there is an oral or performance aspect of the Gospel of Mark that the author recognized when he wrote the book. This was a story to be heard and not read silently. The story began as a performance piece in Peter's preaching and ended as a story to be performed and heard as was common

---

20. Mark 1:22; 2:15; 3:10; 5:8, 28, 42; 6:14, 17, 20, 31, 48, 52; 7:3; 9:6, 31; 11:13, 18, 37; 12:12; 14:2, 56; 15:10; 16:4, 8. See Robert H. Stein, *Mark* (Grand Rapids: Baker Academic, 2008), 78.

21. Mary Ann Beavis, *Mark's Audience: The Literary and Social Setting of Mark 4:11–12* (Sheffield: Sheffield Academic, 1989), 19–20. Whitney Shiner reminds us that "in the ancient Mediterranean world, writing was largely understood as representing oral speech. In most cases it was understood as a poor substitute for oral speech" (*Proclaiming the Gospel: First-Century Performance of Mark* [Harrisburg, PA: Trinity, 2003], 14). Silent reading was done, but literary texts were regularly read aloud. Longinus (*[Subl.]* 26.1–3) instructs the reader not to "talk to all of the audience, but to one person only ... you will make him more emotionally stirred and at the same time more attentive and more full of a sense of the struggle, waking him up by these personal addresses." It might have come as a shock to the public reader of Mark to hear the author addressing him. See also Longinus *[Subl.]* 15.1–2; 30.1–2; Gamble, *Books and Readers in the Early Church*, 203–5; Brian J. Incigneri, *The Gospel to the Romans: The Setting and Rhetoric of Mark's Gospel* (Leiden: Brill, 2003), 47–51; Terence C. Mournet, *Oral Tradition and Literary Dependency: Variability and Stability in the Synoptic Tradition and Q* (Tübingen: Mohr Siebeck, 2005), 100–149. However, the "reader" for Apuleius (*Metam.* 1.1) becomes the person who *hears* this Greek tale which the author composed in Latin: "Lector intende: laetaberis" ("Pay attention, reader, and you will find delight"). The "reader" in Mark could likewise be the *hearer* whom the author addresses in an attempt to grab his attention. Understood either way, Mark geared his Gospel toward oral recitation that captured the attention of the audience. On a side note, our contemporary method of teaching students to *read* instead of *listen to* and *speak* Classical and Koiné Greek distances them from these oral traditions embedded in the New Testament and other Greek literature. While learning to listen and speak is essential for learning any other language, ancient Greek texts remain as objects on a page. Much the pity since the texts we so diligently teach were designed to be *heard* not merely parsed, diagramed, and woodenly translated.

with the great epic poems by Homer.[22] For our present purposes, the inclusion of this gloss about the reader is another indicator of the author's redactional hand and his audience awareness.

Mark may have colored the story along the way as he worked with the material that he received from Peter. We cannot tell what these hues might be nor where they might appear. Mark takes Peter's testimony and interprets it in translation for his audience. Papias's account of Mark's role evokes the language of testimony. He "became Peter's interpreter" and "wrote accurately" all that "he remembered." Papias doubles-up this last point in his note that Mark wrote down things "as he remembered them" (*Hist. eccl.* 3.39.15; cf. Cicero, *Topica* 1.5). As seen previously, the emphasis upon memory was commonplace in discussions about reliable testimony. Papias's remarks are not just about recall but also identify the epistemological category of testimony. Peter gave testimony about Jesus, and Mark presented testimony about Peter's *chreiai*. Given that testimony always includes interpretation and audience awareness, we may expect that Mark shaped Peter's testimony. But Peter's role as interpreter of Jesus' life and teaching was Mark's prime interest. The early church occasionally pointed out Peter's role in the composition and final approval of the document. The assessment of the Fathers was that Mark was restrained, more so than even Hengel would acknowledge. He states:

> Now the bond between Mark and the Peter tradition does not mean that Mark simply hands on the Jesus tradition in the framework of the Petrine mission preaching. Mark, whose theological and literary capacities form criticism have [sic] failed to recognize, is far too sovereign an author for that. We can only say that Peter plays a central role in his Gospel, that with good reason we have to regard him as the decisive mediator of tradition, and that the report in the early church that he was a pupil of Peter and that his Gospel was presumably written in Rome five or six years after Peter's martyrdom also deserves a degree of historical trust.[23]

If Peter was indeed alive at the time of writing, then the possibility of the apostle's involvement in the final composition increases quite dramatically. But even if he were deceased when Mark wrote, the Fathers acknowledge Mark's faithfulness to Peter's preaching, which he and others had heard. Mark's hand is evident in this Gospel, but the principle impress is that of Peter.

Any attempt to locate the theology of Peter must be tempered by the recognition that, at best, we hear the *ipsissima vox* of Peter but not necessarily the *ipsissima*

---

22. See the discussions on the performance of Mark in Shiner, *Proclaiming the Gospel*; Antoinette Clark Wire, *The Case for Mark Composed in Performance* (Eugene, OR: Cascade, 2011); Rob Starner, *Kingdom of Power, Power of Kingdom: The Opposing World Views of Mark and Chariton* (Eugene, OR: Pickwick, 2011). See also L. Michael White, *Scripting Jesus: The Gospels in Rewrite* (New York: Harper One, 2010), 87–105. On Mark as a Christian epic, see below.

23. Hengel, *The Four Gospels and the One Gospel of Jesus Christ*, 87.

verba of the apostle. Testimony from Peter was recorded and sometimes translated by others, whether in Mark or Acts or the epistles, and their hand shaped the final form of the testimony. The *vox Petri* is in no way detached and unsullied by its mediators, whether they be translators, compilers, or even an amanuenses. In the end, we should be able to locate some common threads which run through parts of the New Testament witness to Peter's theology. But this does not mean that we can only accept as Petrine those aspects of the testimony which find support through multiple attestation. That Mark has in some ways colored Peter's testimony does not detract from the authenticity of the *vox Petri* but rather presents a living witness to the way that Peter's words were brought home with clarity to the ones who were the first readers/hearers of the Gospel of Mark. He wrote for them and, as he did so, he sought to be faithful to Peter's witness. There is humanity here and true communication, which can be successful only if there is a personal and subjective exchange of ideas, reaching to the heart in the language of the ones who read and hear.

MARK'S AUDIENCE

The question of Mark's compositional practice becomes important upon considering the way the Gospel of Mark reflects the particular interests and needs of his audience. Mark is acutely aware of his audience and presents his portrait of Jesus in a way that takes into account their social location. We assume that as Peter proclaimed he was mindful of his hearers and their needs as well. The line, therefore, between Mark's hand and Peter's voice is impossible to discern, but the principal player in shaping the story of Jesus in a way which responded to the audience's needs was Peter himself.[24] Given the role of hearers/readers in communication, some understanding of Mark's audience is an essential concern for anyone wishing to understand him well.

Early Church Testimony on Mark's Audience

The testimony of the early church located both Peter and Mark in Rome, where the first recipients of this Gospel also resided. Papias does not record this association between this Gospel and Rome, but later, in the second century, the Anti-Marcionite Prologue linked Mark and his book with Italy: "He was the interpreter of Peter. After the death of Peter himself he wrote down this same gospel in the regions of Italy."[25] Sometime later that century, or perhaps during the first decade of the third, Clement of Alexandria places Peter and Mark together at Rome, as recorded by Eusebius: "When Peter

---

24. As argued previously, this is not Papias's point when he remarks ὅς πρὸ τὰς χρείας ἐποιεῖτο τὰς διδασκαλίας. See chapter 1 on "Peter and the Gospel of Mark." Although we may understand the words to mean, "who [Peter] used to give teaching as necessity demanded," Papias's remark is more likely about the anecdotal nature of Peter's teaching in χρεία.

25. Vincent Taylor, *The Gospel According to Mark* (Grand Rapids: Baker, 1966), 3. The Muratorian Canon is the outlier in identifying the time of composition as after Peter's death.

had proclaimed the word publicly at Rome, and declared the gospel under the influence of the spirit; as there was a great number present, they requested Mark, who had followed him from afar, and remembered well what he had said, to reduce these things to writing, and that after composing the gospel he gave it to those who requested it of him. Which, when Peter understood, he directly neither hindered nor encouraged it" (*Hist. eccl.* 6.14.6–7).[26] Peter was at Rome and those there requested that Mark write what he remembered from Peter's preaching. Mark obliged and gave this Gospel to the Roman church, which had requested it.

Earlier in his history, Eusebius located both Mark and Peter at Rome, the place where this Gospel was composed (*Hist. eccl.* 2.15). Discussing the First Epistle of Peter, Eusebius remarks that these were together at Rome, where also Peter wrote his first letter: "Peter made mention of Mark in the first epistle, which he is also said to have composed at the same city of Rome, and that he showed this fact by calling the city by an unusual figure of speech, Babylon." Eusebius here refers to 1 Peter 5:13, which not only places Mark with Peter but also indicates that they were together at "Babylon," a code word for the city of Rome known in Jewish and rabbinic literature[27] as well as the Book of Revelation (14:8; 16:19; 17:5, 9, 18; 18:2, 10, 21). Elsewhere Eusebius relates that Peter was crucified and buried at Rome, appealing to the testimonies of Gaius and the bishop of Corinth, Dionysius (*Hist. eccl.* 2.25.5–8). In the same way Ignatius locates Peter at Rome (*Rom.* 4.3), as do Irenaeus (*Adv. Haer.* 3.1, 3), Tertullian (*Praescr.* 36; *Marc.* 4.5), and Clement of Alexandria (*Hist. eccl.* 2.14.3–2.15.1).[28] Independent witness of Mark's early presence in Rome comes from the Pauline corpus (Col 4:11; Phlm 24; 2 Tim 4:11). The association between Peter and Mark—and between them, the city of Rome—enjoys very strong testimonial support. Mark, therefore, was most likely written to the Roman church, the same community which had encouraged him to pen the memoirs of Peter.

---

26. On the discrepancy between the Anti-Marcionite Prologue and Clement on the time of Mark's composition, see chapter 1 on "Peter and the Gospel of Mark."

27. John H. Elliott assembles the evidence well (*1 Peter: A New Translation with Introduction and Commentary* [New York: Doubleday, 2000], 882–84).

28. See F. J. Foakes-Jackson, *Peter: Prince of Apostles* (London: Hodder & Stoughton, 1927), 151–63; Cullmann, *Peter: Disciple-Apostle-Martyr*, 71–157; Daniel William O'Connor, *Peter in Rome: The Literary, Liturgical, and the Archeological Evidence* (New York: Columbia University Press, 1969); Carsten Thiede, *Simon Peter: From Galilee to Rome* (Grand Rapids: Zondervan, 1988), 171–84; Richard Bauckham, "The Martyrdom of Peter in Early Christian Literature," *Aufsteig und Niedergang der römischen Welt* 2.26.1 (1992) 539–95; Michael Grant, *Saint Peter: A Biography* (New York: Scribner, 1994), 147–58; Pheme Perkins, *Peter: Apostle for the Whole Church* (Edinburgh: T. & T. Clark, 2000), 168–71; Carsten Thiede, *Geheimakte Petrus: Auf den Spuren des Apostels* (Stuttgart: Kreuz, 2000), 249–56.

Internal Testimony for Mark's Audience

The internal evidence from the Gospel does not itself compel the conclusion that this Gospel was written for the Roman church, but it does provide corroborating support for the early church's testimony. For one, Mark has an abundance of Latinisms which leave testimony about the linguistic environment of the readers. The letter's Greek is marked by any number of Latin words which have been transliterated into Greek, and his syntax likewise betrays Latin influences.[29] The extent of the Latin influence over Mark lead Turner to the conclusion: "That they are probably more frequent in Mark than in other NT texts, except the Pastoral Epistles, may raise the question whether Mark was written in Italy in a kind of Greek that was influenced by Latin. However, supposing that his language is influenced in that way, we presume that it could have happened as well in the Roman provinces."[30] One curious feature of the Latinisms in Mark is the way he translates a Greek numismatic term into transliterated Latin for his audience. Referring to the small copper coins the widow threw into the temple treasury, he says that she ἔβαλεν λεπτὰ δύο, ὅ ἐστιν κοδράντης (she "cast in two *lepta*, which means a *quadrans*" [12:42]). A *quadrans* was one of the smallest-denomination Roman bronze coins and was worth a quarter of an *as* (hence the name "quadr-ans").[31] It was minted in Italy and also circulated in Latin colonies such as Corinth.[32] This was small change, the coin which crossed the palm of the poor.[33] With a *quadrans* you could gain admission to a public latrine. The *lepton* was also a small bronze coin

---

29. See *BDF* §5–6; Taylor, *Gospel According to Mark*, 44–45; E. C. Maloney, *Semitic Interference in Marcan Syntax* (Chico, CA: Scholars, 1981); Raymond E. Brown and John Meier, *Antioch and Rome: New Testament Cradles of Catholic Christianity* (Ramsey, NJ: Paulist, 1983), 196; Peter Dschulnigg, *Sprache, Redaktion und Intention des Markus-Evangeliums: Eigentümlichkeiten der Sprache des Markus-Evangeliums und ihre Bedeutung für die Redaktionskritik* (Stuttgart: Katholisches Bibelwerk, 1984); Gundry, *Mark*, 1043–44; Hengel, *The Four Gospels and the One Gospel of Jesus Christ*, 78–79; Ben Witherington, *The Gospel of Mark: A Socio-Rhetorical Commentary* (Grand Rapids: Eerdmans, 2001), 20–21; Incigneri, *The Gospel to the Romans*, 100–103; Stein, *Mark*, 11–12.

30. Nigel Turner, "Style," in *Style*, ed. James Hope Moulton (Edinburgh: T. & T. Clark, 1976), 29. Taylor notes that the Latinisms in Mark are found in Koine "but their frequency in Mark suggests that the Evangelist wrote in a Roman environment" (*Gospel According to Mark*, 45).

31. Smaller coins were the *sextans*, valued at one-sixth of an *as*, and the *uncia*, one-twelfth of an *as* (Edwin W. Bowen, "Roman Currency Under the Republic," *CJ* 47 [1951] 97). But during the era of Augustus, the smaller denominations were eliminated, leaving the *quadrans* as the smallest Roman coin (Richard Reece, "Roman Coinage in the Western Empire," *Britannia* 4 [1973] 234).

32. Joan E. Fisher, "Corinth Excavations, 1977, Forum Southwest," *Hesperia* 53 (1977) 236; John D. MacIsaac, "Corinth: Coins, 1925–1926 the Theater District and the Roman Villa," *Hesperia* 56 (1987) 97–157.

33. As Reece notes, "in the *Cena Trimalchionis* of Petronius (43, 4) one of the diners defines the financial care and craft of a recently deceased friend with the words 'he started off with an As and didn't mind picking a quadrans out of a muck-heap with his teeth,' giving the clear judgement that only the poor and mean would do such a thing: the rest could afford to leave that smallest of coins for the later excavator" ("Roman Coinage in the Western Empire," 247).

commonly used in Judea[34] and worth half of the Roman *quadrans*,[35] a detail which Mark does not miss in his exchange of the Greek currency into the rough equivalent in Roman coin. The conversion and translation was necessary since the *lepton* was not part of the Roman currency system.[36] The point is not as small as the coins, however. Mark's audience, while knowing Greek, was not fully aware of Greek numismatic terminology or the value of some coinage common in Palestine. Of course, Mark's Latinisms and currency conversion in and of themselves do not compel the conclusion that the recipients of this Gospel lived in Rome.[37] They may have been located in any one of the Roman colonies of the empire, such as Philippi or Corinth, where Latin predominated, but the possibility is left open. They certainly did not live in Palestine, including Galilee, since the explanation of the value of λεπτὰ δύο would be entirely unnecessary there given the wide circulation of *lepta* even among the poorest.[38] The curious feature here, however, is not the presence of Latin loan words but the fact that the book was composed in Greek in the first place. Why not in Latin, a question that may be asked about Romans as well? The most likely answer for Mark at least is that the author and the readers, while bilingual, shared Greek as their common tongue.

On the other hand, Aramaic and Hebrew influences color Mark's language. The Semitic stamp on the Gospel is much more marked than the modest Latin presence and most likely points to the linguistic home of the author and, perhaps, his source. If Mark was indeed Peter's translator, we would expect his writing to show some linguistic interference from Mark and Peter's mother tongue, a phenomenon heard in most bilingual people's speech.[39] At times Mark lets his audience listen to transliterations of Aramaic terms as he then turns and translates the concept for them (3:17; 5:41; 7:11, 34; 9:43; 10:46; 14:36; 15:22, 34). Occasionally Mark utilizes the phrase "which is translated" (ὅ ἐστιν μεθερμηνευόμενον [5:41; 15:22, 34]) to introduce the concept in Greek and at times substitutes it with the elliptical phrase "which is" (ὅ ἐστιν [7:11, 34;

---

34. Giraud V. Foster, et al., "News and Short Contributions," *JFA* 16 (1989) 245–55.

35. Daniel Sperber, "Mark 12:42 and Its Metrological Background: A Study in Ancient Syriac Versions," *NovT* 9 (1967) 181, 185. The *quadrans* was the smallest monetary unit in Rome currency (Sperber, "Mark 12:42 and Its Metrological Background," 180).

36. Sperber, "Mark 12:42 and Its Metrological Background," 182.

37. A point rightly made by Joel Marcus ("The Jewish War and the *Sitz Im Leben* of Mark," *JBL* 111 [1992] 444; *Mark 8–16: A New Translation with Introduction and Commentary* [New Haven, CT: Yale University Press, 2009], 858).

38. Contra Willi Marxsen, *Mark the Evangelist: Studies on the Redaction History of the Gospel* (Nashville: Abingdon, 1969), 54–116; Werner H. Kelber, *The Kingdom in Mark: A New Place and a New Time* (Philadelphia: Fortress, 1974), 138–44; Hendrika Nicoline Roskam, *The Purpose of the Gospel of Mark in Its Historical and Social Context* (Leiden: Brill, 2004), 95; Ched Myers, *Binding the Strong Man: A Political Reading of Mark's Story of Jesus* (Maryknoll, NY: Orbis, 2008), 39–87.

39. On the Aramaic and Hebrew influences in Mark, see C. E. B. Cranfield, *The Gospel According to Saint Mark* (Cambridge: Cambridge University Press, 1959), 21; Taylor, *Gospel According to Mark*, 45–52; Matthew Black, *An Aramaic Approach to the Gospels and Acts* (Oxford: Oxford University Press, 1967); Turner, "Style," 11–25; Casey, *Aramaic Sources of Mark's Gospel*; Chilton, et al., *A Comparative Handbook to the Gospel of Mark*.

15:16, 42]). While the fundamental linguistic orientation of the author is Semitic, he makes a true attempt to communicate as effectively as he can with a Greek-speaking Gentile audience that knows Latin. As Taylor concludes, "The sympathies of Mark are Gentile in their range, but his tradition is Jewish Christian to the core."[40]

The Location of Mark's Audience

Mark's audience is comprised of Gentiles who needed some orientation to Jewish customs. The internal evidence from the Gospel informs us that they were people who not only knew Greek but also Latin, themselves likely being bilingual. The presence of Romans throughout the empire, and the particular Latin cultural and linguistic overlay in the provincial colonies, does not necessarily push us to identify Rome as the place where this Gospel was first read and heard. But an audience located within the imperial city is at least a possibility. The early Christian witnesses regarding the origins of this Gospel, however, unanimously point to Rome as the place where both the author and the readers were located. A Palestinian/Galilean origin is highly unlikely despite the strong Semitic elements in the language of the Gospels. The explanations the author includes about Jewish customs and currency valuation push us away from identifying the first readers as people living anywhere within Palestine.

The other possible location of the first readers of Mark is Syria. Joel Marcus has been this position's strongest advocate, although he does not stand alone as its champion.[41] The core of Marcus's argument is that the apocalyptic discourse in Mark 13 appears to be a response to the events of the Jewish revolt (AD 66–74), a position he supports by interpreting the reference in Mark 11:17 to the temple being a "den of brigands" as an identification of those who were "members of the Jewish revolutionary bands that operated in the time leading up to and including the revolt against the Romans in AD 66–74." The "abomination of desolation" in 13:14 is, then, a reference to "the occupation of the Temple by Eleazar son of Simon in the winter of 67–68."[42] The revolutionaries had appealed to the messianic expectations of the people, with the "Davidic hopes crystallized around two revolutionary leaders, Menachem the son of Judas the Galilean and Simon bar Giora."[43] Mark, on the other hand, "fashioned the 'Davidic' section of his narrative (10:46–12:37) with the claims of figures like Simon and Menachem before his eyes."[44] Marcus argues that the date of the Gospel is,

---

40. Taylor, *Gospel According to Mark*, 65.

41. Marcus, "The Jewish War and the *Sitz Im Leben* of Mark"; Joel Marcus, *Mark 1–8: A New Translation with Introduction and Commentary* (New York: Doubleday, 2000), 25–39; Howard Clark Kee, *The Community of the New Age: Studies in Mark's Gospel* (Philadelphia: Westminster, 1977), 77–105; Gerd Theissen, *The Gospels in Context: Social and Political History in the Synoptic Tradition* (Minneapolis: Fortress, 1991), 236–49.

42. Marcus, "The Jewish War and the *Sitz Im Leben* of Mark," 449, 454.

43. Marcus, "The Jewish War and the *Sitz Im Leben* of Mark," 458.

44. Marcus, "The Jewish War and the *Sitz Im Leben* of Mark," 459.

therefore, sometime around AD 70—perhaps as early as 69 or as late as 74 or 75: "The position adopted here is that for Mark and his community the abomination of desolation, which is the occupation of the temple by the Zealots in 67–68, and the flight of the Christians from Jerusalem shortly thereafter, are events of the recent past. For these events appear to have inaugurated the time of great tribulation in which Mark and his addressees feel themselves to be now living (cf. 13:14–19)."[45] He does not favor Galilee as the home of Mark's audience but rather holds "a location in one of the Hellenistic cities that Josephus tells us were attacked at the beginning of the war, since in such places it is easy to imagine a predominantly Gentile Christian community with bitter feelings toward non-Christian Jews." Pella may have even been the location, a place to which Judean Christians had fled before Jerusalem was taken.[46]

The threads that hold together Marcus's conclusion for a Syrian origin are thin, lacking any testimonial support to make a strong case. Mark composed his Gospel for Christians who were undergoing persecution, but, as Marcus admits, the weakest point in his argument "is the lack of direct evidence for persecution of Christians in the Jewish War."[47] Also, he presents a Syrian location as a possibility without any more evidence than showing that "the war in Palestine spilled over into Syria, and there were frequent massacres there of Jews by Gentiles and vice versa." But the first readers of the Gospel of Mark were Gentiles who needed explanations about Jewish customs and translations of Aramaic terms. They were not displaced Jews from Palestine. To this Marcus can only say, "Christians, who were perceived to be a group standing somewhere between Jews and Gentiles, *may have* become targets to both sides."[48] This hardly constitutes a compelling argument, as Marcus's own language shows. Marcus states that the description of the woman in 7:26 as "'Syrophoenician' may point toward Syrian composition, since it may be intended to distinguish her home from the Coele-Syrian part of the province."[49] But on the other hand, it may distinguish her as a Phoenician from Syria as opposed to one from North Africa around Carthage.[50] The use

---

45. Marcus, *Mark 1–8*, 38.

46. Marcus, "The Jewish War and the *Sitz Im Leben* of Mark," 461; Eusebius, *HE* 3.5.3; Ephiphanius, *Panarion* 29.7.7–8; 30.2.7; *Weights and Measures* 15.

47. Marcus, *Mark 1–8*, 34.

48. Marcus, *Mark 1–8*, 36 (emphasis mine).

49. Marcus, *Mark 1–8*, 36.

50. Hengel, *Studies in the Gospel of Mark*, 29, 137–38; Witherington, *The Gospel of Mark*, 21; John R. Donahue and Daniel J. Harrington, *The Gospel of Mark* (Collegeville, MN: Liturgical, 2002), 233; Stein, *Mark*, 10. Be sure to see the good discussion on the name in Theissen, *The Gospels in Context*, 245–47. Theissen shows that the way Mark identifies the woman does not preclude a Syrian origin of the Gospel. But, on the other hand, it in no way leads to that conclusion either. Theissen notes how the descriptor "Syrophoenician" could be used pejoratively but rejects this possibility in Mark 7:26. But with the note that the person who comes to Jesus is a *woman*, a *Gentile*, someone of *Syrophoenician* origin, and a *dog*, Mark shows the first readers how extremely outside this person was—yet "she went home, found the child lying on the bed, and the demon gone" (Mark 7:26–29). The Gospel is strikingly inclusive of those who were socially excluded.

of the term does not get us very far towards identifying the place where the readers of the Gospel were located. It does not by any means compel us to read it as a document written to Christians in Syria. Marcus's arguments in favor of a Syrian origin do not fully account for the abundance of Latinisms in the document, nor does his mapping enjoy the kind of support from the early church that the traditional identification of a Roman origin receives. We do not have any testimony which locates either Mark or Peter in Syria while the evidence for their presence in Rome is broad and compelling.

Although Rome remains the most probable place of origin for Mark's Gospel, Richard Bauckham has raised important questions about whether or not the Gospels, including Mark, were written for *specific* Christian churches. In the edited volume *The Gospel for All Christians*, Bauckham asks, "Were the Gospels written for a specific Christian audience or for a general Christian audience? ... Are a Gospel's implied readers a specific Christian community (consisting of one or more specific local churches), or are they the members of any and every Christian community of the late first century to which that Gospel might circulate?"[51] The assumption which underlies most contemporary studies of the Gospels is that they were composed with particular communities in mind and we can reconstruct the character of those communities through reading the Gospels themselves. The identification of the community then becomes an essential hermeneutical key for unlocking the central concern and message of each particular Gospel. But as Bauckham notes, contemporary Gospel studies are based upon "the unargued assumption in every case ... that each Gospel addresses a localized community in its own, quite specific context and character." He registers surprise that "nearly all the literature of the last few decades that makes this assumption and increasingly builds large and highly sophisticated arguments upon it seems to regard this assumption as completely self-evident, as though no alternative could ever have occurred to anyone."[52]

Bauckham argues to the contrary, his lively presentation becoming a must-read for anyone studying the Gospels these days.[53] The first plank in his argument is that the Gospels are not like the Pauline Epistles, which were written for specific Christian communities. Second, the genre of the Gospels fits most closely the Greco-Roman *bios*, and such lives were not written to address the particular needs of a small community.[54] The third plank he nails down is that authors do not write for communities who have heard their preaching but for those at a distance, who do not have the privilege of receiving their oral teaching. Fourth, the early Christian communities were not isolated and introverted but rather connected given the high level of mobility in the

---

51. Richard Bauckham, "For Whom Were Gospels Written?," in *The Gospels for All Christians: Rethinking the Gospel Audiences*, ed. Richard Bauckham (Grand Rapids: Eerdmans, 1998a), 10.

52. Bauckham, "For Whom Were Gospels Written?," 11.

53. Bauckham, "For Whom Were Gospels Written?," 26–44.

54. Mary Ann Tolbert makes a similar point but appeals to the function of narrative (*Sowing the Gospel: Mark's World in Literary-Historical Perspective* [Minneapolis: Fortress, 1989], 303–4).

first-century Roman empire.⁵⁵ Moreover, the early Christians understood themselves as part of a worldwide movement, and many of the main characters traveled between the various Christian communities and sent letters from one community to another. Given these considerations, Bauckham concludes that "the attempt by the current consensus in Gospels scholarship to give the so-called Matthean, Markan, Lukan, and Johannine communities a key hermeneutical role in the interpretation of the Gospels is wholly mistaken."⁵⁶ True, a community where the author wrote may have influenced the writing of his Gospel, but the Gospels were not written for that particular church or group of churches. The enterprise to reconstruct these communities has no *hermeneutical* value in Bauckham's eyes.

The audiences for these writings were "any and every church," yet the Gospels are not detached fully from their historical context. Bauckham argues that they were intended for circulation and their context "is the early Christian movement in the late first century." The diversity of perspectives among the Gospels "does not imply that its intended readers were a highly distinctive branch of early Christianity, different from the readership of other Gospels."⁵⁷ Peterson likewise mounts a strong critique of the assumption that the best hermeneutical tool for interpreting the Gospels is the identification of their respective audiences, but disconcertingly offers no alternative perspective as did Bauckham.⁵⁸

The internal evidence from the Gospel of Mark points to the author's keen audience awareness, as we have already seen. He knows that he needs to explain some Greek and Aramaic terms for his readers, he uses an abundance of Latinisms which his readers would have known, he points out the value of unknown currency, and he casually refers to certain figures like Rufus and Alexander without noting who they are since his first readers apparently knew these characters (15:21). Indeed, the author mentions them in order to identify another character not well-known to his readers, Simon of Cyrene. The first readers were located somewhere, and Mark accommodated his Gospel to them, as occurs in all human communication. He is not

---

55. Bauckham references the stellar study by Lionel Casson, a text which helps us understand mobility during this period (*Travel in the Ancient World* [Baltimore: Johns Hopkins University Press, 1994]).

56. Bauckham, "For Whom Were Gospels Written?," 44.

57. Bauckham, "For Whom Were Gospels Written?," 46–47.

58. Peterson's conclusion is that "At the very least, the present state of affairs should make it impossible simply to assume that reconstructed communities behind Gospels are hermeneutically necessary to read Gospels rightly. Perhaps, however, we are approaching a time in which the historical reconstruction Gospel communities will be considered an endeavor not worth the trouble. Time will tell" (*The Origins of Mark: The Markan Community in Current Debate* [Leiden: Brill, 2000], 202). Recent studies on Mark, however, have not abandoned this quest (see, for example, Marcus, *Mark 1–8*, 25–37; France, *The Gospel of Mark*, 35–41; Edwards, *The Gospel According to Mark*, 3–6; Donahue and Harrington, *The Gospel of Mark*, 41–46; Roskam, *The Purpose of the Gospel of Mark in Its Historical and Social Context*, 27–142; Stein, *Mark*, 9–12.).

simply broadcasting to the whole Christian movement, as Bauckham suggests, but has identified his readers' interpretive abilities and adapted his writing to their cultural limitations.

On the other hand, Bauckham rightly argues that the Gospels—especially this Gospel—have a universal message which was intended for wide circulation well beyond a particular local group of Christians who entertained certain questions and had specific needs. There are strikingly particular and local elements in this book which point to a Roman origin, as argued above, but it is also a document which displays the kind of breadth and universality which Bauckham highlights. The message of Mark echoes broad Christian concerns, such as the character and mission of Jesus and the problem of Christian suffering, while maintaining its local color and focus. The history it records is local (Palestinian), and the audience it addresses is local (Roman), but, starting with the prologue of the book (1:1–14), the message and concerns are universal, for all Christians.[59] Jesus is the Christ, "The Son of God," who not only fulfills the Davidic messianic hopes but also presents a challenge to the imperial claim to the title "son of god" (1:1; 15:39; and comments below on Mark's Christology). In his ministry a new age has dawned for all, embodied in the principle proclamation of the Gospel—the advent of the Kingdom of God (1:14). The final consummation in the Mark 13 apocalypse includes the gathering of God's elect "from the four winds, from the ends of the earth to the ends of heaven" (13:27).

The appeal of this Gospel is so broad that both Matthew and Luke found it useful and, through *mimesis/imitatio*, absorbed and adapted a large portion of its contents into their telling of the gospel of Jesus Christ.[60] The author of the Gospel of John apparently wrote for readers who knew the characters in Mark and was circulated "among churches in which Mark's Gospel was already being widely read."[61] Mark's Gospel represents the foundational teaching about Christ, his mission, and his followers that echoed through the Empire. The story was universal from the start and did not become so when Mark recorded Peter's testimony since the apostle had already proclaimed this message widely on his journeys from Galilee to Rome. Subsequently, the

---

59. Adam Winn (*The Purpose of Mark's Gospel: An Early Christian Response to Roman Imperial Propaganda* [Tübingen: Mohr Siebeck, 2008], 3–4) questions Bauckham's exclusive focus on the universal nature of this Gospel: "It seems that Bauckham is creating an unnecessary dichotomy—namely that gospels were either written for a narrow audience or a broad audience. However, me must consider the possibility that an evangelist could have composed a gospel with one eye on his particular community and one on the church empire-wide. A gospel tailored to speak to the needs of a particular community is not precluded from speaking to a broader audience, especially if that broader audience might be facing or might soon face challenges similar to those of the evangelist's particular community."

60. See below on the relationship between Mark and the other canonical Gospels. On ancient literary borrowing and the Synoptic Problem, see R. A. Derrenbacker Jr., *Ancient Compositional Practices and the Synoptic Problem* (Leuven: Leuven University Press; Dudley, MA: Peeters, 2005).

61. Richard Bauckham, "John for Readers of Mark," in *The Gospels for All Christians: Rethinking the Gospel Audiences*, ed. Richard Bauckham (Grand Rapids: Eerdmans, 1998c), 171. See also Ian D. MacKay, *John's Relationship with Mark: An Analysis of John 6 in the Light of Mark 6–8* (Tübingen: Mohr Siebeck, 2004), 300–303.

book circulated and became widely known, although its first readers lived in Rome. This telling of the Jesus story is both universal and local in its focus, or, as we might say today, "glocal." If Papias and others are correct about the connection between this Mark's Gospel and Peter's preaching, then in Paul's interview with Peter (Gal 1:18) he most likely heard the outline of Jesus' story recorded here. This was the first, principle, and foundational telling of the gospel of Jesus Christ.

Recognition of the universal nature of this Gospel rolls us back to consider Peter's place in its origin. Peter, as Mark, ended up in Rome, and the preaching which he delivered in the imperial city echoed what he proclaimed over and again throughout his itinerant ministry before arriving at the imperial city. The story which Mark *received*, and not merely that which he *circulated*, was not primarily tied to any particular Christian community. However, according to early testimony Mark wrote what Peter had preached in Rome and elsewhere, but he composed the book in response to the request of the Roman church. Bauckham argues that such books were not written for communities that have access to oral proclamation. But Clement of Alexandria presents a contrary opinion, stating that the church in Rome, which had heard Peter's *oral* teaching, requested a *written* copy (*Hist. eccl.* 2.15.1–2). The written document allowed the church to *hear* again the gospel Peter preached upon every occasion that Mark was read aloud. A single hearing would not do, and other churches could benefit likewise when they heard it.

The Gospel was intended for the Roman church but then became apt "for study in the churches" or, perhaps, "for recitation in the churches"[62] and so circulated widely. Clement notes that Mark wrote at the behest of those in Rome and then "distributed the Gospel among those that asked him" (*Hist. eccl.* 6.14.6). Clement also commented on Peter's itinerant preaching before Mark composed this Gospel. The apostle "brought the costly merchandise of the spiritual light from the east to the dwellers in the west, preaching the Gospel of the light itself and the word which saves souls, the proclamation of the Kingdom of Heaven" (*Hist. eccl.* 2.14.6; 6.14.6). Our earliest sources that give an account of the Gospel's composition point to both the wide spread of the message Peter preached and the Gospel of Mark while also showing how the composition of the Gospel was in response to the Roman church's request.[63] The request from the Roman church that Mark compose the Gospel marks it as his literary patron who, in the end, would be responsible not only to defray Mark's costs of

---

62. Clement's statement identifies this book as "Scripture" which was to be "read" in the churches (τὴν γραφὴν εἰς ἔντευξιν ταῖς ἐκκλησίαις). Ἔντευξις may refer to the oral reading of the text (*TDNT*, 8:244) that is a necessary component of corporate engagement with its message.

63. See also Margaret M. Mitchell's response to Bauckham in which she outlines how patristic views show an awareness that the Gospels were originally written for particular audiences. She begins her essay with a quotation from Gregory of Nazianzus (*Carmina dogmatica* 1.12.6–9), which says, "Matthew wrote the marvels of Christ for the Hebrews, Mark for Italy, Luke for Achaia, But John, the great herald, the heaven-wanderer, wrote for all" ("Patristic Counter-Evidence to the Claim that 'The Gospels Were Written for All Christians,'" *NTS* 51 [2005] 36).

composition but also for payment for the copying and distribution of the letter. Such patronage would also bind Mark to the Roman church as they, like any literary patron, would have exercised a certain influence over his writing, such as suggesting the topic of his composition.[64] The Roman church's level of involvement is quite high as there is more going on here than putting pen to papyrus.

MARK'S AUDIENCE AND PETER'S MESSAGE

The question remains whether or not identifying the community that first received the Gospel of Mark helps us in any way interpret its message. And, if the Gospel is for a particular community *and*, at the same time, a story told widely and then circulated broadly after being penned, does this provide any useful information as we outline the book's message and theology? Peterson has responded negatively to these questions.[65] The position taken here regarding the universal aspect of Mark's message, however, is not far from the conclusion, voiced by Bauckham, that the Gospel contemplates a general Christian audience in the first century. The route taken here to arrive at this position, however, is different than the one mapped by Bauckham. The Gospel reflects the *testimony* of Peter, and that of Mark derived from Peter, so we should expect that its message is not crafted exclusively with respect to its original audience, however defined, but also with deference to its source. In other words, the Gospel presents faithful testimony, which the author and his immediate source have adapted to the needs of the hearers. As all testimony, it combines not only a witness to the significant events—in this case, Jesus' life—but also includes interpretation of those events. Those offering testimony are not objective observers but rather involved participants who bear witness to events and their meaning. Instead of being a mere record of the facts, it is an act of interpretation or a theological movement which joins fact and meaning. Such interpretation is always for someone and presented in a way that is mindful of the audience's particular understanding and needs. Indeed, all theology is contextual. Ancient historians who based their accounts on testimony needed to represent their subject faithfully *and* recognize the concerns of their audience. We should, therefore, expect that Mark's Gospel bears the traits of the author's interpretive art in addressing his audience's concerns while presenting faithful testimony. The source, the author,

---

64. See the discussion and summary of literary patronage in Barbara Gold's work on the topic (*Literary Patronage in Greece and Rome*, 173–76). The role of patrons warrants further exploration since composition is not simply about authors and readers but patrons who influenced the whole process from composition to distribution. As she concludes, "The presence of a patron in a work of literature ensured that the work would be public in its nature. This was perhaps the ultimate value of the patron: he forced a writer to focus his thoughts outward and thus to create a work worthy of immortality" (Gold, *Literary Patronage in Greece and Rome*, 176). The role of the Roman church in the preservation, development, and distribution of the Gospel merits closer attention.

65. Peterson, *The Origins of Mark*, 20.

the first audience who served as patrons, and the wider Christian community all stand present.[66]

The first readers/hearers of the Gospel of Mark were, as we have seen, Gentiles who knew both Greek and Latin. They most likely resided in the city of Rome and personally knew some of the people mentioned in the Gospel, such as the sons of Simon of Cyrene (15:21). They were also familiar with characters in the story itself whom the author presents with no introduction since he assumes that the readers knew who they were. Mark introduces John simply as the baptizer (1:4), Herod Antipas as King Herod (6:14), and Pontius Pilate as Pilate (15:1). These were widely known figures, but Mark also includes some lesser-known people within the story without introduction, such as Mary Magdalene and the other Mary, who is identified as the mother of "James the younger and of Joses, and Salome" (15:40, 47; 16:1). Many well-known cities appear, such as Jerusalem, Sidon, and Tyre, along with recognizable, regional names, such as Galilee, Judea, Idumea, and the land "beyond the Jordan" (3:7–8). Mark expected that his readers held sufficient geographical and cultural understanding to know that people sought Jesus from considerable distances to the north, south, and east, and that those who sought him were both Jews and Gentiles. His readers could understand the references to Pharisees (2:16) and Herodians (3:6). The intensity of citations from the prophets suggests that the readers were familiar with some content from the Hebrew Scriptures, at least in translation, starting with "the prophet Isaiah" (1:2). They could recognize figures from the Jewish story, such as Moses (1:44), and understand certain Jewish customs, such as Sabbath-keeping (1:21) and festival observance (14:1).

On the other hand, the explanatory clauses in the Gospel, such as the translation of Aramaic terms and the sometimes extensive explanations of other Jewish customs (3:17; 7:1–4, 11, 34; 15:42), point to a readership that knew about several Jewish practices but was not entirely familiar with their meaning. While they could recognize Jewish groups, they occasionally needed an explanation of their beliefs, such as those of the Sadducees (12:18). Stein's opinion is that "all this suggests that the original audience of Mark consisted primarily of gentile Christians, familiar with both the gospel traditions and the Judaism of the first century."[67] He adds that they had been "God-fearers" who were attached to the synagogue (Acts 10:2, 22; 13:16, 26). But they could just as easily have been Gentile Christians who had become familiar with the roots of their faith through hearing Scripture and the gospel message in their gatherings (1 Tim 4:13).

The kind of understanding that Mark assumes his readers held regarding Judaism is similar to that which many Romans already possessed. Knowledge about Jews, their history, customs, and beliefs was widespread due to the presence of Jews throughout the cities of the Empire and the Roman involvement in the affairs of Palestine since

---

66. See chapter 1, "Sources of a Petrine Theology," for elaboration of these points.
67. Stein's discussion of these features forms the basis of the preceding (*Mark*, 9–10).

the conquest of Pompey in 63 BC.[68] The level of understanding about Jewish matters that Mark assumes his readers possessed is not unlike that found in the discussion about Jewish history and customs in Tacitus (*Hist.* 5.1–5). Cicero harbors considerable prejudice against the Jews, which germinated through knowing their customs and history (*Flac.* 66–69), and Juvenal's satire displays a mixture of understanding and incomprehension about the Jews (3.14; 6.155–60, 542–50; 8.159–62; 14.96–106).[69] The readers of this book need not have been God-fearers but only Gentiles who had come into the faith without necessarily passing through the synagogue. We need not assume that they had extensive orientation to Jewish customs and literature apart from the common perspectives about Jewish affairs. To put this another way, the story in Mark does not assume that the hearers had received particular teaching about Judaism either in the gatherings of the church or through having previously assembled with Jews in the synagogue. Despite the particular obscure references to figures such as Rufus and Alexander, we may conclude that the shape of the story would have been comprehensible even to a non-Christian audience. The testimony of the early church regarding the composition of the Gospel was that Mark wrote for the Roman church and that his story was that which Peter had preached. If this reflects a significant part of the compositional history of the book, it accounts for both the marked particular and local features of this Gospel as well as the way the bulk of the message was comprehensible to a wider audience. In other words, this Gospel may be viewed as a document having both an *evangelistic* and *didactic* orientation. The material tells the universal Christian story and, at the same time, acknowledges the community for whom it was originally written. We need not conclude that the content is *either* for Christians *or* for non-Christians. Both are in view.

Unsurprisingly, commentators are divided over this question of whether Mark's Gospel was written for Christians or as an evangelistic tract for non-Christians. Stein, for example, declares that "the original audience of Mark consisted primarily of gentile Christians, familiar with both the gospel traditions and the Judaism of the first century," adding that they had been Gentile "God-fearers."[70] Guelich likewise focuses on the ecclesial side of the message, concluding that "Mark wrote the Gospel pastorally to address a community under duress. This duress had given rise to questions about who Jesus was and the nature of the 'Kingdom' he had come to inaugurate."[71] Likewise, Marcus asserts that the author "seems to have written his work first and foremost for the Christian community of which he himself was a member."[72] So, too, Witherington

---

68. See Irina Levinskaya, *The Book of Acts in Its Diaspora Setting* (Grand Rapids: Eerdmans, 1996).

69. See J. N. Sevenster, *The Roots of Pagan Anti-Semitism In the Ancient World* (Leiden: Brill, 1975); Hans Conzelman, *Gentiles, Jews, Christians: Polemics and Apologetics In the Greco-Roman Era* (Minneapolis: Augsburg Fortress, 1992); Peter Schäfer, *Judeophobia: Attitudes Toward the Jews in the Ancient World* (Cambridge, MA: Harvard University Press, 1997).

70. Stein, *Mark*, 10.

71. Robert A. Guelich, *Mark 1–8:26* (Dallas: Word, 1989), xliii.

72. Marcus, *Mark 1–8*, 25.

sees the readers as "Gentile converts to the Christian faith," yet, contrary to Stein, as "Gentiles who had not first been Jewish proselytes or synagogue adherents."[73] Donahue and Harrington identify them as Christian readers in Rome but leave open the possibility that the book circulated more widely among the churches.[74]

On the other end of the spectrum, Gundry regards Mark primarily as an evangelistic document.[75] Others, however, see both audiences on the landscape. Bauckham opens the possibility of a non-Christian readership while noting that had any of the evangelists contemplated "reaching non-Christian readers, they would surely have had to envisage reaching them via Christian readers, who could pass on copies of Gospels to interested outsiders through personal contact." The primary, though not exclusive, audience in this view was Christian.[76] Cranfield cannot lock down the book exclusively to one group or another since it is an attempt "to supply the catechetical and liturgical needs of the church in Rome, to support its faith in face of the threat of martyrdom, and to provide material for missionary preachers."[77] Beavis is a vigorous supporter of a "both/and" understanding of the Gospel's first audience, stating that "The Marcan sect, which defined itself over and against society, had nevertheless to remain open to 'outsiders.'" She points to the way that "the Gospel, with its distinction between private teaching for disciples and public teaching to the crowds, reflects this kind of ambiguity, to the point that often non-disciples display more faith and insight than the twelve." Beavis concludes that:

> the question should be seriously considered whether Mark was directed not only to the evangelist's church, but to the more general audience of early Christian missionary teaching/preaching; as noted earlier, in Mark, διδάσκειν and κηρύσσειν are synonyms, and early Christian meetings could be open to unbelievers (1 Cor 14:23). We have seen that, rhetorically, the Gospel is framed in a manner that would have been attractive to and understood by a first-century audience, and . . . the portrayal of Jesus as suffering teacher-king would also have been admired. Mark's teaching may thus have been directed not (or not only) to converts, but to *potential* converts. The social alienation ('suffering') resulting from following Jesus would have been as relevant to would-be 'disciples' as to committed Christians, since a general audience, even more than converts, would have feared the rejection by family, friends, and

---

73. Witherington, *The Gospel of Mark*, 26.

74. "That Mark wrote primarily (though not exclusively) for the church at Rome seems likely . . . in light of the content of the gospel, which appears to address a community that has suffered persecution from the outside and division from the inside" (Donahue and Harrington, *The Gospel of Mark*, 42).

75. "Mark's taking for granted little if any knowledge of Jesus . . . favors that Mark writes apologetically not to keep Christians from apostatizing out of shame for the Cross . . . but to convert non-Christians despite the shame of the Cross. . . . So this gospel is for people who are afraid to believe in a world that despises weakness and esteems power" (Gundry, *Mark*, 1026).

76. Bauckham, "For Whom Were Gospels Written?," 10.

77. Cranfield, *The Gospel According to Saint Mark*, 15.

society entailed by embracing the new religion, and have needed the assurance that Christians, contrary to appearances, were the 'insiders' in God's design. Throughout the Gospel, the characters of whom Jesus consistently approves are the kind of 'common people' (the poor, the sick, Gentiles, women) who might well have made up the audiences of the early missionary preaching.... They are the ones who consistently show faith in Jesus—an attitude necessary to the reception of the teaching of Christian missionaries. Mark's emphasis on mission (1:4, 14–15, 16–20; 2:13–14; 3:13–19; 4:15–20; 6:7–13, 30; 9:38–41; 13:10; 14:9) supports the suggestion that the Gospel originally functioned as propaganda. We should not, however, make too sharp a distinction between Christian and non-Christian audiences; the evangelist may well have had both in mind as he composed his Gospel.[78]

The position taken here aligns with Beavis's assessment, but looks at the way the Gospel of Mark combines the universal appeal of Peter's evangelistic preaching and Mark's concern for the needs of the Roman Christian community. The Gospel speaks to those in the empire during the first century and also to the particular realities of the Roman and other churches where the Gospel eventually circulated. If we acknowledge the testimony of the early church, the verbal aspect of the Gospel finds its primary roots not in the way the Gospel would be used but rather in the nature of its source material, that is, in "Peter's oral narration."[79] In other words, it is *kerygmatic* but also served the needs of the nascent Christian community. Mark's focus on the person of Jesus and the nature of discipleship, including the theology of suffering, make this a Gospel for all people, Christians and non-Christians alike. As Hengel notes, Mark "takes a model 'kerygmatic-missionary' form which is indebted to a concrete tradition tied to a person. The special feature of the earliest Gospel is that nothing is narrated here which is not intended as proclamation, and nowhere is there mere 'proclamation' without a concern to offer a dramatic narration of the 'story' and a selection of 'sayings' of Jesus."[80] The early church was a missional church, and its mission cannot be unhooked from its theology. Understanding both the Gospel's *kerygmatic* and *didactic* character helps bring into focus the contours of Mark's theology.

If the Gospel of Mark points to both a Christian and non-Christian audience and also envisions both a local Roman and universal or empire-wide audience, why then does the Gospel place such strong emphasis upon persecution and suffering? While relevant for the Christian community in the Roman Empire of the first century, the persecution theme does not seem to fit within the *kerygmatic* purposes of the document. Telford rightly highlights Mark's "interest in *persecution, suffering* and

---

78. Beavis, *Mark's Audience*, 171–72. Tolbert (*Sowing the Gospel*, 304) surprisingly concludes that the book was meant for individuals, not groups. She does, however, see the document as being for Christians undergoing persecution and for people not quite persuaded to become Christians. "Mark's rhetorical goals are exhortation and proselytizing."

79. Bauckham, *Jesus and the Eyewitnesses*, 179.

80. Hengel, *The Four Gospels and the One Gospel of Jesus Christ*, 85.

martyrdom, and the true nature of *discipleship.*"[81] At numerous points in the narrative, Mark takes up the topic of opposition to Jesus and his disciples, including their suffering and martyrdom.[82] The opposition against Jesus appears as early as chapter 2, in the way that questions swirl around the character of Jesus' person, words, and actions (2:7-8, 16, 18, 24). Questions soon turn into contention as the Pharisees and Herodians want to destroy him (3:6), Judas is introduced as the one who will betray him (3:19), his family regards him as beside himself (3:21), the people consider him to be out of his mind (3:21), and the scribes ridicule him as someone demon-possessed (3:22, 30). Gentiles petition him to leave them (5:17), and some people laugh at him (5:20). He is rejected by his hometown and family (6:3), and the beheading of John the Baptist prefigures his own destiny (6:17-29). Controversy rages over his violation of Jewish customs (7:1-8, 14-15). Unsurprisingly, from early on persecution becomes a topic in Jesus' teaching (4:17; 10:30). He makes it clear that those who follow him will not be well-received (6:11) and may expect to suffer, especially before the final consummation (13:9-27). Betrayal and death will be the disciples' lot. The way of Jesus and his disciples is one of suffering and deadly cross-bearing (8:31-9:1; 9:12, 31; 10:28-40). In the end, Jesus is betrayed, tried, and crucified (14:1-15:47). Mark exalts the power and glory of the Son of Man and portrays him as the true Son of God but also paints a graphic picture of how Jesus and his disciples meet with deadly opposition. Why does this Gospel include such extensive teaching on suffering and persecution if the story's intent is not only to orient Christians but also to gain disciples?

Early Christians faced persecution from the beginning, as the Book of Acts shows repeatedly. The mission was marked by suffering, so much so that part of Paul's basic instruction to the believers was, "It is through many persecutions that we must enter the kingdom of God" (Acts 14:22). The news about how Christians were the cause of social unrest spread widely, sometimes arriving in a city ahead of the preaching of the gospel (17:6). Before Paul walked into Rome, news about the gospel circulated, generating the comment among the Jewish leaders in the city that "with regard to this sect we know that everywhere it is spoken against" (28:22). The expulsion of Jews in Rome during the reign of Claudias may have been precipitated by the clashes between those Jews who accepted that Jesus was the Messiah and those who did not (Acts 18:2). In his book *The Deified Claudius*, Suetonius says, "Since the Jews constantly made disturbances at the instigation of Chresto, he expelled them from Rome" (*Claud.* 25.4). He may have mistaken the Latinized Greek title "Christus" for the common Latin name "Chresto."[83] As we know, Nero persecuted the Christians in Rome whom people

---

81. William R. Telford, *The Theology of the Gospel of Mark* (Cambridge: Cambridge University Press, 1999), 154.

82. See below on the theology of suffering in Mark.

83. Tacitus (*Ann.* 15.44) correctly transliterates the title *Christus* and tags any who follow him as *Christianos*. Tertullian derides the Romans for mispronouncing the Christian name as *Chrestianus* (*Apol.* 3). Justin remarks on the same confusion (1 *Apol.* 4), echoed also in Lactantius (*Inst.* 4.7). The problem with identifying *Chresto* with Christ in Suetonius's comment about the Jews during the reign

considered a class of people "given to a new and mischievous superstition" (Suetonius, *Nero* 16). The antipathy towards Christians predated the punishment Nero inflicted on this community. Tacitus also commented on this persecution (*Ann.* 15.44), noting that Nero found Christians to be a convenient scapegoat since they were "a class of men loathed for their vices." Theirs was, according to Tacitus, a "pernicious superstition" and a "disease" that had come to Rome, "where all things horrible or shameful in the world collect and find a vogue." Christians were charged with "hatred of the human race" and subsequently tortured by being bound in skins and tossed to dogs, crucified, and burned as lamps to illumine the night. The Christian way was one of suffering, not only in Rome but throughout the Empire. First Peter, sent to the churches in the northern half of Anatolia (1 Pet 1:1), addresses the suffering that the believers in those provinces endured but also reminds the first readers that Christians "in all the world are undergoing the same kinds of suffering" (1 Pet 5:9). Mark may have written in response to the persecution which the believers in Rome endured during the Neronian persecution, but the emphasis on persecution in this Gospel do not compel this conclusion. It may have been anytime around that event since dishonoring Christians was commonplace in the imperial city and elsewhere. The teaching on persecution had both local and universal significance. It was relevant for believers in Rome and scattered through the provinces.

For non-believers, the theology of suffering was important as well. How could one contemplate becoming a disciple of Christ without some explanation regarding why Christ and his disciples had become such social pariahs in Rome and throughout the Empire? The message of the gospel included testimony about Christ's suffering as well as his triumph. As Ladd said, "The primitive kerygma had its focal point in the death and exaltation of Jesus."[84] The word to potential followers included not only a vision of the crucified and exalted Christ but also the call to discipleship, which meant entering into the dishonor and pain that Jesus had endured (Mark 8:34–38). Buried within the *kerygma* is the call to discipleship, which entailed suffering as Christ suffered. This was a central and not secondary component of the gospel.[85] To become a

---

of Claudius is that he later correctly identifies the followers of Christ as *Christiani* (*Nero* 16).

84. George Eldon Ladd, *New Testament Theology* (Grand Rapids: Eerdmans, 1993), 366.

85. Studies on the kerygma have not much explored the relationship between early Christian proclamation of the gospel and the theology of suffering for Christ's followers, a topic commonly regarded as part of early Christian teaching. See C. H. Dodd, *The Apostolic Preaching and Its Developments* (New York: Harper & Row, 1964); Robert H. Mounce, *The Essential Nature of New Testament Preaching* (Grand Rapids: Eerdmans, 1960); James I. H. McDonald, *Kerygma and Didache: The Articulation and Structure of the Earliest Christian Message* (Cambridge: Cambridge University Press, 1980); Eugene E. Lemcio, "The Unifying Kerygma of the New Testament," *JSNT* 33 (1988) 3–17; Eugene E. Lemcio, "The Unifying Kerygma of the New Testament, Pt. 2," *JSNT* 38 (1990) 3–11. McDonald, however, reminds us that the shape of the kerygma was not entirely uniform and we cannot draw a neat line between kerygma and didache (*Kerygma and Didache*, 126–27). The proclamation of the gospel of Christ always included the message of the cross and was framed within the early Christian reality of suffering (Acts 14:22; 1 Thess 1:6; 2:2; 2 Tim 1:8; 1 Pet 5:1). The pattern of suffering and glory is never broken (1 Pet 1:10–12; see James M. Robinson, "The Possibility of a New Quest," in *The Historical*

follower of Christ means to follow him to the cross. The wonder is that anyone would join the company of believers given the dishonor and suffering that discipleship entailed. Paul saw in the weakness and foolishness of the cross the wisdom and power of God (1 Cor 1:23), so he preached "Christ crucified." In the same way, Mark proclaims a gospel which entails both the suffering and glory of Christ and the sufferings and honor that his disciples may expect. The promise of life included the loss of life.

Jesus: Critical Concepts in Religious Studies, ed. Craig A. Evans [London: Routledge, 2004], 193-94). The connection between kerygma and suffering has become a topic in *minjung* theology (Andreas Anangguru Yewangoe, *Theologia Crucis in Asia: Asian Christian Views on Suffering in the Face of Overwhelming Poverty and Multifaceted Religiosity in Asia* [Amsterdam: Rodopi, 1987], 139-45).

CHAPTER 4

The Theology of Peter in the Gospel of Mark

The theological message of the Gospel of Mark centers on Jesus Christ and his gospel, as Mark announces in the opening line (1:1) of his book: "The beginning of the good news of Jesus Christ, the Son of God" (Ἀρχὴ τοῦ εὐαγγελίου Ἰησοῦ Χριστοῦ [υἱοῦ θεοῦ]). Jesus proclaimed the gospel of God, which was about the advent of God's kingdom, summarized in 1:15: "The time is fulfilled, and the kingdom of God has come near; repent, and believe in the good news" (Πεπλήρωται ὁ καιρὸς καὶ ἤγγικεν ἡ βασιλεία τοῦ θεοῦ· μετανοεῖτε καὶ πιστεύετε ἐν τῷ εὐαγγελίῳ). The kingdom of God has come near at this time of fulfillment through Jesus' person and deeds. Embedded within this central message is the call to respond to the proclamation of the new events transpiring. Buried within the indicative of the kingdom is an imperative—the summons to discipleship. Those who hear and see must turn and believe and thereby become disciples. Discipleship becomes an additional central theological focus of this Gospel which cannot be sundered from the opening declaration. Each of these pivotal themes in Mark's theology—Jesus, the kingdom of God, and discipleship—is developed extensively throughout the book as Mark elaborates who Jesus is and what he did, how the kingdom has and will come, and what constitutes true discipleship. These themes make their first appearance in the preface of the book (1:1–15) and are woven throughout the narrative. In his treatise on writing history, Lucian urged that in the preface of a historical work the author "will make what is to come easy to understand and quite clear, if he sets forth the causes and outlines the main events. The best historians have written prefaces of this sort" (*Hist.* 53). Though he is no Herodotus or Thucydides, in this regard, at least, Mark writes as one of the "best historians."

Gundry argues that Mark has no hidden agenda; the meaning of the narrative may be found on the surface, not buried below it. He states, "We will look for the meaning of Mark's gospel primarily in its text to avoid the referential fallacy of thinking that we can discern its meaning outside the text in the subject matter to which it refers. For the text itself is our main source of information concerning the external subject matter to which it refers."[1] Gundry is right to call us back to the text of Mark if we seek to understand the message he wished to communicate to his first readers in Rome, but this is just the starting point. In all human communication, meaning is not simply encoded in the sign system of a language, but rather the sign system provides evidence of a speaker or writer's informative intent. The communication of meaning is an inferential process which depends upon a hearer or reader's ability to infer relevant information from that which is salient within his or her cognitive environment. The speaker or writer not only depends upon this ability but also provides evidence which directs the inferential process. What we mean by what we say is larger than what is encoded in the sign system, and hearers/readers have the capacity to understand both the explicit and implicit information in the process of understanding another's utterances. In all communication there is always more going on than encoding into the sign system and decoding the message from the linguistic code. A gap exists between what is said and what is meant by what is said. In other words, while the code is strong, Mark and his source made assumptions about what type of contextual information was salient to their hearers and expected them to draw from that proper inferences given the evidence of their communicative intent contained in the code. There is more going on in Mark than what is contained in the text.[2]

Consequently, we must not forget that Mark, as any author, wrote for an audience and interacted with his and his readers' cognitive environment. In this process he engaged the issues on the ground that his readers faced and were familiar with. At the same time, Mark has inherited a story from Peter, and he offers faithful witness to Peter's testimony about Jesus. The Gospel of Mark is in dialogue with its source and its audience, both of which are in view as the story unfolds. The narrative therefore evokes concepts which were common currency for the Gospel's source and first audience. Such concerns may not always be evident to us as secondary readers of texts given our temporal and cultural distance from them.

---

1. Gundry, *Mark*, 15. Peterson (*The Origins of Mark*) shares Gundry's dissatisfaction with the multiple attempts to understand Mark's message by seeking to unearth the Gospel's setting. See above.

2. "Relevance Theory," based upon Gricean pragmatics, explains the inferential nature of communication or, more properly, ostensive/inferential communication. See Gene L. Green, "Relevance Theory and Biblical Interpretation," in *The Linguist as Pedagogue: Trends in the Teaching and Linguistic Analysis of the New Testament*, ed. Stanley E. Porter and Matthew Brook O'Donnell (Sheffield: Sheffield Phoenix, 2009), 217–50; Dan Sperber and Deirdre Wilson, *Relevance: Communication and Cognition* (Oxford: Blackwell, 1995).

MARK'S THEOLOGICAL FRAMEWORK
God's New Exodus

From the outset Mark frames his story about Jesus and the kingdom within the prophetic hope of a New Exodus, promised in Isaiah and inaugurated by God in the proclamation of John the Baptist. The Exodus was the "founding moment" for Israel, and this event became "a model for her future hope."[3] The hope is for "Yahweh's future victory over the power of evil,"[4] which is now coming to pass through the gospel of Jesus Christ. Mark repeatedly evokes this scriptural framework, beginning with his opening biblical citation in 1:2–3: "See, I am sending my messenger ahead of you, who will prepare your way; the voice of one crying out in the wilderness: 'Prepare the way of the Lord, make his paths straight.'" Despite the fact that Mark indicates that he is appealing to Isaiah ("As it is written in the prophet Isaiah"), the first quotation comes from Exodus 23:20a ("And look, I am sending my angel in front of you"; Mark omits the emphatic ἐγώ found in the LXX). Exodus 23:20 is a promise made to Israel that God's angel or messenger will "guard you on the way in order to bring you into the land that I prepared for you" (LXX). Mark does not cite this second part of Exodus 23:20; nevertheless, the Exodus event is in mind sans this reference to entering the land. The first line of the quotation in Mark also echoes Malachi 3:1, "Behold, I am sending my messenger," a text already brought together with Exodus 23:20 in Jewish tradition.[5] The second part of Mark's quotation ("Who will prepare [κατασκευάσει] your way") is not taken directly from the LXX of either Exodus 23:20b ("In order to guard [φυλάξῃ] you on the way") or Malachi 3:1b ("And he will oversee [ἐπιβλέψεται] the way before me") but rather is an independent translation from the Hebrew of Malachi 3:1.[6]

While Exodus 23 recalls the entry into the land of promise after the liberation from Egypt, the focus in Malachi 3 is on the coming of the messenger of the covenant who will arrive for judgment: "And who will endure the day of his arrival, or who will withstand in his appearance?" (3:2). The warning carries with it a call to repentance (3:6–12). Mark's quotation of Malachi 3:1 evokes Exodus 23:20b, which is bound with the expectations of a New Exodus (NE). In the same way, Malachi's "conditions of

---

3. Rikki E. Watts, *Isaiah's New Exodus in Mark* (Grand Rapids: Baker Academic, 1997), 90. Commenting on Isaiah 40:3 Watts notes, "If Israel's founding moment was predicated on Yahweh's redemptive action in the Exodus from Egyptian bondage, then surely a second deliverance from exilic bondage, this time of Babylon, could scarcely be conceived of in other terms except those of the first Exodus?" (*Isaiah's New Exodus in Mark*, 80).

4. Joel Marcus, *The Way of the Lord: Christological Exegesis of the Old Testament in the Gospel of Mark* (Louisville: Westminster John Knox, 1992), 22.

5. Jacob Mann, *The Bible as Read and Preached in the Old Synagogue: A Study in the Cycles of the Readings from Torah and Prophets, as Well as from Psalms, and in the Structure of the Midrashic Homilies* (New York: KTAV, 1971), 1:479; Marcus, *The Way of the Lord*, 13n4.

6. Marcus, *The Way of the Lord*, 13. The variation hangs on whether פנה is understood as *qal* as in the LXX or *pi'el* as in Mark.

failed crops (3:11f) and the famous 'intermarriage' crux (2:10ff) reflect the promises and commands of Exodus 23:24ff."[7] Moreover, "the historical setting of Malachi is one of disappointment and frustration in the light of the Return having failed to meet the expectations fuelled by the pictures of NE redemption offered in Isaiah 40–55/66 and the prophecies of Haggai and Zechariah." The cause of the delay was the "nation's sin," but "the subsequent call for preparation reaffirms the certainty of Yahweh's coming (2:17–3:5)."[8] In Mark's understanding, the gospel brings both promise and warning as this New Exodus begins. These citations, which follow Mark's opening declaration ("The beginning of the good news of Jesus Christ, the Son of God"), frame that statement within God's redemptive act in the Exodus, his coming judgment, and the repeated promise of a New Exodus. The opening quotations serve as an *exordium* that introduces the subject Mark will elaborate in his narrative.[9]

Although Mark draws the opening citations from Exodus and Malachi, his primary orientation is to Isaiah 40:3, which he quotes in 1:3, saying, "The voice of one crying out in the wilderness: 'Prepare the way of the Lord, make his paths straight.'" The quotation follows the LXX almost exactly, save for the final word in Mark 1:3. By substituting αὐτοῦ ("his") for τοῦ θεοῦ ἡμῶν ("our God") in the LXX of Isaiah 40:3b, Mark gives the quotation a christological focus.[10] Mark quotes and references Isaiah by name. In doing so he "is not just identifying the source for what follows in 1:3 but rather is hinting more broadly that his whole story of 'the beginning of the gospel' is to be understood against the backdrop of the Isaian themes."[11] He frames the whole

7. Watts, *Isaiah's New Exodus in Mark*, 72.

8. Watts, *Isaiah's New Exodus in Mark*, 67.

9. Aristotle, *Rhet.* 3.14.1–7. "But in speeches and epic poems the exordia provide a sample of the subject, in order that the hearers may know beforehand what it is about, and that the mind may not be kept in suspense, for that which is undefined leads astray; so then he who puts the beginning, so to say, into the hearer's hand enables him, if he holds fast to it, to follow the story" (3.14.6). Lucian elaborates the point with reference to history writing (*How to Write History*, 53). In the preface, the historian "will make what is to come easy to understand and quite clear, if he sets forth the causes and outlines the main events."

10. The voice of the messenger cries out, "Prepare the way of the Lord" (1:3b), with Jesus as the Lord whose way is being prepared. "His paths" (1:3c) are those of "the Lord."

11. Marcus, *The Way of the Lord*, 20. Marcus and Watts's analysis of this passage in light of Exodus themes is more convincing than the critique in Thomas R. Hatina, *In Search of a Context: The Function of Scripture in Mark's Narrative* (London: Sheffield Academic, 2002), 138–83. He concludes, "In our reading, Mark's composite quotation does not function to introduce the Isaianic theme of the new exodus, nor is the quotation regarded as the hermeneutical key for the rest of the narrative" (*In Search of a Context*, 181). Hatina fails to appreciate the intensity of the Exodus imagery in Mark 1:1–15 and how the quotations and geographical notes evoke that seminal event for both Israel and the church. The quotations and language of Mark's prologue evoke great events in Israel's history. As Marcus notes, Mark "can expect these biblically literate Christians to be aware of other themes associated with Isa 40:3 in the larger Isaian context: the wilderness, the way of the Lord, the enlightening of the blind, the festal procession to Jerusalem" (*The Way of the Lord*, 46). See also the discussions in Richard Schneck, *Isaiah in the Gospel of Mark 1–8* (Vallejo, CA: BIBAL, 1994), 27–42; Tom Shepherd, "The Narrative Role of John and Jesus in Mark 1:1–15," in *The Gospel of Mark*, ed. Thomas R. Hatina (London: T. & T. Clark, 2006), 151–68, as well as the argument below.

within the hope of a New Exodus as presented in Isaiah: Yahweh is coming through the wilderness and it is time to prepare his way. From Mark's perspective, the time of his coming has arrived with John acting as the herald, the anticipated Elijah (Mal 4:5). He was the forerunner of God's coming kingdom in the last day. But although John is a prominent figure here and throughout the Gospel, as with any herald, the focus is not on him. Jesus, on the other hand, is the Lord, whose coming evokes the call for preparation.

The New Exodus imagery is not isolated to the opening quotations in the prologue of Mark.[12] This section of the Gospel is replete with geographical and other markers which evoke the Exodus. Both the citations from Malachi 3:1 ("Who will prepare your way") and Isaiah 40:3 ("Prepare the way of the Lord") in 1:2–3 focus on the "way of the Lord." The Isaiah quotation in 1:3c interprets this "way" as paths which need straightening ("Make his paths straight"). The references to the "way" and the "path" refer back to Yahweh's great redemptive act in the Exodus. In Isaiah 43:16–17, the prophet identifies the Lord as the one "who provides a way in the sea, a path in the mighty water, who has brought out chariots and horse and a mighty throng together; they have lain down and will not rise" (cf. Exod 13:17–18, 21; 14:1–31). The earliest events of the narrative in Mark transpire in the wilderness, a theme picked up in the Isaiah 40:3 quotation in 1:3 ("The voice of one crying out in the wilderness"). John the Baptist "appeared in the wilderness" to proclaim and baptize (1:4), and Jesus himself was driven by the Spirit "out into the wilderness" and "was in the wilderness forty days" (1:12–13). The location recalls Israel's sojourn in the wilderness at the time of the Exodus (Exod 8:20, 27; 15:22; etc.), a theme remixed in Isaiah's vision of a New Exodus ("I will make a way in the wilderness" [Isa 43:19–20]; 48:21). For any informed hearer, the "forty days" of testing that Jesus spent in the wilderness recall the image of Israel being tested in the wilderness for forty years (Exod 16:35; 20:20; Deut 2:7; 8:2; Acts 7:36). The water imagery, which evokes the Exodus, also appears in Mark's prologue. John the Baptist is out in the wilderness, where he preaches the "baptism of repentance for the forgiveness of sins" (1:4, 5, 8, 9). His ministry took place at the Jordan River (1:5, 9–10), the same river which Israel crossed to enter into the promised land after the Exodus from Egypt (Josh 3). The figure of John himself points to the New Exodus typology as well. Mark identifies John by describing him as one outfitted in the prophetic garb of Elijah: "Clothed with camel's hair, with a leather belt around his waist, and he ate locusts and wild honey" (1:6; 2 Kgs 1:8; cf. Zech 13:4). Elijah was the harbinger before the day of the Lord (Mal 4:5). As noted above, Mark evokes Malachi 3:1 in 1:2, a text tied with New Exodus. As Watts comments on Malachi 3:1, "Given that the terminology is characteristic of the NE motif in the book of Isaiah . . . this suggests that Malachi is referring in particular to the Isaianic expression

---

12. See the thorough discussion of the particularly Isaianic New Exodus themes in Mark's prologue in Watts, *Isaiah's New Exodus in Mark*, 96–121.

of the hope of Yahweh's NE coming."[13] As Israel had gone out from Egypt to Moses (Exod 13:4, 8; 14:8; 40:17; Deut 11:10; 23:5; Josh 2:10; all using forms of ἐκπορεύομαι) so now "the whole Judean countryside and all the people of Jerusalem were going out to him" (ἐξεπορεύετο). Surprisingly, instead of *going into* Judea and Jerusalem, they are *going out* in response to John's call to repent and pass through the waters.

The New Exodus theology also includes allusions to the new covenant being inaugurated. The blessings of the New Covenant, which Jeremiah ties with the old covenant made at the time of the first Exodus, included moral renewal and forgiveness of sins (Jer 31:31–34). John's call to repentance and promise of forgiveness is the first flush of New Covenant language in Mark (1:4). The coming of the Spirit, which "the one who is more powerful" will give (1:7), recalls Ezekiel's promise of washing for moral renewal and transformation by the Spirit (Ezek 36:25–27). As Marcus notes, this passage "is immediately followed by a classic expression of the wilderness theme (Ezek 36:33–36)." Jesus' own reception of the Spirit (1:10) evokes the language of the Servant Song in Isaiah 42:1: "Here is my servant, whom I uphold, my chosen, in whom my soul delights; I have put my spirit upon him; he will bring forth justice to the nations." The announcement from heaven, "You are my Son, the Beloved; with you I am well pleased" (Mark 1:11), makes firm the identification of Jesus with the Servant in Isaiah. Mark combines the words spoken upon the enthronement of the king, "You are my son" (Ps 2:7; cf. 2 Sam 7:14), with an allusion to Abraham's son, the beloved (Gen 22:2, 12, 16), as well as the Servant of Isaiah (42:1). The figure of the Servant is prominent in Isaiah's vision of the New Exodus. Even the introductory scene in Mark 1:10, when Jesus "was coming up out of the water" and "saw the heavens torn and the Spirit descending like a dove," evokes Isaiah 63:11—64:1. While the prologue of Mark centers upon Jesus Christ, with John serving as his harbinger, Mark begins his narrative by evoking the language and imagery of the Exodus, especially the New Exodus as envisioned by Isaiah and others. This Exodus includes the blessings of the new covenant and the call to participate through repentance and baptism. This master theme of the prologue continues throughout the Gospel of Mark as one of its principle theological streams, as discussed below.

The Gospel Epic

Mark narrates the story about Jesus, the kingdom of God, and discipleship within a framework his audience knew and understood—the New Exodus. However, he also appears to have in mind the wider context of the Roman world and, from the beginning, interacts with Roman imperial claims to power and sovereignty. Mark and Peter were provincials from Galilee and Judea who knew too well the way the Roman forces had subjugated their people and exercised control over their land through taxation, military presence, and the threat of crucifixion for anyone who directly challenged

---

13. Watts, *Isaiah's New Exodus in Mark*, 73.

that rule. Those who had political, economic, and religious power had aligned themselves with the Roman interests that were played out graphically in the crucifixion of Jesus. Some coinage that passed through Mark and Peter's hands bore the image of Caesar (Mark 12:14–17). These monetary instruments were part of the Roman "newspaper" system, which kept all peoples within the empire apprised of the emperors' ruling power and the majesty of their deeds. Some denarii minted during Augustus's reign bore the image of the emperor with a comet on the reverse or in the field beside his image, a symbol of his father Julius's divinization. Upon his death, Halley's Comet appeared. Reference to the "star" and its relation to Augustus are many. Virgil, for example says that "on his head dawns his father's star" (Aeneid 8.681). A later issue with the image of Nero on the obverse showed the temple of Janus with closed doors on the reverse, indicating that Nero had secured peace throughout the Empire.

Roman history and that of the Jewish people were inextricably bound together despite the varied attempts to liberate the Jews from Roman domination as did the Maccabeans when they revolted and threw off Seleucid rule (Acts 5:36; 21:38). Peter and Mark had also journeyed to the heart of the Roman power, where, as argued above, this letter was composed and first read by the church. On every side they saw the majesty and story of Rome told vividly.[14] No doubt they had passed the Mausoleum of Augustus on the Campus Martius and had seen the bronze inscription of the *Res Gestae Divi Augusti*, which spoke of the great deeds of the divine Augustus. The "Queen of Inscriptions" testified that through politics, benefaction, and military prowess, he had merited the title Augustus.[15] The Ara Pacis Augustae, built to celebrate Augustus's victories in Spain and Gaul upon his *adventus* in 13 BC, was surrounded by images depicting Rome's imperial story and the role that Augustus had played in unfolding history and establishing peace.[16] Unsurprisingly, images of scenes from Virgil's *Aeneid*, a text well-known, were chiseled there, along with those of Homer, which gave Augustan rule its epic tale. Augustus was said to have descended from Aeneas, and on the altar's reliefs both have their heads covered with the toga as officiants in the sacred rites.

Although both the *Res Gestae* and the *Aeneid* were Latin texts, their story was widely known and clearly visible. The imperial story which surrounded Peter and Mark in Rome celebrated the dawn of the golden age that Augustus had inaugurated, but the history continued to speak loudly in the stone reliefs, public texts, common coinage, and political reality. The greatness of the Augustan era was embraced by the then emperor Nero, whose *imitatio Augusti* was well-known as he attempted to

---

14. See, for example, Paul Zanker, *The Power of Images in the Age of Augustus* (Ann Arbor: University of Michigan Press, 1988).

15. Alison E. Cooley, *Res Gestae Divi Augusti: Text, Translation, and Commentary* (Cambridge: Cambridge University Press, 2009).

16. Peter J. Holliday, "Time, History, and Ritual on the Ara Pacis Augustae," *The Art Bulletin* 72 (1990) 542–57; Diane Atnally Conlin, *The Artists of the Ara Pacis: The Process of Hellenization in Roman Relief Sculpture* (Chapel Hill: University of North Carolina Press, 1997).

portray himself as one who followed in the footsteps of Augustus.[17] The period when Peter and Mark were in Rome was draped with high imperial claims that harkened back to the establishment of empire, visible throughout the city center. Mark wrote his gospel in that milieu. Since all theology is contextual, we should not be surprised if his theology interacted with the story in front of his eyes, one which deeply affected the Christians in the imperial city as the coming persecution of Christians in AD 64 was soon to illustrate. Augustus's arrival in Rome was given eternal significance in the Ara Pacis. But now, Christian heralds announce the *euangelion* of Jesus Christ in the imperial city.

The narrative in Mark opens with the declaration, "The beginning of the good news of Jesus Christ, the Son of God" (1:1). At the very end of the Gospel, a Roman centurion recognizes Jesus as he hangs upon the cross and exclaims, "Truly this man was God's Son!" (15:39). These two texts, which identify Jesus as the "Son of God," form an inclusio around the intervening narrative. Mark asserts that Jesus Christ, and not the emperor Augustus, laid true claim to the title *divi filius*. Augustus had been hailed as "Emperor Caesar Augustus son of God" (*Imperator Caesar divi filius Augustus*), "Caesar, son of god, Emperor" (Καίσαρος θεοῦ υἱὸς αὐτοκράτωρ), and "Emperor Caesar, son of God, Zeus the liberator, Augustus" (Καίσαρος αὐτοκράτωρ θεοῦ υἱὸς Ζεὺς ἐλευθέριος Σεβαστός). Tiberius was likewise called "Emperor Tiberius Caesar Augustus, son of god" (Τιβέριος Καῖσαρ Σεβαστὸς θεοῦ υἱὸς αὐτοκράωρ). Even Nero was called "the son of the greatest of the gods" (τὸν υἱὸν τοῦ μεγίστου θεῶν).[18] Virgil's *Aeneid* celebrates Augustus's rule and empire with the words, "Here is Caesar and all the seed of Iulius destined to pass under heaven's spacious sphere. And this in truth is he whom you so often hear promised you, Augustus Caesar, son of a god, who again establish a golden age in Latium amid fields once ruled by Saturn" (6.789–94). Various denarii issued under Augustus identified him as the adopted son of the divinized Julius Caesar and called him DIVI F., that is, *divi filius* or "son of god."

The Gospel of Mark opens with a challenge to that imperial claim and ends with a confession that the crucified Jesus was the Son of God, which came from the mouth of a centurion who represented Rome's imperial power. These proclamations form an inclusio around Mark's narrative, indicating how the gospel writer wanted his readers to bracket the story. Mark was about Jesus Christ and the Kingdom of God, a universal kingdom which stands as a challenge to Rome's empire. To be sure, Mark's development of the theology of Jesus' divine sonship has its roots deep within Hebrew Scriptures, but it also stands as a counterpoint to the well-known public proclamation regarding the emperor. For Mark, Jesus is the Davidic monarch (2 Sam 7:14; Ps 2:7), whose divine sonship trumps that of the emperor (Mark 1:11).

---

17. Edward Champlin, *Nero* (Cambridge, MA: Harvard University Press, 2003), 140.

18. Craig A. Evans, *Mark 8:27–16:20* (Nashville: Thomas Nelson, 2001), lxxxii. *LAE*, 338–78. See below on the title "Son of God."

Moreover, Mark starts his work with the declaration that this is "the beginning of the good news" (εὐαγγελίου), an affirmation which also co-opts imperial language of the period (1:1, 14–15). Josephus said that Vespasian was on his way to Rome, and "quicker than thought, rumor spread the news of the new emperor in the east. Every city kept festival for the good news (εὐαγγέλια) and offered sacrifices on his behalf" (*J.W.* 4.618, 656). Using similar language, the well-known Priene decree extols the emperor, saying, "But the birthday of the god was the beginning of the good news, on his account, for the world" (ἦρξεν δὲ τῶι κόσμωι τῶν δι' αὐτὸν εὐαγγελίων ἡ γενέθλιος ἡμέρα τοῦ θεοῦ).[19] The "good news" was a term often associated with victory in the Greek-speaking world, a note sounded in this decree as well: "Augustus, whom she has filled with *arete* ('virtue') for the benefit of humanity, and has in her beneficence granted us and those who will come after us [a Savior] who has made war to cease and who shall put everything [in peaceful] order."[20] It is unsurprising, therefore, that "good news" was the LXX lexeme of choice to translate the announcement of Yahweh's victory, salvation, and sovereignty (Isa 40:9; 52:7; 60:6; 61:1–3). In the LXX this announcement of God's salvation is not only proclaimed to Zion, Jerusalem, and the cities of Judah (Isa 40:9–10) but also goes out beyond to the nations: "Sing to the Lord; bless his name; tell (εὐαγγελίζεσθε) of his deliverance (σωτήριον) from day to day.... Say among the nations, 'The Lord became king!'" (Ps 95:2, 10, LXX [96:2, 10]). Mark appears to take up the language of Isaiah regarding the proclamation of God's victory and sovereignty and places it as an alternative narrative to the imperial claims that focused upon the emperor. This is "the beginning of the good news of Jesus Christ, the Son of God" (Mark 1:1, 11). Roman readers/hearers would have understood Mark's concept εὐαγγελίον, which brings together the proclamation from Isaiah and Mark's understanding of Jesus as the Son of God, as a counter claim to Rome's absolute sovereignty.

The opening proclamation of Jesus in the prologue of Mark forwards another counterpoint to Roman imperial power. Jesus came to Galilee "proclaiming the good news of God," which Mark summarizes in the words: "The time is fulfilled, and the kingdom of God has come near; repent, and believe in the good news" (1:14–15). The proclamation of the kingdom of God is the realization of Jewish hopes for the advent of the messianic kingdom. What was promised and anticipated is now coming to pass (Dan 2:44; *Ps. Sol.* 17). Jesus' kingship became a central topic in his trial (15:2, 9, 12, 18), and when he was crucified, the inscription that placarded the charge read, "The King of the Jews" (15:26). The title "Christ" was understood as a claim to kingship even by those who mocked him as he hung on the cross (15:32). After his

---

19. Evans, *Mark 8:27–16:20*, lxxxiv. See also Frederick W. Danker, *Benefactor: Epigraphic Study of a Graeco-Roman and New Testament Semantic Field* (St. Louis: Clayton, 1982), 215–22; *LAE*, 366–67; *TDNT*, 2:721–25; John Dickson, "Gospel as News: εὐαγγελ—From Aristophanes to the Apostle Paul," *NTS* 51 (2005) 214–15.

20. Leander E. Keck, "The Introduction to Mark's Gospel," *NTS* 12 (1966) 361; *TDNT*, 2:722; Dickson, "Gospel as News," 213.

crucifixion, the one who came to claim his body—Joseph of Arimathea—is identified for the readers/hearers as one who was "waiting expectantly for the kingdom of God" (15:43). The kingdom and the kingship of Jesus were central confessions that Mark recorded and that hardly went unnoticed or unchallenged by the Roman authorities. Mark develops the theology of the kingdom and Jesus' kingship in conjunction with his message of the cross, a principle instrument in the establishment and maintenance of Roman imperial power.[21] Jesus was crucified by the Romans, yet he rose from the dead. Recognizing the challenge to Roman power in the proclamation of the kingdom of God and the triumph over the cross does not mean that the theology of the kingdom developed in Mark cast Jesus as a political ruler, at least at the present time (cf. Mark 13). Mark understands the proclamation of God's kingdom as an affirmation of his universal dominion and not the first move in establishing a political realm.[22]

On the other hand, to evacuate all the political meaning from the proclamation of the kingdom of God and the claims made about Jesus' kingship decontextualizes Mark from its setting, where the conquest of kingdoms and the maintenance of imperial rule over subjugated states was a principle issue of the day. This was especially true in Palestine, a region where vassal kings rose and fell at the hands of the Romans. Claims to kingship did not go unnoticed, as the failed attempt by Agrippa I to acquire the title "king" for himself illustrates (Josephus, *Ant.* 18:240–44; *J. W.* 2.181–82). Mark tells the story of the true Sovereign and his dominion in dialogue with the imperial movements that vigorously sought to maintain control over all the realms of the circum-Mediterranean. It constitutes a protest against Roman colonial domination while proclaiming the true sovereignty of Jesus and the advent of God's kingdom.[23]

Mark frames his narrative of the gospel of Jesus Christ within the prophetic hope of a New Exodus. As argued above, this theme appears within the opening prologue of the narrative and is developed throughout the Gospel. At the same time, Mark narrates the gospel story of Jesus Christ in dialogue with the story of Rome's imperial power that dominated the political, social, and religious landscape of the era. The claims made about Jesus and his kingdom and the developing story of his authority and advent, including the cross, all rotate around the Roman realities that early Christians faced in the imperial city and throughout the empire. This is a gospel written for those Christians who resided in Rome and were undergoing social ostracism and even

---

21. Martin Hengel, *Crucifixion in the Ancient World and the Folly of the Message of the Cross* (Philadelphia: Fortress, 1977), 46–50.

22. Marcus, *Mark 1–8*, 172; Joel Marcus, "Entering Into the Kingly Power of God," *JBL* 107 (1986) 663–75. Witherington reminds us of the debate that has "raged over the term βασιλεία. Does it refer to a realm or a reign, a state or a divine activity?" (*The Gospel of Mark*, 78). Surprisingly, while this issue has received considerable attention in the commentaries on Mark, most often discussion about the meaning of the claims concerning kingdom and kingship in the Roman environment, where this Gospel was produced, is entirely off the radar.

23. Simon Samuel examines the post-colonial dimensions of Mark's theology (*A Postcolonial Reading of Mark's Story of Jesus* [London: T. & T. Clark, 2007]).

physical suffering due to their allegiance to Christ. It is also a message to the church throughout the empire that confronted realties not unlike those the Christians faced in Rome (1 Pet 5:9). Mark roots his theology deeply within Jewish prophetic hopes and, at the same time, sows it in the soil of the early Christians' social realities. This is a contextualized theology that has a firm grip upon both the testimony handed down by Peter and the challenges these early disciples faced daily. The message is transcendent and yet relevant, historic yet contemporary. Mark is a story about the struggle with a colonial power and the preservation of traditional hopes and outlooks. There is not one single thing going on in Mark but rather a complex and hybrid story that perhaps may be best understood by those who have sought to live out the faith in the face of political hostility or colonial rule. Mark asserts God's sovereignty and offers hope even in the midst of the sufferings that these believers, caught between worlds, endured.

The great story of the Rome *imperium* was embodied in the epic tale of Virgil known as the *Aeneid*. Not a few authors have argued that the Gospel of Mark is a Christian epic that tells a rival tale to that which Virgil developed to exalt the golden age of Augustus. The *Aeneid* tells the story of Aeneas and his journeys to Italy (chapters 1–6) and his battles (chapters 7–12). Virgil modeled his epic on Homer's *Iliad* and *Odyssey*, which deal with war and wandering respectively, and presented a rival Latin narrative to these great Greek tales. In this process of *imitatio*, Virgil draws the line between his story and the opening line of the *Odyssey*, which says, "Tell me, Muse, of the man of many devices, driven far astray after he had sacked the sacred citadel of Troy" (1.1–2). Near the very beginning of the *Aeneid*, we hear the echo: "Tell me, O Muse, the cause: wherein thwarted in will or wherefore angered, did the Queen of heaven drive a man, of goodness so wondrous, to traverse so may perils, to face so many toils?" (1.8–11). Virgil introduces his protagonist Aeneas as the one who comes from Troy to Italy: "Arms and the man I sing, who first from the coasts of Troy, exiled by fate, came to Italy and Lavine shores" (1.1–2). Virgil's story about Aeneas identifies him as a man driven by "Juno's unforgiving wrath," who comes to "build a city"—that is, Rome—"and bring his gods to Latinum." The tale is about beginnings, for from this "came the Latin race, the lords of Alba, and the lofty walls of Rome" (1.4–7). But there is more to the story since this epic from the past is really about empire and the place which Rome occupies over the nations. As Alder remarks, "In the myth of the *Aeneid*, Rome's conquest, unification, and rule of the world is represented in small by Aeneas's conquest, unification, and rule of Italy."[24] The center of the story is really about Augustus and the establishment of Rome's empire. Virgil had incorporated Aeneas, a figure in the *Iliad*, into his story and placed him as the primary protagonist in his epic, a fitting figure who prefigured Augustus.

---

24. Eve Adler, *Vergil's Empire: Political Thought in the Aeneid* (Oxford: Rowman & Littlefield, 2003), 194; Marianne Palmer Bonz, *The Past as Legacy: Luke-Acts and Ancient Epic* (Minneapolis: Augsburg Fortress, 2000), 23.

The picture which graphically portrays Virgil's gospel is the shield of Aeneas. It represents Augustus's triumph and the subjection of all peoples who are led in procession into Rome: "But Caesar, entering the walls of Rome in triple triumph.... The streets were ringing with gladness and games and shouting.... He himself [Caesar Augustus], seated at the snowy threshold of shining Phoebus, reviews the gifts of nations and hangs them on proud portals. The conquered peoples move in long array, as diverse in fashion of dress and arms as in tongues" (8.714–28). Virgil attributes the universal empire and the glory of Rome to Augustus: "And this in truth is he whom you so often hear promised you, Augustus Caesar, son of a god, will again establish a golden age in Latium amid fields once ruled by Saturn; he will advance his empire beyond the Garamants and Indians to a land which lies beyond our stars, beyond the path of year and sun, where sky-bearing Atlas wheels on his shoulders the blazing star-studded sphere" (6.791–97). As the descendent of Aeneas, he is "equated with the destiny of the Roman people, divinely ordained and divinely justified."[25] Anyone who knows the story of Jesus Christ, the Son of God, who proclaims the advent of the kingdom of God, will hear the counterpoint to Virgil's epic story of empire.

Although Virgil wrote his tale in Latin, its contours were hardly obscure or unknown to those whose primary tongue was international Greek. One did not need to understand Latin to know the story of Aeneas.[26] As noted, scenes from Virgil's *Aeneid* were on public display in the Ara Pacis in Rome. And, as Tarrett reminds us, "Verses and characters from his poetry appear in wall-paintings and graffiti, mosaics and sarcophagi, even the occasional spoon, in locations ranging from Sommerset to Harlicarnassus."[27] That Virgil was parodied and even "honored" in graffiti witnesses to his prominent place in the social consciousness.[28] Those who were educated would know both Homer and Virgil, who became "true companions of life in Antiquity."[29] These were the primary canonical texts students would read (Quintilian 1.8.5; 10.1.46–51, 85–86). Cicero considered these two poets to be *sancti* (*Arch.* 18), and sometime later than our period, Augustine told about memorizing Virgil (*Civ.* 1.3).[30] As Bonz notes, it "celebrate[s] Rome's divine election and elevate[s] *Romanitas* (the Roman way) to ascendancy as the universal human ideal for the new millennium

---

25. James E. G. Zetzel, "Rome and Its Traditions," in *The Cambridge Companion to Virgil*, ed. Charles Martindale (Cambridge: Cambridge University Press, 1997), 198.

26. Did Mark know Latin? The Latinisms in the Gospel may indicate that he had some capacity to understand the Roman tongue.

27. R. J. Tarrant, "Aspects of Virgil's Reception in Antiquity," in *The Cambridge Companion to Virgil*, ed. Charles Martindale (Cambridge: Cambridge University Press, 1997), 56–57.

28. Scott McGill, *Virgil Recomposed: The Mythological and Secular Centos in Antiquity*, American Classical Studies 48 (Oxford: Oxford University Press, 2005), 53–70.

29. Karl Olav Sandnes, *The Gospel 'According to Homer and Virgil': Cento and Canon* (Leiden: Brill, 2011), 6.

30. Sandnes, *The Gospel 'According to Homer and Virgil,'* 6–7.

of Roman power."[31] Many authors appropriated and interacted with Virgil,[32] so we should not be surprised if early Christian authors attempted to present their own epic story.

MacDonald has suggested that Mark was modeled on the Greek epics of Homer. In his study, *The Homeric Epics and the Gospel of Mark*, he attempts to lay out the ways that the Gospel imitates the general story and many of its details in the Homeric epics.[33] MacDonald begins with the premise that "prose authors imitated the *Odyssey* more frequently than any other book of the ancient world. It was supplemented, parodied, burlesqued, dramatized, prosified, and transformed to serve an array of un-Homeric values." Such imitations also appear in Jewish writings, such as the Book of Tobit.[34] Although the ancients often engaged in *imitatio*, some wrote rival narratives, practicing *aemulatio*.[35] MacDonald outlines the various points where Mark consciously imitates Homer while, on the other hand, Sandnes argues that Mark and other NT authors had both Homer and Virgil in mind as they composes their Gospels.[36] This field of study, known as Mimesis Criticism, enables us "to see how biblical texts communicated against the background of the foundational stories of the culture."[37] In this intertextual process, one could borrow directly from an extant literary work or combine worthy elements from various literary pieces (*mimesis* and *emulatio*). As Sandnes notes, "Mimesis Criticism argues that emulation in the Gospels (and Acts) aims at interpreting, excelling, transforming, and eventually replacing the model by embedding it into a new context. *Emulatio* then appears as a cultural struggle in which Christian texts become alternatives (*Ersatz*) to the dominant texts of the culture."[38] Comparison between things that differ was a favorite pastime in antiquity, and the penchant for this practice unsurprisingly appears in examples of *emulatio*. So, "the Christianizing of Virgil and Homer implied some kind of 'conquest.'"[39] According to MacDonald, Mark

---

31. Bonz, *The Past as Legacy*, 19.

32. Bonz, *The Past as Legacy*, 61–86.

33. Dennis Ronald MacDonald, *The Homeric Epics and the Gospel of Mark* (New Haven, CT: Yale University Press, 2000). See also Dennis R. MacDonald, *Does the New Testament Imitate Homer? Four Cases from the Acts of the Apostles* (New Haven, CT: Yale University Press, 2003).

34. MacDonald, *The Homeric Epics and the Gospel of Mark*, 5.

35. D. A. Russell, "De Imitatione," in *Creative Imitation and Latin Literature*, ed. David Alexander West and Tony Woodman (Cambridge: Cambridge University Press, 1979), 1–16; David West and Tony Woodman, *Creative Imitation and Latin Literature* (Cambridge: Cambridge University Press, 1986); Conte, *The Rhetoric of Imitation*; Derrenbacker Jr., *Ancient Compositional Practices and the Synoptic Problem*; Baban, *On the Road Encounters in Luke-Acts*.

36. Sandnes, *The Gospel 'According to Homer and Virgil.'* Bonz looks at Luke-Acts in the light of Ancient Epic (*The Past as Legacy*) while MacDonald's later work looks at Acts through the lens of epic (*Does the New Testament Imitate Homer?*).

37. Sandnes, *The Gospel 'According to Homer and Virgil,'* 17.

38. Sandnes, *The Gospel 'According to Homer and Virgil,'* 41.

39. Sandnes, *The Gospel 'According to Homer and Virgil,'* 43–44.

transvalues Homer "by making Jesus more virtuous and powerful than Odysseus and Hector."[40] This is *aemulatio* as its best. Mark presents *the* rival story.

While Mark may indeed echo Homer, he develops his story over against the ideology of the Roman epic, with its laudation of Augustus, and the emphasis on the virtues of the Roman's empire. Jesus is the true protagonist, who overcomes all obstacles and whose labors and power are the foundation of the kingdom of God. Mark's Gospel tells of the divine plan that was prophesied and now fulfilled in Jesus Christ (Mark 1:14–15) as the *Aeneid* tells of Rome's founding as the fulfillment of Jupiter's prophecy (1.254–96). The Romans would become "lords of the world, and the nation of the toga. Thus it is decreed" (1.281–82). There was a coming one prophesied: "From this noble line shall be born the Trojan Caesar, who shall extend his empire to the ocean, his glory to the stars, a Julius, name descended from great Iulus! Him, in days to come, shall you, anxious no more, welcome to heaven, laden with Eastern spoils; he, too, shall be invoked in vows" (1.286–91). Mark's Gospel is about the advent of the kingdom through Jesus Christ and its final consummation, which Jesus predicted (13:3–4). This will come to pass after wars and great distress (13:5–8), but the Son of Man's coming signals the end of these initial labor pains (13:24–27). This is a marker of epic. As Quint notes, "Epic draws an equation between power and narrative: a power able to end the indeterminancy of war and to emerge victorious, showing that the struggle had all along been leading up to its victory and thus imposing upon it a narrative teleology—the teleology that epic identifies with the very idea of narrative."[41] The Son of Man also overthrows the cosmic powers when he comes with his angels in great power and glory: "The sun will be darkened, and the moon will not give its light, and the stars will be falling from the heaven, and the powers in the heavens will be shaken" (13:24–27). Speaking of the cosmic extent of Augustus's rule in the *Aeneid*, Alder says, "The link between earth, ocean, heaven, and the underworld is the stars. In natural terms, the stars are the visible measure of the sea and all lands: they correspond to or mark the places on the earth. In mythical terms, the region of the stars is the region of the gods: to measure one's glory by the stars means to be as glorious as a god. In natural terms, then, Jupiter says that Roman rule will extend to the ends of the inhabited earth; in mythical terms, that it will, like the rule of the gods themselves, extend to all the four quarters of the world: earth, ocean, heaven, underworld."[42] But the Son of Man is over all the powers, even these cosmic ones, as his coming attests. This is an advent which Augustus's could not match, portrayed here in Mark's *aemulatio*.

The basic question in the *Aeneid* is, "Who will rule the nations?" The book's opening marks out this central concern: will it be Carthage or Rome (1.12–22)? Rome is the city Juno "loved above all other lands" and "here was her armor, here her chariot; that he should be the capital of the nations, should the fates perchance allow

---

40. Dennis Ronald MacDonald, *The Homeric Epics and the Gospel of Mark*, 3.
41. David Quint, "Epic and Empire," *Comparative Literature* 41 (1989) 27.
42. Adler, *Vergil's Empire*, 194.

it, was even then the goddess's aim and cherished hope." Alder unpacks this vision of universal rule, saying:

> It is presupposed that some city will be ruler over the nations, though at the outset the reason for this rather surprising presupposition, and the exact sense of 'the nations,' are obscure. As the poem unfolds it becomes clear both why there must be a single ruler over the nations and why it is Rome rather than Carthage that is by rights that ruler; and simultaneously it becomes clear that 'the nations' means *all* the nations—the entire human race and the whole inhabited world. The reason why the rule of one nation over all the others is presupposed lies in the object of government. Human happiness in both its forms, the felicity of the few and the fortunateness of the many, requires peace. But the secure maintenance of peace against the ineradicable incursions of immortal furor or divine anger onto souls and cities can be achieved only as universal peace; and the universal peace can be achieved only through the unification of all the nations under a single regime.[43]

Rome was the place from which rulers would come "to hold the sea and all lands beneath their sway" (1.236–37). Caesar "will extend his empire to the ocean, his glory to the stars" (1.286–87). The universal peace that this reign brings will be the time when "wars shall cease and savage ages soften" and "the gates of war, grim with iron and close-fitting bars, shall be closed" (1.291–94). The question of universal rule was on the table at this time, both for the Romans and the Jews. Would the ruler be Jewish or Roman?[44]

Mark's counterpoint to such claims is that the kingdom of God is the true eternal government (10:17, 30; 13:30–31) that will come when the Son of Man returns to sit on his throne in glory (10:37), a fact not undone by the message of the cross since Christ rose from the dead (16:6). The coming of his kingdom is the fulfillment of ancient prophecy (1:15; 14:49). Conflict will characterize the nations until the final end (13:5–8), when Christ will come to establish his universal rule, which extends from heaven to earth and out to all lands (13:24–27). Chapter 13 challenges Virgil's claim "that glorious Rome extend her empire to earth's ends, her ambitions to the skies, and shall embrace seven hills with a single city's walls" (6.781–83; 8.99–100). Mark's

---

43. Adler, *Vergil's Empire*, 173.

44. Josephus tells the story of a Jew named Jesus, son of Ananias, who cried out for seven years against Jerusalem before its destruction in AD 70. In reflecting on the resistance to Rome and the destruction which finally came, Josephus says, "But what more than all else incited them to the war was an ambiguous oracle, likewise found in their sacred scriptures [which specific text was in mind is not indicated], to the effect that at that time one from their own country would become ruler of the world. This they understood to mean someone of their own race, and many of their wise men went astray in their interpretation of it. The oracle, however, in reality signified the sovereignty of Vespasian, who was proclaimed Emperor on Jewish soil" (*J. W.* 6.312–13). The question of who held ultimate sovereignty was not limited to the time of Rome's conflict with Carthage, or even Macedonia or Egypt for that matter. The large question of universal rule made Rome nervous in the face of any messianic claim which would emerge from one of her provinces.

turn in this *aemulatio* is that the conquest begins in the present time, well before the final consummation, and embraces the cross, which was the token of Rome's imperial control. Although this era is marked by rejection and suffering (13:9–13), the gospel of Christ goes out to all the nations (13:10) as the Jerusalem temple had been established in God's plan as "a house of prayer for all the nations" (11:17; Isa 56:7, the wide embrace of the nations is part of the Isaiah's vision of the New Exodus). In this present age, Christ has begun to take control over the powers of wind and sea (4:37, 39, 41; 6:48, 51), bringing chaos to an end as Virgil had said of Augustus. Zetzel observes, "The victory of Augustus is not merely the achievement of peace, but the achievement of order in the cosmos itself, the restoration of a golden age of harmony on earth and in the universe, the beginning of empire without end."[45]

Mark repeatedly speaks of the kingdom (1:15; 11:10; 13; 14:25; 15:43) and Jesus' role as the King (15:12, 18, 26, 32), who demonstrates his authority in a myriad of ways (1:22, 27; 2:10; 3:15; 6:7; 11:28, 29, 33). The universal message proclaimed is his gospel (1:1, 14, 15; 8:35; 10:29; 13:10; 14:9; 16:15). The announcement of his rule runs "from east to west," according to the shorter ending of Mark, while the longer ending tells of the gospel proclaimed "to the whole creation" (16:15). Although neither ending was a Markan composition, both capture the message of Mark in the context of the epic claims of empire made by Virgil. Indeed, the other Synoptic Gospels—especially Luke—pick up this theme from Mark and develop it more fully.[46] The hero for Mark is not Odysseus or Aeneas but Jesus Christ, the Son of God, who overcomes more than the obstacles of Fate and Necessity; he conquers death itself. He is not limited by the flux of things. He shows true courage and virtue in all his deeds and words.[47]

Both Isaiah's New Exodus and Virgil's Roman epic play a role in framing Mark's Gospel of Jesus Christ, the Son of God. Neither story, however, can contain the message that Mark received from Peter and preserved for the Roman and other churches. The theme of fulfillment dominates here as Jesus' ministry brings to pass all the hopes of the New Exodus and challenges the aspirational claims of empire contained in the *Aeneid*. Yet the story that Mark tells goes beyond either of these to show that the greater Exodus includes the conquest of death and the redemption of humanity (16:6; 10:45). The universal claims of empire are transcended in the Son of Man's absolute sovereignty over all the powers, and his gospel extends to all peoples as the fulfillment of ancient hopes. No force, not even demonic (1:39; 3:11, 22; 5:12–13; 6:13; 16:9, [17]), can stand before him and obstruct him—not even death itself. The way Peter develops his theology within these frameworks will be the concern of the following sections.

---

45. Zetzel, "Rome and Its Traditions," 199.
46. Bonz, *The Past as Legacy*.
47. Cf. Adler, *Vergil's Empire*, 233–51.

The Development of the New Exodus Theology

As noted above, starting with the opening verses, the New Exodus theme is one of Mark's unifying frameworks for his presentation of the gospel of Jesus Christ. The Exodus was the nation of Israel's founding moment, which filled their memory and informed their existence. The hope of a New Exodus became the paradigm for their thinking about God's salvation, especially in the context of being subjugated by the Roman empire. The Second Exodus theme had three fundamental components: "(A) Yahweh's *deliverance* of his exiled people from the power of Babylon and her idols, (B) a *journey* along the 'way' in which Yahweh leads his people from their exile to Jerusalem, and (C) *arrival* in Jerusalem where Yahweh is enthroned in a gloriously restored Zion."[48] But since the glory of this Exodus was not fully achieved, hope remained for a New Exodus as outlined in the final chapters of Isaiah. The deliverance, the journey, and the establishment of the kingdom would become key elements in this new story of redemption. To put this another way, the Exodus of old was the pattern for Israel's future hope. And from Mark's perspective, "the long-awaited coming of Yahweh as King and Warrior had begun, and with it, the inauguration of Israel's eschatological comfort: her deliverance from the hands of the nations, the journey of the exiles to their home, and their eventual arrival at Jerusalem, the place of Yahweh's presence."[49]

The longing for this new deliverance drove an Egyptian Jew out into the wilderness, from where he and 4,000 of his followers turned to face Jerusalem[50] as they attempted to march against it with the hope that its walls would fall as had those of Jericho (Acts 21:38; Josephus *J.W.* 2.261–363; *Ant.* 20.167–72). Luke's account of this event in Acts employs language evocative of the wilderness wanderings and the Exodus (ἐξαγαγὼν εἰς τὴν ἔρημον). Mark's rendition of the New Exodus story does not anticipate the fall of Jerusalem but only refers to the destruction of the temple and the distress in Judea (13:1–2, 14–20; cf. Matt 23:37–39; Luke 13:34–35; 21:20–24).[51] Mark does not understand Jesus' fulfillment of the "King and Warrior" theology in Isaiah as this kind of conquest.[52] His mission is unlike that of the Egyptian Jew in this regard. The New Exodus would be a time when God would gather his people who had been scattered among the nations (Isa 43:1–7; 54:4–8; Tob 13:1–6; 2 Macc 2:16–18), and at

---

48. Watts, *Isaiah's New Exodus in Mark*, 81.

49. Watts, *Isaiah's New Exodus in Mark*, 90.

50. Josephus notes that he had 30,000 followers all told (*J. W.* 2.261) but that 4,000 were slain by Felix (*Ant.* 20.171).

51. The parable of the withered fig tree (11:20–24) is couched amidst Mark's theology of the temple (11:1–13:37) It forms part of Jesus' critique of the temple cultus and also serves as a prediction of its destruction. For a full discussion, see William R. Telford, *The Barren Temple and the Withered Tree: A Redaction-Critical Analysis of the Cursing of the Fig-Tree Pericope in Mark's Gospel and Its Relation to the Cleansing of the Temple Tradition* (Sheffield: JSOT, 1980).

52. So also 1 QS 8:12–16, which shows that the Qumran community understood that they should prepare the way of Yahweh in the desert by the study of the law. See also 1 QS 9:16–21; 10:21.

times this hope includes the gathering of the Gentiles as well (Isa 56:1–5; 66:18–21).[53] Mark anticipates the gathering of God's people in his account of Jesus' eschatological discourse (13:27), and the gospel is on offer to all nations (13:10; 11:17). But the gathering has already begun as his ministry is a point of gathering not only for his apostles (6:30) but the crowds as well (2:2, 13; 4:1; 5:21; 6:34; 7:1; 10:1). Although Israel had already been gathered and returned from exile in Babylon during that second Exodus, "Israel remained in thrall to foreigners," notes Wright. He continues, "Worse, Israel's god had not returned to Zion," and so, "Israel clung to the promises that one day the Shekinah, the glorious presence of her god, would return at last" (Isa 52:8; cf. 1 Kgs 8:10–11).[54] A New Exodus was still coming, during which the hopes of the nation would be truly fulfilled. But the coming cross would also result in a scattering, away from the Shepherd of Israel (14:27).

The entry into Jerusalem and the temple, with its crowd scene and kingly imagery, combines the theology of the Exodus with a counterpoint to Roman imperial claims. Jesus sends his disciples to procure a colt (11:2, 4–7), which he sits upon. His disciples threw their cloaks on the animal as Jesus mounts up (11:7) for the journey from Bethphage and Bethany near the Mount of Olives, down from the edge of the wilderness, and up to Jerusalem and the Temple Mount. Many people spread cloaks on the road along with branches "cut in the fields" (11:8), and those who went ahead and followed behind Jesus shouted the words of Psalm 118:25–26, the closing Psalm of the Egyptian Hallel: "Hosanna! Blessed is the one who comes in the name of the Lord! Blessed is the coming kingdom of our ancestor David!" (11:9–10). Although the "Stone" would be rejected presently by the "builders" (Ps 118:22), Jesus here enters into Jerusalem as royalty, the one who should have been blessed "from the house of the Lord" (Ps 118:26b). This kingly procession echoes the royal scenes of Solomon, who rides King David's mule, and Jehu, hailed as "king" (1 Kgs 1:38–40; 2 Kgs 9:13). The people hail Jesus, the King, as the one who brings salvation: "Hosanna!" ("Save now!" [11:9a, 10b]). In the context of Mark's theology, it becomes much more than a mere "expression of joy and jubilation,"[55] as the repetition of "Hosanna" forms an inclusio around "the one who comes in the name of the Lord!" and "the coming kingdom of our ancestor David!" This royal procession, which leads to Jerusalem and the temple, is about entry and kingship, not mere excitement and diversion. The people elaborate on the cry from Psalm 118:26a by hailing Jesus, saying, "Blessed is the coming kingdom of our ancestor David" (Mark 11:10a). This part of the crowd's exclamation is not a citation of the Psalm nor any other extant text for that matter, although

---

53. Kelly R. Iverson, *Gentiles in the Gospel of Mark: 'Even the Dogs Under the Table East the Children's Crumbs'* (London: T. & T. Clark, 2007), 182–86. Mark's portrayal of the Gentiles "envisions a time beyond the story line, on the other side of the cross, when the ministry initiated by Jesus among Gentiles will be completed by his followers" (*Gentiles in the Gospel of Mark*, 186).

54. N. T. Wright, *The New Testament and the People of God* (Minneapolis: Fortress, 1992), 269.

55. Contra Stein, *Mark*, 505.

Mark includes the ascription as it identifies Jesus once again as the King of the Davidic line (10:47–48) and the one through whom the kingdom now comes. But the King's coming will end not in triumph but tragedy as this King's radiant crown will consist of thorns, which he will wear to the cross (15:16–20). The scene almost looks like the Ides of March, the Day of Parricide, though this story ends with a true resurrection to life and not the comet's sign of Divus Julius's apotheosis (Suetonius, *Jul.* 88; cf. Mark 16:6–7).[56]

With the narration of Jesus' royal entry into Jerusalem, Mark plays a theme familiar to his Roman readers' ears, as he had introduced his opening quotations with imperial language: the *euangelion* of the Son of God. Within this conceptual schema, the coming and entry announced in the quotations from Exodus and Isaiah (1:2–3) and visualized in the royal entry into Jerusalem (11:1–11) evoked well-known images of imperial procession (cf. Josephus, *J. W.* 4.618–21, 656; Diodorus Siculus 37.26.1; Dio Cassius 51.19.2; Suetonius, *Cal.* 4; *Nero* 25).[57] Starting with the first announcement about the coming of the Lord in the way prepared for him, Mark reengineers his readers' cultural understanding of royal procession. Jesus is the King, and his coming is part of the New Exodus. Such processions in the ancient world would frequently end at a temple, and Jesus' coming follows that pattern (Mark 11:11; Josephus, *Ant.* 11.325–45; Suetonius, *Nero* 25).[58] Exodus, procession, and entry open this Gospel and inform his readers' understanding of its central message. The imagery is multiplex, with colors combined from two distinct palletes.

Within the pericopae that precede the procession, Mark calls his readers to see and understand. Blind Bartimaeus, son of Timaeus, saw who Jesus was (10:46–48). The intended response is heard in Bartimaeus's cry, which acknowledges Jesus' royal line: "Jesus, Son of David, have mercy on me!" But it is also illustrated in his healing. The crowds took up Bartimaeus's claim and amplified it with their shouts so that everyone could hear, and Mark later turns to discuss the ascription "Son of David" (12:35–37; see 2 Sam 7:12; Isa 9:6–7; 11:1; Jer 30:9; Ezek 34:23–24; *Ps. Sol.* 17:21; Eighteen Benedictions 14). This does not mean that Mark has created the exalted claim made by the people[59] but rather shows his attention to the word on the street regarding Jesus' identity. But the claim becomes especially significant in his procession—here

---

56. See Larry Kreitzer, "Apotheosis of the Roman Emperor," *BA* 53 (1990) 210–17.

57. Brent Kinman, *Jesus' Entry Into Jerusalem in the Context of Lukan Theology and the Politics of His Day* (Leiden: Brill, 1995), 25–47. Kinman's study demonstrates that Luke does not view Jesus' entry as a military triumph but as an imperial παρουσία. The same may be said of Mark. Kinman, however, misses the intensity of the royal imagery in Mark's account of Jesus' entry (*Jesus' Entry Into Jerusalem*, 98–103).

58. Kinman, *Jesus' Entry Into Jerusalem*, 33–34.

59. Gundry, *Mark*, 631. Kelber surprisingly claims that "the combined features of the Markan text do not effect a royal entrance scenario." However, from start to finish, the kingship of Jesus and his coming kingdom is one of Mark's principle themes and is hardly "un-Markan" (*The Kingdom in Mark*, 93–94).

comes the King to Jerusalem, as the emperor would make his entry into Rome. Those who recognize him as the King accompany him on the way. They are in procession, going ahead and following behind (11:9-10). The royal entry is the gospel in miniature, compressed along the road that descends down the Mount of Olives and ascends to the Zion's temple. Here we read, hear, and see the gospel enacted, and there is nothing secret about it. Those whose eyes are opened see and understand it. This arrival is the culmination of the Exodus journey, but for Mark the pinnacle event is still steps away: the King's cross. The royal one who comes is the one who will die. And those now following in procession will flee.

The "way of the Lord" is one of the dominant themes in the New Exodus as Mark presents it. From the outset, Mark has turned his readers and hearers attention to the "way," which John prepares. As noted above, Mark strategically locates the announcement of the Isaian New Exodus at the head of this book. The opening quotation conflates Exodus 23:20 and Malachi 3:1 (1:2b—"See, I am sending my messenger ahead of you, who will prepare your way") with Isaiah 40:3 (1:3—"The voice of one crying out in the wilderness: 'Prepare the way of the Lord, make his paths straight'"). These quotations, however, stand under Mark's introductory formula, "As it is written in the prophet Isaiah," which indicates that Mark's primary orientation is toward this Isaian New Exodus, whose antitype was the Exodus of Israel out of Egypt. The messenger calls people to prepare "the way" for the coming Lord who will enter into the promised land, but, at the present moment, the setting is out in the wilderness. Mark evokes this Exodus imagery as he begins to tell the "good news of Jesus Christ, the Son of God" (1:1). The other gospels introduce the Isaiah quotations a bit later in their narratives (Matt 3:3; Luke 3:4-6; John 1:23). But their preservation in those works underscores their importance in the gospel Mark received from Peter. He highlights the role John plays as the herald who prepares the way (1:4-8), just as Peter began his proclamation of the gospel in the house of Cornelius by referencing John's ministry (Acts 10:37). There is a common voice here.

Marcus has argued that the "way" is not primarily an ethical concept but rather Yahweh's way or his return to Zion, although it clearly has ethical implications for those that walk after him as he carves out his way.[60] In Mark's high Christology the

---

[60]. "In Isaiah 'the way of the Lord' means Yahweh's *own* way through the wilderness, his victory march, which indeed carries the returning people in its wake and so has implications for human action, but in which his own mighty demonstration of saving power is the center of attention and the source from which all 'ethics' flow. A similar interpretation may be suggested for the Markan use of the phrase" (Marcus, *The Way of the Lord*, 29; see Marcus, *Mark 1-8*, 143, 147). Marcus does not say that there is *no* ethical dimension to "the way of the Lord," only that it is secondary to the Lord's own way. Oddly, Marcus does not include a section in this study on the procession into Jerusalem (11:1-11), a central event in Mark's understanding of the way of the Lord. He does, however, recognize that the emphasis on the "way" in the middle section of the gospel marks his journey up to Jerusalem (8:27; 9:33-34; 10:32, 52). See also Kelber, *The Kingdom in Mark*, 67-85; Willard M. Swartley, "The Structural Function of the Term 'Way' (Hodos) in Mark's Gospel," in *The New Way of Jesus: Essays Presented to Howard Charles*, ed. William Klassen (Newton, KS: Faith & Life, 1980), 73-86; Ernest

one who comes in the way is the Lord Jesus himself (2:28; 11:3; 12:36–37). Watts states that "The 'Way'" is the theme of the second of three major sections in the Gospel (8:22/8:27–10:45/11:1), which comes after Jesus' journey that begins in "Galilee" (1:14/1:16–8:21/8:26) and precedes his journey on the "way" to "Jerusalem" (10:45/11:1–16:8). Half of Mark's references to the "way" appear in the middle section (8:27; 9:33–34; 10:17, 32, 46, 52), with questions about Jesus' identity that arise along the "way" serving as an inclusio around it (8:27–30; 10:46–52).[61] Gundry, on the other hand, views the "way" language in the middle section as merely Mark's mapping: "'The way' is simply the road on which an event takes place as Jesus and others travel between localities, whatever the direction or destination of their travel."[62] Mark's "way" is geographical not theological. Gundry also points out that the "way" is used outside this central section, and, he concludes, "More often than not, we should translate ὁδός with 'road' to avoid unintended theological connotations associated with 'way.'"[63] Watts counters that Mark does indeed develop the theology of the "way" outside this middle section, but the thematic note sounded in 1:2–3 finds its fullest elaboration in the middle section of the Gospel.

Gundry pays insufficient attention to this thematic use of the "way" in the opening of the Gospel (1:2–3), which he ties with the New Exodus. To be sure, Mark talks about the "road" Jesus walks on, going from place to place, but his Gospel is replete with sacred geography, which goes down to the Jordan river, climbs the mountain, traverses wilderness and sea, and goes up to Zion and the temple (10:32–33; cf. "And the Lord whom you seek will suddenly come to his temple"[64] [Mal 3:1b]). The places are, at once, real and symbolic. The way is prepared in the wilderness; the keynote sounded in the prophecy from Isaiah 40:3 in 1:3; and John the harbinger carries out his ministry in the wilderness (1:4) and baptizes in the Jordan River—the same river that Israel crossed when entering the land (1:5; cf. 3:8, 10) and that the magician-cum-prophet Theudas had said he could part to allow people to cross over (Josephus, *Ant.* 20.97–99). The procurator Fadus, understanding the messaging, slew him and his followers. This was not just about a crowd gathering to watch cheap tricks. John baptized Jesus in the Jordan (1:9–10), from where Jesus went to the wilderness to be

---

Best, *Following Jesus: Discipleship in the Gospel of Mark* (Sheffield: Sheffield Academic, 1981), 15–18; Watts, *Isaiah's New Exodus in Mark*, 123–26.

61. The other references to the "way" are: 1:2, 3; 2:23; 4:4, 15; 6:8; 8:3; 11:8; 12:14.

62. Gundry, *Mark*, 442.

63. Gundry, *Mark*, 442.

64. See above on the opening quotations in Mark and the relationship between Mal 3:1 and Exod 23:20. As Watts notes, Malachi has the Exodus in mind as the similarities between these two texts suggests. Unsurprisingly, they were joined together in Jewish tradition. *Exodus Rabbah* 32:9 strings together texts of God's angel or messenger, including Exod 23:20 and Mal 3:1, the latter prefaced by a comment on eschatological deliverance: "In the millennium, likewise, when he [the angel] will reveal himself, salvation will come to Israel, as it says, *Behold, I send My messenger, and he shall clear the way before me* (Mal 3:1)" (H. Freedman and Maurice Simon, eds., *Exodus, Leviticus* [London: Soncino, 1939], 413; see Watts, *Isaiah's New Exodus in Mark*, 71–76).

tested for forty days (1:12–13), evoking the image of Israel's forty years of wilderness wandering (Num 14:33–34; 32:13; Deut 8:2; Acts 7:36; 13:21). The healing of the deaf man who could not speak (7:31–37) echoes Isaiah 35:5–6, an Isaianic prophecy linked to the wilderness (35:1, 6), the way (35:8), and even Lebanon (35:2), where Jesus had just been in the region of Tyre and Sidon (Mark 7:31). And according to Isaiah, all this occurs on the holy way going up to Zion (35:8–10). The miraculous feedings in Mark takes place in deserted places (6:31, 32, 35; 8:4) as it was during the wilderness wanderings (Exod 16; Num 11). Bartimaeus the blind "was sitting by the roadside" (10:46), but when Jesus restored his sight, he "followed him on the way" (10:52). "Following" is the archetypical action of the disciple, as Mark informs his readers in 10:34. Many follow him in the "way" as the journey on the road becomes the living metaphor of discipleship.

Following Jesus in the way means recognizing his kingship as he enters Jerusalem and goes into the temple (11:9–11). The New Exodus geography also goes up to the mountain where Jesus calls his disciples (3:13) and where he retires to pray (6:46). The mountain is where he reveals his glory to Peter, James, and John (9:2–9; cf. Exod 19; 24) and, as Marcus has noted, the "mountain setting and description of transfiguration are reminiscent of contemporary Jewish accounts of Moses' enthronement."[65] There he is revealed again as God's Son (9:7; cf. 1:1; 15:39). He also begins and carries out his ministry by the sea (1:16–20; 2:13–14; 3:7–12; 4:1; cf. Exod 14:2, 9) and crosses the sea on various occasions, showing his power over it (4:35–5:1; 6:45–52; cf. Exod 14; Isa 43:15–19). Jesus' teaching about those who cause others to stumble and mountains being thrown into the sea (9:42; 11:23) echoes the Exodus theme of judgment celebrated in Moses' song (Exod 15:1, 21). The river, the sea, the wilderness, and the "way" are key theological elements in Mark's presentation of the New Exodus. "I am about to do a new thing; now it springs forth, do you not perceive it? I will make a way in the wilderness and rivers in the desert," says Yahweh to Isaiah (43:19). He "makes a way in the sea, a path in the mighty waters" (43:16). Mark sees the fulfillment of the promise in Jesus. The sacred geography in Mark evokes the images of the Exodus and show that this is now the time of God's New Exodus. There is more happening here than orienteering.

Over and again, Mark weaves together the "literal events" with his theology, and if we stop with the events themselves, we miss the rich texture of the gospel's message. For example, the healing of the blind man (8:22–26) occurs just after Jesus teaches the disciples about understanding or seeing (8:14–21). Indeed, Mark brackets the whole section from 8:22 to 11:1 with two healings of the blind (8:22–26; 10:46–52). These miracles stand as summons to believe and see. Jesus' authority over sin is demonstrated by his authority to heal the human body (2:1–12). Mark frames the question of Jesus' authority in the temple (11:27–33) with scenes of his kingly authority in the royal entry (11:1–11), the cursing of the fig tree (11:12–14, 20–21), and his cleansing

---

65. Marcus, *Way of the Lord*, 201.

the temple (11:15-19). The colt he rode from Bethphage and Bethany was not just a means of transport but also a message about his rule and entry into Jerusalem as part of the New Exodus (cf. Zech 9:9).[66] Mark links events and localities with revelations about Jesus' person and mission, a point which Gundry has not adequately appreciated. Indeed, at the heart of the problem is the question of methodology. Traditional exegetical techniques at times begin and end with questions of history, geography, discourse, and lexicography, failing to recognize that while these are indeed important considerations, they are not final considerations. The Gospel of John has taught us that, and the Synoptics do as well. Theology and history walk together on the road, and we may affirm the latter as we engage the former.

THE KINGDOM IS COMING
The Proclamation of the Kingdom

Mark's theology ascribes a central place to the proclamation of the kingship of Jesus and the advent of the kingdom, and in the memory of the early church this was a key theme in Peter's preaching in Rome (Eusebius, *Hist. eccl.* 2.14.6). The prologue in the Gospel of Mark begins with an announcement of the *euangelion* of Jesus Christ, the Son of God, and then immediately moves into an introduction of the New Exodus announced in Isaiah and the prophets (1:1-4). The Lord is coming, prepare his way. The coming Lord is Jesus Christ himself. Mark's Gospel introduces the harbinger, John (1:4-8), who points to the one "more powerful" who "will baptize you with the Holy Spirit." John meets Jesus as he comes to be baptized, and there the divine voice from heaven declares who he is: "You are my Son, the Beloved; with you I am well pleased." After his forty days of temptation in the wilderness (1:12-13), Jesus returns to Galilee announcing the central call of the gospel: "The time is fulfilled, and the kingdom of God has come near; repent, and believe in the good news" (1:14-15). This announcement of the good news, the New Exodus wilderness setting (1:12-13), and the proclamation of Jesus as the Son (1:11) close Mark's prologue with an inclusio that reiterates the themes set forth at the very beginning (1:1-3). The topic of God's royal rule and Christ's kingship have been implicit up to the end of the preface. Now we hear from Jesus' own mouth the announcement of the key theme: "The kingdom of God has come near!" The coming of the Lord in the way means that God's rule is right at hand, the deliverance of the New Exodus has been inaugurated.[67] As Marcus has correctly observed, the "way" is God's "own extension of kingly power." The gospel call is an invitation to human beings "to *enter into*—that is, participate in—this divine

---

66. Mark does not quote Zech 9:9, as do Matt 21:5 and John 12:15. What those Gospels make explicit is implicit in Mark.

67. Watts, *Isaiah's New Exodus in Mark*, 102.

extension of power."⁶⁸ The alignment with God's way is what it means to "repent and believe in the good news" (1:15).

At the opening of Jesus' ministry, Jesus takes the role of the one who preaches the εὐαγγέλιον τοῦ θεοῦ, the gospel of God⁶⁹ (1:14; cf. 1:1 and the comments above). The "good news" is language which Mark's Roman readers would have understood well since it was used of imperial announcements, especially of accession.⁷⁰ But Mark's primary source is Scripture, and here especially Isaiah, whose message he then contextualizes in his Roman milieux. So the announcement has to do with the "good news" of God's advent and rule, as proclaimed in Isaiah 40:9: "Get you up to a high mountain, O Zion, herald of good tidings (εὐαγγελιζόμενος); lift up your voice with strength, O Jerusalem, herald of good tidings (εὐαγγελιζόμενος), lift it up, do not fear; say to the cities of Judah, 'Here is your God!'" Jesus comes as the messenger "who announces (εὐαγγελιζομένου) peace, who brings good news (εὐαγγελιζόμενος), who announces salvation, who says to Zion, 'Your God reigns'" (Isa 52:7). The proclamation is about God's liberation and restoration (Isa 61:1–2), the exercise of his rule, and this through Jesus Christ. Therefore, responding positively to the "good news" becomes the weightiest matter in human existence, and the only way to save one's life (Mark 8:35; 10:29), whatever losses may come in the present time. God's reign proclaimed is universal, not limited to Israel but rather extended out to all the nations of the earth before the final consummation (13:10). This is empire on steroids, an extensive rule that recognizes one divine sovereign over all nations. There is nothing tribal or boundaried here, with the *limes* of the kingdom nowhere to be found (cf. Velleius Paterculus 2.120.2).

The subject of Jesus' proclamation is "the kingdom of God" (ἡ βασιλεία τοῦ θεοῦ; 1:15). "Kingdom" is not a static concept as we may think of a territorial "realm" (as in the Kingdom of Jordan or the United Kingdom), but in the New Testament the conceptual weight is on the powerful rule or dominion of God.⁷¹ The dynamic nature of the concept of ἡ βασιλεία becomes evident through the announcement that it "has come near." God is the true sovereign and his rule is at hand, whatever claims were made during the era to the contrary. Upon the first Exodus, Moses celebrated God's victorious liberation in song, which ended with the proclamation: "The Lord

---

68. Marcus, *The Way of the Lord*, 33.

69. Here the genitive is objective—the announcement is about God and, as the next verse shows, his rule.

70. *SIG³* 458; *NIDNTT*, 2.108; *LAE*, 366; *TDNT*, 2:724–25; Richard A. Horsley, *Paul and Empire: Religion and Power in Roman Imperial Society* (Harrisburg, PA: Trinity, 1997), 140–41, 148–49.

71. We could translate the phrase ἡ βασιλεία τοῦ θεοῦ as "God's rule," with ἡ βασιλεία understood as a verbal noun and the genitive τοῦ θεοῦ as subjective, the agent in the action of ruling. See 1 Sam 12:12; Ps 110:2; Isa 52:7; Marcus, "Entering Into the Kingly Power of God"; R. T. France, *Divine Government: God's Kingship in the Gospel of Mark* (Vancouver: Regent College Publishing, 1990), 12–13; Marcus, *Mark 1–8*, 172; Donahue and Harrington, *The Gospel of Mark*, 71. Perhaps it may be best to abandon the translation "kingdom" in favor of "rule" or "dominion" to keep this concept before contemporary readers.

will reign for ever and ever" (Exod 15:1–18). Edwards reminds us of the link between God's rule and the Exodus: "The reign of God was initially manifested in Israel's history in the exodus from Egypt and the giving of the Torah at Mt. Sinai, but it would be supremely manifested in the advent of the future Messiah, whose reign would usher in the eternal and heavenly reign of God."[72] That time, promised in Isaiah 52:7 ("Your God reigns"), has come.

Jesus declares in Mark 1:15, "The time is fulfilled, and the kingdom of God has come near; repent and believe in the good news." As any student of New Testament lexicography knows, discussions about the exact sense of the verb "come near" (ἤγγικεν, perfect of ἐγγίζω) have been vigorous. As France has noted, the lexical debate goes hand in hand with the interpreter's theological orientation: does this verb mean "has drawn near" or "has arrived," corresponding respectively to a "futurist" or "realized" eschatology?[73] The key to answering the question does not reside simply in the verb tense or the dictionary entry for the word but rather in the development of the kingdom theology in Mark that informs its use. The prophets anticipated a new era when God would exercise his ruling power, and that time has come. Now is the time of fulfillment (1:15a—πεπλήρωται ὁ καιρὸς) since the kingdom is arriving. Mark testifies to this fact through the multiple healings Jesus effects, his power over nature through stilling the storm, his conquest over demonic forces through exorcism, and his parables, which indicate that the rule of God has begun, albeit witnessed in small ways. What starts small in the present, however, will continue to grow to amazing proportions (4:26–32). Now they hail Jesus as the King in the line of David (10:47–48; 11:9–10), yet his rulership exceeds that of David or his progeny (12:35–37). The inner circle of three become eye and ear witnesses of the transfiguration of Jesus and the divine testimony to his Sonship, which bear witness to the present reality of Jesus' kingship (9:2–8).

Even on the cross he is recognized as the Sovereign, the Son of God (15:39), an echo of the divine testimony that Jesus is God's regent (1:11; 9:7). Joseph of Arimathea, an aristocratic member of the ruling council (βουλή), who had been "waiting for the kingdom of God" (15:43), receives the body of the crucified King. In Mark, the cross is not a denial but an affirmation of Jesus' kingship. Joseph did not understand

---

72. Edwards, *The Gospel According to Mark*, 46.

73. France, *Divine Government*, 23–25; and see the discussions over the debate in all the major commentaries on Mark. The classic expression of "realized" eschatology was penned by C. H. Dodd (*The Parables of the Kingdom* [New York: Scribner's Sons, 1961], 28–40). For a summary, see Kebler (*The Kingdom in Mark*, 7–11), who rightly concludes: "As regards 1:14–15, the exclusive reliance upon a single word led to remarkably inconclusive results. When taken by itself, the ēngiken is a subtle and ambiguous phrase, devoid of any self-explanatory power. The verb's intended delivery will have to be inferred from the contextual unit made up by the two verses. Yet, what will emerge as the plausible contextual meaning cannot be fully determined until it is viewed as an organic ingredient in an even larger unit, the entirety of Markan theology–eschatology." Kebler is right that relying exclusively on the linguistic code will often leave us in theological confusion. An approach to interpretation rooted in pragmatics rather than semantics is preferable.

what was going on at the moment, but Mark and his readers do. Even Jesus' rejection is the eschatological fulfillment of ancient prophetic Scripture (14:49). So in taking Jesus' body, Joseph's hope and fulfillment meet. Therefore, now is the time to repent and believe (1:15) and thereby enter the kingdom, receiving it as a child (4:16; 9:43, 45, 47; 10:15). This is something the rich can do only with difficulty due to their loyalties (10:23–27). The astute scribal interpreter receives the commendation from Jesus: "You are not far from the kingdom of God" (12:34). The kingdom of God has indeed come.

Yet for all the kingdom's "presence," the hope remains for the future advent, which is the climax of Jesus' eschatological discourse (13:24–27). Since one does not know when the final hour will come, staying wakefully vigilant and alert is necessary in the conflicted times before the end (13:32–37). The present banquet of the Lord anticipates the final kingdom feast (14:22–25). The transfiguration of Jesus (9:2–8), while powerfully displaying Jesus' present status, anticipates the final revelation when "he comes in the glory of his Father with the holy angels" (8:38–9:1). The eschatology reflected in Mark is both realized and futurist, with a developmental aspect as well as a final crisis. The kingdom has come; the kingdom is growing; the kingdom will come. Long live the King!

Jesus' Authority and the Kingdom

The advent of the kingdom of God becomes evident, in the first instance, through Jesus' authority over demons, disease, and sin. His healings take a prominent and primary place in the Gospel, and his authority over demonic forces receives considerable attention in proportion to the length of Mark's story.[74] Jesus comes "with authority," the kind expected from the King as he silences and casts out demons from the very outset of his ministry in Capernaum (1:21–28). Following on immediately, Mark shows his authority over disease by healing none other than Simon Peter's mother-in-law, who had a fever (1:29–31). All told, Mark includes four exorcisms (1:21–28; 5:1–13; 7:24–30; 9:14–29), eight healing miracles (1:29–31, 40–45; 2:1–12; 3:1–6; 5:25–34; 7:31–37; 8:22–26; 10:46–52), and numerous summaries about his healings and exorcisms (1:34, 39; 3:11–12; 6:53–56; cf. 6:7, 13; 9:38). He overcomes fever, leprosy, paralysis, bodily deformity, deafness and speech impediment, hemorrhaging, and blindness. When he casts out demons, he is able to silence them (1:25, 34; 3:12). In response to these miraculous deeds, the press of the crowds became unimaginable, necessitating some crowd management (2:4, 13; 3:9, 20, 32; 4:1, 36; 5:21, 24, 27, 30, 31; 6:34, 45; etc.). In one healing, the story identifies an unclean spirit as responsible for the human ailment. Jesus' response is to liberate a man's son from the demon, ending his inability to speak and his convulsions (9:14–19). In another healing, Jesus

---

74. "One of the arresting features of Mark's Gospel is the disproportionate distribution of Jesus' miracles" (Watts, *Isaiah's New Exodus in Mark*, 139).

shows his authority to forgive the sins of the one who then was healed of his paralysis (2:1–12). As in some Jewish and Christian texts, transgression may be linked with physical malady (Deut 28:15–24; Ps 107:17–20; Isa 42:16–17; 57:17–18; Jas 5:14–16), the two being linked in the Servant Song (Isa 53:4–6, 12; see 1 Pet 2:24–25). Healing and forgiveness join hands.[75] From the outset of the gospel, Jesus comes as the liberator. Jesus is on the offensive against the powers that bind humanity—disease, demons, and sin.

Throughout the gospel Jesus' power over disease demonstrates his authority, which was anticipated by the announcement that the reign of God had begun through him. The healings are part of Mark's New Exodus theology (Isa 29:18–19; 32:1–4; 35:1–10; 42:6–7, 16–17; 53:4–5; 57:18; cf. 2 Bar. 73:1–3). Restoring sight, as in the healing of Bartimaeus, son of Timaeus, and healing ears and tongue, as in the case of the deaf mute man, were acts of the righteous king who reigns according to Isaiah 32:1–4: "Then the eyes of those who have sight will not be closed, and the ears of those who have hearing will listen . . . and the tongues of stammerers will speak readily and distinctly." The hope bore repetition, so, in a distinct New Exodus passage that highlights God's coming, the wilderness, and salvation, Isaiah prophesies, "Then the eyes of the blind shall be opened, and the ears of the deaf unstopped; then the lame shall leap like a deer, and the tongue of the speechless sing for joy" (Isa 35:1–10). The paralytic let down through the roof was a beneficiary of this New Exodus.[76] Jesus' healings in Mark would also have communicated a powerful message to Mark's Roman audience, which recognized such acts as divinely inspired. The cult of Asclepius, the god of healing, was well-known throughout the Roman Empire. Though the principle sanctuary located in Epidaurus, the Asclepions were scattered from Jerusalem (on the site of the Pool of Bethesda) to Rome.[77] In contrast to Asclepius, Jesus' healings require only a word or a touch and not a night's sleep in the Abaton of the Asclepion nor the intervention of a priest. Not long after the publication of this Gospel, healings were attributed to the Emperor Vespasian as well, including the restoration of sight and healing a man's withered hand (Tacitus, *Hist.* 4.81). These occurred even when he "yet lacked prestige and a certain divinity, so to speak," since he was a new emperor (Suetonius, *Vesp.* 7). Unlike this later story, Jesus' healing is a manifestation of his own power. He is not shrouded with doubts about his ability. Healing and healers were known in the empire. Jesus trumps them all as the healer supreme.[78]

---

75. For additional texts and discussion, see Marcus, *Mark 1–8*, 221. See below for further discussion on sin and redemption in Mark.

76. Watts, *Isaiah's New Exodus in Mark*, 169–77. He says, in summary, "Jesus' healings of the blind, deaf/dumb, and lame (the resuscitation may reflect Isa 65:20) display substantial and unique parallels with those prophesied in the book of Isaiah as being characteristic of the INE."

77. *OCD*, 187–88; *ABD*, 1.475–76; *New Pauly*, 2.c101–5.

78. See below on Mark's Christology. He should not simply be cast as another "divine man," as is sometimes suggested. Mark's understanding of Jesus is oriented along other lines, although he co-opts the place occupied by ancient healers of various kinds. For a discussion of healers and other miracle

The lead miracle in Mark is an exorcism (1:21–28), although the conflict with Satan and the initial conquest of his power begins in the temptation of Jesus (1:12–13). In the opening exorcism we see Jesus clearing out demons. At this critical moment in his ministry and Mark's narrative, the demons raise the central and revealing question, "Have you come to destroy us?"[79] Jesus' dominion means their defeat. The exorcisms in Mark, according to Watts, stand within the conceptual frame of the New Exodus theology as well. In these Jesus comes as the Yahweh-Warrior who triumphs over his enemies.[80] In the New Exodus, Yahweh will be victorious over his people's oppressors so that all will know "that I am the Lord your Saviour, and your Redeemer, the Might One of Jacob" (Isa 49:24–26). Jesus is the one who is stronger than the "strong man," i.e., Satan, and has the ability, as the "stronger one" (Mark 1:7), to bind him up and plunder his house (Mark 3:27, in the context of the controversy of vv. 22–27). Jewish expectation included the concept of a priestly messiah who would receive revelation, spread the knowledge of God, "And Beliar shall be bound by him. And he shall grant to his children the authority to trample on wicked spirits" (*T. Levi* 18:12; cf. *CD* 6:10–11; Beliar is Satan, the leader of demonic forces[81]). Indeed, "The Lord himself will arise upon you" to heal and "liberate every captive of the sons of men from Beliar, and every spirit of error will be trampled down" (*T. Zeb.* 9:8). The one "from the tribe of Judah" will be "the Lord's salvation," and "He will make war against Beliar" (*T. Dan.* 5:10–11; cf. *T. Sim.* 6:6). The anointed one, according to Isaiah, will liberate the oppressed and the captives (Isa 61:1; cf. Luke 4:16–21) who are understood not simply as the politically oppressed but those bound by evil demonic powers. Within this context, the demonic question in the first exorcism pericope snaps into focus: "Have you come to destroy us?" The one recognized as the Holy One of God has come to do just that (Mark 1:24; cf. John 6:69; Acts 3:14; 4:27, 30).[82] Though Satan would tempt him to divert from his mission (1:13; 8:32–33), his coming means Beliar's overthrow. Resistance is futile (1:23–24; 5:7–8; 9:20). "His end has come" (3:26b, ἀλλὰ τέλος ἔχει), as evidenced in Jesus' multiple exorcisms.[83] Mark sets up the contrast between the

---

workers in relation to Mark's testimony about Jesus, and a critique of the view that Mark viewed Jesus as another "divine man," see Barry Blackburn, *Theios Anēr and the Markan Miracle Traditions: A Critique of the Theios Anēr Concept as an Interpretive Background of the Miracle Traditions Used by Mark* (Tübingen Mohr Siebeck, 1991).

79. Marcus, *Mark 1–8*, 190.

80. As Watts notes, "In keeping with the INE motif, Mark presents Jesus' deliverance of those in bondage to the demons as the equivalent of both the Yahweh-Warrior's and the enigmatic 'servant's' deliverance of the Isaian captive. Similarly, Jesus' healing of the blind, deaf/dumb and lame, his forgiveness of sins, and his feeding of the multitudes signals the inauguration of the Isaianic NE" (*Isaiah's New Exodus in Mark*, 137).

81. In *Mart. Ascen. Isa.* 1:8–9, Nero may be identified as Beliar (*ABD* 1.655).

82. The phrase "holy one of God" was not a title but was language "used for people who were in a special close relationship with God (2 Kgs 4:9; Ps 106:16)" (France, *The Gospel of Mark*, 104).

83. France, *The Gospel of Mark*, 172; Gundry, *Mark*, 173; Marcus, *Mark 1–8*, 282. On the Beelzebul controversy (3:22–27), see Joel Marcus, "The Beelzebul Controversy and the Eschatologies of Jesus,"

coming of the kingdom of God (1:14-15) and Jesus' temptation by Satan (1:12-13), who cannot drawn him into his power. Satan's kingdom is unified but it cannot stand against the king and the kingdom of God (3:22-27). The collapse of Satan's kingdom does not come through the internal conflict of a divided kingdom but by external conquest.

Jesus' conquest of demonic powers evoked familiar images among his Roman audience as well, serving to authenticate his authority among them. Exorcism was not limited to Christians but also was practiced among the Jews, who were well-known among the Gentiles for their ability to cast out demons through invocations (see Acts 19:11-17).[84] Solomon, the son of David, was remembered not only as the king but also the magician supreme, whose ability to cast out demons was legendary (*T. Sol.* 1-26)—a fact which hardly escaped Gentile recognition (Josephus, *Ant.* 8.45-49).[85] Exorcism was not limited to the Jews, however (Philostratus, *Vit. Ap.* 4.20; 3:38; Lucian, *Philops.* 16, 34). Jesus' ability exceeds that of the common exorcist because in liberating the demonic oppressed he used no spells, no ring or herbs to draw out demons through the nose. He silences the demons and casts them out with a simple command since they are underneath his authority (Mark 1:27; 9:25). The opening exorcism frames the understanding of the rest as it reveals that there is something unique and transcendent about Jesus: He is the Holy One of God (1:24).

The exorcism given the largest place in Mark's narrative occurs on Gentile soil—the liberation of the demoniac in "the country of the Gerasenes," located in the predominantly Gentile area southeast of the Sea of Galilee.[86] The pericope (5:1-20) includes narrative elements drawn from the first Exodus (Exod 14:1-15:22). The exorcism, as the liberation of Israel from Egypt, includes the crossing of the sea (5:1; Exod 14:22), the overthrow of the binding power (5:3-4; Exod 14:28; 15:4, 6, 13), the exaltation of God (5:7; Exod 15:2), the drowning (5:13; Exod 14:28-30; 15:19), the flight from the scene (5:14; Exod 14:27), fear (5:15, 17; Exod 15:14-15), and the proclamation of the great deed of God (5:19; Exod 14:31; 9:16).[87] The passage may also echo Isaiah 66:1-7, 11 (LXX) with its mention of demons in the idol cult and tomb-dwelling.[88] New Exodus realities echo through the passage. Mark underscores the Gentile setting of this overthrow of demonic power by noting the location of the

---

in *Authenticating the Activities of Jesus*, ed. Bruce Chilton and Craig A. Evans (Leiden: Brill, 1999), 247-77.

84. See the oft-quoted exorcism formula in *LAE*, 255-63.

85. For a good review of the texts, see Dennis C. Duling, "Solomon, Exorcism, and the Son of David," *HTR* 68 (1975) 235-52.

86. On the textual problem regarding the name Γερασηνῶν, and the location of the region, see especially Guelich, *Mark 1-8:26*, 275-77; Gundry, *Mark*, 255-58; Edwards, *The Gospel According to Mark*, 153-54; Bruce M. Metzger, *A Textual Commentary on the Greek New Testament* (Stuttgart: German Bible Society; New York: United Bible Societies, 1994), 84.

87. See the comparative analysis in Marcus, *Mark 1-8*, 348-49.

88. So Gundry, *Mark*, 258-59.

liberation and Jesus' commissioning of the man to go home to his friends and tell. Obedient to Jesus and not now driven by demons, he "began to proclaim in the Decapolis how much Jesus had done for him" (5:20). He became Jesus' first missionary to the Gentiles as was restored to kith and kin. Not only the geography but also the corporate name of the demons cues the readers about the overthrow of Gentile powers: "My name is Legion" (5:9, 15). A Roman military legion, at full complement, was 5,000 soldiers strong, though the number could run as low as 4,200 and upward to 6,000[89] (cf. 5:13, which mentions 2,000 pigs, though we should not calculate one demon per swine!). The "military might" of these demons was manifest in the way the man could not be restrained, breaking all chains that had been used in vain attempts to bind him (5:3-4). Pigs play a prominent role in this scene as domestic animals, creatures who receive the demons exorcised from the man, and animals who rush headlong to their own destruction (5:11-13, 16). The Romans used pigs for sacrifices as well as food (Varro, *Rust.* 2.4.9-12; Isa 65:3-4),[90] so in Mark's symbolic world the passage may speak not only about the liberation from demonic power but also suggest, on a secondary level, the challenge Jesus and the kingdom bring to the pagan cult, which was driven by demonic forces according to Jewish and early Christian theology (LXX Deut 32:17; Isa 65:3-4, 11; 1 Cor 10:20-21).[91] But his primary message is about the liberation offered not only to Jews but Gentiles as well, a point reinforced by the exorcism of the unclean spirit from the little daughter of a woman who was "a Gentile, of Syrophoenician origin" (7:24-30).[92]

The message to the readers was clear: As many and powerful as the satanic forces are that surround the church and assail humanity ("We are many" [Mark 5:9]), Christ has mastery over them. Käsemann's comment on Mark is that Jesus' coming "drives out the powers of evil, and so sets free the things of earth and takes them into the kingdom of God's peace."[93] Mark's gospel of the kingdom and New Exodus includes the overthrow of demonic powers, but in this exorcism in particular there are overtones of Christ's superiority over and challenge to Roman power.[94] Jesus trumps their claim to autonomy and authority (5:7), and Mark lets his readers know that the power that oppressed inflicts wounds on the possessed (5:5). The oppressive power's occupation

---

89. *OCD*, 839. In the narrative, the message communicated is that the man was possessed with an enormous number of demons, evidenced in his self-destructive and anti-social behavior.

90. *New Pauly* 11.243-247.

91. Alternately, the swine may allude to the Roman military power, which in Palestine used the wild boar as its ensign (Marcus, *Mark 1-8*, 351).

92. On the place of daughters in Mark's portrayal of Jesus' ministry, see Iverson, *Gentiles in the Gospel of Mark*.

93. Ernst Käsemann, *Jesus Means Freedom: A Polemical Survey of the New Testament* (London: SCM, 1969), 56.

94. Richard A. Horsley, *Hearing the Whole Story: The Politics of Plot in Mark's Gospel* (Louisville: Westminster John Knox, 2001), 136-48; Myers, *Binding the Strong Man*, 190-94.

is not the final word, however—liberation has come through "Jesus, Son of the Most High God" (5:6).

Mark includes two pericopae that bear witness to Jesus' power over nature as he calms the storm upon the sea (4:35–41; 6:47–52), showing that in the face of his authority even the wind and the sea must obey him (4:41). He is the Master over all powers bent on the destruction of humanity—chaos must yield to him. Significantly, the first of these miracles in Mark occupies a place in the narrative immediately before the exorcism of the demons possessing the man in the country of the Gerasenes. His command to the sea, "Peace! Be still!" (4:39) is, more precisely, a silencing of the sea. Mark uses the same verb here (πεφίμωσο) as in 1:15, where Jesus silenced the demon. There is a complex of "natural" and "supernatural" powers over which Jesus shows his authority. The sea could be deadly, as all knew, and the disciples recognized that even on the Sea of Galilee they were in mortal danger due to the violence of the storm that had come down upon them (οὐ μέλει σοι ὅτι ἀπολλύμεθα; "Don't you care that we are going to die?" [4:38]; cf. the verb in and outside seafaring contexts in LXX Jonah 1:6, 14; 3:9; Mark 3:6; 9:22; 11:18; 12:9; see Acts 27).[95] The overlay of Roman themes is not as evident in this part of the narrative as in the following exorcism. However, in Virgil's Roman epic, the *Aeneid*, the imperial power of Augustus overcomes the hoards and forces of the East, embodied in Cleopatra and Antony, whose chaos was subdued on the sea at the Battle of Actium. Aeneas's shield tells the story (8.675–728). As Augustus engages the sea battle with Antony, "the whole sea foams, torn up by the sweeping oars and triple-pointed breaks" (8.691–92). Antony and the queen from Egypt (never named by Virgil) bring chaos as the battle is not simply between captains but becomes a clash of divine powers: "Monstrous gods of every form and barking Anubis wield weapons against Neptune and Venus and against Minerva" (8.698–700). Wind and waves join the fury (8.710).[96]

It would be a bridge too far to say that Mark's narrative is dependent upon the *Aeneid* at this point. But the sea's chaos had a particular resonance with Roman seafarers and figured metaphorically into the story of empire.[97] The imagery of the Augustan conquest as a calming of the sea appears also in Philo, who says of the emperor that "from the moment that he had charge of the common weal took in hand the troubled and chaotic condition of affairs . . . the whole human raced exhausted by mutual slaughter was on the verge of utter destruction, had it not been for one man and leader Augustus whom men fitly call the averter of evil. This is the Caesar who calmed the torrential storms on every side, who healed the pestilences common to Greeks and

---

95. Casson, *Travel in the Ancient World*, 160–62.

96. See Quint for the comparison of the powers of West and East ("Epic and Empire," 4).

97. Also Plutarch, *Cat. Maj.* 14.4; Peter G. Bolt, *Jesus' Defeat of Death: Persuading Mark's Early Readers* (Cambridge: Cambridge University Press, 2003), 139–43. On seafaring and travel in the ancient world, the excellent tomes by Lionel Casson (*Ships and Seamanship in the Ancient World* [Baltimore: Johns Hopkins University Press, 1995]; *Travel in the Ancient World*) are worth consulting, although his work on seafaring deals mainly with the mechanics of travel.

barbarians, pestilences which descending from the south and the east coursed to the west and north sowing the seeds of calamity over the places and waters which lay between" (*Legat.* 143–45). The question was, "Who calms the sea?" For Mark, it is not Augustus nor his successors, but Jesus Christ. He has dominion over all powers, a sign of the advent of the kingdom of God. The multiple sea crossings in Mark, though only over the lake we know as the Sea of Galilee, likely evoke images of the New Exodus as well, and, indeed, this is likely Mark's primary orientation in such scenes. As Moses and Israel crossed over so, too, Jesus and his disciples—sometimes miraculously, as in this pericope (4:35–41; 6:35–44, 45–52; 8:1–9; 11:12–14, 20–25). The particular focus of the first crossing is the way he calmed the sea, although the drowning of the swine in the following pericope may suggest that even in this preceding miracle the New Exodus imagery is not absent (5:13; Exod 14:28–30; 15:4–5).

Most importantly, Mark presents Jesus as the one who has power over nature, so this event becomes a christological revelation. Jesus, as Yahweh, has power over the sea. The disciples rightly pose the question at the end, "Who then is this, that even the wind and the sea obey him?" (5:41). Who, indeed! Mark expects the reader to ponder the question as well, and he busies himself with providing direct answers as throughout the following narrative. The informed reader or hearer, however, may have recalled Psalm 107:23–32, which proclaims the Lord's power over the treachery of the sea: "He made the storm be still, and the waves of the sea were hushed" (107:29). The triumph of the Lord celebrated in the song of Moses was likewise attributable to his power over the sea (Exod 15:8, 10, 19).

Jesus not only has power over disease, demons, and the tumultuous sea that threatened disaster but also over death itself. Immediately after stilling the sea and exorcising the demons, Jesus raises a young girl of twelve, the daughter of Jairus, who was one of the leaders of a synagogue (5:21–24, 35–43). Sandwiched between Jairus's appeal to Jesus to heal his daughter and the girl's demise and restoration to life, Mark recounts Jesus' healing of an impossible case, the woman who suffered from hemorrhages for twelve years, the lifetime of the young girl who died.[98] This incident includes a less than complementary comment on ancient health care providers: "She

---

98. On intercalation in Mark (3:20–35; 5:21–43; 6:7–32; 11:12–25; 14:1–11; 14:52–72), see James R. Edwards, "Markan Sandwiches: The Significance of Interpolations in Markan Narratives," *NovT* 31 (1989) 193–216; Tom Shepherd, "The Narrative Function of Markan Intercalation," *NTS* 41 (1995) 522–40. Shepherd emphasizes the way intercalations in Mark are "dramatized irony," an analysis that has trouble rising above the level of rhetorical analysis. Edwards, on the other hand, observes the theological thrust of intercalation, with the middle story providing the theological key for the sandwiched incidents. While irony is an element of the stories about Jairus, a known and named synagogue leader who is called to faith, and the nameless woman who had extraordinary faith, the theological weaving is noteworthy, as Edwards observes. Both situations are utterly hopeless, and Jesus overcomes them both. It may be too much to say, however, that the sandwiched-in narrative is the "key" to understanding (Edwards, "Markan Sandwiches," 196), since the inner story in Mark 5:24b–34 only reinforces and does not unlock the hopeless reality of the surrounding story about the girl who was about to die and then died.

had endured much under many physicians, and had spent all that she had; and she was no better, but rather grew worse" (5:26). Her situation was hopeless by reason of time, malpractice, and economic ruin.[99] So, too, the condition of Jairus's daughter. His "little daughter" was "at the point of death," but on the way back to her the dreadful news arrived: "Your daughter is dead" (5:23, 35). Those who brought the news punctuated the announcement with their question devoid of hope, "Why trouble the teacher any further?" Both females had impossible situations, but Jesus reversed their fortunes. The hemorrhaging woman had a death sentence in her body[100] and the girl was "at the point of death," then died. The restoration of the girl's life is particularly important in this study of Peter's theology since, according to Acts 9:36–43, this raising became a model for his own ministry. Tabitha had died. Peter restricted the audience as had Jesus (Peter went in alone in Acts 9:40), and he spoke to the deceased saying, "Tabitha, get up" (Ταβιθά, ἀνάστηθι), words that echoed Jesus' command to Jairus's daughter, "'Talitha cum,' which means, 'Little girl, get up!'" (ταλιθα κουμ ... ἔγειρε; Mark 5:41).[101] But, as will become evident as the narrative of Mark progresses, raising the dead girl becomes a prelude to Mark's central concern—the death and raising of Jesus (Mark 14:28; 16:6). John serves a similar function. As the King's harbinger, he was executed by the ruler, Herod Antipas, as Jesus' death was the act of the Roman prefect, Pilate. Both were innocent, and their executions were a great injustice. Herod Antipas had surmised, twice over in Mark, that Jesus was John raised (6:14, 16). John's life, ministry, and death were paradigmatic, anticipating that of "the one who is more powerful than I." Although Herod surmised that John might have been raised, he was not—but Jesus indeed was. Mark's story is about the defeat of death, anticipated in the girl's restoration to life and even in Herod's words. Both were fulfilled in Jesus and the empty tomb.[102]

Death's pall draped dark and foreboding over ancient life, not hidden behind hospital and nursing-home doors nor dressed well by the undertaker's art. Death was

---

99. The poor suffer the worse in the face of inadequate health care, both in ancient and modern times. Jesus' ministry was a model of accessibility to health care not based on income but need.

100. Bolt, *Jesus' Defeat of Death*, 170–75. In this Jewish setting, the woman did not turn to gods associated with healing women's ailments, such as Isis and Asclepius. There is no suggestion either that she had turned to magicians for a cure.

101. Mark's preservation of the Aramaic command should not be read in the context using foreign words in magic (Marcus, *Mark 1–8*, 363) since the common incantations and practices of ancient magic are strikingly absent in Jesus' exercise of power. The preservation of the Aramaic in this Greek Gospel points rather to the bilingualism of the author and his source and, moreover, to the importance of even linguistic memory in the early church (cf. Mark 14:36; Rom 8:15; Gal 4:6).

102. On the topic of death's defeat in Mark, see Bolt, *Jesus' Defeat of Death*. He concludes that, "in Mark, Jesus deals with death and its many invasions into human life." His study suggests that "this message would have had a high potential impact on early readers, since their world provided ample occasion to feel the distress inflicted by human mortality, since, as depicted by Seneca (4 BC/AD–AD 65): 'Most men ebb and flow in wretchedness between the fear of death and the hardships of life; they are unwilling to live, and yet they do not know how to die' (E4.6)" (*Jesus' Defeat of Death*, 10).

a hopeless state (1 Thess 4:13).[103] The hopelessness generated by death was expressed in the common epitaph found frequently in both Greek and Latin: "I was not, I was, I am not, I care not."[104] Life expectancy, though notoriously difficult to estimate, was likely under 30 years, although some attained *gravitas* (50–70 years of age) and even *senectus* (over 70). Infant mortality was high, with a 30 to 40 percent death rate in the first year. Only 50 percent of the population survived until their early twenties.[105] Infectious diseases were common and their fever was, as Bolt says, "a force for death which could be wielded by the forces of the dead" (Mark 1:29–31).[106] Illness was unchecked and could even become worse in the hands of medical practitioners (Mark 5:26; Tob 2:10; *m. Qidd.* 4.14), although some received high praise (Sir 38:1–15).[107] Magic stood alongside physicians as a means to cheat death. Iphis's lament for his children in Euripides (*Suppl.* 1080–1113) speaks of those "which seek to lengthen out life's span by meats and drinks and magic philtre-spells to turn life's channel, that they may not die." The dance between death and the demonic fixed Mark's readers'/hearers' attention as they heard of the multi-demon possessed man who "lived among the tombs," which were hewn openings in the rock the size of caves (Mark 5:2–3). So, also, a man's son was afflicted with a spirit that had tried to destroy him by throwing him into fire or water (9:14–29). In the provincial home of Mark and Peter, the Romans did not come with any promise of life but dealt death to thousands, as Josephus describes in *Jewish Wars*. Crucifixion was the central instrument of death and subjugation to imperial control as prisoners were hung along the roadways on public display.[108]

Jesus, on the other hand, defeats death and brings life, as seen through the many healings that rescued people from their deadly conditions, through the raising of a dead youth, and, most importantly, through his own resurrection (16:6). Jesus' raising the young suggests that Peter understood him to be the one who will raise the dead in the last day, just as he healed disease, liberated people from demonic power, and calmed the sea. When challenged by the Sadducees about the resurrection of the dead, a doctrine which they denied, he affirmed the general resurrection (12:18–27; cf. Acts 23:7–8). In Peter's narrative, which Mark recounts, no explicit connection between Jesus' resurrection appears as found later in Paul (1 Thess 4:13–18; 1 Cor 15).

103. Gene L. Green, *The Letters to the Thessalonians* (Grand Rapids: Eerdmans, 2002), 213–29.

104. *MM*, 382; Everett Ferguson, *Backgrounds of Early Christianity* (Grand Rapids: Eerdmans, 2003), 248. See also *LAE*, 187; Richmond Lattimore, *Themes in Greek and Latin Epitaphs* (Urbana: University of Illinois Press, 1942), 218.

105. Bolt, *Jesus' Defeat of Death*, 27–29.

106. Bolt, *Jesus' Defeat of Death*, 76–88.

107. Marcus, *Mark 1–8*, 358. Later than Mark, Soranus of Ephesus and Galen of Pergamon contributed greatly to ancient medical art, following in the footsteps of Hippocrates (460–370 BC).

108. For the details on Roman crucifixion, see Hengel, *Crucifixion in the Ancient World and the Folly of the Message of the Cross*; Gunnar Samuelsson, *Crucifixion in Antiquity: An Inquiry into the Background of the New Testament Terminology of Crucifixion* (Gothenburg: University of Gothenburg, 2010). Samuelsson argues from Greek and Latin literature that the form of execution varied and should be simply labeled a "suspension."

However, his Gospel weaves together Herod's question concerning the possibility of John, the harbinger, being raised, the raising of a young girl, and Jesus' own death and resurrection. The coming kingdom means the defeat of death. The latter part of the narrative reinforces the connection. The conflict with the Sadducees over the resurrection, framed ostensively within a question about Levirate marriage (Deut 25:5-10), appears in the narrative after the Son of David arrives as royalty in Jerusalem and goes up to the temple (10:46—11:19). The narrative highlights Jesus' authority (11:27-33), which is set over against the usurpation of authority highlighted in the parable of the vineyard (12:1-12). Herein Jesus presents the epic quotation from Ps 118:22-23: "The stone that the builders rejected has become the cornerstone." The authority in question here is Jewish (12:12), but the question of Roman imperial authority follows hard on the heels (12:13-17).

After the Sadducees' question of the resurrection, the subject of the kingdom appears again ("You are not far from the kingdom of God" [12:28–34]) and the true character of the Messiah, the Son of David, who is called "Lord" (12:35–37; see below). In short, the question of the resurrection posed by the Sadducees is couched in a section of the Gospel where the issues of the kingdom of God and the kingship of Jesus take central place. The resurrection of the dead is woven through the fabric of that royal message and promise. For Jesus' part, although "he poured out his life unto death," there was hope: "He will see the light of life and be satisfied" (Isa 53:11–12, NIV). The anticipation of the reversal of death's fortune appears in the penultimate chapter of Isaiah as God's New Exodus spells the defeat of the most powerful human enemy (66:20). God breaks the human cycle of death and despair by defeating death and bringing life. The young girl's restoration to life anticipates the central theme of Jesus' story and the theology developed in the church. The defeat of death is one of Mark's central concerns, as evidenced not only in the clear case of restoration of life but also in the multiple healings from conditions that would commonly end life and in the rescues from mortal danger.[109] The kingdom of God has drawn near. This is the message Mark received from Peter.

CHRISTOLOGY IN MARK

That Jesus is the center of Mark's theology is beyond dispute. The opening of his story puts Jesus in tack-sharp focus: "The beginning of the good news of Jesus Christ, the Son of God" (1:1). He remains in focus and at the center of the frame from start to

---

109. Somewhat surprisingly, theologies of Mark often do not take up the defeat of death as a central concern in this Gospel. Indeed, this is the focal issue in Christian theology of salvation. Before he died in April of 2010, Rev. Mark Ashton, the vicar of St. Andrew the Great in Cambridge, England, wrote, "It is my relationship with him [Christ] that can take me through death and which is the only hope we have of eternal life. He alone is the destroyer of death" (*On My Way to Heaven: Facing Death with Christ* [Chorley, UK: 10Publishing, 2011], 17–18. Jesus anticipated the general resurrection of the dead (Mark 12:24–27), knowing that God is the God "of the living." Mark Ashton lives, and will live.

finish. Any exposition of Mark, whether printed or oral, academic or popular, that does not locate Jesus at the center is not faithful to the message Peter preached and Mark penned.

"Your God Reigns!" Jesus the King

The opening declaration of the book (Ἀρχὴ τοῦ εὐαγγελίου Ἰησοῦ Χριστοῦ υἱοῦ θεοῦ) appears to be a temporal reference. This is where the story of Jesus Christ begins (ἀρχὴ; 10:6; 13:8, 19) as Mark reels through the Isaianic prophecies, the ministry of John the Baptist, Jesus' baptism and temptation, and then his proclamation after John's arrest (1:2–14). Mark starts his story neither from before creation (John 1:1) nor with an infancy and childhood narrative about Jesus (Matt 1–2; Luke 1–2) but rather with the prophecies fulfilled in John and Jesus, John's prophecy about Jesus, and the preparatory events leading up to Jesus' public ministry. But the meaning of ἀρχὴ in 1:1 may be more than an announcement about the opening matter as it draws upon the wider literary context. To be sure, we have various examples of its use to mark "the beginning, i.e., initial account, in a book."[110] But the closest parallel in Scripture is Hosea 1:2 (LXX): "The beginning of the word of the Lord to Hosea." Read within this frame, the opening in Mark prepares the informed reader to hear the book as a revelatory and transcendent text, although it is unlikely to evoke Genesis 1:1, as does John 1:1, which speaks about the beginning of God's creative acts. But ἀρχὴ may suggest something more in tagging Mark as an original or first account (Diod. S. 17.1.1; Diog. L. 3.37; Ael. Arist. 23.2K=42 p. 768D) of the "gospel of Jesus Christ," in which case Mark could be aware that this is a first or principle telling of the Jesus story. This is, as argued previously, Peter's account, which, under a Markan priority solution to the Synoptic problem, was the one from which Matthew and Luke drew.[111] Wikgren's article on the opening words of Mark approvingly explores suggestions such as "summary" in the sense of elemental instruction, a first catechism, or a gospel "designed from the first or beginning step of the 'heilsgeschichtlichen' instruction about Jesus"[112] (cf. Heb 5:12). We are likely not far off center if we understand Mark's heading to indicate that this is a (the?) foundational telling of the gospel. There is more going on here than the simple disclosure, "This is how the story begins."

Under a literary reading of the opening, we should understand "the gospel of Jesus Christ" as that announcement which has him as its object rather than reading the genitive "of Jesus Christ" as subjective ("Jesus Christ is the one who proclaims the good news").[113] Jesus is the topic and concern of the good news, although he is a

---

110. BDAG, 137.

111. On the Synoptic problem and *imitatio* in literary borrowing, see Derrenbacker Jr., *Ancient Compositional Practices and the Synoptic Problem*.

112. Allen Wikgren, "ΑΡΧΗ ΤΟΥ ΕΥΑΓΓΕΛΙΟΥ," *JBL* 61 (1942) 19. See also *MM*, 81; *LSJ*, 252.

113. Guelich, *Mark 1–8:26*, 9; France, *The Gospel of Mark*, 53. The "good news" is something proclaimed (13:10; 14:9) and the content of that proclamation is placed in the genitive (1:14; and so 1:1).

herald as well (1:14). In the first instance, we hear the name "Jesus," which, unlike in Matthew 1:21, is given no discernible theological significance here or elsewhere in the Gospel. Many parents in Palestine and the Jewish diaspora called their son "Jesus" since it was the name of the great Jewish leader, Joshua (יְהוֹשֻׁעַ often translated Ἰησοῦς as in LXX Exod 17:9–10 and elsewhere).[114] Since so many went by that name, Jesus is often differentiated from the others by identifying his home town.[115] He is "Jesus of Nazareth" (1:46), the one who hailed "from Nazareth" (1:9). So strong was the connection between Jesus and his home in Galilee (1:24; 10:47) that he becomes known as "the Nazarene, Jesus" (14:67; 16:6). Various titles also adhere to his name that serve to widen the reader's understanding of who he is and differentiate him from others known by the name "Jesus." He is "Jesus, Son of the Most High God" (5:7) and "Jesus, Son of David" (10:47). The longer ending of Mark, not an original part of the Gospel, identifies him by a title well-known later in the church, "the Lord Jesus" (16:19). The name "Jesus," unqualified, simply marks him as a common Jew, one among many. The name was not used among the Greeks.

"You Are the Christ"

As Mark opens, Jesus is called "Christ," which is clearly a title throughout this Gospel (8:29; 9:41; 14:61; 15:32, are ascribed directly to Jesus; 12:35; 13:21, are the title in general).[116] In the first verse, Mark's Roman audience could have heard "Christ" as part of a proper name, "Jesus Christ," although any notion that it was simply that would soon be dispelled as the story unfolded. Indeed, titles were sometimes attached directly to names as is the case here.[117] Latins did not always grasp the titular significance of the Greek title "Christ," however, as evidenced in their misconstrual of it as "Chrestus," a common Latin name (Suetonius, *Claud.* 25:4; Lactantius, *Inst.* 4.7.5;

---

114. Tal Ilan, *Lexicon of Jewish Names in Late Antiquity, Part I: Palestine 330 BCE–200CE*, TSAJ 91 (Tübingen: Mohr Siebeck, 2002), 126–33, 449; Tal Ilan, *Lexicon of Jewish Names in Late Antiquity, Part III: The Western Diaspora 330 BCE–650CE* (Tübingen: Mohr Siebeck, 2008), 103–5.

115. A common enough practice (Ilan, *Lexicon of Jewish Names in Late Antiquity, Part I*, 34).

116. The discussions are multiple. See for example Jack Dean Kingsbury, *The Christology of Mark's Gospel* (Philadelphia: Fortress, 1983), 42–155; Telford, *Theology of the Gospel of Mark*, 35–38; Frank J. Matera, *New Testament Christology* (Louisville: Westminster John Knox, 1999), 5–26; Morna D. Hooker, "'Who Can This Be?' The Christology of Mark's Gospel," in *Contours of Christology in the New Testament*, ed. Richard N. Longenecker (Grand Rapids: Eerdmans, 2005), 79–94; Robert D. Rowe, *God's Kingdom and God's Son: The Background to Mark's Christology from Concepts of Kingship in the Psalms* (Leiden: Brill, 2002); Hengel, *Studies in Early Christology*, 1–72; George F. Moore, *Judaism in the First Centuries of the Christian Era* (New York: Schocken, 1971), 2.276–323; Oscar Cullmann, *The Christology of the New Testament* (Philadelphia: Westminster, 1963), 111–36; J. D. G. Dunn, *Christology in the Making: An Inquiry Into the Origins of the Doctrine of the Incarnation* (Grand Rapids: Eerdmans, 1996); Edwards, *The Gospel According to Mark*, 249–52; Joel Marcus, *Mark 8–16: A New Translation with Introduction and Commentary* (New Haven, CT: Yale University Press, 2009), 1104–7.

117. Ilan, *Lexicon of Jewish Names in Late Antiquity, Part I*, 33–34, a point Matera misses when he comments on 1:1 that Christ "functions as part of Jesus' name" (*New Testament Theology: Exploring Diversity and Unity* [Louisville: Westminster John Knox, 2007], 16).

Tertullian, *Apol.* 3.5).[118] But calling Jesus "Christ" was anything but common since the title marked him as royalty, the king of Israel descended from David (12:35; 15:32). Though "Christ" translates the Hebrew מָשִׁיחַ, which means "anointed," and could refer to one who was ritually anointed as a priest (Lev 4:5, 16: 6:5), Mark's understanding is clearly royal since he regards Jesus as the anointed ruler of King David's line (see 2 Sam 7:12-17; 22:51; Ps 2:2; 18:50; Mark 12:35; 15:32; *Ps. Sol.* 17:32). In Jewish literature, the title on its own suggested royal rule and not priestly ministry.[119]

The opening verse of Mark, therefore, is the starting point for the theology of the kingdom or reign of God in Mark. Jesus is the one anointed as its ruler.[120] At the end of Mark's prologue (1:15), Jesus proclaims, "The time is fulfilled, and the kingdom of God has come near; repent, and believe in the good news." The reason for this proclamation of the good news of the kingdom is that the Christ has appeared (1:1). Mark uses "Christ" strategically at the very beginning of the narrative (1:1), in the central confession by Peter (8:29), and at the very end in Jesus' trial (14:61) and crucifixion (15:32). Although the title "Christ" does not appear with great frequency in Mark, the concept of Jesus' kingship is certainly given prominence.

The Jewish expectations that circulated regarding the coming Davidic king were varied. Although multiplex, "two prominent strands of the Messianic hope do stand out. In the first place," notes Telford, "the term 'Messiah' was used of an earthly, political figure, a warrior-king who by his military exploits and passion for justice would lead his people into victory over their Gentile overlords, establish God's Kingdom, and restore the land of Israel to his chosen people, the Jews" (cf. *Ps. Sol.* 17-18). Another strand of Messianic hope "was the belief entertained in apocalyptic Judaism in an exalted, transcendent, heavenly figure . . . who would appear at the end-time to judge the world, punish the wicked, and vindicate the righteous" (as Daniel; 1 Enoch; 4 Ezra).[121] The title "Christ" comes from the first framework.[122] As Watts has shown, Mark portrays Jesus as Yahweh's Warrior-King whose coming marks the New Exodus anticipated in Isaiah. The coming kingdom draws near in him (1:15; cf. Isa 46:13), as is seen not only in the title Jesus bears and the content of his preaching but also in his kingly power over disease, demons, disaster, and even death itself (see above).[123] He is the king who enters Jerusalem in royal procession (11:1-10) and whose inquisition

---

118. Levinskaya, *The Book of Acts in Its Diaspora Setting*, 177-81. The mistake even occurs thrice in codex Sinaiticus (א) where "Christian" appears as Χρηστιανός (Acts 11:26; 26:28; 1 Pet 4:16).

119. Marcus, *Mark 8-16*, 1104-5. See also 1 Sam 2:10; *Ps. Sol.* 17:32; 18:5; 2 Bar. 39.7; 40:1; 72:2.

120. Cf. the interplay between God's reign and his appointed king in Ps Sol 17:1a ("Lord, you are our king forevermore"), 17:3b ("And the kingdom of our God is forever over the nations in judgment"), and 17:4a ("Lord, you chose David to be king over Israel"), and so throughout the chapter (which ends in 17:46, saying, "The Lord Himself is our king forevermore").

121. Telford, *Theology of the Gospel of Mark*, 35-36.

122. Although the Qumran sectarians also expected a ruler of Aaronic or priestly lineage (1 QS 9:11). See also *T. Levi* 18:1-14; *T. Judah* 21:1-5.

123. Watts, *Isaiah's New Exodus in Mark*, 137-82.

before the Sanhedrin and trial before Pilate pivoted around the claims made to kingship (14:53–65; 15:1–10).

While Jesus fulfills the expectations about the coming Anointed One, the concept of kingship undergoes an *ad hoc* reformulation as Mark modifies his readers' understanding of kingship by showing Jesus hanging upon the cross, the instrument of imperial power, which was the very antithesis of the claim that Jesus was the Ruler (15:26, 32). The irony of the claim to kingship and the casualty of the cross is wrenching and requires the reader to reconsider the very nature of kingship.[124] How can the King hang there, of all places? And how can Mark affirm so vigorously that the reign of God has begun (cf. Isa 43:15; 44:6; 52:7)? The Anointed One was to come with great hope for liberation and the promise of joy (Isa 61:1–7). Mark is able to present Jesus as the crucified Christ through the irony of the event. What is going on here? What is he thinking? The collision of concepts shows that Mark sees no incompatibility between understanding that Jesus is the Christ and the theology of the cross.

Significantly, the first full discussion about Jesus being the Christ does not appear until 8:27–30, when we hear this central confession from the mouth of Peter. This pericope stands at the beginning of the second major section of the Gospel (which may begin in either 8:22 or 8:27—see above), immediately after the healing of the blind man in Bethsaida (8:22–26). Following the question to the blind man, "Can you see anything?" (8:23), comes the query about popular opinion and the disciples' understanding about Jesus' person ("Who do people say that I am? . . . But who do you say that I am?" [8:27, 29]). Popular opinion is not clear ("John the Baptist; and others, Elijah; and still others, one of the prophets" [8:28]), just as the blind man's perceptions are not clear at first but then improve after a second intervention by Jesus ("I can see people, but they look like trees, walking", "And he saw everything clearly," [8:24–25]). Immediately preceding the healing, Jesus repeatedly poses questions about seeing and understanding (8:17–18, 21), indicating once again that the miracle of sight is not only about physical healing. The healing of the blind occurs one other place in Mark: before the royal entry into Jerusalem, which is another moment of revelation where Jesus is hailed as the Son of David, both by Bartimaeus son of Timaeus and the crowd (10:42–43; 11:9–10). These two events stand at the head of the third major section of the Gospel (see above). The restoration of sight is both a healing miracle and a prelude to revelation about Jesus. And both revelations point to Jesus' royalty and occur along the "way," that is, the road which becomes the metaphor for God's way (8:27; 10:46, 52; 11:8; cf. 1:1–3).

The confession in 8:29, in response to Jesus' question to his disciples about their understanding of who he was, came from Peter: "You are the Christ" (ἀποκριθεὶς

---

124. On the irony in Mark, see Glyndle M. Feagin Jr., *Irony and the Kingdom in Mark: A Literary-Critical Study* (Lewiston, NY: Mellen Biblical, 1997). For a more contemporary approach to irony within the domain of pragmatics, see Deirdre Wilson, "Irony and Metarepresentation," *UCL Working Papers in Linguistics* 21 (2009) 183–226.

Πέτρος λέγει αὐτῷ· σὺ εἶ ὁ χριστός). Previously in the narrative similar questions had been voiced by others (1:27; 2:7; 4:41; 6:2; 11:28), and now, as Jesus turns to the disciples, he asks the question repeatedly as they walk in the way (8:27, 29; the imperfect ἐπηρώτα suggests an iterative action). The questioning suggests that the answers are not ready on their tongues. The pericope narrows dramatically as the first question is about popular opinion ("Who do people say that I am?") and the second is about the twelve's opinion ("But who do you [plural ὑμεῖς] say that I am?"). The proper response, we discover, comes neither from the confused populace nor the silent twelve but rather from the one, Peter himself.[125] He takes the theological lead and confesses that Jesus is indeed the Christ, as Mark had announced in the opening of this Gospel (1:1) and has shown through Jesus' deeds and words throughout the first section of the Gospel (1:16—8:21; 8:26; see the discussion above on the rule of God in Mark). The confession from Peter should not be read within the framework of our knowledge about Peter's impetuosity but rather as an indicator of Peter's theological insight and the divine revelation received. This latter point becomes explicit in Matthew's Gospel ("For flesh and blood has not revealed this to you, but my Father in heaven" [Matt 16:17b]) but is implicit here as Peter's confession stands immediately after the miracle of restored sight (8:22–26). Peter does not always get it right, but he stands ahead of the rest and even becomes their principle spokesman (8:32–33; 9:5–7). Jesus repeatedly draws him in close as a disciple who would receive special insight and revelation into God's purposes (9:2; 13:3; 14:33–34; 16:7). Although his failure can be stunning (14:66–72), he returns and maintains the lead in understanding just who Jesus is and what he is about. Peter's is the central confession of the book, though it does not stand alone in revealing who Jesus is. Indeed, it requires some modification.

The opinions of the people which the disciples register (8:28) are more out of focus than just flat wrong. As Marcus notes, "But while the opinions reported by the disciples contain some elements of truth, they are not, from Mark's point of view, the whole truth."[126] These same popular opinions about Jesus had been voiced earlier in the scene about Herod Agrippa and John the Baptist (6:14–16). All three possible identities named in the Herod pericope and by the populace had prophetic ministries, as did Jesus (6:4; 14:65), and each had suffered persecution, as would Jesus (6:4, 17–29; 9:13; 1 Kgs 19:1–18; Matt 23:29–36; 1 Thess 2:15). As an eschatological figure, John is the fulfillment of the hope that Elijah would come before the end (Mal 4:5–6; Matt 3:7–10; Luke 3:7–9; Mark 1:2–8).[127] And as the harbinger of Jesus, it should not go unnoticed that John had been beheaded. The opinion that Jesus might be John the Baptist redivivus underscores the general belief in the resurrection and, more specifically, points to Jesus' resurrection as made clear by Herod Agrippa's twice repeated

---

125. The "answering . . . says" formula (ἀποκριθεὶς Πέτρος λέγει αὐτῷ) implies that Peter got it right (Marcus, *Mark 8–16*, 612).

126. Marcus, *Mark 8–16*, 611.

127. See the discussion in Marcus, *Mark 8–16*, 611.

opinion (Mark 6:14, 16; 8:28). John, Elijah, and the prophets prefigured Jesus and embodied the realities of his life, death, and even resurrection. But Jesus transcended them all—only he is the Christ (cf. John 1:19-28). The contrast between the popular opinion and Peter's revelation should not obscure the fact that the word on the byways about Jesus was leaning in the right direction by regarding him as a transcendent figure. Speculation arose, but reality exceeded it. The curious feature, however, is the prohibition Jesus imposes upon the disciples against circulating the confession publicly (8:30; see below on "The Messianic Secret"). There is no denial of the confession, only restraint regarding its wide dissemination.

Between Peter's confession and the trial and crucifixion of Jesus, where he is again identified as "Christ" (14:61; 15:32), Mark recounts the question Jesus asked about scribal theology, which said that the "Christ" would be "the Son of David" (12:35-37).[128] He queries, "How can the scribes say that the Messiah is the son of David?" The question comes after two pericopae (discussed above) in which Jesus is identified as David's descendant: the healing of Bartimaeus son of Timaeus (10:46-52) and Jesus' royal entry in to Jerusalem (11:1-10). Bartimaeus recognized him as "Jesus, Son of David," and the bystanders hailed him, saying, "Blessed is the coming kingdom of our ancestor David!" (the cry is conflated with Ps 118:25-26), implying Jesus is the Son of David, whose coming signals the advent of his rule. Both Bartimaeus and those entering with Jesus raise the volume as they "shout" and "were shouting" (10:47; 11:9)—there is something here that must be heard. Jesus is the King of the royal line of David, as the title Christ implies (see above). But the Anointed One is more than the Son of David, as Jesus shows in 12:35-37. The extant concept of Davidic kingship was inadequate to describe Jesus fully, just as Peter's confession that Jesus is the Christ needed modification in light of the cross (8:31-33). In this pericope, Mark reveals the common scribal knowledge that the Messiah was of Davidic descent, but Jesus steps further by citing the Davidic Psalm 110:1, in which David himself calls the Messiah "Lord." Jesus prefaces the quotation by ascribing divine inspiration to David ("David himself, by the Holy Spirit, declared"). What then follows is more than Jesus' claim, or even that of Peter or Mark. Its warrant is divine, as the voice from heaven at the baptism and transfiguration where God called him "Son" (1:11; 9:7). Mark's point is that Jesus is indeed the Messiah, but the current messianic categories do not reveal fully who he is.

The final places where the title Christ is ascribed to Jesus occur at his trial and crucifixion, as noted above.[129] These, as the confession of Peter, which was followed by the announcement of his death and resurrection, broaden the concept of messiahship to include suffering and death. This is the truly unique contribution of Christian theology since none of the Jewish authors who read Scripture realized that the Messiah would suffer and die. This messianic understanding originated with Jesus himself and

---

128. On the "Son of David," see Marcus, *Mark 8-16*, 1119-20.

129. The title also appears in 9:41, a passage considered under Mark's understanding of discipleship.

was clearly difficult for even his disciples to grasp, including Peter (8:31–33). As the Petrine confession that Jesus is the Christ is juxtaposed with the announcement of his death, so also the final confessions that he is the Christ are juxtaposed with Jesus' condemnation by the high priest and the cross (14:61; 15:32).

The highest Jewish authority, along with the chief priests and Sanhedrin, looked for testimony against Jesus (14:53–60). The testimony was confused and Jesus maintained silence (14:61a). The high priest asked directly, "Are you the Messiah, the Son of the Blessed One?" (14:61b). Surprisingly, Jesus answers directly, "I am" (ἐγώ εἰμι), which almost appears as lightning out of a Johannine sky. But the truly striking point in the context of Mark is that the same Jesus who had restricted the proclamation of his messiahship (8:30) here affirms it publicly. Jesus adds a conflated quotation from Daniel 7:13 and Psalm 110:1: "'You will see the Son of Man seated at the right hand of the Power,' and 'coming with the clouds of heaven'" (14:62). Mark leaves no doubt that Jesus embraced his messiahship fully, a fact suggested by the absence of a rebuttal to Peter's earlier confession. Whatever reason may be offered for why he was reluctant to have it broadcast (8:30) should not be traced to his own absence of messianic consciousness. The high priest found sufficient cause here to condemn him on the charge of blasphemy (14:63–64), likely due to his claim of divine sonship and not simply claim that he was the Messiah.[130] Bock suggests that his "claim to possess comprehensive authority" and his attack on the Jewish leadership "by implicitly claiming to be their future judge" were the root causes of the charge.[131] The claim to authority is surely present in the citations he pulls from the OT. We should understand these as modifications of his assertion that he is the Messiah that extended the scope of their understanding of who the Messiah would be. He is enthroned on God's right hand, the exalted Son of Man of Daniel 7:13–14 who has an everlasting dominion. And, as such, they condemned him.

The juxtaposition of Jesus' condemnation and the exalted claim to kingship appears again around the cross where he is mocked with the words, "Let the Messiah, the King of Israel, come down from the cross now" (15:32). The crucifixion took place at the third hour (nine in the morning), and the charge against Jesus was inscribed as "The King of the Jews" (15:26, cf. 15:2, 9, 12, 18). The title, "King of the Jews," is that which the Gentiles use whereas "King of Israel" comes from the mouth of fellow Jews (15:31–32), although the former could be voiced by Jews as well (Josephus, *Ant.* 14.36; 15.373; 16.311). The inscription identifying the one crucified between two thieves was, again, extremely ironic as it unveiled the truth about Jesus. He is indeed who the inscription says he is. The taunting rejection likewise bears the truth about his identity: The Messiah, the King of Israel. The royal scene is set with purple cloak, thorny

---

130. Evans, *Mark 8:27–16:20*, 453–58; Marcus, *Mark 8–16*, 1008–9.

131. Darrell L. Bock, *Blasphemy and Exaltation in Judaism and the Final Examination of Jesus: A Philological-Historical Study of the Key Jewish Themes Impacting Mark 14:61–64* (Tübingen: Mohr Seibeck, 1998), 236.

crown, and reed scepter, as the soldiers ironically honor him by saying, "Hail, King of the Jews" (15:16–20), a greeting that plays on the Latin imperial salute, "Ave, Caesar!"[132] Jesus' royal character is played over against the Roman imperial power, which did not tolerate anyone who claimed the title "King," especially in the unruly provinces. The Romans sent Herod Antipas into exile when he sought the title for himself at the provocation of his wife Herodias (Josephus, *Ant.* 18.240–52). Only the emperor had the authority to make someone King, yet Jesus bore the title. Mark's message is that Jesus is indeed the fulfillment of the Jewish hopes for a restored monarchy, a challenge to the Roman imperial claims to sovereignty. At the same time he redefines the nature of Jesus' rulership to include the ignominy of the cross.[133]

We should not underplay the significance of the title "Christ" in Mark as a means by which Jesus' character is revealed to the readers/hearers. Mark places the confessions of Jesus' kingship strategically at the center of his exposition, showing how Jesus announces and inaugurates the reign of God and is therefore acknowledged rightly as the Christ by Peter. But the concept of kingship undergoes a transformation: the traditional category cannot hold the fullness of who he is nor of his proclamation of the kingdom of God. He is greater than David, he suffers and dies on the cross, and his rule embraces realities not anticipated in the extant conceptions of the coming kingdom. The readers' understanding of his royal person and his kingly mission undergo considerable broadening, starting with the other titles and their concepts that, while affirming his rule, unveil a fuller reality in striking ways. Noteworthy also is the concept narrowing that occurs since the advent of the kingdom via the professed King does not entail an armed overthrow of Roman colonial rule. The cross is full of royal meaning in Mark, as we will see, but it is not exchanged for a sword or spear. The claims Jesus made were understandably seditious from Pilate's point of view, but even he recognized that Jesus' profile did not fit with the claims about him. He was not the leader of an armed insurgency movement as the others that arose during the era and, whatever reports and accusations were presented, there was clearly nothing that called for military suppression of Jesus or his disciples. Pilate recognized as much. Jealousy motivated the Jewish leaders to hand him over to the Roman authority (15:10), and Pilate's condemnation of Jesus was instigated by pressure from the crowd who took to shouting against Jesus (15:11–14). The volume is turned up here again in Mark. Pilate handed him over for crucifixion to meet the crowd's demand (15:15).[134] There is no guilt here, nothing worthy of the condemnation Jesus received. In this tribunal, justice was nowhere found. And though accused and innocent, Jesus remained silent

---

132. Stein, *Mark*, 708.

133. This is even implied in Jesus' response to Pilate's question regarding whether he was the King of the Jews (15:2). "You say so" (σὺ λέγεις) is not a rejection of the title, nor does refuse to commit to it, but "implies that his understanding of the title is not the same as Pilate's" (Stein, *Mark*, 698).

134. τῷ ὄχλῳ τὸ ἱκανὸν ποιῆσαι, here meaning "to satisfy," as when demands are met (Polybius 32.3.13); *LSJ*, 825; *BDAG*, 472.

(15:5). Jesus was not causing social unrest, nor were his disciples, an important point for Christian readers and others who heard the message in the volatile environment in Rome during the early seventh decade.[135]

The Son of God

Mark uses other titles that reveal Jesus' kingship and nuance it in significant directions as he answers the question, "Who is this?" The first of these is "Son of God," which appears in the opening verse of the Gospel (1:1, according to significant textual witnesses[136]) and elsewhere in the book (3:11; 5:7; 15:39). At times a variant of "Son of God" appears, such as "Son, the Beloved" (1:11; 9:7; and in the parable 12:6), "Son of the Blessed One" (14:61), or simply "Son" (13:32). The title "Son of God" and its variants do not appear in Mark with great frequency, but like the title "Christ" they are located strategically in the narrative as they reveal aspects of Jesus' person and kingly rule. In fact, confessions of his sonship appear at the very beginning of the book (1:1) and as the final confession in the narrative (15:39), forming an inclusio around the whole and thus framing the christological development throughout. Moreover, the confessions about Jesus' sonship come from supernatural revelatory sources. The demons recognize that he is the Son of God (3:11; 5:7) and, more importantly, God calls him this (1:11; 9:7). Although Jesus' most common self-designation is the "Son of Man," he does not hesitate to call himself the "Son" (13:32; 12:6). With this self-consciousness, he addresses or speaks of God as "Abba, Father" (14:36), or simply "Father" (8:38; 13:32). While the high priest questions him about whether he is the "Son of the Blessed One," the Roman centurion recognizes that he is truly "God's Son" (15:39). Jesus' sonship occupies a significant place in this Gospel.

Two main streams run into Mark's presentation of Jesus' sonship. The first was the use of "son of God" to denote God's king. This nuance may be suggested in the opening verse of the book, which juxtaposes the title "Christ" with "Son of God," the two possibly being in apposition (Χριστοῦ υἱοῦ θεοῦ [1:1]; cf. Matt 16:16; 26:63; Luke 4:41; John 11:27; 20:21). The coming Messiah of the line of David was called God's son (2 Sam 7:14), a name also given to David, the anointed king (Ps 2:7). Both 2 Samuel 7 and Psalm 2 spoke about the Lord's anointed king (2 Sam 22:51; 23:1; Ps 2:2, 6), juxtaposing the "anointed one" with royal sonship in a way not unlike Mark 1:1. Both texts underscore the "son's" dominion (2 Sam 7:12–13, 16; Ps 2:6). The same title for

---

135. Roskam, *The Purpose of the Gospel of Mark in Its Historical and Social Context*, 238.

136. Omitted in ℵ*, Θ, 28c, but it enjoys broad and deep mss. support, including B, D, L, W. We best understand it as original. See the discussions in Jan Slomp, "Are the Words 'Son of God' in Mark 1:1 Original?," *BT* 28 (1977) 143–50; Guelich, *Mark 1–8:26*, 6; Gundry, *Mark*, 33; Metzger, *A Textual Commentary on the Greek New Testament*, 62; Edwards, *The Gospel According to Mark*, 25–26; France, *The Gospel of Mark*, 49; Tommy Wasserman, "The 'Son of God' Was in the Beginning (Mark 1:1)," *JTS* 62 (2011) 20–50. On the other hand, Peter Head ("A Text-Critical Study of Mark 1:1 'The Beginning of the Gospel of Jesus Christ," *NTS* 37 [1991] 621–29) and Marcus (*Mark 1–8*, 141) dissent.

the Davidic monarch appears within Judaism. For example, 4Q174 1:10–12 cites 2 Samuel 7:14 and adds its interpretation: "'I will be a father to him and he will be a son to me.' This (refers to the) 'branch of David,' who will arise with the Interpreter of the law who [will rise up] in Zi[on in] the last days" (so 4Q246 2:1).[137]

Mark's understanding of Jesus' divine sonship draws directly upon Psalm 2 as the divine voice in 1:11 declares: "You are my Son, the Beloved; with you I am well pleased" (σὺ εἶ ὁ υἱός μου ὁ ἀγαπητός, ἐν σοὶ εὐδόκησα). "You are my Son" quotes Psalm 2:7 (LXX υἱός μου εἶ σύ), which was addressed to the king. The second part of the divine announcement, however, derives from Genesis 22:2, a reference to Abraham's beloved son Isaac, "the Beloved" (LXX τὸν υἱόν σου τὸν ἀγαπητόν). The point is not simply that he is the object of his father's love but that he is unique, "beloved" in the LXX rendering the Hebrew "only" (יָחִיד). The final part of the divine declaration, "with you I am well pleased," draws upon Isaiah 42:1 where the Servant is the chosen one in whom God delights. Here is an allusion to the Hebrew, which says: "my chosen, in whom my soul delights" (בְּחִירִי רָצְתָה נַפְשִׁי) rather than a quotation of the LXX.[138] As in Isaiah 42:1, the declaration in Mark 1:11 is linked with the coming of the Spirit ("I have put my spirit upon him"; cf. Mark 1:10). He is the Anointed One, the King (Isa 61:1). In sum, the title "Son of God" refers to Jesus' place as God's King who, according to the divine declaration, is both unique and fulfills the role of the Servant from Isaiah 42. Jesus is not simply one of many, nor is his kingship divorced from his mission as the Servant.

The second stream that runs into Mark's Christology of Jesus' sonship comes from the Roman environment of his readers, where "son of god" had become a title ascribed to Augustus. Augustus was the adopted son of the divinized Julius Caesar and, as such, was known as *divi filius*, the "son of god." Coinage from the period as well as inscriptions bore the title in abbreviated form (DIVI F), while provincial inscriptions in Greek acknowledged him as θεοῦ υἱός, "son of god" (see above). The title was well circulated, appearing even in the provinces of the empire, so the recipients of this message would have had little trouble mentally accessing salient conceptual information about "son of god." This was especially the case when hearing 15:39, where a Roman centurion, the representative of Rome's imperial power, sees Jesus dying and exclaims, "Truly this man was God's Son" (ἀληθῶς οὗτος ὁ ἄνθρωπος υἱὸς θεοῦ ἦν). The title was originally ascribed to Augustus.[139] On the other hand, Tiberius's inscriptions

---

137. "He will be called son of God, and they will call him son of the Most High." These and other Qumran texts from Florentino García Martínez, *The Dead Sea Scrolls Translated: The Qumran Texts in English* (Leiden: Brill, 1994). See also Adela Y. Collins, "Mark and His Readers: The Son of God Among Jews," *HTR* 92 (1999) 393–408.

138. The LXX of Isa 42:1 reads Ισραηλ ὁ ἐκλεκτός μου προσεδέξατο αὐτὸν ἡ ψυχή μου ("Israel is my chosen, my soul has accepted him").

139. For a good collection of texts, see Tae Hun Kim, "The Anarthrous υἱὸς θεοῦ in Mark 15:39," *Bib* 79 (1998) 228–32; Adela Y. Collins, "Mark and His Readers: The Son of God Among Greeks and Romans," *HTR* 93 (2000) 94–97.

designate him as "son of Augustus" or a "new Augustus" but not "son of god," and others followed suit. Caligula called himself "son of Augustus" or "new god," Claudius was "Claudius god" or "Augustus god," and Vespasian could be called "Vespasian god." Nero comes the closest to the Augustan title by being called "the son of the greatest of the gods." The numismatic evidence is somewhat more robust for a continued use of DIVI F with five issues bearing the title with reference to Tiberius, four to Nero, and twenty eight to Domitian. Yet the coins that bear the title often do so with a mix of other names, including that of Augustus.[140] The inscriptions and coins show an attempt to be associated with Augustus, who was honored as the "son of god," one who had built the empire (see the acclamations in the *Res Gestae*).

The centurion's exclamation stands as a counterpoint to the claims about Augustus and goes beyond simply appropriating Augustan honors. Jesus is the true Son of God and, as such, he is the sovereign ruler. While "Son of God" finds its conceptual roots within Jewish Davidic theology of the monarchy (2 Sam 7:14; Ps 2:7), the contextualization of the gospel in the Roman world resulted in an appropriation and adaptation of an imperial title for Christ.[141] The way the centurion frames the title ("Truly this man") makes the "Son of God" title a counterpoint and challenge to any imperial claim. The one who does deeds expected of God's Son is Jesus Christ, not Augustus or any of his successors. Yet just as the concept of sonship underwent a modification in Mark as it became associated with the Servant (1:11; Isa 42:1), so the centurion's confession shows that Jesus' divine sonship embraces the theology of the cross. It is as Jesus "breathed his last" that the centurion recognized him for who he was. The royal Son suffers and dies. Mark appears to underscore the revelatory character of the moment as the previous verse discloses that "the curtain of the temple was torn in two, from top to bottom" (15:38).[142] As at the transfiguration, Jesus' sonship is revealed as he is transformed and is seen in dazzling white (9:3–4, 7). The revelation to the centurion occurs at a moment of darkness (15:33), but the revealed message is the same: that Jesus is "God's Son."[143]

140. Kim, "The Anarthrous υἱὸς θεοῦ in Mark 15:39," 234–37.

141. Mark does not present a "divine man" Christology, however. See the discussion in Carl H. Holladay, *Theios Aner in Hellenistic-Judaism: A Critique of the Use of This Category in New Testament Christology* (Missoula, MT: Scholars, 1977); James R. Edwards, "The Son of God: Its Antecedents in Judaism and Hellenism and Its Use in the Earliest Gosepl" (PhD diss., Fuller Theological Seminary, 1978); Blackburn, *Theios Anēr and the Markan Miracle Traditions*; Edwards, *The Gospel According to Mark*, 105–9.

142. An early Christian interpolation into The Testament of Benjamin has a surprisingly similar understanding of the tearing of the veil and the revelation of God's glory: "And the temple curtain shall be torn, and the spirit of God will move on to all the nations as a fire is poured out" (9:4). See Marcus, *Mark 8–16*, 1067.

143. Marcus reminds us that "the Philonic association of 'king' with 'god' in *Life of Moses* 1.158 should warn us against seeing royalty and divinity as necessarily separate categories," as is the case when God calls Jesus "Son" in Mark 1:11 (*The Way of the Lord*, 91). Philo, *Moses* 1.158: "Again, was not the joy of his partnership with the Father and Maker of all magnified also by the honor of being deemed worthy to bear the same title? For he was named god and king of the whole nation, and

The title "Son of God" serves as an inclusio around Mark's Gospel and presents his royal Christology in a way that was relevant for both Jews and Gentiles. Mark also shows how the advent of the kingdom of God through Jesus, the Son of God, means the overthrow of hostile demonic forces. In two exorcisms, the demons recognize him as the Son of God. In the first account, Mark summarizes Jesus' ministry of healing and exorcism, which drew large crowds (3:7–12). He notes that when the demons saw him they recognized him. Those possessed prostrated themselves and shouted (Mark is intrigued with the volume!), "You are the Son of God!" But Jesus silenced them. The message is that the royal Son has authority not just as king over Israel and in the face of imperial power but also exercises authority over the supernatural realm. They prostrate before him, a sign of obeisance and submission. There is no sphere of power that is autonomous and not subject to his authority. But the demons' cry also is revelatory as they have supernatural insight into who he is. Jesus silenced them but did not deny their claim that he was the Son of God. The other loud announcement from the demonic realm regarding Jesus' sonship is the cry of the Gerasene demoniac, "What have you to do with me, Jesus, Son of the Most High God?" (5:7). Jesus' authority is again in view, and the multiple demons recognize who he is. In this case, however, the name is somewhat different as it echoes Gentile use of "Most High" to refer to the supreme deity (Gen 14:18–20; Num 24:16; Isa 14:14; Dan 3:26, 42; Acts 16:17),[144] but it also refers to Israel's God who was sovereign over all (Deut 32:8; Isa 14:14; 2 Sam 22:14). Calling him "Son of the Most High God" is a recognition of his sovereignty, which Gentile hearers of this story would not have missed.

Jesus is the one through whom God's kingdom advances, and this fuses a missional dimension into the title "Son of God." The mission becomes evident early through the divine approval given the Son as the Servant (1:11) and then again in the call to "listen to him" at the transfiguration (9:7). He accomplishes God's mission and proclaims God's message of the kingdom. That mission embraced both his kingly role as the Christ, which Peter recognized (8:27), and his suffering, which Peter did not understand (8:31–33). Both are true: "Listen to him!" Jesus is not just one of the prophets (8:28), nor is he merely on a par with the great prophets Moses and Elijah as Peter suggested (9:5). The divine exhortation at the transfiguration identifies Jesus as The Prophet who was greater than Moses ("You shall hear him" [Deut 18:15]), and as such his message must be heeded (Deut 18:18–19). Mark recounts that the transfiguration occurred "six days later" when Jesus, with Peter, James and John, went "up a high mountain" and then "a cloud overshadowed them" (Mark 9:2, 7). The scene vividly recalls Moses' encounter with God on Mt. Sinai, which occurred after "the cloud covered it for six days" and "Moses entered the cloud" (Exod 24:15–17). Jesus was transfigured as "his clothes became dazzling white" (Mark 9:3), which may

---

entered, we are told, into the darkness where God was, that is into the unseen, invisible, incorporeal and archetypical essence of existing things."

144. For Greek texts, see Marcus, *Mark 1–8*, 343; *LSJ*, 1910.

suggest the scene on Sinai when the "glory of the Lord was like a devouring fire on the top of the mountain" (Exod 24:17).[145] The event on Mt. Sinai was a time of revelation and unveiling God's glory to Moses, just as the transfiguration revealed to Peter and the others Christ's nature as they saw his glory and heard the divine voice on the holy mountain. In the transfiguration Jesus receives honor while Peter and the ones with him receive revelation from God in the form of the divine disclosure of Jesus' sonship, "This is my Son, the Beloved," and the command to hear him (9:7). Peter knows by revelation that Jesus is God's royal Son, as he knew Jesus was the Christ (8:29), whatever misunderstanding led him to place Moses and Elijah on a par with Jesus (9:5; cf. Peter's misunderstanding in 8:31-33). The divine voice repeats the revelation at Jesus' baptism recorded earlier for Mark's readers: "You are my Son, the Beloved" (1:11). Not only does the transfiguration look back to the baptism, but there is an eschatological element here since the forerunner Elijah has already come (9:11-13; cf. 15:35-36) and the promise through Moses about the greater prophet has been fulfilled (see also Mal 4:4-5). That eschatological dimension was anticipated in Jesus' prelude to the story (9:1): "Truly I tell you, there are some standing here who will not taste death until they see that the kingdom of God has come with power." The transfiguration also anticipates the glorious appearing of "the Son of Man coming in clouds with great power and glory" (13:26). What Peter and the rest see now anticipates the appearing that will be seen by all.

Mark's theology of Jesus' sonship preserves the claim to kingship found in the title "Christ" but expands upon the understanding of the Messiah's rule. We have seen that the "Christ," the anointed King of the Davidic line, is also the Lord, and his being transcends that of an earthly king (12:35-37). And while "Son of God" is another title for "Christ" according to Mark's sources (2 Sam 7:14; Ps 2:7), the notion of divine sonship outstrips the extant messianic categories. The category extensions appear in the divine revelations about Jesus' person at his baptism and the transfiguration. There is not only evidence of his rule through the testimony of his deeds but also direct verbal divine testimony regarding his special relationship to the Father. The sonship of Jesus moves beyond a functional description of his rule into ontology. This aspect of his sonship is especially evident in the transfiguration where the Voice from heaven

---

145. While various background images feed into the transfiguration account (Marcus, *Mark 8-16*, 1108-18; see, for example, 1 En. 14:20; 2 En. 22:8-9; 3 En. 12:1; Ps 104:1-2), the divine revelation on Sinai and the promise of a coming prophet are the most prominent. See also John Paul Heil, *The Transfiguration of Jesus: Narrative Meaning and Function of Mark 9:2-8, Matt 17:1-8, and Luke 9:28-36* (Rome: Editrice Pontificio Istituto Biblico, 2000), 151-99; Pierre-Yves Brandt, *L'identité de Jésus et l'identité de son disciple: Le récit de la transfiguration comme clef de lecture de l'Evangile de Marc* (Göttingen: Vandenhoeck & Ruprecht, 2002), 253-76; Andrew Wilson, *Transfigured: A Derridean Rereading of the Markan Transfiguration* (London: T. & T. Clark, 2007), 52-85; Simon S. Lee, *Jesus' Transfiguration and the Believers' Transformation: A Study of the Transfiguration and Its Development in Early Christian Writings* (Tübingen: Mohr Siebeck, 2009), 9-48. Although the word "glory" is absent from the account, the note that Jesus' clothes were dazzling white suggests the idea of glory, or at the least supernatural or even divine presence (Mark 16:5; Dan 7:9).

identifies him as the Prophet greater than Moses ("Listen to him!"). Most significantly, he becomes transformed before Peter, James, and John. They also receive a visible revelation of his person as his radiance can no longer be contained. There is glory here, which speaks of divinity (cf. John 17:5; 1:14), a hint then more fully developed in later theology. In the transfiguration we witness the significance of the divine pronouncement, first heard at his baptism, that Jesus is truly the Son of God.

The use of "son of god" within the Roman imperial cult also suggests the divine character of his person since the emperor's character transcended normal human categories. Mark's theology of Jesus' sonship challenges the imperial claims but, at the same time, affirms that Jesus is truly the *divi filius* who has genuine power and honor and whose word is revelatory. In discussing the question of the high priest in Mark 14:61, "Are you the Messiah, the Son of the Blessed One," Marcus arrives at a similar conclusion: "At the beginning of the Christian era, then, the title 'Son of God' was ambiguous enough to be open not only to a low, Davidic interpretation but also to a high, quasi-divine interpretation. When used to distinguish a figure from the Davidic Messiah, as we have shown to be the case in the phrase 'Messiah-Son-of-God' it would have fallen on Jewish ears as a claim to commensurability with God."[146] Jesus was more than anyone expected. But he also did not fit the extant categories because, as the beloved Son of God, he was killed (12:6–7). Sonship and suffering unto death are not incompatible categories in Mark, as the centurion realized at the very end of Mark's Gospel (15:39).[147] Although messianic theology is undergoing significant shifts in Mark, there are aspects of later formulations that do not appear here. As Telford notes, "Notions of the Son of God's pre-existence, mediatorial role in creation, descent from heaven, incarnation or sinlessness are as yet undeveloped."[148] Mark's Christology is one in development, with the theology of Jesus' sonship being a significant step in the expanded understanding of the Messiah and his mission.

The Son of Man

As often noted, the way Jesus preferred to speak himself was via the expression "Son of Man." It appears only on his lips in Mark as is the case elsewhere the Gospels. The only other reference to Jesus as the Son of Man is Stephen's confession at his martyrdom (Acts 7:56), which looks back to the teaching in the Gospel (Luke uses the expression twenty five times) and merges the title with Psalm 110:1 as occurs here in Mark

---

146. Joel Marcus, "Mark 14:61: 'Are You the Messiah-Son-of-God?,'" *NovT* 31 (1989) 141.

147. As Richard Hays notes, "The cross becomes the controlling symbol for interpreting Jesus' identity. Thus, the question, 'Who do you say that I am?' finds its final answer in the confession, 'Truly this man was the Son of God,' a confession that can be rightly uttered only at the foot of the cross" (*The Moral Vision of the New Testament: Community, Cross, New Creation* [San Francisco: HarperSanFrancisco, 1996], 80).

148. Telford, *Theology of the Gospel of Mark*, 41.

(14:62).[149] In Stephen's vision the Son of Man stands, not sits, as he who is about to come (cf. Mark 13:26).[150] This title[151] appears fourteen times in Mark (2:10, 28; 8:31, 38; 9:9, 12, 31; 10:33, 45; 13:26; 14:21 [2x], 41, 62). Jesus derives the expression and the concept from Daniel ("There before me was one like a son of man, coming with the clouds of heaven. . . . He was given authority, glory and sovereign power" [Dan 7:13-14, NIV]), as suggested by the eschatological discourse in Mark 13 ("They will see 'the son of Man coming in clouds' with great power and glory" [Mark 13:26]), Jesus' testimony before the high priest ("'You will see the Son of Man seated at the right hand of the Power,' and 'coming with the clouds of heaven'" [14:62]), and his statement about judgment ("When he comes in the glory of his Father with the holy angels" [8:38]). The title "Son of Man" appears not only in Daniel 7:13 but also elsewhere in Jewish literature. The most prominent of these is 1 Enoch 37–71, known also as the Parables of Enoch, and 4 Ezra 13, the "Sixth Vision" of that apocalypse. This latter text comes from the late first century AD (3:1 marks the time of composition: "In the thirtieth year after the destruction of our city") and could not have served as a source of the "Son of Man" sayings. Dating the Parables of Enoch is notoriously difficult, with most contemporary scholars suggesting that it was composed between 34 BC and AD 135. Those who participated in the Third Enoch Seminar at Camaldoni, however, identified the time of writing as around the end of the reign of Herod the Great, that is, late first century BC or early first century AD.[152] The Herodian date makes it possible that Jesus knew the text, and that Peter and Mark were acquainted with it either

---

149. Delbert Burkett suggests that "the absence of the title 'Son of Man' in the New Testament outside of the Gospels and Acts can best be explained if the title had currency primarily in Palestinian Christianity. . . . If the title 'Son of the Man' arose in a Palestinian context, it should appear precisely where it does" (*The Son of Man Debate: A History and Evaluation* [Cambridge: Cambridge University Press, 1999], 123).

150. For a discussion on the interpretations of the Son of Man's standing, see C. K. Barrett, *The Acts of the Apostles* (Edinburgh: T. & T. Clark, 1994), 1:384-85. On the title, see, for example, Morna D. Hooker, *The Son of Man in Mark: A Study of the Background of the Term 'Son of Man' and Its Use in St. Mark's Gospel* (London: SPCK, 1967); Douglas R. A. Hare, *The Son of Man Tradition* (Minneapolis: Fortress, 1990); Ulrich Kmiecik, *Der Menschensohn im Markusevangelium* (Würzburg: Echter, 1997); Burkett, *The Son of Man Debate*; Simon Gathercole, "The Son of Man in Mark's Gospel," *ExpTim* 115 (2003-4) 366-72; Gabriele Boccaccini, ed., *Enoch and the Messiah Son of Man: Revisiting the Book of Parables* (Grand Rapids: Eerdmans, 2007); Mogens Müller, *The Expression 'Son of Man' and the Development of Christology: A History of Interpretation* (London: Equinox, 2008), 390-402; Larry W Hurtado and Paul L. Owen, eds., *Who is This Son of Man? The Latest Scholarship on a Puzzling Expression of the Historical Jesus* (London: T. & T. Clark, 2011).

151. Not all would agree that "Son of Man" was originally a title or quasi-title (see Kingsbury, *The Christology of Mark's Gospel*, 157-79; Casey, *Aramaic Sources of Mark's Gospel*, 255-56; and the discussions in Kmiecik, *Der Menschensohn im Markusevangelium*, 11; Burkett, *The Son of Man Debate*, 82-96). However understood within Judaism, it became a title in Christian use.

152. Darrell D. Hannah, "The Elect Son of Man of the Parables of Enoch," in *Who is This Son of Man? The Latest Scholarship on a Puzzling Expression of the Historical Jesus*, ed. Larry W Hurtado and Paul L. Owen (London: T. & T. Clark, 2011), 134. See the discussions in Boccaccini, *Enoch and the Messiah Son of Man*, 415-96, 505-11.

directly or indirectly.[153] However, Mark consistently refers back to Daniel 7 and does not show clear evidence of dependency on The Parables of Enoch. Mark, as do the other Gospels, betrays the influence of Daniel 7 as their primary background, so the most we can say is that the "Son of Man" concept in the Parables of Enoch and the Gospels both developed from the same source and within the same milieu.[154]

The way Jesus speaks of himself as the "Son of Man" evokes associations that indicate that he understands the expression as something more than a substitute for the pronoun "I" or a way to call himself "man" or "a man."[155] As used in Mark, "Son of Man" is a title that identifies Jesus as a heavenly figure who has authority: "In my vision at night I looked, and there before me was one like a son of man, coming with the clouds of heaven. He approached the Ancient of Days and was led into his presence. He was given authority, glory and sovereign power; all nations and peoples of every language worshiped him. His dominion is an everlasting dominion that will not pass away, and his kingdom is one that will never be destroyed" (Dan 7:13–14, NIV).[156] In evoking imagery from Daniel 7:13–14 Jesus makes the claim that, as the "Son of Man," he has "dominion and glory and kingship" (NRSV) and "everlasting dominion," that is, "his kingship is one that shall never be destroyed." As indicated by the titles "Christ" and "Son of God," Jesus understands himself as a kingly figure who comes to rule. Indeed, "Christ" and "Son of Man" are frames that share a considerable amount of conceptual information (cf. 8:29, 31). He is, in other words, the King whose coming marks the advent of the Kingdom of God, which is proclaimed through both his deeds and words (Mark 1:15).[157]

The title "Son of Man" becomes a principle way to express the realities of the kingdom of God in Mark, including his present authority on earth, his future coming

---

153. Both 1 and 2 Peter were acquainted with 1 Enoch.

154. Chrys C. Caragounis, *The Son of Man: Vision and Interpretation* (Tübingen: Mohr, 1986), 84–119, 172. On the other hand, Ben Witherington leaves open the possibility of some influence on the Gospels, though perhaps not directly. Jesus' use of the Son of Man (*bar enasha*) "often reflects his understanding of himself in light of Daniel 7, but supplemented by the sort of ideas expressed in the *Similitudes* of Enoch" (*The Christology of Jesus* [Minneapolis: Fortress, 1990], 269, 243–48).

155. See the summary of the discussion in Burkett, *The Son of Man Debate*, 82–96, including the use of the Aramaic (א)נש(א) בר (*bar enasha*).

156. There does not appear to have been a unified understanding of the "Son of Man" within Judaism (Burkett, *The Son of Man Debate*, 120). Its prominence in the Gospels most likely stems from the fact that Jesus indeed used the expression to speak about himself (Larry W. Hurtado, "Summary and Concluding Observations," in *Who is This Son of Man? The Latest Scholarship on a Puzzling Expression of the Historical Jesus*, ed. Larry W. Hurtado and Paul L. Owen [London: T. & T. Clark, 2011], 159–77. See Bock on the Daniel roots of the expression (Darrell L. Bock, "The Use of Daniel 7 in Jesus' Trial, with Implications for His Self-Understanding," in *Who is This Son of Man? The Latest Scholarship on a Puzzling Expression of the Historical Jesus*, ed. Larry W Hurtado and Paul L. Owen [London: T. & T. Clark, 2011], 78–100).

157. Kingsbury (*The Christology of Mark's Gospel*, 159–66) mistakenly states that "there is no evidence that he employs 'the Son of Man' to explain to the reader 'who Jesus is.'" The way Jesus uses "Son of Man," however, points back unmistakably to the celestial royal figure in Daniel 7:13–14 and thereby develops the understanding of who Jesus is significantly.

in the clouds of heaven, but also his sufferings and death. He shows the Son of Man's kingly rule by declaring that he has authority on earth to forgive sins and heal (2:10) and that he is Lord of the Sabbath (2:28). His authority to forgive and heal are not derived directly from the Son of Man concept as developed in Daniel 7:14 but extensions of the vision that declares his "dominion and glory and kingship."[158] The one who is "coming with the clouds of heaven" is exercising authority "on earth" now (Mark 2:10) by acts of forgiveness and healing. The concept broadening in this pericope moves in the direction of Jesus' redemptive mission. The scene in Daniel 7 is one of final judgment (7:10, 26), but here in Mark the Son of Man comes to forgive. Similarly, the "Son of Man" is the Lord of the Sabbath. Here, as previously, Jesus uses "Son of Man" as a title and not as a generic reference for a human being. His point is not that humans have authority over the Sabbath but that the Son of Man's authority extends even over the Sabbath laws.[159] This is a further extension of the concept of dominion and kinship found in Daniel 7:14. In Mark's passage on the Sabbath controversy, the prototype for plucking grain on the Sabbath was what David and his companions did in the face of hunger. They went into the house of God and ate the bread of the Presence (2:25–26; 1 Sam 21:1–7). Jesus likewise allows for compassionate acts that respond to human need (2:27), and so he acts as the one who is greater than David, as "lord of the sabbath." We have here then a hint that Jesus merges the Son of Man of Daniel 7 with the promise made to David about the messianic rule of his greater Son (see above). And we again recognize that his dominion as the Son of Man is a present reality and not only a future hope.

As one with sovereign authority, the Son of Man will be "seated on the right hand of the Power" (14:62), a declaration that merges the language of Daniel 7:13 with the royal Psalm 110:1: "The Lord says to my lord, 'Sit at my right hand until I make your enemies your footstool.'" Mark combines this Davidic Psalm with both the royal titles "Christ" (12:35–37) and "Son of Man" (14:62). Jesus has responded positively to the question of the high priest, "Are you the Messiah, the Son of the Blessed one?" (14:61), by juxtaposing the title Son of Man (14:62) with the royal titles, "Messiah" and "Son." The scene is deep with irony since Jesus stands trial before the high priest and the council who are looking for testimony to condemn him to death (14:55–59). In response, Jesus cites Daniel 7:13, which points not only to the Son of Man's advent but also evokes his authority (7:14) and the coming judgment (7:9), a combined concept

---

158. On the Son of Man's authority in Daniel 7:14 (3x ἐξουσία) and Mark, see Frank J. Matera, *The Kingship of Jesus: Composition and Theology in Mark 15* (Chico, CA: Scholars, 1982), 105–8. In addition to Mark 2:10, see 1:22, 27; 3:5; 6:7; 11:28–29, 33. Hooker notes that the Son of Man sayings share in common Jesus' authority and binds together the three types of Son of Man texts: "all are expressions of this authority, whether it is an authority which is exercised now, which is denied and so leads to suffering, or which will be acknowledged and vindicated in the future" (*The Son of Man in Mark*, 180).

159. Guelich, *Mark 1–8:26*, 125–26; Marcus, *Mark 1–8*, 246; France, *The Gospel of Mark*, 147.

also present in Psalm 110.[160] The striking claim is that he, the accused, will come to judge the leaders of his people.

The "Son of Man" is a title tied with Jesus' future advent both here and in 13:26. He will bring in a new age, but that age is already dawning, as his present authority in forgiveness and healing reveals. When he comes, the old order marked by distress in the earth and human conflict will come to an end (13:3-23). Where other regimes have failed and fell into dreadful, deadly conflict (13:8), he will establish "an everlasting dominion that shall not pass away, and his kingship is one that shall never be destroyed" (Dan 7:14). And although the present age is marked by the conflict of nations (Mark 13:8), the Son of Man's rule extends over them all: "that all peoples, nations, and languages should serve him" (Dan 7:14). The universal extension of his rule began to be realized through Peter's proclamation of the gospel to the Gentiles (Acts 10) in (belated) response to Jesus' command (Acts 1:8). That act in the house of Cornelius anticipated the future exercise of the Son of Man's dominion over "all peoples, nations, and languages." Moreover, his advent will affect the very cosmos (Mark 13:24-25) as sun and moon fail to illuminate, stars fall from heaven, and "the powers in the heavens will be shaken," imagery which was not unfamiliar to those who knew the claims to empire that Virgil ascribed to Augustus. The shield of Aeneas depicted Augustus's battle with the opposing forces of Antony and Cleopatra, who brought chaos from the East. The battle that raged was not only upon the sea but had a cosmic dimension (*Aeneid* 8.671-713). Rome celebrated the victory of Augustus as he entered "the walls of Rome in triple triumph" and "the conquered peoples move in long array, as diverse in fashion of dress and arms as in tongues" (8.714-28; see the discussion above on Mark and epic). But a universal rule that extends to all nations is the true promise of the Son of Man. His coming will shake the very cosmos. One greater than Augustus is coming to rule!

Jesus not only understands himself as the fulfillment of the promise in Daniel 7:13-14, but he expands significantly upon the concept presented by the prophet. The most striking extension of the concept is the unfolding story of the Son of Man's suffering, death, and resurrection. Immediately after Peter's confession that Jesus is the Christ, Jesus "began to teach them that the Son of Man must undergo great suffering and be rejected" (8:31). The Son of Man "is to go through many sufferings and be treated with contempt" (9:12), which includes the awful realization that he, as the Son of Man, will be "betrayed into human hands" (9:31) and "betrayed into the hands of sinners" (14:41). The betrayal by Judas will occur "as it is written" (14:21), and so, too, "it [is] written about the Son of Man" that he would suffer and be dishonored (9:12). According to Jesus, Scripture predicts these events, although the passage in Daniel 7 gives no hint of the Son of Man's passion. Jesus pulls together the realities found in texts that refer to the Righteous Sufferer (Ps 22, 41, 69) and the Suffering

---

160. See the discussion in Evans, *Mark 8:27-16:20*, 451. During the era, rulers had a judicial function since there was not the separation of powers as in modern states.

Servant (Isa 50:4-9; 52:13—53:12) and applies them to the Son of Man.[161] In other words, the dishonor and suffering of the Son of Man is part of the divine plan. Mark 10:33 sketches the extent of his dishonor by saying that he "will be handed over to the chief priests and the scribes; and they will condemn him to death; then they will hand him over to the Gentiles." Both the leaders of his people and the Gentile occupiers of their land will conspire against him, adding abuse on top of condemnation: "they will mock him, and spit upon him, and flog him" (10:34). Because of his public dishonor and teaching, some will be ashamed of him (8:38). The Son of Man will then be killed (8:31; 9:31; 10:33), but he willingly gives up his life for the redemption of others. He came "to give his life a ransom for many" (10:45). Jesus' condemnation and death are the antithesis of the message communicated by the portrayal of himself as the royal and triumphant Son of Man of Daniel 7. The cross is the symbol of conquest and, for the Romans, a sign of their empire since it was used to maintain control and subjugation. But the Son of Man sayings also anticipate his resurrection (8:31; 9:9, 31; 10:33) as well as his triumphant advent (8:38; 13:26; 14:62). His betrayal, condemnation, suffering, and death are not his final destiny. As Hooker has noted, in Mark Jesus' authority "is in turn proclaimed, denied and vindicated."[162] The Son of Man sayings hold together the central realities of Mark's Christology.

According to Daniel 7:14, the Son of Man has honor as the one to whom the Ancient of Days gives "glory" and whom "all peoples, nations, and languages" serve. His ascribed honor contrasts sharply with the dishonor he faces through the disloyal betrayal, contempt, mocking, and spitting. The Son of Man statements show the extent of his dishonor, which, in the end, causes some disciples to buckle under the weight of shame. He was treated as if he were nothing (9:12, ἐξουδενηθῇ[163]), as those who held the highest honor in Jewish society reject him (8:31). The rejection (8:31) was predicted in Psalm 118:22, cited in Mark 12:10: "The stone that the builders rejected has become the cornerstone." He was drummed down through mocking, spitting, and physical abuse (10:34; 14:65; 15:15-25, 29-30). The scourging deepened the humiliation of the verbal abuse, and being spat upon was "an ultimate form of contempt."[164] The humiliation he endured is that of the Suffering Servant in Isaiah 50:6: "I gave my back to those who struck me, and my cheeks to those who pulled out my bear; I did not hide my face from insult and spitting." The many things that he suffered (8:31; 9:12) culminated in his death after he was delivered over by Judas and by the Jewish leaders (3:19; 9:31; 10:33; 14:10-11, 18, 21, 41-42, 44; 15:1, 10, 15; Isa 53:6, 12). He follows John's fate (Mark 1:14) and marks out the way for his disciples (13:9, 11-12). The Son of Man was murdered on the cross (8:31; 9:31; 10:34; 12:5, 7-8; 14:1), as

---

161. So Marcus, *Mark 8-16*, 645, and see Matera, *The Kingship of Jesus*, 116-19; France, *The Gospel of Mark*, 360, 567; Edwards, *The Gospel According to Mark*, 274, 424.

162. Hooker, *The Son of Man in Mark*, 181.

163. BDAG 352.

164. Edwards, *The Gospel According to Mark*, 448n92 (Num 12:14; Deut 25:9; Job 30:10).

John had been unjustly murdered (6:19). The utter violence and injustice perpetrated against Jesus fixates Mark as over and again the language and scenes of rejection, suffering, and death fill out the story. But Mark also focuses upon the significance of the Son of Man's death. He "came not to be served but to serve, and to give his life a ransom for many" (10:45). As will be discussed below, this Son of Man declaration draws from Isaiah 53:12, "he bore the sin of many" (also 53:6).[165] The Son of Man is the sacrificial sin-bearer. In Mark, Jesus is the Son of Man of Daniel 7 but, at the same time, he becomes identified with the rejected Stone of Psalm 118 and the Servant who suffers of Isaiah 50 and 52–53. As Maartens notes, "The correlation of the son of man and the suffering righteous one is characteristic of the Gospel of Mark."[166] The Son of Man theology in Mark draws together Jesus' cross and kingship.

Jesus the Lord

The "way of the Lord" occupies a central place in Mark's theology. We meet John the Baptist as God's harbinger, who calls out in the wilderness, "Prepare the way of the Lord, make his paths straight" (1:3). The prophecy from Isaiah 40:3 announces God's New Exodus, which the Lord leads (see above on the New Exodus in Mark). This text from Isaiah sets the direction for the whole Gospel refers to Yahweh's coming (פַּנּוּ דֶּרֶךְ יְהוָה). Mark follows the LXX, which translates the divine name as "the Lord" (ἑτοιμάσατε τὴν ὁδὸν κυρίου). This LXX translation of YHWH transforms "the Lord" (κύριος) into the name of God for the Greek-speaking Jew. The surprise is that the Lord whose coming John heralds is "Jesus Christ, the Son of God" (1:1). To strengthen the identification, Mark alters the LXX of Isaiah 40:3 slightly as he says "make his paths straight" instead of "make straight the paths of our God." Mark's narrative leaves no doubt that the Lord of Isaiah 40:3 is Jesus himself. Jesus is the "more powerful" one who is coming (1:7), suggesting that he is the deliverer of his people from exile. From the outset, Mark presents a high Christology that would have fixed the attention of any Gentile or Jew who heard this message.[167]

There are places in Mark, however, where κύριος (lord) appears to be no more than the polite address "sir" (7:28), or means simply "master of the house" (13:35) or "owner" of a vineyard (12:9). But less exalted concepts attached to the lexeme "lord" become Mark's gateways that open to a fuller understanding of the title ascribed to Jesus. The Syrophoenician woman, a Gentile, begs him to cast the demon out of her daughter, recognizing that he has more power than a common rabbi who has come

---

165. Evans, *Mark 8:27–16:20*, 122; Marcus, *Mark 8–16*, 750. See below for a fuller discussion of Mark 10:45.

166. J. Maartens, "The Son of Man as a Composite Metaphor in Mark 14:62," in *A South African Perspective on the New Testament: Essays by South African New Testament Scholars Presented to Bruce Manning Metzger During His Visit to South Africa in 1985*, ed. J. H. Petzer and J. Hartin (Leiden: Brill, 1986), 82.

167. See Daniel Johansson, "*Kyrios* in the Gospel of Mark," *JSNT* 33 (2010) 103–5.

up from Galilee to the region of Tyre.[168] She humbles herself before him by asking for "the children's crumbs," but in so doing exercises faith in his powerful ability as the one she addressed as κύριος (7:28). As "Lord" he has authority over demons (5:19). Similarly, in the parable at the end of the eschatological discourse in Mark 13, the "master of the house" who comes (13:35) is none other than "'the Son of Man coming in clouds' with great power and glory" (13:26). And in 12:9, Jesus tells a parable about some wicked tenants in which "the owner" (κύριος) of the vineyard is God himself, the one who has sent his son whom they seized, killed, and threw out of the vineyard. While not ascribed to Jesus here, the "lord" in the story represents God. Were there any question about who the "lord" is, Jesus clarifies in 12:10-11, where he cites Psalm 118:22-23: "This was the Lord's doing, and it is amazing in our eyes." Even in the passages that are part of mundane discourse, κύριος may point to the exalted Lord who is either Jesus or God himself. Although the latter comes as no surprise, as when Jesus repeats the Shema, which identifies God as the single Lord (12:29-30), the ascription of the title to Jesus as a marker for his supernatural power and divinity is theologically breathtaking.

Jesus' exalted status as the "Lord" appears in a variety of settings. When Jesus instructs his disciples to requisition a colt for the royal entry into Jerusalem, he tells them to respond to anyone who questions their action by saying, "The Lord needs it and will send it back here immediately" (11:3). Marcus suggests that "he may be exercising a right of impressment, as other influential and powerful people, including teachers."[169] In this setting, where preparations are made for Jesus' royal entry into Jerusalem, the "Lord" would be understood as a high governing official who has authority to impress the animal for his service. In the same passage, those who accompanied Jesus in the royal entry into Jerusalem extol him in the words of Psalm 118:25: "Blessed is the one who comes in the name of the Lord!" (Mark 11:9). The Psalm does not ascribe the title "Lord" to Jesus but simply identifies him as the king who comes in the Lord's name as his agent. Luke makes this point explicit as he interprets Mark for his audience (Luke 19:38, "Blessed is the king who comes in the name of the Lord!"). Jesus is God's regent, as Mark 11:10 likewise suggests: "Blessed is the coming kingdom of our ancestor David." He is the Lord's regent, but elsewhere he also is called "Lord" in a setting that acknowledges his kingship. Mark 12:36 quotes Psalm 110:1: "The Lord said to my Lord, 'Sit at my right hand, until I put your enemies under your feet.'" The

---

168. The Jews, however, were known for their power as exorcists (cf. Acts 19:11-17), a fact that could have prompted the woman to solicit Jesus' help. Mark, however, points to her special knowledge about Jesus' ministry (7:24-25; 3:8).

169. Marcus, *Mark 1-8*, 773. See the proclamation of Germanicus Caesar: "and for boats or animals which we requisition I command that hire be paid in accordance with my schedule.... And I forbid beasts of burden to be forcibly appropriated by those who meet them traversing the city" (Hunt and Edgar §211). Evan's comment that Mark "never calls Jesus ὁ κύριος" (*Mark 8:27–16:20*, 143) requires clarification. Mark frequently ascribes the title "Lord" to Jesus, but, on the other hand, he is not called "The Lord" as in later Christian literature save in the longer ending (16:20).

setting, once again, is royal as David himself calls his son, the Messiah, "Lord." The Lord who speaks to his Lord and gives him dominion is God himself. But the fact that David's son, the Messiah, is addressed as Lord affirms that his status is above that of a mere descendant of David, a point made in Jesus' interpretive question in 12:37. Jesus is not denying that the Messiah is the son of David but evokes Psalm 110:1 to show that the Messiah stands as "Lord" beyond the category of kingship. While his status is not fully defined in this verse, within the frame of Mark's theology he is exalted beyond the categories current during his time. For that reason, he is also known in Mark as the Lord of the Sabbath since his authority supersedes that of the Mosaic Sabbath laws (2:28). Although this passage sets up a comparison between the actions of Jesus and David (2:25–26), as in 12:36–37, Jesus transcends the Davidic royal category again since he is the one who even has authority over the divinely given Sabbath law. He is more than an interpreter of that law since, as the Son of Man, he is Lord of the Sabbath. And as such, he is greater than what the titles "Son of David" and "Messiah" would suggest.[170]

The lordship of Christ became one of the principle confessions of the early church (Rom 10:9; 1 Cor 12:3; Phil 2:11). In the ascription of the title to Jesus, the church confirmed its faith in both his sovereignty and divinity. For the Greek-speaking Jewish authors and readers of the NT, "Lord" was the name of God in the LXX. Texts ascribed to YHWH in the OT (LXX κύριος) are occasionally turned and ascribed to Jesus, who is called "Lord" (cf. 1 Pet 3:15; Isa 8:13). This movement begins in the first chapter of Mark, although the bulk of the narrative points to his transcendent status rather than forwarding a full confession of his divine lordship. Mark is a significant step along the road of christological development, which flourishes fully in later NT books. Indeed, the latter addition of the longer ending of Mark reflects this fuller development as it calls him "the Lord Jesus" (16:19) or simply "Lord" (16:20). But Mark not only draws from Jewish sources that shed considerable light on Jesus' person. He consciously writes for a Greek-speaking audience in Rome, which had their own understanding of the title Lord as a title for divinity (1 Cor 8:5), including the emperor.[171] The Lord who casts out demons (5:19; 7:28), requisitions a colt (11:3), and who has control of history's outcomes (13:20) stands as the most exalted divine ruler. Although not expressed directly but only suggested in Mark, the true Lord is Jesus, not Caesar or any other image of divinity that claims the title lord. Mark's understanding of Jesus' lordship goes beyond to a level of exaltation that transcends mundane categories.

---

170. Donahue and Harrington, *The Gospel of Mark*, 35; Matera, *New Testament Theology*, 17.

171. *LAE*, 353–57; I. Howard Marshall, *The Origins of New Testament Christology* (Leicester, UK: Apollos, 1990), 97–99.

The Shepherd of Israel

In two texts, Mark refers to Jesus as a Shepherd. Although this is not the most prominent piece of Mark's Christology, it occupies a significant place in his understanding of Jesus' role in the New Exodus (see above). In the middle of the story of the feeding of the 5,000 men (6:30-44),[172] Mark comments that when Jesus saw the large crowd following him, "he had compassion for them because they were like sheep without a shepherd." Jesus demonstrated his compassion for those gathered through his didactic ministry (6:34) and by miraculously feeding them (6:37-44). Although Mark does not directly call him "Shepherd," he shows through Jesus' actions that he is indeed that. The comment in 6:34 that "they were like sheep without a shepherd" evokes Numbers 27:17, where Moses appeals to the Lord to assure that someone would be placed over Israel "so that the congregation of the Lord may not be like sheep without a shepherd." Joshua was commissioned for this service (Num 27:18), and now Jesus, the true Joshua, takes up this role as the congregation's shepherd. Mark's New Exodus theology comes into focus in this feeding miracle since it occurs at "a deserted place" (Mark 6:31-32, 35). Moreover, the prophetic announcement of the New Exodus (Mark 1:2-3, citing Exod 23:20; Isa 40:3) included the promise that God "will feed his flock like a shepherd; he will gather the lambs in his arms, and carry them in his bosom, and gently lead the mother sheep" (Isa 40:11). Jesus shows such compassion for the flock (6:34; 82). The promise to those coming out of Egypt was that they would be filled (Deut 8:10), as has now occurred as Jesus feeds this multitude (Mark 6:42). The event anticipates the felicity of the age to come when God will set a banquet for his people (Isa 25:6-9). The meal provided for the 5,000 also looks forward to the banquet the Lord will later share with the disciples, which brings together the wine and bread of covenant salvation (Mark 14:22-25). Jesus becomes the Shepherd-Messiah who provides the feast, that is, manna in the wilderness (cf. 2 Bar. 29:3, 8; John 6:5-15).[173] Images of salvation pervade the event.

But the Shepherd Christology in Mark also embraces the cross. The one who gathers and provides is also crucified as the sheep scatter (Mark 14:26-31). On the

---

172. Mark only mentions the men (ἄνδρες), not the women or children who may have accompanied him as well (6:44; Luke 9:14). Elsewhere in the passage, Mark mentions the many (πολλοί) that met Jesus as he disembarked (6:33). Matthew 14:21 counts the number as 5,000 men but adds "besides women and children." John (6:1-13) tells the story without gender markers. Marcus believes that Mark is either communicating that no women and children were present or "is echoing the OT passages by only counting the men; in view of the strong exodus typology of our passage, the latter is more likely" (see Exod 12:37; Marcus, *Mark 1-8*, 414). France, on the other hand, argues that only men were present since this was possibly "a gathering of patriots with an insurrectionary motive," and, for that reason, the women and children would not be present (France, *The Gospel of Mark*, 268). During an era when women and children were on the margins, leaving them out of the count is no surprise. What is striking in Mark, as in the other Gospels, is how often they move from the margins to more central roles (Mark 5:45; 7:25-26; 14:3; 15:40-41). But these are steps in a process of revising women's place within religious society.

173. Watts, *Isaiah's New Exodus in Mark*, 232-33.

Mount of Olives Jesus announces his death and the scattering of the disciples by quoting Zechariah 13:7: "I will strike the shepherd, and the sheep will be scattered." The prediction in Zechariah includes the anticipation of betrayal (Zech 13:7a), a point not lost on Mark, who includes the announcement of Judas's betrayal just before the prediction of the shepherd's demise (Mark 14:17–21). But the most intriguing aspect of the Zechariah quotation is that Mark has changed the quotation from an imperative ("Strike the shepherd," in both the MT and LXX) to the first person singular ("I will strike the shepherd"). The "I" here is God himself, as indicated by Zechariah 13:7b ("I will turn my hand against the little ones") and by the whole passage in Zechariah which begins with God's declaration about "my shepherd." Although there is betrayal and denial, God himself has become involved in the death of the Shepherd. In the end, the cross is not mere misfortune but part of the divine plan.[174] The theme of God's will and the cross finds development in the following scene in Gethsemane: "remove this cup from me; yet not what I want, but what you want" (14:36).

Significantly, Peter plays a central role in this story. Jesus announces that the disciples will desert him, but Peter rejects the suggestion: "Even though all become deserters, I will not." The other disciples affirm that they, too, will remain faithful. The passage is particularly relevant for Mark and Peter's audience in Rome since they faced persecution themselves and the prospect of desertion (Mark 4:17; 10:30). Judas and Peter are differentiated, however, since the one betrays Jesus and the other becomes one of the scattered sheep who had denied him. For the latter, Jesus offers the hope, which he announces after the Zechariah prophecy: "But after I am raised up, I will go before you to Galilee" (14:28). The hope of restoration shines into the dark corner of denial. The end of this story appears in 16:7, where the angelic figure says to the women, "But go, tell his disciples and Peter that he is going ahead of you to Galilee; there you will see him as he told you." While the Shepherd will be struck down and the sheep scattered, he will lead the way, and the disciples will be restored and gathered again. The Shepherd-Messiah is the crucified and resurrected Messiah who gathers and feeds his community.

Jesus the Teacher

Although lacking some of the extensive teaching sections found in the other Gospels, such as the Sermon on the Mount, Mark presents Jesus as the teacher.[175] This theme, as Mark's Shepherd-Messiah Christology, finds its roots in the New Exodus theology, where the Servant of the Lord will teach God's people in the way (48:17) and so act as God's agent (Isa 42:4, 21; 50:4; 51:4, 7). His teaching will reach the Gentiles and they

---

174. Peter G. Bolt, *The Cross from a Distance: Atonement in Mark's Gospel* (Downers Grove, IL: InterVarsity, 2004), 107–8.

175. See especially C. F. Evans, *The Beginning of the Gospel: Four Lectures on St Mark's Gospel* (London: SPCK, 1968), 43–61; Ralph Martin, *Mark: Evangelist and Theologian* (Grand Rapids: Zondervan, 1972), 111–17; Telford, *Theology of the Gospel of Mark*, 33–35.

will put their hope in him (LXX 42:4; 51:4). In Mark, Jesus is addressed in the vocative as "Teacher" (διδάσκαλε) or "Rabbi" (ῥαββί) a full thirteen times (4:38; 9:5, 17, 38; 10:17, 20, 35; 11:21; 12:14, 19, 21; 13:1; 14:45), and is called "the Teacher" twice, one of which is his self-designation (5:35; 14:14). His ministry consists of teaching, a point made in the Gospel over and again (1:21–22; 2:13; 4:1–2; 6:2, 6, 34; 8:31; 9:31; 11:17; 12:14, 35). Mark occasionally makes a summary statement about his teachings (1:22, 27; 4:2; 11:18; 12:38). Teaching was Jesus' "custom" (10:1), and he reminded the Sanhedrin that he taught in the temple precincts "daily" (14:49) when in Jerusalem. As he went through the towns and villages, he taught there as well (6:6) and could frequently be found teaching in the synagogues (1:21; 6:2). His prominence as a teacher in spaces which were the domain of the scribes must have caused some consternation. Mark tells us nothing about Jesus working, which suggests that he, as a true scribe, had time to acquire wisdom (see the reflection on labor and wisdom in Sir 38:24–34; see also 39:1–11; Ezra 7:10). Mark does not appear to differentiate sharply between Jesus' teaching and his proclamation (1:14, 38–39, 45), which may be due to the fact that this Gospel contemplated audiences both inside and outside the church (see above).

Unsurprisingly, Jesus commissioned his disciples to teach (3:14; 6:12, 30; 13:10) and upbraided the Pharisees and scribes, in the words of Isaiah 29:13, for "teaching human precepts as doctrines" (7:6–7; 12:38). Jesus not only teaches but stands against false instruction. In response, those who had set themselves as teachers among the Jewish people sought to trap him via his teaching (12:14, 19) but were unsuccessful. His teaching provoked the chief priests and teachers of the law to find a way to kill him (11:18). Jesus was deeply concerned that people would hear or receive his teaching (4:3, 9, 11–12, 15–16, 18, 20, 23–25, 33–34) since their destiny depended upon it. It is all about hearing and seeing (8:22–26; 10:46–52). Those who respond to his teaching become disciples or learners (4:34, and see below).

Mark is not devoid of teaching material and, at times, includes extensive sections of Jesus' instruction such as his parables of the kingdom (4:1–34) and the eschatological discourse (13:1–37). The Gospel comes short, however, of presenting a fulsome corpus of Jesus' oral teaching.[176] His preferred form of teaching among the crowds was to use parables (4:2, 11, 33–34), although he gave more direct teaching to the disciples and explained the parables to them (4:11, 13, 34; 7:17). Jesus' teaching, however, is not limited to his oral instruction, but also embraced his miraculous works, which proclaimed the same message of the kingdom (1:27; 6:2). The gospel of the kingdom of God came in both word and deed (1:14–15).[177] If we include the miracles as part

---

176. Martin, *Mark: Evangelist and Theologian*, 113. On the arrangement of the teaching material in Mark, see C. F. Evans, *The Beginning of the Gospel*, 49–53.

177. René Padilla, "Evangelism and the World," in *Let the Earth Hear His Voice: International Congress on World Evangelization Lausanne, Switzerland*, ed. J. D. Douglas (Minneapolis: World Wide, 1975), 116–45.

of Jesus' instruction regarding the kingdom of God, our evaluation of the amount of Jesus' teaching Mark includes will change considerably.

His teaching was authoritative and not derivative as that of the scribes (1:21–22), and so it caused tremendous astonishment among those who heard him and contributed to his overwhelming popularity (1:22; 6:2; 11:18; cf. 7:37). He consistently gave the authoritative interpretation of Scripture (2:23–3:6; 7:1–23; 10:1–12; 12:18–37) and places his words on a par with Scripture (13:31). Jesus shows an awareness that his words are divine instruction and so are authoritative and enduring. The line between his ministry as the Teacher and as the Prophet predicted by Moses (Deut 18:15, 18–19; Mark 9:7) blurs at this point as his prophetic and didactic ministries merge. The fact that Jesus is the Teacher occupies a significant place in his Christology if understood within the Gospel's theology of the New Exodus and the advent of the kingdom of God. Indeed, the Jewish community could regard the teacher as a station of greater honor than either king or priest ('Abot 6.6). Moreover, the story that Mark presents is itself a fulfillment of the commission of the Teacher that his disciples should teach and, at the same time, avoid the teaching that does not have God as its source. Jesus hands down his teaching to the disciples as they then carry out his teaching ministry in deed and word (6:6b–13, 30). Mark's Gospel is part of the process of handing down the authoritative teaching of Jesus, as both Matthew and Luke recognized.

The Rejected Stone

Mark presents Jesus as the Rejected Stone who then becomes the foundation for a new temple. The Stone theology stands as the counterpoint to the anti-temple polemic in the Gospel. In 11:15–19 Jesus comes to Jerusalem, enters the temple, and cleanses it by challenging the way it had been turned into an emporium. The temple's purpose was to be "a house of prayer for all the nations," but it had been turning into a place of injustice. Jesus shows his authority over the temple by driving out merchants and consumers alike, overturning the tables of those engaged in monetary exchange, and prohibiting carrying burdens through its precincts. Mark places the incident between the Parable of the Withered Fig Tree (11:12–14) and its interpretation (13:1–2). This sandwiching places the temple at the center of Jesus' prediction of coming judgment. The anti-temple polemic continues in 13:1–2, where Jesus predicts the building's destruction. This prediction later became a plank in the case against Jesus as a temple destroyer (14:49) and a cause for mockery (15:29). In the end, upon Jesus' death the temple veil is torn from top down (15:38), symbolizing at once the way God was bringing the present temple order to an end and opening a new way of access to him. The veil separated the Holy Place from the Most Holy Place and, according to Josephus, it was symbolic of the heavens (Exod 26:31–35; Josephus, *Ant.* 8.71–72; *BJ* 5.212–14). The older order is passing away, and a new means of access to God has begun as Jesus dies and the centurion recognizes him as the true Son of God (15:37–39). The term that Mark uses to describe the tearing of the curtain appears also at the very beginning of the Gospel, when John baptized Jesus. John saw "he heavens torn apart and the Spirit descending like a dove on him" (1:10). The temple curtain symbolized the heavens and now, access is opened to God through Jesus' death. A change in temple order is occurring.

Likewise, Mark connects the parable of the vineyard (12:1–12) with the temple. Jesus tells the story of the tenets who attempted to lay claim to the vineyard themselves in total disregard for the one who owned and planted it. They had leased it from him, but when the owner sent messengers they took and abused them. The first sent was a slave, who was beaten and dishonored (12:2–3). Then another slave was sent, who was killed upon arrival (12:4–5). Finally, the owner sent his "beloved son," who they likewise killed in order to gain his inheritance for themselves (12:6–8). At this point in the parable, the reader understands that the story is about Jesus, who has twice been proclaimed by God as "my Son, the Beloved" (1:11; 9:7). The parable becomes, in the first instance, part of the fabric of Mark's Christology about Jesus as the Suffering Son of God (see above).

But Jesus also joins the parable in 12:10–11 with Psalm 118:22–23, and in so doing merges the theology of the Son with the Stone testimony of the Psalm: "The stone that the builders rejected has become the cornerstone; this was the Lord's doing, and it is amazing in our eyes."[178] The "chief priest, the scribes, and the elders" who confronted Jesus in the temple (11:27; 12:1) rightly recognized that he had "told this parable against them" (12:12). Just previously he had leveled a stinging critique against their temple management by combining the New Exodus testimony of Isaiah 56:7[179] along with Jeremiah 7:11: "My house shall be called a house of prayer. . . . But you have made it a den of robbers" (Mark 11:17). Jesus has not only made an accusation against their labors in Jerusalem and in the temple on the behalf of the people, but he forwards the messianic claim that he, the one they have rejected by seeking to arrest and then kill him (12:12, 7), is the central figure in God's plan. Jesus' rule is placed as the counterpoint to their usurpation of authority. At the heart of the incident is this question of divine authority (11:27–33). John was commissioned by God and has his authority. Now Jesus is here, the one with the greater authority, which is likewise divine (1:7–8). He is the Son who has been sent by the owner of the vineyard and as such is the legitimate heir (12:6). But the readers of Mark would have also understood the parable and psalm as another testimony regarding the Son's rejection and exaltation. The Son will be rejected, but he will be vindicated by God: "This was the Lord's doing, and it is amazing in our eyes." Jesus' use of the passage anticipates the resurrection.

---

178. See R. J. McKelvey, "Christ the Cornerstone," *NTS* 8 (1962) 352–59; Bertil Gärtner, *The Temple and the Community at Qumran and the New Testament: A Comparative Study in the Temple Symbolism of the Qumran Texts and the NT* (Cambridge: Cambridge University Press, 1965), 133–36; J. Duncan M. Derrett, "The Stone Which the Builders Rejected," *SE* 4 (1968) 180–86; Marcus, *The Way of the Lord*, 111–29.

179. Watts, *Isaiah's New Exodus in Mark*, 319.

The parable of the wicked tenants and the stone testimony in 12:10–11 are set within the temple (11:27; 12:35, 41; 13:1) after Jesus' royal ride into Jerusalem and initial entries into the temple (11:11, 15). The temple setting helps account for the shift in the parable from the vineyard to the temple imagery of Psalm 118. Jesus contemplates the construction of the temple, in which God places the rejected stone as the essential building stone of the whole structure.[180] Once again, the literal setting becomes mixed with Mark's theological understanding. The citation of Psalm 118:22–23 contemplates a new temple, with Jesus as its foundation.[181] Psalm 118 appeared in Jewish tradition in relation to the construction of a new temple (*T. Sol.* 22:6–23:4). The Qumran scrolls associated "stone" texts with the community (1 QH 6:25–29; 7:8–9; 1 QS 8:4).[182] Along with other "stone passages" (Isa. 28:16; 8:14) it continued to occupy a central place in texts associated with Peter (Acts 4:11; 1 Pet 2:4–7; Acts Pet 24) and likely gave rise to Paul's use (Rom 9:33). In particular, Mark frames the whole within the anticipation of the coming of the Davidic king, whose entry into Jerusalem is hailed using the words of Psalm 118:25–26 (Mark 11:9–10).[183] Indeed, the Targum of Psalm 118:22 gives the text a Davidic interpretation: "The architects forsook the youth among the sons of Jesse, but he was worthy to be appointed king and ruler" (see *Tg. Psa.* 118:23–28). In other words, the Stone testimony from Psalm 118:22–23 in Mark 12:10–11 stands at the intersection of the hopes for the Messianic age, the beginning of the New Exodus, and the building of God's new temple, all while embracing the cross and resurrection of Jesus. The passage hints that the current order, administered by the "builders," will come to an end. Here the theological symphony builds to a breathtaking crescendo.

The new temple will embrace not only the Jewish people but "others" as well.[184] In his previous rebuke about temple management in 11:17, Jesus cites Isaiah 56:7, which opens the door to the inclusion of the Gentiles: "My house shall be called a house of prayer for all the nations." Mark sounds the same note about Gentile inclusion in 12:9: "He will come and destroy the tenants and give the vineyard to others." These "others" are defined by the previous reference to "all the nations" and, indeed, would have been a strong statement of inclusion for Mark's first Roman readers. Jesus, the Stone, is the one around whom the new community, consisting of both Jews and Gentiles,

---

180. The stone in 12:10 is "the head of the corner" (κεφαλὴν γωνίας), which may be either a foundation or elevated cornerstone, or it may be a keystone in an arch. See the discussion on 1 Pet 2:4–7. For our purposes here it suffices to observe that this was the essential building stone that had been rejected by the builders.

181. Nicholas Perrin suggests that Mark may even contemplate that Jesus will become the temple-builder (*Jesus the Temple* [Grand Rapids: Baker Academic, 2010], 104). For additional reflection on the temple in Mark's Gospel, see Telford, *The Barren Temple and the Withered Tree*; Timothy C. Gray, *The Temple in the Gospel of Mark: A Study in Its Narrative Role* (Tübingen: Mohr Siebeck, 2008).

182. Gärtner, *The Temple and the Community at Qumran and the New Testament*, 133–36.

183. The omitted sentence from the Psalm (118:26b) joins the whole with the temple: "We bless you from the house of the Lord." Hearers who knew the psalm would get the point.

184. Morna D. Hooker, *The Gospel According to Mark* (Peabody, MA: Hendrickson, 1991), 22; Marcus, *The Way of the Lord*, 123; France, *The Gospel of Mark*, 35.

is oriented. Although the universal rule of the Son of Man is not directly suggested in this passage, the development of the Stone testimony in Mark is consonant with the expectation at the heart of Daniel 7:13–14.[185] The Son of Man comes, and "to him was given dominion and glory and kingship, that all peoples, nations, and languages should serve him." While Psalm 118:10–12 speaks of the demise of the nations ("In the name of the Lord I cut them off! . . . In the name of the Lord I cut them off! . . . In the name of the Lord I cut them off!") that had oppressed the psalmist ("All nations surrounded me. . . . They surrounded me, surrounded me on every side. . . . They surrounded me like bees"), the psalm turns into a denunciation of the Jewish leadership in Mark (12:12) while it anticipates the new temple wherein the Gentiles will be welcome. The way is open for the Gentile mission.

Jesus the Priest

As noted above, Jesus is the foundation for a new temple, which opens the way to God for all the nations. Jesus not only cleanses the temple and predicted its destruction, but he also critiqued the practices carried on in its precincts that were under priestly supervision (11:15–19) and spoke the parable of the wicked tenants against them (12:1–12). While in the temple, the chief priests, scribes, and elders questioned his authority (11:27–33), after which he spoke against them in the parable. As Broadhead states, "Jesus represents a clear threat to their status and to their place."[186] On the other hand, Jesus is the one who opens the way to God through his death since he becomes the foundation for the new temple. We also encounter the language of priesthood. Mark portrays Jesus as one who engages in priestly service.[187] In Mark 7:1–23, for example, Jesus assumes priestly responsibilities: "He declares a leper clean, he offers God's forgiveness, he interprets Sabbath and food laws, he labours on the Sabbath."[188] Jesus also heals a leper and declares that he is cleaned (1:40–45), taking on the role of a priest who pronounced lepers clean (Lev 14:2–9). He also offers forgiveness to the paralytic (2:1–12) as would a priest who makes atonement for sin (Lev 16:29–34). Unlike the people who rest on the sabbath, the priest serves. In the same way, Jesus

---

185. Seyoon Kim suggests that we should read the Son of Man passage in Daniel 7:13–14 in the light of the previous testimony in Daniel 2:34–35, 45, regarding the "stone," thus suggesting the link between Daniel and Psalm 118 as well as the Servant of Yahweh section in Isaiah 42–53 ("Jesus-The Son of God, the Stone, the Son of Man, and the Servant: The Role of Zechariah in the Self-Identification of Jesus," in *Tradition and Interpretation in the New Testament: Essays in Honor of E. Earle Ellis for His 60th Birthday*, ed. Gerald F. Hawthorne and Otto Betz [Grand Rapids: Eerdmans, 1987], 134–48).

186. Edwin K. Broadhead, "Jesus and the Priests of Israel," in *Jesus from Judaism to Christianity:. Continuum Approaches to the Historical Jesus*, ed. Tom Holmén (London: T. & T. Clark, 2007), 132.

187. Edwin K. Broadhead, "Christology as Polemic and Apologetic: The Priestly Portrayal of Jesus in the Gospel of Mark," *JSNT* 47 (1992) 21–34; Edwin K. Broadhead, *Naming Jesus: Titular Christology in the Gospel of Mark* (Sheffield: Sheffield Academic, 1999), 63–74; Broadhead, "Jesus and the Priests of Israel," 133.

188. Broadhead, "Jesus and the Priests of Israel," 133.

heals on the sabbath as part of his ministry of doing good (3:1–6). Mark portrays Jesus as the one who does priestly service as a counterpoint to his polemic against the priesthood in Israel. He fulfills their function although he is rejected by them. In Mark, Jesus is both God's true priest and temple. Though not as highly developed as in Hebrews, the concept is present in this Gospel.

The Messiah's Revelation and Concealment

In his 1901 publication entitled *Das Messiasgeheimnis in den Evangelien*,[189] William Wrede observed that in the Gospel of Mark, Jesus repeatedly attempts to keep his identity a secret: "During his earthly life Jesus' messiahship is absolutely a secret and is supposed to be such; no one apart from the confidants of Jesus is supposed to learn about it; with the resurrection, however, its disclosure ensues."[190] But Wrede believed that the prohibitions were unhistorical. The church came to consider that Jesus was the Messiah and read back his messiahship into his life story. After an extended argument, Wrede concludes, "Thus hardly any possibility remains other than the suggestion that the idea of the secret arose at a time when as yet there was no knowledge of any messianic claim on the part of Jesus on earth; which is as much as to say at a time when the resurrection was regarded as the beginning of the messiahship." In other words, the secret messiahship of Jesus "did not merely arise *after* the future messiahship but out of it." The later church filled the life of Jesus with "*messianic content*." Wrede concludes that "*Jesus actually did not give himself out as messiah*."[191] The reasons for the messianic secret emphasis in Mark are, therefore, theological rather than historical.

Most studies on Mark discuss the messianic secret. All agree that the secrecy motif is a prominent aspect of Mark's Christology which, while most pronounced in Mark, is not entirely absent in Matthew and Luke.[192] They differ, however, on the reasons for and significance of this particular emphasis. The question remains whether it is proper to call this a specifically *Messianic* secret given the broad scope of the concealment theme in the Gospel, as Dunn notes. Moreover, Wrede's conclusion that the motif was read back into the life of Jesus, who did not himself claim to be the Messiah,

---

189. D. William Wrede, *Das Messiasgeheimnis in den Evangelien: Zugleich ein Beitrag zum Verständnis des Markusevangeliums* (Göttingen: Vandenhoeck & Ruprecht, 1901). English: *The Messianic Secret*, trans. J. C. G. Greig (Cambridge: James Clarke & Co., 1971).

190. William Wrede, *The Messianic Secret*, 68.

191. William Wrede, *The Messianic Secret*, 228–30.

192. See the bibliographies on the Messianic Secret in J. L. Blevins, *The Messianic Secret in Markan Research 1901–1976* (Washington: University Press of America, 1981); William R. Telford, *Writing on the Gospel of Mark* (Dorset, UK: Deo, 2009), 442–45. Commentaries, theologies, and articles provide ready summaries, for example, J. D. G. Dunn, "The Messianic Secret in Mark," *TB* 21 (1970) 92–117; Martin, *Mark: Evangelist and Theologian*, 91–97; Telford, *Theology of the Gospel of Mark*, 41–54; Marcus, *Mark 1–8*, 525–27; Edwards, *The Gospel According to Mark*, 63–65; Evans, *Mark 8:27–16:20*, lxx–lxxii.

has come under considerable criticism.[193] Back to back with the concealment theme is Mark's emphasis on Jesus' revelation. The Gospel highlights both of these within the frame of Jesus' ministry. Any theory that seeks to account for the secrecy motif must also embrace the topic of revelation.

In Mark we find from the start that Jesus frequently required no one should announce publicly what had occurred (1:40–45; 5:35–43; 7:31–37; 8:22–26). Jesus' disciples are told not to disclose the revelations about his person that they had heard and seen (8:27–30; 9:2–10). Demons are commanded to be silent, although they knew who he was (1:21–26, 32–34; 3:7–12). Instead of seeking fame, Jesus withdraws from the crowds (1:35–37; 6:30–32, 45–46; 7:24, 33; 8:23; 9:30). When there are disclosures or revelations, the audience is sometimes limited. He gives a private interpretation of the parables to his disciples (4:10–12, 33–34; 7:17–23), instructs them privately about their inability to cast out a demon (9:28–29), reveals himself in the transfiguration to the select three (9:2–8), and gives a considerable amount of private teaching to the disciples (9:30–50; 13:3–37). The efforts to maintain privacy and conceal himself are not fully successful, however. The crowds continue to gather; he cannot escape their notice (6:31–34; 7:24–25; 10:1), and those he told not to tell do tell (1:43–45; 7:36–37). He rejects the demand to give a sign (8:11–13) and refuses to reveal the source of his authority (11:27–33). Jesus holds his cards close.

On the other hand, there is a considerable amount of open revelation occurring in this story, and not just for those who are listening to or reading the narrative. The whole is about the open proclamation of the kingdom of God, which begins with the public announcement by John in the wilderness (1:4–8) and is then taken up by Jesus as he begins his itinerant ministry (1:14–15). On various occasions Jesus does not call for secrecy (2:1–12; 3:1–6). He even exhorts the liberated demoniac to proclaim what had happened to him (5:14–20). While Peter and the other disciples are told not to tell that he is the Messiah (8:27–30), he publicly confesses that he is the Messiah before the High Priest and the council (14:61–62) and does not seek to conceal his identity from Pilate (15:1–5). He does miracles and even forgives openly (2:1–11; 3:1–6; 6:53–56; 8:1–10; 10:46–52) and teaches publicly (6:1–13). There is no mistaking who he is when he rides into Jerusalem (11:1–10). Mark recounts the attempts to conceal who Jesus is through silencing demons, telling people not to report miracles, and limiting what his disciples may disclose. On the other hand, the crowds had heard and seen enough so that they flocked to him. In the end, the accusations against him were based on his public pronouncements (14:53–65). This was, in Lesslie Newbigin's words, a very "open secret."[194]

Wrede has explained the so-called "messianic secret" by saying that its roots are theological, not historical. I would suggest that the theme of concealment and

---

193. Dunn, "The Messianic Secret in Mark," 93–110.

194. Lesslie Newbigin, *The Open Secret: An Introduction to the Theology of Mission* (London: SPCK, 1995).

revelation that has Jesus as its main object is both historical and theological in nature. Mark writes his Gospel on the basis of Peter's testimony, and so we expect that the document traces genuine historical occurrences. But these events are interpreted, as is the case in all testimony. The rhetorical concerns of the one who offers the testimony is the stuff of theology. The blind see and the reader understands. So, too, with the theme of concealment and revelation. On the first layer, Jesus calls for secrecy and withdraws as a means of crowd control. Over and again Mark links concealment with the need to manage the throngs that constantly gathered to have their needs filled in a world where resources were truly scarce. So when the leper who was healed went out and, contrary to Jesus' command, announced his healing, the result was that "Jesus could no longer go into a town openly" (1:45). He had a mission to complete, and were he controlled by the crowd's demands he could not spread the message of the kingdom as thoroughly as he did (1:37–39). He also attempted to help the disciples avoid the fatigue that came with responding to the crowd's demands (6:31). Jesus occasionally took a particular person in need away from the crowd to perform his healing (7:33; 8:23). His attempts at crowd control, however, were not very successful, but he consistently responded to those who managed to reach him (6:30–34; 7:24–30). The "messianic secret" in Mark is about crowd management in the face of Jesus' immense popularity. But it also reveals for the reader how exceptional and noteworthy Jesus' life and ministry were.

On a second historical level, Mark demonstrates over and again how Jesus consistently redefined the category of messiahship. He called himself the heavenly Son of Man of Daniel 7 and merged this title with images of the Suffering Servant. In the same way, while accepting the title "Christ" when Peter confessed him as such, he redefined the concept in terms of his suffering and death. "Christ crucified" is a Pauline oxymoron that captures Mark's theology well. The secrecy surrounding the particular confession of Peter is most noteworthy since the concept "Messiah" was extremely charged and would have been one most difficult to redefine publicly. Jesus repeatedly gives the disciples insight into his messiahship through the announcements of his impending death and resurrection (8:31–33; 9:30–32; 14:22–25). Unsurprisingly, the "messianic secret" becomes public just before and during Jesus' crucifixion. He rides into Jerusalem as the kingly Son of David (11:1–11), confesses that he is the Messiah openly before the high priest and the council (14:61–62), and intimates the same to Pilate (15:2). He is crucified publicly with the inscription stating the charge against him declaring to all that he is "The King of the Jews" (15:26). The messianic message is complete at the end of the story. The Messiah suffers and dies, and the centurion embraces this confusing juxtaposition (15:39). Significantly, the bulk of the material in Mark on concealment occurs before the final events leading up to the cross. So the "messianic secret" becomes Jesus' means of redefining the nature of his messianic ministry in the face of existing expectations about the Messiah's role as found in texts like Psalms of Solomon 17–18. We should not overstate, however, his attempt to avoid the political statements since Jesus repeatedly made claims that challenged the *imperium* of Rome. The proclamation of the "kingdom of God," the gathering of disciples and crowds that followed Jesus, and Jesus' own demonstrations of power placed him within the frame of the well-known revolutionaries that arose during the era. And for the readers/hearers in Rome, the centurion's words were a direct challenge to imperial claims.

The theme of concealment and revelation holds another theological dimension. It characterizes something essential within Jesus' ministry: the way those who are inside receive and understand his revelation while those on the outside do not. The crux here is his statement about the parables of the kingdom, which becomes paradigmatic for the whole of his approach to concealment and revelation: "To you has been given the secret of the kingdom of God, but for those outside, everything comes in parables," after which he quotes Isaiah 6:9–10 (Mark 4:10–12). The irony in Mark runs along this same line. The public inscription that mocks him as "the King of the Jews" reveals the truth. Only the one inside understands this. Hiddenness and concealment are the counterpoints to openness and revelation, and the road between them is the way of faith and discipleship. One "sees" if one has faith, as Bartimaeus son of Timaeus reminds us. If someone believes, they see that the crucified Jew is truly the Son of God. This is not magic, which maintains itself through a studied attempt to keep secrets hidden.[195] Through the theme of concealment and revelation Mark presents the reader with an essential element of Christian understanding about how God interacts with humanity. His theology is woven together tightly with his history. The two cannot be separated—a lesson for those who would deny the historical, as did Wrede, and for those who affirm the historical but fail to move beyond it.

Peter's Christology in Mark

Peter's Christology in the Gospel of Mark is intimately tied with the overarching themes of the New Exodus and the kingdom of God. Jesus is the anticipated Messiah who acts as the deliverer for his people as he shows his authority in kingly acts. The Gospel emphasizes Jesus' kingship through a variety of titles, from Son of Man to Son of God. The level of Jesus' kingly authority is extraordinary as we see him cast out demons, calm the sea, and deliver from disease. He teaches with authority and commissions his disciples to spread his revolutionary message and power. The character of his royal office cannot be contained, however, in any one extant category. Each of the images of his kingship expressed through various titles becomes subject to change and modification, especially as they are joined with Jesus' sufferings and crucifixion. He is the Suffering Servant King. After Peter recognizes that he is the

---

195. See, for example, Georg Luck, *Arcana Mundi: Magic and the Occult in the Greek and Roman Worlds* (Baltimore: Johns Hopkins University Press, 1985), 23; Georg Luck, *Ancient Pathways and Hidden Pursuits: Religion, Morals, and Magic in the Ancient World* (Ann Arbor: University of Michigan Press, 2000).

Christ, Jesus declares his rejection, crucifixion, and resurrection. After Jesus enters into Jerusalem in royal procession, he is taken, tried, and crucified. The juxtaposition of his kingship and cross becomes the central message of the book, which Mark begins to announce in the opening verse and which the centurion proclaimed as he bears witness to Jesus' death: "Truly this man was God's son!" (15:39) Mark steers near to the Johannine understanding of the cross as Jesus' hour of glorification. In one go the centurion's proclamation lays out a challenge to Roman imperial claims and redefines Jewish expectations regarding the Messiah's work. In Mark, Herod is not the genuine king; Jesus is the true royal who offers a miraculous banquet. Jesus is not John raised from the dead; John is the harbinger of the one who is the coming Lord of the New Exodus. Both Herod and John serve as foils to help the reader understand more fully who Jesus is. Although he is the King crucified, he is also the one who conquers death. Mark anticipates Jesus' resurrection through the miracles when Jesus raised the dead and through Herod's musing that perhaps Jesus is John raised.

The final theme in this christological symphony, however, is the testimony of the man in white ("He has been raised; he is not here"), and the invitation to become a witness there at the tomb ("Look, there is the place they laid him") and in Galilee ("There you will see him"; 16:6–7). The Gospel ends with the invitation to "see," and so ends the theme of concealment that has occupied much of Markan research. There is promise and hope at the end, which calls for faith on the part of the women who came to the tomb (16:1), of the wider body of disciples, and of Mark's readers. The ending is redemptive even for Peter, the one who fails ("But go, tell his disciples and Peter"). He offers his personal and poignant testimony, remembered for us in Mark.

SOTERIOLOGY IN MARK
Jesus' Rule and Salvation

The message of salvation Peter proclaims in Mark begins with the announcement of the kingdom of God and the theology of the New Exodus. Any reflection on how this Gospel envisions Jesus Christ's salvific work must begin here. The New Exodus and the kingdom's advent center upon the person of Jesus Christ and his conquest of demons, disease, and death, culminating in his own death and subsequent resurrection. Since Mark inextricably binds the message of salvation with the overarching themes of the Gospel and with the person of Jesus, most of the observations made up to this point about his theology may be subsumed under the category of soteriology. The whole is about how God brings deliverance and order to the chaos of this world through the person of Jesus Christ. Jesus is the beloved Son whom God has sent (Mark 12:6; 1:11; 9:7) to save through healing (3:4; 5:28, 34; 6:56; 10:52), by rebuking demons (1:25; 9:25) and winds of disaster (4:38–39), and in rescuing people from death (5:23). He keeps people from perishing from demons or disaster (9:22; 4:38), both present signs that he is the one who can keep people from perishing eternally (8:35). His acts of salvation as the King of the kingdom of God are of one piece with the ultimate salvation that he offers those who come to him (8:35; 10:26; 13:13). By virtue of the advent of the kingdom of God and the New Exodus, which has begun in the person of Jesus, salvation has come. Mark testifies to his liberating power repeatedly and so reveals just who Jesus is. Demons, disaster, disease, and death are no match for him. But the way that he accomplishes this ultimate salvation is not simply through his acts of power that flow from his person but by losing his own life (15:30–31). He perishes so that others may live. This constitutes salvation as Mark understands it and as Peter preached it. It is bound with both his power and being overpowered.

Jesus' Sufferings and Salvation

The central expression of the kingdom of God and Jesus' royal rule, demonstrated in his deeds and teaching, is found in Peter's confession: "You are the Messiah" (8:29). The reader knows Jesus as the Christ from the beginning (1:1) and has seen through the miracles and teaching that he is indeed the one who exercises messianic authority. The array of titles used to describe Jesus before the confession point the reader toward Peter's theology: Jesus is the beloved Son of God, the Son of Man, the Lord who comes in his way, and the Holy One of God. The hearer of the text is not surprised when Peter makes the messianic confession—we were waiting for it. Mark does not preserve Jesus' response save for the call not to disseminate the news that he was the Messiah (8:30). Although he enjoins the disciples not to tell anyone that he is the Messiah, the prohibition is an assent to and not a denial of Peter's confession. Matthew, however, elaborates on the assent (Matt 16:17). In the face of the confession, Jesus announces his forthcoming suffering, rejection, death, and resurrection: "Then he began to teach them that the Son of Man must undergo great suffering, and be rejected by the elders, the chief priests, and the scribes, and be killed, and after three days rise again" (8:31). Over and again in Mark, Jesus connects the royal titles with the proclamation of his deadly demise and subsequent defeat of death. Even the centurion is able to recognize Jesus as the Son of God when he breathes his last (15:39). His confession coalesces with the Father's confession at Jesus' baptism and transfiguration (1:11; 9:7). Mark's readers also anticipate the white robed young man's announcement, "He has been raised" (16:6). The facts of his suffering, death, and resurrection occupy much of the narrative, but what does it all mean? How does Mark understand the significance of the sufferings, crucifixion, and resurrection of Jesus? Are these just the "facts on the ground" that become the raw data for subsequent Christian theology, or does Mark's Gospel theologize on the meaning of these events? Does Mark have a theology of salvation and the cross?[196]

---

196. See, for example, Bolt, *Jesus' Defeat of Death*; Bolt, *The Cross from a Distance*; Kelli S. O'Brien, *The Use of Scripture in the Markan Passion Narrative* (London: T. & T. Clark, 2010).

Mark 10:45 offers the clearest statement of Mark's theology of the cross: "For the Son of Man came not to be served but to serve, and to give his life a ransom for many." As Marcus says, 10:45 "is of central importance in Mark's narrative because it is the clearest Markan reflection on the saving purpose of Jesus' death (cf. 14:24)."[197] But this explanation of the meaning of Christ's death, which we will return to later, by no means stands alone as the theological unveiling of the event. Mark's theology of salvation through the cross develops through various explanations of Jesus' death, including both statements and symbolic acts and times. The first announcement of Jesus' death points the way not only to the fact of his demise but also to the theological meaning of the event. Jesus taught the disciples that he, as the Son of Man, "must undergo great suffering" (8:31). Jesus understands his suffering, as well as his rejection, death, and resurrection, as a divine necessity (δεῖ, "it is necessary"). These all are part of the fabric of salvation and not a twisted form of divine abuse of the Son by the Father. What Jesus endured was not a mere travesty of justice either, an unfortunate string of circumstances, or even the outworking of destiny, but part of the divine plan for him and for us. Elsewhere this understanding of his sufferings and death finds expression in the affirmation that the Scriptures are being fulfilled. What was predicted by divinely inspired canonical authors is now coming to pass: "How then is it written about the Son of Man, that he is to go through many sufferings and be treated with contempt" (9:12; so 14:21, 49). What stands written (γέγραπται) indeed comes to pass since God has planned and spoken it, revealing his will to the biblical writer.[198] A surprising expression, the divine plan appears in the quotation from Zechariah 13:7, which was reworked to show God's plan being worked out in Jesus' sufferings and death: "I will strike the shepherd" (Mark 14:27; see above on "The Shepherd of Israel").[199] Before his betrayal, Jesus prayed in a garden called Gethsemane for the removal of the "cup" from him, but concedes, "not what I want, but what you want" (14:36; cf. Matt 6:10). Were there another way to accomplish this salvation, Jesus would welcome it. But as there was not, he submitted completely to the Father's will. The divine plan and the Son of God's subordination to it are central to Mark's understanding of the cross. Salvation would not come simply by an exercise of power but through a loss of everything, even life. Jesus willingly embraces that plan that God has ordained. Suffering and salvation run on the same rails.

In Mark 8:31 we discover that the Son of Man must "suffer many things" (NIV) (πολλὰ παθεῖν; see 9:12). Mark's theology of redemption includes Jesus' sufferings and not only his death. These, as his death, were predicted and part of the divine will in carrying out the plan of redemption (see above). The sufferings to which Mark

---

197. Marcus, *Mark 8–16*, 757.

198. Marcus, *The Way of the Lord*, 96–97; Marcus, *Mark 8–16*, 645.

199. The rejected stone prophecy of Psalm 118:22–23 in Mark 12:10–11 likewise includes a statement of divine agency: "this was the Lord's doing." Stein suggests that this is a reference perhaps not only to his vindication but his rejection as well (*Mark*, 538).

refers are not limited to being nailed to the cross; they began sooner in the narrative. As Evans notes, the sufferings included all the adversities he faced as enumerated in 10:33–34: "The Son of Man will be handed over to the chief priests and the scribes, and they will condemn him to death; then they will hand him over to the Gentiles; and they will mock him, and spit on upon him, and flog him" (cf. 14:43–15:37).[200] The composite picture of his sufferings includes the physical blows that he endured and also the intense humiliation of having been accused and condemned falsely, being forsaken by the disciples and even denied by Peter, the mocking and derision, being stripped and humiliated both before and then during the time when he hung upon the cross. Within the frame of *minjung* theology, Jesus experienced han. As Park says, "When the heart is hurt so much, it ruptures symbolically; it aches. When the aching heart is wounded again by external violence, the victim suffers yet a deeper pain. The wound produced by such repeated abuse and injustice is *han* in the heart."[201] Jesus' han, or sufferings, were social and physical, and included the agony of dereliction also as he cried out in the lament of Psalm 22:1, "My God, my God, why have you forsaken me?" (15:34). When being prepped for crucifixion, he endured dishonor and shame, as well as the flagellation that ripped his flesh bone-deep.[202] Those crucified "draw the breath of life amid long-drawn-out agony" (Seneca, *Epistulae Morales ad* Lucilium, 101.14) since "the cross tortures for a long time those who are fixed to it" (Isidore of Seville, *Etymologia* 5.27.34; Apuleius, *Metam*. 8.22.5). The suffering before and during crucifixion was unrivaled by other means of torture.

But the sufferings, as his death, were not only about injustice but identified him in word and deed as the Suffering Servant of Isaiah: "He was despised and rejected by other; a man of suffering and acquainted with infirmity; and as one from whom others hide their faces he was despised, and we held him of no account" (Isa 53:3). As the Suffering Servant and Righteous Sufferer of the Psalms, his sufferings and humiliation were predicted in Scripture (9:12; cf. Ps 22:7; Isa 53:3; Acts 3:18; 1 Pet 1:10), a fact which Peter came to understand well. As the Son of Man of Daniel 7, he not only has dominion but becomes identified with his people, who themselves suffer at the hands of the "fourth beast" (Dan 7:23–25).[203] The suffering of the one is tied with the sufferings of the many. Mark presents a vivid picture of the glorious Son of God who

---

200. Evans, *Mark 8:27–16:20*, 16. Evans mentions the interesting parallel in the Testament of Moses 3:11, which says that Moses "suffered many things ... in Egypt and at the Red Sea and in the wilderness for forty years." But the sufferings in these Markan passages are oriented to the Suffering Servant and not Moses.

201. Andrew S. Park, *The Wounded Heart of God: The Asian Concept of Han and the Christian Doctrine of Sin* (Nashville: Abingdon, 1993), 20; Byung-Mu Ahn, "Jesus and the Minjung in the Gospel of Mark," in *Voices from the Margins*, ed. R. S. Sugirtharajah (Maryknoll, NY: Orbis, 1997) 85–104.

202. Plato, *Gorg*. 473B–C; *Res*. 361E–362A; Dio Chrysostom 4.67; Philo, *Flaccus* 72; Josephus, *J.W.* 2.306; 5.449–551; Hengel, *Crucifixion in the Ancient World and the Folly of the Message of the Cross*, 22–32.

203. Marcus, *Mark 8–16*, 613.

is transfigured before the three disciples (9:1–8) but also of the Suffering Servant who endures humiliation, grief, and deep pain before vindication. The Suffering Servant is, then, the one who "has borne our infirmities and carried our diseases" as "he was wounded for our transgressions, crushed for our iniquities" (Isa 53:4–5). The point is not simply that he is the predicted sufferer but the Suffering Servant who bears the others' pain and punishment. The suffering and death are vicarious or "place-taking" as he was "stricken for the transgression of my people" (53:8).[204] While Mark does not play out all the implications of the identification of Jesus as the Suffering Servant in this Gospel, he points to those text that help the hearer understand what she or he hears. He is also the Righteous Sufferer of the Psalms of Lament, with Psalm 22 playing a significant role in the discourse.[205] Psalm 22 not only expressed the lament of dereliction but also the promise of salvation: "In you our ancestors trusted; they trusted, and you delivered them. To you they cried, and were saved; in you they trusted, and were not put to shame" (22:4–5). The sufferings of Christ, insofar as Mark understands them in terms of the psalm, are surprisingly filled with the hope in God's salvation, which resolves the dissonant notes of lament.[206]

In Mark 8:31 Jesus furthermore tells the disciples that he, as the Son of Man, must "be rejected by the elders, the chief priest, and the scribes." As noted above, he explains this rejection in the Parable of the Wicked Tenants (12:1–2), which he then interprets in light of Psalm 118:22–23. He is the stone the builders rejected but has now become the principle building stone. That psalm is foreshadowed in 8:31 and finds its primary fulfillment in 14:1—15:1 as Jesus is taken, tried, and handed over by the "builders" in the nation (cf. 1 Pet 2:4). The reader becomes aware with Pilate that the motivation of the "builders" was self-interest: "For he realized that it was out of jealousy that the chief priests had handed him over" (15:10). The rejection identifies Jesus as the principle Stone in God's building, the temple, whom God honors after the humiliation of rejection. The leaders act as representatives of the whole as they stir the chorus of the crowd to call for his crucifixion (15:11). "Ask for Barabbas, the murderous insurrectionist instead of the King." The rejection speaks of the dishonor and also anticipates the vindication of Christ by God. He, then, is placed as the principle building Stone in God's temple. This is the temple that God constructs, but the reader sees from 8:31 onward that the way God will do this is through the irony of rejection by those charged with building. They tested Jesus but did not approve him; they should have honored him as the Son but did not (12:6). God tested Jesus and found him worthy of great honor. The way Jesus frames the rejection in terms of Psalm 118:22–23 means also that the way the builders dishonored him anticipates the vindication or resurrection of Jesus. On a first hearing, this was not evident, as Peter's initial response

---

204. Bolt, *The Cross from a Distance*, 132.

205. O'Brien, *The Use of Scripture in the Markan Passion Narrative*, 68–74, 76–96.

206. Craig A. Evans, *Mark 8:27–16:20*, 507; Donahue and Harrington, *The Gospel of Mark*, 451; France, *The Gospel of Mark*, 652–53.

showed (8:32). But it became abundantly evident to the apostle upon reflecting on Jesus' words (1 Pet 2:4–8). Rejection by the builders and resurrection by the Builder were conjoined realities in Mark's theology of salvation.

The penultimate note in Mark 8:31 is that the Son of Man must "be killed." This killing was done on the road outside Jerusalem, out on an ancient Highway 61,[207] where all could witness as they passed by. As Paul said, "this was not done in a corner" (Acts 26:26). The announcement in 8:31 to the disciples comes as no surprise to the reader since the controversies and questions about Jesus have been mounting up to this point. The plot to destroy him was hatched early (ἀπόλλυμι in 3:6 and later in 11:18). Mark has also carefully underlined the relationship between the harbinger, John, and Jesus, whom he heralds. John was vocal and was jailed by Herod Antipas, who was maneuvered into killing John by beheading (6:17–29) as Pilate was pressured into killing Jesus (15:6–15). Mark discloses the confusion about Jesus' identity by showing how "King" Herod surmised that Jesus was John raised from the dead (6:14–16). John's death and the speculation about Jesus' identity serve to prepare the reader for the announcement in 8:31 and Jesus' subsequent reiterations that he would be killed and Mark's disclosure of the plot to carry that out (9:31; 10:34; 11:18; 14:1). In the parable of the Wicked Tenants, the son who the tenants kill stands for Jesus himself (12:5, 7, 8). Killing someone in that place at that time is no remarkable event. In his *Jewish Wars*, Josephus records, almost casually, the slaughter of countless people during the first century up through the mass suicide at Masada. The surprise is that Jesus' death captured anyone's attention and its story survived for millennia. The theological significance of this killing is what turns this from common occurrence into the story of redemption besides which all others are shadows when compared to it. Mark notes, first off, that the killing was done to an innocent since there was no justification for it beyond envy (φθόνον) and a desire to placate popular demand (15:6–15).[208]

Mark notes that the killing took place at the time of the Passover (14:1–2, 12, 14, 16), also the time of the festival of Unleavened Bread. During this festival the custom was to grant clemency to a prisoner (15:6), but Jesus was not the one chosen for this act of mercy.[209] The Passover was the time when the Jews sacrificed the Passover lamb and ate the meal that commemorated the Exodus (14:12; Exod 12:1–32). Only unleavened bread was consumed at this time in memory of the hasty retreat out of Egypt (Exod 12:15–20; 13:6–7; Deut 16:1–8; 1 Esd 1:19; Josephus, *Ant*. 14.21; 17.213). The Passover initiated the Exodus out of Egypt and then became the paradigm for the anticipated New Exodus that God would bring to pass. The festival was filled with

---

207. Bob Dylan, "Highway 61 Revisited."

208. A. C. Hagedorn and Jerome H. Neyrey, "'It Was Out of Envy That They Handed Jesus Over' (Mark 15:10): The Anatomy of Envy and the Gospel of Mark," *JSNT* 69 (1998) 15–56.

209. Robert L. Merritt, "Jesus Barabbas and the Paschal Pardon," *JBL* 104 (1985) 57–68. Although Merritt rejects the historicity of Mark's account, he chronicles the models from the ancient world that frame the event in this Gospel within a known custom. His skepticism is not entirely warranted.

expectation of a new deliverance (Hos 6:1–2; Mark 14:1), especially as the city of Jerusalem swelled in population for this event.[210] Redemption occurred through the Passover sacrifice as the Israelites were protected from death through the blood of the Passover lamb (Exod 12:21–27). During the subsequent yearly celebration of the Passover, the Hallel was sung (Ps 113–118), "whose main themes are praise and thanksgiving for deliverance, both national and personal."[211] The timing of Jesus' death fills the cross with the meaning of the Passover event as Mark portrays Jesus as the new Passover Lamb, whose killing means redemption. If the timing of the event were not enough to secure the theological connection, Mark notes that Jesus took the Passover *seder* with his disciples and identified himself with both the wine and the bread, which recalled the horror and liberation of the first Exodus (14:22–25). The Passover lamb killed is now Jesus (cf. Ezra 6:20; 1 Esd 1:1, 6). The New Exodus deliverance has now begun.

The Passover *seder* began with questions posed by the youngest family member: "Why is this night different from other nights?"[212] In response the father or, as in the case of Mark 14:17–21, the host Jesus rehearses the story of the Exodus, beginning with the words, "A wandering Aramean was my father" (*m. Pes.* 10.4; Deut 26:5–9).[213] An explanation of the elements in the symbolic meal was offered to all gathered. In this meal the bread is Jesus' body, which he then offers to the disciples: "Take; this is my body" (14:22; σῶμά). The words of institution are surprisingly stark when heard by ears accustomed listening to the fuller, theologically charged language found elsewhere (Luke 22:19; 1 Cor. 11:24; John 6:51). The reserve and simplicity makes this a compelling testimony that, according to the later biblical tradition, is latent with meaning.[214] The unleavened bread, called the "bread of affliction," recalled the hasty redemption from Egypt (Deut. 16:3; *m. Pes.* 10.5). Jesus broke the bread, as he would be broken for redemption. As Stein, following Gundry, points out, "The close association

---

210. Marcus, *Mark 8–16*, 938. Marcus says, "Ceremony commemorated a great and joyful event of liberation in the past and anticipated an ever greater and more joyful one in the future" (*Mark 8–16*, 966). On the festival and the swell of crowds in Jerusalem, see E. Sanders, *Judaism: Practice and Belief 63 BC–66 CE* (Philadelphia: Trinity, 1992), 132–38. Roman nerves were on edge.

211. Sanders, *Judaism*, 135.

212. For a discussion of the meal as a Passover feast, see Joachim Jeremias, *The Eucharistic Words of Jesus* (London: SCM, 1966), 41–62, 84–88. On the words of institution, see his discussion as well. Jeremias argues that "the *Markan tradition* is linguistically the most ancient one" but that the Markan and Pauline/Lukan forms go back to a common source in Aramaic or Hebrew (*The Eucharistic Words of Jesus*, 186–91).

213. For a brief description, see Stein, *Mark*, 649–50.

214. *How* the bread and wine *are* Jesus' body and blood has given subsequent theologians a considerable opportunity for reflection and debate. I would suggest that in Mark's symbolic world, to level the event down to a mere symbolic representation would be to under-read his theology. Events are more pregnant with meaning than that in Mark, and events also connect on a deeper level than anticipation and symbolism. The resurrection of a young girl is part of the fabric of Jesus' resurrection, for example. Healing the eyes is a revelatory event. Mark is more about continuity and identification than simple symbolism.

of the cup with the bread indicates that 'body' should be interpreted in light of the sacrificial imagery of Mark 14:24."[215] The body of Jesus soon hung on the cross during the Passover.

Joseph of Arimathea, who himself was a member of the council, asked for his body (σῶμα) and then "laid it in a tomb that had been hewn out of the rock. He then rolled a stone against the door of the tomb" (καὶ ἔθηκεν αὐτὸν ἐν μνημείῳ ὃ ἦν λελατομημένον ἐκ πέτρας καὶ προσεκύλισεν λίθον ἐπὶ τὴν θύραν τοῦ μνημείου [15:43–46]). The "stone" imagery is vivid in this passage: Jesus's body is laid in a rock tomb and a stone seals the door, all arranged ironically by one of the very "builders" in the nation, who expected the coming kingdom of God and did not reject the Stone (cf. 12:10). While the extensive description of Jesus' burial may be explained simply with reference to archaeology and Jewish burial customs, the cacophony of imagery that is familiar to Mark's readers brings theology into the process of disposing his body, as also when the disciples are given the bread that is his body. Within the frame of Mark's theology, the body of Jesus anticipated the New Exodus, was killed in sacrifice, and became the rejected stone.

He also offered the cup of wine all drank from as he said to them, "This is my blood of the covenant, which is poured out for many" (14:24). The Passover meal was traditionally celebrated with four cups of wine passed around among the participants. Jesus identifies the wine that he shares with the disciples as the "blood of the covenant." While the symbolism of the meal evokes the theological realities of the Passover and Exodus, the language Jesus employs as he passes the cup draws from Exodus 24:8 when Moses instituted the covenant between God and his people: "Moses took the blood and dashed it on the people, and said, 'See the blood of the covenant that the Lord has made with you in accordance with all these words'" (cf. Zech 9:11). The sacrifice, here of oxen, results in a pouring out of blood, part of which is showered over God's people to seal the covenant. The wine of Jesus' supper now stands in representation of his own sacrifice to seal this new covenant that had been promised by God, a point made explicit in later eucharistic texts (Luke 22:20; 1 Cor 11:25). This is the covenant anticipated in Jeremiah 31:31–34 and fulfilled in Jesus' sacrifice (2 Cor 3:6; Heb 8:8, 13; 9:15; 12:24). Once again, Mark's description of the event is stark and does not explicitly state that this is a "new" covenant.[216] The informed reader would understand, however, that this is the covenant that had been anticipated by Jeremiah, and that Jesus' "blood of the covenant," which will be shed, establishes it. But Exodus 24:8 was also understood in the Targumim Onqelos and Psuedo-Jonathan as being an atoning sacrifice. This aspect of Jesus' "blood of the covenant" has been woven into the fabric of Mark's theology.[217] This is more than a conjecture since Jesus' words

---

215. Stein, *Mark*, 650; Gundry, *Mark*, 831.

216. Although some mss., such as A, but the weight of the testimony favors its exclusion. See Metzger, *A Textual Commentary on the Greek New Testament*, 95.

217. Tg. Onq Exod. 24:8: "Whereupon Moses took the blood and sprinkled it *on the altar to atone*

additionally join this Passover *seder* with the language of the Suffering Servant in Isaiah 53:12, which points to atonement. His blood of the covenant, represented in the wine, "is poured out for many" (τὸ ἐκχυννόμενον ὑπὲρ πολλῶν) as with the Servant, who "bore the sin of many" (αὐτὸς ἁμαρτίας πολλῶν ἀνήνεγκεν). Indeed, the word "poured out" evokes the language of atonement through sacrifice (cf. Lev 4:7, 18, 25, 30, 34; 8:15; 9:9).[218] The cup Jesus offers the disciples brings together the theology of the covenant and atonement, all bound together with the sacrifice of the Servant and the theme of God's New Exodus.

The most well-known statement of the theological meaning of Jesus' death appears in 10:45: "For the Son of Man came not to be served but to serve, and to give his life a ransom for many." The statement functions, in the first instance, as a call to the *imitatio Christi* in discipleship (see below). Those who are in leadership are not to be like the Gentiles who oppress others even with violence, acting like slave masters (κατακυριεύουσιν αὐτῶν: cf. 1 Pet 5:3), nor should they seek to have dominion or act tyrannically over others (κατεξουσιάζουσιν αὐτῶν).[219] Rather, the great disciple is one who serves others as would a low slave (10:42–44). In this context, Jesus forwards his own example as one that they should follow. He, as the Son of Man who has dominion and authority, comes not to be served but to serve. As noted in the section on the Son of Man, Jesus turns the vision of Daniel 7:14 inside out. Instead of being one who is "given dominion and glory and kingship, that all ... should serve him," Jesus comes with authority yet serves "all peoples, nations, and languages." He acts as a slave in this regard ("And whoever wishes to be first among you must be slave of all" [10:44]) since his mission is to serve others.

The second clause of 10:45 brings us to the heart of Mark's theology of the cross, although this is not the only place where he reveals the theological significance of Jesus' death. The Son of Man came to serve "and to give his life a ransom for many" (δοῦναι τὴν ψυχὴν αὐτοῦ λύτρον ἀντὶ πολλῶν). As in the institution of the covenantal meal (14:24; see above), the death of Jesus is "for many," harkening back to the Servant's sacrifice in Isaiah 53:11–12: "The righteous one, my servant, shall make many righteous," and "he bore the sin of many."[220] He gives his life in death as the Servant

---

for the people, and he said, '*Here, this* is the blood of the covenant which the Lord has established with you in accordance with all these words." Tg. Ps.-J. Exod. 24:8: "Then Moses took *the half of* the blood *that was in the dashing-basins* and dashed (it) *against the altar to make atonement for* the people; and he said, 'Behold, *this is* the blood of the covenant which the Lord has made with you in accordance with all these words.'" See Marcus, *Mark 8–16*, 966.

218. Evans, *Mark 8:27–16:20*, 394.

219. Evans, *Mark 8:27–16:20*, 118; Marcus, *Mark 8–16*, 784; *BDAG*, 519, 531; *LSJ*, 924.

220. For a discussion of the dependency of Mark 10:45 on Isaiah 53:10–12, see Douglas J. Moo, *The Old Testament in the Gospel Passion Narratives* (Sheffield: Almond, 1983), 122–27. O'Brien, however, doubts the allusion in her comprehensive attempt to bring into question this and other connections between Mark and Isa 52:13–53:12 (*The Use of Scripture in the Markan Passion Narrative*, 84–87). O'Brien's methodology, however, is too narrow since allusions may be both verbal and conceptual. As in all communication, the lexemes themselves suggest larger conceptual worlds. Finding allusions,

of God and in so doing brings benefit to others, the "many," bearing their sins and making them righteous. The "many" are defined slightly earlier in Isaiah 52:14-15, a passage Jesus and Mark knew. There the "many" are those who witness the Servant's suffering and includes the "many nations." All have access to him as the universal redeemer, a relevant piece of theology for the Roman hearers of this Gospel. Isaiah saw the Gentile mission from afar (Isa 49:6-7; 52:10, 15; 60:3).[221] This eschatological event is now coming near, as Peter and the first hearers of this Gospel knew.

Jesus identifies his death as a "ransom," a term applied to Jesus' death only here and in Matthew 20:28, which is dependent upon the present passage. Mark is the first place where this theology of the cross appears. Titus 2:14 uses the verb "to redeem" (λυτρόω) with reference to Jesus' death as well.[222] The verbal form likewise appears in 1 Peter 1:18-19, where the apostle specifies that the redemption effected came through Jesus who died as the sacrificial lamb ("You know that you were ransomed . . . with the precious blood of Christ, like that of a lamb without defect or blemish"; see the chapter on theology of 1 Peter). Mark 10:45, as 1 Peter 1:18-19, understands that a price was paid for redemption, which he identifies as the life offered ("Give his life," δοῦναι τὴν ψυχὴν αὐτοῦ), which in the context of Mark's Gospel means giving himself over to death (Mark 14:34). The language here reflects Isaiah 53:10: "When you make his life an offering for sin" (אִם־תָּשִׂים אָשָׁם נַפְשׁוֹ),[223] a passage which underlies 1 Peter 1:18-19 as well. While Mark follows the vocabulary of the LXX Isaiah 53:10, the thought translated is closer to the Hebrew text than the LXX. Although Isaiah 53 does not refer to the Servant as a "ransom" nor indicate that his service "redeems," the language of redemption is shot through the Servant Songs (Isa 41:14; 43:1, 14; 44:22-24; 51:11; 62:12). God is the Redeemer of the redeemed. He has paid a price for that redemption (45:13; 52:3; and recall 1 Pet 1:18-19). These passages are relevant for our understanding of Mark 10:45 since Jesus' words have their roots in the theology of the Servant. The divine redemption in Isaiah has to do with the liberation or New Exodus, which God effects. That liberation is understood in its connection with

---

therefore, is not simply a process of comparing the lexemes shared by particular texts. Moreover, a thorough discussion of the question must bring into play the way the early Christian communities turned repeatedly to this passage to understand what occurred in Jesus' death. The language of Servant Songs in Isaiah permeated the early church as this was one of the key "go to" texts for the development of early Christian theology. For a quick summary of the debate surrounding the echoes of Isaiah 53 in Mark 10:45, see Witherington, *The Gospel of Mark*, 288-90.

221. The "many" does not mean "all" as in contemporary universalism, nor is it limited to the community (contra Marcus, *Mark 8-16*, 750).

222. Jesus' effects redemption (ἀπολύτρωσις) according to Rom 3:24; 1 Cor 1:30; Eph 1:7, 14; Col 1:14; Heb 9:15. Redemption is seen occasionally as an eschatological good (Luke 21:28; Rom 8:23; Eph 4:30; Heb 11:35). These texts communicate a concept similar to the one Mark and 1 Peter work over, but the lexeme is different.

223. The LXX reads slightly different: ἐὰν δῶτε περὶ ἁμαρτίας ἡ ψυχὴ ὑμῶν ὄψεται σπέρμα—"If you give an offering for sin, your soul shall see a long-lived offspring." The language is similar to Exodus 21:30 (LXX): "He shall pay a ransom for his life"—δώσει λύτρα τῆς ψυχῆς αὐτοῦ.

the sacrifice of the Servant, who is crushed as the sin offering (53:10–12). Neither in Isaiah nor in Mark or 1 Peter does any discussion arise regarding to whom or what the payment for redemption is given, leaving ample space for subsequent theological reflection. Through 10:45 we learn that Jesus' death is an atoning sacrifice which is efficacious beyond the confines of Israel. Christ's death is redemptive. It liberates from the bondage of sin. His sacrifice as the Servant effects the New Exodus. Once again, his theology of the cross is deep and wide.

They killed Jesus by crucifying him. He was not beheaded as John the Baptist (6:27), nor run through with a sword (14:47).[224] Mark tells his readers that the cry of the crowd got him crucified (15:13–15) as the final move of the chess game instigated by the "builders" who had accused him before Pilate. Mark is careful to explain that the crucifixion did not mean he was guilty of criminal offense. When Pilate asked the charge ("What evil has he done?"—τί γὰρ ἐποίησεν κακόν;), all he heard in response was the call for crucifixion. There is no hint that Jesus has done evil; the reader knows that he has done good instead. Pilate simply felt compelled to appease the crowd. He, as Herod before him, was trapped by the offer made (15:6, 8–9, 12; 6:22–23). The scene points up Jesus' innocence, contrary to the implicit message of crucifixion, which publicly tagged him as a criminal. Mark offers an apologetic here to anyone who knew the story and would have assumed Jesus' guilt. Mark identifies Jesus as the innocent victim, or in the words of Isaiah 53:7, "By a perversion of justice he was taken away." He is indeed "the righteous one, my servant" (Isa 53:11). Not only does Mark evoke the Suffering Servant but also the theology of the Righteous Sufferer, whose clothes were divided (15:24; Psalm 22:18). In addition to his innocence and righteousness, the theme of Jesus' royalty plays throughout the crucifixion, as noted previously. His trial centers around the question of his kingship (15:1–15), he is mocked as King (15:16–20, 32), and the charge publicly displayed was that he was King. The crucifixion is, ironically, the very place where his kingship, first recognized by Peter, is most prominently displayed. Moreover, the crucifixion is replete with temple imagery, again as noted above. While hanging on the cross he was derided by those who said, "Aha! You who would destroy the temple and build it in three days" (15:29). When he does die, the temple veil is torn top to bottom, signaling the end of one temple's ministry and suggesting the opening way via a new temple (15:38). Finally, the theme of salvation is the river that runs through it: "Save yourself. . . . He saved others; he cannot save himself" (15:30–31). As he hangs between two bandits, those who are in true need of salvation, he is bringing salvation as the atoning sacrifice anticipated in the cup he shared with the disciples. Jesus' innocence, righteous

---

224. Mark may record a "miss," though the description only highlights the effect that would have rendered the person unsuitable for temple service (Evans, *Mark 8:27–16:20*, 425). John notes that the person was Peter himself (John 18:10). Peter's intent was to die with Jesus (14:31). With the stakes this high, and the plot to kill Jesus unfolding, preacher-wisdom about this being a miss is probably nearer the mark than Evans permits.

suffering, kingship, and salvation all gather around the cross. Here is redemption and Mark's theology of the cross.

The cross as the means of Jesus' death has another theological dimension connected with Mark's purposes in writing to the church located in Rome. Throughout the Gospel, Mark has shown that Jesus not only inaugurates the New Exodus as he heralds the kingdom of God in both his deeds and words, but he also comes to inaugurate the rule of God in contradistinction to the imperial claims made during the period. Rome's authority and power spread broad and wide around the Mediterranean basin as she conquered nations and peoples of every tribe and tongue. The colonial power of Rome was imposed through an effective army, savvy engineers, and administrative acumen of a kind that Alexander III would have envied. But a centerpiece of Rome's domination was the cross, which the empire used effectively to assure the kind of order necessary to hold the political behemoth together. Crucifixion was prominent and, at times, massive. It was not hidden behind prison walls but carried out on public thoroughfares. Roman citizens were exempt from the supreme penalty, which, Cicero notes, is not even the topic of conversation among polite Roman company.[225] It was both cruel and barbaric, but also very effective. It was used politically and militarily, it focused on the lower classes in the provinces, and it served as a deterrent against any form of insurrection. The cross was deeply political and served Rome's imperial machinery effectively. It is no small matter that Jesus was crucified instead of being simply the victim of a violent skirmish, as was Sitting Bull in America's colonization, or an unfortunate prophet condemned to beheading due to jealousy. He was the King, the true Son of God instead of Caesar. The crucifixion of Jesus Christ was a means of absorbing Rome's imperial power and claims to absolute sovereignty and subverting them through working out salvation that triumphs over Rome's claims. The tomb will soon be empty since Rome's cruelty, torture, and death cannot hold him. And he will come in glory as the Son of Man to establish his dominion, which shall reign forever and ever (Mark 14:62). Through Jesus' killing on the cross the new order advances: The kingdom of God has come at the moment it appears to end. This is a cruel and sweet irony.

Jesus' Resurrection

In the very first announcement of his sufferings, Jesus concluded with a final and surprising note: "And after three days rise again." As his sufferings, rejection, and death were necessary so, too, his rising after three days. The resurrection of Jesus completes the predictions and story of his passion and completes the theology of salvation in Mark. Without the resurrection, the Jesus story is one of injustice and tragedy, no more. If there was no resurrection, the gospel of the kingdom of God would come

---

225. Cicero, *Pro Rab. Post.* 16; and see the fulsome discussion in Hengel, *Crucifixion in the Ancient World and the Folly of the Message of the Cross*, 22–90.

apart. Though announced first in 8:31, the resurrection is anticipated prior to this point in the narrative. As part of Mark's theology of the kingdom of God and Jesus' kingship, Jesus conquers demons, disease, and death itself through raising Jairus's daughter (5:21–24, 35–43). This event prefigures Jesus' own resurrection as in the narrative the same language is used of both events (ἔγειρε and ἀνέστη; see the discussion on Jesus' kingship above). The young girl raised and returned points to the risen King. The one who rode into Jerusalem as the King (11:1–11) and who was condemned, mocked, and killed as the King (14:53—15:39) is now vindicated through the resurrection. The resurrection announced in 16:6 seals the kingdom's claim, which otherwise could be called into question. The theology of the resurrection in Mark is the first finale of the gospel of the kingdom of God (cf. 14:62).

Hints of Jesus' resurrection likewise appear in the scene of John the harbinger's beheading as Herod ponders whether Jesus could be John raised from the dead (6:14, 16). What Herod thought might have occurred with John happened in deed with Jesus. Moreover, Jesus cites Psalm 118:22–23 as evidence that, though rejected, the stone "has become the cornerstone" (Mark 12:10–12). The reader of Mark's Gospel would understand the rejection spoken of in the Psalm in terms of the trials, sufferings, and cross of Jesus. God's vindication of the rejected stone becomes then a prediction of the resurrection (cf. Acts 4:10–11). Mark's Gospel, therefore, anticipates the resurrection in passages other than Jesus' direct predictions of the event. But in Mark Jesus also affirms the belief in the general resurrection of the dead, as discussed above (12:18–27), finding the theology rooted in the nature of God himself: "He is God not of the dead, but of the living" (12:27). As we cannot understand the raising of Jairus's daughter entirely separate from Jesus' resurrection, neither is it possible to separate Jesus' underlying theology of the resurrection from the event he himself would soon experience. Although the belief in the general resurrection is not rooted specifically in the resurrection of Jesus in Mark (cf. 1 Thess 4:13–18; 1 Cor 15), the two events are threads of the same theological fabric in this Gospel. Jesus' resurrection is linked with the general resurrection of the dead due to God's character. Mark takes the matter no further, however. He stops short of exploring this theological landscape.

Jesus continued to predict his resurrection in the passion prophecies after 8:31, indicating on two more occasions that the event would occur after three days (9:31; 10:34). The reference to "three days" likely hearkens back to Hosea 6:2: "After two days he will revive us; on the third day he will raise us up, that we may live before him." Rabbinic interpretation understood this passage from Hosea "as a prophecy of eschatological resurrection."[226] Jesus' resurrection would occur shortly after his death and it would be the fulfillment of this hope for God's final resurrection. The affliction

---

226. Marcus, *Mark 8–16*, 606; Evans, *Mark 8:27–16:20*, 17–18. Most commentators seek to work out the timing of the "three days" between Jesus' death and resurrection. Marcus is one of the few who minimizes the importance of the clock, arguing on the basis of 8:2 and elsewhere that the three days is "a general term of a short period of unspecified duration" (*Mark 8–16*, 605). He wisely points instead to the theological significance of the repeated phrase.

of Hosea 6:1 ("he has struck down") yields to the hope of resurrection ("And he will bind us up ... on the third day he will raise us up") so that life and service to God may begin ("that we may live before him"). The future hope, so lyrically expressed in Hosea, leads to turning to God in the present ("Let us know, let us press on to know the Lord; his appearing is as sure as the dawn; he will come to us like the showers, like the spring rains that water the earth"). The resurrection in "three days" means that the eschatological age has begun and that salvation has come from God. The anticipation of Jesus' resurrection in three days signals hope for the ones rejected who are now outside (Hos 1:10).

The disciples did not understand Jesus' talk about his resurrection (9:9–10). The hope did not control them at the critical moment of Jesus' arrest, trial, and crucifixion. They deserted him (14:50), and Peter denied him (14:66–72), plummeting the apostle into despair (14:72). At his crucifixion, Mark notes that the two Mary's were "looking from a distance" (15:40). Yet they watched to see where his body was laid and after the Sabbath came to prepare it properly for burial since it had been laid in the tomb hastily (15:47—16:1). They, as the disciples previously, did not understand his predictions about the resurrection. Burial spices were not needed (2 Chr 16:14; *T. Ab.* 20:10–11; *m. Šabb.* 23:5). Joseph of Arimathea did a good deed by asking for the body of Jesus, purchasing the burial cloth used to lower his body from where it was impaled and wrap him up, and securing the tomb to bury Jesus' body. Though he anticipated the kingdom of God, he did not anticipate that the kingdom meant resurrection at this time. The stone was rolled in front of the mouth of the tomb (15:42–47). The story, the reader assumes, has ended. It appears that despite the thick theology of the resurrection that Jesus showed, announced, and repeated, nobody understood.

However, the announcement made by the young man in white snaps all the predictions of Jesus' exaltation and resurrection into focus since each one pointed to this moment: "He has been raised; he is not here. Look, there is the place they laid him." Jesus does not appear at this moment as in the other Gospels. There is only the promise of seeing him in Galilee: "But go, tell his disciples and Peter that he is going ahead of you to Galilee; there you will see him, just has he told you" (16:6–7). Readers since ancient times have considered this ending to be incomplete and, unsurprisingly, have added their own shorter and longer endings to the Gospel. Many consider that the final note about the women fleeing in fear from the tomb marks this as an incomplete story (16:8).[227] Given that Papias noted that Mark was an unfinished literary work (see chapter 1), this may indeed be the case. Even if the Gospel is not a final and complete literary piece, the story is complete with the announcement of Jesus' resurrection and the promise of seeing him in Galilee. What was promised regarding

---

227. On the ending of Mark, see the commentaries, especially Evans, *Mark 8:27–16:20*, 540–51; France, *The Gospel of Mark*, 685–88; Adela Yarbro Collins, *Mark: A Commentary* (Minneapolis: Fortress, 2007), 802–18; Marcus, *Mark 8–16*, 1088–96, and Metzger, *A Textual Commentary on the Greek New Testament*, 102–7.

resurrection and meeting him in Galilee has now been fulfilled (14:28; 16:7). If this Gospel was indeed written for the church in Rome, which had heard Peter's preaching and then solicited a written edition, they would have known the rest of the story. No doubt, however, is left in the mind of the reader about the meaning and outcome as the evidences of the fulfillment, angelic witness, and empty tomb are all available witnesses. The women hear the witness, see the empty space, and remember Jesus' prophetic testimony. Mark's resurrection scene is about testimony that will be verified as the disciples journey to Galilee and see him there. Jesus has indeed risen and is alive; now they must go and tell (16:5–7). As in all the materials associated with Peter, we are brought back to the power of testimony. And although there is no ascension promise or scene in the Gospel, the advent of the Son of Man in the clouds of heaven predicted in Mark 13:26–27 presupposes the ascension (cf. Acts 1:9–11; 2:32–35). What is implicit in Mark, both with regard to the resurrection appearances and ascension, is made explicit by subsequent Gospel writers.

The salient features of the resurrection scene at the end of the Gospel for Mark's theology of salvation begin with the identification of the crucified one. He is "Jesus of Nazareth," the name heard first in 1:9 and repeated somewhat infrequently in the Gospel (1:24; 10:47; 14:67). In the first instance, the very one who came from Galilee and was identified as the Christ is the very person resurrected. The address is right, the identity is not mistaken. There are hints here of the later Pauline theology of the continuity between the mortal and resurrected immortal person (1 Cor 15:35–41). Furthermore, there is a note about redemption and forgiveness here, one that was especially poignant for Peter: "But go, tell his disciples and Peter that he is going ahead of you to Galilee" (16:7). The disciples had deserted him, and Peter had denied him. The hopeless, broken tears of Peter are turned to hope and mercy as Jesus is consistent with his promise and offers continued fellowship with him after the resurrection (cf. 1 Pet 1:3). This is a word of forgiveness and the living witness of the new covenant that Peter and the disciples had drunk with Jesus before their utter failure (14:24; Jer 31:34). The promise that follows, "there you will see him," ties the resurrection with the advent of Christ, when "they will see 'the Son of Man coming in the clouds' with great power and glory" (13:26). The resurrection appearance anticipates the final appearance of the Son of Man at the end of the age. The resurrection is itself the beginning of the final eschatological act (see above on "after three days"), which anticipates the final scene of his advent.[228] Finally, the resurrection in Mark is filled with a call for faith in the midst of continued ambiguity and fear. The women flee, gripped with terror and amazement to the extent that they become mute, and they are afraid (16:8). There is a striking contrast between what they had seen and their present state, not unlike the believers in Rome who were torn between promise and persecution, testimonial evidence yet not seeing. Mark ends in the midst of the Christian reality of the first century AD. The vast majority of believers were not present and did not go to

---

228. Marcus, *Mark 8–16*, 1081.

Galilee since they lived scattered through the empire and in Rome. They had heard, they knew the story, but they had not seen the risen Christ with their own eyes. These first disciples, at least at the end of Mark as it stands, were like them. How would they respond (cf. 1 Pet 1:8–9)? Would they believe, go, and tell, or would they flee in fearful silence? The resurrection scene in Mark is a call to faith on the basis testimony, and this in the midst of utter fear and confusion.

The full cycle of the theology of salvation in Mark associated with the sufferings, rejection, death, and resurrection of Jesus leads us into a rich, breathtaking tapestry of theology. His passion and resurrection are resonant with the theology of the Son of Man and the Suffering Servant, whose death inaugurates the new covenant as part of the promise of the New Exodus. The theology of the kingdom of God enters. The advent of the kingdom ushers in salvation with all its benefits. But the kingdom only comes through the death and subsequent triumph of the King. The theology of salvation includes the promise of life and the defeat of all those powers that assail humanity: disease, demons, and death. The suffering of Jesus and the travesty of the cross give way to triumph, as per Jesus' promise, and anticipate the final glorious advent of the Son of Man when all will see him. He was the innocent sufferer who brings redemption, his death being an atonement that will, in the end, make many righteous. The new covenant, with all its blessings, has come. So in the middle of this story of salvation we discover the promise of forgiveness and the call to faith based on testimony in the midst of uncertainty and fear. The promise is personalized for Peter, the bearer of this testimony, but is open to all disciples who do not see yet believe. Though Mark's telling of the key events in the story of salvation is surprisingly stark at times, later Christian authors rightly understood the richly colored textures of his theology and sought to make explicit for their readers what they had recognized in Mark. They do not so much add to Mark as explain him. He laid down the theological foundations and blueprinted the whole structure. What remains is to see how the realities of salvation give way to the understanding of discipleship. Just as Christology holds within it Mark's theology of salvation so, too, does this understanding carry in its bosom the nature of discipleship to Jesus Christ. These are simply various areas within his single tapestry of the kingdom of God.

DISCIPLESHIP IN MARK

Discipleship and Christology

As noted above, the focal point of Mark's message is the gospel of Jesus Christ, the Son of God (1:1), whose mission is to proclaim the advent of the kingdom of God: "The time is fulfilled, and the kingdom of God has come near; repent and believe in the good news" (1:14). Mark understands that the inauguration of the reign of God is inextricably bound with the ministry of the Messiah, who is the promised and true Son of God. But no sooner does Jesus announce the coming kingdom that he calls the first four disciples—Simon, Andrew, James, and John—to follow him (1:16–20). Mark's presentation inextricably binds discipleship with the person of Jesus and his mission, and, as such, it becomes a central theological theme in the Gospel. Donahue remarks, "The gospel of Mark tells us not only who Jesus is, but what it is to be involved with him." Mark is, as he says, "the proclaimed good news of Jesus; it is also the narrative of what it means to hear and to respond to this good news."[229] The character of discipleship in Mark has received considerable comment and continues to generate debate, especially the obtuseness of Jesus' followers and their negative portrayal in the Gospel.[230] Whatever explanation might be given to the question of why the disciples appear to be cast in a negative light should not, however, obscure the fact that they are placed in alignment with Jesus and his mission. The relationship between Jesus and his disciples is marked "by both *presence* and *practice*," as Henderson observes. The disciples "are summoned to remain in Jesus' presence as they bear witness to Jesus' christological mission," and they "are meant to continue Jesus' *practice* of wielding the power associated with God's apocalyptic reign." As such, they are authorized participants in Jesus' mission.[231] Over and again Mark emphasizes his disciple's participation in Jesus' mission (3:13–19; 4:15–20; 6:6b–13, 30; 9:38–41; 13:10–11; 14:9). Jesus not only commissioned the disciples but endowed them with power over demonic forces

---

229. John R. Donahue, *The Theology and Setting of Discipleship in the Gospel of Mark* (Milwaukee: Marquette University Press, 1983), 2–3; Suzanne Watts Henderson, *Christology and Discipleship in the Gospel of Mark* (Cambridge: Cambridge University Press, 2006), 6.

230. See, for example, Joseph Tyson, "The Blindness of the Disciples in Mark," *JBL* 80 (1961) 261–68; Hans Dieter Betz, *Nachfolge und Nachahmung Jesu Christi im Neuen Testament* (Tübingen: Mohr Siebeck, 1967); Theodore J. Weeden, "The Heresy That Necessitated Mark's Gospel," *ZNW* 59 (1968) 148–58; Robert Meye, *Jesus and the Twelve: Discipleship and Revelation in Mark's Gospel* (Grand Rapids: Eerdmans, 1968); Gunter Schmahl, *Die Zwölf im Markusevangelium* (Trier: Paulinus, 1977); Robert C. Tannehill, "The Disciples in Mark: The Function of a Narrative Role," *JR* 57 (1977) 386–405; Martin Hengel, *The Charismatic Leader and His Followers* (New York: Crossroad, 1981); Best, *Following Jesus*; Frederick H. Borsch, *Power in Weakness: New Hearing for Gospel Stories of Healing and Discipleship* (Philadelphia: Fortress, 1983); Morna D. Hooker, *The Message of Mark* (London: Epworth, 1983); Donahue, *The Theology and Setting of Discipleship in the Gospel of Mark*; Ernest Best, *Disciples and Discipleship: Studies in the Gospel According to Mark* (Edinburgh: T. & T. Clark, 1986); C. Clifton Black, *The Disciples According to Mark: Markan Redaction in Current Debate* (Sheffield: Sheffield Academic, 1989); Beavis, *Mark's Audience*; Joong Suk Suh, *Discipleship and Community: Mark's Gospel in Sociological Perspective* (Claremont: Center for Asian-American Ministries, School of Theology at Claremont, 1991); Stephen C. Barton, *Discipleship and Family Ties in Mark and Matthew* (Cambridge: Cambridge University Press, 1994); Henderson, *Christology and Discipleship in the Gospel of Mark*; James Dawsey, *Peter's Last Sermon: Identity and Discipleship in the Gospel of Mark* (Macon, GA: Mercer University Press, 2010).

231. Henderson, *Christology and Discipleship in the Gospel of Mark*, 4. Donahue and Harrington say, "The two essential elements of the call to discipleship are 'being with' Jesus and doing the things of Jesus" (*The Gospel of Mark*, 31). René Padilla adds that, "existe una estrecha relación entre la vida y misión de la iglesia, por un lado, y la vida y misión de Jesucristo, por otro lado. Sin negar el carácter singular de la obra de Jesucristo por medio de sus 'eventos salvíficos,' podemos afirmar sin temor de equivocarnos que esa obra se prolonga y se hace efectiva en la historia, por el poder del Espíritu, por medio de la vida y misión de la iglesia. El señorío de Jesucristo constituye la base de la misión de la iglesia" ("Una Visión Bíblica de la Iglesia," *El Blog de Bernabé* (blog), August 7, 2012).

(3:14–15; 6:7; 9:38) and assured them of the Holy Spirit's witness through them as they faced persecution (13:9–11).

The bond between Jesus and his disciples begins with him calling those whom he wants to follow him and join in his ministry. In contrast with the rabbinic practice of receiving disciples who took the initiative to attach themselves to the teacher, Jesus summoned people to follow him. Hengel observes, "There are no rabbinical stories of 'calling' and 'follow after' analogous to the pericope in Mark and Q, nor did the summons 'follow me' resound from any rabbinical teacher in respect of entry into a teacher-pupil relationship. Whereas in the Gospel the decisive 'call' came from Jesus, entry into a rabbinical school was generally on the basis of an initiative on the part of the pupil."[232] The disciple is not simply a student who attends class instruction but who makes an unequivocal commitment to Jesus in response to his summons. Following Jesus "has primarily the very concrete sense of following him *in his wanderings and sharing with him his uncertain and indeed perilous destiny*, and becoming pupils only in the derivative sense."[233] While following a philosopher was common enough in the wider Mediterranean world, those traditions do not correspond with the portrayal of discipleship in Mark either. After examining the philosopher/student relationships depicted in the writings of Xenophon, Iamblichus, Philostratus, and Ben Sira and comparing them with Mark, Shiner concludes, "Unlike the followers of philosophers and wisdom teachers, the disciples of Jesus are shown to have no apparent merit. While other teachers draw their students from an intellectual and moral elite, Jesus gathers an undistinguished group, and Mark emphasizes the inclusion of the tax collector Levi among them (2:14–17). They are not the elite but representative of those on the margins of Jesus society. Yet the audience knows that this seemingly undistinguished group, because of its connection with Jesus, is the real elite, part of the elect of God whom the Son of Man will gather from the four winds when he returns from heaven (13:26–27)."[234] The first disciples were fishermen, and others who followed him had no particular social and economic standing. They hardly augmented Jesus' honor in anyone's eyes. Discipleship in Mark shares elements with both Hellenistic and Jewish models, including the concepts of following and learning. But the calling, the personal commitment to the exalted person of Jesus, the framing within the advent of the

---

232. Hengel, *The Charismatic Leader and His Followers*, 50–51. Instead of "following after" the pupil would take to "learning Torah" (לָמַד תּוֹרָה). Hengel continues, "It is significant that the New Testament equivalent (μανθάνειν) for this term which is extremely frequent in rabbinical sources appears only once in the Synoptics, Namely in Mark, in an entirely different context—'from the fig tree learn this parable' (Mark 13:28//Matt 24:32)." Hengel's work is a response to Betz who regards rabbinic practice as the model Jesus followed (Betz, *Nachfolge und Nachahmung Jesu Christi im Neuen Testament*).

233. Following Hengel in differentiating the rabbinic pupil from the disciple of Jesus are Witherington, *The Gospel of Mark*, 86; Edwards, *The Gospel According to Mark*, 49–50; France, *The Gospel of Mark*, 96; Stein, *Mark*, 78.

234. Whitney Taylor Shiner, *Follow Me! Disciples in Markan Rhetoric* (Atlanta: Scholars, 1995), 290.

kingdom of God, and the absolute sacrifice involved make the concept here truly *ad hoc* since it cannot be attributed to a single source, save Jesus himself.[235]

As Jesus passed along the shore of the Sea of Galilee, he saw the brothers Simon and Andrew and summoned them: "Follow me and I will make you fish for people" (1:17). Their response was immediate—they "followed him" (1:18). Down the beach further he called James and John, and they likewise "left . . . and followed him" (1:20). From the beginning Mark shows that following Jesus entails participation with him in the fishing expedition for people, but it also includes leaving and loss. Peter and James "left their nets" (1:18), while James and John "left their father Zebedee in the boat with the hired men" (1:20). The followers leave their place, labor, and family, all that is familiar and provides identity. While they will be in Jesus' presence, they will also experience the loss of those things in life which constitute security as they follow Jesus in the way. Following Jesus in this new way is the living metaphor for discipleship. Becoming a disciple means responding to Jesus' call to come after him (δεῦτε ὀπίσω μου) and follow him (ἀκολουθέω; 1:17–18, 20; 2:14; 6:1; 8:34; 10:21, 28, 52), that is, to walk down the road with him.[236] But as noted above, the road or way is at once both a literal byway and a metaphor for the way of the Lord, a piece of Mark's New Exodus theology (8:27; 9:33; 10:32, 52; 11:8–9). Those who follow Jesus become participants in this New Exodus of salvation that Jesus has initiated, and this includes women as well as men (15:41). As noted above, following Jesus in the way is the living metaphor for discipleship. Discipleship entails being involved in this central movement of salvation. They are caught up in this moment when God inaugurates his kingdom through the ministry of Jesus (1:14–15) and participate in its mission with Jesus.

While the ones who follow Jesus are, in the first instance, people called to be disciples (μαθηταί), Mark makes his readers aware that there was a larger company of followers who were distinguished from those whom he designates this way (2:15; 3:7–8; 5:24b–34; 10:1, 10; 11:1, 7–10). They were the many who had been attracted to Jesus because of what he was doing and pressed in on him. Mark refrains from calling these crowds "disciples," although they have access to his company (2:15) and have heard the sacrificial call to surrender their lives entirely to him (8:34; cf. 10:28). Mark shows that people had "varying degrees of commitment" to Jesus, some weak, some strong.[237] But a person could move through the crowd to him as the woman who touched Jesus in faith and was healed. She was not like the rest who simply pressed in on him (5:30–31). Mark further differentiates a smaller group of twelve who received the special commission to be his apostles (3:13–19a; 4:10; 10:32). Mark draws three

---

235. Donahue and Harrington, *The Gospel of Mark*, 29–30; Hengel, *The Charismatic Leader and His Followers*, 87. On *ad hoc* concept formation, see Gene L. Green, "Lexical Pragmatics and Biblical Interpretation," *JETS* 50 (2007) 799–812; Gene L. Green, "Lexical Pragmatics and the Lexicon," *BBR* 22 (2012) 315–34.

236. See Best, *Following Jesus*, 15–16.

237. I. Howard Marshall, *New Testament Theology: Many Witnesses, One Gospel* (Downers Grove, IL: InterVarsity, 2004), 88.

"concentric circles" around Jesus,[238] although at times it is difficult to distinguish in a particular verse whether Mark speaks of the twelve or the larger group of disciples (e.g., 10:10, 13, 23–24, 32). In either case, becoming one of Jesus' disciples entailed being a member of the Jesus community. Indeed, John remarked on one person who cast out demons but was not "following *us*,"[239] an unusual condition. But even though attachment to Jesus was the mark of discipleship, his followers could become the deserters (14:27–31). Abandoning Jesus and his way was an option in the time of tension, and this was true even for his closest adherents—even Peter (see below).

Those who believe in him and receive the benefits of the coming kingdom need not be Jewish, as illustrated through the healing of the Syrophoenician woman's daughter (7:24–30) and the Roman soldier's confession (15:39). Those far outside may respond to Jesus with extraordinary faith, heralding the day when the door giving access to the Gentiles would swing open fully (see 3:7–8). Notably, in Mark, "only the women are consistently shown in a positive light (5:25–34; 7:24–30; 12:41–4; 14:3–9; 15:40f., 47), and even here there is one surprising exception—his own mother (3.31)."[240] On the other hand, the ones the readers would expect to be on the inside such as family (3:31–35; 6:4), people from his hometown (6:1–6), and the religious leaders (11:27–33) fail to respond to him in faith.[241] Mark draws the circle of discipleship around unlikely adherents and leaves his readers to marvel at who remains outside of it, looking in. The inclusion of Gentiles and women and the conflict with those who are near likely resonated deeply among Mark's first Roman readers.

Following Jesus as a disciple means being with him. At times, however, Jesus instructs a person to go on their way instead of accompanying him. More often than not, this occurs when someone is healed or delivered from demonic oppression and is sent home (2:11; 5:18–19, 34; 7:29–30) or to the priest (1:44). The command to go could, in the end, result in a person returning to following Jesus (10:21, 51). Jesus could, on the other hand, send someone out on a mission (11:2; 5:18–19). Obedience to Jesus' call may entail going out to do kingdom work as well as following him in the way. Those who are in Jesus' presence for a limited time may participate in his mission since when they go they proclaim what the Lord has done (1:44; 5:19). Although the concept of following Jesus is fundamental to Mark's understanding of discipleship, above all else Jesus summons people to obedience. Following is the principle way this obedience manifests itself, but going on a mission may also be part of the call. In both cases, the disciple becomes one who participates with Jesus in his work.

Whether someone remains with him or he sends the person away, the disciple is one who has responded to the message of the kingdom of God by repentance and faith

---

238. Marcus, *Mark 8–16*, 744.

239. Occasionally the early church refers to Mark as a follower of the Elders or Peter (Eusebius, *HE* 3.39.4, 15; 6.14.6–7; Clement of Alexandria, *Adumbr. in 1 Pet* 5:13).

240. Hooker, *The Gospel According to Mark*, 21.

241. Edwards, *The Gospel According to Mark*, 17.

in the gospel (1:15; 6:15). Although Mark uses the language of repentance infrequently in his Gospel, the concept is implied within the call to follow Jesus. The one who turns in repentance becomes the follower of Jesus (1:15, 16–20). Such turning and commitment to Jesus is an act of faith in him and the gospel of the kingdom of God that he proclaims. That faith, in turn, opens a person to the benefits of the kingdom of God (2:5; 5:34, 36; 9:23–24; 10:52). Mark portrays the rich complex of repentance, faith, and following bundled together in discipleship. The disciples are those who believe in Jesus (9:42[242]; 11:23–24), as even those who were not disciples recognized (11:31; 15:32). On the other side, one may believe, receive, and then disobey (1:40–45). True discipleship entails obedience.

Discipleship and Suffering

After Peter's confession that Jesus is indeed the Messiah (8:27–30) and Jesus' announcement of his suffering, rejection, death, and resurrection (8:31–33), Jesus' announces to both the crowd around him and his disciples the level of commitment required for discipleship: "If any want to become my followers, let them deny themselves and take up their cross and follow me. For those who want to save their life will lose it, and those who lose their life for my sake, and for the sake of the gospel, will save it" (8:34—9:1). As noted previously, from the beginning the call to follow Jesus entailed loss and sacrifice (1:16–20). The commitment to Jesus included the loss of that which was most important in life for identity and honor. Family, labor, and land became subordinate to Jesus, whom the true disciples follow. But their commitment to him goes even deeper than what the disciples first realized since it includes being present with him and participating in his ministry to the point of cross-bearing sacrifice. Jesus announced his own great suffering and dishonor, and now the disciples are called to share with him in the same. While the disciples are compelled by the revelation that Jesus is the Messiah, as seen in his deeds and witnessed in Peter's words (8:29), they also heard Jesus announce his defeat and death (8:31–33). As Jesus reworks their understanding of what his messiahship entailed he must, at the same time, draw the concept of discipleship into this frame. The commitment to Jesus required for discipleship is the resolve to deny oneself as he denied himself (14:36–39) and suffer as he suffered, even to the point of death. Mark lets his readers understand that discipleship may include both the shame and agony of bearing a cross and being hung upon the gibbet.

Mark's readers in Rome would come to understand the literal nature of that commitment soon enough as Nero tortured and killed Christians after the great fire of Rome. Tacitus said, "Mockery of every sort was added to their deaths. Covered with the skins of beasts, they were torn by dogs and perished, or were nailed to crosses, or were doomed to the flames and burnt, to serve as a nightly illumination, when daylight

---

242. The "little ones who believe in me" refers to the disciples (see the preceding context in 9:38–41; cf. Matt 10:40–42; Marcus, *Mark 8–16*, 689).

had expired" (*Ann.* 15.44; cf. Mark 13:12–13). The cruel and agonizing injustices Jesus suffered would also become the disciples' lot in Rome. But this cross bearing, while literal, becomes metaphorical in Mark for "falling in behind" Jesus as he is persecuted (implied in the call to deny oneself in 8:35 and made explicit in Luke's redaction in 9:23—καθ' ἡμέραν).[243] The one who follows Jesus in the way of sacrifice subordinates their interests to those of Jesus and, like him, serves others rather than serving self (10:42–45). The call to cross-bearing discipleship "reaches beyond the confines of the Markan scene at Caesarea Philippi and challenges the believing community. Who is the true disciple?"[244]

So fundamental is the relationship between Jesus' and the disciples' sacrificial suffering that the denial of Jesus' suffering that Peter vocalized (8:32–33) could also unravel the commitment to Jesus necessary for any who respond to the call to follow him. To deny the cross of Jesus is, in the end, to end the relationship of the disciple with him. To refuse one's own cross-bearing would, in the same way, break the bond between disciple and Master. The message was compelling for the crowd and the disciples who surrounded Jesus since it moved them to weigh the cost of discipleship. Indeed, to dishonor Jesus by denying him will result in Jesus being ashamed of that person in the final assize (8:38). To be ashamed of Jesus may refer to "interrogation before magistrates, in which Christians were called upon to curse or deny Jesus or else be martyred," suggests Marcus.[245] This is precisely the kind of situation Pliny the Younger later describes in his correspondence with the Emperor Trajan when he was governor of Bithynia (AD 112): "Those who denied that they were or had been Christians, when they invoked the gods in words dictated by me, offered prayer with incense and wine to your image, which I had ordered to be brought for this purpose together with statues of the gods, and moreover cursed Christ–none of which those who are really Christians, it is said, can be forced to do–these I thought should be discharged. Others named by the informer declared that they were Christians, but then denied it, asserting that they had been but had ceased to be, some three years before, others many years, some as much as twenty-five years. They all worshipped your image and the statues of the gods, and cursed Christ" (*Letters* 10.96). But 8:38 could refer to a wider range of responses to Jesus that were signs of being ashamed of him. As Marcus continues, "8:38 probably also contains a reference to a tendency both within and outside the Christian community to gloss over, down-play, or take offense at Jesus' crucifixion"[246] (cf. Isa 52:14; 53:3, 8). If this kind of response to the cross was in mind, Jesus' words in 8:38 may be viewed as a comment on Peter's rejection of the cross (8:32–33) and a warning to anyone who would deny Jesus and the message of

---

243. Best, *Disciples and Discipleship*, 8–9.
244. Dawsey, *Peter's Last Sermon*, 37.
245. Marcus, *Mark 8–16*, 629.
246. Marcus, *Mark 8–16*, 629.

the cross by either word or action (cf. Matt 10:32–32; Luke 12:8–9).[247] To turn against Jesus was a distinct possibility, especially for those who experienced great social pressure because of their commitment to him.

Peter's response to Jesus stands as a paradigm of true discipleship and of the possibility of denying Jesus rather than self (cf. 8:34).[248] Peter becomes the first to respond to the call to follow Jesus as a disciple (1:16–18) and the first to step forward among the disciples to confess Jesus as the anticipated Messiah (8:27–30). But Peter also becomes the first disciple to reject how Jesus framed his messiahship as including rejection, dishonor, and death (8:31–33) and is the first to deny him publicly (14:26–31; 66–72). On the other hand, he is also the first to repent of his failure (14:72). Although Jesus predicted that all would become deserters (14:27, 31, 50), Mark focuses on Peter's denial (14:66–72) as well as Judas's betrayal (14:43–46). Unlike Peter, Judas stepped beyond denial to becoming a participant with those who killed Jesus (14:1–2, 10–11, 17–21). Unlike Judas the betrayer, Peter becomes paradigmatic as the disciple who fails (14:50) yet is restored after the resurrection (16:7). Moral lapse and final ruin are both possibilities for the follower of Jesus. But the example of Peter becomes a message of hope and renewal for those who fail when faced with the temptation to deny him. Renewal before the end is indeed possible. Borrell even dares to call Peter's denial "good news."[249] The demands of discipleship are great, but the one who calls them also summons them back into relationship with him after failure. As Borrell notes:

> Apropos of the denial, we have seen how the disciples personify the human difficulties in being faithful to Jesus until death. They also show that a positive continuation in the relationship with Jesus depends solely on him: the denial of Peter is, in fact, the last word *of* the disciples in the disciples in Mark, but the last word *about* them is the invitation to reunite given by Jesus, despite their failure. Jesus alone can prevent the human story, composed of weakness and incoherence, from ending in failure. He alone can overturn it and change it into a story of hope.[250]

The story of discipleship in Mark includes renewal and hope and not only the summons to obedient faith (cf. 1 Pet 1:3). Jesus goes before the disciples into Galilee (16:7), echoing how he led them in the way before the crucifixion (10:32). They would meet him again at the place where their discipleship began (1:14–20). As Jesus had predicted Peter's and the disciples' failure (14:30), so also he anticipated the restoration of Peter and his fellow followers in Galilee (14:28). The resurrection of Jesus is the

---

247. Stein, *Mark*, 410.

248. First Clement 5:1–6:1 places Peter among those who are examples of enduring persecution and contending for the faith unto the end. Clement's attention fixes upon Peter's strength and endurance rather than his failure.

249. Agustí Borrell, *The Good News of Peter's Denial: A Narrative and Rhetorical Reading of Mark 14:54.66–72* (Atlanta: Scholars, 1998), 214.

250. Borrell, *The Good News of Peter's Denial*, 214.

story about the Messiah's restoration and the restoration of the disciples. Renewal to participation with him comes even after failure to follow him.

The Disciples' Incomprehension

Peter's denial and his initial rejection of Jesus' declaration about his crucifixion are part of a larger story of how the disciples failed to comprehend Jesus. This is a characteristic feature of Mark's portrayal of the first followers. Hooker observes, "If Mark's story is a story about the meaning of discipleship (barely understood), it is also a story about misunderstanding and opposition, incomprehension and rejection."[251] Kingsbury concurs:[252] "The cardinal problem besetting the disciples is incomprehension."[253] Repeatedly the disciples fail to understand Jesus' revelation and do not respond in faith. They are given revelatory insight into the secret of the kingdom of God (4:11–12), but they fail to understand his parable (4:13) despite their special privilege. When Jesus reveals his power over nature (4:39), the disciples show a lack of faith and do not comprehend who he is (4:40–41). They do not grasp his ability to supply food for the multitude (6:35–37), and they could not even work out the implications of this miracle after he showed his authority over the raging sea (6:51–52). The second time Jesus was faced with a hungry crowd they still did not comprehend (8:4), and he was highly exasperated with their inability to perceive (8:17–21). Jesus upbraided them for not understanding a parable (7:14–19) although he had previously explained everything to the disciples (4:34). After Jesus revealed that he, as the Messiah, would suffer and die, Peter failed to understand and rebuked him (8:32). Even when Jesus was transfigured the meaning of the event remained opaque to Peter (9:5–6). Jesus openly declared his resurrection, but the disciples had no idea what he meant (9:9–10). Neither the crucifixion nor the resurrection were understandable concepts for them (9:31–32). His teaching on the wealthy likewise shot straight past them (10:32–37). The reader is not surprised to discover that, in the end, they failed to remain awake to watch with him (14:32–42). Jesus predicted that they would desert him, and so it happened. Peter denied him three times. Judas betrayed him. The disciples' final response to Jesus graphically displayed their inability to comprehend him, his message, and his mission.

The significance of the disciples' inability to comprehend Jesus and his mission has garnered considerable debate. Weeden, for example, argued that Mark is a polemic against the disciples of Jesus, a position which has found sympathy with authors as recent as Telford, although they differ in their explanation of the reason for the

---

251. Hooker, *The Gospel According to Mark*, 20.

252. Jack Dean Kingsbury, *Conflict in Mark: Jesus, Authorities, Disciples* (Minneapolis: Fortress, 1989), 96.

253. Hooker, *The Gospel According to Mark*, 20; Kingsbury, *Conflict in Mark*, 96; Mary R. Thompson, *The Role of Disbelief in Mark: A New Approach to the Second Gospel* (Mahwah, NJ: Paulist, 1989), 172; Shiner, *Follow Me!* 292; Watts, *Isaiah's New Exodus in Mark*, 221; Henderson, *Christology and Discipleship in the Gospel of Mark*.

polemic.[254] In Weeden's view, the disciples in Mark held a divine-man (*theios anēr*) Christology (see above), which did not embrace the cross. The reason the author of Mark wrote the Gospel was to combat this heretical view of the disciples. They regarded Jesus as a miracle worker while Mark showed that his suffering and death were redemptive through his *theologia crucis* (theology of the cross). Telford affirms the polemic purpose of the author and that "the Gospel reflects the tension between opposing Christologies in the early church." But it is doubtful, in his opinion, that the early disciples would have held a Christology that was rooted in Hellenistic thought.[255] Instead, he supports the stance of Tyson, who proposed that Mark's disciples had embraced the theology that Jesus was the royal Messiah of the line of David, but they could not accept the notion that, as such, he would be crucified. As he says, "The point is this: Mark is not here saying that the disciples understood that Jesus was the Messiah and were commanded not to broadcast it; rather he is saying that they completely misunderstood the nature of Jesus' Messiahship, not understanding it as a suffering Messiahship but as a royal Messiahship which would issue in benefits for themselves."[256] Telford comments, "This theory has much to commend it, although one has to add that an equally primitive view of Jesus as the exalted, apocalyptic son of Man shortly to return in glory is in addition being modified by the evangelist in light of his *theologia crucis*."[257] Tyson's view has much to commend it since the disciples, beginning with Peter, failed to understand the necessity of the Messiah's suffering.

However, Best correctly notes that Mark does not reflect a community that is divided against itself but rather "the community as a whole is being instructed through the failure of the disciples and the teaching they are given."[258] Mark does not portray a particular group as those who had embraced an errant Christology. But Best affirms there is a problem, that being the nature of the disciples' faith in light of the cross. "Faith is necessary," he notes, "but faith which is unrelated to the cross only misleads. The nature of discipleship becomes apparent only in the light of the cross, and not in the light of Jesus' mighty acts."[259] Henderson, on the other hand, takes on the topic of the disciples' lack of comprehension and shows that the motif is part of the earliest encounters they had with Jesus. Their misunderstanding is not simply due to an inability to embrace the theology of the cross, but "their faltering gains momentum *prior* to Jesus' teachings about the necessity of his impending suffering (see Mark 6:52; 8:17–21). Thus to infer that their later failings derive from a deficient understanding

---

254. Weeden, "The Heresy That Necessitated Mark's Gospel"; Theodore J. Weeden, *Mark-Traditions in Conflict* (Philadelphia: Fortress, 1971), 52–69; Telford, *Theology of the Gospel of Mark*, 135–36.

255. Telford, *Theology of the Gospel of Mark*, 136. See Best, *Following Jesus*, 237–45.

256. Tyson, "The Blindness of the Disciples in Mark," 262.

257. Telford, *Theology of the Gospel of Mark*, 136.

258. Best, *Following Jesus*, 244.

259. Best, *Following Jesus*, 13–14. This position has almost become axiomatic. See, for example Samuel, *A Postcolonial Reading of Mark's Story of Jesus*, 132.

of Jesus' suffering messiahship either leaves out of account these earlier instances of success and failure or views them as merely provisional."[260] Instead, Henderson understands their misunderstanding in relation to the advent of the rule of God (as 6:47–52): "Jesus consistently expects his followers to wield authority that stems from God's sovereign dominion—not on their own as self-designated 'divine men,' but as those empowered by Jesus for the collective extension of his Christological witness. Thus where they emulate his paradigmatic exposition of God's rule, the disciples have properly grasped not just Jesus' true messianic identity but also their own call to participate in the new age of God that he proclaims and embodies. Where they fall short, they have failed to trust the prevailing promises of God's coming dominion."[261] The King's power and not the Servant's pain is what the disciples fail to grasp. And they themselves come short of operating fully in the kingdom's power.

While Henderson's analysis brings a fresh breeze into the debate about the disciple's failure, she limits her study to the opening chapters of the Gospel and offers an incomplete analysis of Mark by not exploring the failure and the redemption surrounding the cross. A more complete analysis would recognize that the disciples' failure is indeed about their inability to grasp the power of Jesus' kingly rule but also includes the way that rule is then merged with his mission to suffer as the Servant. In addition, the disciples not only fail to enter into the power of the kingdom but also fail to embrace the pain of the cross. They are confused by both, and in the end they flee. But the message of Mark includes redemption—their failure on both counts is not the final word. They will meet him in Galilee. That is the promise predicted before the cross and repeated after the resurrection. In Mark, the disciples see and are called to participate in Jesus' suffering and glory.

THE COMMUNITY OF DISCIPLES

While the center of Mark's theology of discipleship is the relationship between Jesus and his followers, the Gospel also focuses the readers' attention on the nature of the community formed by Jesus. Those who follow Jesus enter into a relationship with one another. While the disciples, as Jesus, are in conflict with their contemporaries in society as people persecuted for the kingdom, their alienation is counterbalanced by their inclusion into the company of disciples (10:28–31). Belonging is just as much of a concern in this Gospel as separation and alienation. The images that appear in Mark to describe the relationship between the disciples are varied and, in the end, not as fully developed as in subsequent New Testament literature. The concepts that express the nature of community are principally familial, religious, pastoral, maritime, and didactic. They are also the people of God of the New Exodus.[262] Mark communicates

---

260. Henderson, *Christology and Discipleship in the Gospel of Mark*, 14.
261. Henderson, *Christology and Discipleship in the Gospel of Mark*, 242.
262. Surprisingly, many studies on Mark's theology focus so much attention on the relationship

that Jesus' intent was not to call individuals into isolated relationship with him but into a community of those who share a common faith and walk. Though the word "church" does not appear in the Gospel (cf. Matt 16:18), Mark betrays a strong ecclesiology. Isolation is not the disciples' lot.²⁶³

The concept of the community as a household appears at various points in the Gospel. The two central texts that define the relationship between the disciples in familial terms are 3:31–35 and 10:29–30. In the first of these, the relationship between Jesus regards those who are at table around him as "my mother and my brothers." Indeed, "Whoever does the will of God is my brother and sister and mother." The declaration regarding the kinship relation between Jesus and his disciples occurs within Jesus' own house (Καὶ ἔρχεται εἰς οἶκον, "Then he went home" [3:19a]).²⁶⁴ This occurs immediately after Jesus' call of twelve apostles on the mountain (3:13–19a). Those who are called now enter into his house and will be declared members of his household. For Mark, geography and space are elements of the theological story (as "the way"; see above). His family tried to restrain him from going out again to the crowd since people were saying, "He has gone out of his mind" (3:21). This first part of a "Markan sandwich" sets the stage for what follows in 3:31–35.²⁶⁵ Surprisingly, "his mother and his brothers came; and standing outside, they sent to him and called him" (3:31). Mark does not indicate which members of his household restrained him, but it was not every member since some appear to be absent from the first scene. However, when his mother and brothers do arrive, they cannot reach him due to the crowd "sitting around him" (3:32). They are on the outside (cf. 4:10–12). Jesus' family does not fare well here in Mark's narrative. They appear to be either in opposition to Jesus' mission or separated from him and not included. Jesus' embrace of those who are with him and do God's will as "my brother and sister and mother" stands in stark contrast to Jesus' family since they, who should have been outside by the household norms of the day, were given the most intimate place in the household. The setting in Jesus' own house, the separation between Jesus and his kin, and the redefinition of kinship in terms of doing the will of God all highlight the central place that kinship plays in Mark's understanding of the community. They partake of the promised restoration of

---

between Jesus and the disciples that they fail to examine the community outcomes of this relationship. In contrast, Donahue pays special attention to the household language in the book (*The Theology and Setting of Discipleship in the Gospel of Mark*, 31–56), while Best recognizes a wider array of imagery to describe the relationship (*Following Jesus*, 208–36).

263. Matera incorrectly states, "The ecclesiology of the Markan Gospel is implicit at best" (*New Testament Theology*, 20). While it is true that the word *ekklēsia* is absent, the concept of a community formed in relation to Jesus is central to Mark's theology. The NT literature associated with Peter does not use the term at all but presents a rich theology of community or ecclesiology.

264. The way that Mark positions Jesus family in relation to this house indicates that this was Jesus' family dwelling. They "went out to restrain him" (3:21) and then appear outside and send a message into him (3:31). See Adela Yarbro Collins, *Mark*, 226, who notes that εἰς οἶκον "is idiomatic for '(going) home.'" Contra Stein, *Mark*, 179.

265. Stein, *Mark*, 187.

kinship ties prophesied in Isaiah 49:18–21 and 60:4 as those related to Jesus and not simply descended from Israel (cf. Ps 22:22–23; Deut 3:18). Moreover, the message for the first Roman readers, who themselves experienced opposition from their families, would have been powerful indeed.[266] They, too, are Jesus' brothers and sisters and mother and, therefore, gather together as true kin.

The loss that Roman believers experienced around the time when Mark was first read aloud to them was vocalized by Peter at the head of the second major paragraph where Jesus defines the community of disciples in familial terms: "Peter began to say to him, 'Look, we have left everything and followed you'" (10:28–31). He and the rest experienced loss of place and family as they responded to the call to follow Jesus (1:16–20), and they and the readers of the Gospel knew the severe corruption of family relations that could come with discipleship (13:12–13). They have not amassed riches (cf. 10:23–28) and have even embraced economic loss (2:13–14). Now what is left for them? Jesus does not dismiss or rebuke Peter for the concern but affirms that even "in this age" the one who has lost will receive "houses, brothers and sisters, mothers and children, and fields, with persecutions" and, on top of that, "in the age to come eternal life." Discipleship appeared to be the loss of familial community and all that sustains life, but following Jesus means a multiplication of all that one needs. The family is not lost but rather extended, and even the life within that community is extended for eternity. At the very heart of Jesus' gospel is the formation of the familial community accompanied with place, security, and sustenance ("houses . . . fields"). But this restoration is joined with opposition as well, that is, "with persecutions." The gospel entails suffering with Jesus (cf. 1 Pet 4:13), yet within the midst of the disciples' loss of family and place stands the promise of *present* community and place with the additional benefit of eternal life. We should not lose sight of the present material promise regarding "houses" and "fields," a point often glossed in the commentaries. The promise regarding restored place and sustenance is part of the social restoration that comes with the gospel. Mark's theology is not only about the restoration of community and the promise of life but also touches on present human needs such as daily bread (cf. Matt 6:11).

A Household

While Mark 3:31–35 and 10:29–30 are the principle places where Mark portrays the disciples as a household, other texts add additional content to the concept. Not insignificantly, numerous healings occur within houses throughout the narrative, beginning with the healing of Peter's mother-in-law (1:29–31; 2:1–12; 5:35–43) and including exorcism (7:24–30). As the "way" is both a place and a metaphor for the way of the Lord, so also the house is both a place and symbol of household renewal. Jesus conducts the mission of the gospel within the house (2:15–17; 14:3–9; cf. 6:6b–13),

---

266. Marcus, *Mark 1–8*, 285–86.

forgives within the house (2:1–12), and repeatedly withdraws with his disciples into a house where he instructs them regarding the kingdom (7:17–23; 9:28–29, 33–37; 10:10–12). He celebrates the Passover with them in the house (14:12–26). As the disciples are regarded as kin, members of a common household related to Jesus, so Jesus carries out the core activities of the gospel mission within the house. In speaking about his coming as the Son of Man, he portrays himself as the coming master of the house to whom those of the household are accountable (13:32–37). They must be watchful and ready for his coming. The household is the central place for the ministry of the gospel and the household Jesus forms can only stand if it remains unified and not divided (3:19b–27).

A Temple

Alongside the household imagery, Mark alludes to the community as a temple.[267] The use of temple imagery to describe the community is not as developed here as in 1 Peter 2:4–10. What is only seminal in the Gospel becomes flowers fully in Peter's epistle. Gray has demonstrated that "the temple plays a vital role in the plot of Mark's gospel and is deeply connected to the story of Jesus. It serves as the stage for the Markan Jesus' conflict with the Jewish authorities, and moreover it is vital reference point for the narrative portrait of Jesus' identity, mission, and eschatological message."[268] Jesus enters into temple towards the end of his ministry (11:11) and there engages in the dramatic acts of cleansing the temple (11:15–19), confronting the authorities gathered in the temple (11:27–12:34), teaching in its precincts (12:35–44), linking the temple with eschatological events (13:1–37), and finally being charged and crucified on the basis of his prediction of the temple's destruction and restoration (14:58; 15:29). Given the nature of Jesus' engagement with the temple, Perrin argues: "Jesus of Nazareth saw himself and his movement as nothing less than the decisive embodiment of Yahweh's eschatological temple."[269] In Perrin's view, Jesus and his disciples "constituted the foundation of this new temple, one which on some level stood in continuity with Herod's temple order, but also, on another level, anticipated an altogether different cultic order," one that embodied justice.[270] Jesus and his disciples constitute a counter-temple movement that stands over against the central institution of Judaism. The temple will meet its end and, as Gray observes, "This old temple will be replaced by a new one consisting of those who, like the centurion, put their faith in the rejected-yet-vindicated cornerstone of God's new eschatological temple, Jesus."[271] Jesus' place within the temple and the temple imagery that he applies to himself bears within it the theology

---

267. Best, *Following Jesus*, 213–25. See the previous discussion in this chapter on Jesus' relationship with the temple.

268. Gray, *The Temple in the Gospel of Mark*, 198.

269. Perrin, *Jesus the Temple*, 12.

270. Perrin, *Jesus the Temple*, 12–13.

271. Gray, *The Temple in the Gospel of Mark*, 200.

later explicitly developed in 1 Peter which regarded the community as the temple of which Jesus was the chief cornerstone.

Mark suggests the connection between the temple and the community through the stone imagery. Jesus is the rejected stone (12:10–11; see above), a citation of Psalm 118:22–23, which Jesus places within the parable of the vineyard (12:1–12). The owner of the vineyard comes and destroys those who are its tenants and, as Jesus says, he will "give the vineyard to others." The parable echoes Isaiah 5:1–7, where Israel is portrayed as the vineyard of God.[272] In this complex of imagery, the leaders Jesus denounces (Mark 11:27–33) will be displaced since they, the builders, rejected "the stone" (12:10). The authority over the vineyard transfers "to others," who may be the "leaders of the church, as in Acts 4:5–6, 11," or could represent a much wider group, those being the "Gentile church that was beginning to see itself as the true Israel."[273] To be sure, "The teaching on the church as the new temple is only incidental to this pericope," as Best says, but it is strongly suggested by the placement of the vineyard imagery for Israel in juxtaposition with the stone testimony, which is so clearly associated with the temple. A new community is formed as the old is rejected. Their destiny is related to the one who is the foundation of the new temple.

The coming change of order appears as a central topic in the trial of Jesus. In 14:58 those who gave false testimony against Jesus reported that Jesus said, "I will destroy this temple that is made with hands, and in three days I will build another, not made with hands." The testimony against him is repeated as Jesus hangs on the cross: "Aha! You who would destroy the temple and build it in three days, save yourself, and come down from the cross!" (15:29–30) The testimony offered is a distortion of Jesus' own teaching in which he had predicted the temple's destruction but did not take responsibility for that act: "Do you see these great buildings? Not one stone will be left here upon another; all will be thrown down" (13:2). The testimony conflates his predication of the destruction of the temple with his teaching on his own death, which would be followed by his resurrection three days hence (8:31; 9:31; 10:34). So while the false testimony was wrong in ascribing the temple's destruction to Jesus itself, Mark and his readers would understand the reference to its rebuilding in three days as true—but with Jesus as the temple. Also, within the testimony against Jesus is a critique of the temple itself, i.e., the one "that is made with hands," in contrast with the raised temple "not made with hands" (14:58). This language echoes the critique of cult idolatry, which was nothing more than the product of human hands (see the LXX of Lev 26:1, 30; Judith 8:18; Isa 2:18),[274] an accusation which later appears in Stephen's speech in Acts (Acts 7:48). The thought that Jesus would construct a new

---

272. See the discussion in the commentaries, such as Evans, *Mark 8:27–16:20*, 215–40; Stein, *Mark*, 530–40; Marcus, *Mark 8–16*, 801–15.

273. Best, *Following Jesus*, 219–20; Hooker, *The Gospel According to Mark*, 276; Marcus, *Mark 8–16*, 805.

274. Marcus, *Mark 8–16*, 1003.

temple not made with hands is most likely a reference to the church, the new temple.[275] The tradition here is strikingly similar to Jesus' declaration to Peter recorded in Matthew that "on this rock I will build my church" (Matt 16:18). In Mark, the temple is called the "house" (2:26) and, as noted above, the house evokes the image of the community of disciples as a household. That house, according to Mark 11:17, "shall be called a house of prayer for all the nations" (cf. Isa 56:7), recalling again the theme of the inclusion of the nations into this new temple community. The building of the new temple suggests the formation of a new temple community that will stand in the place of the old temple, which will be destroyed. The main actor in this drama is Jesus himself who will be rejected but, in the end, will become the principle cornerstone of this new structure. Once again, the identity of the community is bound tightly with Jesus who is also the new temple.

A Flock

Mark also presents the community of disciples as the flock of God.[276] As noted above, Mark presents Jesus as the Shepherd-Messiah of Israel (6:24; 14:26–28), who shepherds the congregation of the Lord and leads them in the way. This aspect of Mark's Christology is tied deeply with his theology of the New Exodus and the cross. The Shepherd will be struck down and his sheep scattered, but he will lead the way and the disciples will be restored and gathered again. The Shepherd-Messiah is the crucified and resurrected Messiah who gathers and feeds his community. The flock are the recipients of salvation. Moreover, the prophetic announcement of the New Exodus included the promise that God "will feed his flock like a shepherd; he will gather the lambs in his arms, and carry them in his bosom, and gently lead the mother sheep" (Isa 40:11). Mark regards the company of disciples as the flock of God that stands in continuity with Israel, which now has its true Shepherd (Num 27:17; Zech 10:3; 13:7) who will protect his own (Isa 40:11; 63:11). As in the previous images of the community of disciples, language that referred to Israel is now attached to the followers of Jesus. They are the sheep whom the Shepherd provides for and leads. Although they may be scattered at the time of persecution, he gathers them (Mark 14:26–28; 16:7).

A Ship

Best argues that the company of the disciples is also envisioned as a ship. While the maritime imagery is not as central as the images of the church as a household, temple, or flock, it is not without precedence in Israel. In the Testament of Naphtali 6, Naphtali recounts a dream in which a ship appears on the sea inscribed with the name "The Ship of Jacob." Jacob instructed the patriarchs to board it and, upon doing so,

---

275. Marcus, *Mark 8–16*, 1004.
276. Best, *Following Jesus*, 210–12.

"a violent tempest arose, a great windstorm." Jacob was tossed overboard as the boat filled with water and broke apart. The patriarchs floated on planks, and "thus we were all dispersed, even to the outer limits." After Levi's prayer, "the storm ceased, the ship reached the land, as though at peace." Jacob approached, unharmed. We cannot say that this story was in the mind of the author when he recounted the story of the storms that arose when the disciples were in the boat (Mark 4:35–41; 6:45–52). In both these cases, Jesus shows his mastery over the elements and saves the disciples who, unlike the sons of Jacob, are preserved together and not scattered. The boat in Mark becomes an image of Jesus' authority but also his salvation, which preserves the community in the midst of disaster. Jesus teaches from the boat in Mark (4:1) and also instructs the disciples while they are in the boat (8:14–21). The boat is a means to separate himself and the disciples from the crowd (3:9). Indeed, Jesus called the first disciples from their own boats before inviting them to journey with him by boat across the Sea of Galilee (1:16–20). The boat then stands for the community that is in the presence of and under the protection and instruction of Jesus. Given the strength of the symbolism of the boat, the later church adopted it as one of its iconic representations.[277]

A Community of Learners

The disciples of Jesus also appear in Mark as a community of learners.[278] The majority of the texts in Mark that speak about Jesus' teaching show him directing his instruction to the crowds who surrounded him in various settings, as this was his usual custom (10:1; 14:49; 1:21–22; 2:13; 4:1–2; 6:2, 6, 34; 11:17; 12:14, 35). Although Mark contains less didactic material than the other Gospels, the reader is left without any doubt that one of Jesus' principle activities was teaching. He did, however, offer special instruction to the disciples since to them "has been given the secret of the kingdom of God, but for those outside, everything comes in parables" (4:11). Jesus unlocks their understanding and also upbraids them when they fail to understand his instruction (4:13–20; 6:52; 7:17–23; 8:14–21; 9:30–32; 10:10–12). Mark is as much about the disciples' obtuseness as it is the Messianic secret! They are not the most ready group of learners. The reader is called to understand as the first disciples should have understood his teaching (13:14). The disciples should understand the parables and the miracles, both signs of the kingdom of God. Jesus also gives the disciples special teaching regarding his forthcoming death on the cross (8:31–33), which they also did not fully comprehend (9:30–32). They received special instruction regarding the end of the age (13:1–37). Jesus calls them not only to hear his teaching but also to engage in the didactic ministry of the kingdom themselves (6:30). They are called inside to receive the complete details of Jesus' mission and are then summoned to

---

277. Best, *Following Jesus*, 232.
278. Best, *Following Jesus*, 235–36.

participate with him in teaching others. The disciples are a company of learners who receive instruction and, in turn, impart the teaching of Jesus to others.

Followers of the Jesus Way

Above all, the disciples of Jesus are those who follow him in the way of the Lord. As such, they are the community of the New Exodus who have experienced the liberation that comes from the Messiah-Servant (see above on the New Exodus in Mark). They take on the role of Israel, inheriting many of the titles ascribed to the holy nation such as "flock" and, as they, the disciples become the household of God. Their identity is consistently bound with their relation to Jesus, who goes before them. The disciples in Mark are not simply individuals who are attached to Jesus but rather form a cohesive community as the new temple and those who gather in the boat with Jesus. They learn, and misunderstand, together. Their mission is corporate as well (6:30). They are the ones who are the closest to Jesus and are present with him at every turn. They then participate with him in both his ministry and his sufferings. When they fail, they are restored as those called to meet the risen Christ in Galilee. Mark's understanding of discipleship includes a robust theology of suffering and, at the same time, the promise of participation with him after his exaltation. The message of discipleship revolves around Jesus' calling and his continuing redemptive work in the lives of his followers. Given Jesus' persistence with them despite their continued failure to understand, Jesus' followers are people who should hope and follow him faithfully. Their salvation is about his persistence and not their ability. The message of grace permeates Mark, even though the language of grace is never found.

THE ETHICS OF DISCIPLESHIP

According to Mark's Gospel, being a disciple of Jesus entails a significant change in conduct. Jesus' coming inaugurates the new era of the rule of God. Jesus goes before and leads the way in proclaiming and acting out the power and the values of this rule. He calls individuals to follow him and put into practice the values of the kingdom as they follow his example. Houlden, however, once remarked that there is a "paucity of ethical material" in Mark and that "even the ethical material which Mark includes is for the most part not present as a result of purely ethical interest."[279] Indeed, Mark includes nothing like the long moral discourse found in Matthew (5–7) and Luke (6:20–49), leading Via to state that while Mark has an ethic the "ethical categories . . . are obviously not formally announced as such."[280] These assessments begin with a western assumption about how ethics should be taught and fail to take into account the way narrative becomes a vehicle for moral instruction. Hays notes that Mark "contains

---

279. J. L. Houlden, *Ethics and the New Testament* (Middlesex: Penguin, 1973), 41–43.

280. Dan O. Via Jr., *The Ethics of Mark's Gospel—In the Middle of Time* (Philadelphia: Fortress, 1985), 81.

very little explicit ethical teaching" but does recognize that "to investigate the ethical import of Mark's story of Jesus, we must look beyond such brief didactic units and attend to the broader contours of Mark's narrative world."[281] Instead of seeing a lack of moral teaching in Mark, Verhey argues that the whole narrative has a moral orientation. In Mark, "the focus is ... on heroic discipleship, but the major premise of discipleship makes the whole narrative a form of moral exhortation. Jesus, who came to serve rather than to be served, who patiently and heroically endured suffering for the sake of God's reign, is paradigmatic in other ways as well. His open sympathy with the ill and helpless, with Gentiles and sinners, his impatience with ostentatious and self-serving piety, his freedom from legalistic code mentality are all in their own way morally instructive."[282] Any examination of Mark's moral world must take into account that his Gospel best fits within the ancient literary category of *bios*, a type of historical writing whose concern is not simply to tell the story of a person's life but to show what kind of conduct is honorable or shameful.[283] This concern for character formation appears in various comments on ancient *bioi*. In Plutarch's *Life of Timoleon* he states, "I began the writing of my 'Lives' for the sake of others, but I find that I am continuing the work and delighting in it now for my own sake also, using history as a mirror and endeavoring in a manner to fashion and adorn my life in conformity with the virtues therein depicted. ... I receive and welcome each subject of my history in turn as my guest, so to speak, and observe carefully 'how large he was and of what mien,' and select from his career what is most important and most beautiful to know" (Tim 1).[284] The purpose of the *bios* is moral formation and not simply the preservation of an historical record. These narratives are, at their core, moral treatises.

Ethics and the Kingdom of God

Houlden is correct, however, in identifying the advent of the rule of God, which was breaking in through the ministry of Jesus Christ as the center of Mark's moral world. As he says, "For Mark, the answer to the question, 'What is my duty with regard to X?' is, 'God is sovereign—live under his rule.'"[285] Houlden rightly recognizes that Mark presents a theological ethic, that is, one that is rooted in the activity of God. The ethic enjoined flows out of the reign of God, a rule that is both a deed and a summons. The

---

281. Hays, *The Moral Vision of the New Testament*, 74. What may be "explicit" will vary from culture to culture and from genre to genre.

282. Allen Verhey, *The Great Reversal: Ethics and the New Testament* (Grand Rapids: Eerdmans, 1984), 78.

283. See, for example, the *bioi* of Plutarch, Suetonius, or Diogenes Laertius. See Burridge, *What Are the Gospels?*; Craig S. Keener, *The Historical Jesus of The Gospels* (Grand Rapids: Eerdmans, 2009), 78.

284. See also Plutarch (*Alex.* 1.1–3), and Cornelius Nepos, who notes the importance of character in writing a *bios*: "I do not know exactly how I should describe his character, and I am afraid that if I begin to tell you of his deeds, I will appear not a biographer but a historian" (*Pel.* 1).

285. Houlden, *Ethics and the New Testament*, 44.

moral imperative, according to Mark, is buried within the indicative of God's reign. The opening announcement of the kingdom is wedded with the call to repent and believe: "The time is fulfilled, and the kingdom of God has come near; repent, and believe in the good news" (1:15; cf. 1:4).[286] The rule of God brings with it radical demands over a person's life, so much so that it is worth the loss of limb and sight if these in any way keep a person from coming under his rule (9:45, 47). The sacrifice required is so great that the wealthy will be enabled to follow only through the miraculous power of God, since their attachment to riches may make demands greater than their commitment to follow Jesus, the King of the kingdom (10:17-22, 23-27). The call of the kingdom requires a total reorientation of life so that a person becomes willing to leave all in order to follow Jesus. Peter understood the implications of the call and said to Jesus, "Look, we have left everything and followed you." This act of leaving and following (cf. 1:16-20) is the paradigm of the moral life because of the advent of the rule of God in Jesus' ministry.[287] Turning away from one's former life through repentance is the first move as a person aligns themselves with the kingdom of God. Faith, then, is not simply a "virtue" but rather "the all-embracing term that describes the moral and ethical life of those who embrace the kingdom of God."[288] Repentance and belief are predicated on God's activity of bringing in the kingdom through Jesus' deeds and proclamation. The imperative only exists because God has acted in a decisive way.

The Ethics of Following Jesus

After the announcement of the kingdom's advent (1:14-15), Jesus calls the first disciples to follow him (1:16-20). Jesus inaugurates the New Exodus and now summons people to be with him and become participants in this Exodus, walking after him in the way (see above on the New Exodus and following Jesus). The disciples' participation in the kingdom includes their moral life. Jesus embraces suffering and the way of the cross as he obeys the will of God ("the Son of Man must [$\delta\epsilon\tilde{\iota}$] undergo great suffering" [8:31]), and so the disciples receive the call to take up their cross as well. Discipleship entails denying oneself and following Jesus even in suffering and death. The only way to gain life is through surrendering oneself for his sake and for the sake of the gospel (8:34-9:1). The moral life entails an absolute commitment to Jesus and his way, living a life of service rather than seeking to dominate and control (9:33-37; 10:35-40). Although Jesus is the Messiah King, he is also the Suffering Servant who forfeits his life on the cross. Although sovereign, he models obedience to God to the point of death. When the disciples show that they have not completely reoriented

---

286. Frank J. Matera, *New Testament Ethics: The Legacies of Jesus and Paul* (Louisville: Westminster John Knox, 1996), 14-15.

287. Matera notes that "at the beginning of the Markan narrative, then, the disciples function as examples of what it means to repent; they leave behind family, livelihood, and possessions to follow Jesus because they perceive the presence of God's kingdom in his ministry" (*New Testament Ethics*, 22).

288. Matera, *New Testament Ethics*, 23.

their lives and argue who will be the greatest among them, Jesus tells them that the greatest must be the servant of all. The pattern they are to imitate is the one that he models: "For the Son of Man came not to be served but to serve" (10:41–45). As Hays says, "The *norm* for discipleship is defined by the cross. Jesus' own obedience, interpreted as servanthood (10:45), is the singular pattern for faithfulness."[289] The indicative of Jesus' life of sacrificial service carries within it the imperative to serve as he served. They must join with him in unwavering service to God and others. But Mark's narrative makes an abrupt turn at this point as Jesus moves from being the imitable model of service to doing that which is inimitable: "And to give his life a ransom for many." The imperative of discipleship is buried within the indicative of Jesus' ministry and service, but the *imitatio Christi* has its limit since the disciples may never become "a ransom for many." Jesus is a moral example to follow, but he is more than that.[290]

Ethics and Eschatology

Although the moral life in Mark is oriented around the in-breaking of the kingdom of God and participation with Jesus as he leads the disciples in the way of the Lord, one eye is firmly fixed on the future. Jesus frames his moral instruction within the promise of his *coming* rule. Eschatology is tightly tied with ethics in Mark. Discipleship brings with it enormous demands, which only seem reasonable to embrace in light of the presence of the rule of God and Mark's high Christology. But the ethics also look forward to the final consummation when the Son of Man comes and sends out the angels to "gather his elect from the four winds, from the ends of the earth to the ends of heaven" (13:26–27). The promise of salvation is for the one who lives now in light of that event, enduring the suffering that comes in the interim: "But the one who endures to the end will be saved" (13:9–13). The present time before the end is one of alert watching (13:32–37). The new kingdom order has begun already with Jesus' ministry. Mark relates how Jesus declared all food clean but called people to abandon the moral defilements of the heart (7:1–23). He relativized the Sabbath law by placing human need as the primary concern and showing himself to be the Lord of the Sabbath (2:23–28). Jesus reoriented people's understanding of the divine sanction of marriage and contradicted current rabbinic teaching on divorce (10:2–9). He also stood against the sovereignty of riches as he taught in favor of giving to the poor (10:17–27). To be a disciple meant receiving the kingdom as a child (10:13–16). Indeed, if someone does not receive it as a child, they "will never enter it." The moral demands that come with following Jesus during the present time, including following him in his sufferings, are also oriented to the final return of the Son of Man and the coming of his kingdom when all powers will be overthrown (13:24–37). The final

---

289. Hays, *The Moral Vision of the New Testament*, 84.

290. Or as Hays observes, "While Mark depicts Jesus' death as a vicarious sacrifice, he stresses even more emphatically its exemplary character: Jesus' death on the cross establishes a pattern for his disciples to follow" (*The Moral Vision of the New Testament*, 80).

reward relativizes the radical demands made on the disciple during the present age (9:42–48). The moral life has an eschatological orientation.

An Ethic of Obedience

The moral life of the disciple is marked by obedience. Jesus presented the model they must imitate. He prayed for deliverance from the suffering of the cross yet submitted himself in obedience to the Father's plan (14:36). And while on the cross, he refused to save his own life though he was taunted to do so (15:25–32), demonstrating the extent of obedience required of the disciple (8:35). Jesus fully submitted to the will of God, and the disciples who follow him must do the same. Those who do the will of God are the true members of Jesus' family (8:31–35). The first disciples in Mark obey Jesus' call to follow (1:16–20), becoming a moral example for the first readers/hearers. But Mark also shows the disciples' failure to obey. They do not stay awake and pray in the middle of trial as Jesus had exhorted them to do (14:32–42). Instead of following him in self-sacrificial service, Peter denied Jesus (14:66–72). Peter had become ashamed of him (8:38). In fact, all the twelve "deserted him and fled" when he was arrested (14:50). Despite their failure to obey, Mark presents a picture of hope and restoration. For his part, Peter "broke down and wept" because of his failure (14:72) and after the resurrection he sends the message to the "disciples and Peter" that he is going ahead to meet them in Galilee (15:7). Grace overcomes moral failure and calls for a renewed commitment to be with Jesus and follow him.

Obeying the will of God entails reorienting one's life in response to Jesus' call. Instead of serving self, one serves God and others. Mark shows that the life of service may also be understood as love for God and others, a characteristic of those who "are not far from the kingdom of God" (12:28–34). When a scribe asked Jesus about the first commandment, Jesus responded by citing the Shema (Deut 6:4–5), saying, "The first is, 'Hear, O Israel: the Lord our God, the Lord is one; you shall love the Lord your God with all your heart and with all your soul, and with all your mind, and with all your strength." He then cited Leviticus 19:18: "The second is this, 'You shall love your neighbor as yourself,'" concluding that "there is no other commandment greater than these." Although this teaching does not come in a formal discourse on the moral life, Mark includes the double love command as a central element in Jesus' moral teaching. It is hardly incidental. Hays misses the way moral teaching is integrated into Mark's narrative when he comments that "nowhere, however, does the Markan Jesus promulgate love as a distinctive mark of discipleship."[291] Love for God and neighbor mark the character of the one who is near the kingdom of God in this new order that Jesus has established (12:34). The sacrificial service to which Jesus calls his disciples is, in the end, a service of love for God and the other, placing their interests ahead of

---

291. Hays, *The Moral Vision of the New Testament*, 84.

one's own. This includes forgiving the other as the disciple has been forgiven (11:25; 2:5, 7, 9, 10; 3:28; 4:12).

The moral vision in Mark centers on the presence of the kingdom and the hope of its future consummation. Jesus is the one who leads the disciples as an example of the moral life, yet his own redemptive service transcends that which the disciples can imitate. The core values in this new reality are obedience to the will of God and loving service to God and others. The ethics of discipleship are not only oriented around God's present work through Christ but also the coming of the Son of Man, making the present time one to stay awake and pray. Temptation is always near, and failure is a possibility. But Mark's ethic includes redemption in the face of moral failure. The moral teaching in Mark includes instruction on marriage and divorce, riches, responsiveness to human need, and childlike humility. These are aspects of what it means to be a follower of Jesus in the present time of the kingdom with its reordering of values. While Mark does not record any of Jesus' extended moral discourses, it does include trajectories of a moral vision centered on the reign of God and its Servant King, Jesus.

PETER'S TESTIMONY IN MARK

As argued in this and the previous chapters, Mark's theology faithfully represents the perspectives of Peter on Jesus' life and theology. Mark presents a reliable testimony of Peter's preaching to his readers/hearers although he only gives the apostle's *ipsissima vox* rather than his *ipsissima verba*. Whatever redactional changes Mark made to Peter's story would have remained conceptually faithful to his source and, to be sure, if this Gospel were written during Peter's lifetime the final edition would have been read and approved by the apostle. Peter played a central role in the early church as one who heard and transmitted the story of Jesus and its interpretation. Our foundational knowledge of Jesus' story comes through him even though Mark would have added his own perspectives as someone who translated and offered testimony to the apostle's preaching.

Mark primarily addressed a Roman audience of Christians, although the Gospel represents both didactic and evangelistic elements. The scope of the message in Mark is universal, due likely to its source in Peter's preaching, but Mark was clearly aware that the first hearers/readers of this book were Roman. Although the audience is Gentile, the foundation of the Gospel is thoroughly Jewish, reflecting both Peter and Mark's roots in Palestine. The message is true to its origins but, at the same time, faithfully contextualized for the new Gentile audience. The Gospel is both Jewish and Gentile in its outlook, universal and particular in its scope. The universal character of the Gospel made it an adequate source for both Matthew and Luke's presentation of the gospel story. Undoubtedly John knew it as well.

Mark centers his theology on Jesus, the advent of the kingdom of God, and discipleship. He places a double framework around these themes, the most important being the theology of the Isaianic New Exodus. Jesus comes and marks out the way of this New Exodus, which includes the establishment of the new covenant through his ministry as the Servant portrayed in Isaiah. But Mark also contextualizes the story of Jesus as an *aemulatio* against the imperial story of the Roman Empire. Jesus, not Augustus or his successors, is the true Son of God, and his kingdom stands over against the claims of imperial Rome. Jesus has authority over all powers, even cosmic powers, and he is the one who in the end will rule the nations. God's agent who brings order to the cosmos is none other than the Davidic monarch (2 Sam 7:14).

The advent of the kingdom of God is played out on the road or the way, all the way up to Jesus' royal entry into Jerusalem. God's reign is seen through the overthrow of demonic powers, in the salvation from disaster, and most significantly in the liberation from sin. Jesus demonstrates the presence of the kingdom through his healings and exorcisms, showing repeatedly his power over nature and even death itself. Through these events and the teaching of the Gospel, the hearer/reader of Mark's Gospel comes to understand that Jesus is the Christ, that is, the King. Peter is the first one to demonstrate divinely inspired theological insight into his true nature. He sees clearly, just as the one who had been healed from blindness (8:22–26, 29). Since Jesus is the Son of God, he has sovereign authority as both the ruler expected by the Jewish people and as the one who stands over against any Roman imperial claim to divine sonship. Jesus is also the Son of Man of Daniel 7:14, whose dominion begins in the present time and is demonstrated in multiple ways, including the forgiveness of sins. But that rule will be brought to completion upon his glorious return with his mighty angels. Mark's presentation of Jesus' rule is also coupled with the theology of the cross. Jesus is both the Suffering Servant of Isaiah and the apocalyptic Son of Man in Daniel. Mark understands that the suffering of Jesus on the cross is not a contradiction of his rule but an essential dimension of his sovereignty.

But the sovereignty of Jesus goes beyond that of any earthly ruler since he is indeed the Lord who prepares the way for his people. He is, moreover, the Shepherd of Israel who leads his flock in this New Exodus. He teaches his people the way, including the way of rejection, dishonor, and suffering. Although he is the rejected Stone, he occupies the principle place in the formation of the new temple. Jesus is rejected and his identity is concealed, but the disciples who follow him in faith receive revelation about his true character and mission through his teaching and deeds. The disciples are offered insight into the nature of the kingdom, although who Jesus is and what his mission entails remains hidden to others.

Mark's understanding of divine salvation flows out of his Christology and his presentation of the advent of the kingdom of God. The story of salvation is that the New Exodus has begun, which culminates in the cross of Christ. Jesus' death as the Suffering Servant is as the Passover lamb who also inaugurates the new covenant and not only the New Exodus. Moreover, his death is vicarious and stands as a ransom for sin. Mark displays a rich theology of atonement, which serves as the foundation for further Christian theological development. His theology of salvation brings together the story of Christ's sufferings, rejection, death, and resurrection.

Mark also presents the readers/hearers with the story of Jesus' disciples who are present with him and who put into practice what he does. They share in his ministry of the kingdom, even including his rejection and sufferings. They are called to follow Jesus in the way, to participate in this New Exodus, taking on the greatest burdens of dishonor and pain through cross-bearing. Some will fail, Mark tells us, but Jesus offers them the hope of restoration after failure. As the resurrection looses the bond of death that held Jesus, so also the resurrection has buried within it the promise of renewal. Failure may face the disciple, but Mark's message is one of restoration and hope. Mark presents a clear moral vision for discipleship that is centered around the advent of God's kingdom and the person of Jesus, who stands as their moral example. The ethics of the kingdom in Mark center on doing the will of God and living a life of loving service toward God and others rather than serving oneself. The disciples are also formed together into a community that is variously described as a household, a temple, a flock, a ship, and a company of learners. The community finds its identity in relationship with Jesus. He is the Shepherd; they are the flock. He is the foundation stone; they become the new temple. He teaches; they learn. The story of Mark is about Jesus and his disciples, those who are called together and participate with him in his ministry of the kingdom of God.

CHAPTER 5

The Acts of the Apostles and the Testimony of Peter

The Acts of the Apostles contains eight speeches ascribed to Peter (1:15–22; 2:14–36 [with the Eleven], 38–40; 3:11–26; 4:8–12, 19–20 [with John]; 5:29–32 [with the other apostles]; 10:27–29, 34–43, 47; 11:4–17; 15:7–11). Do these speeches contain the perspectives of the apostle Peter, or are they creative compositions that reflect the theology of the author of Luke-Acts? Can they be regarded as a reliable source for understanding Peter's theology? The argument of this book is that the discourses are not simply free Lukan creations but faithful representations of Peter's perspectives.[1] Luke is a competent historian who presents testimony that was handed down to him. But he is more than a scribe who simply records since his rhetorical concerns lead him to reshape the testimony, thus offering his readers his own perspectives on transpired events and delivered speeches. Faithful representation and rhetorical shaping go hand in hand. The speeches, we would expect, betray the author's viewpoint and are accented with his rhetoric, while at the same time offering a recognizable rendering of the apostle's thought. As a credible historian of his age, Luke pens Peter's *ipsissima vox* but not the apostle's *ipsissima verba*. He is like Thucydides who "adhered as closely as possible to the general sense of what was actually said" (Thucydides 1.22.1). This is a far cry from Timaeus, who "shows off is oratorical power, but gives no report of what was actually spoken" (Polybius 12.25a.5). While it may not be possible to isolate which rhetorical elements Luke introduced into the Petrine speeches in Acts, we can be

---

1. For a discussion of the historicity of the speeches in Acts, see chapter 2.

assured that the speeches summarize Peter's thoughts just as his history sought to represent faithfully the places, people, and events portrayed. Luke adhered to the meaning of the apostle's ideas, staying faithful to both the person and the setting to which he bears witness. The author of Acts wrote one history with one approach to his sources, whether he was dealing with deeds or words. Given the qualifications discussed previously, we can affirm that we hear the particular theology of Peter in the speeches recorded in Acts.

In his survey of the Petrine speeches in Acts, Ridderbos argued that Luke's concern is not, however, to offer his readers a presentation of Peter's theology. Ridderbos is far from skeptical about the historical reliability of the speeches, but he refrains from regarding them as a source for Peter's thought. "Possibly we would like to learn from Acts more about Peter and his 'theology,'" he states, "but we must realize that Peter's speeches are not given us for this purpose. Luke is not interested in what is specifically Petrine or Pauline. Their joint significance in the service of Christ and the gospel is more important to his purpose than anything which is peculiar to the one or to the other. That is why the speeches in Acts cannot serve as a primary source for the 'theology' of Peter and Paul."[2] Bayer, voicing a view similar to Ridderbos, argues that the author of Acts regarded Peter as a representative voice for the "collective apostolic group."[3] In other words, Peter simply stands as a cipher for the company of the apostles and their proclamation. He is representative but hardly unique. Luke's purposes are indeed wider than presenting a compendium of the apostle Peter's teaching. The balanced presentation of the respective ministries of Peter and Paul, which form the backbone of his second volume, betrays his wider purposes. He elaborates on the spread of the gospel of Christ from the parochial confines of Jerusalem to the heart of the Roman Empire, a program laid out in Acts 1:8. Luke's purpose in his two-volume work is to show how God's salvation came into the world through Jesus Christ and how that salvation spread from the Jewish people in the heart of their world to the Gentiles extending to the center of the Roman empire. In other words, his overarching purpose outstrips his particular portrayal of Peter and Paul.

But if Luke penned a faithful representation of Peter's theology for his readers it may be an overstatement to say that he is solely concerned with the apostolic witness in general terms. As previously discussed at some length in chapter 1, history writing in the ancient world was a matter of recording both πράξεις καὶ λόγοι (deeds and words).[4] Speeches formed an essential part of the history, which, as Polybius noted, served to "sum up events and hold the whole history together" (12.25a.3). Through

---

2. Herman N. Ridderbos, *The Speeches of Peter in the Acts of the Apostles* (London: Tyndale, 1962), 7. Nonetheless he states, "For even though Luke's book may not be a biography of Peter of Paul, none the less the value of it depends upon the historical character of the information. For it is his purpose to depict the confirmation of the Gospel in the deeds and in the preaching of the apostles" (*The Speeches of Peter*, 9).

3. Hans F. Bayer, "The Preaching of Peter in Acts," in *Witness to the Gospel: The Theology of Acts*, ed. I. Howard Marshall and David Peterson (Grand Rapids: Eerdmans, 1998), 261–62, 269.

4. Conrad Gempf, "Public Speaking and Published Accounts," in *The Book of Acts in Its Ancient Literary Setting*, ed. Bruce W. Winter and Andrew D. Clarke (Grand Rapids: Eerdmans, 1993), 264.

the speeches of Peter and others in Acts, the events described are interpreted so that the reader may understand the meaning of those events. While this is truly a general function of speeches in ancient historiography, the observation does not detract from the particular commitment to the *ipsissima vox* of particular speakers in that history. The speeches in Acts contribute to the whole fabric of apostolic theology in the book, but they are not thereby divorced from the particular contributions of the respective speakers, whether they be Peter, Paul, or Stephen. Although we may assemble a composite picture of Luke's understanding of apostolic theology when we bring together the various voices represented, this should not distract us from seeing the way each of the protagonists made their own peculiar contribution to the whole. In this composite witness Peter is the first to speak and, indeed, his testimony provides the groundwork for subsequent contributions.

PETER AND THE BEGINNINGS OF CHRISTIAN THEOLOGY

The concerns of Ridderbos and Bayer, however, may bring us into a deeper understanding of the placement of Peter's speeches in the weave of apostolic witness. By all accounts Peter was the representative apostle who, over and again, served as spokesman for the apostolic company. Strauss comments: "It is significant that Peter is the one who delivers the [Pentecost] speech. For Luke, Peter will be the leading character of the first twelve chapters of Acts." Luke views him "as representing the apostolic preaching as a whole." Regarding Peter's Pentecost discourse, Strauss adds, "The speech of Acts 2 may therefore be seen as representing for Luke the apostolic kerygma *par excellence,* and is likely to be introductory and programmatic for his proclamatory message throughout Acts."[5] We should not pass by the fact that it is *Peter*, and none other, whom Luke casts in this representative role. The question arising from these observations is whether Peter only serves to represent the apostolic testimony or whether he was responsible for giving early Christian theology its shape. Should we consider him as simply the narrative voice for developing Christian theology regarding Christ and salvation or did he hold a principle position in shaping the character of that testimony? Are Peter's speeches in Acts witness to the apostle's constructive theological work in the early church?

Peter's primacy is a principle element in the story of Jesus and the early church. As argued previously, Peter played a central role in the development of the Gospel of Mark.[6] Bauckham says that in Mark "there is sufficiently frequent reestablishment of the Petrine perspective for it to be the dominant form of internal focalization, just as there are sufficient references to Peter to keep readers aware of Peter's special

---

5. Mark L. Strauss, *The Davidic Messiah in Luke-Acts: The Promise and Its Fulfillment in Lukan Christology* (Sheffield: Sheffield Academic, 1995), 132; and so others such as Paul Schubert, "The Final Cycle of Speeches in the Book of Acts," *JBL* 87 (1968) 2.

6. See chapters 3 and 4.

relationship to this narrative."⁷ Acts records the relationship of Peter with Mark as well (Acts 12:12). If this is indeed the case, then we may regard Peter not only as the bearer of the Christ tradition from which the other Synoptic Gospels drew but also the first Christian theologian. The story of Jesus and the earliest interpretation of that story can be traced back to Peter's telling.

The primacy of Peter within the apostolic company was not lost on Luke in the first volume of his work. Luke portrays Simon the fisherman as the first disciple called and commissioned (5:1–11). His name unsurprisingly stands at the head of the company of the twelve apostles (6:13–16). He is among the inner circle of three along with John and James (8:49–56; with John in 22:8) and becomes the principle spokesman among them (9:28–36) and the rest of the apostles (8:45; 9:20; 12:41; 18:28). Peter is the first disciple to recognize his sinful condition and to prostrate himself before Jesus (5:8). The scene is reminiscent of Isaiah's commissioning, when the prophet saw the exalted Lord Almighty and became fearfully cognizant of his moral failing (Isa 6:5).⁸ The account of Peter's conviction is laced with grace since Peter, as Isaiah, received a call instead of chastisement (Luke 5:10b; Isa 6:8–13). The event also evokes a christological confession. Peter had addressed Jesus using the title of respect ἐπιστάτα ("master"), which placed Jesus in the position of authority over the activities being carried on in the boat (Luke 5:5).⁹ But upon recognizing his sinfulness, Peter prostrated himself before Jesus and implored him to withdraw from him and addressed Jesus as κύριε ("Lord"). While the address may have meant no more than a respectful "Sir," in this context where a miracle had been performed (5:6–7) and Peter becomes cognizant of his own sinfulness, we must conclude that he understood the transcendence of the one who stood before him. Although it is highly unlikely that Peter confessed Christ's deity at this point (cf. Luke 8:25), he at least recognized Jesus as a divine agent.¹⁰ Indeed, according to Luke, Peter is the first disciple to address Jesus as κύριος, a title that would fill with meaning beyond imagination (cf. 2:11). Peter was also the first disciple to recognize that Jesus was none other than the Davidic "Messiah of God" (τὸν χριστὸν τοῦ θεοῦ [9:20]; cf. 1:32–33, 69; 2:11).¹¹ This central confession was "the first creed of the Church"¹² and again marks Peter as a theologian who understands that Jesus is

---

7. Bauckham, *Jesus and the Eyewitnesses*, 164. As he says, "Taken together, these features make Mark a Gospel that presents, to a far larger degree than the others, a Petrine perspective on the story of Jesus" (*Jesus and the Eyewitnesses*, 171).

8. Joseph A. Fitzmyer, *The Gospel According to Luke (1–9)* (Garden City, NY: Doubleday, 1981), 567; John Nolland, *Luke 1–9:20* (Dallas: Word, 1989), 222; Robert H. Stein, *Luke* (Nashville: Broadman & Holman, 1992), 168; Green, *The Gospel of Luke* (Grand Rapids: Eerdmans, 1997), 238.

9. Green, *The Gospel of Luke*, 232.

10. Darrell L. Bock, *Luke* (Grand Rapids: Baker, 1994), 1:459; Green, *The Gospel of Luke*, 233; contra I. Howard Marshall, *The Gospel of Luke: A Commentary on the Greek Text* (Grand Rapids: Eerdmans, 1978), 204; Fitzmyer, *The Gospel According to Luke (1–9)*, 568.

11. Mark 8:29, "You are the Messiah"; Matt 16:16, "You are the Messiah, the Son of the living God."

12. F. J. Foakes-Jackson, *Peter: Prince of Apostles* (London: Hodder & Stoughton, 1927), 60.

the fulfillment of the Davidic promise. In counterpoint, Luke points to Peter as the first to deny Jesus as well (22:31–34, 54–62). Despite his failing, Peter walks the road of rehabilitation when he becomes the first of the twelve to respond to Mary, Joanna, and Mary's testimony about seeing the risen Christ (Luke 24:1–12). The first to turn away was the first to return.

Peter's primacy is also evident in the first chapters of Acts since Peter becomes the leader of the church (1:12–14) and directs the process for replacing Judas (1:15–26; 2:32) as a witness to the life, death, and resurrection of Jesus. He responds to the crowd's amazement and question at Pentecost, becoming the first public witness for Christ (2:14–41). Peter was the principle in the first miracle after Pentecost (3:1–10). He explained the miracle to the gathering crowd (3:11–26) and offered a defense and explanation of the miracle before the Sanhedrin (4:5–17). Peter confronted the first recorded sinners in the early church (5:3–9)[13] and served as God's agent to confirm the testimony of Philip to the Samaritans. He also judged the errant Simon the Sorcerer (8:9–25) and thereby became the first person to correct doctrinal error that surfaced in the church.[14] Peter was the first to preach the gospel to the Gentiles (10:1–48) and to make the case before the Jerusalem church that God had truly accepted them (11:1–18). At the Jerusalem Council, Peter was the first to speak as he reaffirmed God's acceptance of the Gentiles (15:6–11), reminding those gathered that he was one among them whom God chose to preach the gospel to them (15:7). James, who voiced the decision of the Council, appealed exclusively to Peter's testimony and regarded it as harmonious with prophetic testimony (15:14–17, citing Amos 9:11–12). Peter stands, therefore, as the primary agent in unifying the Jewish and Gentile church.[15] The author of Acts portrays Peter as the primary leader of the church, the

---

13. Is this a story of excommunication that demonstrates Peter's role as the one who holds the keys of the kingdom of heaven and can therefore bind and loose (Matt 16:19)? See Henriette Havelaar, "Hellenistic Parallels to Acts 5:1–11 and the Problem of Conflicting Interpretations," *JSNT* 67 (1997) 63–82.

14. As Pheme Perkins says, "Peter's victory over Simon demonstrates the superiority of orthodox Christianity" (*Peter: Apostle for the Whole Church* [Edinburgh: T. & T. Clark, 2000], 91). Simon attempted to reduce the gospel to the level of magic by trying to purchase power (Acts 8:18–24; cf. 19:19). Peter resisted Simon's overture as he affirmed the gospel of grace (8:20). Peter was so remembered in the early church. Irenaeus and Eusebius regarded Simon the Magician as "the one from whom all sorts of heresies derive their origin" and "the first author of all heresy" (Irenaeus, *Adv. Haer.* 1.23.2; Eusebius, *HE* 2.13.6).

15. Hengel, *Saint*, 91; Perkins, *Peter*, 184–85. Perkins regards Peter as a unifier in the midst of the diversity in the early church. Bauckham recalls that "It was Peter who successfully pioneered the view that Gentile Christians did not need to be circumcised and to observe the whole Torah, and it was James who finally secured a permanent agreement this effect. That is how Acts portrays the history, and a careful reading of Galatians shows that Paul says nothing to contradict it. Paul did not have standing, in Jerusalem or even in Antioch (as Gal 2:11–14 shows), to carry the most influential parts of the early Christian movement with him. *Peter and James did* [emphasis mine], and, contrary to the many scholars still influenced ultimately by F. C. Baur, they did not use their authority to fight a conservative Jewish rearguard action against Paul's Gentile mission" (Richard Bauckham, "James, Peter, and the Gentiles," in *The Missions of James, Peter, and Paul. Tensions in Early Christianity*, ed.

one who gives direction to the church's mission as the first preacher to both Jews and Gentiles, and the pivotal theological leader in the early church. Peter is the principle apostle who speaks for the eleven (2:14) and who stands in the company of the other two "pillars" of the Jerusalem church, John (3:1–10; 4:1–4, 13; 8:14, 25) and James (12:17; 15:6–11, 13–14). Moreover, Peter stands closest to Jesus as the one who leads the Jerusalem church, leads the selection of the twelfth apostle, preaches the gospel, performs extraordinary miracles of healing and raising the dead (3:1–10; 5:12–16; 10:36–43), and confronts evil (5:1–11; 8:14–24). As Jesus, he suffers and is arrested for his testimony (4:1–4; 12:1–5; cf. 5:17–42). He also experiences miraculous liberation (12:6–19). Peter is the one commissioned by Jesus as the principle actor in establishing and leading the church.[16]

Paul arrived on the scene after the foundational work of Peter. Despite his importance, Paul was an apostolic latecomer by his own admission (1 Cor 15:8–9). Although he encountered the risen Christ on the Damascus Road (Acts 9:1–30), after three years in Arabia and Damascus he finally went to Jerusalem to speak with Peter and not the other apostles (Gal 1:17–18). Paul says that he went "to visit Cephas" and that he was with Peter for two weeks. During this time he got to know Peter, but he most likely received information from him about Jesus. Paul uses the term ἱστορῆσαι to describe the encounter. While it may signify no more than "to make the acquaintance of," it could mean here "to get information from."[17] Given that Peter had walked with Jesus and was recognized at this time as the leader of the church, Paul likely received the Jesus story from him. Paul's statement that he "stayed with him [Peter] fifteen days" leads us away from the idea that all Paul did was make Peter's acquaintance. Time spent implies stories shared. This is not to say that the formulation of the gospel Paul preached came from Peter (1:11–12)[18] but that Paul would have heard a significant amount of Peter's narrative about Jesus. Although Paul has his own voice in Acts, the Peter/Paul story Luke develops places Peter on par with Paul; indeed, Peter precedes him as the foundational apostle.[19]

Bruce Chilton and Craig Evans [Leiden: Brill, 2005], 139).

16. Reflecting on the portrayal of Peter in the Gospels, Hengel says, "For the evangelists he serves as the *authoritative disciple*; one could even say that he stands in, as the 'Rock,' on behalf of the large crowd of disciples. By this means he becomes *the decisive 'apostolic witness,'* who almost takes on the character of one who functions as a mediator. One could thus describe him as the one who holds the keys of the kingdom of God, or, with a grain of salt, as *mediator ad Mediatorem*, mediator to the Mediator" (Hengel, *Saint Peter*, 82).

17. *BDAG*, 483.

18. Douglas J. Moo, *Galatians*, BECNT (Grand Rapids: Baker Academic, 2013), 109.

19. Hengel makes much of the rift between Peter and Paul. He underscores the split between Peter and Paul as a result of the conflict at Antioch (Gal 2:11–14) and states, "The deep divide that was signified by the dramatic, public, drawn-out dispute between Peter and Paul is something we cannot portray deeply enough" (Hengel, *Saint Peter*, 63). With regard to Acts, he says, "With some awareness of what he is doing, Luke presents Paul as the successor to Peter, even though the 'Cephas party' in Corinth and the further expansion of Petrine authority both show that his role outside of Eretz

The consistent placement of Peter as the leader of the apostolic band and the head of the early church, the portrayal of him as the first to understand who Jesus was, and the presentation of him as the one who interprets and explains God's plan together point to Peter as the earliest and leading theologian of the early church. Hengel heads in this direction saying, "Because of the leading role played by this authoritative disciple of Jesus, who was also the first witness among the Twelve to the resurrection in the original community, one must assume that he was also a participant in giving shape to the beginnings of the 'teaching of the apostles' (Acts 2:42)."[20] Peter is the innovator who is not only the first to follow but the first to witness and theologize. The picture painted is of a man who is more than a voice for the many; he is the leader who offers insight into God's acts, whether before the gathered crowd at Pentecost or the assembled believers in Jerusalem. The theology expressed in Peter's speeches was that of the early church but it appears to be *his* theology that was accepted by all. The theology of Peter became foundational for subsequent Christian theological reflection. Peter was the Rock for the church's theology and not solely its first leader. We would expect no less from the first apostle who had been uniquely charged to feed Jesus' flock (John 21:15-17).

Not a few students of Peter's life and thought have also recognized his central role in the development of Christian theology. Although refraining from calling Peter a "theologian," Cullmann states, "But I do not believe that Paul was the first one to understand the death of Jesus as an atoning death for the forgiveness of sins. On the contrary, I am inclined to ascribe to Peter this particular and fundamental insight. . . . I think that here, too, he should be given a place of honor at the beginning of all Christian theology."[21] Similarly, Hengel affirms a wider theological role for Peter than is often recognized: "Based on everything that has been said to this point, the Galilean fisherman ought not to be underestimated or brushed to the side with respect to his activities in both the church and theological-historical matters."[22] Perkins likewise highlights the foundational role ascribed to Peter: "Peter is not depicted as the

---

Israel increased, not decreased. This means that Luke—unfairly in terms of history—allows Peter to be pushed aside by Paul" (Hengel, *Saint Peter*, 78). The debate about the conflict in Antioch is long and drawn (see, for example, Michael Goulder, *St. Paul Versus St. Peter: A Tale of Two Missions* [Louisville: Westminster John Knox, 1994]), and this is not the place to engage it in detail. Hengel's position ignores the rhetorical effect on the Galatians of Paul's account of the Antioch incident and does not take into account the affirmation of Peter in Galatians (1:18-20; 2:1-10) or the common opinion of Peter, Paul, and James on the inclusion of the Gentiles (Acts 15:6-21). Paul's concerns about the Corinthian church centered on the way the church framed Paul, Apollos, and Peter as rhetors with their own disciples (1 Cor 1:10-17; 3:1-23). Paul does not critique his fellow workers as his opponents. The rift between Peter and Paul has been overdrawn.

20. Hengel, *Saint Peter*, 85. He goes on to say, "Concerning Mark, but then also concerning Luke and Matthew, in fact in some partial sense concerning Paul and John, one could even say, *concerning the apostolic witness*, that he is—without having left us with a single sentence that he himself wrote—the teacher of us all" (*Saint Peter*, 89).

21. Cullmann, *Peter: Disciple-Apostle-Martyr*, 67.

22. Hengel, *Saint Peter*, 96.

founder of any particular churches. The canon itself might be viewed from this Petrine perspective. With the attribution of Mark to Peter's oral tradition and the addition of Peter as shepherd in John 21:15–17, all four Gospels as well as Acts have some connection to Petrine tradition."[23] Although not going as far as to regard Peter as the first Christian theologian, Brown, Donfried, and Reumann see him as "the confessor of the true Christian faith" and "a guardian of the faith against false teaching."[24] Both Meyendorff and Kessler underscore the primacy of Peter in the early church, adding support for the view that he contributed significantly to the church's theological development.[25] This Peter was an "uneducated fisherman," as Bockmuehl notes, but this does not diminish his intelligence or creative theological power. Bockmuehl, as others, recognizes the apostle's pivotal position in the early church: "Peter is the rock, an eyewitness to the passion and resurrection of Jesus, and he is a witness, healer, miracle worker, and martyr. Beginning as a fisherman from Capernaum, the apostle became a centrist, bridge-building, and uniting figure in the early church, often pictured with Paul as the twin pillars of the Roman church. A sincere, if flawed, disciple of Jesus."[26] This sympathetic portrayal, however, stops too short. Peter was all this, and more: he was the apostle who, after Jesus, gave the church its theological direction.[27]

---

23. Perkins, *Peter*, 184.

24. Raymond E. Brown, et al., eds., *Peter in the New Testament: A Collaborative Assessment by Protestant and Roman Catholic Scholars* (Minneapolis: Augsburg, 1973), 165–66.

25. John Meyendorff, ed., *The Primacy of Peter* (Crestwood, NY: St. Vladimir's Seminary Press, 1992); William Thomas Kessler, *Peter as the First Witness of the Risen Lord: An Historical and Theological Investigation* (Rome: Editrice Pontificia Università Gregoriana, 1998).

26. Markus Bockmuehl, *Simon Peter in Scripture and Memory* (Grand Rapids: Baker Academic, 2012), 179–80. Somehow we have become snared in our perceptions of Peter as a benign and endearing figure at the expense of seeing his creative theological power and leadership. Helyer, for example, summarizes his legacy as that of "Pastor and Practical Theologian of the Earliest Church," yet he softens the portrait saying, "Perhaps no figure from the earliest years of what became Christianity is more approachable and endearing than Peter. There is something about Peter that resonates in the soul of most Christians whether ancient or modern" (*The Life and Witness of Peter* [Downers Grove, IL: IVP Academic, 2012], 302). This popular image passes over the boldness of his theological statements about Christ and who may be included among the people of God. It fails to accurately describe the one who faced off against Simon the Sorcerer.

27. Although not committed to the possibility of recovering a comprehensive understanding of Peter's theology, Hengel asks: "Is it possible that the decisive foundational insights for their faith within the earliest (i.e., pre-Pauline) community, which means the first two or three years of existence for this new movement, could have taken place without the significant participation of the first witness to the resurrection and the leader of the earliest community in Jerusalem? He could have played a decisive, if not *the decisive*, role in the development of the earliest kerygma" (Hengel, *Saint Peter*, 88). Hengel adds, "It is certainly not just by chance that Paul, a few years after his conversion, visited with Peter alone in Jerusalem and that he stayed with him for fifteen days—that is, not an extremely short period of time. During this two-week period, they would each have learned from the other, but at the time Paul would have certainly learned more from Peter than vice versa" (*Saint Peter*, 88). The development of the earliest theological traditions of the church was not simply in the hands of "anonymous collectives," as form critics would have us believe, but "authoritative personalities were connected as bearers of the tradition" (*Saint Peter*, 89). By all indications, Peter was the principle bearer of the tradition.

VOX PETRI

PETRINE SPEECHES IN ACTS AND EARLY CHRISTIAN THEOLOGY

From the time of C. H. Dodd's pivotal work on *The Apostolic Preaching and Its Developments*, many have recognized within the early chapters of Acts an outline of the early church's *kerygma* or preaching.[28] While numerous scholars in Dodd's wake accepted his thesis that the early Acts speeches represented a primitive strain of Christian theology, subsequent theologians began to regard them as witness to the author of Acts' theology at the end of the first century rather than that of the early church. Here we hear Luke, not the apostles. Subsequent studies have focused on the role of the speeches in the narrative of Acts without troubling much over the historical question of whether or not the speeches faithfully represent the apostolic testimony.[29] All three of these positions have their merit. Luke is an able historian who has his own point of view and theology, which he weaves into the narrative of Acts and which finds its expression in the deeds and words he records. We need to read Acts as a complete narrative with distinct theological concerns and not simply a compendium of words and deeds as they occurred.[30] But Luke is also a competent historian who is faithful to his sources while, at the same time, being faithful to his audience. Rhetoric and history meet as he gives testimony to developments in the early church. The position of this study is that we may regard the Petrine perspectives represented in the speeches as *faithful* representations without needing to divine whether this or that particular aspect of the speech may be Lukan or Petrine. Luke is present, but so also Peter in

---

28. The *kerygma*, Dodd states, "signifies not the action of the preacher, but that which he preaches, his 'message,' as we sometimes say" (C. H. Dodd, *The Apostolic Preaching and Its Developments* [London: Hodder & Stoughton, 1944], 7). Dodd's work was first published in 1936.

29. See the brief summaries in Richard F. Zehnle, *Peter's Pentecost Discourse: Tradition and Lukan Reinterpretation in Peter's Speeches of Acts 2 and 3* (Nashville: Abingdon, 1971), 13-17; I. Howard Marshall, *The Acts of the Apostles: An Introduction and Commentary* (Grand Rapids: Eerdmans, 1980), 39-42; Eugene E. Lemcio, "The Unifying Kerygma of the New Testament," *JSNT* 33 (1988) 3-5; Marion L. Soards, *The Speeches in Acts: Their Content, Context, and Concerns* (Louisville: Westminster John Knox, 1994), 1-17; Darrell L. Bock, *Acts* (Grand Rapids: Baker Academic, 2007), 20-23. See also Hengel, *Acts and the History of Earliest Christianity*, 59-68. This study leaves to one side the question of whether there is a unified *kerygma* in the New Testament or multiple *kerygmata* (see James D. G. Dunn, *Unity and Diversity in the New Testament: An Inquiry Into the Character of Earliest Christianity* [Philadelphia: Trinity, 1990], 11-32; David G. Peterson, "Kerygma or Kerygmata: Is There Only One Gospel in the New Testament?," in *God's Power to Save: One Gospel for a Complex World?*, ed. Chris Green [Leicester: Apollos, 2006], 155-84). The focus here is upon the testimony regarding Peter's early preaching.

30. Noteworthy studies on Luke's theology in Acts include J. C. O'Neill, *The Theology of Acts in Its Historical Setting* (London: SPCK, 1970); Jacob Jervell, *The Theology of the Acts of the Apostles* (Cambridge: Cambridge University Press, 1996); I. Howard Marshall and David Peterson, eds., *Witness to the Gospel: The Theology of Acts* (Grand Rapids: Eerdmans, 1998). See the commentaries on Acts for summaries, such as C. K. Barrett, *The Acts of the Apostles*, ICC (Edinburgh: T. & T. Clark, 1998), lxxxii-cx, 2; Ben Witherington, *The Acts of the Apostles: A Socio-Rhetorical Commentary* (Grand Rapids: Eerdmans; Carlisle: Paternoster, 1998), 68-76; Bock, *Acts*, 32-42; Richard I. Pervo, *Acts: A Commentary* (Minneapolis: Fortress, 2009), 22-25.

these speeches. Luke consistently recognizes Peter as the leader of the church and its first theologian. In representing Peter he highlights the way the apostle took the theological lead, and this suggests that in his mind Peter was the main protagonist in shaping the early Christian *kerygma*. The accounts of the earliest Christian preaching hold within them the foundations of Christian theology. The key tenets of *kerygma* appear to have received their early shape from Peter.[31]

More than one commentator has noted that the early speeches in Acts appear to represent primitive forms of Christian theology. Instead of mirroring later developments in Christian theology, they stand out as unique and early conceptions of the church's faith. Selwyn, for example, comments on the early Petrine speeches, saying, "At the same time we cannot rule out the possibility that some of the speeches in Acts are dependent on written sources or oral information; and the rough Semitic style and the primitive doctrine which mark parts of St. Peter's speeches (notably that in Acts 10:34–43) suggest that this is so in their case."[32] Hilgert similarly observes, "While the speeches are certainly his own composition and are intended to advance his own theological point of view, yet in chapters 2 and 3 he uses a number of primitive, though not always thoroughly integrated, Christian understandings, some of which may indeed reflect authentic Petrine traditions."[33] Instead of Acts presenting a fully synthesized theology, the early speeches in Acts present an early Christology and primitive eschatology. Lane sounds the same note, saying, "A careful analysis, moreover, reveals shades of difference between the speeches of Peter and Paul in Acts which should not be minimized. The archaic Christology of the Petrine speeches has no parallel in the sermons for Paul, nor in his epistles. The expectation that the parousia of Jesus will be conditioned by a national repentance on the part of the Jews appears only in the earliest expressions of Peter (Acts 3:19–21). These characteristics can be ascribed plausibly to a primitive source."[34]

---

31. Fitzmyer pushes in a similar direction but stops short of tracing the core of the speeches to Peter. After discussing Dodd, he states, "Haenchen's skepticism about that view and his preference for Dibelius's judgement, that 'Peter's speeches go back to Luke himself,' ... do not resolve the problem, because the pattern in the early speeches of Peter and that of Paul in Acts 13 argues at least for something that Luke has inherited and has worked into the speeches that he has composed. They are not simply the way Luke would have preached or the way the church in his day would have proclaimed the kerygma.... Each speech has to be analyzed for traces of pre-Lucan material, as with Peter's speeches in general.... [Luke] seems to be dependent on some possibly Palestinian oral tradition" (Joseph A. Fitzmyer, *The Acts of the Apostles* [New York: Doubleday, 1998], 249). The evidence we have points to Peter as the one behind the tradition. No other source can be plausibly suggested. As Ridderbos notes, Peter's speeches "bear the hallmark of foundation-laying apostolic preaching" (*The Speeches of Peter*, 18).

32. Edwin Gordon Selwyn, *The First Epistle of Peter: The Greek Text with Introduction, Notes and Essays* (London: Macmillan, 1947), 33.

33. Earle Hilgert, "Speeches in Acts and Hellenistic Canons of Historiography and Rhetoric," in *Good News in History: Essays in Honor of Bo Reicke*, ed. Ed. L. Miller (Atlanta: Scholars, 1993), 109. See also Zehnle, *Peter's Pentecost Discourse*, 17.

34. William L. Lane, "The Speeches in the Book of Acts," in *Jerusalem and Athens: Critical*

For example, the title παῖς (Servant) "is used of Jesus four times in Acts, twice in Peter's speech in Solomon's porch (3:13, 26) and twice in the context of prayer (4:27, 30)" and was a primitive designation "which was soon abandoned apart from the conservative language of liturgy in which it lay embedded from earliest times."[35] Likewise the eschatology in the Petrine speeches appears to date very early. Barrett contends that the expectation of the restoration of Israel may contain the most primitive eschatology of all.[36] Bruce similarly argues that "the eschatology of Acts 3:19–21 is neither Luke's nor Paul's. It implies that early repentance on the part of the people of Jerusalem would speed the parousia," and that "it might well be argued that we do indeed have the most primitive *eschatology* of all."[37] These theological turns in Peter's speeches will be discussed in detail below under their respective headings. The point here is simply that many have recognized in the Petrine speeches traces of the church's earliest theological thinking. Late theological developments are not simply read back into Peter's speeches. In these early speeches we recognize the *vox Petri*, which expresses the emerging theological development of the church. Peter, the Rock, laid the foundations.[38]

Discussions on the Philosophy and Apologetics of Cornelius Van Til, ed. E. R. Geehan (Phillipsburg, NJ: Presbyterian & Reformed, 1971), 264. Ridderbos similarly notes, "The speeches of Peter in particular show very characteristic 'old' elements. . . . These speeches are, therefore, of untold significance for our knowledge of early Christianity, and in particular the original apostolic *kerygma*" (*The Speeches of Peter*, 11).

35. Lane, "Speeches in the Book of Acts," 268–69.

36. C. K. Barrett, "Faith and Eschatology in Acts 3," in *Glaube und Eschatologie: Festschrift für Werner Georg Kümmel zum 80. Geburtstag*, ed. Erich Gräßer and Otto Merk (Tübingen: Mohr Siebeck, 1985), 14–15.

37. F. F. Bruce, "The Speeches in Acts–Thirty Years After," in *Reconciliation and Hope: New Testament Essays on Atonement and Eschatology Presented to L. L. Morris on His 60th Birthday*, ed. Robert Banks (Carlisle: Paternoster, 1974), 68. At the same time, Bayer ties this eschatology with the rest of Acts: "Considering the theme of eschatology as a test case, we see that the foundation laid in the Petrine speeches within the initial three chapters of Acts sets the tone of the eschatological framework for the entire book" ("The Preaching of Peter in Acts," 260).

38. Given the Petrine primacy portrayed in Acts, Pervo's development of his claim that "Luke appropriated more than a little from Paul" is overstated (Pervo, *Acts*, 23). Pervo attributes Luke's theology of the cross to Paul, as well as Acts' emphasis on the Spirit, even tracing Luke's theological emphases in Peter's discourse in 2:33 to Paul. For him there is no *vox Petri* but only the *vox Pauli*.

CHAPTER 6

The Theology of Peter in the Acts of the Apostles

Although the speeches represent primitive strains of Christian theology, they are also part of the theological framework of Luke's two-volume work. Luke had particular purposes in writing his work to Theophilus and his circle,[1] and he selectively integrated his sources into his larger framework. This is not to say, however, that his sources had no influence upon his understanding of the early history of the church. As Luke gives testimony to his readers he, at the same time, is informed by the received testimony. We can observe this dual phenomenon in the way he allows the primitive aspects of early Christian theology to stand while simultaneously portraying parallel pictures of Peter and Paul, the two main human protagonists in his story.[2]

Luke's purpose in writing has been variously described, though it may not be possible to isolate one single purpose for the composition. Powell summarizes a variety of suggestions made over the years. Some have regarded Acts as an *irenic* document that attempts to harmonize two streams of early Christianity, one represented by Peter and

---

1. Theophilus may have served as the literary patron who offset the publication of these volumes for a group of associates. See Gold, *Literary Patronage in Greece and Rome*; Luke Timothy Johnson, *The Acts of the Apostles* (Collegeville, MN: Liturgical, 1992), 24; and the questions about this view in Loveday Alexander, *The Preface to Luke's Gospel: Literary Convention and Social Context in Luke 1:1-4 and Acts 1:1* (Cambridge: Cambridge University Press, 1993), 50-63, 187-200.

2. See, for example David Moessner, "'The Christ Must Suffer': New Light on the Jesus—Peter, Stephen, Paul Parallels in Luke-Acts," *NovT* 28 (1986) 220-56; James D. G. Dunn, *The Acts of the Apostles* (Valley Forge: Trinity, 1996), 14-15; Witherington, *The Acts of the Apostles*, 72-73.

the other by Paul. F. C. Bauer and the Tübingen School were the main proponents of this view, recently revived by Goulder.³ Others saw the book as *polemical* in its attempt to combat false teaching such as Gnosticism. The position was held by Charles Talbert in his *Luke and the Gnostics*, but Talbert has minimized this view in his later work on Acts.⁴ It could be that Acts is an *apologetic* work that forwards the position that Christianity should be regarded as a legitimate religion by the Roman government, or that it seeks to alleviate the tensions between the Christian and Jewish communities.⁵ Still others view Acts as *evangelistic* since it attempts not only to defend Christianity against its detractors but to convert them.⁶ But the book appears to be directed at the church rather than the wider world in which the church lived. So it may have had a *pastoral* purpose as it sought to strengthen the faith of early believers.⁷ This view is not entirely incompatible with the possibility that the book is *theological*, that is, it attempts to help Christians understand the eschatological tension between the present and the future. The book, on the other hand, could present the theology of salvation, as Marshall and others argued.⁸

Although the views regarding the purposes of the book are varied, the casual reader observes that Acts presents a continuous story about Jesus and his disciples as the gospel of Jesus Christ spread beyond the confines in Judea (to use Luke's term) to the wider Roman Empire, arriving at its very heart—Rome. Talbert focuses on the first part of this story, arguing that the second volume of Luke's work serves to legitimate the work of the apostles, especially Peter and Paul, by presenting a succession narrative. The work and teaching of Jesus' disciples carries forward that of their master in a way similar to Diogenes Laertius's *Lives of Eminent Philosophers*, which shows the succession of various schools of philosophers. Aristoxenos's *Life of Pythagoras* tells of Pythagoras and the Pythagoreans, and Andronicus's *Life of Aristotle* is not only about the great philosopher but also his successors. As Talbert says, "Succession narratives used for philosophers were numerous in Mediterranean antiquity," and Luke-Acts appears to be one of the many such works which elevated the honor of a founder's followers. The divine hand is evident in the succession.⁹ Pervo likewise sees Acts as a "legitimating narrative," that is, it is a story that shows "the legitimacy of Pauline Christianity

---

3. Mark Allan Powell, *What Are They Saying About Acts?* (Mahwah, NJ: Paulist, 1991), 13–14; Goulder, *St. Paul Versus St. Peter*. Echoes of Tübingen appear in Hengel, who states: "The deep divide that was signified by the dramatic, public, drawn-out dispute between Peter and Paul is something we cannot portray deeply enough" (Hengel, *Saint Peter*, 63).

4. Powell, *What Are They Saying About Acts?* 14–15; Charles H. Talbert, *Reading Acts: A Literary and Theological Commentary on The Acts of the Apostles* (New York: Crossroad, 1997).

5. Powell, *What Are They Saying About Acts?* 15–16.

6. Powell, *What Are They Saying About Acts?* 16–17.

7. Powell, *What Are They Saying About Acts?* 17–18.

8. Powell, *What Are They Saying About Acts?* 18–19; I. Howard Marshall, *Luke: Historian and Theologian* (Downers Grove, IL: InterVarsity, 1988).

9. Talbert, *Reading Acts*, 6–17.

… or generally as the claim of the Jesus-movement to possess the Israelite heritage."[10] Although Pervo views the legitimation along different lines than Talbert, he notes that, in general, "Since Aristotle a major reason for composing a history of a subject has been the bestowal of legitimacy upon it."[11] We may affirm that Acts' purpose is "to explain and defend a body that has existed for some time and whose identity has been challenged rather than, for example, to nurture a young and fragile body grappling to discover its identity."[12]

The author of Acts directed it toward Theophilus and others who have learned the fundamentals of the faith but who needed to know the certainty of what they received (Luke 1:1–4) as the message spread from the confines in Judea to the heart of the empire and from the small circle of the first Jewish disciples out to the wide sphere of the Gentile world. The narrative of Acts sets the seal on the church's master narrative about Jesus and the spread of his message to the "ends of the earth" (Acts 1:8) as it embraced the Jews in Judea, the Samaritans in Samaria, and then Gentiles from the Roman centurion Cornelius to the heart of Rome itself. Divine agency is at the heart of the story since the spread of the message was directed by Jesus and empowered by the Holy Spirit (Acts 1:8). Witherington highlights the second part of this narrative of legitimation, arguing that Acts "focuses on its horizontal universalization (to all peoples throughout the Empire)."[13]

THE FRAMEWORK OF PETER'S THEOLOGY IN ACTS

The narrative of Acts tells the master story of the gospel of Jesus Christ. The story is epic in its scope since it shows the divine activity in the establishment of the message of Christ's salvation and the spread of that message throughout the empire. "Jesus is the *one* savior for *all* peoples and this is why he must be proclaimed *to* all peoples."[14] There are no small plans here, only small cameos that contribute to the larger plan of God. As may be expected, Luke's framing of the story would have been familiar to his readers, whether they were Jews or Gentiles. He tells the Christian epic and wraps it around the story of the New Exodus, which had become Israel's eschatological hope. As noted previously in the discussion of this theme in Mark, the Exodus was the "founding moment" for Israel, and this event became "a model for her future hope."[15]

---

10. Pervo, *Acts*, 21.

11. Pervo, *Acts*, 21; Roger French, "General Series Introduction," in *Ancient Astrology*, by Tamsyn Barton (London: Routledge, 1994), xvi–xvii. Pervo notes, however, that "'Legitimating' is, from the social-scientific perspective, a proper task of the second and later generations of a movement, although it may well begin at the time of origin" (*Acts*, 21n134).

12. Pervo, *Acts*, 22.

13. Witherington, *The Acts of the Apostles*, 69.

14. Witherington, *The Acts of the Apostles*, 70.

15. Rikki E. Watts, *Isaiah's New Exodus in Mark* (Grand Rapids: Baker Academic, 1997), 90. Commenting on Isaiah 40:3, Watts notes that "if Israel's founding moment was predicated on Yahweh's redemptive action in the Exodus from Egyptian bondage, then surely a second deliverance from exilic

The New Exodus in Acts and the Petrine Speeches

As in the Gospel of Mark, one of the principle theological frameworks in Acts is the New Exodus of Isaiah 40–55.[16] Anderson summarizes the theology of the New Exodus in Isaiah this way: "The fall of Babylon would be followed by a new exodus, more marvelous than the Exodus under Moses, and by the restoration of Zion. This new event would prompt the whole world to recognize that Yahweh is God alone and that his salvation extends to the ends of the earth. Significantly, Second Isaiah's prophecy begins (40:3–5) and ends (55:12–13) with the theme of the new exodus."[17] The New Exodus becomes the subject of numerous passages that evoke the story of the first Exodus.[18] Anderson outlines the New Exodus motifs found in Second Isaiah, which include "the promises to the fathers," "the deliverance from Egypt," "the journey through the wilderness," and "the re-entry into the Promised Land."[19] Pao takes up the topic of the New Exodus theme in Acts and focuses on how the author reworks the Isaianic promise to focus on four principle themes: "The restoration of Israel, the word of God, the anti-idol polemic, and the salvation offered to the nations/Gentiles."[20] Pao contends that while all four of these New Exodus themes are present in Acts, "the restoration of Israel is the foundational one upon which the other three can be developed."[21]

Surprisingly, however, Pao's study principally examines the programatic text Acts 1:8 and the presentation of Paul in Acts while almost completely passing over the portrayal of Peter as the principle theologian in the development of the New Exodus motif. For example, Pao draws attention to ὁδός (way) as a marker for the New Exodus and notes that the travel narratives tie into the New Exodus theme of the "way of the Lord." He states, "In Acts, the importance of traveling is even more apparent when apostolic journeys become the single most important organizing principle of its content. The journeys of Philip (Acts 8:4–10), Peter (Acts 9:32–11:18), and Paul

---

bondage, this time of Babylon, could scarcely be conceived of in other terms except those of the first Exodus" (*Isaiah's New Exodus in Mark*, 80).

16. See the extensive discussion of the theme in David W. Pao, *Acts and the Isaianic New Exodus*, Biblical Studies Library (Grand Rapids: Baker Academic, 2002) and, more briefly, in Jindrich Mánek, "The New Exodus in the Book of Luke," *NovT* 2 (1957) 8–23.

17. Bernhard W. Anderson, "Exodus Typology in Second Isaiah," in *Israel's Prophetic Heritage: Essays in Honor of James Muilenburg*, ed. Bernhard W. Anderson and Walter Harrelson (New York: Harper & Brothers, 1962), 182.

18. Anderson's list ("Exodus Typology in Second Isaiah," 181–82) includes 40:3–5 (highway in the wilderness); 41:17–20 (transformation of the wilderness); 42:14–16 (Yahweh leads his people in a way they know not); 43:1–3 (passing through the waters and the fire); 43:14–21 (a way in the wilderness); 48:20–21 (exodus from Babylon); 49:8–12 (new entry into the Promised Land); 51:9–10 (new victory over the sea); 52:11–12 (new exodus); and 55:12–13 (Israel shall go out in joy and peace).

19. Anderson, "Exodus Typology in Second Isaiah," 182–84; Watts, *Isaiah's New Exodus in Mark*, 135.

20. Pao, *Acts and the Isaianic New Exodus*, 111.

21. Pao, *Acts and the Isaianic New Exodus*, 111.

(Acts 12:25–28:16) form the framework in which the story of Acts develops."[22] Yet his study lacks any major discussion of the Petrine travel narrative or any other aspect of the New Exodus in the Petrine speeches. Pao's works through Isaiah 40:1–11 as the introduction to Isaiah's New Exodus and identifies the key themes that are then developed in Acts: "The restoration of Israel, the power of the word of God, the anti-idol polemic, and the concern for the nations."[23] As noted above, the theology of Acts has been shaped by its author, yet he is using source materials that represent the voice of the actors indicated in the narrative. Luke's New Exodus theology is part of the fabric of Pauline thought, to be sure. But it is also part of Petrine theology as evidenced in Mark, 1 Peter, and in the Petrine speeches in Acts. Pao misses this point and appears to be under the spell of the dominant Pauline scholarship, which gives no place to Peter in its vision of theological developments in the early church.

Pao identifies Acts 1:8 as one of the programmatic texts in Luke's second volume: "But you will receive power when the Holy Spirit has come upon you; and you will be my witnesses in Jerusalem, in all Judea and Samaria, and to the ends of the earth." He correctly locates the background to Jesus' commission as Isaiah 32:15 ("Until a spirit from on high is poured out on us"), a text that anticipates the coming of the new era of God's salvation in a New Exodus. Being God's witnesses picks up the Isaianic theme in 43:10 ("You are my witnesses, says the Lord") and 43:12 ("And you are my witnesses, says the Lord").[24] The New Exodus witness goes out through Jerusalem, Judea, Samaria, and onward "to the ends of the earth," which is part of the Isaianic vision: "It is too light a thing that you should be my servant to raise up the tribes of Jacob and to restore the survivors of Israel; I will give you as a light to the nations, that my salvation may reach to the end of the earth." Although the only other place where Acts picks up Isaiah 49:6 is in Paul's sermon in Antioch (13:47), Pao ignores the fact that Peter is the apostle who is the principle apostolic presence in Jerusalem and Judea (Acts 2–5), Samaria (8:14–25, after the preaching of Philip), and then with the Gentile Cornelius and those gathered with him, who are the first from the "ends of the earth" to receive the gospel (Acts 10:1–18). Peter's preaching begins with the restoration of Israel (the programmatic concern in the apostles' question in Acts 1:6) in the promise of salvation held out to "the entire house of Israel" (2:36, 37–42) and the hope that, upon their repentance, "times of refreshing may come from the presence of the Lord, and that he may send the Messiah appointed for you, that is, Jesus" (4:20). The restoration continues in Samaria (8:14–17) before Peter is led by the Spirit to tell the Gentile Cornelius and those gathered with him that "in every nation anyone who fears [God] and does what is right is acceptable to him" (10:34). Paul then picks up this Gentile mission begun by Peter. Luke portrays Peter as the one who first works out

---

22. Pao, *Acts and the Isaianic New Exodus*, 1–2.
23. Pao, *Acts and the Isaianic New Exodus*, 13.
24. Pao, *Acts and the Isaianic New Exodus*, 92–93.

the programmatic themes in Acts 1:8 as he journeys to bear witness of Christ. Peter's actions become theology of the New Exodus as it is lived out on the road.

The themes identified with the Isaianic New Exodus are threads in the fabric of Peter's preaching as portrayed in Acts.[25] Following Pao's outline, the first of these is *the restoration of the people of God*. The theme begins in Acts with the selection of Matthias to fill the place left by Judas. The twelve apostles stand for the twelve tribes of Israel, now beginning to be restored. Peter takes the lead in outlining the need to find a replacement for Judas who would become, with the eleven, a witness to the resurrection of Christ (1:15–22). Peter takes the theological lead at this point. The restoration of Israel theme includes the gathering of God's people who had been exiled (Isa 40:1–2, 10–11; 43:5–7; 49:6, 13) and the call to return and repent from their sins (43:24–25; 44:21–22; 50:1–3; 59:1–19). Peter focuses on the gathering and restoration of Israel in his call for all Israel to repent (Acts 2:14, 36, 38), including the promise of restoration for those who are both near and far (2:39), and holds out the promise of restoration if the people of God turn to him (3:19–20). Peter delivers this call and promise to the Jews who had gathered together in Jerusalem from the nations (2:5–13). The gathered exiles now have hope.

The hope of restoration of Israel was also tied tightly with the restoration of the Davidic kingdom (Isa 55:3; cf. 9:6–7; 16:5). The restored Davidic monarchy through Jesus Christ is central to Peter's preaching (Acts 2:25–36; 1:16; 4:25). The promise of God's Spirit is also an essential aspect of Israel's restoration, for it is the Spirit who will restore the nation (Isa 44:1–5; cf. 32:14–15). Peter takes this New Exodus theme and develops it extensively with the quotation from Joel 2 and the promise that those who repent will receive the Spirit (Acts 2:14–21, 38–39).

The second aspect of the New Exodus Pao identifies is *the Word of God*, regarded as the "agent of the New Exodus."[26] Isaiah 2:2–4 highlights how God's word will run: "For out of Zion shall go forth instruction, and the word of the Lord from Jerusalem." The theme is taken up again in Isaiah 40:8–9, the prologue to the New Exodus theme. This is the word that does not wither or fade but as the word of God it "will stand forever." So the call goes out: "Get you up to a high mountain, O Zion, herald of good tidings (LXX ὁ εὐαγγελιζόμενος), lift up your voice with strength, O Jerusalem, herald of good tidings, lift it up, do not fear; say to the cities of Judah, 'Here is your God!'" Peter's proclamation in the house of Cornelius references this theme, where he states, "You know the message (τὸν λόγον) he sent to the people of Israel, preaching peace by Jesus Christ—he is Lord of all." Peter echoes Isaiah 52:7: "How beautiful upon the mountains are the feet of the messenger who announces peace, who brings good news, who announces salvation, who says to Zion, 'Your God reigns.'" This word, however, is

---

25. While the key themes are outlined here, the development of the details of each will be part of the discussion in the following sections on Peter's theology.

26. Pao, *Acts and the Isaianic New Exodus*, 147.

not limited to the house of Israel but extended to the Gentiles, as Peter makes clear in testimony before the Jerusalem Council (Acts 15:15).

The third dimension of the New Exodus is the recognition that *Yahweh is the Lord of the nations,* a theme that includes *the anti-idol polemic.* The preaching of Peter does not include a vigorous denunciation of idolatry as found in Isaiah (Isa 40:12–31; 41:1–10; 44:9–20; 46:1–13) and in the Pauline speeches in Acts (14:14–18; 17:22–31), but given the geographic scope of Peter's ministry this should not be a surprise. When Peter moves to the Gentile city of Caesarea in Acts 10, his ministry is to the God-fearer Cornelius and those gathered with him. Peter does, however, evoke the polemic against idols in his condemnation of Simon Magus in Acts 8:23: "For I see that you are in the gall of bitterness and the chains of wickedness." Simon was regarded as having divine status since people knew him as "the power of God that is called Great" (8:10).[27] Peter's denunciation of Simon in 8:23 is an allusion to Deuteronomy 29:17–18 (LXX "And you have seen their abominations and their idols, wood and stone, silver and gold, that were among them. Who is there among you, man or woman or family or tribe, whose mind has turned away from the Lord our God, to go to serve the gods of those nations? Who among you is a root growing up with gall and bitterness?"). Peter stands against idolatry, a theme more fully developed in Paul's writings and his speeches in Acts (14:8–18; 17:22–31). Luke refrains from ascribing to Peter a vigorous anti-idol polemic and only shows how Peter raised the issue in one instance.

The counterpoint to the anti-idol polemic in the New Exodus theme is that *Yahweh is Lord of the nations,* an Isaianic theme (Isa 42:10–12; 45:22–23; 49:6; 51:4–5; 55:5; 66:18) that is particularly embraced by Peter. Peter is the one who acknowledges Christ's lordship over all in Acts 2:32–36, where he evokes Psalm 110:1 in the affirmation of his universal sovereignty ("The Lord said to my Lord, 'Sit at my right hand, until I make your enemies your footstool'"). When Peter stands before the Sanhedrin in Jerusalem, he cites the Stone testimony from Psalm 118:22, which affirms that Jesus, the Stone, "has become the cornerstone," and proceeds to proclaim: "There is salvation in no one else, for there is no other name under heaven given among mortals by which we must be saved" (4:11–12). Luke's inclusion of this testimony anticipates the mission to the Gentiles, those who are "far away, everyone whom the Lord our God calls to him" (2:39; cf. Isa 57:19). Moreover, the prayer of the church in Acts 4:24–30 acknowledges his universal sovereignty. This prayer, though not ascribed particularly to Peter, includes his voice as one of the gathered apostles (4:23–24). Most significantly, the Lord's sovereignty over the nations becomes a principle topic in Peter's proclamation to the Gentiles in the house of Cornelius: "You know the message he sent to the people of Israel, preaching peace by Jesus Christ—he is Lord of all" (10:36). This affirmation follows Peter's recognition that "in every nation anyone who fears him and does what is right is acceptable to him" (10:35). After Peter's account of the ministry to

---

27. C. K. Barrett, *The Acts of the Apostles,* ICC (Edinburgh: T. & T. Clark, 1994), 1:406–8; Pervo, *Acts,* 209–10.

the Gentiles, the apostles and believers in Judea praised God and said, "Then God has given even to the Gentiles the repentance that leads to life." God's sovereignty over the nations issues in their salvation (2:17a, 21). This is precisely Peter's point at the Jerusalem Council ("We believe that we will be saved through the grace of the Lord Jesus, just as they will" [15:11]), one that James endorses ("Simeon has related how God first looked favorably on the Gentiles, to take from among them a people for his name" [15:14; cf. the use of Simeon in 2 Pet 1:1]). Peter traces God's blessing of the Gentiles back to the promise given to Abraham that "in your descendants all the families of the earth shall be blessed" (3:25). Peter understands that God shows no partiality in his dealings with humanity (10:34–35; 11:12, 18; 15:8–9, 11 and 15).

In sum, Luke identifies Peter as the principle theologian who interprets early Christian experience in light of the New Exodus. Although Peter does not quote Isaiah at every turn, the fundamental themes of the New Exodus pervade his teaching. The New Exodus is the framework for the theology of Acts, as Pao argues, but that framework is developed through the preaching of Peter and not only Paul. Luke artfully pieces together the narrative and speeches in Acts but, at the same time, preserves the integrity of the *vox* of the respective protagonists in the story. Given the strong emphasis on the New Exodus in Mark and 1 Peter (as will be seen), we are not surprised by this strain in the account of Peter's preaching in Acts.

Acts and Epic

While the story in Acts wraps around the theme of the New Exodus, with Peter being one on the leading voices in developing this theology, the Book of Acts also presents the church's founding epic.[28] The best known of ancient epics were the writings of Homer and Virgil, and, due to their pervasive presence, many works in antiquity imitated the themes found therein. As argued previously, the Gospel of Mark shows traces of epic in its presentation of the gospel as a rival to Virgil's *Aeneid*. In a similar way, Acts shows evidence of being part of the epic tradition. Epic tales, such as the *Aeneid*, "were considered the repositories of genuine wisdom concerning the meaning of the past and its implications for the present."[29] The gospel story in Luke-Acts, as

---

28. Previously I argued that Acts fits within the canons of ancient historiography ("Peter and The Acts of the Apostles" in chapter 1, "Sources for a Petrine Theology"). But historiography and epic are not mutually exclusive categories, especially as we consider that ancient historians sought to present and interpret the deeds and words in their historical narratives. For a discussion on the overlap of the genres, see Raymond F. Person Jr., "Biblical Historiography as Traditional History," in *Oxford Handbook of Biblical Narrative*, ed. Danna Nolan Fewell (New York: Oxford University Press, 2015), 73–83.

29. Marianne Palmer Bonz, *The Past as Legacy: Luke-Acts and Ancient Epic* (Minneapolis: Augsburg Fortress, 2000), 16, 19, 23. On Acts and epic, see also Dennis R. MacDonald, *Does the New Testament Imitate Homer? Four Cases from the Acts of the Apostles* (New Haven, CT: Yale University Press, 2003); Dennis R. MacDonald, *The Gospels and Homer: Imitations of Greek Epic in Mark and Luke-Acts* (London: Rowman & Littlefield, 2015); Dennis R. MacDonald, *Luke and Virgil: Imitations of Classical Greek Literature in the "Aeneid" and Luke-Acts* (London: Rowman & Littlefield, 2015b). Discussions on epic are found in Aristotle, *Poetics* 23–26 (1459a–1462b); Katherine Callen King,

that in Mark, ties together Israel's founding story—the Exodus—with the founding story of the church presented as a New Exodus. It is a narrative epic that shares the fundamental traits of epic, save for the fact that the emerging Christian epic lacked the classic poetic form. However, in *mimēsis* (*imitatio* or imitation) of the epic tradition an author could employ prose instead of meter and verse.[30]

Apart from poetic form, Aristotle's expectation was that "epic poetry must tell a long but focused story with the same kinds of reversals, disasters, and recognitions that we find in tragedy; its language must be highly adorned with metaphors and exotic words; and the poet must not speak in his own voice, but must keep himself in the background.... Lastly, the subject of epic must be the deeds of heroes."[31] The epics of the ancient world emerged "only at significant inaugural moments in a community's or a society's corporate life,"[32] so we are not surprised that this literary genre was adopted and adapted by the early church at its founding moment, much the way that Virgil's *Aeneid* appeared early in the Augustan era. Of particular concern in Roman epic was the community and empire.[33] Epic does not simply state the facts of history but interprets them to show how actions are part of a unified and universal story. Moreover, "epic has more scope for the irrational (the chief cause of awe), because we do not actually see the agent" (*Poetics* 24.11–14), that is, "the epic convention of gods interacting with human beings as central to the poem's dramatic motivation and plot narration gives the poet more ways of explaining what in historiographical narratives is generally left unexplained or dismissively attributed to τύχη or *fortuna* (chance, fortune)."[34] In Acts the stage is set by God, the invisible protagonist in almost every scene.

The studies on Luke-Acts that identify these volumes as an early Christian epic focus primarily on Peter and Paul as protagonists in the second volume. Peter's role

---

Ancient Epic (Oxford: Wiley-Blackwell, 2009); Catherine Bates, ed., *The Cambridge Companion to the Epic* (Cambridge: Cambridge University Press, 2010). See the apologetic for mimesis criticism in Dennis R. MacDonald, *The Gospels and Homer*, 7–19.

30. MacDonald, *The Homeric Epics and the Gospel of Mark*, 4–5. Richard Martin notes that some epic is presented as prose and not poetry ("Epic as Genre," in *A Companion to Ancient Epic*, ed. John Miles Foley [Oxford: Blackwell, 2005], 9).

31. King, *Ancient Epic*, 4. William Harmon (*A Handbook to Literature* [Upper Saddle River, NJ: Prentice Hall, 2003], 185) summarizes the characteristics of epic: "(1) The hero is of imposing stature, of national or international importance, and of great historical or legendary significance; (2) the setting is vast, covering great nations, the world, or the universe; (3) the action consists of deeds of great valor or requiring superhuman courage; (4) supernatural forces—gods, angels, and demons—interest themselves in the action; (5) a style of sustained elevation is used; and (6) the poet retains a measure of objectivity." Acts contains these elements, although it is written as a prose and not poetic piece. It does, however, employ "middlebrow" *koinē* that imitates the style of the LXX, which contains the founding stories of Israel. The style of Acts improves on Luke (Pervo, *Acts*, 7–8).

32. Bonz, *The Past as Legacy*, 17.

33. Peter Toohey, "Roman Epic," in *The Cambridge Companion to the Epic*, ed. Catherine Bates (Cambridge: Cambridge University Press, 2010), 35–39.

34. Bonz, *The Past as Legacy*, 21.

in the epic presentation is in his person and deeds as interpreted by Luke. However, his speeches are an integral part of the story as well since in all forms of ancient history, including epic, deeds and words are bound inseparably.[35] So, for example, Luke includes a catalog of the gathered nations Acts 2:9–11 as Vergil includes a catalog of conquered peoples (*Aeneid* 8.722–28). From the start of the narrative in Acts, Luke begins to show "the eschatological fulfillment of a divinely ordered Mission and of promises of the establishment of a kingdom without temporal or spatial limits" (cf. Luke 24:47; Acts 1:8; 13:47).[36] Following hard upon the outpouring of the Spirit on Pentecost, Luke includes Peter's sermon, which outlines the meaning of that event (Acts 2:14–40). Bonz adds that the speech "also reveals the Lukan perspective concerning the fate of the house of Israel and the importance of the incorporation of the gentiles in the reconstituted people of God. It is the dramatic presentation of this theme of the reconstitution of the people as the eschatological fulfillment of the divine plan that affords the most significant agreement between Virgil's presentation and Luke's."[37] The conclusion of Peter's sermon, where he states that the promise of God is "for all who are far away," is tied tightly with the restoration of Israel, that "the promise is for you, for your children" (2:39).

MacDonald lays out the parallels between Luke-Acts, the Homeric epic, and Virgil's *Aeneid* in some detail with some reference to Peter's roll in this narrative.[38] Of special note are Peter's vision (Acts 10:9–23; cf. Homer, *Iliad* 2.305–319; Virgil, *Aeneid* 2.199–227), his escape from prison (Acts 12:1–17; cf. Homer, *Iliad* 24), and the Jerusalem Council (Acts 15; cf. Homer, *Iliad* 9).[39] Although Peter comes on the stage as a second protagonist after Jesus and before Paul in Luke's Christian epic, Luke's hand in shaping the narrative is primary rather than Peter's direct contribution. That is to say, Luke uses the Petrine story in his presentation of this epic while the speeches of Peter as presented by Luke focus primarily on the New Exodus. Luke picks up aspects of that story as part of his understanding of the epic of Christian foundations.

The New Age Has Come—The Gospel of the Kingdom

"This is what was spoken through the prophet Joel: 'In the last days it will be, God declares, that I will pour out my Spirit upon all flesh'" (Acts 2:16–17). Peter's Pentecost sermon begins with the declaration that what was promised prophetically is now fulfilled and that the fulfillment of the prophetic hope for the outpouring of the Holy Spirit indicates that "the last days" have arrived. The theme of fulfillment is a

---

35. See the discussion on "Peter and The Acts of the Apostles" in chapter 1, "Sources for a Petrine Theology."

36. Bonz, *The Past as Legacy*, 109.

37. Bonz, *The Past as Legacy*, 110–11.

38. Dennis R. MacDonald, *Luke and Virgil*, 125–204. See also Dennis R. MacDonald, *The Gospels and Homer*, 30–31; Bonz, *The Past as Legacy*.

39. Dennis R. MacDonald, *Luke and Virgil*, 150–51, 163–65, 182–83.

dominant feature in the Petrine speeches in Acts. Peter believed that events transpiring within the community were part of God's plan that he had predicted through the prophets (cf. 1 Pet 1:10–11). The fulfillment of the prophetic hope was, in the first instance, a sign that a new age had already arrived.[40] "These days" (3:24) are "the last days" (2:16). The notion that the coming of Jesus Christ began a new era in history can be traced back to the earliest strata of Christian theology in Jesus' preaching (Mark 1:15). The first to record this preaching was Mark who, as argued previously, translated Peter's preaching.[41] Peter, however, is not the innovator of this eschatological perspective on history but one who integrates this theology deeply into his proclamation. The declaration that prophetic hopes are now fulfilled is also part of the fabric of testimony. As Aristotle noted, witnesses who offer testimony may be "ancient or recent" (*Rhet.* 1.15.13, 15–16), but witnesses can also be "interpreters of oracles for the future" (1.15.14). Fulfilled prophecy serves as testimony alongside that of eye and ear witnesses (cf. 1:21–22; 4:20; 5:32; 10:39–43).[42]

The first Petrine speech in Acts recalls the apostle's leadership in guiding the post-ascension community into the selection of a person to replace Judas as a member of the Twelve. Peter interprets the prophetic oracle through David as a prediction about Judas, the betrayer: "Friends, the scripture had to be fulfilled, which the Holy Spirit through David foretold concerning Judas, who became a guide for those who arrested Jesus" (1:16). The reference is likely to the scriptural citations in 1:20 which are taken from Psalm 69:25 and 109:8.[43] Peter regards the fulfillment of Scripture as a

---

40. On the theme of fulfillment in Acts, see David Peterson, "The Motif of Fulfilment and the Purpose of Luke-Acts," in *The Book of Acts in Its Ancient Literary Setting*, ed. Bruce W. Winter and Andrew D. Clarke (Grand Rapids: Eerdmans; Carlisle: Paternoster, 1993), 83–104; John T. Squires, *The Plan of God in Luke-Acts* (Cambridge: Cambridge University Press, 1993), 121–54; Strauss, *Davidic Messiah in Luke-Acts*, 130–93; William Kurz, "Promise and Fulfilment in Hellenistic Jewish Narratives and in Luke and Acts," in *Jesus and the Heritage of Israel: Luke's Narrative Claim Upon Israel's Legacy*, ed. David Moessner (Harrisburg, PA: Trinity, 1999), 147–70. Squires emphasizes the way the fulfillment theme points to the divine plan, especially with reference to the crucifixion and the mission to the Gentiles. The theme also serves an apologetic purpose, as Peterson also contends. Kurz likewise focuses on God's providence and plan, which are demonstrated by the fulfillment of prophecy. Epicureanism raised considerable doubt about the existence of any divine plan, so Luke's inclusion of this theme may be part of a response to their views, which were widely known (see Green, *Jude and 2 Peter*, 155–57, 327–28). The fulfillment theme, however, is about God's plan brought to fruition at a particular moment, that being "the last days" (2:16). God's purpose and plan has come to a decisive climax, the dawning of the Messianic age. See Dodd, *The Apostolic Preaching*, 21; Ridderbos, *The Speeches of Peter*, 13.

41. Chapter 1.

42. See chapter 1 and the discussion in McConnell, who concludes, "In the case of previously received oracles which are fulfilled by current events, the context must determine if the oracle is the gods' testimony for or against a character receiving the oracle" (James R. McConnell Jr., *The "Topos" of Divine Testimony in Luke-Acts* [Eugene, OR: Pickwick, 2014], 105).

43. Barrett, however, suggests that the text Peter references in 1:16 is Ps 49:9 (49:10 LXX): "Even my bosom friend in whom I trusted, who ate of my bread, has lifted the heel against me" (Barrett, *The Acts of the Apostles*, 1:96–97). Given the following citation of Davidic psalms in 1:20, reference to Ps 49 is unlikely. See Fitzmyer, *The Acts of the Apostles*, 223.

divine necessity (ἔδει; cf. 1:21; 3:21; 4:12; 5:9).⁴⁴ The focus of the first prophecy is the fate of the land Judas purchased, now left desolate because of his death (1:18–19): "Let his homestead become desolate, and let there be no one to live in it."⁴⁵ Although Peter underscores the relation of Psalm 69 to Judas's demise, the whole psalm was mined as a source of testimony about Jesus (for example, Ps 69:4 [LXX 68:5]; John 15:25; 69:9 [LXX 68:10]; John 2:17; 69:21 [LXX 68:22]; Mark 15:36; 69:22–23 [LXX 68:23–24]; Rom 11:9–10). Peter's concern is christological and does not simply concern Judas's fate and replacement. Jesus was arrested through Judas's agency (Acts 1:16), the betrayer amidst the apostolic company (1:17), and Judas's replacement would be a witness of the resurrection of the Lord Jesus (1:22). Peter regards the second citation from Psalm 109:8 [LXX 108:8] as a directive to replace Judas: "Let another take his position of overseer." The one chosen would become "a witness with us to his resurrection" (Acts 1:22). The focus is, once again, on the Lord Jesus and not only upon Judas's replacement. As Christ is anticipated in the Davidic psalms, so David's enemies in Psalms 69 and 109 prefigure Judas. The fulfillment of the Davidic psalms marks the advent of a new age when what was predicted now comes to pass. The age of the Messiah has come, a point made repeatedly in Peter's preaching.

Although the theme of fulfillment in Peter's first speech has a distinct christological purpose, the replacement of Judas as the twelfth member of the apostolic company is part of the fabric of the restoration of Israel. As Pao states, "Israel's restoration forms the foundation of the Lukan New Exodus program."⁴⁶ Matthias replaces Judas, who "was numbered among us" (Acts 1:17), and as such he was one of the twelve (Luke 22:3) who "will sit on thrones judging the twelve tribes of Israel" (Luke 22:30) to whom God made his promise (Acts 26:6–7). Matthias's election should therefore be regarded as "the beginning of the restoration of Israel" and therefore "the foundation and the starting point of the New Exodus in Acts," that is, "the arrival of the new era in which the hope of Israel is beginning to be fulfilled."⁴⁷ The betrayer is replaced and the restoration continues as the new age dawns anew.

The theme of prophetic fulfillment at the dawn of a new is at the head of the second Petrine speech in Acts. Peter stands to interpret the meaning of the outpouring of the Spirit on Pentecost (2:1–4) via a quotation from Joel: "This is what was spoken through the prophet Joel: 'In the last days it will be, God declares, that I will pour out my Spirit upon all flesh'" (Acts 2:16–21; citing Joel 2:28–32; LXX 3:1–5). Peter views the advent of the Spirit as a direct fulfillment of Joel's prophecy ("This is what was spoken") and as a sign that the last days have arrived. The phrase "in the last days" is an interpretive gloss on Joel's prophecy, which simply says, "And it shall be after these

---

44. Soards, *The Speeches in Acts*, 187–88.

45. Barrett, *The Acts of the Apostles*, 100; Craig S. Keener, *Acts: An Exegetical Commentary* (Grand Rapids: Baker Academic, 2012), 1:766.

46. Pao, *Acts and the Isaianic New Exodus*, 122, and see the discussion on the New Exodus above.

47. Pao, *Acts and the Isaianic New Exodus*, 125–26.

things" (Joel 2:28). The advent of the Spirit is a sign of "God's final act of redemption"[48] which then leads up to "the coming of the Lord's great and glorious day" (Acts 2:20). The scope of God's redemption is "all flesh" (2:17). He gives the Spirit to everyone who calls upon him without distinction (2:21). In the first instance, this restoration is for the house of Israel without distinction of gender, age, or social class: "Your sons and your daughters . . . your young men and your old men . . . my slaves, both men and women" (2:17–18). But there is also a universal note in the citation from Joel: "Everyone who calls on the name of the Lord shall be saved" (2:21). This theme is picked up again in Peter's promise at the end of the sermon where he states that "the promise is for you, for your children, and for all who are far away, everyone whom the Lord our God calls to him" (2:39). Those who are "far away" harkens back to Isaiah 57:19: "Peace, peace, to the far and the near, says the Lord." While the Jewish diaspora may be in mind, Luke likely understands Peter's words as anticipating a wider mission to the Gentiles—a perspective Peter later fully embraces (Acts 10).[49]

The theme of fulfillment continues in the body of Peter's sermon. The resurrection of Christ was prophetically anticipated through David. Bruce notes that "for those who believed that Jesus was the Messiah of David's line, this meant that many of the experiences of the psalmist (David) were understood as prophetically applicable to Jesus (cf. 2:25–31, 34–36)." Peter cites Psalms 16:8–11 and 110:1 (LXX 15:8–11 and 109:1) in which David predicts the resurrection of Christ. Peter's theology has a sharp christological focus, which finds confirmation in the prophetic testimony of David. Peter combines the Davidic prophecy with the eyewitness testimony of the apostles: "This Jesus God raised up, and of that all of us are witnesses" (2:32).

The third Petrine speech in Acts similarly focuses on the prophetic testimony about Christ, highlighting the way his suffering (3:18) was "foretold through the prophets." This theme picks up Jesus' teaching as first heard, though not immediately understood, by Peter (Mark 8:31–33; 9:12). ThecChristological orientation of the prophecies expands here to include the anticipated "time of universal restoration that God announced long ago through his holy prophets" (3:21). The time of restoration is when God will "send the Messiah appointed for you, that is, Jesus" (3:20). The restoration of Israel's rule was part of the apostles' expectation after seeing the resurrected Christ (1:6) and was an essential thread in the fabric of the New Exodus theology. Peter, however, understands the prophetic witness to include a broader "universal restoration" (3:21) when all his enemies are subjected to him (cf. 2:34–35) and the cosmos would be restored in a new creation (cf. 2 Pet 3:13). Peter envisions a restoration that transcended Israel's national hopes.[50] The golden age and renewal of heavens and earth, anticipated in the New Exodus (Isa 65:17; 66:22; cf. Josephus, *C. Ap.* 2.218;

---

48. David G. Peterson, *The Acts of the Apostles* (Grand Rapids: Eerdmans, 2009), 141.

49. Barrett, *The Acts of the Apostles*, 1:155–56; Pao, *Acts and the Isaianic New Exodus*, 230–31; Bock, *Acts*, 145; Pervo, *Acts*, 85; Keener, *Acts*, 1:987.

50. See the discussion in Keener, *Acts*, 2:1109–12.

Philo, *Eternity* 85; *Mos.* 2.64)[51] and also a central concern of ancient epic, appears here as a significant tenet of Peter's theology.

This speech also picks up the prophetic hope of the coming of the Prophet like Moses (3:22–23; citing Deut 18:15–20), whom Peter identifies as Jesus (3:20). Once again, Peter understands the present time of fulfillment as the inauguration of the New Exodus, which one like Moses leads. Moses's testimony stands with that of all the prophets from Samuel onward who "predicted these days" (3:24). Possibly the original version of the sermon included the litany of prophetic testimony here compressed into this general affirmation. For Peter, Jesus is the Prophet whose words people must heed. Those who do not listen "will be utterly rooted out from the people" (3:23b). The rejection of Moses and his words (Deut 18:19) finds its counterpart in the rejection of Jesus. In Peter's view, the time of fulfillment is a sword of two edges, one for salvation and the other of judgment. Response to the resurrected Christ, who is the predicted Prophet, determines a people's end. Christ is the center of God's plan to deliver and to judge. Therefore, the present is the beginning of the end of time, the dawn of the messianic age, which anticipates the final time of restoration and judgment brought to pass when the Messiah returns. Peter understands the present fulfillment of the divine promise as a call to heed God's messenger since the final age has dawned.

The theme of fulfillment likewise informs Peter's citation of Psalm 118:22 in Acts 4:11: "This Jesus is 'the stone that was rejected by you, the builders; it has become the cornerstone.'" The stone testimony from Psalm 118 is a centerpiece in Petrine theology (Mark 12:10; 1 Pet 2:7). The testimony "in each case vindicates Jesus against his rejection by the Jewish leaders, and sees him become 'the keystone in God's new temple.'"[52] Peter announces this particular prophetic testimony within the confines of or near the temple (4:1–7),[53] just as Jesus evoked this text while within the temple (Mark 11:27). Jesus' rejection by the leaders of the nation (Acts 4:6) does not mean that he is forsaken by God. Indeed, in God's plan the Rejected Stone has become the cornerstone (or capstone).[54] As noted previously, the Stone testimony, "stands at the intersection of the hopes for the Messianic age, the beginning of the New Exodus, and the building of God's new temple, all while embracing the cross and resurrection of Jesus. The passage hints that the current order, administered by the 'builders,' will come to an end."[55] The rejection of Christ, the Stone, does not mean that God's plans have been thwarted since Christ has become "the cornerstone" and, as such, is the foundation for universal salvation (4:12), a principle theme of the New Exodus.

Central to Peter's theology in Acts is the belief that the time of fulfillment has come. A new golden age has dawned and the New Exodus has begun, making present

51. Keener, *Acts*, 2:1111.
52. Hilgert, "Speeches in Acts," 110.
53. Keener, *Acts*, 2:1139.
54. Keener, *Acts*, 2:1149.
55. See chapter 4.

the inauguration of the eschatological age. Peter's prime concern, however, is not simply the times but the person of Jesus who, as the new Moses, determines a peoples' destiny according to their response to him and his words. The new age ushers in the advent of the Spirit, the renewal of Israel, the inclusion of the Gentiles, and the renewal of all things. The central event predicted and fulfilled is the resurrection of Christ, the one who had been rejected, suffered, and died. God's predicted plan could not be thwarted even by death. Now, therefore, is the time of repentance in anticipation of the final restoration of all things. Peter understands that God makes sweeping plans that he revealed through his prophets and are now coming to pass.

The Plan of God

The dominant theme of fulfillment in Peter's theology is a piece of his overall understanding of the plan of God. In the midst of a world where Pharisees and Sadducees, Stoics and Epicureans, debated their differences regarding divine providence, Peter stands within the biblical tradition that God's plans supersede all others. God purposes, predicts, and executes—views contrary to those of the Sadducees and Epicureans of Peter's day. According to Josephus, the Sadducees did not believe in fate and the Epicureans denied any form of divine providence (*Ant.* 13.173; 10.277–80; *BJ* 2.164).[56] Greek and Latin authors who affirmed providence said that the gods themselves were subject to "the fixed decrees of Fate" (Ovid, *Metam.* 15.808–9).[57] But in Peter's theology God is the one who predetermines. Divine providence becomes a central motif in both epistles ascribed to Peter (1 Pet 1:1–2, 10–12, 20; 2 Pet 3:1–10). History is not simply the stage upon which human plans play themselves out but where God's purposes are brought to pass even in the face of human resistance. God's plan cannot be thwarted by human sin, nor do his purposes make him an agent of evil. According to Peter, God not only knows what will come to pass and then reveals events to his prophets, but he also plans events in accordance with his will. His providence is most clearly evident in the unlikeliest of places: the cross of Christ. Peter declared that "this man, handed over to you according to the definite plan and foreknowledge of God, you crucified and killed by the hands of those outside the law" (2:23). The human verdict against Jesus could not stand since "God raised him up, having freed him from death, because it was impossible for him to be held in its power" (2:24). Peter juxtaposes the divine purpose in the death of Jesus with human responsibility without flinching. His purpose is not to resolve the tension between human and divine agency

---

56. Contra Jonathan Klawans (*Josephus and the Theologies of Ancient Judaism* [Oxford: Oxford University Press, 2012], 63–64), who argues that the Sadducees did indeed have a doctrine of divine providence. But see David Flusser, who convincingly argues that the Sadducees rejected the doctrine since it seemed to implicate God in evil (*The Jewish Sages and Their Literature* [Grand Rapids: Eerdmans, 2009], 11–14). See Keener's extensive discussion on the topic of providence and fate (*Acts*, 927–38).

57. Keener, *Acts*, 1:929.

but, as Ridderbos remarks, here we witness "the terminology of the history of salvation, of the great eschatological drama, which is now being enacted."[58]

Peter employs strong language when speaking of God's plan, which centered on Jesus' crucifixion. Jesus was handed over by God's "determinate counsel" (τῇ ὡισμένῃ βουλῇ). According to Peter, Christ was crucified according to God's determined (ὁρίζω)[59] design or decree (βουλή),[60] just as he determined that Jesus should become the "judge of the living and the dead" (10:32). Peter adds that Jesus was handed over for crucifixion "according to the . . . foreknowledge (προγνώσει) of God" (2:23). This foreknowledge is not simply prescience (as in 2 Pet 3:17) but has a determinative element (cf. 1 Pet 1:2; and the verbal form in 1:20; Rom. 8:29; 11:2). Peter is a principle actor in developing the Christian understanding that the cross was not simply a travesty of justice, or an enormous dishonor that produced shame, but rather was Christ dying by divine design. God's took a lawless action (2:23b) and accomplished his purpose through it. And, in the end, he reversed the deadly deed (2:24). Roman and Jewish powers (2:23) did not have the final word since God's designs were fully accomplished even through the ignominy of his death.

According to Peter, God's purposes include calling people to himself. God prepared the blessings of the New Covenant, i.e., forgiveness and the gift of the Spirit (2:38; Jer 31:31–34), for those gathered at Pentecost, their children, and "all those who are far away" (2:39). This latter group is made up not simply of those who are geographically dispersed but of the Gentiles who are "far away" (22:21; Isa 57:19; Sir 24:32). All of these are ones "whom the Lord our God calls to him," a point Peter picks up from the prophecy in Joel (Joel 2:32b). They must call upon him (Joel 2:32a; Acts 2:21), but the human call to God is predicated on his initiative and call (προσκαλέσηται). God's plan includes summoning people to become part of it.[61] God's plan is centered in Christ, but his work is to bless those whom God summons to himself.

---

58. Ridderbos, *The Speeches of Peter*, 13. Or as Susan Garrett ("Exodus from Bondage: Luke 9:31 and Acts 12:1–24," *CBQ* 52 (1990) 678) says, "For Luke, historical events are the window through which one can discern the trans-historical plan of God (Acts 2:23; 4:27–28)."

59. *MM*, 457; *TDNT*, 5:452–53. The term is Lukan (Luke 22:22; Acts 17:26, 31), and its use could betray the presence of Luke's hand in the redaction of Peter's speech. However, the concept of God's determinate plan in the cross is commonplace in Petrine thought (Mark 8:31–33; 1 Peter 1:20). Moreover, the specific expression of God's determined or predetermined plan (ὁρίζω or προορίζω βουλή) appears only in the Petrine strata (2:23; 4:28).

60. Although βουλή may mean "counsel" (*BDAG*, 181–82; *LSJ*, 325; *MM*, 115), that concept implies that there are multiple agents who consider a matter together (hence the term's use to speak of a "council" that gives "counsel"). Here the emphasis is on the divine sovereign decree. God's deliberation is only with himself, a point Peter makes by coupling the term with ὁρίζω. It is "the final result of inner deliberation" (*TDNT*, 1:633).

61. The term often appears where people are being summoned to gather (Acts 5:20; 6:2; 13:7; 20:1; 23:17–81, 23), or when God summons someone to engage in some service (13:2; 16:10). In this instance, however, the divine summons to salvation, or his election, is in view (cf. the use of "call," καλέω in 1 Pet 1:15; 2:9, 21; 3:9; 5:10; 2 Pet 1:3).

The coalescence of God's plans for Christ and those whom he calls appears in the second Petrine speech, where the apostle anticipates the time when God will send again "the Messiah appointed for you, that is, Jesus, who must remain in heaven until the time of universal restoration that God announced long ago through his holy prophets" (3:20b–21). Jesus is "the appointed Christ" (τὸν προκεχειρισμένον ὑμῖν χριστὸν Ἰησοῦν), that is, the one who was preordained or appointed for them (cf. Exod 4:13; Josh 3:12; 2 Macc 3:7; 9:9; 14:12; Acts 22:14; 26:16). As Spicq notes, the term used here is noble "because those entrusted with a mission have been elected or appointed on account of their competence and integrity."[62] As the one previously appointed by God, Christ is invested with high authority. But Peter wraps up God's plan in Christ with those who hear the sermon—the Messiah was appointed "for you." Peter consistently places people in the center of God's plans in Christ (cf. 1 Pet 1:12, 13; 2:7). The apostle understands that God not only will send Christ but grants (δοῦναι) Israel both repentance and forgiveness of sins (5:31; cf. 11:18 of the Gentiles; Sir 12:10, 19). Peter's thought may mean nothing more than God offers an opportunity for repentance. But given his strong theology of divine agency he may mean that God enables or grants both Jews (and Gentiles in 11:18) repentance. Under either reading, the divine plan, centered in Christ, brings those called into this river. The divine plan should not, therefore, be hindered (11:17). Peter showed that he was in step with God's plan by baptizing the Gentiles whom God had filled with his Spirit at the house of Cornelius. This is precisely what we would expect from one who himself had been appointed to this mission by God (15:7). God's plan includes his choice of messengers (cf. 1:2, 27). Peter is conscious of his own particular place in God's plan.

In his preaching Peter betrays his deep belief that present events, which God has brought to pass, are in continuity with his past dealings with his people. None other than "the God of Abraham, the God of Isaac, and the God of Jacob, the God of our ancestors" has glorified Jesus by raising him from the dead (3:13, 15). Peter touches this point again in 5:30, where he declares, "The God of our ancestors raised up Jesus." God was with Jesus (10:38b) just as he had been with their ancestors Abraham, Isaac, and Jacob.[63] Instead of being an aberration in God's plans, the divine presence with Jesus and his resurrection and glorification stand in continuity with God's past actions with his people. Indeed, the allusion here to Exodus 3:6 and 15 ties together the past Exodus with God's New Exodus in Christ. Peter's New Exodus theology appears here also in the reference to Jesus as God's Servant, whom God glorifies (Acts 3:13; Isa

---

62. *TLNT*, 3.207; cf. *TDNT*, 4:863. The term itself appears only in Luke in the NT but expresses a part of Peter's theology insofar as he links God's plan for Christ with that of his people.

63. The reference is, in the first instance, to the burning bush (Gen 3:6), but the idea that God is with them and the ancestors embraces a wider circle of those who knew his presence. Joseph, Moses, and David are evoked as well. See, for example, Gen 26:3, 24; 28:15; 1 Sam 18:12, 14; Barrett, *The Acts of the Apostles*, 2:525.

52:13; 53:11-12; cf. 49:3).⁶⁴ There is one story that God has played out since the time of the patriarchs and is now being played out in Christ.

Peter does include references to the incarnation in Acts, following the theological pattern in the Gospel of Mark (cf. Matt 1:20-23; Luke 1:30-35; John 1:14-18). He does, however, stress that God "anointed Jesus of Nazareth with the Holy Spirit and with power" (10:38; cf. Mark 1:9-11; 1:21-2:12). As a result of this anointing and empowerment he "went about doing good and healing all who were oppressed by the devil, for God was with him" (cf. Acts 4:27; Luke 4:18; Isa 61:1). For Peter, God empowered the whole of Jesus' ministry through the agency of the Holy Spirit, enabling him to become a benefactor to all whom he encountered (εὐεργετῶν, "doing good") as a benefactor.⁶⁵ Jesus is, therefore, the Christ or Anointed One. When Christ's empowered mission was apparently thwarted by death, God raised Jesus (3:13; 10:40). God carried out his plan through Christ, whom he empowered and, in the end, glorified (3:15; 5:31). This is the very one whom God will send (3:20) to consummate his divine plan. The arc of God's plan in Christ is unbounded. What God planned he brought to pass and will bring to pass in the future. According to Peter, God made large plans, and he empowered Christ and acted so that those plans would be accomplished. The overarching plan of God becomes a central tenet in Peter's theology.

THE JESUS STORY

According to Peter, Jesus stands at the center of the plan of God. As argued previously, the fullest expression of the Jesus story told by Peter is in Mark.⁶⁶ Mark's rendition of the gospel is rooted in Peter's proclamation, and we may assume that Peter related to Paul the contours of the story found there when the two met (Gal 1:18).⁶⁷ Although

---

64. See below on Peter's use of the Servant Songs in this sermon. See also David Moessner, "The 'Script' of Scriptures in Acts: Suffering as God's 'Plan' (Βουλή) for the World and the 'Release of Sins,'" in *History, Literature, and Society in the Book of Acts*, ed. Ben Witherington III (Cambridge: Cambridge University Press, 1996), 228; Keener, *Acts*, 2:1085. Peter shares his understanding of the way the Servant Songs point to Jesus, but his understanding of their applicability appears to be foundational for the church. See "The Testimony of Peter in the Gospel of Mark."

65. For discussions on the language of benefaction, see the chapter on the theology of 1 Peter and Frederick W. Danker, *Benefactor: Epigraphic Study of a Graeco-Roman and New Testament Semantic Field* (St. Louis: Clayton, 1982); Bruce W. Winter, *Seek the Welfare of the City: Christians as Benefactors and Citizens* (Grand Rapids: Eerdmans, 1994); *TLNT* 2.107113. Barrett comments that "the ministry [of Jesus] regarded as a whole was made up of a continuous series of acts of beneficence. εὐεργετεῖν (cf. Luke 22:25) is the action of a public benefactor ... but here *doing good* is a strong enough rendering. Luke describes it in terms of healing, of the overthrow of the devil, and of the presence of God himself" (*The Acts of the Apostles*, 1:525). The language of benefaction was also used of rulers and deities. As Spicq notes, "Thus it is attributed first of all to the gods and goddesses who are benefactors of their faithful" (*TLNT*, 2.110). Given the nature of Jesus' benefaction (see also Acts 4:9), Peter points to the supernatural agency in Jesus' benefaction.

66. See the chapter on the theology of Mark.

67. While the purpose of the visit could have been simply to get to know Peter as Hofius ("Gal 1:18: Historesai Kephan," *ZNW* 75 (1984) 73-85) suggests, we can hardly imagine that Paul spent time with

we do not have a complete description of that encounter, the fact that Paul states that he only met with Peter and James (1:19) before he laid out his gospel to the "pillars" fourteen years later (2:1–10) suggests that his understanding of the *story* of Jesus came principally from Peter and, likely, the Lord's brother. Paul's theological understanding of the Christ event came from God (1:13–17), but the Jesus story was mediated to him (cf. 1 Cor 15:1–11). The contours of that story are also present in the Petrine sermons in Acts. None of the Petrine speeches tells the full story in narrative form, but aspects are highlighted throughout. Luke has already given a full account of Jesus' life in the first volume of Luke-Acts (Acts 1:1), so for his purposes he only needed to reference briefly events his readers already knew.

As in the Gospel of Mark, the story of Jesus begins with the baptism of John (Acts 1:22; 10:37), mentioned as part of the qualifications for the apostolic replacement of Judas and as the beginning of the *kerygma* proclaimed in Cornelius's house. The speeches also include summary statements about Jesus' ministry. According to Peter, Jesus performed miracles, which were part of the divine testimony. He was "a man attested to you by God with deeds of power, wonders, and signs that God did through him among you, as you yourselves know" (2:22). Peter later summarizes the miracles as acts of divine benefaction ("doing good") empowered through the Holy Spirit. These included healing "all those who were oppressed by the devil" (10:38). God was with him, as testified in Mark. Jesus' ministry was marked by preaching as well as miraculous deeds (10:36–37). He was sent first to the people of Israel (3:26), starting in Galilee where Jesus was from, and extending to Judea and Jerusalem (10:37–39).

Other details of his life and ministry are only suggested in statements like "the Lord Jesus went in and out among us" (1:21), but the events are not discussed in detail. However, a considerable portion of the Petrine speeches of Acts tell of his rejection, suffering, and crucifixion. Peter names Judas as the one who led those who arrested Jesus (1:16). He was handed over and rejected before Pilate, who wanted to release him (3:13). Over and again Peter underscores that his own people had rejected, crucified, and killed Jesus (2:23–24, 36; 3:13–15; 4:10–11; 5:30). Though the Jewish people were responsible, they acted in ignorance (3:17). However, Peter notes that Jesus' execution was carried out by non-Jews or "those outside the law" (2:23). The form of death was crucifixion by hanging Jesus "on a tree" (5:30; 10:39; cf. 1 Pet 2:24; Deut 21:23), a description of the cross that may originate with Peter but was not unique to him (Acts 13:29; Gal 3:13). Peter focuses on the way Jesus, the Christ, suffered (3:18).

The story does not end with Jesus' death. Peter testified that God raised him from the dead (2:32; 3:15, 26; 4:10; 5:30; 10:41) on the third day (10:40). He was freed from death (2:24) and was not abandoned by God though people had rejected him

---

Peter and did not hear the story of Jesus from the one who had been named as the Rock. See George D. Kilpatrick, "Galatians 1:18: *Historēsai Kēphan*," in *New Testament Essays: Studies in Memory of Thomas Walter Manson, 1893–1958*, ed. A. J. B. Higgins (Manchester: Manchester University Press, 1959), 144–49; James G. D. Dunn, "The Relationship Between Paul and Jerusalem According to Galatians 1 and 2," *NTS* 28 (1982) 463–66.

(2:26–28). The testimony about his resurrection was quite ample. The apostles were witnesses of the resurrected Jesus (1:22; 2:32), supported by the prophetic testimony (2:26–31). The apostles saw the resurrected Jesus and even ate and drank with him (10:40–41). The resurrection was the beginning of Jesus' glorification by God (3:13). He was taken up into heaven (1:22), where he was seated at the right hand of God (2:33–35; 5:31), where he is enthroned (2:30). There he remains until God sends him again (3:20–21). Given Christ's exaltation, the apostles proclaimed that "in Jesus there is the resurrection of the dead" (4:2), that is, it anticipates the final resurrection.[68] The Petrine speeches in Acts summarize Jesus' story, which Luke's readers already knew. But they step further by developing a theology of Jesus' person and deeds.

Petrine Christology in Acts

The center of Peter's proclamation is the person of Jesus Christ and the significance of his life, death, and glorification. His Christology is not abstracted but wraps around the story of Jesus. The very first Petrine speech in Acts, which addresses the problem of Judas's defection (1:15–22), is highly Christocentric, beginning with a compressed narrative about Jesus' arrest (1:16) and culminating in a call to seek a replacement for Judas who would become "a witness with us to his resurrection" (1:25). Peter demonstrates his leadership of the church in this call and his guidance of the selection process. None other steps into this role. His primary concern, however, is not ecclesial order but the testimony about Jesus. As expected, he seeks the twelfth member of the apostolic community who would be a witness ($μάτυρα$) of the resurrection. As argued previously, testimony is a central motif in early Christian reflection about Peter, and this also becomes a prime component of Peter's own theological concern. Acting as a witness and giving testimony is not only about affirming the veracity of events that have occurred but also offering relevant interpretation of those events. For this reason Peter requires that Judas's replacement be someone who "accompanied us through the time that the Lord Jesus went in and out among us, beginning from the baptism of John until the day when he was taken up from us" (1:21–22). Only someone who had participated in the full arc of Jesus' ministry and had seen and heard from the Lord himself could offer testimony as a "witness with us to his resurrection." More was at stake than testifying that Jesus was no longer entombed since witnesses offered interpretation. Peter participates in the testimony about Jesus, presenting his understanding of who he is through the names ascribed to him. Names attach to concepts about both Jesus' person and work. The honorific titles spring from the deep well of Peter's Christology.

---

68. Barrett, *The Acts of the Apostles*, 1:219–20; Keener, *Acts*, 2:1131–32.

Jesus Christ of Nazareth

Simon Peter's first encounter with Jesus was at the Sea of Galilee (Mark 1:16–21), in the region where people called him Jesus of Nazareth (Mark 1:9, 24). Peter commonly refers to Jesus as either being from Nazareth (Acts 3:6; 4:10; 10:38) or as the Nazarene (Acts 2:22), although Stephen (Acts 6:14) and Paul (Acts 26:9; cf. 22:8) at times identify him by his place of residence.[69] Peter recalls the man he knew (2:22), the one through whom God had worked "deeds of power, wonders, and signs" during his earthly ministry (2:22b, ἄνδρα) and through whose name miracles still occurred (4:10). Among Cornelius's household Peter declares that this Jesus of Nazareth was the one whom "God anointed . . . with the Holy Spirit and power" (cf. Isa 61:1; Luke 4:18), thereby enabling him to carry out a ministry of benefaction by "doing good and healing all who were oppressed by the devil" (10:38). The lame man at the Beautiful Gate received healing "in the name of Jesus Christ of Nazareth" (Acts 3:6), and the apostle said to Aeneas, a paralytic bedridden for eight years, "Jesus Christ heals you; get up and make your bed!" (9:34). Peter's Christology thus begins with the person of Jesus, one who was fully human and then divinely empowered to accomplish miraculous deeds and "a prophet elevated by God."[70] As Barrett observes, "It is from this starting-point that the Christology of Acts proceeds, not from the notion of a divine being who by some kind of incarnation or *kenosis* accommodated himself to the human world."[71] Peter's perspective accords with Jewish expectations that the Messiah would be fully human (*Ps. Sol.* 17:21, 32) but endowed with power through God's Spirit (*Ps. Sol.* 17:37).[72] The miracles God did through him marked Jesus as God's designated agent ("A man attested to you by God," ἄνδρα ἀποδεδειγμένον ἀπὸ τοῦ θεοῦ εἰς ὑμᾶς [2:22]). These miracles gave testimony to this man's place in God's plan and purposes (cf. Heb 2:4).

Peter distinguished this Jesus[73] from others so named by identifying him as being "from Nazareth" (Ἰησοῦν τὸν ἀπὸ Ναζαρέθ [10:38]) or as "the Nazarene" (2:22). The name somewhat surprises since, as Kilgallen observes, to call him the Nazarene "separates Jesus from the heritage and even the physical territory of David"[74] (cf. 2:29–30 where Peter argues that Jesus is of the Davidic line). Theophilus and the other readers of Luke-Acts would have already known that Jesus was the son of David and associated

---

69. *TDNT*, 4:874–75.

70. Pervo, *Acts*, 81.

71. Barrett, *The Acts of the Apostles*, 140.

72. Emil Schürer, *The History of the Jewish People in the Age of Jesus Christ (175 BC–AD 135)* (Edinburgh: T. & T. Clark, 1979), 518–19.

73. See Tal Ilan's "phone book" of those named Jesus (*Lexicon of Jewish Names in Late Antiquity, Part I: Palestine 330 BCE–200CE* [Tübingen: Mohr Siebeck, 2002], 129; Bauckham, *Jesus and the Eyewitnesses*, 85). It was the sixth most popular male name during the period.

74. John J. Kilgallen, "'With Many Other Words' (Acts 2:40): Theological Assumptions in Peter's Pentecost Speech," *Bib* 83 (2002) 78.

with Bethlehem (Luke 2:4–7). But this fact, which arises from the infancy narrative in Luke, is of little concern to the audiences Peter was addressing when he identified him as Jesus of Nazareth.[75] This is how Peter's hearers would have known him.

Peter recognized that this man from Nazareth was the Christ and so calls him "Jesus Christ of Nazareth" (4:10). Peter was the first to realize that the Nazarene was indeed the Anointed one, the Christ (Mark 8:29; Acts 10:38).[76] As in the Gospel of Mark, in Acts Peter understands that Jesus is the long-awaited Messiah who was foretold through the prophets (3:18), displayed miraculous healings (3:6; 9:34), suffered and was crucified (3:18; 4:10), was raised from the dead (2:31; 4:10), is exalted as Lord over all (2:36; 10:36), and will return in God's time (3:20). Christ came preaching peace with God (10:36), and so now all—both Jews and Gentiles—should believe in him and be baptized for the forgiveness of sins (2:38; 10:48; 11:17). Cullmann reminds us that Peter was the first to preach that Jesus was the Christ in Jerusalem and that as the "leader of the first church" he "was not merely the organizer with only practical interests, as we usually conceive him. Here too the picture of the Prince of the Church is incorrect. He certainly possesses a much greater significance in the foundation of Christian theology than we are accustomed to assume."[77] This fundamental confession of the Christian faith can be traced to him.

Peter proclaimed that the suffering Jesus endured as the Christ was the result of ignorance on the part of the people of Israel and their leaders. But it was also the fulfillment of God's plan predicted through the prophets: "In this way God fulfilled what he had foretold through all the prophets, that his Messiah would suffer" (3:17–18). Soards notes, "The cross is not cast as a scandal, for the crucifixion of Jesus at the hands of the lawless is viewed as part of the fulfillment of God's plan"[78] (cf. 2:23; 1 Pet 1:10–11). That the Messiah would come was the consistent expectation within the OT (2 Sam 7:12–16; Isa 9:7; Jer 23:5–6) and Judaism (*Ps. Sol.* 17.21–34; 4Q252 5.1–4; 1 En 48:10; 52:4), although Jewish expressions of that hope were variegated.[79] Absent from the streams of Jewish Messianism, however, was any thought of a suffering Messiah who would die as an atoning sacrifice for sin.[80] Peter's rejection of Jesus' announcement of his sufferings was conditioned by contemporary notions about a triumphant

---

75. Kilgallen, "'With Many Other Words' (Acts 2:40)," 79.

76. See the section "You are the Christ" in chapter 2, "The Testimony of Peter in the Gospel of Mark."

77. Cullmann, *Peter*, 69.

78. Soards, *The Speeches in Acts*, 34. See above on *The Plan of God*.

79. See Schürer, *The History of the Jewish People in the Age of Jesus Christ (175 BC–AD 135)*, 488–554; Richard N. Longenecker, *The Christology of Early Jewish Christianity* (London: SCM, 1970), 109–10; N. T. Wright, *Jesus and the Victory of God* (Minneapolis: Fortress, 1996), 481–89; William Horbury, "Jewish Messianism and Early Christology," in *Contours of Christology in the New Testament*, ed. Richard N. Longenecker (Grand Rapids: Eerdmans, 2005), 3–24; Keener, *Acts*, 1:964–68.

80. The notion of a righteous man who would suffer and atone for the sins of the nation was present, however (Schürer, *The History of the Jewish People in the Age of Jesus Christ [175 BC–AD 135]*, 549).

Messiah (Mark 8:27–33). His confession that Jesus was the Christ was juxtaposed with Jesus' prediction of his death, thus generating profound theological dissonance in the apostle's mind. But now in Acts Peter regards Christ's death as the true fulfillment of ancient hopes and contemporary expectations. Peter was capable of theological adjustment (cf. Acts 10:28).

Peter did not believe that the crucifixion was the end of the Messiah's story. He boldly proclaimed the crucified one was resurrected. God raised Jesus from the dead (2:24) in fulfillment of the same prophetic hope: "David spoke of the resurrection of the Messiah, saying, 'He was not abandoned to Hades, nor did his flesh experience corruption'" (2:31; citing Ps 16:10). Peter focuses sharply on the testimony of David (2:25–28; Ps 16:8–11; cf. Acts 1:16; 2:34–35; 4:25), from whom the Messiah descended (Mark 12:35–37) and to whom God had sworn that his descendent would sit on the throne of Israel forever (Acts 2:30, citing Ps 132:11; 2 Sam 7:13).[81] Peter's citation of Psalm 16:8–11 establishes the unique perspective that the Messiah was not only crucified but was raised from the dead. This, then, is the prelude to the claim in Acts 2:34–35 that Jesus is the exalted and enthroned Messiah. Peter places the Davidic prophetic testimony regarding the resurrection of the Messiah (2:25–28) alongside the apostolic witness that Jesus was indeed alive: "This Jesus God raised up, and of that all of us are witnesses" (Acts 2:32; cf. 1:22; 5:32; 10:39, 41). Peter disavows that the resurrection of the Messiah was merely an existential experience detached from what occurred. There were, in fact, multiple witnesses. As Ridderbos said, "The original *kerygma* rests upon what has *happened*. And the resurrection forms the very heart of this."[82] Peter contrasts the deadly decision of the Jewish leaders with the life-giving action of God. Jesus Christ is the one "whom you crucified" but "whom God raised from the dead" (4:10). The resurrection of Jesus the Messiah is not a secondary but a central tenet in Peter's theology (see also 2:31; 3:15, 36; 5:30; 10:40–41). This is God's planned and miraculously executed act to assure that his promise regarding the Davidic Messiah, the ruler of Israel, would be fulfilled.

The resurrection of Jesus Christ is the first stage of his exaltation. Peter was a witness of the ascension (1:9–11) and he now proclaims Jesus the Messiah is the exalted Lord. Peter not only appeals to the prophetic word from David to explain the resurrection of Christ (2:31) but cites David once again as the prophetic witness regarding Christ's exaltation. Quoting Psalm 110:1, he reminds those gathered at Pentecost that "David did not ascend into the heavens, but he himself says, 'The Lord said to my Lord, "Sit at my right hand, until I make your enemies your footstool"'" (2:34–35; cf. 5:31). Jesus had previously interpreted Psalm 110:1 as a prophetic testimony about himself (Mark 12:35–37; 14:62),[83] a teaching Peter now proclaims to all. Jesus is the *enthroned* Messiah. Strauss points up that Peter "wishes to prove not just that Jesus

---

81. Strauss, *Davidic Messiah in Luke-Acts*, 147.
82. Ridderbos, *The Speeches of Peter*, 18.
83. Also see its use in the longer ending of Mark (16:19).

was the Davidic messiah, but that he has already been exalted to the Davidic throne. In the climax of the sermon in verse 36, he will proclaim both conclusions together, that Jesus is both the Christ and the reigning Lord."[84] Peter understands that Jesus is "exalted at the right hand of God" and as the exalted Lord he received and poured out the Holy Spirit upon those gathered at Pentecost (2:33). The enthroned Messiah is the exalted Lord who gives gifts to his subjects. Indeed, the outpouring of the Spirit demonstrates that "both God and the exalted Christ are actively 'present.'"[85] The prophetic testimony, the apostolic witness, and the evidence of the presence of the Holy Spirit ("This that you both see and hear") lead to only one conclusion: "God has made him both Lord and Messiah, this Jesus whom you crucified" (2:36). At this stage his sovereignty is marked out and made certain for "the entire house of Israel," but later Peter's understanding widens to include his universal sovereignty (10:36).

Peter's theology of Jesus the Christ includes robust affirmations about his life, death, resurrection, and exaltation. But Peter also looked forward to the time when the Christ would return and restore all things. After speaking about the Messiah's sufferings as a fulfillment of the prophetic promise (3:18), calling for repentance, and offering the promise of forgiveness ("So that your sins may be wiped out" [3:19]), he looked further ahead. Israel should repent "so that times of refreshing may come from the presence of the Lord, and that he may send the Messiah appointed for you, that is, Jesus, who must remain in heaven until the time of universal restoration that God announced long ago through his holy prophets" (3:20–21). Peter binds the advent of Christ with his exaltation, recalling the angelic announcement after Jesus' ascension: "Men of Galilee, why do you stand looking up toward heaven? This Jesus, who has been taken up from you into heaven, will come in the same way as you saw him go into heaven" (1:11). At present Jesus remains in heaven. He is absent, yet exercises his sovereign presence through the Spirit (2:33).

The proclamation of the message is intended to bring about repentance in Israel (as 2:38) "so that times of refreshing may come from the presence of the Lord" (3:20; cf. Jub 1:15–18). The term translated "refreshing" (ἀναψύξεως) could refer to various forms of relief, such as relief from torrid heat by cooling or liberation from some evil.[86] It may be that "times of refreshing" refers back to the Pentecost experience or holds out the promise of current eschatological blessings or seasons of refreshment in the present that anticipate the return of the Messiah.[87] Here Peter most likely refers to the final age when the Messiah returns as the "times of relief," that is, "the eschatological

---

84. Strauss, *Davidic Messiah in Luke-Acts*, 140; Kilgallen, "'With Many Other Words' (Acts 2:40)," 80–81.

85. Max Turner, *Power from on High: The Spirit in Israel's Restoration and Witness in Luke-Acts* (Sheffield: Sheffield Academic, 1996), 303.

86. *TDNT*, 9:664.

87. Barrett, *The Acts of the Apostles*, 1:205; James D. G. Dunn, *The Acts of the Apostles*, 46–47; Pao, *Acts and the Isaianic New Exodus*, 133; Pervo, *Acts*, 108.

redemption which is promised to Israel if it repents."[88] The following clauses point to the "times (καιροὶ, plural) of refreshing" as the time when God will send the "Messiah appointed for you" (v. 20) and "the time (χρόνων, plural) of universal restoration that God announced long ago through his holy prophets" (v. 21; cf. 3:18; Ps 110:1). Peter points to the final eschatological liberation at the time of the Messiah's advent. If Israel repents, the Messiah will come and all things will be restored. The restoration of Israel is a principle theme of the New Exodus, as discussed above. Corporate repentance will lead to corporate redemption.[89]

The Lord

Peter does more than embrace the theology of a suffering and exalted Messiah. The apostle takes one further theological step when he identifies the resurrected Christ as Lord. He proclaims to those gathered at Pentecost and beyond to everyone in the house of Israel that "God has made him both Lord and Messiah, this Jesus whom you crucified" (2:36; 11:17). The lordship of the Messiah was part of Peter's testimony from Jesus in Mark (Mark 12:35–37; from Ps 110:1) and appears again here in Acts for the first time on Peter's lips (1:21; 2:25, 34–36). The lordship of the Messiah was also part of the Jewish expectation (*Ps. Sol.* 17:32). Through the resurrection God appointed ("made") Jesus to the office of Lord and Messiah. Keener notes, "The language of 'appointing' refers to status, not ontology, and hence is appropriate for Jesus beginning only at his exaltation. This sort of 'Messiah-designate-until-enthroned' Christology seems to have been an early one in the church."[90] The messianic lordship of Jesus finds its roots in the OT promise and Jewish hopes, has its definitive expression in Peter's testimony regarding Jesus' teaching, and then is fully proclaimed publicly in the preaching of Peter.

On a personal level, Peter is accustomed to addressing Jesus as Lord. He recounted "how the Lord had brought him out of prison" (12:17), how he remembered "word of the Lord" (11:16), and how he even resisted the Lord's direction when beckoned to eat what was regarded as unclean food ("By no means, Lord" [10:14; 11:8;

---

88. *TDNT*, 9:664–65; Hans Conzelmann, *Acts of the Apostles* (Philadelphia: Fortress, 1987), 29; F. F. Bruce, *The Book of the Acts* (Grand Rapids: Eerdmans, 1988), 84; F. F. Bruce, *The Acts of the Apostles: Greek Text with Introduction and Commentary* (Grand Rapids: Eerdmans, 1951), 111; Witherington, *The Acts of the Apostles*, 187; *BDAG*, 75. Note that Peter uses the plural to speak of both the "times (καιροὶ) of refreshing" and "the time (χρόνων) of universal restoration," although many translations render the second in the singular (NRSV, NIV, *ESV, NASB*). The plural may be used "to denote what is long or wide, or mysterious powers" (*BDF* §141) but be rendered as a singular (as in Heb 12:23, where the plural is rendered "heaven," or 1:2, where the plural is translated by some by the singular "world" (*NASB*) or "universe" (NIV)).

89. "Repentance has personal and corporate aspects and is called for in the present; the blotting out of sins is similarly both personal and corporate, and in its personal aspect belongs to the present; the coming of the Messiah means corporate redemption in the future" (Barrett, "Faith and Eschatology in Acts 3," 10; Keener, *Acts*, 2:1112).

90. Keener, *Acts*, 1:964; Barrett, *The Acts of the Apostles*, 1:151.

cf. Mark 8:32; Matt 16:22]). Peter's use of the title Lord is very personal and betrays the developed relationship he enjoyed with Jesus even beyond the ascension. Yet he understands Jesus' ultimate sovereignty as the Lord who offers salvation to all who call upon him. The Lord is also the one whose day of salvation will dawn: "The sun shall be turned to darkness and the moon to blood, before the coming of the Lord's great and glorious day" (2:20). Salvation comes to "everyone who calls on the name of the Lord" (2:21). These quotations from Joel 2:31-32 referred originally to the coming of Yahweh.[91] But Peter turns them to refer to the resurrected Jesus, who is himself Lord (2:25-36). The one they call upon for salvation is none other than Jesus (2:38), the divine Lord.[92] Ontologically, the title Lord is an ascription of divinity to Jesus (Ps 110:1), which may be traced back to the use of *kyrios* as the translation of the divine name *Yahweh* in the LXX. He is the universal, divine Lord who offers salvation to all (Acts 2:21; 10:36).[93] The confession that Jesus is Lord was a foundational tenet in earliest Christian theology (1 Cor 16:22; Phil 2:11; Rev 22:20), which had its origin in the teaching of Jesus. But the first to proclaim Jesus' divine Lordship after the resurrection was neither the Jerusalem church nor Paul; it was Peter (Acts 1:21, 24; 2:20-21, 34-36; 10:36; cf. 1 Pet 1:3; 3:15; Mark 1:1-4). Peter's expression of Christ's lordship became a central confession of early Christian Christology just as his revelation that Jesus was the anticipated Messiah.

The Suffering Servant Jesus

Peter's speeches identify Jesus as the Messiah and Lord but also describe him as the suffering Servant of Isaiah, as intimated above. The third Petrine sermon recorded in Acts was delivered in Solomon's Portico in the temple (3:11) after the healing of the lame man at the Beautiful Gate (3:1-10). This spontaneous address begins with a denial that Peter and John had performed the deed by their "own power or piety" (3:11-12), then quickly attributes the miracle to Jesus (3:16). Peter's address, however, starts with a litany of christological affirmations beginning in 3:13: "The God of Abraham, the God of Isaac, and the God of Jacob, the God of our ancestors has glorified his servant Jesus, whom you handed over and rejected in the presence of Pilate, though he had decided to release him." Jesus is the "Servant," the "Holy and Righteous One" (v. 14), "the Author of life" (v. 16), the "Prophet" (3:22-23), and it was through faith "in his name" that the lame man was healed (v. 16). These affirmations are set over against

---

91. As the LXX, the Hebrew יְהוָה (Yahweh) is translated κυρίου (Lord) in the Pentecost sermon.

92. Barrett, *The Acts of the Apostles*, 1:139; Bock, *Acts*, 118; Keener, *Acts*, 1:920-21.

93. Oscar Cullmann, *The Christology of the New Testament* (Philadelphia: Westminster, 1963), 195-237; Longenecker, *Christology of Early Jewish Christianity*, 120-47; I. Howard Marshall, *The Origins of New Testament Christology* (Leicester, UK: Apollos, 1990), 97-110; I. Howard Marshall, *Jesus the Saviour* (London: SPCK, 1990), 197-210; Fitzmyer, *The Acts of the Apostles*, 260-61; Larry Hurtado, *Lord Jesus Christ: Devotion to Jesus in Earliest Christianity* (Grand Rapids: Eerdmans, 2003), 179-84; I. Howard Marshall, *New Testament Theology: Many Witnesses, One Gospel* (Downers Grove, IL: InterVarsity, 2004), 175; Keener, *Acts*, 1:922-23, 963.

the injustice foisted upon Jesus and God's vindication of him. Those gathered in the temple "handed over and rejected Jesus" in the face of Pilate's decision to free him (v. 13), they repudiated Jesus and asked for a murder's freedom (v. 14), and they "killed the Author of life" (v. 15). But God reversed their judgment by raising him from the dead (v. 15) and glorifying him (v. 13). The apostle's sermon stands at the forefront of christological development in the early church. Peter was not only the community leader of the early church but its theological innovator.

Peter is the first in Acts to identify Jesus as the Suffering Servant of Isaiah. The servant Christology forms an inclusio around the whole Petrine sermon in Acts 3. At the beginning Peter declares that God "glorified his servant Jesus" (3:13) who had been rejected by the people, and at the end he states that "God raised up his servant" (3:26). Peter links the first declaration with the hearer's culpability ("Whom you handed over and rejected") and the second with God's promise ("He sent him first to you, to bless you by turning each of you from your wicked ways"). In v. 13 Peter draws from the Servant Song in Isaiah 52:13: "See, my servant shall understand, and he shall be exalted and glorified exceedingly." As the Servant, Jesus suffered and was subsequently glorified, as was foretold by the prophets (see 3:18, 21, 24–25; Isa 52:13–53:12: 1 Pet 1:11, 21). According to Moessner, Peter not only refers to Isaiah's Suffering Servant in 3:13 and 26 but echoes the Servant Songs throughout the address ("glorified" [3:13; Isa 49:3, 5; 52:13]; "handed over" [3:13; Isa 53:6, 12]; "Righteous One" [3:14; Isa 53:11]; apostles as "witnesses" [3:15; Isa 43:9–12]; "covenant" [3:25; Isa 42:6; 49:6, 8]; "make" a covenant [3:25; Isa 61:8]).[94] Over and again Peter's sermon echoes the Servant Songs, thus demonstrating he understands the whole as a prophetic witness to Jesus. Later in Acts the Ethiopian eunuch reads from Isaiah 53, and Philip explains the passage as a reference to Jesus' humiliation (Acts 8:26–35). But Peter stands as the first in Acts to make the identification of Jesus with the Servant who bore the sins of many (cf. the use of Isa 53 in 1 Pet 2:21–24; Mark 9:12; 10:45; 14:24, 61; 15:27). He knows that through God's Servant, Jesus, "their sins may be wiped out" (3:19; Isa 53:4–6, 10–12).

Cullmann comments: "We come straight to the heart of New Testament Christology with the title *ebed Yahweh*. . . . The 'Servant of God' is one of the oldest titles used by the first Christians to define their faith in the person and work of Christ."[95] In this title the early church understood the vicarious nature of Jesus' death. Cullmann takes a step further, stating that Peter was a "*theological* anchor" in his understanding of Christ's person and work:

> This was in the understanding he achieved that Christ's death was the atoning death. Perhaps he was the first one to grasp this after Jesus' resurrection. It

---

94. David P. Moessner, "The 'Script' of Scriptures in Acts," 228.

95. Cullmann, *The Christology of the New Testament*, 51. See Walther Zimmerli and Joachim Jeremias, *The Servant of God* (London: SCM, 1965); Marshall, *Jesus the Savior*, 121–23; George Eldon Ladd, *New Testament Theology* (Grand Rapids: Eerdmans, 1993), 330–31; Sigurd Grindheim, *Christology in the Synoptic Gospels: God or God's Servant* (London: T. & T. Clark, 2012), 27–29.

is true that it has become common custom to regard the apostle Paul as the creator of the theology of the cross.... But I do not believe that Paul was the first one to understand the death of Jesus as an atoning death for the forgiveness of sins. On the contrary, I am inclined to ascribe to Peter this particular and fundamental insight.[96]

Jesus the Servant had been "handed over and rejected" in an act of betrayal by his people (3:13), but the use of παρεδώκατε ("handed over") in the context of a sermon woven around the Servant Songs suggests that his death was vicarious for their sins ("And the Lord gave him over to our sins" [Isa 53:6]; "Because his soul was given over to death . . . and he bore the sins of many, and because of their sins he was given over," using παραδίδωμι three times [53:12]). Peter, therefore, calls his hearers to "turn to God so that your sins may be wiped out" (Acts 3:19). The apostle's proclamation of God's Servant Jesus brings us to the core of Peter's theology of the cross as an atonement for sin. His understanding of Isaiah 53 was rooted in the teaching of Jesus, who had said that the Son of Man came "to give his life a ransom for sin" (Mark 10:45, alluding to Isa 53:10–12). But Peter was the first apostle to testify to this teaching and then utilize it in his proclamation of Christ.[97]

God's Servant Jesus was not only delivered over in dishonor but was vindicated by God, who "glorified his servant Jesus" (3:13) and "raised up his servant" (3:26). The resurrection of Jesus was the beginning of Jesus' glorification. Not only the humiliation of the Servant but also his glorification were part of the fabric of the Isaianic hope: "See, my servant shall understand, and he shall be exalted and glorified exceedingly" (Isa 52:13). Peter's theology focuses upon the themes of rejection/dishonor at the hands of people and vindication/honor by God (3:13, 26). The dual themes of suffering and glory for the Messiah and his followers became a centerpiece in Peter's theology (cf. 1 Pet 1:7, 10–12, 21; 4:13, 16; 5:1, 10). As noted above, the revelation of God's glory is a piece of the Isaianic New Exodus theology that marks the Petrine speeches in Acts as well as the underlying Petrine theology in Mark: "Then the glory of the Lord shall appear, and all flesh shall see the salvation of God, because the Lord has spoken it" (Isa 40:5; 42:10, 12; 44:23; 49:3; 52:13). The glorification of God's Servant, Jesus, is central in this salvation, the New Exodus, and as such is the eschatological fulfillment of the prophetic hope. But it also anticipates the final era of glory when God sends

---

96. Cullmann, *Peter: Disciple-Apostle-Martyr*, 67; Ridderbos, *The Speeches of Peter*, 31; Hengel, *Saint Peter*, 86–89. Cullmann concludes his discussion of the *ebed Yahweh* in Acts saying, "We may conjecture, by way of summary, that the *ebed Yahweh* concept very probably dominated the Christology of the Apostle Peter—if we may really speak of a 'Christology' of Peter in spite of the small amount of direct information we possess about his thought. If this is the case, he, who had wanted to divert Jesus from the way of suffering, who had denied him at the decisive moment of the passion story, would be the first after Easter to grasp the necessity of this offence. He could not express this conviction better than with the designation *ebed Yahweh*, especially since he must have known what great importance3 Jesus himself had attributed to the ideas related to it" (Cullmann, *The Christology of the New Testament*, 75). Cullmann calls out the injustice of placing Peter "in the shadow of Paul."

97. See the discussion in chapter 4.

Jesus the Messiah in the time of restoration (Acts 3:20–21). That restoration is itself another part of the hope for the New Exodus, which God is now bringing to pass in Christ and which will be consummated upon his return.[98] The Servant has been and will be glorified according to Peter's understanding.

The coming of Isaiah's Suffering Servant is the fulfillment of the prophetic hope (3:18, 21, 24–25) but also the consummation of the covenantal promise to Abraham and his descendants. The one who glorified God's Servant Jesus is none other than "the God of Abraham, the God of Isaac, and the God of Jacob, the God of our ancestors" (3:13). The promise of his salvation is for God's people in accordance with his prophetic promise and covenant with Israel (3:25). God fulfills his covenant with Israel, but Peter is quick to point up that the covenant with Abraham included blessing beyond those who were descendants of the ancestors Abraham, Isaac, and Jacob. Peter cites the covenantal promise to Abraham in Genesis 22:18, which says, "And in your descendants all the families of the earth will be blessed" (Acts 3:25), and couples it with the saving activity of the Servant (3:26). Although Peter's focus is on his people, the sermon anticipates a wider ministry to the Gentiles, which Peter will lead (Acts 10). The New Exodus includes within it the covenantal promise that the Gentiles will also receive God's blessing (Isa 49:6, 8; 55:3–4). Peter will eventually understand and embrace the full import of this hope.[99]

The Holy and Righteous One, The Author of Life, The Prophet

As noted above, Peter binds together a Servant Christology with other functional titles for the Messiah. He is "the Holy and Righteous One," whom the people rejected when they asked that a murderer, a person neither holy nor righteous, be granted amnesty (Acts 3:14; cf. Mark 15:6–15). While Peter seeks to heighten their understanding of the depth of their culpability, he also evokes the Isaianic Servant Song. Isaiah 53:11 calls the Servant "the Righteous One who serves many well" (LXX δικαιῶσαι δίκαιον εὖ δουλεύοντα πολλοῖς), or "the Righteous One, my Servant" (צַדִּיק עַבְדִּי). In his first epistle, Peter likewise identifies Jesus as the Righteous One, whose death atones for the unrighteous many (1 Pet 3:18). The designation "Holy One" is not found within the Servant Songs, but, as Barrett says, "[It] is probably a term of Christian origin, resting upon the moral character of Jesus and the conviction that he was the one set apart by God to act as his Servant, to accomplish his will"[100] (cf. 4:27). Peter's Christology underscores the high moral character of Jesus and serves to offer an apologetic to his audience who only knew Jesus as one condemned as a criminal who suffered the

---

98. Pao, *Acts and the Isaianic New Exodus*, 46–54.

99. The Servant Christology also appears in the prayer of the Jerusalem church (Acts 4:27, 30), where Christ is called "your holy servant Jesus," who was opposed by the Gentiles and Israel but whom God had anointed. He is the one in whose name miracles occur. While the prayer is not attributed to Peter, it is likely that the invocation is influenced by Peter's Servant Christology.

100. Barrett, *The Acts of the Apostles*, 1:196.

ignominy of the cross. Those culpable were the ones who had rejected "the Holy and Righteous One," the very people who stood before him.

Peter uses the unique title, "Author of life" (τὸν ἀρχηγὸν τῆς ζωῆς), to describe the one whom they had not only rejected but killed ("you handed over and rejected," "you rejected," "you killed" [3:13–15]). Peter proclaims the painful irony of the cross—the life-giver has his life extinguished unjustly. In Acts only Peter calls Jesus the ὁ ἀρχηγός, (3:15; 5:31; cf. Heb 2:10; 12:2), a title that had a variety of uses in the ancient world. Most likely it designates Jesus as the leader or founder of life, eternal life, who himself had been raised from the dead (cf. 1 Cor 15:20).[101] Pervo remarks: "The meaning may be that Jesus is leader by virtue of his standing as the first to rise from the dead."[102] While correct, Peter's thought likely includes the notion that the crucified Jesus not only has life (Acts 3:28) but offers life as well (5:20; 11:18; cf. "the grace of life" [1 Pet 3:7]). In this sense, he is the Founder of life who opens the way of life for others.

According to Peter, Jesus is also the Prophet who fulfills the promise given to Moses in Deuteronomy 18:15, 18–19. Peter quotes the promise at some length saying, "The Lord your God will raise up for you from your own people a prophet like me. You must listen to whatever he tells you" (Acts 3:22–23). Peter charged his hearers with culpability but offered the promise of the forgiveness of sins (3:19), God's eschatological gift of refreshing and the Messiah (3:20), life (3:15), and blessing (3:25). Peter calls the people to "repent, therefore, and turn to God" (3:19, 26) and to "listen to whatever he (the Prophet) tells you" (3:22–23). The parallel between Jesus and Moses as the messengers of God rejected by the people later becomes a central tenet in Stephen's speech (7:35–44). While that particular nuance of the Moses typology may be latent in Peter's sermon, his principle point is that the one whom Moses spoke about has come and, therefore, the people must heed what he says. Now is the time when God fulfills the promise given to Moses and, indeed, to all the prophets (3:24; cf. 2:16). They all, from Moses onward, "predicted these days." Instead of rejecting Jesus, the Prophet, they must "listen" (3:22) or face the dire consequence: "Everyone who does not listen to that prophet will be utterly rooted out from the people" (3:23; cf. the Moses typology in the transfiguration account recorded in Mark 9:2–8). By referencing the prophecy given to Moses, Peter once again evokes the New Exodus, which has now begun with Jesus.[103] Peter joins together the Servant Christology with the Moses typology. Indeed, the Suffering Servant is a New Moses, or "Moses *revdivivus*." The unique blending of the Moses typology of the Prophet and the Servant Christology

---

101. Barrett, *The Acts of the Apostles*, 1:197–98; Keener, *Acts*, 2:1096–99; *TDNT*, 1:487–88.

102. Pervo, *Acts*, 105. He also states, "The word ἀρχηγός ('the one who opens the way to life') comes from the world of Hellenism, which had a great interest in founders, inventors, discoverers, and origins of all sorts."

103. See above and David Moessner, "Luke 9:1–50: Luke's Preview of the Journey of the Prophet Like Moses of Deuteronomy," *JBL* 102 (1983) 582; Zehnle, *Peter's Pentecost Discourse*, 78.

appears to be attributable to Peter.[104] The Moses typology may also appear in the Pentecost blessing of the Spirit and the promise of the New Covenant outlined in Acts 2:33.[105] Jesus has gone up and given the promised Holy Spirit as Moses had gone up has given the law (Exod 19:3).

The Rejected Stone

As in Mark, in his sermon Peter cites Psalm 118 as a reference to Jesus, the Rejected Stone.[106] Peter, as Jesus, was in the temple when he cited the Psalm, saying, "This Jesus is 'the stone that was rejected by you, the builders; it has become the cornerstone'" (Acts 4:11; cf. Acts 4:5–7; Ps 118:22; Mark 12:10–11). As in Mark, the citation of the Stone testimony from the psalm is set within a challenge to the temple and its authority. Peter stands before a gathering of "*their* rulers, elders, and scribes" along with priestly authorities. Luke describes the Sanhedrin, which met within the confines of the temples or near it (4:15).[107] Peter lays the culpability for Jesus' death at their feet ("whom you crucified" [v. 10]) but contrasts their verdict and execution with God's verdict ("whom God raised from the dead"). These authorities had heard how Jesus used the psalm against them (Mark 11:27ff) within the context of the parable of the Wicked Tenants (Mark 12:1–12). They now hear the parable's conclusion from Psalm 118:22, cited again in a second scathing accusation. The Sanhedrin's hostile reaction was predictable (Acts 4:13–22).

---

104. See Richard J. Dillon, "The Prophecy of Christ and His Witnesses According to the Discourses in Acts," *NTS* 32 (1986) 547–51, although Dillon points to Luke's hand rather than Peter.

105. Garrett, "Exodus from Bondage," 658; Hilgert, "Speeches in Acts," 97–98; Strauss, *Davidic Messiah in Luke-Acts*, 193; Jud Davis, "Acts 2 and the Old Testament: The Pentecost Event in Light of Sinai, Babel and the Table of Nations," *CTR* 7 (2009) 43–45; and the chapter on the Theology of Mark. Strauss rejects the idea that the promise of the Spirit in 2:33 is "meant to recall the giving of the Law at Sinai and hence to portray Jesus as a new Moses" since there are no contextual references to Moses or Sinai (*Davidic Messiah in Luke-Acts*, 145–47). But Turner notes that "Luke combines this Davidic Christology with a prophet-like-Moses motif, which alone explains the strong Moses/Sinai parallels in 2:1–13 and the remarkable statement in 2:33. Acts 2 thus not only present Jesus as attaining the exalted throne of David, but also as a greater Moses who ascends to God in order to grant a foundational gift to Israel. The gift of the Spirit would appear to be portrayed as the power of Israel's covenant renewal" (Turner, *Power from on High*, 267; Hilgert, "Speeches in Acts," 95). Turner's case appeals to the multiple parallels such as the fulfillment of the longing for the Spirit on all God's people in Numbers 11:29, the apocalyptic language of "signs and wonders," the evocation of Sinai in the fire, Peter's appeal to the audience to save themselves from this "crooked generation" (2:40), and the coming of the Spirit from the ascended Jesus in 2:33. According to Turner, this latter point echoes the Targum of Psalm 68:19, which says, "You have ascended to heaven, that is Moses the prophet. You have taken captivity captive, you have learned the words of the Torah, you have given them as gifts to men" (Turner, *Power from on High*, 285–89).

106. See "The Rejected Stone" in the chapter on the theology of Mark.

107. Schürer, *The History of the Jewish People in the Age of Jesus Christ (175 BC–AD 135)*, 2:212–14; Barrett, *The Acts of the Apostles*, 1:223–24; Steve Mason, "Chief Priests, Sadducees, Pharisees, and Sanhedrin in Acts," in *The Book of Acts in Its Palestinian Setting*, ed. Richard Bauckham (Grand Rapids: Eerdmans, 1995), 115–77; Fitzmyer, *The Acts of the Apostles*, 299; Keener, *Acts*, 2:1139.

In the setting of the temple and its authorities, the quotation of Psalm 118:22 anticipates a new temple whose foundation is Jesus.[108] Psalm 118 had become part of the Jewish tradition that anticipated the construction of a new temple (*T. Sol.* 22:6–23:4). Psalm 118:22 occupies a central place in Peter's Christology (1 Pet 2:4–7; cf. Acts Pet 24), and his use of it likely gave rise to Paul's citation (Rom 9:33). As in Mark, Peter frames his temple theology together with the anticipation of the coming of the Davidic king, "Jesus Christ of Nazareth" (Acts 4:10; cf. Mark 11:9–10). In the same way, the Targum of Psalm 118:22 gave the text a Davidic interpretation: "The architects forsook the youth among the sons of Jesse, but he was worthy to be appointed king and ruler" (and see *Tg. Psa.* 118:23–28). The Stone testimony stands at the beginning of the Messianic age and anticipates the building of God's new temple. It also frames the rejection of the cross and the resurrection of Jesus and anticipates the end of the current order administered by the "builders." A new age is dawning, and Peter proclaims that Jesus is its foundation.

The Leader and Savior

In 5:31 Peter proclaims that God has exalted the crucified Jesus "at his right hand as Leader and Savior." The declaration echoes Peter's previous citation of Psalm 110:1 in his Pentecost sermon (Acts 2:34–35). The apostle had also proclaimed that Jesus was the "Leader" or "Author of Life" (3:15). Here the term (ἀρχηγὸν) "stands . . . nearer to the simple meaning *leader* or *prince*; that is, it would not differ widely from κύριος [Lord] (cf. 2.36)."[109] Peter's proclamation here is therefore quite similar to his Pentecost declaration that "God has made him both Lord and Messiah, this Jesus whom you crucified" (Acts 2.36). Once again Peter challenges the authority of the Sanhedrin (5:21b, 27) by claiming Jesus' sovereignty. The apostle here adds that he is the Savior, a title that was commonly used of rulers with authority[110] who delivered their people and served as their benefactors.[111] The designation Savior comes close to the title "Founder of Life" (3:15) and points to his miraculous beneficence (10:38). He is, as Peter previously proclaimed, the only one who offers salvation (4:12), given that he is the crucified and risen one (5:31). As its "Leader and Savior," he therefore becomes

---

108. Nicholas Perrin suggests that Mark may even contemplate that Jesus will become the temple-builder (*Jesus the Temple* [Grand Rapids: Baker Academic, 2010], 104). For additional reflection on the temple in Mark's Gospel, see William R. Telford, *The Barren Temple and the Withered Tree: A Redaction-Critical Analysis of the Cursing of the Fig-Tree Pericope in Mark's Gospel and Its Relation to the Cleansing of the Temple Tradition* (Sheffield: JSOT, 1980); Timothy C. Gray, *The Temple in the Gospel of Mark: A Study in Its Narrative Role* (Tübingen: Mohr Siebeck, 2008).

109. Barrett, *The Acts of the Apostles*, 1:290; Bruce, *Book of the Acts*, 113.

110. Pervo, *Acts*, 145; Keener, *Acts*, 2:1219.

111. Keener, *Acts*, 2:1219.

God's agent to "give repentance to Israel and forgiveness of sins" (5:32; cf. 11:18) instead of vengeance.[112]

The Name

The "name" of Jesus holds great significance in Peter's Christology in a way not unlike Mark (9:37-41, 13:6, 13). In the Pentecost sermon, Peter picks up Joel 2 and concludes the citation with the declaration that "everyone who call on the name of the Lord shall be saved" (2:21). In this context the "Lord" is Jesus (cf. 2:36, 38).[113] Over and again the apostle evokes the "name." He calls on his hearers to "Repent, and be baptized every one of you in the name of Jesus Christ so that your sins may be forgiven" (2:38). Through the name of "Jesus Christ of Nazareth" Peter bids the lame man to rise and walk (3:6) and then proclaims that "by faith in his name" the man was restored (3:16). Salvation comes uniquely through Jesus' name; no other name under heaven has saving efficacy (4:12). The apostles' preaching and teaching were all in the name, and the authorities deemed their activity a threat (4:18). Peter boldly declares that everyone who believes, whether Jew or Gentile, may receive forgiveness through faith in his name (10:43). Peter's evocation of the name was so prominent that James echoes it in his address to the council at Jerusalem: "Simeon has related how God first looked favorably on the Gentiles, to take from among them a people for his name" (15:14). The salvific activity of God comes to people through the "name" of Jesus and includes forgiveness of sins and healing. His name is the only one with power to save both Jew and Gentile. Peter's ministry of preaching and healing was carried out in the "name" and was calculated to evoke repentance and faith, both evidenced in obedience and baptism.

Barrett cautions that we should not interpret Peter's use of the name within the frame of ancient magic. In magic "the name itself is an active power which can be employed by those who know how to use it."[114] Magical formulas that invoked powerful names were common enough during the era.[115] But Peter does not speak out the name as a kind of talisman. Rather, the "name" stands for the person. On the one hand, Peter takes the role of a divinely commissioned prophet who speaks "in the name of the Lord" (cf. Exod 3:13-15).[116] But more than this is in play. Keener recalls:

---

112. Barrett, *The Acts of the Apostles*, 1:290.

113. See above on the title "Lord."

114. Barrett, *The Acts of the Apostles*, 1:139, 182.

115. John G. Gager, *Curse Tablets and Binding Spells from the Ancient World* (Oxford: Oxford University Press, 1992); Fritz Graf, *Magic in the Ancient World* (Cambridge, MA: Harvard University Press, 1997); Everett Ferguson, *Backgrounds of Early Christianity* (Grand Rapids: Eerdmans, 2003), 227-35; Hans-Josef Klauck, *The Religious Context of Early Christianity: A Guide to Graeco-Roman Religions* (Minneapolis: Fortress, 2003), 209-31; Stephen Llewelyn, *New Documents Illustrating Early Christianity* (Grand Rapids: Eerdmans, 1997-98), 1:33-36; 2:45-46.

116. Hilgert, "Speeches in Acts," 97-98.

"The divine name was powerful, and strictly pious hearers might rend their garments when hearing it blasphemed."[117] The name stood for God's presence and power, which suggests that speaking in "the name of Jesus" was to invoke the powerful presence of Jesus himself.[118] Peter's use of Jesus' name in the context of the layers of salvation parallels Jewish use of the divine name, thus underscoring the exalted nature of Peter's Christology. Jesus is indeed the man from Nazareth, but he is also the divine Lord who is the only way of salvation for both Jew and Gentile. In his name people receive forgiveness and healing. Calling upon his name they find the divine resources that meet human need.

PROCLAMATION AND RESPONSE

The public proclamation of Jesus Christ's person and work "begins only after the Spirit has come," notes Jennings, "It is a second word after the words of praise have been given by God. Before the Spirit came, Peter had little to say. His words will now and forever be ony commentary on what the Spirit is doing, and what God has done for us in Jesus."[119] Peter's preaching elicits a response from those who have heard. Peter had no interest in conducting an information session about Jesus, the Christ. The indicative of his sovereignty bears within it the imperative to acknowledge him as such. Jesus, as the promised Messiah who was crucified, buried, resurrected, and is now the glorified Lord becomes the one in whom the hearers of this message must put their trust. When Peter told the story of the outpouring of the Spirit on the Gentiles to the Jerusalem church, he recalled their own moment of faith: "God gave them the same gift that he gave us when we believed in the Lord Jesus Christ" (11:17). Later at the Jerusalem Council, Peter recalled how God chose him as the one through whom "the Gentiles would hear the message of the good news and become believers" (15:7). God gave them the Holy Spirit and cleansed "their hearts by faith" (15:9). Faith is the response (15:7) that issues in salvation by God's grace ("We believe that we will be saved through the grace of the Lord Jesus, just as they will" [15:11]).

Although Peter uses the name "believers" to describe fellow disciples of Christ (12:17), his summons embraces the whole complex of conversion and initiation. When asked by those who heard his Pentecost proclamation what they should do, his response was, "Repent and be baptized every one of you in the name of Jesus Christ so that your sins will be forgiven; and you will receive the gift of the Holy Spirit" (2:38, 41; 10:43–48). The Petrine kerygma calls for a response, described as belief and manifested in repentance and baptism. This requirement held for the Jews in Jerusalem and the Gentiles in Caesarea. Peter asked, "Can anyone withhold the water for baptizing these who have received the Holy Spirit just as we have?" (10:47). They were

---

117. Keener, *Acts*, 1:921, 982–83.
118. *TDNT*, 5:242–81.
119. Willie James Jennings, *Acts* (Louisville: Westminster John Knox, 2017), 34.

then "baptized in the name of Jesus Christ" (10:48).[120] The common act of faith and baptism for both Jews and Gentiles points to Peter's understanding of the formation of a new community or people that includes all ethnicities. Community formation into the people of God (λαός) becomes a part of the process of conversion.[121] The other movement in this complex response to the proclamation about Jesus Christ was repentance, the turn to God that finds visible expression in the act of baptism (3:19; 2:38). True repentance includes turning from "wicked ways" (3:26). Peter exhorted Simon to "repent therefore of this wickedness of yours" (8:22). Peter's theology of conversion finds its roots within the Christ event, which carries within it the call to turn, believe, and be baptized.

Although Peter calls for a response of faith, repentance, and baptism, he recognizes that repentance is a gift of God for both Jews and Gentiles. Human response is placed alongside divine agency. God gives "repentance to Israel" (5:31). Similarly, the Jerusalem church concluded with Peter that "God has given even to the Gentiles the repentance that leads to life" (11:18). God is actively involved in the hearers of the gospel "by turning each of you from your wicked ways" (3:26). Peter comfortably juxtaposes human response with divine initiative. God is the one who calls people to himself (2:39), and he chooses those whom he wants as his people, including Gentiles (15:14, echoing Peter's preaching). God also chooses his messengers (15:7), including Jesus (10:36), and directs his messengers by the Holy Spirit (11:12), although Peter could talk about his own agency (10:23, 29). Divinely ordained mission is a thread in the fabric of Peter's theology. Surprisingly, the dominant call of discipleship in Mark—"follow me"—does not appear in Acts. In the post-resurrection era, the commitment to Jesus Christ finds expression in the language of repentance, faith, and baptism. Both calls, however, demonstrate the fundamental commitment to the person of Jesus, the Christ.

Salvation and Inclusion

The result of repentance, faith, and baptism is the promise of forgiveness of sins (2:38; 5:31; 8:22) and "cleansing their hearts by faith" (15:9; cf. 1 Pet 1:22), whether the person is Jewish, Samaritan, or Gentile. All hear the message of Jesus the Christ, everyone must turn in faith to God and be baptized, and each receives the promise of forgiveness, renewal through the Holy Spirit (2:38), and life (11:18). Throughout the discourse Peter proclaims God's inclusion of those who were not Jewish without insisting they submit to the outward Jewish identity markers of dietary laws or circumcision

---

120. G. R. Beasley-Murray, *Baptism in the New Testament* (Grand Rapids: Eerdmans, 1973), 93–122; Everett Ferguson, *Baptism in the Early Church: History, Theology, and Liturgy in the First Five Centuries* (Grand Rapids: Eerdmans, 2009), 166–85.

121. As Zhelne says, "Thus a community of believers in Acts is the new people of God to whom salvation has been given. Whoever wishes to be saved must join himself to this community by a profession of faith in Jesus Christ, signified by baptism in his name" (*Peter's Pentecost Discourse*, 66).

(15:1, 6–11).[122] God's blessings through Jesus, the Christ, are open to all without proselyte conversion. Commenting on Peter's contribution to the Jerusalem Council in Acts 15:6–11, Kilgallen says, "The key to interpreting Peter's speech is to see in its logic that faith in Jesus achieves all that one could hope for by circumcision and obedience to the Mosaic Law."[123] Peter stands for Gentile inclusion in the community of faith via baptism without imposing upon them the cultural signs of Jewish identity.

Peter understands that Jesus' messianic lordship is not limited to the "house of Israel." Although he does not reflect on the experience in his Acts speeches, Peter acknowledged the work of God among the Samaritans to whom Philip had proclaimed Jesus as the Messiah (8:25; Acts 1:8[124]). Although Peter did not open the mission to the Samaritans, he, along with John, acknowledged God's work among them and prayed that they, too, might receive the Holy Spirit (8:14–17).[125] The question of the Samaritans' ethnicity was a subject of debate during the era.[126] On the one hand Josephus calls them "apostates of the Jewish nation" (*Ant.* 11.340) but then remarks that they self-identified as both Jews and Gentiles depending on the prevailing winds (*Ant.* 11.341; 9.291). Their ethnicity was ambiguous and the subject of considerable rabbinic debate. We can say of surety with John that, as a rule, "Jews do not associate with Samaritans" (John 4:9, NIV). In sanctioning the mission to the Samaritans under Philip, Peter recognizes that the gospel is open to those who are on the margins of Judaism and who were considered "other."

---

122. Udo Schnelle (*Theology of the New Testament* [Grand Rapids: Baker Academic, 2009], 200) lays out the Council's questions: "What criteria must those fulfill who would belong to the elect people of God in continuity with the first covenant? Should circumcision as the sign of God's covenant (cf. Gen 17:11), and thus of membership in the elect people of God, also be a general requirement for Christians in the Greco-Roman tradition? Must a Gentile who wants to become a Christian first become a Jew?"

123. John J. Kilgallen, "Peter's Argument in Acts 15," in *"Il Verbo di Dio è vivo": Studi sul Nuovo Testamento in onore del Cardinale Albert Vanhoye, SI*, ed. José Enrique Aguilar Chiu, et al. (Rome: Pontifical Biblical Institute, 2007), 246.

124. While not outlining the book of Acts, 1:8 underscores Jesus' concern for both the geographic and ethnic expansion of the gospel (Acts 8:9, 25; 13:47; Isa 49:6; Keener, *Acts*, 1:702–11;).

125. Marshall (*The Acts of the Apostles*, 157) notes that Luke's parenthetical statement in 8:16 ("for as yet the Spirit had not come upon any of them; they had only been baptized in the name of the Lord Jesus") "is perhaps the most extraordinary statement in Acts. Elsewhere it is made clear that baptism in the name of Jesus leads to the reception of the Spirit (2:38)." While puzzling over the reason for the delay, Pervo (*Acts*, 213) rightly observes that "the (remedial?) action includes prayer and the imposition of hands. All was then well. Samaria had a 'Pentecost' of its own, and the unity of the community with that in Jerusalem, as well as the authenticity of the conversions, is established beyond doubt." For a full discussion of the conundrum, see Turner, *Power from on High*, 360–75.

126. See 2 Kgs 17; Talbert, *Reading Acts*, 83; Keener, *Acts*, 2:1490. On Samaritan history, identity, and theology, see Robert T. Anderson and Terry Giles, *The Keepers: An Introduction to the History and Culture of the Samaritans* (Grand Rapids: Baker Academic, 2001); V. J. Samkutty, *The Samaritan Mission in Acts* (London: T. & T. Clark, 2006); Gary N. Knoppers, *Jews and Samaritans: The Origins and History of Their Early Relations* (Oxford: Oxford University Press, 2013).

Peter steps further by acknowledging that God's salvation and Christ's sovereignty extends beyond to all the Gentiles. Speaking to the household of Cornelius, the Roman centurion, he announces that Jesus Christ "is Lord of all" (Acts 10:36). This proclamation fully opens the gospel to the Gentiles. The resurrected Messiah is not only the king and sovereign of Israel but of all peoples. Peter, once again, is the theological innovator who begins to grasp the full implications of Jesus' messiahship. No ethnic boundaries delimit the proclamation of the gospel of peace since Jesus Christ's sovereignty is universal, extending to every ethnicity. God had opened the way for Peter to eat with Gentiles by telling him that he had cleansed all food (10:14–15). Jewish dietary laws prohibited Peter from eating with Gentiles, as the apostles and others in Jerusalem recognized after Peter went into Cornelius's house (11:1). Jennings comments, "The disciples who came with Peter should not be in the same room with Cornelius's family and close friends, his household, but there they are together. The cultural codes and social rules and theology that normally apply are being suspended in this encounter, and no one knows what will happen next."[127] The common theology of separation meets the gospel challenge. Yet Peter did not arrive at a new theology of inclusion easily. González notes, "Peter enters the house and does not show great tact. His interest is not in winning the good will of those who are present. On the contrary, his first statement is that from his own religious perspective it is 'unlawful' for him to visit Cornelius, and that he acceded to this only because he has had a vision in which God has told him 'that I should not call anyone profane or unclearn'—in other words, that if it were up to me that is precisely what I would call you!"[128] Peter innovates theologically, but not easily. His new understanding comes in fits and starts under the divine initiative.

Peter embraced inclusion and defended his move by recounting the heavenly vision (11:8–9). Peter then took another step by recognizing that not only had God declared all food clean but that no person should be regarded as common or unclean (10:28). We see the walls begin to come down when Peter offered Cornelius's messengers hospitality (10:23)—he was on the verge of understanding that God welcomes all without partiality (10:34; cf. Rom 15:7). Peter's vision and open proclamation were then confirmed by God, who gave the Gentiles the Spirit as he had the disciples of the Jewish community (10:44; 11:12, 15–18). Peter reaffirms God's inclusion of the Gentiles when he stood before the council at Jerusalem. He reminded those gathered that God gave the Gentiles the Spirit and made no distinction between them and the Jewish believers (15:8–9).

---

127. Jennings, *Acts*, 109. He continues, "This moment schools us in divine transgression. God brings Peter to one outside of the covenant, transgressing God's own established boundary and border. We must not weaken the radical implications of this epic meeting" (110).

128. Justo L. González, *Acts: The Gospel of the Spirit* (Maryknoll, NY: Orbis, 2001), 132–33; González, *Hechos* (Miami: Caribe, 1992), 174.

Peter's proclamation stands in stark contrast to the expectation that the coming Messiah would only bring judgment to Gentile nations. God's Anointed was expected to assail those powers hostile to Israel (Ps 110:1–2; 2:1–11; 4 Ezra 12:31–33; 13:32–38; 1 En. 46:4–6; 52:4–9).[129] For Peter, the Messiah himself suffers instead of making the enemies of God's people suffer. God had indeed sent his message "to the people of Israel, preaching peace by Jesus Christ," a foundational promise within the New Exodus (Isa 52:7). But as soon as Peter announces the promise of peace for Israel, he proclaims that Christ "is Lord of all" (Acts 10:36), thus bringing the gathered Gentiles and those beyond into the sphere of God's promise through the Suffering Servant of Isaiah 52:13–53:12. They, too, are recipients of the promise of God's peace (see Isa 57:19; Acts 2:39[130]). God had demonstrated to Peter via the rooftop vision (10:9–16) that "God shows no partiality, but in every nation anyone who fears him and does what is right is acceptable to him" (10:35). Salvation for both Jew and Gentile is "through the grace of the Lord Jesus" (15:11), an affirmation anticipated in Peter's Pentecost citation of Joel 2 ("Everyone who calls on the name of the Lord shall be saved" [Acts 2:21]). Peter understands God's message of inclusion and again takes a bold theological step in both word and deed as he preaches Jesus Christ the Lord to the Gentiles. He even does this in front of the centurion Cornelius, a representative of the occupying Roman power, which was the recognized enemy of Israel. No less than James acknowledged Simeon Peter's leadership in showing the church "how God first looked favorably on the Gentiles, to take from among them a people for his name" (15:14).

While we commonly think of Paul's fisticuffs with the Judaizers in Galatia and at the Jerusalem Council as the beginning of the heated discussion regarding circumcision, Peter is the one who initially laid out the terms of Gentile inclusion without the "works of the law" (Gal 2:16; 3:2, 5).[131] Peter could eat with Gentiles and made no distinction between them and his fellow Jews. Upon witnessing the way God gave the Holy Spirit to the Gentiles he then only commanded baptism as a rite of conversion initiation as he had learned from Jesus (Acts 10:44–48). Peter, not Paul, is the one who first stood for unencumbered Gentile acceptance. This was a moment of the apostle's theological innovation stands second only to his confession that Jesus was the Christ. Peter was the theological innovator both in bringing the gospel to the Gentiles (15:7)[132] and in affirming their inclusion in the people of God without the works of

---

129. Schürer, *The History of the Jewish People in the Age of Jesus Christ (175 BC–AD 135)*, 2:526–29.

130. While Acts 2:39 appears to echo Isa 57:19, it appears that Peter did not fully grasp the implications of the allusion at Pentecost. Luke, however, would have. See Keener's discussion of Acts 2:39 (*Acts*, 1:987).

131. Marshall, *New Testament Theology*, 210–13; N. T. Wright, *Paul and the Faithfulness of God* (Minneapolis: Fortress, 2013), 1:852–60. The conflict between Paul and Peter in Antioch was not a matter of Peter's understanding of the gospel but rather a question of living in conformity with what he himself believed (Gal 2:1–2, 7–9, 11–14).

132. "By reference to 'my mouth' Peter at once establishes his preeminence in this matter: he was the means (and eye-witness), not the others, whom God used for what God wanted" (Kilgallen,

the law. Peter's withdrawal from table fellowship with the Gentiles in Antioch was a scandal precisely because his behavior did not conform to the gospel that he himself had preached (Gal 2:1–14). According to Paul, Peter habitually ate with the Gentiles (Gal 2:12), as was the case in Acts 10 (see also Acts 11:1). By withdrawing from breaking bread with the Gentiles he stood, as Paul said, "self-condemned" because he did not act in accordance with "the truth of the gospel" they had all agreed upon (Gal 2:7, 11–14). Peter's failing at Antioch should not detract from his theological innovation. Peter was known for theological leadership, but also failure and restoration.

Peter's vision of inclusion extends beyond the Jew/Gentile divide. Starting with his quotation of Joel 2 in the Pentecost sermon, Peter stands for salvation that extends to all people regardless of their gender, age, or social class. Sons and daughters, old and young men, male and female slaves are all embraced by the gospel (2:17–18). Indeed, the extent of God's blessing is not limited by time since the promise is "for you, for your children" (2:39).[133] While the principle focus Peter's theology of inclusion is the way God reaches out to those who are not Jewish, Acts retains repeated traces of the apostles' wide understanding of the gospel's embrace of people of all genders, ages, and social classes. Peter was with the women in his ministry (1:14) and saw that the door of the gospel was open to them. He appears at the side of the deceased Tabitha, who is also called Dorcas in Greek, and raises this beloved disciple from the dead by saying to her, "Tabitha, get up" (9:40; cf. Luke 8:40–42, 49–56; Mark 5:21–24, 35–43). He then "called the saints and widows" and "showed her to be alive" (9:42). On the other hand, he made no distinction between Ananias and his wife Sapphira, who colluded in their embezzlement of funds from the sale of land that had been dedicated to God. He asked Sapphira, "Tell me whether you and your husband sold the land for such and such a price?" (5:7) and, upon discovering her duplicity, pronounced judgment upon her, saying, "Look, the feet of those who have buried your husband are at the door, and they will carry you out" (5:9). Peter regarded women as equally responsible as men in their obligations before God. On a more positive note, he proclaims salvation at the house Cornelius for all those who believe and then orders baptism for everyone who had received the Holy Spirit (10:43, 47). Those gathered were Cornelius's "relatives and close friends" (10:24), a group that would have included women as well as children.[134] While children do not figure prominently into the Petrine story and speeches in Acts, Peter clearly affirms that the young have a part in this gospel and may receive the blessing of forgiveness and the Holy Spirit (2:17, 38–39). Peter also crossed the boundary of social class by going to the house of Simon, a person who engaged in the profane trade of tanning (9:43), so considered by Jews and hardly respected by Gentiles. Keener comments: "Polite Roman society looked down on

---

"Peter's Argument in Acts 15," 7).

133. Barrett states that those "far away" are distant in time (*The Acts of the Apostles*, 1:155), but it is more likely a reference to the Gentiles (Isa 57:19).

134. Barrett, *The Acts of the Apostles*, 1:513.

tanners as well as smiths and butchers."[135] Cornelius brought together his "friends," a term that could embrace those who were clients of Cornelius, the patron hosting this gathering (10:24).[136] Male and female slaves were likewise worthy candidates to receive God's salvation and Spirit (2:18, 21). Regardless of gender, age, or social class, Peter demonstrates through his preaching and *praxis* that the gospel is open to all who call upon the name of the Lord.

The Human Condition

In the Petrine speeches in Acts, the apostle uses the language of covenant, forgiveness, and salvation to speak about God's work for humanity through Christ. Peter understood that sin was at the heart of the human condition and problem. Peter describes two of the most sinful characters in Acts, Judas and Simon, as people bound by wickedness. Judas's betrayal was an act of wickedness that gained him a monetary reward (ἐκ μισθοῦ τῆς ἀδικίας [1:18]; cf. ἐκ μισθοῦ τῆς ἀδικίας [2 Pet 2:13, 15]; a Semitic expression—2 Macc 8:33; Wis 2:22). Peter describes Simon, one who attempted to buy the ability to confer divine blessing, as a person who was bound by "chains of wickedness" (σύνδεσμον ἀδικίας [8:23]), an expression that parallels Peter's charge in 8:22 that Simon needed to repent "of this wickedness" (ἀπὸ τῆς κακίας; cf. 1 Pet 2:1, 16). His heart was "not right before God" (8:21; cf. Ps 78:37; Isa 40:3), that is, he was not "*straightforward, frank, honest.* Simon is attempting to cheat God, to infringe the divine prerogative of bestowing the Spirit in accordance with his own will."[137] Avarice motivated both Judas and Simon and was, by some tellings, the source of Balaam's sin as well (2 Pet. 2:15; Jude 11). Peter regards their sin as an injustice that, in the case of Judas, rose to the level of a criminal act.[138] Sin, in Peter's eyes, is a vice, the opposite of virtue (ἀρετή) and, as Selwyn notes, embraces "the whole wickedness of the pagan world."[139]

Peter also confronts the populace about their sin in his appeal, "Save yourselves from this corrupt generation" (2:40, σώθητε ἀπὸ τῆς γενεᾶς τῆς σκολιᾶς ταύτης; cf. 2:21; Deut 32:5; 1 Pet 2:18). Peter regarded those of his day (the reference is temporal not ethnic) as "twisted" or "crooked," as also the Exodus generation (Deut 32:5; Ps 78:8). Only through repentance and baptism in the name of Jesus Christ could they become straight (Acts 2:38). Soon Peter would turn to again denounce their sin while recognizing that God sent his Servant Jesus "to bless you by turning each of you from your wicked ways" (3:26). Peter calls people to repent "so that your sins may be wiped

---

135. Keener, *Acts*, 1:1725. See Joachim Jeremias, *Jerusalem in the Time of Jesus* (Minneapolis: Fortress, 1969), 310; Talbert, *Reading Acts*, 104; Lev 11:39–40; *m. Ketubim* 7:10; *m. Megillah* 3:2.

136. Barrett, *The Acts of the Apostles*, 1:513; Keener, *Acts*, 2:1780.

137. Barrett, *The Acts of the Apostles*, 1:415.

138. *BDAG*, 20.

139. *BDAG*, 500; Selwyn, *The First Epistle of Peter*, 152.

out" (3:19) but recognizes at the same time that Christ turns people from evil, here described as "wicked ways" (ἀπὸ τῶν πονηριῶν ὑμῶν) or "evil."[140] Peter says that God sent Jesus "first to you" to turn his people from evil, language that suggests that others—the Gentiles—would be similarly blessed.

The apostle stood against the lies of Ananias and Sapphira, who skimmed funds from the sale of their land that had been dedicated to God. In this act they not only attempted to deceive the community but had also lied to the Holy Spirit (5:3), which meant lying to God (5:4). As with Achan and his family in Joshua, the judgment upon them was swift and terrible although not carried out by the community itself as in the case of Achan (Acts 5:1–11; Josh 7:1–26).[141] According to Peter, Ananias and Sapphira had "put the Spirit of the Lord to the test" (5:9), language that echoes Exodus 17:2 and 7 where Israel put God to the test in the wilderness (see the memory of the event in Deut 6:16; Ps 78:18; 95:9). Peter's charge against the couple underscores the seriousness of his concern at the Jerusalem Council where he viewed the Judaizers' attempt to insist on circumcision for the Gentile converts (Acts 15:1) as "putting God to the test" (15:10). Peter stood against sin and was willing to denounce its many forms, both individually and corporately. At the same time, he understood the depth of God's forgiveness and salvation through Christ Jesus. As a faithful Jew, Peter was concerned about ritual purity (10:14, 28; 11:8; cf. Lev 11:1–47; 1 Macc 1:47, 62–63), but his reaction towards sins against God's work in Christ was profoundly deeper.

God's Salvation

Peter's speeches betray a robust understanding of the nature of God's salvation. The theme of salvation is woven throughout the fabric of Luke's narrative (Luke 1:69, 71; 2:11; 19:10; Acts 2:47; 16:30–31). As Bonz suggests, the theme of salvation in Luke/Acts may be regarded as "a powerful and appealing rival to the ubiquitous and potentially seductive salvation claims of imperial Rome."[142] It is also a dimension of the New Exodus theology that permeates Luke's second volume.[143] But "salvation" is, at the same time, a strong thread in Petrine theology (2:21, 40; 4:12; 5:31; 11:14; 15:11; Mark 8:35; 13:13; 1 Pet 1:5, 9–10; 2:2; 3:21; 4:18; and also see 2 Pet 2:1, 20; 3:2, 15, 18). Starting with his citation of Joel 2, Peter proclaims that "everyone who calls upon the name of the Lord shall be saved" (2:21). Peter's *pesher* interpretation of the prophecy spells out clearly that the last days have already arrived, as evidenced by the outpouring of the Spirit, which all gathered saw and heard (2:17, 1–4). The dawning of a new era has begun and, with that, "God's final act of salvation has begun to take place."[144]

140. *BDAG*, 851, equivalent of "sins" in 3:19.

141. The verb νοσφίζω (*BDAG*, 679) describes the sin in both narratives as a "skimming operation" (Acts 5:2, 3; Josh 7:1).

142. Bonz, *The Past as Legacy*, 86, and see above.

143. Pao, *Acts and the Isaianic New Exodus*, 47, and see above.

144. Marshall, *The Acts of the Apostles*, 73. The LXX text of Joel 3:1 (2:28 in the Hebrew) says

The offer of salvation to all who call on the name of the Lord (understood by Peter as Jesus) in v. 21 is set over against the prophecy's proclamation of the signs that will herald "the coming of the Lord's great and glorious day" (2:20). "*The great day* of the Lord," Barrett reminds us, "is the last day, of salvation for his people and destruction for his enemies; the day of judgment therefore"[145] (cf. 2 Pet 2:9; 3:7, 10, 12; 1 Thess. 5:2; 2 Thess 2:2). In this context, the promise of salvation offered in v. 21 would signify deliverance from final judgment. As noted above, this salvation is held out for "everyone" who calls upon the name of the Lord, regardless of gender, age, social class, or ethnicity.

After the Pentecost proclamation of Christ, Peter exhorts his people, saying, "Save yourselves from this corrupt generation" (2:40). Peter hardly means that his hearers could effect their own salvation but rather that they should respond to the offer of salvation outlined in his sermon and "call upon the name of the Lord" (2:21, 38). Barrett cites a similar plea in Plato, where Crito exhorts Socrates, saying, "Take my advice and make your escape" (*Crito* 44b, using the verb in the passive as does Peter: σώθητι).[146] Peter believes his hearers are embedded in "this corrupt generation" (τῆς γενεᾶς τῆς σκολιᾶς ταύτης), not a reference to their ethnicity but rather their social era, which was morally twisted or bent (cf. Deut 32:5; 1 Pet 2:18).[147] Peter's call is part of the New Exodus theology that recalls the corrupt wilderness generation (Ps. 78:8).[148] Those of his day had fallen into the same pattern of unfaithfulness to God. The apostle presents the gospel of Christ as an alternative to the moral failure of his times.

In 4:12 Peter makes the surprising claim that "there is salvation in no one else, for there is no other name under heaven given among mortals by which we must be saved." In the context of the Greco-Roman world, where the title "savior" was ascribed to multiple deities and even the emperor as part of the imperial cult, we understand the relevance of this claim.[149] To be sure, Luke had an eye on his Gentile audience when choosing to include Peter's words at this point. At this stage in the narrative, however, the exclusive claim that salvation is only found in the name of Jesus is juxtaposed with the healing of the lame man (3:1–10), about which the leaders of the nation question Peter, "By what power or by what name did you do this?" (4:5–7). Peter's response first focuses on the healing, which is part of the fabric of salvation (4:8–10a; cf. 1 Pet 2:24), but then moves on to speak of all the salvific benefits of Christ's death and resurrection (4:10b–11). Healing is particularly prominent in Peter's ministry and teaching. The lame man was healed (3:1–6), and Peter comments that it was through

---

simply "after these things" (μετὰ ταῦτα), but Peter's citation substitutes the words "in the last days" to clarify that the time of fulfillment has arrived and that the new era, "the last days," has arrived.

145. Barrett, *The Acts of the Apostles*, 1:138.
146. Barrett, *The Acts of the Apostles*, 1:156. Barrett renders Peter's call: "*Accept your salvation.*"
147. BDAG, 930.
148. Keener, *Acts*, 1:990.
149. See, for example, the range of uses of "save," "salvation," and "savior" in *TLNT*, 3:344–57.

Jesus that he was made strong and enabled to walk (3:13, 16). He regards healing as divine benefaction given through Jesus Christ (4:9–10, εὐεργεσίᾳ denoting benefits that may come through divine agency[150]). While Peter's shadow somehow brings healing (5:15) and through his words even the dead are raised (9:40), he consistently attributes healing to Jesus (9:34), whose ministry of benefaction consisted of "doing good (εὐεργετῶν) and healing all who were oppressed by the devil, for God was with him" (10:38). According to Peter, Jesus not only brings physical health but liberation from the Satanic oppression. He understands Satanic agency both in bringing physical adversity and moral impurity (5:3, 9). But he also recognizes benevolent supernatural agents (12:11).

Jesus is God's exclusive agent of salvation (4:12), and Peter describes him in a way similar to Isaiah's claims about Yahweh (43:11; 45:20–21). This, then, is the surprise: Jesus occupies a place exclusive to Yahweh. Although the title was ascribed to various deities and emperors (see above), Peter's understanding in this Jewish context is most likely informed by the way the Old Testament describes Yahweh as Savior (Ps 24:5; 25:5; Isa 12:2; 17:10; 45:15, 21; 62:11; cf. Luke 1:47). This is the first time in Acts where Jesus is designated as Savior, later followed by Paul (13:23). Peter underscores that God's exaltation of Jesus to his right hand (cf. Acts 2:34–35; Ps 110:1) qualifies him as Savior: "God exalted him at his right hand as Leader and Saviour, so that he might give repentance to Israel and forgiveness of sins" (5:31).[151] Only one so exalted can save from sin. As his people's Savior, he offers repentance and forgiveness of sins (2:38; 10:43; cf. Mark 2:7, 10; Ps 79:9).

The language of salvation is woven into the narrative about the way the gospel came to Cornelius and those Gentiles gathered with him in Caesarea. Peter recounts the angel's words to Cornelius about the need to send for Peter: "Send to Joppa and bring Simon, who is called Peter; he will give you a message by which you and your entire household will be saved" (11:13–14). In recounting the story of bringing the gospel to those Gentiles, Peter tells the Jerusalem Council that "we believe that we will be saved through the grace of the Lord Jesus, just as they will" (15:11). According to Peter, God's salvation is open to both Jew and Gentile alike without distinction, as already seen. He also understands that the proclamation of Christ is an essential component in bringing salvation to people. Moreover, Peter regards salvation as a gift of grace given by the Lord Jesus. Grace is not only a Pauline concept but also is part of Peter's understanding of the gospel, even becoming a dominant theme in 1 Peter (1:2, 10, 13; 3:7; 4:10; 5:5, 10, 12; cf. 2 Pet 1:2; 3:18). Grace (χάρις) emerges from the context of benefaction where benefactors, whether human or divine, bestow their favor

---

150. *TLNT*, 1:107–113.

151. Cullmann, *The Christology of the New Testament*, 238–45; Longenecker, *Christology of Early Jewish Christianity*, 141–44. Conzelmann's contention that the title "Savior" "only belongs to the Hellenistic stratum of christology" is ill-founded (*An Outline of the Theology of the New Testament* [London: SCM, 1969], 86). Peter utilizes an OT title for God to describe Christ.

and benefits. As Spicq notes, "Any gift, present, pardon, or concession that is granted freely, out of one's goodness, is called a *charis*," with the deity being the greatest of all benefactors.[152] At Cornelius's house, Peter proclaimed Christ as the benefactor (10:38), and before the council he affirms that the boon Christ confers is nothing less than salvation. The benefits he confers are multiplex, including healing and liberation from evil powers as part of the gift of salvation.

A central component of God's salvation in Peter's preaching is the forgiveness of sins through Christ, a new covenant blessing (2:38). He calls upon his people to repent and turn to God "so that your sins may be wiped out" (3:19), that is, so that "the list of accusations against them will be obliterated (*cf.* Col. 2:14). This is simply another way of saying that their sins are forgiven (2:38)."[153] The call, as the promised eschatological "refreshing" (3:20), is corporate and not merely individual. The nation of Israel and not just its members are called to respond. The promise of forgiveness in this context includes pardon for the sin of clamoring for Christ's crucifixion (3:17). But forgiveness is not for Jews only but also for Gentiles who believe in Jesus (10:43). Peter links forgiveness with God's turning people from their past ways (3:26). As noted above, Peter understands Christ's death as an atonement for sin. He is the Servant of God who bears their sin (3:13; Isa 53:6, 12) and through whom they enter into the new covenant with God (2:38).

The apostle's theology of conversion includes a call to the initiatory right of baptism. He harkens back to John's baptism by water and the promise of the greater baptism by the Spirit (11:16), but he does not deny the importance of water baptism for those who turn to Christ Jesus. He calls those who heard his Pentecost sermon to "repent, and be baptized every one of you" (2:38, 41), baptism being the sign of faith. He gave the promise of the new covenant, that is, their "sins may be forgiven" and they would "receive the gift of the Holy Spirit" (Jer 31:31–34; Ezek 36:26–27). Barrett adds that "baptism in or into the name of Jesus means a rite in which the person concerned becomes the property of Jesus. He (and no doubt the person baptizing too) will call upon him by name, trusting him for salvation, and the baptized person in doing so surrenders himself into the hands of the one whom he invokes, so as to become his."[154] Peter, therefore, ordered that the Gentiles who received the Spirit be baptized since they, too, received the promise predicted by John (Acts 10:44–48; 11:15–17). Peter links baptism with faith, the reception of the Spirit, the blessings of the new covenant, and inclusion in the community of faith.

Peter is deeply concerned with people's sinful condition but also regards salvation as including a restored relationship with God as indicated in his covenant language. When at Cornelius's house he notes that God sent his message to Israel, "preaching peace by Jesus Christ" (10:36). The promise of peace is yet another blessing of Peter's

---

152. *TLNT*, 3:501–6.
153. Marshall, *The Acts of the Apostles*, 93.
154. Barrett, "Faith and Eschatology in Acts 3," 7–8.

New Exodus theology, which exalts the reign of God (Isa 52:7). That promise is offered now to the Gentiles since Jesus Christ "is Lord of all." Peace is not an existential experience but rather the restoration of a harmonious relationship, the fruit of reconciliation (cf. Rom 5:1).[155] Peace, then, is another way to describe salvation, but with a particular focus on the restoration of right relationship with God. Insofar as the proclamation of peace through Christ stands at the head of Isaiah's prophecy about the Suffering Servant (Isa 52:13—53:12), we may assume that Peter understands peace-making as part of the atoning sacrifice of Christ. The Gentiles as well as the Jews now receive the benefit ("Peace, peace, to the far and the near, says the Lord; and I will heal them" [Isa 57:19]).[156]

THE COMING OF THE SPIRIT

Peter ties the coming of the Spirit closely with his theology of salvation. The quotation from Joel 2 in his Pentecost sermon begins with the last-days promise of the Spirit ("I will pour out my Spirit upon all flesh" [Acts 2:17]) and ends with the offer of salvation ("Then everyone who calls on the name of the Lord shall be saved" [2:21]). The coming of the Spirit was an anticipated eschatological event now fulfilled at Pentecost. But Peter's theology of the Spirit does not begin with Pentecost but rather the ministry of Jesus. Peter tells those at the house of Cornelius that "God anointed Jesus of Nazareth with the Holy Spirit and power" (10:38). He assumes that even the Gentiles gathered there had heard about the ministry of John the Baptist and the baptism that he preached (10:37; cf. 19:3–4). Their understanding may have included not only John's prophecy about the coming of the Spirit (Mark 1:7–8 and plls.) but also the claim that Jesus himself was baptized by the Spirit (Mark 1:9–11 and plls.; Luke 4:18; Isa 61:1). This latter point may be implied in Acts 10:36–38 since Peter assumed that they knew "the message" about Jesus starting from the baptism of John (10:36–37; cf. 26:26). Indeed, the title "Christ" contains within it the vivid memory of that anointing (4:26; Ps 2:2; and see above on Peter's Christology in Acts). Jesus was empowered by the Holy Spirit[157] for a ministry of benefaction and deliverance. While Peter's preaching is in harmony with Luke's overall theology regarding the way Jesus was empowered by the Holy Spirit (Luke 4:18–19), we should not conclude that Luke simply ascribed this idea to Peter. All the Petrine materials in the New Testament point to Peter's own understanding of Jesus' association with the Spirit of God, and, as Dunn notes, the

---

155. Marshall notes that "*peace* is used here in its full sense as a synonym for 'salvation' (Luke 1:79; 2:14; Rom 5:1; Eph 2:17; 6:15), and denotes not merely the absence of strife and enmity between man and God but also the positive blessings that develop in a state of reconciliation" (Marshall, *The Acts of the Apostles*, 191; see *NIDNTT*, 2:776–83).

156. See the discussion in Keener, *Acts*, 2:1798–1801.

157. "Holy Spirit and power" is a "hendiadys which identifies the Spirit as the power in his ministry" (Turner, *Power from on High*, 263).

idea was "already implicit in the traditions that he [Luke] himself had been able to draw on."[158] Peter framed those traditions.

Peter brings into focus the prophetic role of John the Baptist in announcing the coming of the Spirit. Repeatedly Peter mentions John's baptism, giving it a place of prominence often overlooked in contemporary discussions of the gospel. Peter begins the gospel with Jesus' baptism by John (1:22; 10:37), as does Mark (Mark 1:2–11).[159] The story about John was so prominent that Peter made it a centerpiece in his preaching to those gathered at Cornelius's house (Acts 10:37) and his explanation to the Jerusalem church about God's inclusion of the Gentiles (11:16). Peter testified to Jesus' words, "John baptized with water, but you will be baptized with the Holy Spirit," recorded prior in Acts 1:5. Once again, while Luke is particularly concerned with the inclusion of the Gentiles and the transcendent significance of the coming of the Spirit upon them, Peter is portrayed as the first person who gives testimony to John's baptism, Jesus' words about him, and their implication for the gospel.

The coming of the Spirit fulfilled not only Jesus' prophecy but that of Joel as well (2:16; Joel 2:28–38a). As noted previously, Peter regarded the Spirit's advent as a sign that the last days, the era of divine fulfillment, had arrived. Joel is not the only prophet to speak of the coming age of the Spirit (cf. Num 11:29; Isa 32:15; Ezek 36:26–27; 37:14), yet Peter keys on Joel's words as the primary promise. He alters the quotation from "in those days" to "in the last days" in order indicate that the Spirit's coming signals the dawning of the eschatological age. The choice of Joel 2 here is quite relevant since it speaks about the Spirit's coming "upon all flesh," which means, in this context, "people of every gender, age, and class"[160] (2:17b–18). In Peter's theology the reception of the Spirit means inclusion and participation in God's people and plan (11:15–17).

Joel's prophecy also focuses upon the inspiration that comes through the Spirit: "Prophesy . . . see visions . . . dream dreams" (2:17b–18). Through the Spirit all his people are endowed with the prophetic gift and they together become an oracular community, the locus of divine revelation.[161] Not only does the Spirit widen the recipients of the prophetic gift to the whole community, but the Spirit bears witness to the gospel in concert with the apostolic witness (5:32). Peter offers testimony but so, too, does the Spirit (cf. 4:8).[162] The community and its leaders are endowed with the Spirit

---

158. James D. G. Dunn, *The Acts of the Apostles*, 143; James D. G. Dunn, *Jesus and the Spirit: A Study of the Religious and Charismatic Experience of Jesus and the First Christians as Reflected in the New Testament* (London: SCM, 1975), 88–94; cf. Turner, who regards the language in Acts 10:38 ("anointed with the Holy-Spirit-and-power") as echoing Luke 4:14 rather than traditional (*Power from on High*, 263). While the language may indeed be that of the author of Luke-Acts, the association of Jesus with the Spirit in his life, ministry, and exaltation is deeply embedded in the earliest strata of the tradition.

159. Barrett, *The Acts of the Apostles*, 1:524; Bock, *Acts*, 397.

160. Bock, *Acts*, 113; and see above.

161. Gene L. Green, "'As for Prophecies, They Will Come to an End': 2 Peter, Paul, and Plutarch on 'the Obsolescence of Oracles,'" *JSNT* 82 (2001) 107–22.

162. As Soards says, the Spirit is "the ultimate 'evidence' or 'witness' to God's will and work" (*The

to serve as agents of God's revelation as had God's ancient prophets (1:16; cf. 10:43; 1 Pet 1:11; 4:10–11). According to Peter, God directed the mission to the Gentiles through both vision and the voice of the Spirit (Acts 10:9–16, 19–20; 11:5–9, 12), but he also recognized angelic agency (11:13).

According to Peter, the sending of the Spirit also witnesses to Jesus' exaltation. He understood that God would baptize his own with the Holy Spirit as Jesus said (Acts 1:4–5; 11:16–17), but he now takes a further step when identifying the exalted Christ as he who sends the Spirit (2:33).[163] This declaration harkens back to the testimony of John the Baptist, which Peter knew (Mark 1:8). Jesus is the exalted Messiah who is at the right hand of the Father and, as God's regent, he gifts humanity with the Holy Spirit. Peter presents the citations from Psalms 16:8–10 and 110:1, the eyewitness testimony of the apostles, and the presence of the Holy Spirit as witnesses testifying to the resurrection and enthronement of Christ (Acts 2:31–36). As the exalted Lord, Jesus receives then sends the Spirit, which all could both see and hear (2:33, 1–4). The manifestation of the Spirit's presence gives powerful witness to Christ's lordship. Strauss's statement that "Peter offers the outpouring of the Spirit as indirect proof of the exaltation and so links his Christological conclusion to the Pentecost event"[164] is correct save for his indication that this is "indirect proof." Peter understands the Spirit's testimony as direct and present testimony alongside Scripture and the apostolic witness. In Luke's overall theology, the presence of the Spirit is a sign of the Kingdom (1:6–8), a concept Peter advances in 2:33 but with different language. Behind Peter's declaration also stands Psalm 68:18 ("You ascended on high; you led captivity captive; you received gifts by a person" [67:19 LXX]; cf. Eph 4:8). Peter regards God as the one who gave Christ the Spirit, either at his baptism (Acts 10:38) or upon his ascension. The context implies the latter.[165] Gifting the Spirit is evidence of Christ's co-regency with the Father and may echo the Sinai hope of the coming of the Spirit (Num 11:29).[166] Acts of giving characterize those who are the greatest of all.

One of the most extraordinary stories regarding the Holy Spirit is the conversion of the Samaritans (8:4–5). Jesus' commission in Acts 1:8 included the extension of the gospel into Samaria. Philip became their gospel messenger. After hearing, believing, and being baptized, the Jerusalem apostles sent them Peter and John "that they might receive the Holy Spirit" (8:15). As noted above, Luke's following parenthetical statement in v. 16 is one of the most extraordinary in Acts: "For as yet the Spirit had not come upon any of them; they had only been baptized in the name of the Lord Jesus."

Speeches in Acts, 36).

163. Turner registers the surprise in this verse: "This statement may in part build upon Jewish expectation that the Davidic messiah would be a figure powerfully endowed with the Spirit, and that others would experience the Spirit's work *through* him, but it goes very substantially beyond such understanding" (*Power from on High*, 276).

164. Strauss, *Davidic Messiah in Luke-Acts*, 141.

165. Barrett, *The Acts of the Apostles*, 1:150.

166. Bock, *Acts*, 131.

What makes the statement unusual is the Petrine theology that those who accepted the gospel and were baptized would receive the Holy Spirit (2:38). Dunn's explanation of this break in order is likely the best: "Only the manifestation that God had accepted them by giving them the Spirit (cf. 10:44–47; 11:17–18; 15:8–9) could validate the major step forward. Only that could break down the barriers which had divided Jew and Samaritan (not least, dispute regarding the Temple). Only the shared participation in the Spirit (cf. 2.42) could make these representatives of divided peoples into one church."[167] Something new was happening that required apostolic witness for the unity of the community.

At Samaria, Peter and John became agents through whom the Samaritans experienced their own Pentecost (8:17). As a magician understood power,[168] Simon asked that he might be empowered to do the same (8:18–19). Peter's response does not add a considerable amount to our understanding of Peter's pneumatology save for the fact that Peter regard the Spirit as "God's gift" (τὴν δωρεὰν τοῦ θεοῦ), which could not be purchased (8:20; cf. 2:38; 10:45; 11:17). Simon's focus is on the empowerment of the Spirit, yet Peter consistently links the Spirit to God's grace of conversion, which Simon apparently lacked (8:21–23). The emphasis on the Spirit as a gift may, as Keener suggests, be in contrast with a Jewish notion "that the Spirit was merited only by the most pious."[169] But more likely Peter points to God as the benefactor who gifts the Holy Spirit to those who believe (cf. the verb in 2 Pet 1:3; 1 Thess 4:8).[170] As such, the language crosses into the conceptual space of "grace" (χάρις; cf. Rom 3:24).

Among the Gentiles at Cornelius's house, as at Samaria, the advent of the Spirit was a Gentile Pentecost, which demonstrated God's embrace of these non-Jews and served to cement together the diverse community of Jews and Gentiles. The Gentiles received the Spirit and, as a sign of that event, spoke in tongues, as had the 120 gathered on the Day of Pentecost (Acts 10:44–46; 2:1–4). Given that they had received the Spirit, Peter recognized them as those who had received the gospel and so ordered they be baptized (10:47–48; 2:38). The order had been upset, as was the case in Samaria, since the reception of the Spirit had occurred before baptism. However, Peter held together proclamation/baptism/reception of the Spirit as the necessary complex of conversion/initiation. In recounting the event to the Jerusalem church, Peter laid out his thoughts regarding what had occurred with these Gentiles. First, he tied the Gentile reception of the Spirit together with the Jewish Pentecost, thus recognizing the common community that had received the same gift of God (11:15). Second, he

---

167. James D. G. Dunn, *The Acts of the Apostles*, 111; and see James D. G. Dunn, *Baptism in the Holy Spirit: A Re-Examination of the New Testament on the Gift of the Spirit* (Philadelphia: Westminster John Knox, 1977), 55–72. Dunn rightly argues that the incident does not provide a basis for classic Pentecostalism's theology of subsequence.

168. See Graf, *Magic in the Ancient World*; Klauck, *The Religious Context of Early Christianity*, 209–31.

169. Keener, *Acts*, 1:986.

170. *TDNT*, 2:166–67; *NIDNTT*, 2:40–41; David A. deSilva, *Honor, Patronage, Kinship and Purity: Unlocking New Testament Culture* (Downers Grove, IL: InterVarsity, 2000), 121–57.

regarded the Gentile Pentecost as a fulfillment of Jesus' promise (11:16; 1:5), which now extends not just to Jews but also Gentiles. Third, he argued that God had given them the Spirit, implying that the Gentiles also had believed (11:17). Peter could not stand in the way of the divine work. Peter reaffirmed this argument at the Jerusalem Council, saying, "And God, who knows the human heart, testified to them by giving them the Holy Spirit, just as he did to us" (15:8). Here Peter adds that the endowment of the Spirit was the demonstrable divine testimony of their inward faith (cf. 11:17). Peter concludes, therefore, that "in cleansing their heart by faith he has made no distinction between them and us" (15:9). With this he affirms that these Gentiles also were members of the New Covenant community (cf. 2:38; Jer 31:31–34). The Gentiles are brought into the New Exodus, which promised salvation for the Gentiles.[171] This, for Peter, includes the reception of the Spirit. Restoration by the Spirit is for them as well as for the Jews. Given that this is God's work, the community should not take measures to try to stop it (10:47; 11:17) but should support it. Peter is insistent on this point.[172]

THE COMMUNITY

As noted previously, one principle piece of the New Exodus theology is the creation of the community of the people of God, including the restoration of Israel and the inclusion of the Gentiles into God's plan and people.[173] The Petrine speeches in Acts take up this New Exodus theme. Although Peter opened up the Gentile mission, he was known as the apostle to the Jewish people (Gal 2:7–8). His Acts speeches reflect this focus of his ministry while, at the same time, highlighting the tensions the apostle experienced with his own ethnic community. Peter addresses his nation's leadership as "rulers of the people (τοῦ λαοῦ) and elders" (4:8) and makes his proclamation to them and "all the people (παντὶ τῷ λαῷ) of Israel" (4:10). The people (λαός) was used repeatedly of Israel in the LXX (Exod 5:1; 7:4; 19:5; Isa 1:3; 52:4; 53:8). The resurrected Jesus appeared to the apostles, not all the Jewish people, and commanded Peter and the rest "to preach to the people and to testify that he is the one ordained by God as judge of the living and the dead" (10:40–42). Peter proclaims that God raised up his Servant and "sent him first to you," his people (3:26), a statement that anticipates a ministry beyond the Jewish people (cf. Rom 1:16) since the promise to Abraham he cited in the previous verse says, "And in your descendants all the families of the earth shall be blessed" (3:25; Gen 12:3; 18:18; 22:18).[174] Peter appears not to have been fully

171. See above on the New Exodus.

172. Barrett makes a good point that Peter could not stop what God had already done, but "the general sense however is clear: God had made plain his intention; who was I to act in a contrary fashion?" (*The Acts of the Apostles*, 1:543).

173. See above on *The New Exodus in Acts and the Petrine Speeches*; Pao, *Acts and the Isaianic New Exodus*, 111–46.

174. Barrett points out that the citation conflates the language of all three verses in Genesis (*The*

aware of the implications of the promise to Abraham, but Luke indeed was. Later Peter understood the full scope of God's plan. He did affirm, however, that the gospel was for those who were "descendants of the prophets and of the covenant that God gave to your ancestors" (3:25).

Although Peter recognizes that God extended the blessings of the Messiah to the people of Israel yet again, he also realized his people's rejection of the gospel of Christ. He warned those gathered in the temple after healing the lame man that God would send his prophet like Moses, and "it will be that everyone who does not listen to that prophet will be utterly rooted out from the people" (3:23; citing Deut 18:19). A distancing from Peter's people begins in this speech. In Acts 12:11 Peter recounts his rescue from Herod Agrippa I and "the people of the Jews" (τοῦ λαοῦ τῶν Ἰουδαίων). Barrett comments on the passage, saying, "Peter, a representative Christian, is now separated from the Jewish people."[175] It should be noted that Peter at no point abandons his identification as a Jew, yet he recognizes a distinction between those of his people who responded to the Prophet and those who did not (Acts 3:22–26). Peter is the one who begins to reinterpret the composition of God's λαός (people), as is the case in 1 Peter (1 Pet 2:9–10; cf. Rom 9–11).

Peter also broadens the concept of God's λαός (people) to include the Gentiles. James cites Peter's position on the matter, saying, "Simeon has related how God first looked favourably on the Gentiles, to take from among them a people for his name" (15:14; cf. Zech 2:11 LXX; 1 Pet 2:4–10). James's language echoes Deuteronomy 14:2 (LXX "and it is you the Lord your God has chosen to be an exceptional people to him out of all the nations on the face of the earth") as well as Exodus 19:5, which Peter cites in 1 Peter 2:9. The language in Acts 15:14 may be simply James's summary of Peter's argument that the Gentiles believed the message, received the Holy Spirit as had the Jewish believers, and that God cleansed their hearts and "made no distinction between them and us." The Gentiles, as the Jews, will all "be saved through the grace of the Lord Jesus" (15:7–11). On the other hand, Luke does not record full transcripts of the speeches, and it may be that Peter himself used the language James cites, that is, that God took from the Gentiles "a people for his name" (15:14). This is entirely

---

Acts of the Apostles, 1:212); cf. Gal 3:8. Note, however, that instead of αἱ φυλαί (tribes in Gen 12:3) or τὰ ἔθνη (Gentiles or nations in 18:18; 22:18), Luke renders Peter's citation with αἱ πατριαί (peoples or nations), which emphasizes either ancestral or sociopolitical connections (*BDAG*, 788).

175. Barrett, *The Acts of the Apostles*, 1:583. Dunn adds, "the movement represented by Peter had become clearly distinct from 'the people of the Jews'" (*The Acts of the Apostles*, 163). See 12:3, where those who celebrated the execution of the apostle James are called "the Jews." Dunn again comments, "Here we see again the tension which runs through Luke's portrayal of the new movement's identity. One the one hand, the new sect was in full continuity with Israel's hope and heritage. But on the other, there was a growing distinction between the movement and those with a more obvious claim to that heritage in national and religious terms. How else better to describe the latter than as 'the Jews'?" (*The Acts of the Apostles*, 162). Peter's language and understanding about his people has begun to shift, and Luke picks up the changes as the mission turns to the Gentiles while not abandoning the Jewish people. See the comments on the community in the chapter on 1 Peter.

possible, if not likely, given Peter's use of this language in his first epistle. Even if the words are not Peter's, James captures the import of Peter's presentation before the Jerusalem Council. The people of God includes those Gentiles whom he has called.

Peter recurs to other concepts to describe of the community as well. He uses the term "disciples," the most common term in the Gospels and Acts used for the followers of Jesus, to speak of the Gentile believers (15:10). According to Luke's narrative in Acts, Peter was not the first to speak of the Gentile believers in this way (11:26, 29; 13:52). Peter also employs the gender-marked "men brothers" when speaking to the Jewish (2:29; 3:7) or the Jewish Christian (1:16; 15:7) communities, as do others in Acts (2:37; 7:2; 13:15; 15:13). The language is traditional Jewish and only appears when a Jewish community is addressed (cf. 4 Macc 8:19). Although gender marked, it appears in contexts where both men and women were present (1:14–16; 2:29, 37). No conclusion should be drawn regarding the gender exclusivity of Peter's proclamation and his understanding of the community since, as noted above, he topicalizes women.[176] Luke does not portray Peter as someone who excludes the women from the community.

The Petrine speeches in Acts show the apostle as someone engaged in the proclamation of the gospel and the integration of those who believe into community. After preaching on Pentecost, he calls for repentance and baptism (2:38). The number of disciples increased dramatically underneath his early ministry (2:41; 4:4). He confirmed the inclusion of the Samaritans and opened the door of the gospel to the Gentiles, a move he defended before the Jerusalem church and Council (11:1; 15:7–11). He worked in concert with the other principle leaders of the church, John (3:1) and James (12:17; 15:13–14), and Paul recognized these three as the "pillars" (Gal 2:6). James acknowledges Peter's special authority when he rendered the decision of the Jerusalem Council (Acts 15:14). Peter stands for community formation, expansion of the community beyond Judaism, and speaks as a conciliatory figure in the most critical decision of the early church. His understanding of the reach of the gospel is matched by his offer and acceptance of hospitality to and from the Gentiles (Acts 10). He stands for inclusion at a pivotal moment in the church's development.

PETRINE ETHICS

The Petrine speeches Luke records offer no more than a glance at Peter's ethical teaching regarding human duty before God and others. His Acts speeches do not relay much of his teaching to the church but rather focus on proclamation. We do, however, overhear the apostle talk about obedience as the primary response to the divine initiative. When charged by the authorities to teach no more in the name of Jesus, Peter's response was to affirm his principle responsibility: "We must obey God rather than any human authority" (5:28–29). Peter regards obedience as a divine necessity (δεῖ)

---

176. See the discussion in Keener, *Acts*, 1:757.

which overrides any human demand.[177] The level of necessity is augmented by the verb Peter uses (πειθαρχεῖν), which, in such contexts, implies the strict obedience that a hierarchical relationship imposes.[178] The statement echoes the position of Peter and John in 4:19: "Whether it is right in God's sight to listen to you rather than to God, you must judge." Peter goes on to affirm that God grants his Spirit "to those who obey him" (5:32b), that is, to those who have been persuaded by the gospel message and have responded in the obedience of faith. Whether coming to faith or being a disciple of Christ, God requires obedience, a theme in Petrine ethics (Acts 4:12; 2 Pet 3:11; 1 Pet 1:22; 3:1, 10; 4:7), although one not absent in other NT authors (Rom. 1:5; 2 Cor. 9:13; Heb 5:9; 1 John 2:3). Peter regards God, not humans, as sovereign, and Peter's ethics are rooted in this premise.

Another high value in Peter's ethics is "doing good," that is, acting as a benefactor within society. As noted above, Peter sees "doing good" (εὐεργετῶν) as a characteristic of Jesus' ministry (10:30), so much so that his summary of Jesus' life placed such Spirit empowered beneficent action as a center piece of his proclamation. Peter also recognized that humans could do righteous deeds and be recognized by God for what they had done, regardless of their ethnicity. In 10:35 he states his new understanding that "in every nation anyone who fears him [God] and does what is right is acceptable to him" (ἐργαζόμενος δικαιοσύνην). Peter's statement is hardly an affirmation that "doing righteousness" obviates the necessity of obeying God and believing in Christ (10:43). But Peter acknowledges that God recognizes the deeds of the "righteous Gentile,"[179] those who do alms-giving and other righteous acts such as showing piety and living in holiness before God and demonstrating humanity and justice to one's fellows.[180] While this is not an example of Peter's ethical teaching to the disciples, it demonstrates the value he places upon righteous deeds (1 Pet 2:24; 3:14). Peter links these deeds with fearing God (10:35), recognizing that people of any nation may indeed honor him in this way. Luke says that Cornelius was "a devout man who feared God with all his household," which likely indicates that he was a "God-fearer," a Gentile sympathizer to Judaism who had not become a full proselyte (10:2).[181] But in 10:35 Peter speaks more broadly of any Gentile who "fears God," which here means acknowledging him and

---

177. δεῖ may refer to that which was necessary or required because of some compulsion, whether it comes from God, law or custom, or a given situation (*BDAG*, 214). Here the compulsion comes from God. Peter's statement contrasts obedience to God's demand from that which humans impose (μᾶλλον ἢ ἀνθρώποις).

178. *TLNT*, 3:63-64.

179. Terence L. Donaldson, *Paul and the Gentiles: Remapping the Apostle's Convictional World* (Minneapolis: Augsburg Fortress, 2006), 65-69; Keener, *Acts*, 1:512-13.

180. Barrett, *The Acts of the Apostles*, 1:520, referencing Philo, *Spec.* 2.63: "two most especially important heads of all the innumerable particular lessons and doctrines; the regulating of one's conduct towards God by the rules of piety and holiness, and of one's conduct towards men by the rules of humanity and justice; each of which is subdivided into a great number of subordinate ideas, all praiseworthy." See Rom. 2:14-15.

181. Levinskaya, *The Book of Acts in Its Diaspora Setting*, 51-126.

honoring him by righteous deeds. Although Peter does not develop the thought as does Paul, he recognizes that Gentiles may have a true knowledge of God and honor him (cf. Acts 17:26–29; Rom 1:19–20; 2:14–16). Peter's ethical teaching places high value on the fear of God (cf. 1 Pet 1:17; 2:17–18; 3:2).

Peter was a person of prayer (1:24; 3:1), and his voice may possibly be heard in the church's prayer of 4:23–31, although Luke does not directly ascribe the prayer to him. By Luke's account and Peter's telling, he was in prayer when the messengers arrived from Cornelius's house (10:9; 11:50), and in that time of communion with God he received a revelatory vision from God (10:9–16; cf. 2:17). When Simon Magnus's request revealed the true character of his heart, Peter exhorted him, saying, "Repent therefore of this wickedness of yours, and pray to the Lord that, if possible, the intent of your heart may be forgiven" (8:22). Simon needed to invoke God in prayer.

Peter understood his and other's dependency on God and that the Holy Spirit's agency was necessary for people's lives (2:38). He was filled with the Spirit (2:4) and through the Spirit's agency proclaimed the gospel (4:8; 1 Pet 1:12). Whatever else may be said about Peter's theology and work, he recognized his dependency on God, and others saw that as well. His theology, in part, arose out of his encounter with God as seen both at Pentecost and in the events surrounding the conversion of Cornelius. Peter's life was marked by divine dependence, leading, and power.

PETRINE ESCHATOLOGY

As other NT authors, Peter regards the final consummation of God's plan to have already begun, as noted above. The coming of the Spirit at Pentecost is a sign that the last days have indeed arrived. Peter reworks the quotation from Joel 2:28, which read: "Then afterwards I will pour out my spirit on all flesh," and, in doing so, lays out how the prophecy explains the Pentecost event. He preambles the quotation, saying, "No, this is what was spoken through the Prophet Joel," then adds the altered quotation: "In the last days it will be, God declares, that I will pour out my Spirit upon all flesh" (Acts 2:17). Peter utilizes the *pesher* form of biblical interpretation, which regards the present era as the time of prophetic fulfillment.[182] As Ellis notes, *pesher* interpretation uses the characteristic formula "the interpretation (*pesher*) is" or "this is," and "uses or creates variant Old Testament text-forms designed to adapt the text to the interpretation of the commentary." Ellis comments further that "As *eschatological exegesis,* it views the Old Testament as promises and prophecies that have their fulfilment within the writer's own time and community, a community that inaugurates the 'new covenant' of the 'last (*'aharit*) days.'"[183] The last days, notes Keener: "Was a biblical phrase for the

---

182. Richard N. Longenecker, *Biblical Exegesis in the Apostolic Period* (Grand Rapids: Eerdmans, 1975), 38–45, 98–103; Daniel Patte, *Early Jewish Hermeneutic in Palestine* (Missoula: Scholars, 1975), 299–308; Maurya Horgan, *Pesharim: Qumran Interpretations of Biblical Books* (Washington: Catholic Biblical Association of America, 1979), 229–59.

183. E. Earle Ellis, "How the New Testament Uses the Old," in *New Testament Interpretation: Essays*

period of Israel's restoration, which Jewish hopes now fixed in the eschatological time (Isa 2:2; Hos 3:5; Mic 4:1; Dan 2:28)."[184] Peter, along with other NT figures, affirms that the eschatological era has dawned (cf. 1 Pet 1:20; 2 Pet 3:3; 1 Tim 4:1; 1 John 2:18). The plan of God is being fulfilled.

Peter regards present events as the eschatological fulfillment of prophetic promises in other places as well (such as 2:25–36, citing Ps 16:8–11; 110:1; 3:22–23, citing Deut 18:15–20; 4:11, citing Ps 118:22).[185] Christ's coming is no new and novel thing but rather the realization of ancient testimony. Ridderbos is correct when he says that Peter's eschatology is the "ground on which all his preaching rests, is the consciousness that the time of eschatological fulfilment has dawned."[186] Bayer is right in noting that eschatology is not dominant in Acts. But he qualifies this observation, saying, "Considering the theme of eschatology as a test case, we see that the foundation laid in the Petrine speeches within the initial three chapters of Acts sets the tone of the eschatological framework for the entire book."[187] Once again, Luke portrays Peter as the person on the forefront of theological innovation.

According to Peter, the last days have already come, though the final consummation still awaits, though one may anticipate it. The apostle holds his "eschatology in a Christ-centered tension between the extremes of near-expectation and far-expectation."[188] Although the last days have already arrived, as evidenced by the fulfillment of prophecies in the advent of Christ and the Spirit, Peter expects the final consummation predicted by Joel: "The coming of the Lord's great and glorious day" (Acts 2:20). This is the "day of the Lord," the eschatological event when the Lord comes to judge the world's inhabitants (Isa 13:6, 9; Ezek 13:5; 30:3; Joel 1:15; 2:1, 11; 3:14; Amos 5:18, 20; Zeph 1:7, 14; Zech 1:14; Mal 4:5) and to bring his people salvation (Joel 2:21–32; 3:18; Obad 15–21; Zech 14:1–21). The epistles speak of it as the "day of the Lord" (1 Thess 5:2; 2 Thess 2:2; 1 Pet 3:10) or as the "day of the Lord Jesus" (1 Cor 1:8; 2 Cor 1:14; and see Phil 1:6, 10; 2:16; 2 Thess 1:6–10). In Peter's eyes the day arrives when the Messiah returns from the heavenly realm (3:20–21; cf. 1:11). That will be "the time of universal restoration that God announced long ago through his holy prophets" (3:21). As noted above, the restoration of Israel is a central tenet of Peter's New Exodus theology. He affirms that the final fulfillment of that hope will be the coming "times of refreshing" (3:20). But he adds that God's restoration of all things (ἀποκαταστάσεως πάντων, echoing Mal 3:22–23) will then occur, that is, "Jesus as God's Messiah will restore God's perverted world."[189] Second Peter argues that this

---

on Principles and Methods, ed. I. Howard Marshall (Exeter: Paternoster, 1977), 206–7.

    184. Keener, *Acts*, 1:878.
    185. See the full discussion above.
    186. Ridderbos, *The Speeches of Peter*, 12.
    187. Bayer, "The Preaching of Peter in Acts," 260.
    188. Bayer, "The Preaching of Peter in Acts," 267.
    189. Barrett, *The Acts of the Apostles*, 1:206.

restoration includes both the destruction of the old order by fire and the establishment of God's new order (see 2 Pet 3:6–7[190]), but Peter focuses on God's renewal according to the speech in Acts. The restoration of Israel is part of a wider hope of the restoration of all things. Commenting on Acts 3:20–21, Bruce adds that here "we may not have 'the most primitive Christology of all,' but it might well be argued that we do indeed have the most primitive *eschatology* of all."[191]

While Peter awaits universal restoration, he also recognizes that his people's destiny is bound with their response to Christ Jesus. He is the Prophet Moses predicted, and as such, "everyone who does not listen to the prophet will be utterly rooted out from the people" (3:23). Both Judas and Simon Magus were under the threat of divine judgment in Peter's view (1:18; 8:20). Indeed, Christ is not only the one who brings salvation, but he is the one God ordained to be the "judge of the living and the dead" (10:42; cf. 1 Pet 4:5; 2 Tim 4:1, 8; Gen 18:25). God controls the process by making Christ the one ordained (ὁ ὡρισμένος) to this judicial office (cf. Acts 17:31). Peter does not shrink from declaring God's judgment both as a present event and a future reality. His eschatology is both present and future and includes divine salvation and judgment.

Peter's eschatology is not highly developed in Acts. He does, however, show clear consciousness of the present and future dimensions of the eschaton. The last days have come, God's people are empowered by the gift of the Spirit, Christ's mission is carried out, and Israel is called to turn to their Messiah in anticipation of his return, the time when refreshing and renewal will come to them and, indeed, the world. Peter's eschatological vision is large, and his ministry and preaching are framed within it.

PETER'S TESTIMONY IN THE ACTS OF THE APOSTLES

Far from presenting a bare narrative of events in the life of Peter, Acts records the apostle's speeches, which contain rich evidence of his theology. Luke did not simply weave his presentation from his own theological store and concerns but integrated the apostle's perspectives into his wider narrative. Peter's speeches reflect the apostle's own concerns and views, which Luke then interprets for his readers. Such is the nature of testimony. The consistent picture throughout the speeches is that Peter was a theological innovator who was responsible for the primitive church's theology about Jesus' person and work. He understands the events that have occurred as part of the overarching plan of God for the salvation not only of Israel but of the nations. Peter's theology is part of the Christian epic that tells of God's New Exodus. A new age has dawned in fulfillment of ancient promises. There are no small plans here.

---

190. Green, *Jude and 2 Peter*, 320–23.

191. Bruce, "The Speeches in Acts—Thirty Years After," 68; Barrett, "Faith and Eschatology in Acts 3," 15.

Peter's theology centers on Jesus, the Messiah, and his cross. He is the Lord as well as the Suffering Servant of Isaiah who suffers and is exalted by God. Peter regards him as the new Moses who is both rejected as the Stone but placed as the cornerstone in God's plan. Peter knows that people must respond to God's saving initiative, and so he leads with a theology of proclamation that expects a response in the obedience of faith evidenced publicly in baptism. Humans are in need of God's salvation and must turn to him. Peter's theology of grace is inclusive of Jews, Samaritans, and Gentiles, and it includes every gender and social class. These are formed into a new community of the people of God. While standing for God's saving grace shown to all, he opposes ethnic divisions within the people of God. Peter is a conciliatory figure who includes and defends inclusion because he understands God's plan based on Scripture, the Spirit, and divine leading. Peter also stands for a strong ethic of obedience to God and orients himself to God's eschatological present and future. Peter knows that a new age has dawned and anticipates the final consummation upon the Messiah's return.

Peter's theology of the cross and the eschaton is the most primitive of all. The apostle stands at the head of Christian theological innovation. Luke's Peter is the church's first theologian from the time of the ascension. Paul is a theological powerhouse, as the latter chapters of Acts and his epistles show. But Peter laid the foundations.

CHAPTER 7

First Peter and the Testimony Peter

The salutation in 1 Peter begins with the author's name and identification: "Peter, an apostle of Jesus Christ" (1 Pet 1:1).[1] Following letter writing conventions of the era, the author of 1 Peter begins by identifying himself by name and apostolic office.[2] He is Jesus Christ's messenger, sent by Christ and invested with his authority.[3] Peter was the first apostle Jesus called (Matt 4:18; 10:2) and the only one Jesus named (Mark 3:16). A few other autobiographical notes are laced through the letter. Peter says to the elders of the Christian communities scattered throughout Asia Minor that he also is an elder (5:1), indicating to the readers/hearers whom he has not met (1:12) that he is a man advanced in years. During Peter's era older people were considered wise, and

---

1. See also chapter 2 on the authorship of 1 Peter and the role of Silvanus in 5:12.

2. The name Πέτρος (Peter) translates the Aramaic Cephas (כֵּיפָא), both meaning either "rock" or "stone" (John 1:42; Joseph A. Fitzmyer, *The Gospel According to Luke [1–9]* [Garden City, NY: Doubleday, 1981], 112–24; Cullmann, *Peter: Disciple-Apostle-Martyr*, 17–21). The Aramaic may also mean a "crag" in the rocks. This noun was used as a name, although rarely (Tal Ilan, *Lexicon of Jewish Names in Late Antiquity, Part III: The Western Diaspora 330 BCE–650 CE* [Tübingen: Mohr Siebeck, 2008], 436). Jesus named Simeon using this Aramaic name (Mark 3:16; Luke 6:14; cf. Matt 4:18; 10:2; 16:17–18; Acts 10:5). Although we know Peter by the Greek form, at times he was called Cephas (Gal 1:18; 2:9, 11, 14; 1 Cor 1:12; 3:22; 9:5; 15:5). The combination of the names "Simon Peter" appears infrequently compared with "Peter" (Matt 16:16; Luke 5:8) apart from John's Gospel (John 6:68; 13:6, 9, 24, 36; 18:10, 15, 25; 20:2, 6; 21:2, 3, 7). The name underscores his derived authority from Jesus (Green, *Jude and 2 Peter*, 172).

3. The Jewish שָׁלִיחַ, an authoritative messenger who spoke with the authority of the person who sent him, underlies the NT concept of apostleship (*TDNT*, 1:422–23; and see Ernest De Witt Burton, *A Critical and Exegetical Commentary on the Epistle to the Galatians* [Edinburgh: T. & T. Clark, 1920], 364–78). As m. Ber. 5.5 says, "the one sent by a man is as the man himself" (*TDNT* 1:414–20).

society granted them greater honor. Consequently elders were invested with authority and named as ambassadors, magistrates, and administrators among their people.[4] Peter writes as an experienced and respected leader. Indeed, the term "elder" became a title given to those who exercised ecclesiastical leadership (Acts 14:23; 20:17; 1 Tim 5:17, 19; Titus 1:5) and were sometimes known as "overseers" or "pastors" (Acts 20:17, 28; Titus 1:5, 7; 1 Pet 5:1, 2). Peter's self-identification underscores both his authority and humility.

PETER'S TESTIMONY

The apostle also tells his readers that he is "a witness of the sufferings of Christ" (5:1). Here as elsewhere in the letter, Peter assumes that the readers knew the gospel story about Jesus (1:12) in addition to Peter's place in that story. He does not elaborate whether he is an "eyewitness" of Christ's sufferings or "one who bears witness" about them.[5] Given the nature of testimony the distinction is artificial since the person who bears witness is precisely the one who has seen something and is therefore qualified to bear witness to those events. He saw Christ's sufferings (μάρτυς [5:1]) and now offers testimony (ἐπιμαρτυρῶν [5:12]) about God's grace. First Peter is the apostle's testimony about Christ and God's grace, shaped for readers in Christian communities scattered throughout Asia Minor (1:2). As noted previously, testimony is a central theme in Petrine theology.

The debate over the letter's authenticity has been vigorous, as discussed in chapter 2. The position taken in this volume is that Peter was indeed the author of the book, but his amanuensis shaped his testimony. While the letter contains the *vox Petri*, we should not expect to hear the unredacted *verba Petri*. Richards argues that the discussion over whether Silvanus was the amanuensis or the messenger of the letter (5:12) has been put to rest. He shows that the language ("Through Silvanus . . . I have written this short letter" [Διὰ Σιλουανοῦ . . . δι' ὀλίγων ἔγραψα]) commonly referred to the messenger who delivered and helped interpret a correspondence and not to the scribe who penned it.[6] But as demonstrated previously, the prepositional phrase δι' ὀλίγων functions adverbially ("briefly" or "in a few words"[7]) and topicalizes the act of composition ("I have written") rather than sending. While Richards is correct that in many ancient texts the phrase "I write through someone" (γράφω διὰ τινος) is a way to identify the letter's courier, in a significant number of instances

---

4. Adolph Deissmann, *Bible Studies* (Edinburgh: T. & T. Clark, 1901), 154–56; *TDNT*, 6:652–53; *NIDNTT*, 1:192–97. See, for example, Luke 7:3; 22:66; Acts 22:5.

5. John H. Elliott, *1 Peter: A New Translation with Introduction and Commentary* (New York: Doubleday, 2000), 819. Aristotle, *Rhetoric* 1375b–1376a; As Antiphon, *Against the Stepmother for Poisoning* 1.28; *Hymn 4 to Hermes* 372; Xenophon, *Cyropaedia* 1.6.16; Plato, *Symposium* 175e.

6. E. Randolph Richards, "Silvanus Was Not Peter's Secretary: Theological Bias in Interpreting διὰ Σιλουανοῦ . . . ἔγραψα in 1 Peter 5:12," *JETS* 43 (2000) 417–32.

7. See the use of δι' ὀλίγων in Plato, *Philebus* 31d: "if I may speak in the fewest and briefest words about matters of the highest import" (εἰ δεῖ δι' ὀλίγων περὶ μεγίστων ὅτι τάχιστα ῥηθῆναι).

it refers to the secretary.[8] We discern the meaning through the context of the phrase and not simply by statistical probabilities. In the case of 1 Peter 5:12 the prepositional phrase δι' ὀλίγων points to the composition of the document and Silvanus's role as the amanuensis.[9] Moreover, Peter references the content of the composition after the phrase: "Through Silvanus . . . I have written this short letter." The topic is the content: "To encourage you and to testify that this is the true grace of God." But even if Richards were correct that Διὰ Σιλουανοῦ referred to the messenger, it would be highly likely that Peter, as Paul, employed the services of an amanuensis who participated in composing or editing the document.[10] When using an amanuensis, the ascribed author commonly included a final greeting in their own hand, sometimes indicating that they were inserting a greeting (1 Cor 16:21; Gal 6:11; Col 4.18; 2 Thess 3:17; Phlm 19) and at other times simply writing the final greeting in their own handwriting without placing any note in the text that the pen had changed hands.[11] Authors maintained control of the composition's content, as these final greetings indicate.[12] In the case of 1 Peter, the apostle's voice is mediated to its readers, yet we should not hesitate to ascribe the theology of the letter to Peter.[13] Peter clearly has confidence in Silvanus, however, since he calls him "a faithful brother," one who is dependable.[14] He dispatched his secretarial duties in a trustworthy manner. Peter stood behind any editorial changes

---

8. My former student, Jeremiah Coogan, makes the point saying, "Of the available examples, seven clearly refer to the delivery of a message by a courier or couriers (POxy 937; Acts 15:23; Rom 16:27, Z 035; *Ign. Philad.* 11:2; *Ign. Smyrn* 12:1; *Ign. Rom.* 10:1; *Poly. Phil.* 14:1). Two, on the other hand, can only indicate a secretary (Rom 16:27, uncial 337; *HE* 4.23.11). Three are uncertain (BGU I33; PFay 123; *EDiog.* 17)." In light of this evidence, Richards's conclusion ("the evidence outside 1 Peter argues rather conclusively that this formula indicates solely the letter-carrier") is "overstated" (Jeremiah Coogan, "Silvanus as Secretary: 1 Peter 5:12 and the Idiom γράφω διὰ τινός" [paper presented at the Annual Meeting of the Midwest Region of the SBL, 2013], 9).

9. Contra Richards, "Silvanus Was Not Peter's Secretary," 429. Selwyn (*The First Epistle of Peter: The Greek Text with Introduction, Notes, and Essays* [London: Macmillan, 1947], 369 makes much of Silvanus's compositional role, ascribing to him the parallels between 1 Peter, the apostolic decree in Acts 15, and the Thessalonian correspondences, which include him (under his Greek name Silas) as co-author of the letters (1 Thess 1:1; 2 Thess 1:1).

10. See the discussion in chapter 2.

11. For example, see *LAE*, 170-73, 179-80; Stanley K. Stowers, *Letter Writing in Greco-Roman Antiquity* (Philadelphia: Westminster, 1986), 60-61; Jeffrey A. D. Weima, *Neglected Endings: The Significance of the Pauline Letter Closings* (Sheffield: Sheffield Academic, 1994), 119. Numerous extant ancient letters clearly show a change in handwriting where the final greeting begins, a feature that obviously disappears in copies of the autographs.

12. E. Randolph Richards, *The Secretary in the Letters of Paul* (Tübingen: Mohr Siebeck, 1991), 14-67, 76-80; E. Randolph Richards, *Paul and First-Century Letter Writing: Secretaries, Composition, and Collection* (Downers Grove, IL: InterVarsity, 2004), 171-75. Richards shows that "an author was held responsible for every word of the letter. The personal handwriting at the end of a letter indicated the author had seen the letter and consequently assumed responsibility for its contents" (*Paul and First-Century Letter Writing*, 171).

13. For the full discussion of the letter's authorship, see chapter 1.

14. John H. Elliott, *1 Peter*, 878.

Silvanus made. Silvanus could also have been the letter's courier, but that is not the primary concern of Peter's commendation in 5:12.

PETER AND THE AUTHORIAL COMMUNITY

Peter does not write alone but is part of what Loubser has called an "authorial community" that included the author, amanuensis, messenger, and readers as active participants in the communication event.[15] Peter is also with others beyond Silvanus, whatever we might consider his role to be. He conveys greetings from the community he is with when writing the letter: "She who is in Babylon, chosen together with you, sends you her greetings" (5:13, NIV). "She" is most likely the church that is with Peter when he writes ("Your sister church in Babylon, chosen together with you," NRSV). They are "the fellow elect one" (ἡ συνεκλεκτή), the noun being feminine. The one identified here could be Peter's wife (Mark 1:30; 1 Cor 9:5; Clement of Alexandria, *Stromata* 7.11.63[16]), an interpretation supported by the fact that Peter next uses kinship language to identify Silvanus as "a faithful brother" and Mark as "my son" (1 Pet 5:12–13). Some ancient scribes and translators, however, added the term "church" (ἐκκλησία and equivalents) to clarify that Peter was speaking about the community and not a person.[17] Under this reading, the language is similar to 2 John 1 and 13, where the churches are called "the elect lady" and "your elect sister."[18] Elsewhere Peter uses filial language to speak of the Christian communities (2:17; 5:9), and the apostle likely does the same here. The final greeting would serve as an inclusio that binds together the recipients who are "the elect" (1 Pet 1:1) with the "fellow elect" community that stands with Peter. The community is "in Babylon," most likely a coded reference to the city of Rome.[19]

Mark was also with Peter when he composed the letter, and Peter includes a greeting from him as "my son" (5:13). As argued previously, Mark was responsible for the Gospel that goes by his name. Ancient tradition identified him as Peter's interpreter as well as the one who penned Peter's preaching. Mark's role in the composition of 1 Peter is not indicated since Peter only conveys greetings from him. Yet his presence at least opens the possibility that he participated at some level in the process of preparing the letter since he did indeed work as Peter's interpreter.[20] Mark's role in

---

15. Johannes A. Loubser, "Media Criticism and the Myth of Paul, the Creative Genius, and His Forgotten Co-Workers," *Neot* 34 (2000) 329–45.

16. "They say, accordingly, that the blessed Peter, on seeing his wife led to death, rejoiced on account of her call and conveyance home, and called very encouragingly and comfortingly, addressing her by name, Remember the Lord. Such was the marriage of the blessed and their perfect disposition towards those dearest to them."

17. Sinaiticus (א) and other Greek mss., Vulgate, Syriac Peshitta, Armenian.

18. Paul J. Achtemeier, *1 Peter: A Commentary on First Peter* (Minneapolis: Fortress, 1996), 353.

19. Cf. Rev 11:8; 2 Bar. 11:1–2; 67:7; Sib. Or. 5.137–43; 159–60; Num. Rab. 7; Midr. Ps. 121; Midr. Meggiloth 1.6 [89a]. See John H. Elliott, *1 Peter*, 882–86.

20. See chapter 2.

composing of the Gospel of Mark from the preaching of Peter points to the strong literary relationship between the apostle and his "son," which could well have issued in Mark being given input into the letter's contents and expression. We cannot prove this suggestion, but the nature of Peter and Mark's relationship at least suggests it.[21] As noted in the discussion of the Gospel of Mark, Peter utilized Mark as his translator and, indeed, the gospel itself was the preaching of Peter. While Peter's influence on Mark was considerable, as a translator Mark would have shaped Peter's testimony. Every translation is an interpretation. The close association between the apostle and John Mark suggests then that John Mark could have left some mark upon this letter given his presence with Peter. While the theology of the letter is Peter's, those with the apostle were in a position to provide input and, indeed, John Mark's presence may account for some parallels between the letter and the Gospel of Mark.

THE RECIPIENTS OF 1 PETER

Unlike the author of 1 Peter, the letter's recipients were not eyewitnesses of the life of Jesus, yet the author recognizes that they both love and believe in him (1:8). They had heard the gospel testimony of Jesus' sufferings and glories through messengers empowered by the Holy Spirit (1:12). Peter was not the person who brought them the gospel since he refers to their evangelists in the third person: "Those who brought you the good news by the Holy Spirit sent from heaven" (1:12). Peter was an itinerant minister (Gal 2:11; 1 Cor 9:5), but we have no early evidence from the New Testament that he carried out gospel work in Asia Minor. Later testimony indicates that he did indeed travel there, but these witnesses appear to base their conclusion on their reading of 1 Peter 1:1 and not on any independent tradition (Eusebius, *HE* 3.1.2; Jerome, *De vir. ill.* 1; Epiphanius 27.6.6[22]). While Peter may have traveled through this area at some point, nothing points to such a regional ministry before the composition of this letter.

As noted previously,[23] the recipients know Peter by name although they are located far from the place of the letter's composition. The Christian communities that first read and heard this letter resided north and west of the Taurus mountains in Asia Minor, a region known as Anatolia.[24] Peter addressed them by referring to their social situation and location. He writes to "the exiles of the Dispersion of Pontus, Galatia, Cappadocia, Asia, and Bithynia" (1:1b). These Roman provinces, as Elliott

---

21. While Elliott does not hold to Petrine authorship of the letter, he affirms that it was composed by a Petrine group after his death. He does, however, state that "the explicit reference in 1 Peter to Mark and Silvanus as intimate associates of Peter indicates that the letter originated not simply with one individual but with a group including Silvanus and Mark, with Peter as its leading figure" (*1 Peter*, 889).

22. Epiphanius, *The Panarion of Epiphanius of Salamis*, trans. Frank Williams (Leiden: Brill, 1994), 1.104.

23. See chapter 2.

24. Stephen Mitchell, *The Celts in Anatolia and the Impact of Roman Rule* (Oxford: Clarendon, 1993), 1, 5.

notes, cover 129,000 square miles,[25] an area populated by native Celts who lived under Roman rule.[26] Hort was the first to suggest that the list of provincial names indicate the route the messenger took when he circulated the letter among the Christian congregations in Asia Minor.[27] The provincial list reads as an ancient itinerary such as those found on mile markers (*miliaria*) along Roman roads.[28] Elliott adds that if the provincial list indeed indicates the route of the messenger we would have an explanation for the separation of Pontus and Bithynia, which were a joint province during this period. The messenger likely took ship on the Black Sea and put in at either the ports of Sinope or Amisus in Pontus.[29] Jobes objects, saying, "Although various proposals have been made, none seem able to describe an itinerary that both follows the list and is consistent with what is known of the network of roads in first-century Asia Minor."[30] However, the archaeological record shows that these provinces were laced with a system of major and minor roads, which would have made following this itinerary entirely possible.[31]

The Recipients' Ethnicity

The ethnicity of these scattered Christian communities is most likely Gentile, although there are reasons to believe they were Jewish. We know from Acts that the Pauline mission focused first upon the synagogues in the diaspora of Asia Minor (Acts 13:14; 14:1; 19:8; and so Apollos, 18:26). The mission was also directed to Gentile God-fearers and proselytes in the synagogue (13:16, 26, 43; 14:1) and then turned directly to the Gentiles (13:46–48; 14:27). The vigorous response of the Gentiles to the gospel should not obscure the fact that there were Jewish converts in the region. First Peter uses an abundance of titles for the Christian communities drawn from the Old Testament, which suggest that the recipients of this letter were primarily Jewish converts (for example, 2:9–10 draws from Isa 43:20–21; Exod 19:6; Hos 1:6, 9; 2:25). He expects them to understand references to the establishment of the covenant (1:2; cf. Exod 24:1–8) and Zion (2:6). Indeed, in the opening address they are identified as members of "the Dispersion" (1:2), a title ascribed to the Jewish community that

---

25. John H. Elliott, *1 Peter*, 84. Elliott argues also that the names are provinces and not regions (John H. Elliott, *A Home for the Homeless: A Sociological Exegesis of 1 Peter, Its Situation and Strategy* [Philadelphia: Fortress, 1981], 51).

26. Mitchell, *The Celts in Anatolia*, 19.

27. F. J. A. Hort, *The First Epistle of St. Peter 1:1–2:17* (London: Macmillan, 1898), 17, 157–84; Colin J. Hemer, "The Address of 1 Peter," *ExpTim* 89 (1977–1978) 239–43.

28. See examples in John H. Elliott, *1 Peter*, 86. Latin *miliaria* are cataloged in *CIL* XVII. On their use, see Lionel Casson, *Travel in the Ancient World* (Baltimore: Johns Hopkins University Press, 1994), 173–74.

29. John H. Elliott, *1 Peter*, 91.

30. Karen H. Jobes, *1 Peter* (Grand Rapids: Baker Academic, 2005), 66.

31. Mitchell, *The Celts in Anatolia*, 130–31, 268–69; Richard J. A. Talbert, ed., *Barrington Atlas of the Greek and Roman World* (Princeton: Princeton University Press, 2000), 62–67, 86–87.

resided outside of Palestine (John 7:35; Jas 1:1; Ps 147:2; 2 Mac 1:27; also of their place of residence as in Judith 5:19). These communities stand differentiated from those who are Gentiles (2:12; 4:3). The abundance of OT texts and allusions in the letter argues for an audience well versed in Jewish Scripture. Church Fathers said the recipients were Jewish converts (Eusebius, *HE* 3.1.2; 3.4.2), a position not without its support in contemporary literature on the letter. Witherington regards the recipients as Hellenized Jews who became Christians, while Liebengood says the epistle is a piece of Jewish restoration theology written to Jewish Christians.[32]

Despite the evidence that the communities to whom Peter writes were ethnically Jewish, certain indicators point more strongly to a predominantly Gentile audience. While the Jewish orientation of the letter cannot be denied, Schelkle rightly questions whether this suggests a Jewish author rather than Jewish readers.[33] When these readers came to Christ, Peter says, they were "ransomed from the futile ways inherited from your ancestors" (1:18). He describes their former way of life (ἀναστροφῆς) as "vain" (ματαίας), employing a term that often appears in both Jewish and Christian critiques of idolatry (LXX Lev 17:7; 2 Chr 11:15; Isa 2:20; Jer 2:5; 8:19; Sir 15:8; Acts 14:15; Eph 4:17). Moreover, they had once participated in "lawless idolatry" with the attendant vices of "licentiousness, passions, drunkenness, revels, [and] carousing" (4:3). Since they were participants in both the banquets and the idolatry of their communities, their contemporaries were "surprised that you no longer join them in the same excesses of dissipation" (4:4). Their shock is combined with considerable displeasure,[34] which we hear in the following observation that "they malign you" (βλασφημοῦντες). Although the Jewish community in Asia Minor may well have been Hellenized, we have no evidence that Hellenistic cultural influence extended to the point that they embraced idolatry. Peter urges that these believers "no longer join them" as they once had. They had ceased running with the crowd in unbridled immorality or "torrent of dissipation" or "debauchery."[35] In contrast, the extant epigraphical and textual evidence from the period demonstrates that the Jewish communities were recognized and distinct. Occasionally calls were made to let them practice their ancestral customs without hindrance.[36] In both the literature and inscriptions, Jews are associated with

---

32. Ben Witherington, *A Socio-Rhetorical Commentary on 1-2 Peter* (Downers Grove, IL: IVP Academic, 2007), 23–33; Kelly D. Liebengood, *The Eschatology of 1 Peter: Considering the Influence of Zechariah 9–14* (Cambridge: Cambridge University Press, 2014), 1–22. Witherington states that "The evidence we have, both literary and archaeological, suggests as well that Jews, perhaps particularly in Asia Minor, were well integrated into the social ethos of the region, having become quite Hellenized" (*Letters and Homilies for Hellenized Christians*, 25).

33. Karl H. Schelkle, *Die Petrusbriefe, Der Judasbrief* (Freiburg: Herder, 1961), 11–15.

34. Elliott notes that the verb ξενίζονται "in the passive voice . . . means 'to be surprised,' 'astonished,' or shocked at something because of its unusual or unexpected nature, with the possible overtone of anger and resentment" (*1 Peter*, 725; cf. 4:12).

35. Elliott, *1 Peter*, 726.

36. Levinskaya, *The Book of Acts in Its Diaspora Setting*, 137–52; Irina Levinskaya, "The Traces of Jewish Life in Asia Minor," in *Neues Testament und hellenistisch-jüdische Alltagskultur: Wechselseitige*

their synagogues and not the various cults of their non-Jewish contemporaries (for example, Acts 13:14; 14:1; 19:8).[37] In other words, it is highly unlikely that the readers of this letter were Jews who had engaged in the immorality and cult practices that characterized the Gentile community. Whatever their level of acculturation, it did not extend to adoption of their communities' religious practices as Jobes appears to suggest.[38]

The former life of these believers was one marked by "ignorance," most likely ignorance of the true God (1:14). The text points to a Gentile readership. At the same time, Peter describes their former "vain way of life" as inherited from their forebearers (1:18).[39] This would be an odd and unique way to describe their Jewish ancestry and its religious practices. Moreover, Peter utilizes the language of alienation to describe the recipients of the letter (πάροικος καὶ παρεπίδημος, alien and exile) and this may well mark them as proselytes to the Christian faith, as argued below. Becoming a proselyte suggests the abandonment of idolatry, separation from family and community, and adhesion to a new kinship community.[40] They had left the life-ways of the Gentile community and joined a new religiously oriented clan. While Peter differentiates the readers from the "Gentiles" (2:12; 4:3), in the NT the concept attached to the term broadened to refer to "non-Christians" rather than "non-Jews" (1 Cor 5:1; 12:2; 1 Thess 4:5; 3 John 7). In other words, the Christians identify with Israel and its history regardless of their ethnicity.[41] "Gentiles," then, are those who are over against the Christian community, those who are "aliens and exiles" (2:12).

The internal evidence from the letter strongly argues for a Gentile audience, although Elliott suggests that it was mixed—"some of Israelite roots and some of pagan

---

Wahrnehmungen: III. Internationales Symposium zum Corpus Judaeo-Hellenisticum Novi Testamenti, 21-24. Mai 2009, Leipzig, ed. Roland Deines, et al. (Tübingen: Mohr Siebeck, 2011), 347-57. Some texts indicate that non-Jews were sometimes confused about the identity of the Jewish God, even confusing him with Dionysos, Jupiter Sabazios. This confusion, however, did not exist among the Jews themselves (Sherman E. Johnson, "Sabaoth/Sabazios: A Curiosity in Ancient Religion" (1978) 97-103.

37. Armin Lange, "Jews in Ancient and Late Ancient Asia Minor between Acceptance and Rejection," *Journal of Ancient Judaism* 5 (2014) 225-26; Gerhard Langer, "Rabbinic References to Asia Minor," *Journal of Ancient Judaism* 5 (2014) 259-69. Jewish communities in Asia Minor were subject to anti-Semitism given their distinct religious practices (Lange, "Jews in Ancient and Late Ancient Asia Minor," 226-44).

38. Jobes, *1 Peter*, 24.

39. The term "designates the positive sense of values, traditions, and customs that are rooted in the past and transmitted by the fathers as a worthy heritage" (John H. Elliott, *1 Peter*, 370). See Diodorus Siculus *Hist*. 5.48.2: "and that we should nevertheless fail to cherish and maintain for the god the pious devotion which has been handed down to us from our fathers," and 15.74.5: "Dionysius the younger on his succession to the tyranny first gathered the populace in an assembly and urged them in appropriate words to maintain toward him the loyalty that passed to him with the heritage that he had received from his father" (cf. 15.74.5; 17.4.1).

40. Torrey Seland, "πάροικος καὶ παρεπίδημος: Proselyte Characterizations in 1 Peter?," *BBR* 11 (2001) 268.

41. *TDNT*, 2:371.

origin."[42] As attractive as this *via media* appears given the Jewish character of the letter and early engagement of the gospel with the Jewish community, the internal evidence of texts such as 4:3–4 appears to make a significant Jewish presence unlikely. Moreover, Pliny the Younger, the governor of Bithynia, wrote to the Emperor Trajan about the Christian problem in the province (10.96–97, written AD 112). The correspondence supposes that the Christians were Gentiles whom the governor wished to turn back to the temples and the ruler cult. Some had indeed abandoned the Christian faith: "It is certainly quite clear that the temples, which had been almost deserted, have begun to be frequented, that the established religious rites, long neglected, are being resumed, and that from everywhere sacrificial animals are coming, for which until now very few purchasers could be found." This kind of abandonment had been occurring for some time: "Others named by the informer declared that they were Christians, but then denied it, asserting that they had been but had ceased to be, some three years before, others many years, some as much as twenty-five years." This points to the strong presence of Gentile churches years prior to Pliny's correspondence. While we cannot open the window fully regarding the ethnic composition of the congregations in Peter's day, this later historical evidence is in line with what we observe within the letter. Peter's first readers were Gentiles who now find themselves identified with the ancient people of God (1 Pet 2:9–10). And in this identification they have become strangers and resident aliens in the communities where they previously participated and enjoyed full acceptance. They were "Christians" (4:16), those loathed because of their allegiance to Christ and their abandonment of the gods of family and community.

Strangers and Resident Aliens

What does their identification as strangers and resident aliens mean for Peter (1:1, 17; 2:11)? Is this a metaphor describing their alienation from the surrounding society due to their conversion or were the readers literal foreigners who became Christians? Elliott has championed the position that the letter's first readers were literally visiting foreigners and resident aliens who became Christians. He stresses the socio-political dimensions of being a foreigner but also recognizes that the language of alienation expresses "an additional religious-historical dimension of the condition of Christian estrangement in society."[43] In other words, the language takes on a metaphorical dimension although the recipients were non-citizens. As he says, "There is neither need nor reason to postulate mutually exclusive literal/figurative options here. As we have already seen, these words in 1 Peter are used to describe religious *as well as* social circumstances."[44] Elliott's work vividly highlights the sociological condition of early

---

42. John H. Elliott, *1 Peter*, 96.
43. John H. Elliott, *A Home for the Homeless*, 48.
44. John H. Elliott, *A Home for the Homeless*, 42. Goppelt was the first to explore the sociological reality of these Christian communities (Leonhard Goppelt, *A Commentary on 1 Peter* [Grand Rapids: Eerdmans, 1993]). The language of alienation marked their status in society and was not simply

Christians by outlining the precarious social situation of non-citizens throughout the Roman provinces. Being strangers and resident aliens "indicates that their political, legal, and social situation was a precarious one, similar to the multitude of the déclassé and homeless strangers, who lacked, or were deprived of, local citizenship and its privileges."[45] Elliott's studies have laid bare the tenuous position of the aliens in society, thus providing a valuable contribution to our understanding of these early Christians' social realities whether or not the readers were literal aliens or those who experienced the status of aliens upon becoming followers of the Christ.

Jobes suggests a variation of Elliott's thesis by arguing that the readers of 1 Peter "had become Christians elsewhere, had some association with Peter prior to his writing to them, and now found themselves foreigners and resident aliens scattered throughout Asia Minor."[46] Jobes points out that we have no evidence of evangelization of the northern regions of Asia Minor where Peter's churches were located. On the other hand, we know that the emperor Claudius vigorously colonized Asia Minor using those who were foreigners residing in Rome. Those deported would have had the social status of aliens in the places where they were relocated. The recipients of 1 Peter were Christian deportees who were somehow within Peter's sphere of influence.[47]

While Jobes effectively shows that deportations and colonization were a grim reality during Claudius's reign (see Acts 18:1–2), her argument suffers for lack of evidence that those displaced were Christians or that the gospel in northern Asia Minor ran along these lines of displacement and colonization. Her suggestion that Peter had some association with these displaced people given his residency in Rome is a tack that does not jibe with Peter's own statement in 1 Peter 1:12 that he had not evangelized them. He talks about "the things that have now been announced to you through those who brought you good news by the Holy Spirit sent from heaven," thereby distancing himself from the readers. Others had brought them the gospel. The distance between Peter, an eyewitness of the Christ, and the first readers is suggested in 1:8: "Although you have not seen him, you love him; and even though you do not see him now, you believe in him and rejoice with an indescribable and glorious joy." The contrast with Peter is striking since in 5:1 he identifies himself as "a witness of the sufferings of Christ." While the distance/proximity theme wraps around seeing Jesus, it also points up the author's attempt to close the gap between himself and his distant readers (cf.

---

theological.

45. John H. Elliott, *1 Peter*, 94. Elliott goes on to note that "*Paroikoi*, 'by-dwellers,' were distinguished legally from complete strangers (*xenoi*) and belonged to an institutionalized class ranked socially below the citizen population and above freed-persons, slaves and complete strangers.... In addition to natives dispossessed of their lands which were annexed to expanding cities, this group included strangers from abroad (tradespersons, artisans, teachers, and travelling missionaries) who had taken up residence for more than thirty days."

46. Jobes, *1 Peter*, 26.

47. Jobes, *1 Peter*, 25–41.

1:1; 5:13). Jobes's thesis remains no more than a hypothesis that does not provide a more plausible explanation of the readers' identification than Elliott's argument.

A more fruitful analysis comes from Seland, who demonstrates that the language of alienation was an indicator that society regarded the readers as proselytes. The terms πάροικος (resident foreigner) and παρεπίδημος (sojourner or one who resides temporarily in a foreign place), he says, should be read as metaphors that draw upon the Jewish institution of proselytism. Given the use of the terms, Seland argues that they "should be considered not just to denote strangers but in some cases to be related to what we may call proselytes." He lays out how these lexemes, as used in 1 Peter, connect with the conceptual world of proselytism, which included "leaving polytheism for monotheism, leaving one's country, family, and kinfolk, becoming enemies of families and friends at the risk of one's own life, and entering a community of fictive kinship and brotherly love."[48] Seland points out that the Hebrew גר (gar) denotes a "'stranger,' 'sojourner,' or 'alien'" and that those such as Abraham and Israel are regarded as having this status (LXX Gen 23:4; Exod 22:21; 23:9; Lev 25:23; Deut 10:19; Ps 39:12; 119:19). Surprisingly, the LXX alternates between rendering גר (gar) as either πάροικος (paroikos, resident alien) or προσήλυτος (proselutos; proselyte; see for example, Exod 12:48–49; 20:10; 22:20; 23:9, 12). Philo likewise depicts Abraham as a model proselyte and places the "alien" and "proselyte" within the same conceptual frame.[49] Applying this linguistic insight to 1 Peter, Seland concludes that "the recipients [of 1 Peter] were not παρεπίδημοι before they became Christians but entered this state upon their conversion."[50] They were regarded as aliens in the communities where they once had complete solidarity.

Seland's conclusion is consistent with the internal evidence from 1 Peter. The readers' alien status in society is linked with their new commitment to Christ. Peter ties their social status with their election ("To the exiles of the Dispersion ... who have been chosen and destined by God the Father" [1:1]). Previously they were full participants in their social networks but are now alienated from them due to their conversion (4:2–3). Since they have given up their previous lifestyle marked by "licentiousness, passions, drunkenness, revels, carousing, and lawless idolatry," Peter urges them "as aliens and exiles to abstain from the desires of the flesh that wage war against the soul" (2:11). The following verse identifies them over against their contemporaries, the non-Christian "Gentiles" (2:12), those among whom they had

---

48. Seland, "πάροικος καὶ παρεπίδημος," 268.

49. Seland, "πάροικος καὶ παρεπίδημος," 249–56. "Philo describes Abraham as a proselyte.... Philo's conclusion runs thus (*Virt.* 219): he is the standard of nobility for all proselytes ... who abandoning the ignobility of strange laws and monstrous customs which assigned the divine honors to stocks and stones and soulless things in general, have come to settle in a better land, in a commonwealth full of true life and vitality, with truth as its director and president" ("πάροικος καὶ παρεπίδημος," 255).

50. Seland, "πάροικος καὶ παρεπίδημος," 257. Horrell affirms Seland's findings and concludes, "As such, *pace* Elliott, the terms describe not the addressees' socio-legal status *prior* to conversion, but their socio-spiritual status *consequent* on their conversion" (Horrell, *Becoming Christian*, 118).

previously engaged in the full gamut of Gentile sin ("You have already spent enough time in doing what the Gentiles like to do" [4:2]). Their social position was as proselytes to Judaism who experienced alienation from their society. Indeed, Peter directs the conceptual understanding of "aliens and exiles" in 2:11 by using the term "as" (ὡς, hōs), which, as Achtemeier reminds us, is "a particle regularly used in 1 Peter to identify a metaphorical word or phrase" (2:2, 5).[51] Seland offers a linguistic insight into a well-known model of religious conversion. Those who became proselytes belonged to a new community but were alienated from their former community. The social alienation Peter's readers experienced was due to their new status as "Christians," those denigrated by the rest of society (1 Pet 4:16).

Peter's readers were recent converts. The break with the life-ways of the rest in their communities brought them into tense conflicts, which were not a distant memory but were a present and real danger (4:1–4). Peter reminds them of their evangelization (1:12), their recent obedience to the gospel message (1:14, 22), their baptism (3:21) and new birth (1:3), and their present existence, which is like that of "newborn infants" who need milk (2:2). Although young in the faith, their communities were in existence long enough to have established leadership (5:1–5) and liturgical traditions such as the holy kiss (5:14).[52] They had God's gifts of grace, which were in use in these new communities (4:10–11).

The Social Orders and the Recipients' Situation

The readers' social status ranged from low to high. Some were slaves (2:18–25), a group large enough in the congregations to receive special attention in the apostle's instruction. Peter does not direct teaching directly at masters but, as Best reminds us, "We dare not assume that there were not masters in the congregation since 2:13–17 is directed to free men who may possibly have had civic duties."[53] The free persons paid tribute (2:17), marking them as persons of means. The exhortation to wives (3:1–6) indicates that a significant number of women were wealthy (especially 3:4). The ages

---

51. Achtemeier, *1 Peter*, 56. Achtemeier traces the language back to figures like Abraham and David, who were aliens in the land God promised (Gen 15:13; 23:4; Ps 39:12; 105:12). "The phrase is therefore not descriptive of the secular political status of the readers, whether before or after their conversion. Rather, the language is chosen once again under the influence of the controlling metaphor of Israel to describe the status of Christians within the world they inhabit. That is not to deny that their religious status as 'exiles and aliens' had social or political ramifications. The suffering they underwent is ample testimony to that fact. It is to affirm, however, that the choice of the terminology grew not from the political vocabulary of the Greco-Roman world but rather from the language of Israel, whose faith and history functioned as the controlling metaphor for the Christian community" (*1 Peter*, 71).

52. Best, *1 Peter*, 19.

53. Best, *1 Peter*, 17. Selwyn (*The First Epistle of Peter*, 49) remarks that the revelries alluded to in 4:2–4 had a significant cost and were "not indulged in for nothing."

of the congregants varied between the young and the old, whatever leadership positions the people addressed in 5:1–5 might have held.[54]

The readers were embedded in established social orders but these did not protect them from the onslaught caused by their conversion to Christ and disengagement from former religious and social life-ways. The social situation of the epistle's first readers was precarious.[55] Christians were now on the margins and became subject to an array of hostile attacks.[56] The persecutions they endured were the common lot of Christians throughout the inhabited world where the gospel had reached (5:9). While the readers suffered "for the name of Christ" (4:14, 16), they do not appear to have been driven by the state. Indeed, the sufferings which Jesus' disciples endured were similarly described from the beginning (Acts 5:41; 9:16; Matt 5:11–12). The persecutions took instead the form of spasmodic social pressure against this non-conforming group. Christians were maligned as evildoers (2:12; 3:16),[57] verbally abused (3:9), blasphemed (4:4), and reviled (4:14). Their contemporaries could call them to account for their faith at any time (3:15–16). When they broke with traditional life-ways, the rest of society rejected them (4:3–4; cf. 2:18, 14). The pressures they faced were extremely acute for slaves and women since they were lived as socially subordinate to their masters and husbands (2:18—3:6). Relations with the governing authorities are not described as tense or strained but could be a potential source of adversity (2:13–17; 4:15). As Williams says, "We must not underestimate the possible threat which governing officials posed to the Anatolian congregations. Because the judicial system of Roman Asia Minor was set in motion by the private accusations of local inhabitants, the general hostility and harassment faced by Christian assemblies could have turned into legal accusations at any moment and with relative ease."[58] Peter endorses peace by giving due honor to everyone in society, especially the supreme authority in the empire (2:17; cf. Prov 24:21; Sir 10:24). Peter calls the readers to engage in honorable social behavior within the extant structures of superordination and subordination (2:13–17).[59]

While the persecutions manifested themselves principally as verbal abuse and social rejection (2:15), in some cases the hostility could overflow and become physical

---

54. See the discussion in Achtemeier, *1 Peter*, 321.

55. On the persecutions Peter's readers faced, see Travis B. Williams, *Persecution in 1 Peter: Differentiating and Contextualizing Early Christian Suffering* (Leiden: Brill, 2012). Williams seeks to frame their suffering "by situating the letter against the backdrop of conflict management in first-century CE Asia Minor" (*Persecution in 1 Peter*, 327).

56. On the persecutions these believers faced, see Edwin Gordon Selwyn, "The Persecutions in 1 Peter," *BSNTS* 1 (1950) 39–50; F. V. Filson, "Partakers with Christ: Suffering in First Peter," *Int* 9 (1959) 400–412; Helmut Millauer, *Leiden als Gnade: Eine traditionsgeschichtliche Untersuchung zur Leidenstheologie des ersten Petrusbriefes* (Frankfurt: Lang, 1976); Williams, *Persecution in 1 Peter*.

57. In 3:16 some mss. add ὑμῶν ὡς κακοποιῶν (א A C K P 049 33 81) to harmonize with 2:12.

58. Williams, *Persecution in 1 Peter*, 330.

59. "Being subordinate is thus explained as a means of showing honor and thereby demonstrating a respect for social order and conventional roles so as to allay any suspicion of Christian disruptive social behavior" (John H. Elliott, *1 Peter*, 501).

(2:20; 4:1; and likely 3:6). This social ostracism brought them profound grief (1:6; 2:19) and fear (3:6, 14). They were bewildered why their faith should meet with such opposition (4:12). Anxiety due to the instability of their situation gnawed at them (5:7). Their reaction to the verbal and physical hostility was that some had become ashamed of their faith (4:16, where the present imperative with μὴ [*mē*] implies that what is already occurring should be stopped). In order to regain honor, retaliation would be a socially expected course of action, one which Peter does not sanction (3:9; cf. 2:23).[60] They were also in danger of turning back to a more socially acceptable lifestyle to relieve these tensions (4:2–3; 1:14; cf. Matt 5:38–41). This was, in fact, the design of their adversary, the devil (5:8–9). Apostasy from the faith knocked at the door.[61]

This is the readers' problem that 1 Peter addresses. The author's antidote is to tell these Christians in northern Asia Minor about the true grace of God and exhort them to stand in it (5:12). Peter directs them how to maintain proper conduct as Christians within a hostile society. Peter frames his practical exhortation, however, within the wide arc of God's plan and their place within it.

---

60. Epstein notes that a humiliated Roman's prestige would suffer "if he showed himself reluctant to respond and retaliate for hostile acts" (David F. Epstein, *Personal Enmity in Roman Politics 218–43 BC* [London: Routledge, 1987], 2). deSilva adds, "The honorable person subjected to insult or to some other challenge to honor is culturally conditioned to retaliate, Christians confronted with such attacks on their honor as verbal challenges, reproachful speech and even physical affronts would be sorely tempted to respond in kind, playing out the challenge-riposte game before onlookers." Christians were called to respond with honorable behavior. Peter's approach, as Jesus', is akin to Plutarch's advice: "'How shall I defend myself against my enemy?' 'By proving yourself good and honorable'" (*Mor.* 88B; 89D-E; 1 Pet 2:12, 15; 3:16) (David A. deSilva, *Honor, Patronage, Kinship and Purity: Unlocking New Testament Culture* [Downers Grove, IL: InterVarsity, 2000], 70–71;).

61. See I. Howard Marshall, *Kept by the Power of God* (Minneapolis: Bethany Fellowship, 1969), 158–71.

CHAPTER 8

The Theology of Peter in 1 Peter

In the midst of their agonizing social rejection, Peter reminds his readers of their participation within the over-arching plan of God. He responds to their precarious situation by counseling a social strategy designed to attenuate the threats against them, but he frames that strategy within a robust understanding of God's person and purpose.[1] This is the heart of 1 Peter's theology. Some years ago Russell pointed to the centrality of Peter's theology proper, saying, "The *foundational principle* is the nature

---

1. While Williams (*Persecution in 1 Peter*) does an admirable job of placing the persecutions of the believers within the social and political forces and norms of Asia Minor, he does not address the intimate relationship between the theology of the letter and the social ethic Peter prescribes. Goppelt's seminal socio-theological analysis of both the reader's situation and the apostle's response offers a more holistic and faithful analysis (Goppelt, *A Commentary on 1 Peter*, 37–45). Although not a robust theological treatment of the situation of Peter's readers and the letter's response, Elliott at least recognizes that "all social and socioreligious movements, including the literature which they produce, involve implicit or explicit ideological perspectives and strategies." By "ideology" he means "'an integrated system of beliefs, assumptions and values, not necessarily true or false, which reflects the needs and interests of a group or class at a particular time in history.'" (John H. Elliott, *The Elect and the Holy: An Exegetical Examination of 1 Peter 2:4–10 and the Phrase βασίλειον ἱεράτευμα* [Leiden: Brill, 1966], 268, citing David Brion Davis, *The Problem of Slavery in the Age of Revolution 1770–1823* [Ithaca: Cornell University Press, 1975], 14). In his commentary on the epistle, Elliott addresses the letter's theology saying, "Since 1 Peter is not a theological treatise but a particular message of encouragement for a particular situation, its theological concepts are not easily isolable but are interwoven into one coherent line of thought" (*1 Peter*, 109). But put another way, Peter's theology is inclusive of his social ethic and strategy. Theology and ethics cannot be drawn asunder. Elliott falls short of recognizing that the indicative and the imperative, theology and ethics, are both parts of the overarching plan of God. Peter's ethic is distinctly theological (Gene L. Green, "Theology and Ethics in 1 Peter" [PhD diss., University of Aberdeen, 1979]).

of God. The statement, 'you shall be holy, for I am holy' (1:15–16), and its explication through the revelation of Christ provide the pivot of the letter's entire theology."[2] Beare likewise remarked that the writer's thought is theocentric.[3] God is the Creator (4:19), Father (1:2, 3, 17), and Judge (1:17). He is living and abiding (1:23), holy (1:15–16), merciful (1:3), gracious (5:10), patient (3:10), trustworthy (4:19), and caring (5:7). Everything Peter says about God is the raw material for a treatise on the nature of God since there are few verses in the letter where God is not mentioned directly or indirectly.

However, the author's purpose is not to present a philosophical discourse on the nature of God, setting his character against current conceptions and misconceptions (cf. Cicero, *De Natura Deorum*). Rather, his concern centers on those theological frames that will encourage and establish his readers in their adversity. Peter's theology focuses on the transcendent *activity* of the living God. He is the God who acts, and because he acts in favor of his people, they can have hope (1:3, 13, 21). Peter understands this activity as a wide and transcendent arc that runs from creation to final consummation. Given this, Peter urges his readers to see the present travails within the wider frame of God's plan and purpose.

THE PLAN OF GOD
Future and Present

Peter first lifts his reader's eyes beyond their present situation by orienting them to the soon-coming final consummation: "The end of all things is near" (4:7). Selwyn noted some years ago that "there is no book in the New Testament where the eschatology is more closely integrated with the teaching of the document as a whole."[4] From the outset the epistle looks to the end of things—God gives Christians a living hope, an imperishable inheritance, and a final salvation (1:3–5). The sufferings these believers endure are compared with the past sufferings of Christ, but Peter contrasts them with the final eschatological glory that God will reveal, the sign of his vindication of the righteous (1:7, 21; 4:13; 5:1, 10). These resident aliens must place their hope on the grace that will be brought to them at the revelation of Christ (1:13), the time when God will grant crowns of glorious honor to his faithful servants (5:4).[5] The end is already near in Peter's view (4:7) since Christ "stands ready to judge the living and the dead" (4:5). But the apostle also reminds the readers that the end is not yet.

2. Ronald Russell, "Eschatology and Ethics in 1 Peter," *EQ* 47 (1975) 83.

3. Francis Wright Beare, *The First Epistle of Peter* (Oxford: Basil Blackwell, 1970), 52. So Selwyn (*The First Epistle of Peter*, 75); Martin Andrew Chester and Ralph Martin (*The Theology of the Letters of James, Peter, and Jude* [Cambridge: Cambridge University Press, 1994], 104); and Davids (*A Theology of James, Peter, and Jude*, [Grand Rapids: Zondervan, 2015], 157), who says, "It is clear that the core category in 1 Peter is God, for all of the teaching in the letter is related to God in one way or another."

4. Edward G. Selwyn, "Eschatology in 1 Peter," in *The Background of the New Testament and Its Eschatology*, ed. W. D. Davies and David Daube (Cambridge: Cambridge University Press, 1964), 394.

5. Alan Hugh McNeile, *New Testament Teaching in Light of St. Paul's* (Cambridge: Cambridge University Press, 1923), 149.

Though still coming, Peter observes that the eschatological hope is already being realized, though it has not fully broken into the present age. The eschatology Peter lays out includes the death, resurrection, presence, and return of Christ, thus embracing a truly realized eschatology. The early church "merged into one divine event all of history as it had become meaningful in all the work of Christ."[6] Peter weaves future and present into a high thread-count fabric. In 1:19–20 he affirms that Christ's redemptive sacrifice occurred at "the end of the ages."[7] Christ's sufferings are the present fulfillment of the hope of grace predicted by the prophets (1:10–11). Peter uses the lexeme "now" (νῦν) to signal that the time of fulfillment is the present (1:12; 2:10; 3:21). God's promised grace has come, but the present is also the time when final judgment begins (4:17). Despite the sufferings Christians endure, the present is the time when they experience the joy of the eschaton (1:6, 8; 4:13). Christ will indeed be revealed in the future (1:13), but he already reigns as the sovereign over all (3:22). Although the end is near, Peter's perspective is that it has already broken into the present (4:7). Commenting on the perfect tense of the verb ἤγγικεν ("has drawn near"), Achtemeier says it "emphasizes not so much the mere approach of the end as its presence in the end time events that are already underway (e.g., 4:17), pointing to the immanence of the consummation."[8] The future event already infuses the present. The future is not a distant hope but rather something that has begun to be realized in the present age.[9]

Peter's eschatology is both future and realized in the present. The poles are in tension from the standpoint of one who lives between the times. He holds the future hope of an inheritance and full salvation that will come at the unveiling of Christ in the last time (1:3–5, 13). Yet Christ has already been revealed in the incarnation, inaugurating the end of times (1:20). The salvation that God has wrought in Christ is a future anticipation (1:5), yet it is even now a present reality in which believers participate (3:21; 1:10–12). A final judgment awaits both the living and the dead (4:5), yet that judgment has already begun in the suffering that the saints endure (4:17). In Peter's view, the judgment for unbelievers has begun as well (2:8). Despite the social

---

6. Julian Price Love, *The First, Second, and Third Letters of John; The Letter of Jude; the Revelation to John* (Richmond: John Knox, 1960), 82. Love's opinion is that "the early church did not long tarry with any literal expectancy of the visible coming of the Lord." But this is clearly not Peter's perspective despite the realized aspects of his eschatology.

7. C. H. Dodd, *The Apostolic Preaching and Its Developments* (London: Hodder & Stoughton, 1944), 44–46.

8. Achtemeier, *1 Peter*, 294. In 4:7, ἤγγικεν does not simply mean "has begun," as Selwyn argued (*The First Epistle of Peter*, 111; C. H. Dodd, *The Parables of the Kingdom* [New York: Scribner's Sons, 1961], 44–45). It may suggest the concept that something "come nearer to a place than before but has not yet reached it" (Werner Georg Kümmel, *Promise and Fulfilment: The Eschatological Message of Jesus* [London: SCM, 1957], 19–21; Oscar Cullmann, *Salvation in History* [London: SCM, 1967], 199; John H. Elliott, *1 Peter*, 745). But the perfect embraces the concept of some form of inauguration, as Jobes notes. Peter's readers "are living in the last stage of God's great redemptive plan, and the goal of that plan is being realized" (Jobes, *1 Peter*, 275; cf. Matt 3:2; 4:17; 10:7; Mark 1:15; Luke 10:11; 21:8).

9. Robert F. Berkey, "*Eggizein, Phthanein*, and Realized Eschatology," *JBL* 82 (1963) 177–87.

ostracism and physical abuse these Christians faced, they currently rejoice with the very joy that will characterize the final age (1:6, 8; 4:13). The glory and honor of the final age is experienced now amidst the social dishonor the community endures (1:8; 4:14; 1:7; 4:13). Future and present are separate yet bound together in Peter's thought. The end begins to break into the present and with that comes the palpable promise of a final and glorious consummation. Peter's weave of time and God's activity in history are not simply linear or circular. Rather, the present is embedded with the past and the future.[10] Peter is not concerned with the way the community marks time but with how past, future, and present intersect.[11]

Peter binds together the present and future, but the future does not fully collapse into the present. The tension between them remains, yet the final resolve is quite near according to Peter's calculation. Peter reminds his readers that their sufferings are just "for a little while" (1:6). After they "have suffered for a little while," God will establish them firmly (5:10). "The end of all things," he says, "is near" (4:7). The Judge already stands ready for the final tribunal (4:5). On the other hand, the last-day salvation is prepared and "ready to be revealed in the last time" (1:5).[12] Although "the time has come for judgement to begin with the household of God" (4:17), that beginning is not the full end. Christians set all their hope "on the grace that Jesus Christ will bring you when he is revealed" (1:13). They anticipate that time when "the chief shepherd appears" from whom these persecuted believers "will win the crown of glory that never fades away" (5:4; cf. 1:7; 4:13; 5:1). The revelation of Christ and the final consummation of all things is imminent. The present time is "the end of the ages" (1:20) since Christ, who will be revealed (1:13; 5:4), has been revealed. As Elliott observes, "The initial (1:19, 20b) and final (5.4; cf. 1:7; 5:1) appearances of Jesus Christ mark the boundaries of the end time."[13]

Hope operates within the tension between future and present (1:3, 13, 21). Adversity besets the readers of this epistle, but they need not despair. Full deliverance is near at hand, and God has set forth Christ as a surety of their final salvation (1:21; 3:18–22). Even amidst unjust suffering, these Christians can commit themselves to the faithfulness of God just as Christ had (4:19; 2:24).

---

10. See, for example, Milič Čapek, ed., *The Concepts of Space and Time: Their Structure and Their Development* (Boston: Reidel, 1976).

11. On the history of marking time, see Samuel L Macey, "The Concept of Time in Ancient Rome," *International Social Science Review* 65 (1990) 72–79.

12. The expectation regarding the end stands in tension with the delay of the promised advent of Christ. For a recent discussion of the purpose of eschatology in relationship to Christian living and existence in the world, see Christopher M. Hays, et al., *When the Son of Man Didn't Come: A Constructive Proposal on the Delay of the Parousia* (Minneapolis: Fortress, 2016).

13. John H. Elliott, *1 Peter*, 377.

Past and Present

The center of Peter's theology in the epistle is the transcendent activity of the Living God. Peter sees this activity as both present and future, "already" and "not yet," with the future currently breaking into the present and the final consummation coming right soon. But the present and future are also linked with the past. Peter looks back to God's agency πρὸ καταβολῆς κόσμου ("before the foundation of the world" [1:20a]; cf. Matt 25:34; Luke 11:50; John 17:24; Eph 1:4; Heb 4:3; 9:26; Rev 13:8; 17:8; *Test. Mos.* 1:14; *Odes Sol.* 41:15), a time connected with the "end of the ages," which has already come in the present with the incarnation of Christ (1:20b). This "combination . . . circumscribes the entire scope of world history from start to close."[14] God, the Creator, so ordained and executed his plan with Christ at the very center since his is the one so foreordained and now revealed. Peter's arc is large and embraces the whole of God's saving history.[15]

God's redemptive activity before creation centered on Christ and his sacrifice (1:19–20) and embraces those who would be its beneficiaries (δι' ὑμᾶς, "for your sake"). To speak of God's redemptive activity before creation is to assert that his providence is independent, thus making the whole redemptive work dependent upon him alone and rooted solely in his nature. The lexeme προεγνωσμένου includes the idea of prescience ("foreknown") but here communicates the concept of foreordination ("destined," NRSV).[16] Peter's thought is similar to the statement in the Petrine speech in Acts 2:23: "This man [Jesus of Nazareth], handed over to you according to the definite plan and foreknowledge of God, you crucified and killed by the hands of those outside the law." God's redemptive plan for these Christians in Asia Minor is not based on any temporal contingency. His care for their eternal welfare is sure, despite what adverse circumstances say to them.

God's past activity links with the present through his election. He chooses his own, those called the "elect" or "chosen" (1:1; 2:9; 5:13), according to his determinate plan expressed as his foreknowledge (ἐκλεκτοῖς . . . κατὰ πρόγνωσιν θεοῦ πατρὸς [1:1–2]), a plan laid down before creation (1:20). Christ, as these Christians, is known as the Elect One (2:4, 6). Election is a "controlling concept" in the book,[17] which "turn[s] their attention away from their historical antecedents to the true cause of their new life in the Christian Church, which was the Will of God."[18] God's plan for

---

14. John H. Elliott, *1 Peter*, 376.

15. While we may speak of "salvation history" in Peter's thought (Cullmann, *Salvation in History*), Peter does not separate the planes between God's saving history and the course of the history of the world. God works within that history that began with his creation (implied in 1:20). See the discussion on past, present, and future in Achtemeier, *1 Peter*, 68–69; Joel B. Green, *1 Peter* (Grand Rapids: Eerdmans, 2007), 36–47.

16. The NIV's rendering "chosen" is unwarranted in its introduction of the idea of election. The focus is upon God's plan and execution of that plan.

17. *TDNT*, 4:190.

18. Edwin Gordon Selwyn, *The First Epistle of Peter*, 66.

Christ and the Christians found expression through the promises given through the prophets that are now fulfilled and proclaimed (1:10–12). In Peter's view both Christ and the believers are the fulfillment of the OT promises and hopes (ὑμῖν). The subject of the prophets' testimony in advance (προμαρτυρόμενος) and their inquiry was the sufferings and glory of Christ. But the benefits accrue to the saints in the present time (1:12). God's eternal plan centers in Christ and brought to realization in the lives of the letter's recipients.

God's plan laid out before history and realized in the present is also linked with his past historical activity. The community of believers stands in an organic relationship with the prophets, who predicted the grace that would be brought to them (ὑμῖν δὲ διηκόνουν αὐτά [1:12]), that is, God ministered to the church through the prophets. Peter does not simply speak of the fulfillment of a promise but the completion of a process rooted in God's plan before creation. He links historical past with the present. For example, the Christian community is the people of God with whom God makes his new covenant (1:2; cf. Exod 24:1–8). As such they are bound with the people of God in the past. They have a promised inheritance as had his people in the past (1:4; cf. Deut 15:4; Ps 16:5; Dan 12:13). The OT is for them (1:10–12, 24, 25, etc.), and they now are the elect (1:1; cf. Gen 23:4; Lev 25:23) and heirs of the titles given to Israel: "But you are a chosen race, a royal priesthood, a holy nation, God's own people" (2:9; cf. Exod 19:5–6; Isa 43:20–21). Unlike Paul, Peter does not struggle with the question of the relationship between Jew and Gentile in God's plan (cf. Rom 9–11). For him, there is only one people of God.

This organic relationship with the past appears in his discussion of ancient women who hoped in God (3:5–6). Faithful women are now Sarah's daughters. Similarly, Peter links Noah and the seven who entered the arc for salvation with those who now pass through the waters of baptism. Those in the past are saved from cataclysmic judgment as are these baptized believers (3:20–21). The "one and the same God is at work in history, bringing the same purpose even fuller realization in the succession of personages and events," remarks Kelly.[19] The OT process continues into the present. Past and present coalesce.

In Peter's view, the central focus of God's plan is Christ. The preexistent and predetermined Christ is the agent of God's salvation for these believers (1:20). He is the living and elect Stone (2:4), and he defines the existence of the believers who are living stones (2:5, 9).[20] His sufferings and subsequent glorification were the subject of the prophetic hope and inquiry (1:10–11), and people's response to him is determinate for people's eternal destiny (2:6–8).

---

19. J. N. D. Kelly, *A Commentary on the Epistles of Peter and Jude* (Grand Rapids: Baker, 1969), 161.

20. "The Old Testament interpretive constant, 'the election of the people of Israel,' remains, of course, the constant for the New Testament as well. But now it becomes the election of one person. Towards this election the whole election of the people of Israel trends, and from it the whole election of the New Israel proceeds" (Cullmann, *Salvation in History*, 100).

The cross and resurrection of Christ serve as the hub of God's plan in Christ, and Peter's epistle is therefore replete with references to these conjoined events (1:2–3, 11, 18–21; 2:21–25; 3:18–22; 4:1, 6, 13; 5:1; and implied in 2:4–8; 3:15–16; 4:11; 5:10, 14). Peter underscores the magnitude of these events by noting that he is a witness and participant in them (5:1; and implied in 1:8). God's saving activity becomes most clear in the sufferings of Christ on the cross, his resurrection, and his exaltation to the right hand of God (3:22). If the community is to make sense of the intersection of God's plan for them and their present adversity, they must do so in light of the Christ event. God's whole redemptive plan is brought to its climax here. Peter speaks of the prophetic witness to "the glories" of Christ (τὰς ... δόξας [1:11]), which include his resurrection (1:21), his exaltation and rule over all (3:22), and his final revelation, the time when he endows his saints with the honor he has received (1:7; 4:13; 5:1, 10). His glorification is meant to inspire faith and hope in God (1:21).

Put another way, the will of God and his plan are part of an eternal, historic, and ongoing plan of God centered in Christ, and he catches up the church into that plan. Peter's theological vision is not simply past and future but also vividly present, tied to all that God has and will do. The letter stresses the will of God, which directs their present circumstances (2:15; 3:17; 4:2, 19). The repeated ὑμῖν ("for you") and related phrases show these believers that they participate in that plan (1:10, 12, 15, 20, 25; 2:5, 7, 9). "Now" (νῦν) is the time of God's saving work for them (1:12; 2:10; 3:21). The present connects with the past. Past is more than memory; it becomes present in their lives amidst adversity. So, too, what God is doing now is part of one whole with the future blessings of God. For example, future and present salvation are inextricably bound together (1:5, 9, 10–12; 3:21), as are present and future judgment (4:5, 17–18). They can, at present, stand in God's grace (5:5, 10), the very grace that will be brought to them in the future revelation of Christ (1:13). Present praise to God will continue through eternity (1:3; 2:5; 4:11) as will the joy of the saints as well (1:6, 8; 4:13). Peter's understanding of God's work in time is holistic and organic rather than being segmented and separated. Past and future penetrate the present in God's plan.

An integral part of God's overarching plan is the reality of suffering and vindication. Though Christ suffered unjustly, God's vindication came through his resurrection and exaltation (1:11; 2:21–24; 3:18–22). God's plan through Christ's sufferings and glorification becomes the model for the believers, whose sufferings and glorification are bound organically with his (4:13; 5:1). They, as he, suffer unjustly (2:12, 15, 19–20; 3:16; 4:14–16, 19), and they will be exalted as he was (1:7; 5:1, 6, 10).

God is the director of history, the sphere of his saving word. His plan is eternal and will be carried on until completion. The plan centers in Christ and catches up into it those to whom Peter writes, the elect saints. Amidst all their adversity, they can have hope since God is faithful in working out his plan. The surety God has given them is the resurrection of Christ (1:21). As he was vindicated so also will be God's elect people. The true grace of God in which they are to stand (5:12) is the salvation of God, the outworking of his plan in history (1:10, 13).

The New Exodus

As noted previously in the study of Mark and the Peter's speeches in Acts, the New Exodus appears to be a prominent theme in Petrine theology, and 1 Peter is no exception. The letter adds texture to this dimension of his theology.[21] The New Exodus themes found in Isaiah include, according to Anderson, "the promises to the fathers," "the deliverance from Egypt," "the journey through the wilderness," and "the re-entry into the Promised Land."[22] Watts isolates three main features of the New Exodus theology: "(A) Yahweh's *deliverance* of his exiled people from the power of Babylon and her idols, (B) a *journey* along the 'way' in which Yahweh leads his people from their exile to Jerusalem, and (C) *arrival* in Jerusalem where Yahweh is enthroned in a gloriously restored Zion."[23] Pao presents four principle themes of the New Exodus as developed in Acts: "The restoration of Israel, the word of God, the anti-idol polemic, and the salvation offered to the nations/Gentiles," noting that "the restoration of Israel is the foundational one upon which the other three can be developed."[24] The New Exodus themes are prominent within Peter's epistle, coupled with abundant references to the first Exodus.

Many of the epistle's allusions to the Old Testament find their roots in the Exodus of Israel out of Egypt, which anticipated Isaiah's New Exodus. God's deliverance is central to Peter's theology. Neither Moses nor the Exodus/New Exodus are mentioned directly, but from the epistle's opening lines, the imagery is present. In 1:18–19 Peter states that the community has been redeemed from their former futile way of life. While the language of redemption (ἐλυτρώθητε) has various Old Testament antecedents, such as the redemption of property (Lev 25, 27), the payment for a fault committed (Exod 21:30), the ransom of the firstborn (Num 3:44–51), or the half-shekel paid by every Israelite (Exod 30:12–16),[25] Peter most likely has in mind Israel's redemption from Egypt (Exod 6:6; cf. Acts 7:35). The reference to the lamb "without defect or

---

21. See, for example, Paul L. Deterding, "Exodus Motifs in 1 Peter," *Concordia Journal* 7 (1981) 58–65; Eric James Gréaux, "'To the Elect Exiles of the Dispersion . . . from Babylon': The Function of the Old Testament in 1 Peter" (PhD diss., Duke University, 2003); Kenny Ke-Chung Lai, "The Holy Spirit in 1 Peter: A Study of Petrine Pneumatology in Light of the Isaianic New Exodus" (PhD diss., Dallas Theological Seminary, 2009); Patrick T. Egan, "'This Word Is the Gospel Preached to You': Ecclesiology and the Isaianic Narrative in 1 Peter" (PhD diss., University of St. Andrews, 2011).

22. Bernhard W. Anderson, "Exodus Typology in Second Isaiah," in *Israel's Prophetic Heritage: Essays in Honor of James Muilenburg*, ed. Bernhard W. Anderson and Walter Harrelson (New York: Harper & Brothers, 1962), 182–84; Rikki E. Watts, *Isaiah's New Exodus in Mark* (Grand Rapids: Baker Academic, 1997), 135.

23. Watts, *Isaiah's New Exodus in Mark*, 81.

24. David W. Pao, *Acts and the Isaianic New Exodus* (Grand Rapids: Baker Academic, 2002), 111.

25. Edwin Gordon Selwyn, *The First Epistle of Peter*, 144.

blemish" (1:19) secures this identification (cf. "Your lamb shall be without blemish" [Exod 12:5]), as also the previous exhortation in 1:13: "Therefore gird up the loins of your mind" (Διὸ ἀναζωσάμενοι τὰς ὀσφύας τῆς διανοίας ὑμῶν; cf. "This is how you shall eat it: your loins girded" [Exod 12:11]). Israel was to be ready for the march out of Egypt, whereas Peter has in view moral preparedness. God's deliverance is central to the Exodus/New Exodus theology and 1 Peter.

The Exodus imagery in 1 Peter comes early in the epistle (1:1–2), where the author echoes the establishment of the old covenant God made with Israel. As a people who have been delivered, he addresses the readers as "the exiles of the Dispersion . . . who have been chosen and destined by God the Father and sanctified by the Spirit to be obedient to Jesus Christ and to be sprinkled with his blood" (εἰς ὑπακοὴν καὶ ῥαντισμὸν αἵματος Ἰησοῦ Χριστοῦ). The combination of the pledge of obedience and the sprinkling of blood echoes Exodus 24:2–8. Moses seals the covenant between God and Israel as the people say they will obey God's requirements, which Moses read from the book of the covenant ("All that the Lord has spoken we will do, and we will be obedient" [Exod 24:7]). Subsequently, Moses dashes the sacrificial blood upon them ("Moses took the blood and dashed it on the people and said, 'See the blood of the covenant that the Lord has made with you in accordance with all these words'" [Exod 24:8]). The recipients of 1 Peter have themselves been called out and now enter into a New Covenant with God through both their pledge of obedience and Christ's death (1:2, 14, 22). In the New Covenant they are restored as the people of God.

Peter centers the New Exodus theology on the suffering and glories of Christ (1:11). The apostle not only harkens back to the establishment of the covenant through the Pascal lamb of Exodus 24 but also draws from Isaiah's New Exodus. He frames God's salvation within the Servant Song of Isaiah 53 (1 Pet 2:21–25 references parts of Isa 53:4–12), showing again that through Christ's death, God effects his salvation. The New Exodus theme is also present with Peter's citation of Psalm 118:22: "To you then who believe, he is precious; but for those who do not believe, 'The stone that the builders rejected has become the very head of the corner'" (1 Pet 2:7). Jesus is the one who is triumphant over his enemies, even the enemies of the communities Peter addresses. They, by contrast, believe in him and "will not be put to shame" (1 Pet 2:6 citing Isa 28:16). Peter previously used Psalm 118:22 in Mark 12:10 and Acts 4:11. In Mark the psalm citation appears as Jesus enters Jerusalem and the temple as the King (11:2–7), journeying from Bethphage and Bethany near the Mount of Olives, down from the edge of the wilderness, and up to Jerusalem and the Temple Mount. Those who went ahead and followed behind Jesus shouted the words of Psalm 118:25–26: "Hosanna! Blessed is the one who comes in the name of the Lord! Blessed is the coming kingdom of our ancestor David!" (11:9–10). Although the "Stone" would be rejected presently by the "builders" (Ps 118:22), Jesus here enters into Jerusalem as royalty, the one who should have been blessed "from the house of the Lord" (Ps 118:26b). Jesus is the King, and his coming is part of the New Exodus. By way of contrast, in Acts 4 Peter stands before the Sanhedrin in Jerusalem and quotes Psalm 118:22, which affirms that Jesus, the Stone, "has become the cornerstone." Although the citation targets these leaders as "you the builders," Peter here wraps the testimony around the restoration of God's people: "There is salvation in no one else, for there is no other name under heaven given among mortals by which we must be saved" (4:11–12). Luke's inclusion of this testimony anticipates the mission to the Gentiles, those who are "far away, everyone whom the Lord our God calls to him" (2:39; cf. Isa 57:19). Peter's use of Psalm 118:22 wraps around the themes of kingship and community.

The theme of becoming God's covenant people is dominant in 1 Peter 2:9, where Peter tags them as "a chosen race, a royal priesthood, a holy nation" (CSB), language taken from Exodus 19:5–6: "And now if by paying attention you listen to my voice and keep my covenant, you shall be for me a people special above all nations. For all the earth is mine. And you shall be for me a royal priesthood and a holy nation" (LXX). They, as Israel in the Exodus, are the elect and holy people of God.[26] Indeed, for Peter, the Christian community is thoroughly identified with Israel, and this, then, becomes a central tenet in Peter's theology. As Achtemeier notes, "1 Peter has appropriated the language of Israel for the church in such a way that Israel as a totality has become for this letter the controlling metaphor in terms of which its theology is expressed."[27] The Exodus and the covenant constituted Israel as the elect people of God (Deut 7:7), a framework Peter now uses to describe the Christian communities throughout Asia Minor. They are the "elect (ἐκλεκτοῖς) aliens of the dispersion" (1:2) and an "elect (ἐκλεκτόν) race" (2:9).

The language Peter uses to describe the Christian community in 2:9 not only derives from the first Exodus but also Isaiah's New Exodus. In this verse the apostle combines Exodus 19:6 with Isaiah 43:21, which says, "My people whom I have acquired to set forth my excellencies" (λαόν μου, ὅ περιεποιησάμην τὰς ἀρετάς μου διηγεῖσθαι) and Isaiah 42:12: "And shall proclaim his excellencies in the islands" (τὰς ἀρετὰς αὐτοῦ ἐν ταῖς νήσοις ἀναγγελοῦσιν). Peter's quotation says they are "a people for his possession, so that you may proclaim the praises of the one who called you out of darkness into his marvelous light" (λαὸς εἰς περιποίησιν, ὅπως τὰς ἀρετὰς ἐξαγγείλητε τοῦ ἐκ σκότους ὑμᾶς καλέσαντος εἰς τὸ θαυμαστὸν αὐτοῦ φῶς [CSB]). The apostle regards the Christian community as a fulfillment of the New Exodus hope for the restoration of Israel. In the following verse (2:10), Peter conflates Hosea 1:6, 9; 2:1, 3, and 25, declaring, "Once you were not a people; but now you are God's people; once you had not received mercy, but now you have received mercy." Hosea spoke of God's rejection of Israel and his readiness to receive them again as part of the people of God's New Exodus from exile. Hosea views their captivity in Assyria as following the pattern of their Egyptian

---

26. John H. Elliott, *The Elect and the Holy*, 434–39.

27. Achtemeier, *1 Peter*, 69. Achtemeier reminds us that, in distinction from Paul, "in 1 Peter, the language and hence the reality of Israel pass without remainder into the language and hence the reality of the new people of God."

exile: "They shall not remain in the land of the Lord; But Ephraim shall return to Egypt, and in Assyria they shall eat unclean food" (Hos 9:3). The prophet weaves together the return to the land with the story of the first Exodus, as Hosea says in 12:9: "I am the Lord your God from the land of Egypt; I will make you live in tents again, as on the days of the appointed festival" (so 13:4–5).

The surprise 1 Peter offers up is that language that described Israel's restoration now applies to these Gentile converts. Perhaps this segue became possible due to the way Deuteronomy 32:21b refers to Gentiles as "no people": "So I will make them jealous with what is no people, provoke them with a foolish nation." The inclusion of the Gentiles was a prominent topos in Isaiah's New Exodus. The New Exodus would be a time when God would gather his people from among the nations (Isa 43:1–7; 54:4–8; Tob 13:1–6; 2 Macc 2:16–18) and would also embrace the inclusion of the Gentiles (Isa 42:10–12; 45:22–23; 49:6; 51:4–5; 55:5; 56:1–8; 66:18–21). Peter's readers were Gentiles who had participated in the cult life of their communities and families but then abandoned those ways upon integration into the people of God (4:3–4). Their former way of life, handed down through their ancestors, is now deemed "vain" (ματαίας [1:18]). Their separation and inclusion places them over against the "gentiles," a term that, in Peter's theology, describes those who are not part of God's elect and holy people (2:12; 4:3). They have separated from the idolatry of their former life and their surrounding community, which, as noted above, is a key theme in the New Exodus theology as outlined in Isaiah (Isa 40:12–31; 41:1–10; 44:9–20; 46:1–13). The proclamation of judgment over the "spirits in prison" may also be part of the anti-idol polemic insofar as these fallen angels were responsible for the idolatry in the world (see the comments on 3:18–22 below).

Although 1 Peter does not speak of the people of God as being in the "way" as in Mark, the language of alienation and exile (1:1, 17; 2:11) suggests that Peter views the community as being on a journey. Their current condition is temporary. Indeed, these elect exiles are being kept by God's power for an inheritance, a metaphorical promised land, currently kept in heaven for them: "An inheritance that is imperishable, undefiled, and unfading, kept in heaven for you" (1:4; cf. Exod 15:17; Isa 58:14). Peter anticipates a final consummation, which will mean the judgment of God's enemies (4:5, 17–18) and the entry into God's inheritance (1:4) upon the time of Christ's revelation (1:7). The fundamental framework of Peter's theology in this letter is the Exodus, alien existence in this age, and the anticipation of final salvation when Christ is revealed (1:5). But the inheritance they receive also finds its present fulfillment in that they now have a living hope (1:3), salvation (1:5; cf. Heb 1:14); the grace of life (3:7; cf. Dan 12:13; Mark 3:7), and a blessing (3:9). Indeed, these communities are themselves God's heritage (τῶν κλήρων [5:3]; cf. οὗτοι λαός σου καὶ κλῆρός σου, "these are your people and heritage" [Deut 9:29]).

The New Exodus is based upon God's promise and calling (Isa 41:8–9; 51:1–2).[28] As noted above, God has chosen Peter's readers (1 Pet 1:2) and had given the promise of salvation through his prophets (1:10–11). God has sent his Word as the promise of the New Exodus. The theme appears in Isaiah 40:8–9, where the prophet proclaims that God's Word will neither wither nor fade but will endure forever: "The grass withers, the flower fades; but the word of our God will stand for ever. Get you up to a high mountain, O Zion, herald of good tidings; lift up your voice with strength, O Jerusalem, herald of good tidings, lift it up, do not fear; say to the cities of Judah, 'Here is your God!'" Peter links God's promise through the prophets (1 Pet 1:10–11) with the proclamation of good news: "Things that have now been announced to you through the those who brought you good news by the Holy Spirit sent from heaven" (1:12). The announcement of God's rule is heralded by his messengers according to the hope embodied in the New Exodus. Isaiah 52:7 picks up the theme again with the words, "How beautiful upon the mountains are the feet of the messenger who announces peace, who brings good news, who announces salvation, who says to Zion, 'Your God reigns.'" Although Peter does not refer directly to this text, his epistle resonates with the theme of the proclamation of God's good news. Indeed, he conflates Isaiah 40:6 and 8 in 1:24: "All flesh is like grass and all its glory like the flower of grass. The grass withers, and the flower falls, but the word of the Lord endures forever." The focus on God's promise and the proclamation of his word in the good news is yet another mark of the New Exodus theology in 1 Peter.

Upon examining the thoughts of the fisherman from Galilee turned apostle, the surprise is that he consistently frames his theology within the large arc of God's work through Christ. First Peter is no exception to that rule. He elevates his readers' eyes to see the scope of God's plan from before the creation of the world until the final consummation at the revelation of Jesus Christ. He understands that through God's call, his readers have become God's people, who are liberated and look forward to an imperishable inheritance. Though at this time they are social aliens in society, they belong to God and constitute a new people. Peter will not allow them to become mired in the painful realities of the moment but makes sure that they understand that they belong to God and to one another. In drawing the large arc of God's salvation in Christ, he lets them know that the present era is not simply a time of waiting but rather a time when God is truly active and present. His great salvation has been proclaimed to them by messengers empowered by the Holy Spirit (1:12), the very Spirit who rests upon them in the middle of their suffering (4:14). God is active now, giving them grace (5:5) and establishing them firmly (5:10). They are not forsaken but in the present enjoy a deep relationship with Christ marked by faith and love (1:8). They experience his salvation now (1:9), the salvation promised through the prophets (1:10) and realized through Christ's sufferings and glories (1:11), which will be finally consummated upon his revelation (1:5–6, 13). Peter lifts his readers' eyes

---

28. Anderson, "Exodus Typology in Second Isaiah," 182–83.

beyond the immediacy of their situation, which has brought them terrible grief (1:6) and has made them perplexed (4:12). He frames their lives within God's eternal plan and lets them know that they have a part and a place. This salvation is for them (1:12). While we may be accustomed to thinking about Peter as an impetuous disciple who sometimes fails, we witness in his reflection here and elsewhere a vision of God's eternal plan. Peter, though "uneducated and ordinary," was Jesus' companion (Acts 4:13).

THE GOD WHO PLANS
God's Transcendence and Immanence

Peter's theology is decidedly theocentric, a fact recognized by many readers of his letter.[29] His teaching about God focuses on the realities of God's person and character that will encourage the readers in the midst of their adversity. Hence the theology of the epistle centers on the transcendent activity of the Living God, as noted above. God acts in favor of his people and, given that, they can have hope (1:3, 13, 21). God orchestrates his transcendent plan, and his hand brings the hope of the New Exodus into a living reality. For Peter, God is not absent or unmoved by human concerns like the Epicureans conceived of the deity.[30] He is present and engaged, working for the welfare of those whom he has called. He has agency, and these believers, as Christ, occupy a central place in his plan. In other words, they are recipients of his grace (5:12).

As Peter lays out the plan of God, he highlights divine sovereignty and transcendence, an understanding of his nature that he balances against his "intimate concern with human life."[31] On the one hand, God is the Creator (4:19), the Planner of the ages (1:20, 2), the Eternal One (implied in 1:23, 25; 4:11; 5:11), the Almighty (5:11; 4:11), and the God of glory (4:11, 14; 5:10). He is in the world above, keeping the inheritance for the saints (1:4) while also standing ready to judge both the living and the dead (4:5[32]; 1:17). Yet despite the emphasis on God's sovereignty and transcendence, Peter knows he is near and present. God is active in the lives of the believers, and they, in turn, are in close relationship with him. God is near to his people since he is the source of their life (1:3, 23) and the one who keeps them for final salvation (1:5). His eyes are constantly upon them and his ears are attentive to their prayers (3:12, citing

---

29. Edwin Gordon Selwyn, *The First Epistle of Peter*, 75; Love, *The First, Second, and Third Letters of John; The Letter of Jude; the Revelation to John*, 70; Beare, *The First Epistle of Peter*, 52; Chester and Martin, *The Theology of the Letters of James, Peter, and Jude*, 104; Davids, *A Theology of James, Peter, and Jude*, 157, for example.

30. The Epicurean view was that "Gods exist . . . but takes no thought for this cosmos or any other, living an ideal life of eternal, undisturbed happiness—the Epicurean ideal. It is good for men to respect and admire them, without expecting favours or punishments from them" (*OCD*, 533).

31. Edwin Gordon Selwyn, *The First Epistle of Peter*, 76.

32. While the primary reference here is to Christ as the Judge, we may assume that God the Father is the one who ordained him as Judge of the living and the dead (see Peter's point of view in Acts 10:42; cf. 17:31).

Ps 34:15). The members of the community engage in mutual service as "stewards of the manifold grace of God" (4:10). They speak his words and serve with the strength he supplies (4:11). God's Spirit rests upon those who suffer (4:14). God gives his grace to the humble (5:5), not simply as a future blessing but also as a lived reality in the present time of trouble. The believers stand in his grace now (5:12). Peter's readers are none other than the very people of God (2:10), and they live and act in consciousness of him (2:19).[33] Christ brought them into covenant with God, as happened to Israel in the first Exodus (3:18; cf. Exod 19:4), and in so doing leads them into his presence.[34] In his presence they pray and trust him to answer (3:7, 12; 4:7; 5:7). Peter speaks to the women about the virtue of a "gentle and quiet spirit, which is very precious in God's sight," that is, "before God" (ἐνώπιον τοῦ θεοῦ [3:4]). God is manifestly present to these believers. Despite the rejection endured in their communities, they live conscious of being in his presence, knowing that he is attentive to them. Although Peter understands that God is both Creator and Judge, he sees God's relationship with his people as profoundly tender and caring. Peter does not explicitly say with John that "God is love" (1 John 4:8), but the apostle understands the concept well. God demonstrates deep concern for them.

Creator, Father, and Judge

Peter utilizes a few titles to speak about God, each of which unveils unique aspects of his person and work in relation to the believers. He is the Creator (4:19; 1:20) and the Father of the community and of Christ (1:2, 3, 17). But the apostle also describes God's role as Judge without utilizing the title (1:17; 2:23; 4:4–6, 17).[35] Peter understands that God is intimately engaged with his people and, indeed, with all people. He also looks back to God's activity from before creation of the world until the final consummation. The apostle goes beyond speaking of divine attributes in the abstract but rather understands that God is actively engaged in the world.

---

33. Συνείδησιν commonly means "conscience" but here attaches to the concept of "consciousness" or "awareness of something," in this case God (Edwin Gordon Selwyn, *The First Epistle of Peter*, 176–78; Charles Anthony Pierce, *Conscience in the New Testament* [London: SCM, 1955], 107–8. *TDNT*, 7:914–16; *BDAG*, 967; as Heb 10:2; 1 Cor 8:7).

34. John H. Elliott, *1 Peter*, 643.

35. Peter says that the Gentiles who have seen the good works of the believers will "glorify God when he comes to judge" (NRSV's rendering) or "on the day he visits us" (NIV's rendering of ἐν ἡμέρᾳ ἐπισκοπῆς). This "day of visitation" may be a time of blessing (as in Gen 50:24–25; Job 10:12; Isa 23:17; 1 Sam 2:21; Wis 3:7; 4:15) or judgment (Isa 10:3; Jer 6:15; 10:5; Sir 18:20). The fact that the Gentiles will honor God suggests that the latter is in view, although the decision is difficult. See the discussion in Eugenio Green, *1 Pedro y 2 Pedro* (Miami: Editorial Caribe, 1993), 149–50; John H. Elliott, *1 Peter*, 470–71.

Creator

God is the Creator (4:19), a divine title that only appears here in all the New Testament writings, although the concept is present throughout (Matt 19:4; Rom 1:25; Eph 3:9; Col 3:10). The title is common enough in Jewish literature, where God as Creator is regarded as the source of all things (2 Macc 7:23; Sir 24:8) and the Sovereign (Jdt 9:12; 2 Macc 1:24; 13:14) deserving of honor (2 Macc 11:5). The Creator is a sure foundation, and his people's salvation comes from him (LXX 2 Sam 22:32, 33–51). The Creator shows them mercy (2 Macc 1:24; 7:23) and sympathy (2 Macc 5:25). Peter emphasizes this latter aspect of God's character as Creator. He cares for his people (as in 1 Pet 5:5) and is faithful towards them (4:19). Those who were suffering for causes other than their own sin (4:15–16) and who were surprised and confused by severe social rejection (4:12) had cause to doubt God's faithfulness. But Peter assures them of the Creator's fidelity (cf. 1 Cor 1:9; 10:13; 2 Cor 1:18; 1 Thess 5:24). He is attentive to them (1 Pet 3:12), gives them grace (5:5), and strengthens them (5:12). They are assured of his care precisely because he is the Creator.[36] The Creator's care is especially evident in Christ, who "was destined before the foundation of the world, but was revealed at the end of the ages for your sake" (1:20). God's plan in Christ for these believers was set in motion "before the foundation of the world." This way of speaking about the beginning of all things[37] appears frequently in the NT (Matt 13:35; 25:34; Luke 11:50; John 17:24; Eph 1:4; Heb 4:3; 9:26; Rev 13:8; 17:8). God planned the great events of salvation for his people before creation, which underscores their greatness (see *Tanh.* 26a; *Pesiq. Rab.* 21.145a). Peter places God's activity as Creator within the arc of his saving activity through Christ, who has now been revealed "at the end of the ages for your sake." The Creator's eternal plan is executed in real time.

Father

Peter's view of God as Creator is not far removed from the title "Father" (1:2, 3, 17). He stands in relation to Christ as the Father (1:3), a relationship that finds its primal expression in the Gospels (see, for example, Mark 8:38; 13:32; 14:36). Here we witness Peter's memory and recognition of the intimate relationship between Jesus Christ and his Father, the one who planned his saving work through him (1:20). But in this title we also witness the beginnings of Trinitarian theology. In 1 Peter 1:3 the apostle speaks of the believers as "chosen and destined by God the Father and sanctified by the Spirit to be obedient to Jesus Christ and to be sprinkled with his blood." Both

---

36. Within Indigenous communities, God is commonly known as Creator, and from that understanding comes a deep and abiding confidence in his care for humanity and all other creatures. Creator remains engaged with all of creation, and his role as Creator is not simply a "back then" event. See the discussions and critique of Western views of God as Creator in Deloria Vine Jr., *God is Red: A Native View of Religion* (Golden, CO: Fulcrum, 2003), 77–96; Randy S. Woodley, *Shalom and the Community of Creation: An Indigenous Vision* (Grand Rapids: Eerdmans, 2012), 25–66.

37. *NIDNTT*, 1:377.

Jesus Christ and the Spirit stand together with the Father as agents of salvation for the believers.

Peter's emphasis in this letter, however, is on the Father's intimate relationship with and care for the believers. He is the one who chose them according to his own plan and purpose (1:2). They were "chosen according to the foreknowledge of God the Father," which does not simply mean that the Father knew them beforehand (κατὰ πρόγνωσιν) but rather had destined them as he had Christ (cf. προεγνωσμένου [1:20]). We may assume that this choosing preceded creation, as was the case in God's plan for Christ. Despite their current situation, they could rest in the assurance that the Father's purposes for them had eternal roots. This plan then issued in their new birth effected through Christ's resurrection ("Blessed by the God and Father of our Lord Jesus Christ! By his great mercy he has given us new birth into a living hope through the resurrection of Jesus Christ from the dead" [1:3]; cf. 1:23, where the agent in their new birth is the message of God). As Father, God has given them new life, and therefore they are now "newborn infants" (2:2). As the giver of life, the Father has formed "the believing community as God's family or household (2:5; 4:17) and 'brotherhood' (2:17; 5:9)."[38] The Father has demonstrated mercy towards them (1:3) as he does as their Creator (4:19). But moreover, he has also brought them into the brother/sisterhood as members of a common household. They know him as Father in community.[39]

Since God their Father has given them life and cares for them, they freely pray to him as Father: "And if you invoke as Father" (1:17a). The communities to whom Peter writes have learned to pray as Jesus had taught his disciples to pray, saying, "Our Father in heaven" (Matt 6:9; Luke 11:2). The disciples were likely taught to address him with the most intimate familial name, "Abba" (Mark 14:26), an Aramaic term preserved even within the Gentile churches (Rom 8:15; Gal 4:6).[40] They offer prayers in confidence that he cares for them (5:7) as a Father is concerned for the welfare of his children.

Judge

In patriarchal society the father was a numinous figure who offered protection and care and exercised ultimate authority.[41] This combination of intimacy on the one side

---

38. John H. Elliott, *1 Peter*, 331.

39. Peter's elaboration of the fatherhood of God should be framed within Roman social history, including the *patria potestas* (Richard Saller, *Patriarchy, Property and Death in the Roman Family* [Cambridge: Cambridge University Press, 1994]). However, "Father" is not gender marked as if God, the Creator, possesses a male and not female gender. "Father" marks God's function and relationship and not sexual identity.

40. See the helpful article by Willem A. VanGemeren, "'ABBĀ' in the Old Testament," *JETS* 31 (1988) 385–89, which serves as a useful corrective to some of the conclusions in Jeremias's work regarding the familial term ʾ*Abbā* (Joachim Jeremias, *New Testament Theology* [New York: Scribner's Sons, 1971], 67–68).

41. John H. Elliott, *1 Peter*, 364; Saller, *Patriarchy, Property and Death in the Roman Family*, 102–32.

and authority on the other meant that the image of God as Father was not separated from his role as Judge. In 1:17 Peter exhorts, "If you invoke as Father the one who judges all people impartially according to their deeds, live in reverent fear during the time of your exile." Reverence for one's father and mother were principle tenets of the Torah (Lev 19:3; cf. Sir 3:1–16). Therefore, the call to respond to him in "reverent fear" would not be out of place with notions of God's care as Father. Indeed, the Father is the one who will judge them (1 Pet 1:17b). Similarly, Sirach 3:1 speaks of the "judgment of your father," a thought not far removed from Peter's reminder in 4:17 about what is occurring in the communities' sufferings: "For the time has come for judgement to begin with the household of God." God begins his judgment with his people, a reference to the testing they endure through suffering rather than their condemnation (4:12; 1:6–7). Over and again, the Old Testament speaks of God's judgment beginning with his people (Isa 10:12; Jer 25:29; Ezek 9:6; Zech 13:7–9; Mal 3:1–6; see 2 Macc 6:12–17). God's judgment is a future reality (1 Pet. 4:6, 17b, 18b) that begins in the present for his household (4:17a, 19a). As in God's salvation, there exists an inextricable link between present (1:9) and future (1:5).

God's role as Judge also becomes a source of comfort for the beleaguered Christians in Asia Minor. Christ had committed himself "to the one who judges justly," and since he did no sin, was vindicated (2:22–23). As Christ was vindicated, so, too, these believers will find favor with God insofar as they suffer for doing good and not evil (2:19–20; 3:14; cf. 5:6). Though they are subject to God's judicial examination (4:19; 1:7), they can cast their care upon him because of his active concern for their well-being (5:6–7).[42] Peter offers comfort to his persecuted readers by informing them that God stands ready to judge the living and the dead and that those who oppose the believers will give account to him (4:5). It is not clear whether Peter has in mind God the Father or Christ as Judge in 4:5. In Acts 10:42 Peter ascribes this role to Christ, and this may be the thought here since the focus has been on Christ's agency as Judge in 3:18–22. However, when Peter speaks explicitly of divine judgment, in this letter, the subject is God the Father. Most likely the apostle has him in mind here. Peter asks the question, "What will be the end for those who do not obey the gospel of God," and, citing Proverbs 11:31, "What will become of the ungodly and the sinners?" (4:17–18). The doom of those who oppose the gospel is clear.

On the other hand, those who had heard the gospel before they died and seem to have been judged like any other human now live before God. This appears to be the thrust of 4:6: "For this is the reason the gospel was preached even to those who are now dead, so that they might be judged according to human standards in regard to the body, but live according to God in regard to the spirit." The verse does not speak about Christ's preaching to those who had died in his descent to hell between his death and resurrection, a traditional interpretation of 3:18–22 (see below). First Peter

---

42. They are under God's "mighty hand," an expression which in the OT at times appears in the context of God's judicial discipline of his people (Jer 21:5; Ps 32:4).

4:6 is not another rendition of Christ's preaching to the "spirits in prison" but recalls rather the proclamation of the gospel (εὐηγγελίσθη) to those who became Christians but then subsequently died.[43] Peter's thought aligns closely with Wisdom 3:1–4, the possible source of his thought: "But the souls of the righteous are in the hand of God, and no torment will ever touch them. In the eyes of the foolish they seemed to have died, and their departure was thought to be a disaster, and their going from us to be their destruction; but they are at peace. For though in the sight of others they were punished, their hope is full of immortality."[44] The assessment of society does not correspond to God's evaluation of his people. While the readers' contemporaries would regard death as the ultimate judgment or punishment, there is hope in the gospel and vindication in his sight (ζῶσι δὲ κατὰ θεόν πνεύματι, "but live according to God in regard to the spirit").

Although the recognition that God will judge the Christians' persecutors provides them comfort, Peter never forgets their need to honor God out of reverent fear (1:17) since, in the end, "it is hard for the righteous to be saved" (4:18a, citing Prov 11:31). God's judgment provides comfort and raises concern. God's role as everyone's Judge serves as a motivation for Peter's ethics. Peter's statements to the believers about God's judicial examination of the household of God and the affirmation from Proverbs that the righteous will only be saved with difficulty (4:17–18) appear within the context of Peter's moral exhortation in 4:12–19. He concludes with the call, "Therefore, let those suffering in accordance with God's will entrust themselves to a faithful creator, while continuing to do good." God's judgment provides motivation for Christian ethics in 1:17 as well. Since the Father judges "all people impartially according to their deeds," these believers should "live in revering fear during the time of your exile."

First Peter does not describe the final judgment of the world in vivid terms like those in 2 Peter 2:1–3:13. The terms are more reserved though hardly less severe. Peter regards God's judgment as stumbling (προσκόπτουσιν [2:8]), and in 4:17–18 he hints at the severity in God's judgment of the disobedient in contrast to the hard road of salvation that the righteous tread. He compares the ultimate judgment of the unrighteous with the flood during Noah's days (3:18–22; cf. 2 Pet 3:5–6). Peter's focus in this passage, however, is upon Christ's proclamation of judgment upon "the spirits in prison, who in former times did not obey, when God waited patiently in the days of Noah, during the building of the ark, in which a few, that is, eight people were saved through water" (3:19–20). In this text Peter contrasts the salvation of Noah and his family with the doom of those beings who disobeyed God's command (see below).[45]

---

43. William Joseph Dalton, *Christ's Proclamation to the Spirits: A Study of 1 Peter 3:18–4:6* (Rome: Pontifical Biblical Institute, 1989), 230–41; Kelly, *A Commentary on the Epistles of Peter and Jude*, 172–76; Grudem, *1 Peter*, 170–72; Eugenio Green, *1 Pedro y 2 Pedro*, 241–42; Achtemeier, *1 Peter*, 286–91.

44. Eugenio Green, *1 Pedro y 2 Pedro*, 242–43.

45. Dalton, *Christ's Proclamation to the Spirits*; Kelly, *A Commentary on the Epistles of Peter and Jude*, 146–64; I. Howard Marshall, *1 Peter* (Downers Grove, IL; Leicester: InterVarsity, 1991), 117–32; Eugenio Green, *1 Pedro y 2 Pedro*, 215–33; Achtemeier, *1 Peter*, 239–74; John H. Elliott, *1 Peter*,

This was the angelic fall. As in 4:17–18, the salvation of the righteous is placed in contrast with the doom of the unrighteous ("Eight people were saved through water" [3:20]; "And baptism, which this prefigured, now saves you" [3:21]). Peter is aware of the supernatural conflict that lays behind the believers' persecutions. In 5:8b the apostle says, "Like a roaring lion, your adversary the devil prowls around, looking for someone to devour." Peter understands, however, that Christ proclaims God's judgment over all supernatural powers (3:19, 22). Peter's readers can rest assured that God has and will call to account those who oppose them.

Peter may also take up God's judgment in 2:12, where he calls these Christians to live honorably before the non-Christian Gentiles "so that, though they malign you as evildoers, they may see your honorable deeds and glorify God when he comes to judge," or, rather, "on the day he visits us" (ἐν ἡμέρᾳ ἐπισκοπῆς, NIV; the language comes from Jesus' teaching as found in Matt 5:16). The "day of visitation" in the Old Testament and Judaism could be a time of punishment (Isa 10:3; Jer 6:15; 10:5; Sir 18:20) or an occasion for mercy, blessing, and salvation (Gen 50:24–25; Job 10:12; Isa 23:17; 1 Sam 2:21; Wis 3:7; 4:15). The basic concept was that God conducts an inquest into people's doings, which may result in punishment or blessing.[46] In Luke 19:44, the day of visitation was the time of salvation, which then turned into a day of judgment. That Peter views the unbelievers as glorifying or honoring God on that day suggests that they had been persuaded to join the company of Christians as they responded positively to the witness of the believers through both word and deed (2:9, 12).[47] Conversion comes through the testimony of Christian conduct (cf. 3:2).

THE CHARACTER OF GOD
The Holy One

Peter knows God as "the Holy One" (1:15) who has called them.[48] God's holy character bears within it the imperative to the communities to be holy: "Be holy yourselves in all your conduct." Peter reinforces his call to holiness rooted in the holy character of God in the following citation from Leviticus 19:2 (see also 11:44–45): "You shall be holy,

---

637–710; Jobes, *1 Peter*, 235–60.

46. Kelly, *A Commentary on the Epistles of Peter and Jude*, 106; John H. Elliott, *1 Peter*, 470–71.

47. John H. Elliott, *1 Peter*, 471.

48. Peter calls him τὸν καλέσαντα ὑμᾶς ἅγιον, "the Holy One who called you." The participle does not serve as a substantive as the NRSV and NIV suggest. See Charles Bigg, *A Critical and Exegetical Commentary on the Epistles of St. Peter and St. Jude* (Edinburgh: T. & T. Clark, 1901), 114; Beare, *The First Epistle of Peter*, 98; Best, *1 Peter*, 86; J. Ramsey Michaels, *1 Peter* (Waco, TX: Word, 1988), 51; John H. Elliott, *1 Peter*, 360. Achtemeier says that either "holy" ("the holy one") or "called" ("the one who called") could be the substantive "without significant change in the meaning of the sentence." That God is "the one who calls" in 2:9 and 5:10 tips the scale in favor of "the one who called you" (*1 Peter*, 121). On the other hand, God is frequently known as "the Holy One" within Isaiah (1:4; 5:16, 19, 24; 10:20; 12:6; 29:25; 31:1; 40:25; 41:16, 20; 43:3, 14–15; 45:1; 55:5), the source of much of Peter's thought.

for I am holy." Peter's focus is on the moral character of God. As Bigg notes, "God is holy because He is separate from all uncleanness."[49] Although the attribute may suggest God's power, might, and greatness, given the way Peter uses the call in his ethics, the focus is on how God is separate from everything that is evil and ethically unclean.[50] Although Achtemeier is correct in noting that the term "does not contain etymologically any necessary connotation of morality," the call to separation "from their former culture" points to the need to be like God, who is separate from evil.[51] Peter regards Christian conduct as a holy "way of life" (1:15b) that emulates the character of God. The roots of the apostle's thought is God's redemption of Israel from Egypt (see Lev 11:44–45) and his subsequent attempt to separate the nation from the cultic and immoral irrectitude of that society. The holiness to which God called the nation was set in contrast with the evil found in the land of Canaan (Lev 18:3; 20:26). Similarly, the readers of this letter had been redeemed from their former way of life (1 Pet 1:18) and were charged to engage in a lifestyle distinct from that of their society (4:2–3). So while "holy" may suggest God's perfection of being and separation from all that is creaturely,[52] he is not simply aloof but rather separate from all that defiles, thereby being ethically perfect.[53]

The God of Grace and Glory

Peter also highlights God's beneficence as one who gives grace (χάρις). "Grace" receives mention ten times in the letter (1:2, 10, 13; 2:19, 20; 3:7; 4:10; 5:5, 10, 12). Best noted some years ago that Peter's concept of grace is not simply about God's favorable disposition. Peter regards grace as "an 'object' of which more or less can be given by God."[54] Grace is the bounty or benefit granted a person or community by a benefactor, whether the benefactor is human or divine. For Peter it means more than having benevolent feelings but rather points to the bounty given by the benefactor. The beneficence of deities was well known in antiquity. Epictetus, for example, said, "What else should we do but sing the divinity, celebrate him, list all his benefits" (1.16.15).[55]

---

49. Bigg, *Peter and Jude*, 115.

50. *IDB*, 616–25; *NIDNTT*, 2:223–32.

51. Achtemeier, *1 Peter*, 121.

52. *TDNT*, 1:91.

53. Hort, *The First Epistle of St. Peter 1:1–2:17*, 69–70; C. E. B. Cranfield, *1 and 2 Peter and Jude: Introduction and Commentary* (London: SCM, 1960), 35–36.

54. Best, *1 Peter*, 73. See Beare, *The First Epistle of Peter*, 91. Selwyn remarks that "χάριν φέρειν τινί, to confer a kindness or boon on anyone, is a phrase common in Attic Greek," a meaning that appears in 1:13. But the concept frames Peter's use of the term elsewhere as well.

55. *TLNT*, 3:503; Frederick W. Danker, *Benefactor: Epigraphic Study of a Graeco-Roman and New Testament Semantic Field* (St. Louis: Clayton, 1982), 35–36, 173–201, 487; deSilva, *Honor, Patronage, Kinship and Purity*, 141–51; B. J. Oropeza, "The Expectation of Grace: Paul on Benefaction and the Corinthians' Ingratitude (2 Corinthians 6:1)," *BBR* 24 (2014) 207–26.

Peter holds up God as the Benefactor who gives his bounty to his people, and in this reciprocal relationship they offer him praise (1:3).

God is the source of grace (implied in 1:2), a benefit that consists of the salvation now bestowed through Christ's sufferings and glories (1:10). He also anticipates its full manifestation at the time of Christ's revelation (1:13). Grace is also God's present help that he offers to the humble, those who in do not merit it (5:5). He is therefore titled "the God of all grace" (5:10) since he is the ultimate Benefactor who strengthens them in the present and who calls them to his eternal glory or honor. His benefit consists of life ("the gracious gift of life" [3:7]). In a move that surprises those unfamiliar with patron-client relationships, God turns these believers into brokers of his grace for the mutual benefit of the community. They are to be "good stewards of the manifold grace of God" (4:10). Each, then, receives a "gift" (χάρισμα), and they then broker these concrete manifestations of God's grace to others (χάριτος).[56]

In his concern to offer his readers encouragement in adversity, Peter shows them how God supplies them what they need in concrete ways. He acts on their behalf. Benefaction sets up a reciprocal relationship between the patron and the client, where the client returns to the patron honor, loyalty, or faithfulness, and shows of gratitude. As Briones explains:

> Patron–client relationships are bound by 'social obligation and the inner force of honor,' which may have been viewed as an exploitative transaction couched in terms of personal loyalty or reciprocity. In any case, it was incumbent upon recipients to express their gratitude, so as not to be considered ignoble and so as to enhance the social prestige and reputation of the patron. Failure to do so was deemed a disgraceful insult and resulted in public opprobrium, as Seneca attests: 'Not to return gratitude for benefits is a disgrace, and the whole world counts it as such' (*De Ben.* 3.1.1; cf. 4.18.1).[57]

The language of thanksgiving and honor may be understood as appropriate responses to the benefactor's bounty. Peter begins the letter with praise for their divine Benefactor while naming the character of his gracious gift: "Blessed be the God and Father of our Lord Jesus Christ! By his great mercy he has given us a new birth into a living hope through the resurrection of Jesus Christ from the dead" (1:3). Peter anticipates that the way believers offer witness to their contemporaries through word and good works will, in the end, issue in honor to God (2:12).

---

56. On the concept of being brokers of a benefactor's bounty, see David Briones, "Mutual Brokers of Grace: A Study in 2 Corinthians 1:3–11," *NTS* 56 (2010) 536–56. He introduces the concept of brokerage in the patron-client relationships, saying, "Broadly speaking, it introduces a third party into the patron–client alliance, an intermediary who distributes the goods of the patron to the client and likewise mediates the reciprocating return of the client back to the patron. It is called brokerage" ("Mutual Brokers of Grace," 537). Brokers served as privileged clients who distributed goods and also served as a conduit for the client to return gratitude and loyalty ("Mutual Brokers of Grace," 541).

57. Briones, "Mutual Brokers of Grace," 541.

Peter honors their Benefactor in the context of the way these believers serve as brokers of his gracious gifts. They speak and serve "so that God may be glorified in all things through Jesus Christ. To him belong the glory and the power for ever and ever. Amen" (4:11). "Glory" often appears in honorific inscriptions lauding a benefactor's gifts.[58] The Benefactor is again eulogized in 5:11: "To him be the power for ever and ever. Amen." The response expected among those who receive benefits from either a human or divine benefactor is sometimes spoken of as πίστις, that is, faith or fidelity (1 Pet 1:5, 9, 21).[59] God is the Benefactor, and "faith" or "faithfulness" is expected among those who receive his bounty. In the context of adversity, where the fidelity of these Christians was under question, this response to God's benefaction is especially important. Their fidelity is tested by adversity but if found genuine would be honored by God (1:7).

Aside from the use of "glory" as a term of honor granted the divine Benefactor, glory is one of God's essential attributes, which expresses "the majesty and wonder of the divine nature and province."[60] Glory may be understood not only as God's brightness and presence (Exod 24:16–17) but also the sum of his moral perfections (Exod 33:18–23; 34:5–8) and therefore is closely related to his holiness.[61] While God may be given honor or glory due to his benefaction, it is also something he possesses (4:11), a characteristic of God that is eternal (5:10). His glory becomes manifest among his people in the midst of their suffering ("The Spirit of glory and of God rest on you" [4:14]). God not only receives glory and has inherent glory, he also gives glory or honor to Christ in the resurrection (1:21; cf. 1:11), a glory that will be revealed upon Christ's final revelation (4:13). In the present social shame, the saints receive honor or glory (4:14; 1:8) as also at the time of the future revelation of Christ (5:1, 4, 10). God overturns their shame and shows them honor. Over and again, Peter links the dishonor of suffering that Christ and the believers endured with God's glory. He honors those who suffer in his name (1:11; 5:1, 10). Future glory now rests on these persecuted believers (4:14), and, as Elliott says, "The glory that is God's (4:11) and Christ's (1:11, 21; 5:1) rests now on the suffering faithful and soon will be revealed in all its fullness (1:7; 5:1, 4)."[62]

---

58. James R. Harrison, "The Brothers as the 'Glory of Christ' (2 Cor 8:23): Paul's *Doxa* Terminology in Its Ancient Benefaction Context," *NovT* 52 (2010) 156–88.

59. Andrew Wallace-Hadrill, "Patronage in Roman Society: From Republic to Empire," in *Patronage in Ancient Society*, ed. Andrew Wallace-Hadrill (London: Routledge, 1989), 63–87. See E. Randolph Richards and Brandon J. O'Brien, review in *Misreading Scripture with Western Eyes: Removing Cultural Blinders to Better Understand the Bible* (Downers Grove, IL: InterVarsity, 2012), 164, 166. Seneca, *De Ben.* 1.1.3.

60. Edwin Gordon Selwyn, *The First Epistle of Peter*, 256, see 250–58; *TDNT*, 2:233–53.

61. Norman Snaith remarks that holiness "is synonymous with *kabod* [glory], in the sense of the burning Splendor of the Presence of the Lord" (*The Distinctive Ideas of the Old Testament* [London: Epworth, 1944], 48).

62. John H. Elliott, *1 Peter*, 782.

The Power of God

Peter's doxologies include affirmations of God's power or κράτος (4:11; 5:11), God's "'power,' 'might,' 'authority,' 'rule,' and 'dominion.'"[63] This divine attribute that would have given assurance and comfort to the suffering Christians. As Beare states, "The thought is probably of the victorious power which ensures the ultimate triumph of the divine purpose for the world."[64] God's power is not occasional or limited but rather enduring and eternal (4:11; "for ever and ever" [5:11]). The exercise of God's power is evident within the community as Peter calls members of the Christian communities to "humble yourselves under the mighty hand of God" (τὴν κραταιὰν χεῖρα τοῦ θεοῦ), a phrase that occurs in the LXX to describe God's power in liberating Israel from Egyptian bondage (Exod 3:19; 6:1; Deut 3:24; 4:34) or God's judgment and discipline (Job 30:21), two senses that combine in Ezekiel 20:34-35. Peter has in mind the sufferings these Christians endure, the "judgment" of God upon them, which proves the character of their fidelity (4:17; 1:6-7; 3:17). While his power plays a role in examining their character, however, Peter's principle concern is to assure the believers that they are kept for final salvation by the very power of God (ἐν δυνάμει θεοῦ [1:5]). Amidst the warnings to remain faithful to God through the adversity and sufferings they faced, Peter reminds them that nothing less than God's power is guarding or protecting them for the final salvation that stands ready to be revealed (1:5). For the present, the power of God, their Benefactor, enables them to be renewed, established, strengthened, and settled firmly in the face of hostility they experience in society (5:10).

God and the Resurrection of Christ

Peter bears witness to the extent of God's power in the resurrection of Christ from the dead. Indeed, in 1 Peter God is the God of the resurrection. Unlike Paul, Peter does not speak about the resurrection of the believers in relation to Christ's resurrection (cf. 1 Thess 4:13-18; 1 Cor 15). He focuses solely on Christ's resurrection by the agency of God the Father (1:3, 21). The resurrection is the first part of God's glorification of Christ after his suffering and death (1:11,[65] 21; cf. Acts 3:13-15; 2:32-33). The salvation that the believers receive comes to them through Jesus Christ's resurrection from the dead (3:18). Through the resurrection of Christ, God grants the believers new birth (1:3) and offers salvation as they pass through the waters of baptism (3:21). By Christ's resurrection, Kelly notes, God "confirms that he is the living God Who

---

63. John H. Elliott, *1 Peter*, 762. The term attaches to the concepts of might and supremacy (*TDNT*, 3:905-10).

64. Beare, *The First Epistle of Peter*, 187.

65. The NRSV obscures the sense of 1:11 by translating "glories" in the singular ("and the subsequent glories") instead of the plural (τὰ μετὰ δόξας, NIV "the glories that would follow). The "glories" include the resurrection of Christ (1:21), his ascension, victory over hostile forces and enthronement (3:19-20, 22), and his final unveiling at the time of his return (4:13).

can impart life to what seems stricken down and dead."⁶⁶ God has triumphed in the resurrection of Christ, and therefore he becomes the object of faith and hope for those who are suffering (1:21, 3).

Peter presents the resurrection of Christ within the context of Christ's death for the unrighteous for their reconciliation with God (3:18a) and his proclamation of victory over hostile supernatural forces (3:19-20, 22). By God's agency Christ was "made alive in the spirit" or "in the spiritual realm" (CSB note on ζωοποιηθεὶς δὲ πνεύματι). Many translations interpret the phrase as a statement of the Holy Spirit's agency in raising Christ from the dead ("made alive in the Spirit" [NIV]; "made alive by the Spirit" [CSB]). However, the expression "in the spirit" grammatically parallels the preceding clause, "put to death in the flesh" (θανατωθεὶς μὲν σαρκὶ)—that is, in the human sphere of existence. This suggests that the following clause should be understood as a statement regarding the Christ's resurrected state (cf. the same contrast in Rom 1:3-4; 1 Tim 3:16). Peter's thought is similar to Paul's in 1 Corinthians 15:42-44, where, when speaking of Christ's death and resurrection, he says, "It is sown a physical body, it is raised a spiritual body. If there is a physical body there is also a spiritual body." This is not a denial of the bodily resurrection of Christ, which Peter himself had witnessed (John 20:26-29; Luke 24:37-43); rather, Peter marks out Christ's resurrected state of existence as possessing properties unlike that of his body that was crucified. We should not, however, entirely bracket out the Spirit's work in the resurrection. As Elliott correctly notes, πνεύματι ("in the spiritual realm") "refers to that state of Christ's existence demonstrably controlled and animated by God's life-giving Spirit."⁶⁷ In this state he ascends to make his proclamation of judgment over the fallen supernatural powers, the "spirits in prison" (3:19, 22). The victory of Christ over the powers is, in the end, God's victory.

THE PERSON AND WORK OF JESUS CHRIST

In this letter Peter appears to have no interest in speculating about the person and work of Jesus Christ. His understanding of Christ resonates with the Petrine kerygma in Acts and the portrayal of Christ in Mark as well. There are unique developments in this letter, however, that go beyond those found in other Petrine sources. Peter speaks extensively and somewhat enigmatically about Christ's proclamation to the "spirits in prison" (3:18-22), a section that finds no parallel in the other theological strains attributed to the apostle or any other author represented in the New Testament. Despite its uniqueness, 3:18-22 reflects some common Petrine thought, albeit developed along new lines. On the main, Peter's understanding of the person and work of Christ brings us to heart of early Christian theology. We witness the most foundational

---

66. Kelly, *A Commentary on the Epistles of Peter and Jude*, 77.

67. See his full argument John H. Elliott, *1 Peter*, 646-47, and Dalton's extensive comments *Christ's Proclamation to the Spirits*, 135-42.

teaching of the early church regarding Jesus Christ. As Cullmann suggested years ago, Peter "should be given the place of honor at the beginning of all Christian theology."[68] This is especially the case with Peter's Christology.

Christ's Role in God's Plan

Christ is the focus of God's saving plan. God's plan through him began before the creation of the world, and his advent marked the beginning of "the last times" (1:20). His future revelation will inaugurate "the end of all things" (4:7, 13). Peter understands Christ as the Pre-existent One who was subsequently "revealed," an affirmation that implies his preexistence (1:20).[69] Ancient prophetic inspiration came through the "Spirit of Christ" (1:11), who previously testified to the sufferings and glories of Christ. Christ's preexistence was part of the fabric of early Christian theology (John 1:1:1-2, 14; 12:41; 1 Cor 10:4). This marks the beginning of Peter's Christology.

God's plan and purpose for Christ's work in history was laid out before creation (1:20a) and was then revealed to the prophets, who anticipated but did not see Christ's sufferings and glories (1:10-11), that honor being held for these believers (1:12). From Peter's perspective the center of God's plan in Christ is in this redemptive activity and not simply in the incarnation (implied in 1:20). Peter witnessed Christ's sufferings and now he offers his testimony (5:1). Peter saw, interpreted, and bore witness, although others brought these readers the news of the events that were predicted and fulfilled (1:12). Over and again, Peter returns to the theme of Christ's sufferings and death (1:2, 18-19; 2:21-24; 3:18).

The historical activity of Christ did not end with his death. God raised him from the dead (1:3, 21; 3:18, 21) and then ascended to the right hand of God to exercise his lordship over all powers (3:22). Upon the ascension, he proclaimed judgment upon hostile supernatural powers (3:19). He now reigns as Lord (3:15), an acknowledgment calculated to assuage the fears and temptation to moral lapse that beset Peter's readers. His lordship over the powers serves to counter concerns about the supernatural dimension of the persecution the believers endured (5:8-9).

As the resurrected and ascended Lord, Christ is never absent from his people. He is only veiled for a season. Peter never speaks of Christ's "coming" (παρουσία) in this letter but only his revelation or unveiling (ἀποκάλυψις [1:7, 13; 4:13; 5:1]). A thin veil hides him from view for the moment, but it will be taken away. At the present time the

---

68. Cullmann, *Peter*, 66.

69. Contra Beare, *The First Epistle of Peter*, 52; John H. Elliott, *1 Peter*, 377. See Schelkle, *Die Petrusbriefe, Der Judasbrief*, 50; Best, *1 Peter*, 91; Michaels, *1 Peter*, 67; Peter H. Davids, *The First Epistle of Peter* (Grand Rapids: Eerdmans, 1990), 74; Eugenio Green, *1 Pedro y 2 Pedro*, 99; Thomas R. Schreiner, *1, 2 Peter, Jude* (Nashville: Broadman & Holman, 2003), 87-88. As Achtemeier says, "Since the two participles (προεγνωσμένου, φανερωθέντος) do in fact describe Christ (Χριστοῦ of v. 19) and not God's plan, it would be strange if Christ's preexistence were not also implied here" (*1 Peter*, 132). 1 Peter 3:18-22 is not about Christ's preexistent preaching in the days of Noah, as shown below.

veil is constantly penetrated through faith and love for Christ (1:8). These believers have tasted the kindness of the Lord (2:3)[70] and have come to him (2:4). Christ, in turn, brings them to God (3:18). Their worship is acceptable to God through Jesus Christ (2:5). The time of Christ's unveiling is not in the far distant future but rather right at hand (1:13; 4:7; 5:4). At that time, the glory given Christ at his resurrection (1:21) will be fully disclosed (4:13). The final salvation that the believers have already received (1:9) stands ready to be revealed (1:5). God's judgment has begun with the household of God (4:17), and the judge stands ready to execute his final judgment upon the living and the dead (4:5). At that time, Christ will share his glory with his own (5:1) who have shared his sufferings (4:13).

Christ is the center of God's saving history, a plan activated and realized in the past, current in the present time, and ready to be consummated at the time of Christ's revelation, which Peter anticipates soon. God's plan, which centers in Christ, cannot be thwarted by humans who have rejected him (2:4, 6–8). Despite the opposition that both Christ and these believers endured, God will bring his plan to completion with great glory and exceeding joy (4:13). The end has drawn near, and with that comes great promise in Peter's view.[71]

The Person of Christ

The person of Christ is not separate from his work since what he does is an outgrowth of who he is. Descriptions of his person, including those in 1 Peter, are functional and not simply ontological. The way Peter describes Jesus Christ in this epistle is consummate with his portrayal in the other New Testament Petrine materials, but there are notable omissions. Peter does not describe Jesus as the Son of Man as in Mark, but this common title in the Gospels is conspicuously absent from the other New Testament letters (cf. Heb 2:6; Rev 1:13; 14:14). Nor does 1 Peter call Jesus the Son of God, a key christological title in Mark (1:1; 15:39; cf. 2 Pet 1:17). Other titles in the epistle, however, share a common understanding of Christ's person with other strata of Peter's theology.

Jesus Christ

In 1 Peter the name "Jesus" never appears by itself, but Peter uses the name "Jesus Christ" thirteen times (1:1–3, 7, 13; 2:5; 3:21; 4:11) and the title "Christ" alone thirteen times (1:11, 19; 2:21; 3:15–16, 18: 4:1, 13–14; 5:1, 10, 14).[72] Peter never refers to

---

70. Kelly suggests that this is a eucharistic reference (*A Commentary on the Epistles of Peter and Jude*, 86–87).

71. On the problem of the delay of Christ's advent, see Christopher M. Hays et al., *When the Son of Man Didn't Come*.

72. Note that "Jesus" appears with "Christ" in some texts of 5:10 and 14. See the discussion in Bruce M. Metzger, *A Textual Commentary on the Greek New Testament* (Stuttgart: German Bible Society; New York: United Bible Societies, 1994), 627–28.

him simply as "Jesus" nor "Christ Jesus" as do Paul and others.[73] Peter believed that Jesus is the promised Messiah of Israel and, indeed, he was the first to confess him as such (Mark 8:29). In Acts he begins to proclaim that this Jesus was the Messiah, or Christ ("That he may send the Messiah appointed for you, that is, Jesus" [Acts 3:20]). Peter starts with the person of Jesus, whom he met in Galilee, but always recognizes him as none other than the long-anticipated Messiah.[74] Achtemeier suggests that Peter's penchant for referring to "Jesus Christ" perhaps indicates "the extent to which the title had already become part of the name."[75] However, the fact that Peter repeatedly calls him simply "the Christ" and never just "Jesus" underscores the importance of the title in Peter's mind. Jesus had confirmed Peter's confession, and the apostle keeps that revelation ever present (Matt 16:17).

Peter knows Jesus as the suffering Messiah (1:11, 19; 3:18; 4:1, 13; 5:1), who was also foreknown (1:20), raised from the dead, and glorified (1:21) at the time of his resurrection and future revelation (4:13). Peter came to understand that the Messiah would suffer, a reality that he had denied when he first recognized Jesus as the Christ (Mark 8:31-33). But 1 Peter bears witness that the apostle subsequently fully embraced the reality and necessity of the Messiah's sufferings and integrated a theology of suffering into his preaching and writing. He knows that the Christ suffered in the flesh (4:1) and realized that his suffering was predicted through the prophets (1:11). His death was that of the paschal lamb, who redeemed them from bondage in this New Exodus (1:19; Exod 12:5; 6:6). Although Peter understands the importance of his sacrifice for redemption (Isa 53:7), the theological significance did not erase the tortured reality of Jesus' death. Jesus shed blood. Peter saw his pain and bears witness to it in this letter and elsewhere (5:1). The believers to whom he writes faced their own pain, even to the point of suffering physically for their faith (4:1). Therefore, the apostle reminds them that they share in the sufferings of the Christ (4:13, 16). Some have suggested that Peter occasionally refers to the Messianic Woes, the travails that were to mark the times before the end (1:10-11; 4:13; perhaps 5:1).[76] While this theological understanding of the "sufferings of the Messiah" may well be in play,[77] the apostle's first concern is to frame his readers' experience within the reality of Christ's crucifixion with all its horror and pain. They suffer with him. As he was rejected, so are they. And as he was subsequently honored by God, so will they be. In no text are the sufferings of Christ divorced from the historic realities of the life of Jesus.

---

73. By contrast, the Paulines never refer to him as Jesus Christ save in Titus 1:1.

74. See the comments on the title and name in chapters 3 and 4.

75. Achtemeier, *1 Peter*, 81.

76. See Dan 7:21-27; 12:1; Joel 2:1-32; 1 QH 11:3-18; Jub 23; Mark 13:3-27; Mark Dubis, *Messianic Woes in 1 Peter: Suffering and Eschatology in 1 Peter 4:12-19* (New York: Lang, 2002), 4-36.

77. Edwin Gordon Selwyn, *The First Epistle of Peter*, 299-303; Best, *1 Peter*, 162-63, 168; John H. Elliott, *1 Peter*, 775; Dubis, *Messianic Woes in 1 Peter*, 96-117.

Peter also regards Jesus Christ as an exalted figure who has been glorified or honored by God despite his rejection, sufferings, and death. The prophets predicted the sufferings and the glories of the Christ (1:11), and his glory shall be revealed to all (4:13). Although Christ died (3:18), he was made alive and in that state went to proclaim judgment upon the spirits in prison (3:19). Peter's theology turns around the resurrection of Jesus Christ (1:3; 3:21), who has now ascended into the heavens with all supernatural powers subjected to him (3:22). Peter anticipates the future glorious appearance or revelation of Christ (1:7, 13; 4:13; 5:1). Christ has authority over all the powers that oppose these believers (cf. 5:8–9). Between the ascension and his appearing, Peter regards Jesus Christ as the mediator through whose agency the spiritual sacrifices of the believers are acceptable to God (2:5). In Peter's theology, Jesus Christ is currently the heavenly Lord whose glory will be revealed to all in short order.

The Lord

The title "Lord" (κύριος) appears eight times in 1 Peter (1:3, 25; 2:3, 13; 3:6, 12, 15). In three occurrences it refers to God (1:23–25; 3:12 uses the title twice)[78] and once to Abraham (3:6), the rest being references to Christ, whom Peter regards as the Lord. Peter cites three Old Testament texts that talk about Yahweh or God and interprets them christologically (2:3, citing Ps 33:9 [LXX]; 3:12, citing Isa 40:8; 3:15, citing Isa 8:13).[79] When he quotes Isaiah 8:13 in 3:15, he emphasizes the identification of Christ with Yahweh by referring to "the Lord Christ" (κύριον ... τὸν Χριστὸν), where the LXX only reads "the Lord himself" (κύριον αὐτὸν). The strong association of Christ with Yahweh/God of the Old Testament leads to the conclusion that Peter regarded Christ as the divine Lord. As Bigg noted years ago, "The writers of the New Testament take no trouble to guard their readers against misapprehension on a subject of such consequence."[80] Peter's readers should therefore show Christ due reverence in their conduct given his divinity. Indeed, their conduct in society should be carried out in subjection to his Lordship (2:13).

The Lordship of Christ plays an especially prominent role in Peter's theology, both here and elsewhere. As in Mark 12:36 and Acts 2:34–35, in 1 Peter 3:22 the apostle understands Psalm 110:1 christologically: "The Lord said to my lord, 'Sit on my right until I make your enemies a footstool for your feet'" (LXX 109:1). Peter does

---

78. κύριος in 1:25 may refer to God, but the citation of Isaiah 40:8 here substitutes κυρίου for the LXX τοῦ θεοῦ ἡμῶν, suggesting that Peter uses the text as a reference to Christ. On the other hand, "Lord" in 3:12 could refer to Christ, but there is no clear indication in the text that Peter here makes this identification. Indeed, as Achtemeier notes, "the phrase 'face of the Lord' (πρόσωπον κυρίου) is so firmly attached to the presence of God in the OT that that is probably the way it should also be understood here (*1 Peter*, 227).

79. The Hebrew of Psalm 33:9 (LXX), i.e., 34:9 MT, and of Isaiah 8:13 reads יְהוָה (Yahweh, LXX κύριος), and Isaiah 40:8 has אֱלֹהֵינוּ (God, LXX θεός).

80. Bigg, *Peter and Jude*, 169; Jobes, *1 Peter*, 229, 233–34. Jobes adds that Peter "claims the divinity of Christ throughout the letter."

not cite the Psalm in 3:22 but echoes it, saying that Jesus Christ "has gone into heaven and is at the right hand of God, with angels, authorities, and powers made subject to him." Peter does not use the title "Lord" here, but the reference to Psalm 110:1 indicates that the concept of Christ's Lordship is present. As the Lord, he is the ruler over his enemies who, in this contextualization of the psalm, are hostile supernatural forces. Jesus Christ the Lord exercises authority over all the powers. The expression "at the right hand of God" is a way to speak of God's divine power (Exod 15:6, 12; Ps 17:7; 20:6; 21:8; 63:8; 118:15; Isa 48:13) but also signifies the place of the one who received the king's favor and received his honor (1 Kgs 2:19; Ps 45:9). Peter and the early church understood Psalm 110:1 as a prophecy regarding the Messianic King who would rule under Yahweh.[81] The ascended Jesus Christ is the Lord over all, the Ruler supreme, and the recognition that he is Lord will raise these persecuted believers above fearing their adversaries (3:14–15).

The Stone

One of the most significant Petrine titles for Jesus Christ in this epistle is λίθος (Stone [2:4–8]).[82] Peter gathered a litany of OT "stone" texts and interpreted them christologically (Ps 118:22 and Isa 28:16 in 2:4; Isa 28:16 in 2:6; Ps 118:22 in 2:7; and Isa 8:14 in 2:8). Jesus had adopted the Stone testimony to describe his own person and work (Mark 12:10–11, citing Ps 118:22–23). Elliott points out, however, the antecedents to Jesus' adoption of the Stone imagery. The Qumran community saw in it a reference to themselves as the people of the last days (1 QS 7.7–8), and the Isaiah Targum on 28:16 gives the text a royal interpretation: "Behold I am establishing in Zion a king, a king mighty and strong." So also the Targum on Psalm 118:22–23 interprets it as a reference to the Davidic king. The "stone" becomes the "youth" David and the "cornerstone" is the "king and ruler."[83] Schelkle comments that where the Stone passages received a Messianic interpretation, the focus was not upon a rejected but an exalted Messiah.[84] This changed with Jesus. As the Stone he is the rejected but exalted Messiah, the King.[85]

---

81. Eugenio Green, *1 Pedro y 2 Pedro*, 226; *TDNT*, 2:37–38.

82. Best mistakenly states, "Peter cannot be said to make much of the stone concept by itself except in so far as it is a foil to Christians as stones" ("1 Peter 2:4–10—A Reconsideration," *NovT* 11 [1969] 279). The Stone testimony is a central feature in Petrine theology.

83. John H. Elliott, *A Home for the Homeless*, 26–28; Andrew C. Brunson, *Psalm 118 in the Gospel of John: An Intertextual Study on the New Exodus Pattern in the Theology of John* (Mohr Siebeck, 2003), 40–42; *TDNT*, 4:268–80. Targum Psalm 118:22–23 says, "The builders abandoned a youth; he was among the sons of Jesse and was entitled to be appointed king and ruler." Psalm 118:22–23 reads, "The stone that the builders rejected has become the chief cornerstone. This is the Lord's doing; it is marvelous in our eyes."

84. Schelkle, *Die Petrusbriefe, Der Judasbrief*, 60.

85. "In every case, without exception, the λίθος image has been applied to Jesus as the Messiah. Thus the messianic/eschatological interpretation begun in pre-Christian Judaism reaches its culmination in its application to Jesus as the Bringing of the Messianic Age, the Last Aeon" (John H. Elliott, *The Elect and the Holy*, 28).

Jesus located the Stone imagery at the center of his own theology and through it framed the rulers' rejection of him and the honor God would subsequently grant him. He was the Stone whom the leaders of his nation rejected but whom God would exalt to the place of honor. Peter subsequently introduced the Stone testimony into the early church (Acts 4:11, using Ps 118:22),[86] again emphasizing both Christ's rejection and exaltation. First Peter develops the testimony more extensively, placing particular emphasis on the election, rejection, and honor of Christ along with that of his community. In Peter's hands, the Stone imagery guides his understanding of the sufferings and glories of Christ (1 Pet 1:11) and also frames the community's suffering, honor granted by God, and the fall of their adversaries (2:4–8).

Elliott's work demonstrates Peter's particular emphasis on God's election of the Stone. "Divine election," he states, "is the overwhelming counter to human rejection. Men have rejected the λίθος Jesus but in God's sight he is elect and precious."[87] Christ is the elect Stone, and his people are elect as well (2:4, 9). Elliott elaborates that 2:4–8 is "an attempt to describe via the motif of *election* the character and responsibility of the eschatological People of God, [and] her bond with Jesus Christ."[88] Peter calls Christ a "living Stone" (2:4), which points to his resurrection from the dead, the time when he was "made alive" (3:18). In that event he was honored as the one who is "precious" (ἔντιμον [2:4, 6]), that is, one who has great value (Luke 7:2; Tob 13:17) and has received the highest honor (Num 22:15; Luke 14:8; Phil 2:19; 1 Clem 3:3).[89] His position is so exalted that people's eternal destiny hinges on whether they receive him or reject him, responding to the message of the gospel in either faith or unbelief (2:6–8). Those who come to him themselves become "living stones" who are built together into a temple or "spiritual house" (2:5). They are formed into a community as a result of their relation to the Stone ("As you come to him" [2:4, NIV, picked up from LXX Ps 33:6 (34:5)]),[90] and he, then, serves as the mediator of their "spiritual sacrifices," which are "acceptable to God through Jesus Christ" (2:5).

---

86. It also appears in Paul (Rom 9:32–33; Eph 2:20), but the roots of this interpretation appear to be Jesus and Peter. Paul, as Peter, combines Isa 26:18 and 8:14 in Rom 9:33, but we should not assume that Peter shaped his teaching on that of Paul. The combination of the two Stone testimonies from Isaiah with Ps 118:22 is unique to Peter. As argued, Peter was the first to introduce Jesus' teaching through his preaching witnessed in Mark and through his testimony recorded in Acts.

87. John H. Elliott, *The Elect and the Holy*, 35.

88. John H. Elliott, *The Elect and the Holy*, 219.

89. BDAG, 340;. John H. Elliott, *1 Peter*, 410–11.

90. The participles should not be interpreted as an imperative as in the NRSV (Eugenio Green, *1 Pedro y 2 Pedro*, 122; John H. Elliott, *1 Peter*, 409). First Peter references LXX Psalm 33 [34] at various points in the letter: 2:3 cites Ps 33:9 [34:8]; 3:10–12 cites Ps 33:13–17a [34:12–16a]. The psalm speaks of the suffering of the righteous, God's judgment of their persecutors, and the necessity of maintaining a righteous life in the midst of suffering, all themes germane to Peter's readers. On the use of the OT in 1 Peter, see Gene L. Green, "The Use of the Old Testament for Christian Ethics in 1 Peter," *TynBul* 41 (1990) 276–89.

The Stone, then, is the Messiah, Jesus Christ (2:4–5), who has been rejected by people but honored by God. The title has soteriological significance since he is the Living Stone who determines people's eternal destiny and who forms those who believe in him into a temple for the worship of God. The centrality of the Stone imagery in 1 Peter stems from the teaching of Jesus but may also be informed by Peter's own consciousness of the way Christ had named and commissioned him (Matt 16:18). The Stone imagery helps Peter's readers understand Christ's and their own sufferings and affirms them in their faith, knowing that God will indeed honor them while dishonoring those who assail them. There is no christological title in 1 Peter that more fully embodies the message Peter wishes to communicate to the rejected Christian communities scattered throughout Anatolia.

The Shepherd and Chief Shepherd

In 2:25 Peter calls Jesus the "shepherd . . . of your souls," and in 5:4 he calls Christ the "chief shepherd." In 2:25 he stands in relation to the sheep while in 5:4 he is the one who rewards the faithful shepherds of the flock (see 5:2–3). As the Shepherd, Christ watches over his people ("guardian" [2:25]), provides for them, and protects them now that they have turned to him. Formerly, as sheep wandering astray, they were in danger, but now that they have returned to him they can rest in safety and confidence. This message offers particular comfort to the slaves who have to endure the injustices of their masters (2:18–25) but holds significance for all the afflicted readers of this letter. By using the Shepherd imagery Peter draws out a paradox: although they are persecuted, they now dwell in safety. In 5:4 the Chief Shepherd is a majestic figure who, when he is revealed (5:4; cf. 1:7, 13, 20; 4:13), will reward the faithful shepherds with "the crown of glory that never fades away." Peter refers to the crowns made of celery, pine needles, or laurel, which were given to victorious athletes but faded with time (1 Cor 9:25). The crown became a symbol of public recognition and honor. The crown these shepherds will receive does not fade with time (cf. 1:4). They, as Christ, will receive glory or honor (cf. Isa 22:18; 28:5; Jer 13:18; 1 Pet 1:7; 5:1). We may infer from Peter's affirmation that they, too, had suffered, although this is not the focal point of the exhortation in 5:1–4. Rather, the reward serves as motivation for proper conduct (5:2–3). We may, then, understand the Chief Shepherd as the Judge of these Christian leaders (cf. Ezek 34), although Peter says nothing about any condemnation of unfaithful shepherds.

In the OT, the title "Shepherd" was one way to speak of God (Ps 23:1; 77:20; 79:13; Isa 40:11; Jer 2:8; 3:15; 10:21; Ezek 34:12) but could also refer to the Davidic Messiah who was to rule (Ps 78:71; Ezek 34:23; 37:24; Micah 5:1–3; *Ps. Sol.* 17:45–47), shepherding his people. The early church picked up the title to refer to Jesus, the Messiah, under the direction of Jesus himself (Mark 6:34; 14:27; John 10:11; Heb 13:20; Rev 7:17). Peter wishes to bring his readers comfort knowing that Christ is the

Shepherd of their souls or lives (2:25), but there is more going on here. The readers had been "going astray like sheep," language which echoes the Servant Song in Isaiah 53:6. Israel in the past had been like lost and scattered sheep (1 Kgs 22:17; 2 Chr 18:16; Jer 50:6; Ezek 34:5–6; Zech 10:2; Matt 15:24). Peter picks up this imagery now to refer to these Gentiles who had been wandering lost before their turning to Christ, their Shepherd. They have "returned" (ἐπεστράφητε), language commonly used to describe the conversion to God (Luke 1:16; Acts 9:35; 11:21; 14:15; 15:19; 26:20; 2 Cor 3:16; 1 Thess 1:9; Jas 5:30). The pastoral language, therefore, is salvific. The Shepherd has saved them through his own sacrifice (see 1 Pet 2:22–24). The fact that these Gentiles have been converted by turning to him implies that he not only "bore our sins in his body on the cross" but also was raised from the dead. He now lives, and they are safe.

The Guardian

In conjunction with the title Shepherd, Peter knows Christ as the Guardian (ἐπίσκοπος). In 2:25 the apostle states that these Gentiles "have returned to the shepherd and guardian of your souls." A guardian is "one who has the responsibility of safeguarding," although in other contexts it may refer to a supervisor or overseer (Acts 20:28; Phil 1:1; 1 Tim 3:2; Titus 1:7).[91] Commenting on the relationship between this title and the previous, Beare says Peter "is bringing out this particular function of Christ as the Shepherd, watching over His flock, His eye ever upon them to guard them from harm, and to keep them for straying yet again."[92] Peter does not use "guardian" as title of ecclesiastical office as does Paul, yet he clearly connects the function of Christian leaders as shepherds with their charge to guard the flock of God (ἐπισκοποῦτες, "exercising the oversight" [5:2]).[93] Christ's roles as Shepherd and Guardian become the paradigm for Christian leadership.

Beyer suggests that the guardianship of Christ may also imply that "Christ is He who has the fullest knowledge of souls."[94] According to Wisdom 1:6, "God is witness of their inmost feelings, and a true observer [ἐπίσκοπος] of their hearts" (so Philo *Mut.* 39.216; *Somn.* 1.91; *Leg.* 3.43, LXX Job 20:29). While the immediate context suggests the concept of protective care rather than omniscience, Peter does stress that God knows and is attentive to his people in the midst of their adverse situation (3:12; 5:7). Peter may also be communicating that the one who watches over them as guardian has deep insight into their situation and being. He sees and protects.

---

91. BDAG, 379.

92. Beare, *The First Epistle of Peter*, 141.

93. Note that the mss. evidence places the inclusion of the participle in some doubt. While found in p72, ℵ², A, P, and Ψ, it is absent from ℵ* and B. See the discussions in Metzger, *A Textual Commentary on the Greek New Testament*, 625–26; John H. Elliott, *1 Peter*, 824n665; Jobes, *1 Peter*, 310.

94. TDNT, 2:615.

The Righteous One

Peter calls Christ the Righteous One in 3:18. While this may simply be a description of his character and not a title, Δίκαιος is found elsewhere as a christological title (Matt 27:19, 24; Luke 23:47; Acts 7:42; 22:14; 1 John 2:1), even in Peter's preaching (Acts 3:14). The Suffering Servant of Isaiah 53:11 is called "the righteous one," and given that Peter makes ample use of Isaiah 53 (1 Pet 2:22–25), we should assume that he has the title in mind in 3:18. In the pre-Christian era, the Messiah was known as the Righteous One (*Ps. Sol.* 17:35),[95] the one whose life is lived in harmony with God's plan and purpose. He does the will of God in contrast with others who are the "unrighteous many" (1 Pet 3:18). As the Righteous One he does not sin (2:22). The Righteous One is the Messiah who suffers unjustly and yet, in the midst of adversity and rejection, maintains a righteous way of life. His death, then, is an atonement—he dies for them in order that they may be reconciled with God. As the Righteous One, he also serves as an example for the believers who themselves are called to maintain a righteous life in the midst of their sufferings (3:17–18).

The Lamb

The title Lamb (ἀμνός) highlights the sacrificial nature of Christ's death. First Peter 1:19 is one of various texts in the New Testament that refer to Christ as a Lamb (John 1:29, 36; 8:32; Acts 8:32–33, citing Isa 53:7–8; see 1 Cor 5:7). Peter highlights the moral perfection of the Lamb, who was "without defect or blemish" (ἀμώμος καὶ ἀσπίλος). The perfect Lamb was sacrificed to bring about redemption: "You were ransomed from the futile ways inherited from your ancestors . . . with the precious blood of Christ, like that of a lamb without defect or blemish" (1 Pet 1:18–19). Peter links his character with the efficacy of his redemption. Christ was like the paschal lamb of the Exodus, which had to be "without blemish" (Exod 12:5). As the deliverance of the first Exodus was made possible through the blood of the lamb (Exod 12:7–13, 21–27),[96] so now Christ the Lamb liberates believers through his death. Peter does not describe the Lamb's redemption as forgiveness or justification but rather as deliverance or ransom from their former way of life (ἀναστροφή) or "from the futile ways inherited from your ancestors." As Israel was delivered from bondage in Egypt, so now these believers are ransomed from their former idolatrous life through the death of Christ, the Lamb (cf. "I will free you from the burdens of the Egyptians and deliver you from slavery to them. I will redeem you with an outstretched arm and with mighty acts in judgment" [Exod 6:6]; cf. 15:13, 16; Neh 1:10).

The redemption of Israel from slavery in Egypt was socio-political. During Jesus' day the Jewish people lived under the imperial power of Rome and longed for similar

---

95. *TDNT*, 2:186–87.

96. Cf. *Rab. Exod.* 12:22: "With two bloods were the Israelites delivered from Egypt, with the blood of the paschal lamb and with the blood of circumcision."

liberation. The seventh of the Eighteen Benedictions, recited daily within the Jewish community, pleaded with God, saying, "Look on our affliction and plead our cause, and redeem us for the sake of your name. Blessed are you Lord, the redeemer of Israel" (cf. 1 Pet 1:3; Luke 24:21; Acts 1:6).[97] While Peter reflects on the moral liberation the Lamb effects for these Gentile believers (1 Pet 1:18–19), the deliverance embraces their whole social matrix since they are now redeemed from a traditional way of life and suffer the social consequences of that Exodus.

The title Lamb finds its roots embedded in Peter's theology of the New Exodus.[98] Given his repeated reference to the chapter, Peter may be drawing upon the thought in Isaiah 53:7: "He was oppressed, and he was afflicted, yet he did not open his mouth; like a lamb that is led to the slaughter, and like a sheep that before its shearers is silent, so he did not open his mouth." Indeed, his statement that they were "ransomed (ἐλυτρώθητε) not with perishable things like silver or gold" (cf. Acts 3:6) may hearken back to Isaiah 52:3: "You shall be redeemed (λυτρωθήσεσθε) without money." Through the Lamb, God effects a powerful deliverance that is accomplished through Christ's sacrifice and not simply a demonstration of divine power. God did indeed exercise his power in the Exodus but sacrifice was required.[99]

Peter's Christology

Peter presents a high Christology that focuses on the rule and authority of Jesus Christ the Lord. Although he suffered, God raised him from the dead and exalted him over the powers. Over and again, the images Peter uses remind his readers that Jesus Christ is the foundation of their salvation and the sacrifice for their deliverance. He also reconciles them to God. People's response to him of faith or unbelief will determine their eternal destiny. The apostle always keeps in mind the realities of his readers, who themselves face suffering and rejection as had Jesus Christ. Christ is the foundation of their hope. Buried within the affirmations of who Jesus Christ is and their relationship with him is an implicit call to rest in the security of his salvation and not return to their former life ways. Peter also points up Christ's character as one who is holy, righteous, and without moral defect. This qualifies him as their liberator but also carries with it the call to live holy and righteous lives. Peter links his Christology with the formation of the Christian community as well. These believers had been alienated from their families and communities, but Christ, the Stone, has formed them into a temple to offer sacrifices that he then mediates to God. Although Christ has died he

---

97. David Instone-Brewer, "The Eighteen Benedictions and the *Minim* Before 70 CE," *JTS* 54 (2003) 30.

98. See further below on salvation through Christ.

99. Beare is unsuccessful in his attempt to understand this redemption as simply an act of God's power. While he admits that in the present text the ransom is costly since it required the precious blood of Christ to effect it, he denies the sacrificial dimension (*The First Epistle of Peter*, 103–4). But the sacrificial language from both Exodus and Isaiah mitigate against this interpretation.

has been raised and lives. The believers, then, can enter together into relationship with him. Peter's theology regarding the person of Christ is intimately linked with his work on their behalf.

The Work of Christ—Sufferings and Glories

Peter summarizes the redemptive activity of Christ in 1 Peter 1:11. Under the inspiration of the Spirit of Christ, the prophets predicted the "the sufferings of the Messiah and the glories that would follow" (NIV). Now is the time of fulfillment. Christ's sufferings and glories served the recipients of the letter, not the prophets themselves. The news of Christ's sufferings and glories "have now been told you by those who have preached the gospel to you by the Holy Spirit sent from heaven" (1:12). According to Peter, the sufferings and the glories of Christ constitute the gospel message. Christ's humiliation and exaltation are events so transcendent that "even angels long to look into these things." Unsurprisingly, this double theme of sufferings and glories occupies a central place in the epistle's theology. The sufferings of Christ (1:11; 4:13; 5:1, 9) become paradigmatic for the persecuted believers in Asia Minor (4:13; 5:1, 9). Christ was given glory, and that glory will be revealed to all (1:21; 4:13; 5:1). And as the believers share his sufferings so, too, they will share his glory (1:7; 5:1, 4, 10).

The Sufferings of Christ

Sprinkled with His Blood (1:2)

Peter begins his letter by evoking covenant language. In the opening greeting he refers to the recipients as "God's elect, exiles scattered" throughout the provinces of Roman Asia Minor. They have been sanctified by the Spirit and chosen by God "to be obedient to Jesus Christ and sprinkled with his blood" (1:1–2). Peter refers neither to the ceremony by which lepers were cleansed through the sprinkling of sacrificial blood (Lev 14:1–7) nor the way blood was sprinkled on priests in their ritual of consecration (Exod 29:21; Lev 8:3). The unique combination of "obedience" and "sprinkling of blood" points rather to the establishment of the covenant between God and Israel (Exod 24:1–8), when sacrificial blood was sprinkled on the altar (v. 6), the law was read, the people pledged obedience (v. 7), and then the blood was sprinkled on the people (v. 8). Peter, as with other NT texts, utilized this text to explain the significance of the new covenant with God (Matt 26:28; 1 Cor 11:15; Heb 9:15–20; 10:29; 12:24). Peter's readers have entered into this new covenant through their pledge of obedience to the gospel (1 Pet 1:22) and the blood of Christ, who through his death, ratified this new covenant (1:19). Through Christ's death and subsequent resurrection (1:3, 21), these Gentiles have been brought into relationship with God in the New Covenant and are therefore now his people (2:10).

Beare argues that the "sprinkling of blood" in 1:2 does not suggest "atonement or vicarious suffering."[100] Beare misses the mark here since Peter evokes Exodus 24 as part of his theology of the new covenant, which offered forgiveness of sins (Jer 31:31–34; Matt 26:28; Mark 14:22–25; Heb 9:19–22).[101] In 3:18 Peter states that Christ's suffering was a death "for sins." It was an atonement for sin and also vicarious since his death was "once for all, the righteous for the unrighteous." Through Christ's atoning death, these Gentiles who had been engaged in the sins of their age, including idolatry (4:3), have entered the new covenant and have found forgiveness of sins. Peter does not speak directly of God's forgiveness of sins, but it is strongly implied in the new covenant and Peter's theology of the atoning death of Christ.

Ransomed . . . with the Precious Blood of Christ (1:19)

Peter continues to reflect on the blood of Christ in 1:18–19, where, as in 1:2, "blood" refers to his death. The blood of Christ effects their redemption: "You know that you were ransomed from the futile ways inherited from your ancestors . . . with the precious blood of Christ, like that of a lamb without defect or blemish." Peter changes the imagery behind the blood of Christ from the blood of the new covenant (1:2) to the blood of the paschal lamb, which delivered Israel from slavery in Egypt (see above on the christological title Lamb). Christ's death is now viewed as the means by which God redeemed these believers from their former way of life inherited from their ancestors, although this event was linked with the soon to be inaugurated covenant (Exod 24). The imagery derives from Exodus 12:5, where the Israelites were instructed to select a lamb without blemish.[102] The lamb was slaughtered (12:6), and the blood was put on the doorposts and lintels of the houses (12:7). The blood was then "a sign for you on the houses where you live: when I see the blood, I will pass over you, and no plague shall destroy you when I strike the land of Egypt." The blood of the lamb was therefore instrumental in effecting their liberation. As Goppelt says, "The comparison with the Passover lamb contributes to the understanding of Jesus' death, which God himself made possible as atonement and thus legally: Jesus' death makes possible the

---

100. Beare, *The First Epistle of Peter*, 77.

101. Edwin Gordon Selwyn, *The First Epistle of Peter*, 120–21; Leon Morris, *The Apostolic Preaching of the Cross* (London: Tyndale, 1965), 188–90; Kelly, *A Commentary on the Epistles of Peter and Jude*, 44; Best, *1 Peter*, 72; W. C. van Unnik, "The Redemption in 1 Peter 1:18–19 and the Problem of the First Epistle of Peter," in *Sparsa Collecta: The Collected Essays of W. C. van Unnik, Part Two: 1 Peter, Canon, Corpus Hellenisticum, Generalia* (Leiden: Brill, 1973), 63; Eugenio Green, *1 Pedro y 2 Pedro*, 57; Daniel G. MacCarney, "The Atonement in James, Peter, and Jude," in *The Glory of the Atonement: Biblical, Historical, and Practical Perspectives*, ed. Charles E. Hill and Frank A. James III (Downers Grove, IL: InterVaristy, 2000), 180–89; *TDNT* 1:172–77.

102. The LXX of Exod 12:5 reads τέλεον, perfect or without blemish. Peter adopts the concept of perfection but places emphasis on the Lamb's moral perfection as one who was "a lamb without defect or blemish" (αἵματι ὡς ἀμνοῦ ἀμώμου). The change also reflects Peter's penchant for using alpha-privatives in this letter, which was read aloud in Christian gatherings. Cf. 1:4: ἄφθαρτον καὶ ἀμίαντον καὶ ἀμάραντον ("imperishable, undefiled, and unfading").

liberating exodus, in accord with God's gracious institution in the Old Covenant."[103] Achtemeier plays down the liberating aspect of the blood, saying, "Yet Israel was not redeemed from Egypt by the blood of the paschal lamb; rather it was by the power of God. The blood of the lamb had apotropaic rather than redemptive value."[104] But as noted above, Peter theologically aligns with Midrash Rabbah 12:22: "With two bloods were the Israelites delivered from Egypt, with the blood of the paschal lamb and with the blood of circumcision."[105] Since Peter has in mind the redemption that came via the paschal lamb, 1 Peter 1:19 is part of the fabric of Peter's New Exodus theology, an Exodus accomplished through the death of Christ.

In 1:18-19 Peter also turns his readers back to Isaiah 53:7, where the prophet proclaims that God's Servant "was oppressed, and he was afflicted, yet he did not open his mouth; like a lamb that is led to the slaughter, and like a sheep that before its shearers is silent, so he did not open is mouth." Peter draws heavily on this chapter from Isaiah in 1 Peter 2:22-25. Indeed, the statement that these believers were redeemed (ἐλυτρώθητε) without silver or gold hearkens back to Isaiah 52:3: "You shall be redeemed (λυτρωθήσεσθε) without money" (cf. 1 Pet 1:18). This text recalls the Exodus from Egypt: "Long ago, my people went down into Egypt to reside there as aliens" (Isa 52:4). As Goppelt notes, this very complex of texts in Isaiah 52–53 about the Servant "stands behind the origin of this Christian tradition, namely Mark 10:45,"[106] which says, "For the Son of Man came not to be served but to serve, and to give his life a ransom (λύτρον) for many."[107] In Peter's theology Christ is the Lamb of God who redeems them from bondage to their former life and whose death, as the Servant of Isaiah, is an atonement for sin. Through him, the New Exodus has begun.

Here we touch the heart of Peter's theology of the cross wherein Christ's death ransoms the many (Mark 10:45), including these Gentiles. Peter's affirmation about the death of Christ brings us to the earliest Christian understanding of the cross, which echoed through the early church (cf. Heb 9:11-14, a text strikingly similar to 1 Pet 1:18-19).[108] Elliott catches the significance of this piece of Petrine theology: "Theologically, vv. 18-19 in their entirety represent a fabric of thought interwoven from several strands of OT and early Christian tradition. The result is a portrayal of the redemption accomplished through Christ that evokes memory of the historic deliverance of Israel from Egypt, the sacrificial system through which atonement between God and Israel was achieved, and the poignant depiction of the Suffering Servant of Isaiah."[109] The point I would dispute with Elliott is the notion that this text

---

103. Goppelt, *A Commentary on 1 Peter*, 116.
104. Achtemeier, *1 Peter*, 128.
105. Hort, *The First Epistle of St. Peter 1:1–2:17*, 79; John H. Elliott, *1 Peter*, 374.
106. Goppelt, *A Commentary on 1 Peter*, 116.
107. See chapter 4.
108. John H. Elliott, *1 Peter*, 374.
109. John H. Elliott, *1 Peter*, 375.

simply weaves in Christian tradition regarding the cross; rather, we witness here the foundational expression of the theology of the cross that first comes through Peter himself. As Cullmann said some time ago, "I do not believe that Paul was the first one to understand the death of Jesus as an atoning death for the forgiveness of sins. On the contrary, I am inclined to ascribe to Peter this particular and fundamental insight. Although he was anything but a theologian, I think that here too he should be given the place of honor at the beginning of all Christian theology." Jesus is the Suffering Servant of God, and, Cullmann continues, "I believe, indeed, that this earliest Christological explanation can be shown to have the apostle Peter as its author."[110] In Acts we also hear Peter's New Exodus theology in the reference to Jesus as God's Servant whom God glorifies (Acts 3:13; Isa 52:13; 53:11–12; cf. 49:3). Here we hear with great clarity the *vox Petri* regarding Christ and his death.

Christ also Suffered for You (2:21–24)

The death of Christ served as an example for domestic slaves, especially for those who suffered unjust punishment at the hands of their masters (1 Pet 2:18–23). As in 3:17–18, Peter moves between Christ's exemplary character in the face of suffering to discussing the redemptive value of Christ's death (2:21, 24–25). He tells the slaves, and all those who heard this letter read, that "Christ also suffered for you" (ἔπαθεν ὑπὲρ ὑμῶν), words that echo 1:11 ("the sufferings destined for Christ," τὰ εἰς Χριστὸν παθήματα), but adds that Christ's death was vicarious, not only exemplary. The substitutionary nature of Christ's death is brought out again in 3:18 ("Christ also suffered for sins," Χριστὸς ἅπαξ περὶ ἁμαρτιῶν ἔπαθεν). Christ's death, here described as his suffering, was not simply an unfortunate and unjust event in history but rather served a broader purpose as a sacrifice for the sins of the many. He suffered unjustly, for, as Peter says, "He committed no sin, and no deceit was found in his mouth" (2:22, citing Isa 53:9). He did not retaliate when being dishonored verbally and suffering, but rather committed his cause to God who judges with justice (2:23; cf. 3:9). The sinless Christ "bore our sins in his body on the cross" (τὰς ἁμαρτίας ἡμῶν αὐτὸς ἀνήνεγκεν ἐν τῷ σώματι αὐτοῦ ἐπὶ τὸ ξύλον), an expression that meant bearing the penalty or consequences of sin (Heb 9:28; Num 14:33–34; cf. Ezek 18:20). His suffering was not the consequence of his own injustice but rather his death was vicarious for the sins of others. "As our representative," Kelly states, "He endured the penalties which our sins merited."[111] Peter's understanding of Christ's death draws from Isaiah 53:4 (LXX "This one bears our sins and suffers pain for us") and 53:12 (LXX "He bore the sins of many, and because of their sins he was given over"). As in Acts 5:30 and 10:39, Peter refers to the cross as an object made of wood (so Gal 3:13; Acts 13:29; Deut 21:23).[112]

---

110. Cullmann, *Peter*, 66.
111. Kelly, *A Commentary on the Epistles of Peter and Jude*, 184.
112. Hengel, *Crucifixion in the Ancient World and the Folly of the Message of the Cross*; John

This wood was not only an instrument of death and Roman imperial control but also the greatest shame that could be endured (Heb 12:2; cf. 1 Pet 4:16).[113] Peter's focus here, however, is on the innocent suffering of Christ, his moral example, and on his vicarious death for sins.[114]

Peter takes a turn in his discussion on Christ's sin-bearing by pointing up the outcome for the believers' moral lives. He bore their sins in his body on the wood "so that, free from sins, we might live for righteousness" (2:24). Christ's atoning death makes possible the moral life to which God calls them (2:18–23). Peter's thought is not the same as Paul's in Romans 6:2 and 11, where the apostle speaks about death to sin viewed as a power controlling life (cf. Rom 7:17). For his part, Peter thinks in terms of concrete transgressions ("sins") and being "dead" to them in the sense of being finished or done with such acts (ἀπογενόμενοι).[115] They now have no part in such behavior, a thought that reappears in 4:3, where Peter reminds the readers, saying, "You have already spent enough time in doing what the Gentiles like to do, living in licentiousness, passions, drunkenness, revels, carousing, and lawless idolatry." On the positive side, the purpose of Christ's vicarious death is so that now, being dead to that way of life, they may "live for righteousness" (2:24). In Peter's ethics, living for righteousness means doing good within the social structures in which they are embedded (2:20; 3:13–14). As in 1:17–19, Christ's death liberates them from their former way of life so that now doing good marks their moral conduct (2:12, 15, 20; 3:11, 13, 16).

The final clause in 2:24 lays out a further effect of Christ's death for their sins: "By his wounds you have been healed." Peter once again draws from the Servant Song, citing Isaiah 53:5: "By his bruises we were healed." The prophet spoke of the physical suffering of the Servant in 53:3 and 4: "A man being in calamity and knowing how to bear sickness," and "This one . . . suffers pain for us." Given the physical abuse the domestic slaves suffered (1 Pet 2:19–20) and the reference to Christ's own suffering under abuse (2:21, 23), even in his body (2:24), we should not dismiss outright the idea that Peter has physical healing in mind (cf. Matt 8:14–17; Mark 5:29; 10:38; Jas

---

Granger Cook, *Crucifixion in the Mediterranean World* (Tübingen: Mohr Siebeck, 2014).

113. See deSilva, *Honor, Patronage, Kinship and Purity*, 43–93.

114. Peter does not speak out against the institution of slavery nor does Paul in his domestic codes or *Haustafeln* (Eph 6:5–9; Col 3:22–25). The question remained whether Peter and Paul believed that slavery was God-ordained or whether the apostles wanted to show believers how to live as followers of Christ within the structures of society as they found them, leaving open the question of whether or not to change those structures. The seeds of abolition, however, are deep within apostolic teaching. Peter elevates the slaves by addressing them and offering them the highest moral example, Christ himself, and reminds them that Christ died for all without distinction. Paul works out the implication of this that there are no slave or free in Christ, thereby nullifying traditional social hierarchies (Gal 3:28). But the full social implications of this theology were worked out in church and society only later (see Mark A. Noll, *The Civil War as a Theological Crisis* [Chapel Hill: University of North Carolina Press, 2006]). On the domestic codes in the NT and Greco-Roman moral philosophy, see James E. Crouch, *The Origin and Intention of the Colossian Haustafel* (Gottingen: Vandenhoeck & Ruprecht, 1972); David L. Balch, *Let Wives Be Submissive: The Domestic Code in 1 Peter* (Chico, CA: Scholars, 1981).

115. *MM*, 59; *TDNT*, 1:686; *BDAG*, 108; *New Docs*, 3.62; Josephus, *Ant.* 19.178; 5.1.

5:16). But the first part of 1 Peter 2:24 deals with liberation from sin through Christ's substitutionary death as also Peter's source, which states, "He was wounded for our transgressions, crushed for our iniquities; upon him was the punishment that made us whole, and by his bruises we are healed" (Isa 53:5). The healing in 1 Peter 2:24 must surely include moral healing from the effects of sin. Perhaps it is best to see this healing as holistic, including physical and moral healing. The bifurcation between the physical and moral illness is a modern construct alien to Peter's thought (see, for example, Mark 2:1–12).[116]

The following verse begins with the explanatory γὰρ (for) and adds another dimension to the declaration in 2:24 that Christ "bore our sins in his body on the cross." Evoking Isaiah 53:6, Peter concludes, "You were going astray like sheep, but now you have returned to the shepherd and guardian of your souls" (1 Pet 2:25). The image of wandering sheep is meant to point to their condition of being lost in sin, as made clear in Isaiah 53:6: "All we like sheep have gone astray; we have all turned to our own way, and the Lord has laid on him the iniquity of us all."[117] But they have now been reconciled to God through Christ, having returned to the "shepherd and guardian." This movement is, as Elliott says, a "collective unification with Christ" as they turn to him (cf. Mark 4:12; Acts 3:19; Jas 5:19–20). "The contrast in v. 25a/b of former alienation and present reconciliation with God recalls the similar double contrast in 2:10."[118] This turning and reconciliation with God is a vital aspect of Christ's salvation for these Gentiles who had once wandered in idolatry and the lifestyle associated with it (4:3; cf. 1 Thess 1:9).

For Christ also suffered for sins once and for all (3:18–22)

Peter again takes up the issue of Christ's sufferings in 3:18–22, a passage many consider the most difficult to interpret in the letter—if not the whole New Testament collection. The passage begins with a further declaration about Christ's sufferings: "For Christ also suffered for sins once for all, the righteous for the unrighteous." But the fundamental controversy surrounding this section is whether 3:19 speaks about Christ's preexistent ministry, his descent into hell between his death and resurrection, or his work upon the ascension. After stating in v. 18b that "He was put to death in the flesh, but made alive in the Spirit," Peter adds, "In which he went and made a proclamation to the spirits in prison" (v. 19a). Whatever the solution to this interpretive enigma, Peter's first concern is to set forth Christ as the supreme example of innocent

---

116. See chapter 4. In various Jewish and Christian texts, transgression may be linked with physical malady (Deut 28:15–24; Ps 107:17–20; Isa 42:16–17; 57:17–18; Jas 5:14–16), as they are linked here and in Isaiah 53. Physical healing and liberation from sin are conjoined. Jesus liberates from the powers that bind humanity, including both disease and sin.

117. Cf. 1 Kgs 22:17; 2 Chr 18:16; Jer 50:6; Ezek 34:5–6; Zech 10:2; Matt 15:24.

118. John H. Elliott, *1 Peter*, 538.

suffering and, as such, present him as an example for his readers to follow. Peter has just declared to his readers that "it is better to suffer for doing good, if suffering should be God's will, than to suffer for doing evil" (3:17), a point made previously when addressing domestic slaves (2:19-20). In that passage Peter also presents Christ as the example of endurance in the face of unjust suffering: "For to this you have been called, because Christ also suffered for you, leaving you an example, so that you should follow in his steps" (2:21). However, just as in 2:19-24, Peter seamlessly moves from the *imitatio Christi* to Christ's work, which was inimitable ("He himself bore our sins in his body on the cross"), so here also Peter quickly moves from Christ's sufferings as an example to his substitutionary death: "For Christ also suffered for sins once for all, the righteous for the unrighteous" (3:18a). Peter does not enlarge upon the exemplary character of Christ's death since its sacrificial nature engrosses him.

Peter states, "For Christ also suffered for sins once for all" (ὅτι καὶ Χριστὸς ἅπαξ περὶ ἁμαρτιῶν ἔπαθεν).[119] Peter regards the suffering of Christ, here understood as his death (cf. 2:23, which focuses his sufferings that lead to his death), as an unrepeatable or once for all sin offering (Rom 6:10). This affirmation underscores the efficacy of Christ's redemptive work. The prepositional phrase περὶ ἁμαρτιῶν was one way the LXX designated sin offerings (Lev 5:5-11; 6:18, 23; 14:19; 16:3, 5) as well as the NT (Heb 10:6, 8, 18, 26; 1 John 2:2; 4:10).[120] Christ's death as a sin offering was for the multiple sins of humanity. He was the Righteous One who became a sin offering for the unrighteous many (δίκαιος ὑπὲρ ἀδίκων), just as the Suffering Servant was a sin offering that makes the many righteous ("When you make his life an offering for sin. . . . The righteous one, my servant, shall make many righteous, and he shall bear their iniquities" [Isa 53:10-11]). Central to Peter's theology is the conviction that Christ's was undeserving of death since he was the Righteous One. Rather, he died as a substitutionary sin-offering, a sacrifice that was extensive in its effect and final in its efficacy. No further sacrifice need be offered, a point not only made by the author of Hebrews (Heb 7:27; 9:12, 26-28) but also the apostle Peter.

The expression δίκαιος ὑπὲρ ἀδίκων ("the righteous for the unrighteous") points to Christ's innocence, a theme Peter touched previously (2:22-23). But it also affirms that Christ's death was vicarious.[121] He did not suffer death for his own injustices but rather atoned for those of the unrighteous (cf. 2 Pet 2:9). While Peter portrays Christ's

---

119. The textual variant ἀπέθανεν (died) enjoys strong mss. support (P72 ℵ A), although the attestation for ἔπαθεν (suffered) is hardly weak (B K P). In this letter, Peter speaks of Christ's death as his suffering (2:21; 4:1) in order to show the connection between him and Peter's readers, who themselves were suffering (2:19-20; 3:14, 17; 4:1, 15, 19; 2:23). The phrase "died for us" or "for sins" was common in Paul, and this may account for the scribal tendency to insert the well-known expression here (Rom 5:6, 8; 1 Cor 15:3; 2 Cor 5:14-15; 1 Thess 5:10). See the discussion in Metzger, *A Textual Commentary on the Greek New Testament*, 622-23.

120. Kelly, *A Commentary on the Epistles of Peter and Jude*, 148; Achtemeier, *1 Peter*, 247.

121. Edwin Gordon Selwyn, *The First Epistle of Peter*, 95; Kelly, *A Commentary on the Epistles of Peter and Jude*, 148; Beare, *The First Epistle of Peter*, 168; Jobes, *1 Peter*, 238.

death as being for the many who are unrighteous, he particularly has in mind the readers of this epistle who have turned to God from their unrighteous life-ways (1:18; 2:24–25; 4:2–4). Peter's focus here is on Christ's mediatorial role as the one who brings his readers and him to God (ἵνα ὑμᾶς προσαγάγῃ τῷ θεῷ; cf. 2:5; Rom 5:2; Eph 2:18; 3:12). He has reconciled them, together with Peter, to God. The thought is communitarian. Together they now have "access to God"[122] through Christ's substitutionary death. Peter's expression also appears in contexts of sacrifice (Exod 29:10; Lev 1:2; 3:12; 4:4; 8:14) and the consecration of priests to divine service (Exod 29:4, 8; 40:12; Lev 8:24; Num 8:9–10). These cultic associations are in mind (see 1 Pet 2:5, 9), but Peter's principle point is that relationship with God is now established. But this access to God brings with it moral effects (3:10–12). Peter suggests the notion of their deliverance from unrighteous lifestyle since now through Christ's mediation they are led to God, having abandoned their profligate lifestyle oriented around idolatry (4:3). Peter does not separate ethics from relationship with God.

Peter takes one step further in 3:18b by affirming not only Christ's substitutionary death but also his exaltation, a topic covered more completely below. "He was put to death in the flesh, but made alive in the Spirit" (θανατωθεὶς μὲν σαρκὶ ζῳοποιηθεὶς δὲ πνεύματι). It is unlikely that the statement affirms that Christ, after his death, was made alive by the Spirit as the NIV and some other translations suggest. The parallel construction of the clauses leads us to understand the datives (σαρκὶ, πνεύματι) as functioning the same. It cannot be said that Christ was "put to death *by* the flesh but made alive *by* the Spirit."[123] Rather, the expression means that Christ died in the human sphere of existence (see 1:24; 4:1) and was made alive in the heavenly or spiritual sphere of existence.[124] Although it may be said with Paul that the Spirit raised Christ from the dead (Rom 8:11), Peter's point is that Christ has entered a new sphere of spiritual existence through the resurrection. Peter is not denying the bodily resurrection of Christ any more than Paul does in 1 Corinthians 15:35–49. Christ's resurrected state is, as Paul says, in a "spiritual body." Peter does not draw out the identification of the believers with Christ in this resurrected state as does Paul. But his affirmation that Christ suffered in the flesh betrays his belief in Christ's identification with humanity, save for participation in sin (2:22–23; 3:18b).

Christ's Sufferings

Central to Peter's theology is the sufferings and death of Christ. These sufferings were not due to Christ's own sin nor did they occur due to the twisted hand of fate. Indeed, a great injustice had been done since Christ is the Righteous One. Peter understands

---

122. Achtemeier, *1 Peter*, 248.

123. Instrumental dative. *BDF* §195.

124. Kelly, *A Commentary on the Epistles of Peter and Jude*, 150–51; Best, *1 Peter*, 139; Dalton, *Christ's Proclamation to the Spirits*, 135–42; John H. Elliott, *1 Peter*, 647; Jobes, *1 Peter*, 242. Dalton calls this a dative of reference.

Christ's sufferings as integral to God's plan for humanity (1:10–12) and, indeed, the central purpose of the incarnation (1:20). Peter's foundational theology is that Christ's sufferings were vicarious and atoned for sins. Through his death he ransomed those whom God had chosen from their former life ways and reconciled them to God. They now have access to God through Christ their mediator. In this he led them in the New Exodus and brought them into a New Covenant with God, with the implied attendant blessing of forgiveness. Peter frames Jesus and his death in terms of the Suffering Servant of Isaiah. His death was final and efficacious universally, even for the most unrighteous. Christ's suffering brings healing, both physical and moral, and carries within it the call to a new way of life, one oriented to the will of God. Peter's theology of Christ's suffering upon the cross (2:24) is kaleidoscopic yet foundational for Christian theology. We cannot assume that Peter's theology of the sufferings of Christ is derivative. Peter lays the foundations for Christian understanding of the cross of Christ. In 1 Peter we encounter the most vital spring for the early church's embrace of the cross. Early believers did not flee from the Christ's cross, suffering, and shame despite the ignominy of even the mention of the cross in Roman society. They drew the cross into the center of the faith, and this under the principle leadership of the apostle Peter.

The Glories of Christ

In 1:10 Peter summarizes the prophetic testimony through the Spirit of Christ as "the sufferings destined for Christ and the subsequent glory." This is the heart of the gospel according to Peter. Unfortunately, the NRSV obscures the meaning of the latter words since Peter speaks about the "subsequent glories" of Christ in the plural (τὰ εἰς Χριστὸν παθήματα καὶ τὰς μετὰ ταῦτα δόξας, translated "the sufferings of the Messiah and the glories that would follow" in the NIV). Unlike the Gospel of John, Peter does not regard the glorification of Christ as having begun with the cross (John 17:1; 21:19). When speaking of Christ's "glories," Peter reflects on Christ's triumphs, which are set over against his humiliation and rejection (2:7).[125] Elsewhere Peter speaks about these triumphs as Christ's "mighty acts" (τὰς ἀρετὰς), which the redeemed community now proclaims (2:9). These "mighty acts" should not be understood as moral "virtues" in 2:9, as the word is commonly used (2 Pet 1:5), but rather they are manifestations of divine power (Isa 43:21; Josephus, *Ant.* 17.130; 2 Pet 1:3).[126] Peter's understanding of Christ's glories runs from the resurrection (1:3, 21; 3:18, 21), his ascension and session at the right hand of God (3:22), to his final revelation (4:13: 5:1).

Peter uses honorific language to speak of these realities. "Glory" is the language of honor, contrasted with "shame" in the ancient world (note the contrast in the *ESV* rendering of 1 Pet 4:16: "Yet if anyone suffers as a Christian, let him not be ashamed,

---

125. Edwin Gordon Selwyn, *The First Epistle of Peter*, 137; Michaels, *1 Peter*, 45.
126. *BDAG*, 130; Deissmann, *Bible Studies*, 95–96.

but let him glorify God in that name"). Christ's cross was a time of deep humiliation and shame (Jesus "endured the cross, disregarding its shame" [Heb 12:2, NRSV]). The early church struggled against the shame of Jesus' rejection and death, yet because of the resurrection of Christ, they understood that Christ's death was truly honorable. Paul was therefore able to say, "For I am not ashamed of the gospel; it is the power of God for salvation to everyone who has faith" (Rom 1:16). Second Timothy 1:8 exhorts Timothy, saying, "Do not be ashamed, then, of the testimony about our Lord or of me his prisoner." The one who believes in Christ, the Stone, will not be put to shame (1 Pet 2:6, citing Isa 28:16). Jesus had called his disciples not to be ashamed of him and his words (Mark 8:38; Luke 9:26). Through the resurrection, ascension, session at God's right hand, and future revelation, Peter reveals Christ's honor, dignity, and renown. Although he suffered rejection and died, Christ has honor as the one who was, is, and will be exalted. God has ascribed honor to him through these mighty acts.[127] Central to Peter's theology is this divine reversal. God honors Christ Jesus whom the rest rejected and dishonored (2:4, 21–25; 3:18–22; 4:1, 13). We could say that the resurrection and the subsequent glories of Christ are God's riposte to the challenge to Christ's honor brought about by his rejection, suffering, and death. Christ's honor accrues to those who suffer because of their identification with him (4:14).

The Resurrection of Christ

Peter speaks directly about Christ's resurrection from the dead four times in this letter (1:3, 21; 3:18, 21), while in other passages his resurrection is implied (1:11; 2:4, 7). Peter regards Christ as the living and exalted Lord over the powers (3:22). According to Peter, the gospel and the sufferings of Christ cannot be understood and experienced apart from the affirmations that he who had died was raised to life and is now fully alive and acting as the exalted Lord.

Four strands of theology are directly connected with the resurrection of Christ in 1 Peter. First, since God raised Christ from the dead, those who believe in him can have hope (1:3, 21) and faith (1:21, 8) in God and Christ. They also love Jesus Christ

---

127. *TLNT*, 1:362–79. John Hall Elliott, "Disgraced Yet Graced: The Gospel According to 1 Peter in the Key of Honor and Shame," *BTB* 25 (1995) 166–78; David A. deSilva, *Despising Shame: Honor Discourse and Community Maintenance in the Epistle to the Hebrews* (Atlanta: Scholars, 1995); deSilva, *Honor, Patronage, Kinship and Purity*, 23–94. As Elliott notes, "'Honor' is a claim to worth (on the part of an individual, family, or group) accompanied by the public acknowledgment of, and respect for, that worth (Prov 3:4; 20:3; 21:21; Demothenes, *Or*. 2.15; 3.24; Josephus, *Vita* 274, 422–29). Honor was a matter of one's *fama*, one's reputation, social standing, and status rating in the eyes of others. 'Honor,' Aristotle comments (*Rhet*. 1.5; 1316A), 'is the token of a man's being famous for doing good.'" Therefore, in collectivist cultures such as the one in which Peter and his readers are embedded, "Defending, maintaining, and enhancing personal or group honor, on the one hand, and avoiding being publicly degraded, demeaned, disgraced, insulted, scorned, and humiliated (i.e., 'shamed'), on the other, were universal and persistent preoccupations of the ancient Mediterraneans in their informal interactions" (John Hall Elliott, "Disgraced Yet Graced," 168–69). Christ's honor demonstrated in his innocence, and divine vindication of him is central to Peter's theological and ethical strategy.

(1:8). Since these persecuted believers see the plan of God worked out in Christ even though he had been rejected by "the builders" (2:7), they can take comfort and have courage in their situation. The resurrection of Christ was the proof of God's power over his enemies, and this, therefore, becomes the pledge of the believer's future glorification. The believer's hope is for the grace and glory that will be brought to them at the time of the revelation of Christ (1:13; 5:1, 4, 10). Peter does not state that the resurrection of Christ is the guarantee of the believer's resurrection (cf. 1 Thess 4:13–18; 1 Cor 15), but in a similar way, he connects Christ's glorification with theirs (1:21; 5:1, 4, 10). Through the resurrection of Christ, these believers can have faith and hope in God, knowing that the divine plan is being worked out even amidst the confusion of social rejection and hostility.

Closely related to this teaching is the affirmation that the resurrection of Christ is God's ultimate vindication of him. Although Christ was rejected by his fellows, God made him the chief cornerstone (2:7). The notion of God's vindication of Christ in the resurrection appears in the liturgical fragment embedded in 1 Timothy 3:16: "He appeared in the flesh, was vindicated by the Spirit" (NIV). This declaration of Christ's righteousness (ἐδικαιώθη ἐν πνεύματι) was part and parcel of the primitive church's catechetical teaching concerning the meaning of the resurrection of Christ. His victory was of such magnitude that "he went and made proclamation" of it "to the spirits in prison" (1 Pet 3:18–19, NRSV), thus showing his power and authority over all supernatural beings (cf. 3:22). The attendant promise is that, in the end, God will vindicate his elect—giving them honor or glory in the place of their current shame—and reverse the verdict of their peers who condemn and malign them as ones who do evil (2:12).

In the third place, the resurrection brings about the new birth in the lives of those who believe in Christ (1:3). As Best remarks, "The new life flowing from the new birth only exists because of the new risen life of Christ"[128] (cf. John 3:3–8). In 1:23 Peter states that "the living and enduring word of God" effects this new birth, and most likely the word he has in mind here is the message of the gospel, the heart of which was the sufferings and the resurrection of Christ (1:11–12). Peter affirms that baptism, the right of Christian initiation and conversion, saves them. Its efficacy resides in the resurrection of Jesus Christ (3:21). There is moral transformation, which is not empowered by the water but by the resurrection of Christ. Only through the power of God manifested in the resurrection of Christ can the believers obtain the new moral orientation that the new birth brings.

Finally, through the resurrection of Christ the believers are led to God and reconciled to him (3:18). Peter does not use the world "reconcile" but simply states that Christ was made alive in the spirit ἵνα ὑμᾶς προσαγάγῃ τῷ θεῷ ("in order to bring you to God"). Through his substitutionary death and his subsequent resurrection, Christ becomes the mediator between God and his people (2:5). Peter may have in mind the

---

128. Best, *1 Peter*, 75.

notion of Christ as the new covenant mediator, theology more explicitly expressed in Hebrews (8:6; 9:15; 12:24).

The Ascension of Christ

Peter's theology revolves around the sufferings and glories of Christ, with Christ's resurrection from the dead being the beginning of his glorification (1:21). But Peter also embraces a robust theology of Christ's ascension, most clearly expressed in 3:22. After his death, God brought Christ to life (3:18b), and now the believers are saved "by the resurrection of Jesus Christ" (3:21b). In that resurrected state he "has gone into heaven and is at the right hand of God, with angels, authorities, and powers made subject to him" (3:22; cf. Acts 1:10; 2:32–35, citing Ps 110:1; Mark 12:35–37). Upon his ascension, the spiritual forces of this age were subjected to Christ, the supreme Lord. These powers lay behind the social rejection and hostility Peter's readers experienced, motivated as they were by Satan, who was determined to overthrow their faith (5:8–9). Peter's word about Christ's exaltation over them in his ascension would have been a source of inestimable comfort. As Achtemeier states, "The readers of the letter are thus assured that the powers still rampant in their world, motivating the suppression of the Christian community, have been robbed of their ultimate power through Christ's resurrection and his assumption of divine authority, an authority that will soon become visible with God's final judgment."[129] Part of Peter's testimony was that Christ had ascended to a place of authority over all powers hostile to God. The sovereign rule of the ascended Jesus finds its earliest expression in the literature ascribed to Peter, and most likely the Christian understanding of this reality is rooted in Jesus' teaching and then given its first full expression in Peter's theology. We may add the ascension to Cullmann's affirmation of Peter's theological innovation.[130]

Peter begins to elaborate his theology of the ascension in 3:18–20, which describes Christ's proclamation of victory over fallen angels and the forces of evil when he ascended after the resurrection. This reading of 3:18–22, one of many suggested through the centuries, was first proposed by Karl Gschwind, later developed by William Dalton, and adopted by many commentators hence.[131] Earlier interpretations

---

129. Achtemeier, *1 Peter*, 274. See Kelly, *A Commentary on the Epistles of Peter and Jude*, 164; Best, *1 Peter*, 148; Rom 8:38–39; Eph 1:19b–23; 6:12; Col 2:8–15. As the late Rev. William "Willie" Still of Gilcomston South Church in Aberdeen said leaning over the pulpit, "Little children, *don't forget the devil!*"

130. Cullmann, *Peter: Disciple-Apostle-Martyr*, 66.

131. Karl Gschwind, *Die Niederfahrt Christi in die Unterwelt: Ein Beitrag zur Exegese des Neuen Testamentes und zur Geschichte des Taufsymbols* (Münster: Aschendorff, 1911); Dalton, *Christ's Proclamation to the Spirits*; Kelly, *A Commentary on the Epistles of Peter and Jude*, 146–64; Michaels, *1 Peter*, 194–222; Marshall, *1 Peter*, 117–32; Achtemeier, *1 Peter*, 239–74; John H. Elliott, *1 Peter*, 637–710; Jobes, *1 Peter*, 235–60. Pierce presents a variation on this view by arguing that the "spirits in prison" are not simply supernatural but human (Chad T. Pierce, *Spirits and the Proclamation of Christ: 1 Peter 3:18-22 in Light of Sin and Punishment Traditions in Early Jewish and Christian Literature* (Tübingen: Mohr Siebeck, 2011). Summaries of interpretive approaches are found in various commentaries. See

followed various lines. Clement of Alexandria believed that the passage referred to the descent of Christ when he preached to those who had previously died, a position that still finds favor. Some who hold this position state that this proclamation was made to deceased souls who, upon hearing the proclamation of Christ, would come to conversion.[132] A variation of this position is that between Christ's death and resurrection he went to preach "good news only to those of Noah's generation who were converted before death (or to all of the OT righteous and patriarchs who died prior to Christ)."[133] Others regard the "spirits in prison" as the deceased in Noah's day to whom Christ proclaimed a message of condemnation.[134] On the other hand, Augustine forwarded the interpretation that Peter's statement that Christ "went and made a proclamation to the spirits in prison" (3:19) referred to his preexistent activity when he made proclamation through Noah (*Epistola* 64.14–17). This view is not commonly held today.[135] Rather surprisingly, the position forwarded by Dalton that the passage speaks of Christ's ascension has garnered the greatest support among contemporary commentators.

The evidence for understanding 3:19 as a description of the ascension is strong. First Peter 3:18 speaks of the death and resurrection of Christ: "He was put to death in the flesh, but made alive in the spirit." Verse 19 begins, "In which he also went" (ἐν ᾧ ... πορευθείς). The immediate antecedent of the prepositional phrase "in which" (ἐν ᾧ) is "in the spirit" (πνεύματι), that is, in his resurrected state.[136] Alternately, as Elliott points out, "in which" may be understood as a reference to the occasion of Christ's going to preach, that being "having been made alive."[137] The difference between these readings is of little importance since the point is that the journey to proclaim to the

---

especially Dalton, *Christ's Proclamation to the Spirits*, 27–50; Achtemeier, *1 Peter*, 258; John H. Elliott, *1 Peter*, 648–51; Jobes, *1 Peter*, 236–37; Chad T. Pierce, *Spirits and the Proclamation of Christ*, 2–20.

132. Bigg, *Peter and Jude*, 162–63; Cranfield, *1 and 2 Peter and Jude*, 85; Schelkle, *Die Petrusbriefe, Der Judasbrief*, 104–8; Beare, *The First Epistle of Peter*, 170–73; Goppelt, *A Commentary on 1 Peter*, 255–60.

133. See the discussions in John H. Elliott, *1 Peter*, 648–49; Dalton, *Christ's Proclamation to the Spirits*, 34–37; Bo Reicke, *The Disobedient Spirits and Christian Baptism: A Study of 1 Pet 3:19 and Its Context* (København: Munksgaard, 1946), 14–27. On recent Roman Catholic discussion of the topic, see Lyra Pitstick, *Christ's Descent Into Hell: John Paul II, Joseph Ratzinger, and Hans Urs von Balthasar on the Theology of Holy Saturday* (Grand Rapids: Eerdmans, 2016).

134. See the arguments in Reicke, *The Disobedient Spirits and Christian Baptism*, 44–45; Dalton, *Christ's Proclamation to the Spirits*, 41; John H. Elliott, *1 Peter*, 648–49.

135. See, for example Grudem, *1 Peter*, 164–69, 211–48.

136. Dalton, *Christ's Proclamation to the Spirits*, 145; Achtemeier, *1 Peter*, 252–53; Jobes, *1 Peter*, 242.

137. John H. Elliott, *1 Peter*, 652. Elliott points out that it is unusual for the dative of reference (πνεύματι) to serve "as antecedent of a relative pronoun (cf. Acts 2:8; Eph 2:2, 3; 2 Pet 1:4; 3:1)." The infrequency of such use is of little consequence since the examples he cites simply prove that a dative of reference can be the antecedent of the relative pronoun. Elliott's stress on the temporal understanding of ἐν ᾧ does, however, find support from Peter's use of the prepositional phrase elsewhere in the letter, where twice it is temporal (2:12; 3:16). In other instances (1:6; 4:4) it is most likely causal (Achtemeier, *1 Peter*, 252).

spirits in prison occurred after the death and resurrection of Christ. The case for interpreting 3:19 as the ascension is bolstered by 3:22, which closes the inclusio begun in 3:19: "Who has gone into heaven and is at the right hand of God, with angels, authorities and powers made subject to him" (ὅς ἐστιν ἐν δεξιᾷ [τοῦ] θεοῦ πορευθεὶς εἰς οὐρανὸν ὑποταγέντων αὐτῷ ἀγγέλων καὶ ἐξουσιῶν καὶ δυνάμεων.). Peter's principle concern is to show how Christ is made sovereign over all powers upon his ascension. Indeed, the lexeme translated "who has gone" (πορευθεὶς) is the same verb used in the same participial form found in 3:19 (ἐν ᾧ . . . πορευθεὶς). In 3:22 Peter makes clear what kind of "going" he had in mind in 3:19—he journeyed "into heaven." In 3:18–22 Peter marks Jesus' journey from his death to his resurrection, ascension, and session at the right hand of God.

For some time scholars have recognized that the backstory of 3:19–22 was the person of Enoch, who, according to Genesis 5:21–24, "walked with God; then he was no more, because God took him." The heart of Jewish reflection on the Enoch story is the pseudepigraphical book of 1 Enoch, which tells of Enoch's ascension when he preached a message of condemnation upon those supernatural beings who had committed sin (1 En. 12:3–13:5). First Enoch was well-enough known in the era that Jude quoted from it (Jude 14; 1 En. 1:9).[138] The story recounted is that Enoch goes to proclaim judgment upon those celestial beings, the Watchers, who had defiled themselves with women, an apparent reference to the account in Genesis 6:1–4 in which "the sons of God went in to the daughters of humans, who bore children to them." These were angels who were trapped in prison ("In the prison [where] they will be locked up forever" [1 En. 10:12–14]; 18:14; 21:10; 2 En. 7:1–5), who had been disobedient to the commands of God ("These are among the stars of heaven which have transgressed the commandments of the Lord and are bound in this place" [1 En. 21:6]; 106:13–15). They had committed their sin in Noah's day ("And call his name Noah, for he shall be the remnant for you; and he and his sons shall be saved from the corruption which shall come upon the earth on account of all the sin and oppression that exited" [1 En. 106:13–19]; T. Naph. 3:5) and were condemned due to their sin with women ("For what reason have you abandoned the high, holy, and eternal heaven; and slept with women and defiled yourselves with women" [1 En. 15:3–12]; 19:1).[139] Peter understands these traditions as the substructure of his theology of the ascension of Christ,

---

138. See the discussion in Green, *Jude and 2 Peter*, 101–3.

139. Jobes, *1 Peter*, 242–45. See the relevant texts in Dalton, *Christ's Proclamation to the Spirits*, 167–76; Achtemeier, *1 Peter*, 252–62; John H. Elliott, *1 Peter*, 653; Jobes, *1 Peter*, 242–45. The most complete analysis of the relevant Jewish texts that form the background of Peter's teaching is Pierce (*Spirits and the Proclamation of Christ*, 25–175), who, on the basis of these texts, contends that the "spirits in prison" should include fallen angels and evil spirits who lead humans into evil. Less convincing, however, is his argument that the group would include human oppressors, given the celestial context of Christ's journey and proclamation (*Spirits and the Proclamation of Christ*, 208–17).

who now himself goes and proclaims judgment upon the forces of evil.[140] What Enoch is said to have done is precisely what Christ accomplished.

Since Peter regards the present persecutions the believers are enduring as supernatural opposition and not simply a social conflict, Peter's announcement of Christ's ascension and proclamation of victory over the powers is highly relevant for his readers. In 5:8–9 he states, "Like a roaring lion your adversary the devil prowls around looking for someone to devour. Resist him, steadfast in your faith." These believers may resist the devil's advances precisely because they know that Christ has risen and ascended, victorious now over the supernatural powers of evil that motivate the persecutions they face (3:22). Christ also "went and made a proclamation to the spirits in prison" (τοῖς ἐν φυλακῇ πνεύμασιν πορευθεὶς ἐκήρυξεν). Peter does not say that Christ preached the gospel to them (εὐαγγελίζομαι, as in 1:12, 25; 4:6) but that he made some kind of proclamation over or to them (ἐκήρυξεν). While this verb can be employed to describe the proclamation of the Christian message (Acts 8:5; 9:20; 19:13; 28:31; Rom 10:8, 14–15; 1 Cor 1:31; Phil 1:15), it can map to the concept of proclamation without the attendant association with the gospel (Luke 12:3; Rom 2:21; Rev 5:2).[141]

The message Enoch was said to proclaim to the fallen Watchers was a proclamation of judgment that did not carry any hope of redemption ("At that moment the Watchers were calling me, And they said to me, 'Enoch . . . go and make known to the Watches of heaven who have abandoned the high heaven . . . and have defiled themselves with women . . . neither will there be peace for them nor the forgiveness of sin"; "There will not be peace unto you; a grave judgment has come upon you" [1 En 12:4–14:8]). Since Peter regards those whom Christ made this proclamation as those "who in former times did not obey" in the days of Noah, we may assume that his was a declaration of judgment as well as the proclamation of his victory over them (3:22). Christ is victorious over the powers and has made his proclamation to them. The particular reference to judgment proclaimed over the disobedience of the spirits in prison due to their sin in Noah's day is particularly relevant since these spirits, according to 1 Enoch, were responsible for the proliferation of malignant spirits in the world ("But now the giants who are born from the [union of] the spirits and the flesh shall be called evil spirits upon the earth. . . . Evil spirits have come out of their bodies" [1 En. 15:8–12]).

---

140. An objection that could be raised against this line of interpretation is that Peter's readers, who were on the main Gentiles, would likely not have known the Enoch traditions. However, as Jobes has pointed out, "Peter's allusion to the tradition of the Watchers does not necessarily require a literary knowledge of the Book of 1 Enoch" (Jobes, *1 Peter*, 245). Citing Trebilco, Jobes forwards the intriguing suggestion that residents of Asia Minor would have known the Noah traditions given that the flood story was known there, and it was even believed that the ark came to rest near the town of Apamea Kibotos, with "*kibōtos*" meaning "ark" (*1 Peter*, 245–47; Paul R. Trebilco, *Jewish Communities in Asia Minor* [Cambridge: Cambridge University Press, 1991], 85–103). The evidence does not point to knowledge of the Enoch story but only suggests how the Noah traditions would have been viewed as relevant for Peter's readers.

141. BDAG, 543–44; LSJ, 949.

Paul was not alone in recognizing the battle with the spiritual forces of evil (Eph 6:12). Peter regarded the ascension of Christ as the time when he was exalted over the powers of evil (1 Pet 3:22) that now assail the church. But the apostle does not focus exclusively upon Christ's journey to proclaim judgment, but his eye is also upon his present session at the right hand of God (cf. Eph 1:20–21; 2:6; Ps 110:1; Mark 12:36; Acts 2:34; Heb 1:13). "The right hand of God" metaphorically expresses the concept of divine power (Ps 17:7; 20:6; 21:8; 63:8; 118:15; Exod 15:6, 12; Isa 48:13) but also was regarded as the place of one who enjoyed the favor of the king and who received his honor (1 Kgs 2:19; Ps 45:9). Peter calls his readers to acknowledge his lordship amidst the social rejection they endured (1 Pet 3:15): "but in your hearts sanctify Christ as Lord." Peter cites Isaiah 8:13, which says of Yahweh, "But the Lord of hosts, him you shall regard as holy." Peter does not call the believers to consecrate Christ as the Lord but to reverence and regard him as holy (cf. Matt 6:9; Luke 11:2; Isa 29:23; Ezek 20:41). Believers are to fear or reverence Christ as the sovereign Lord (cf. Isa. 8:13) instead of fearing their adversaries (1 Pet 3:14b). They should hold this reverence for Christ the Lord in the deepest recesses of their being (cf. 1:22; 3:4).

The call to regard Christ as Lord brings these believers assurance in adversity but also carries a call to right conduct. Peter juxtaposes the call to sanctify Christ as Lord with his exhortation to do good (3:13), to respond to questioning accusations with meekness and reverence (3:15–16a), and to keep a good conscience as they maintain a good way of life (3:16b; 2:12).[142] Peter develops his theological ethics around Christ's present lordship. Though ascended into heaven, Christ is not absent from his people. Indeed, in the present time they are in a relationship of love with him and believe in him. This relationship is the source of present inestimable joy (1:8). Peter acknowledges the distance between his readers and Jesus and the differences between him and them. Unlike the apostle, who walked with Jesus, they "have not seen him" and they "do not see him now" (1:8). However, the bond between Christ and them is firm: they love him and believe in him. Given that relationship, they now receive "the salvation of your souls" through him (1:9). These believers in the provinces of Asia Minor have "tasted that the Lord is good ($\chi\rho\eta\sigma\tau\grave{o}\varsigma$)," that is "kind" or "benevolent" and perhaps even "loving,"[143] in the present hour (2:3; citing Ps 34:9). Given that Christ is alive and reigning as Lord, the believers now "come to him, the living Stone" (2:4). The expression may be cultic since it appears in contexts of offering sacrifice to God (Lev

---

142. "Conscience" appears in three passages in 1 Peter: 2:19; 3:16, 21. It is closely connected with "doing good." In 2:19 he points the slave to the concept of being conscious of God. Their life is lived before him. Pierce and Kelly note that the consciousness is the community's common or shared knowledge of God and his will (Charles Anthony Pierce, *Conscience in the New Testament*, 107; Kelly, *A Commentary on the Epistles of Peter and Jude*, 117). The "good conscience" in 3:16, 21, includes abstaining from sin but also something more. It involves positive moral action (cf. 3:17), doing good in society (2:15). Mauer is right in saying that a good conscience is "a formula for the Christian life" (*TDNT*, 7:918; see Johannes Stelzenberger, *Syneidesis Im Neuen Testament* [Paderborn: Schöningh, 1961], 66).

143. *BDAG*, 1090.

9:7–8; 21:17–18, 21, 23; Num 18:3–4, 22). But it may also mean to come near to God (Exod 16:9; Lev 9:5; Deut 5:27), and, as Elliott points up, the language may suggest the way proselytes are those who have "drawn near to God."[144] Peter regards his Gentile readers as proselytes who have come to Christ, the living Stone (see above). They have entered into alliance with him, the one who then brings them to God (3:18). In the present Christ, the living Stone, serves as the mediator. They, now constituted as a holy priesthood, "offer spiritual sacrifices acceptable to God through Jesus Christ" (2:5).

Christ's ascension and present session at the right hand of God brings various realties of Peter's theology to the forefront. Christ is the Lord over all the powers of evil which now assail the persecuted believers in Asia Minor. Whatever the opposition they face, in all its spiritual, social, and physical dimensions, they can rest in the assurance that Christ has indeed overcome all opposition and that he currently reigns as sovereign. But his present life means that these believers may enter into a relationship with him marked by faith, love, and joy. They experience the sweetness of his benevolence. On the other hand, his lordship carries within it a call to life marked by recognition of his position over their lives with holy living as its outcome, even amidst the dishonor they endured in their communities. They have come to him and are assured of his mediation as he brings them and their spiritual sacrifices of worship and service to God. Such worship God finds acceptable through Christ.

The Revelation of Christ

The glories of Christ (1:11) include Christ's final revelation. Nowhere does Peter speak about Christ's coming (παρουσία) as does Paul (1 Cor 15:23; 1 Thess 2:19; 3:13; 4:15; 2 Thess 2:1), James (Jas 5:7–8) or even 2 Peter (2 Pet 1:16; 3:4). For Peter, Christ is very present but simply not seen at this time (1 Pet 1:8). Peter reminds the believers that Christ will be revealed (1:7, 13; 4:13; 5:4) and that the time draws near (4:7; cf. 1:5; 4:5). The glory bestowed on the resurrected and ascended Christ (1:21) has yet to be revealed to all.

Peter ties a number of theological threads to the future glorious revelation of Christ. First, at that time he will bring salvation in its fullest extent. At present these believers are "protected by the power of God through faith" (1:5). God is the one who guards them and watches over them (cf. 2 Cor 11:32; Josephus, *Vit.* 53, 240), securing them "for a salvation ready to be revealed (ἀποκαλυφθῆν) in the last time." The salvation begun (1:9; 3:21) will be fully completed at the time of Christ's revelation. For Peter, salvation includes moral transformation in the present time (3:21) and deliverance from God's judgment in the future (4:18). Peter also speaks of salvation as "the grace that Jesus Christ will bring you when he is revealed" (1:13). "Grace" is the comprehensive term Peter uses to describe the full extent of God's benefaction (5:12b; 1:2b).

---

144. John H. Elliott, *1 Peter*, 409; see Philo, *Spec.* 1.51, 309; *Praem.* 152.

Peter regards the revelation of Christ as the time when Christ's glory will be revealed and they will participate in the glory of God in Christ (4:13; 5:1, 10; 1:11). The revelation of Christ will be the event when Christ, the one rejected and dishonored (2:7), will be honored before all. The honorific language touches upon a key element in the realities Peter's readers faced within their communities. Campbell rightly notes that "conflict in 1 Peter is best seen in light of the honor contest. The suffering experienced by the Christians whom Peter addresses is not an official persecution on any scale, but primarily defamation of the community. Defamation in the Mediterranean world is a challenge to honor. If not properly answered, its recipient is dishonored."[145] Throughout the letter Peter demonstrates that Christ's honor was challenged through his rejection and sufferings but that, in the end, God responded to the challenge to his honor by the "glories" of Christ, including his resurrection, ascension, session, and revelation (1:11; 2:6–8). The revelation of Jesus Christ will be the ultimate honoring of Christ. His glory/honor will be revealed publicly, and believers "will be glad and shout for joy" in celebration (4:13). God's glory in Christ will no longer be challenged since it is eternal (5:10). Moreover, just as the believers share in the sufferings of Christ (4:13) they, as Peter, will share in this glorious honor (5:1). They, too, have been called "to his eternal glory in Christ" (5:10). Final honors will be afforded them given their solidarity with Christ through faith. Peter could have the resurrection of believers in mind given Peter's discourse about Christ's glorification. While the point may be implied, it is far from clearly stated (cf. Luke 24:26; 1 Cor 15:43; Rom 8:17). Peter's central concern is that as these believers identified with Christ in his suffering and dishonor, they will share with him in his glory and honor. As he says to them, "The genuineness of your faith—being more precious than gold that, though perishable, is tested by fire—may be found to result in praise and glory and honor when Jesus Christ is revealed" (1:7).

Given that Christ has been raised these believers now have a living hope (1:3). That hope is bound up with their future inheritance made ready and secured for them (1:4) and the salvation that will come when Christ is revealed (1:5). They now live in hope and joy (1:6), the very joy that shall be theirs when Christ is revealed (4:13). Once again we see that in Peter's theology the future, present, and past are joined tightly together in an eschatology that is both realized and future.

On the other side, the revelation of Christ is the time when those who oppose the new believers will have "to give an accounting to him who stands ready to judge the living and the dead" (4:5). The unbelievers had demanded an explanation of the believers' conversion (3:15) and had condemned them as evildoers in the public realm (3:16; 4:3, 14). Upon Christ's revelation they, then, must give account before the Judge. They will not stand (2:8). Elsewhere in the New Testament, Christ is named as the one who executes judgment over the living and the dead (Acts 10:42; 2 Tim 4:1). In 1

---

145. Barth L. Campbell, *Honor, Shame, and the Rhetoric of 1 Peter* (Atlanta: Scholars, 1998), 27. See David A. deSilva, "Honor, Shame, and the Rhetoric of First Peter," *ATJ* 32 (2000) 129–32.

Peter God is identified as the Judge (1 Pet 1:17; 2:23; 4:6), but in 3:18–22 Christ takes this role. Whether Peter has in mind God the Father or Christ as the Judge here is not the primary concern of the passage, which simply announces that the Judge "stands ready to judge" in the context of the discussion of the nearness of the end (4:7). Just as salvation is ready to be revealed (1:5) so, too, is divine judgment. Both will occur at the time of Christ's revelation.

Christ's Sufferings and Glories

Christ is the center of God's plan. He has endured suffering and dishonor, but God has and will honor him fully while bringing to shame those who rejected and dishonored him. Those who believe in Christ share in his suffering and his shame, but they "will not be put to shame" (2:6). Rather, they will receive ascribed honor and glory with him. In the present time the believers receive honor since "the spirit of glory, which is the Spirit of God, is resting on you" (4:14). Sufferings and glories mark the arc of Christ's existence from the time of his revelation in the incarnation (1:20) up to the final event of his glorious revelation. Christian existence in the present time patterns itself on these sufferings and glories. With him they suffer and will be glorified. Peter's prescription for these socially ostracized believers in the Roman provinces of Asia Minor is framed within the large perspective of God's saving history, which began before the foundation of the world (1:20), was predicted through the prophets (1:10–11), proclaimed by the Christian messengers, and received by these believers (1:12). They have been caught up into this plan of God, known in its entirety as God's grace (5:12). While at the present time they are perplexed because of their ordeals (4:12), Peter lets them know that God's plan prevailed in Christ and will prevail in them. The time is short; the end of all things is at hand. For the present, then, Peter calls them to stand in this grace, this whole arc of God's plan. They may do so since "the God of all grace, who has called you to his eternal glory in Christ, will himself restore, support, strengthen, and establish you" (5:10). He holds all power forever and ever (5:11). Amen.

THE HOLY SPIRIT IN 1 PETER

First Peter speaks of the Holy Spirit in only a few texts (1:2, 11–12; 2:5; 4:14), yet the Spirit's role in the epistle's development of salvation history is significant.[146] The

---

146. In 3:18c πνεύματι may mean "in the Spirit" (NIV) or "by the Spirit" (NIV 1984), but, as argued above, Peter's thought is that Christ was made alive "in the sphere of the spirit." The meaning of πνεύματι is similar to πνευματικός in 1 Cor 15:44–46, where Paul places two spheres of Christ's existence in contrast, the physical body and the spiritual body (σπείρεται σῶμα ψυχικόν, ἐγείρεται σῶμα πνευματικόν, "It is sown a physical body, it is raised a spiritual body"). See Eugenio Green, *1 Pedro y 2 Pedro*, 217–19; John H. Elliott, *1 Peter*, 646–47. We cannot bracket out the Holy Spirit's agency in the resurrection of Christ (cf. Rom 8:11), but Peter's emphasis does not lie here. Achtemeier demurs, however, arguing that we should see the Spirit's agency in 3:18 since he reads Peter as saying

language of baptism in or by the Spirit (cf. Mark 1:8; John 1:33; Acts 1:5; 11:16) is absent from 1 Peter, yet the letter holds a robust theology of the Spirit that focuses on the nature of God and his saving history.

Sanctified by the Spirit (1:2)

In the opening verses of the letter, Peter recounts God's saving activity accomplished in the lives of the believers found in the Roman provinces. He addresses his readers as "the exiles of the Dispersion . . . who have been chosen and destined by God the Father and sanctified by the Spirit to be obedient to Jesus Christ and to be sprinkled with his blood" (ἐκλεκτοῖς παρεπιδήμοις διασπορᾶς . . . κατὰ πρόγνωσιν θεοῦ πατρὸς ἐν ἁγιασμῷ πνεύματος εἰς ὑπακοὴν καὶ ῥαντισμὸν αἵματος Ἰησοῦ Χριστοῦ). This verse contains an early Trinitarian affirmations as Peter places God the Father, the Spirit, and Jesus Christ as co-actors in the work of salvation (cf. Matt 28:19; 2 Cor 13:14; Eph 4–6; Jude 20–21). Achtemeier notes that "this construction . . . displays the kind of reflections that eventuated in the Trinitarian formulations embodied in the Nicene Creed, but it is probably anachronistic to refer here to 'trinitarian formulations.'"[147] We must not overstate Peter's understanding of the relationship between God the Father, the Spirit, and Jesus Christ. Speaking of the several Trinitarian passages in the New Testament, Hort reminds us that "in no passage is there any indication that the writer was independently working out a doctrinal scheme," but then proceeds to affirm that "a recognized belief or idea seems to be everywhere presupposed."[148] Best puts the matter this way: "We have here the beginnings of Trinitarian doctrine."[149] Peter's focus is on the function and work of God the Father, the Spirit, and Jesus Christ, not on ontology, but his ability to place the collaboration of the three implies a high Christology and Pneumatology. Indeed, elsewhere Peter ascribes the divine title "Lord" to Jesus Christ (2:3; 3:15) and affirms that "the Spirit of glory and of God" rests on these persecuted believers (4:14, NIV). The elevated understanding of both Christ and the Spirit as divine was coursing through the early church, and Peter is an early witness

---

that Christ was "put to death by unbelieving humanity" (σαρκί) and not by "the flesh," and then he was "raised by (God's) Spirit" (1 Peter, 249–51). While σάρξ may signify humans or humanity in 1 Peter (1:24), it also refers to the human condition (3:21; 4:1–2, 6). The contrast between "flesh" and "spirit" in this verse has to do with Christ and his being (cf. 4:6; 1 Cor 5:5; 2 Cor 7:1; Col 2:5; Heb 12:9) when he was crucified and when he was raised from the dead. Peter topicalizes two stages of Christ's existence as 1 Timothy 3:16 ("He was revealed in flesh, vindicated in spirit"), although in other NT texts the contrast can also be between the human condition and the Spirit of God (John 3:6; 6:63; Rom 8:4–6; Gal 3:3; Phil 3:3). In Christ's resurrected condition (πνεύματι) Christ then went to preach to the spirits in prison.

147. Achtemeier, 1 Peter, 86, citing Schelkle, Die Petrusbriefe, Der Judasbrief, 24. Achtemeier also references Hort, who says the verse sets forth "the operation of the Father, the Holy Spirit, and the Son respectively" (The First Epistle of St. Peter 1:1–2:17, 18).

148. Hort, The First Epistle of St. Peter 1:1–2:17, 18.

149. Best, 1 Peter, 72.

to the foundations of this Trinitarian theology. In the apostle's theology all three are actors in the drama of divine redemption.

In 1:2b Peter focuses on the Spirit's agency in sanctifying those who have been chosen by God (ἐν ἁγιασμῷ πνεύματος). A number of commentators regard the expression as a reference to the conversion and baptism of the readers.[150] Elliott supports this reading, saying, "The combination of *sanctifying action* with *Spirit* together with the triadic form of 1:2a–c, suggests the influence here of primitive Christian baptismal tradition (Rom 6:1–11, 19, 22; Matt 28:19; cf. 1 Cor 6:11)." Peter focuses intently on Christian baptism in 3:21, so the suggestion of the baptismal context for this Spirit's sanctifying work cannot be placed to the side. In Acts 2:38 Peter exhorts his hearers at Pentecost, saying, "Repent and be baptized, every one of you, in the name of Jesus Christ for the forgiveness of your sins. And you will receive the gift of the Holy Spirit." In 1 Peter the most likely context of the initial sanctifying work of the Spirit is baptism as well. Moreover, as noted previously in the chapter on Acts, Peter employed covenantal language when speaking of the promise of the Spirit in the context of baptism (cf. Acts 2:38; Jer 31:31–34). Here also Peter juxtaposes the Spirit's agency in sanctifying these believers with the New Covenant in the following clause: "To be obedient and to be sprinkled with his blood" (see above; Exod 24:1–8). Peter recognizes the Spirit's agency in the conversion/initiation of these believers at the time of their baptism, a time when they enter the New Covenant with God through Jesus Christ.

However, moral renewal is not outside the frame in 1:2 since ἁγιασμός almost exclusively speaks of moral cleansing in the New Testament (Rom 6:19, 22; 1 Thess 4:3–4, 7; 1 Tim 2:15; Heb 12:14).[151] The concepts of conversion/initiation and moral renewal are hardly antithetical since separation to God, symbolized in baptism, is the beginning of a life of holiness (cf. 1 Cor 1:30; 2 Thess 2:13). One of Peter's principle concerns is sanctification (1:13–16) as he exhorts his readers, saying, "As he who called you is holy, be holy yourselves in all your conduct; for it is written, 'You shall be holy, for I am holy'" (citing Lev 11:44–45; 19:2). Peter does not develop the concept of the Spirit's enabling agency in the moral life as does Paul (Rom 8:1–17), but he understands the key role that the Spirit plays in bringing these Gentiles out of their former way of life and into obedience to God (1 Pet 1:14–16; 4:1–4).

The Testimony of the Spirit of Christ (1:11)

As argued in chapter 2, central within the witnesses to Peter's theology is the concept of testimony. Offering testimony stands at the center of Peter's mission according to this letter (5:1, 12). Peter is both an eyewitness and one who bears testimony. Since he witnessed Christ's sufferings, Peter can offer the kind of proofs that characterized valid

---

150. Edwin Gordon Selwyn, *The First Epistle of Peter*, 119–20; Schelkle, *Die Petrusbriefe, Der Judasbrief*, 21; Kelly, *A Commentary on the Epistles of Peter and Jude*, 43; Best, *1 Peter*, 71.

151. See *TDNT*, 1:113.

testimony (Aristotle, *Ars Rhetorica* 1.2.2). Moreover, the content of his testimony was identical with that of the prophets, which centered on Christ's sufferings and glories (1:10–12). Multiple witnesses had great value (Plato, *Gorgias* 471e). As argued earlier, oracular utterances and their interpretation were deemed valid testimony (cf. 2 Pet. 1:19). Aristotle said that "interpreters of oracles for the future" (1.15.14) could serve as witnesses. Peter places the prophetic testimony regarding the sufferings and glories of Christ alongside his own testimony (1:11; 5:1). The apostolic and prophetic witness to Christ ground Peter's Christology and soteriology.

Both Jewish and Christian theology held that the Spirit of God inspired the prophetic witness (2 Sam 23:2; Isa 59:21; 61:1; Acts 1:16; 28:25; Heb 3:7; 9:8; 10:15; 2 Pet 1:21). Early Christians affirmed that the Spirit's testimony through the prophets centered on Christ's person and work (Luke 24:25–27; Acts 3:24; 8:32–35; 17:2–3; cf. John 15:26). But in 1 Peter 1:11, Peter ascribes the source of prophetic inspiration to "the Spirit of Christ in them." The early church did not distinguish between the "Spirit of God," the "Spirit of the Lord," and the "Spirit of Christ" (1:12; Acts 16:6–7; Rom 8:9; Gal 4:6 with Rom 8:14–16; Phil 1:19; 2 Cor 3:17–18).[152] It is unlikely that Peter regards "Christ" in 1:11 as the object of the Spirit's testimony. The phrase "Spirit of Christ," as "Spirit of God" and "Spirit of the Lord," is a statement of the Spirit's identity and does not refer to the content of the Spirit's testimony. Peter presupposes that Christ was preexistent (cf. 1:20) and that through his Spirit the prophets offered testimony of Christ's sufferings and glory. These are not Christian prophets, as Selwyn argued,[153] but rather Old Testament prophets who "testified in advance" (προμαρτυρόμενον) about Christ's passion and glories.

The Gospel Proclamation through the Holy Spirit (1:12)

Peter identifies the Spirit of Christ who testified through the prophets (1:11) with the Holy Spirit who now inspires those who bear witness to the gospel: "The things announced to you through those who brought you good news by the Holy Spirit sent from heaven" (1:12). The message of the Spirit of Christ through the prophets is the same as that proclaimed by those who preach the gospel, in 1:12 simply summarized as "these things" (αὐτά). Peter lays emphasis on the eschatological nature of this proclamation through the Holy Spirit. What was previously witnessed (προμαρτυρόμενον) through the prophets are "the things that have *now* been announced to you" (αὐτά, ἃ νῦν ἀνηγγέλη ὑμῖν; cf. 2:10, 25; 3:21). Indeed, even the prophetic witness about the sufferings and glories of Christ was for them. The witness of the "prophets who prophesied about the grace that was to be yours" (εἰς ὑμᾶς) is now brought home "to you (ὑμῖν)" in the gospel proclamation. The Spirit's work ties together the prophetic witness with the gospel testimony, both of which centered on Christ and those who are

---

152. Best, *1 Peter*, 81; Eugenio Green, *1 Pedro y 2 Pedro*, 75–76.
153. Edwin Gordon Selwyn, *The First Epistle of Peter*, 134, 259–68.

the beneficiaries of salvation. The fulfillment of God's plan in Christ embraces Peter's readers.

Peter's affirmation stands together with other New Testament witnesses that the proclamation of the gospel was empowered by the Holy Spirit (Luke 24:46-49; Acts 1:8; 5:32; 1 Cor 2:4-5; 1 Thess 1:5; Heb 2:3-4). Peter adds the additional note that the Holy Spirit was "sent from heaven" (1 Pet 1:12), that is, he came from God the Father (John 14:26; Acts 1:4-5; 2:17) or Christ himself (John 15:26; Acts 2:33). "Heaven" here is a circumlocution for "God" (Luke 15:18, 21; Matt 21:25; Mark 1:15). Peter's statement in 1:12 may allude to the sending of the Spirit at Pentecost,[154] but Peter more likely includes this statement "to reinforce such divine origin and initiative," as Achtemeier says.[155]

The Spiritual House (2:5)

One of the several ways Peter describes the Christian community is as "living stones" who are "built into a spiritual house" (λίθοι ζῶντες οἰκοδομεῖσθε οἶκος πνευματικὸς). They are also a "holy priesthood" whose duty is "to offer up spiritual sacrifices acceptable to God through Jesus Christ" (εἰς ἱεράτευμα ἅγιον ἀνενέγκαι πνευματικὰς θυσίας εὐπροσδέκτους [τῷ] θεῷ διὰ Ἰησοῦ Χριστοῦ). Scripture contains abundant references to the temple or tabernacle as God's house and, given the cultic ideas of priesthood and sacrifices associated with the "house" in 2:5, Peter clearly has in mind the temple as a metaphor for the community (Judg 18:31; 2 Sam 12:20; 1 Kgs 5:5; Isa 56:7; Matt 12:4; 21:13; Mark 2:26; Luke 6:4; 11:51; John 2:16-17; Heb 10:21). In Greek literature, non-Jewish temples could also be called a "house,"[156] and the Qumran sectarians likewise employ the "house" metaphor to speak of their community as a temple.[157] Elliott, however, argues that the "house" metaphor does not refer to the community as a temple but rather a household (cf. 4:17). He states that "the sense of *oikos* as 'house(hold)' is consistent with the depiction of the believing community in familial metaphors throughout the letter," and concludes, "*Oikos pneumatikos (oikos tou theou)* constitutes the root metaphor for Christian community in 1 Peter, the fundamental concept that identifies the collective identity of the Christians, their relation to God and to one another, and the basis of their behavior as a family or brotherhood."[158] While Elliott is correct in viewing the "household" metaphor as a primary conceptual frame in 1

---

154. Bigg, *Peter and Jude*, 111; J. W. C. Wand, *The General Epistles of St. Peter and St. Jude* (London: Methuen, 1934), 52.

155. Achtemeier, *1 Peter*, 111-12; Kelly, *A Commentary on the Epistles of Peter and Jude*, 63.

156. *MM*, 443.

157. Bertil Gärtner, *The Temple and the Community at Qumran and the New Testament: A Comparative Study in the Temple Symbolism of the Qumran Texts and the NT* (Cambridge: Cambridge University Press, 1965), 22-44; Best, *1 Peter*, 102; Achtemeier, *1 Peter*, 156. See 4QFlor. 1:1-7; 1 QS 5:5-7; 8:4-6; 9:3-5.

158. John H. Elliott, *1 Peter*, 417-18; John H. Elliott, *A Home for the Homeless*, 200-237.

Peter, the juxtaposition of the building, priestly, and sacrificial imagery in 2:5 and the temple imagery with Christ as the cornerstone in 2:6–7 mitigate against his view (see below).[159] The Christian community is a temple indwelt by the Spirit of God, a "spiritual house."[160]

"Spiritual" in 2:5 does not mean "metaphorical" but rather that the Spirit is within the community in its collective existence and service to God (cf. 1 Cor 3:16; Eph 2:22). No idol indwells these communities, but rather the Spirit of God is in their midst. Similarly, the "spiritual sacrifices" offered to God are those "that are controlled and animated by God's sanctifying Spirit."[161] The gathered people of God is where the Spirit dwells, and through the same Spirit they offer sacrifices to God.

The Spirit of Glory and God (4:14)

Peter encourages the persecuted believers by reminding them that "if you are reviled for the name of Christ, you are blessed, because the spirit of glory, which is the Spirit of God, is resting on you" (ὅτι τὸ τῆς δόξης καὶ τὸ τοῦ θεοῦ πνεῦμα ἐφ᾽ ὑμᾶς ἀναπαύεται). The Spirit's presence with God's people in times of adversity is a common NT theme (Matt 10:19–20; Mark 13:11; Luke 12:11–12; Acts 7:55), but Peter's affirmation finds its roots in Isaiah 11:2 (LXX—καὶ ἀναπαύσεται ἐπ᾽ αὐτὸν πνεῦμα τοῦ θεοῦ πνεῦμα σοφίας καὶ συνέσεως πνεῦμα βουλῆς καὶ ἰσχύος πνεῦμα γνώσεως καὶ εὐσεβείας, "And the spirit of God shall rest on him, the spirit of wisdom and understanding, the spirit of counsel and might, the spirit of knowledge and godliness"). In Isaiah the promise is that the Spirit of God was the particular possession of the stem of Jesse (11:1), a reference to the Messiah. Peter applies the text to the persecuted believers, most likely since they share the sufferings of Christ (4.13). As they share his reproach so, too, they now share the blessing of the Spirit resting upon them.

The designation of the Spirit as "the spirit of glory, which is the Spirit of God" (literally "the of glory and the Spirit of God") presents an interpretive problem. We may understand "of glory" as a reference to the Shekinah glory of God. Selwyn follows this line and translates the clause, "The Presence of the Glory, yea the Spirit of God, rests upon you."[162] But it is doubtful that Peter would have referred to the Shekinah glory of God in a way that would be so obscure for his readers. On the other hand, "of glory" and "of God" may both modify "Spirit." Given that the Spirit is associated with God's glory (2 Cor 3:17–18; Acts 7:55), it is more likely that Peter understands the glory inherent in the presence of the Spirit of God. Elliott accordingly translates the phrase: "the divine Spirit of glory."[163] The emphasis on "glory" may possibly suggest the notion

---

159. Achtemeier, *1 Peter*, 158–59.

160. BDAG, 678.

161. John H. Elliott, *The Elect and the Holy*, 154; Achtemeier, *1 Peter*, 155–56; John H. Elliott, *1 Peter*, 418; Giácomo Cassese, *Epístolas Universales* (Minneapolis: Augsburg Fortress, 2007), 48.

162. Edwin Gordon Selwyn, *The First Epistle of Peter*, 223–23; Best, *1 Peter*, 164.

163. John H. Elliott, *1 Peter*, 782.

of the divine presence with the believers in the midst of their social rejection, a reading Achtemeier suggests but does not fully endorse.[164] But given that both "glory" and "God" qualify "Spirit," it would be best to understand this as a statement that "the divine Spirit of glory" rests upon them. Throughout this section and the letter as a whole, Peter is concerned with the dishonor of suffering, both that which Christ and the believers endure, and the honors that God attributes to Christ. He shares that glory with his suffering people (5:1). As Elliott says, "The glory that is God's (4:11) and Christ's (1:11, 21; 5:1) rests now on the suffering faithful and soon will be revealed in all its fullness (1:7; 5:1, 4). Thus 'the Spirit turns reproach into glory.'"[165] In the midst of their shame (4:14a, 16) the presence of the Spirit now rests upon them with all the honor his glory entails. They now have the glory of God through the Spirit upon them, the very glory God gave to Christ (1:11), which shall soon be revealed to all (5:1).

The Holy Spirit in Peter's Theology

Peter holds a robust theology of the Holy Spirit, although it is not as developed as in Paul's writing. Although Peter touches on the Spirit's role in sanctification, for example, he does not develop this theology as Paul did extensively in Romans 8:1–27. Peter focuses on the Spirit's role in conversion and the New Covenant as well as his agency in separating these Gentile believers unto a holy life. Peter focuses on the Spirit's work through the prophets and links the Spirit with the preexistent Christ. The same Spirit who inspired the prophetic testimony then offers his witness through those who preached the gospel. The Spirit is an identifying feature of the community who inspires their worship. His presence rests upon them even though they are persecuted. The Holy Spirit is the divine presence with the community in the present time when they do not see him (1:8). Christ is not absent but only veiled. They are not forsaken, for the Spirit abides among them.

CHRISTIAN COMMUNITY IN 1 PETER

The ecclesiology of 1 Peter is robust, although the apostle does not use the term ἐκλησία ("church") to describe the communities of Christians. Peter's thought is not Pauline, and this is most evident in his theology of the people of God. His ecclesiology develops against the backdrop of the social rejection these new believers endured in their cities and villages. They were reviled and maligned (2:12; 3:16; 4:14), accused of being evildoers or criminal elements in society (2:12; 3:16). Peter's readers faced public denigration and questioning about their new allegiance to Christ (3:15). We can

---

164. "The additional attribution of 'glory' to the Spirit may reflect a further linguistic usage in the LXX, namely, the translation of the word designating the visible brightness or glory (Heb כבוד) that was the sign of God's presence with the word δόξα. The author will then have wanted to emphasize the actual presence of God through his Spirit with the suffering Christians" (Achtemeier, *1 Peter*, 308–9).

165. John H. Elliott, *1 Peter*, 782, citing Bigg, *Peter and Jude*, 177.

hear the clamor against them (2:15). The situation they faced was intimidating (3:14) as they fell out of step with their contemporaries because of their non-participation in banquets and idolatry, both in public and in their households. They became an enigma in their communities (4:3–4) since conformity was valued above all else. These Christ followers broke with the traditions of their fathers and ancestors (1:18). Slaves did not follow the religion of their masters and women broke from the worship of their husbands, placing them in precarious, even dangerous, positions (2:18–20; 3:1–6). Those who once fully belonged within their social networks were ostracized and became disconnected. Due to their conversion, they have the social status of aliens and exiles (πάροικοι καὶ παρεπίδημοι).[166]

In their study on the profile of ancient personality, Malina and Neyrey forward the hypothesis that "first-century Mediterranean persons were strongly group-embedded, collectivist persons. Since they were group-oriented, they were 'socially' minded, as opposed to 'psychologically' minded. They were attuned to the values, attitudes, and beliefs of their in-group, with which they shared a common fate due to generation and geography."[167] Those in collectivist, also called dyadic, cultures display a dyadic personality. This kind of person

> needs another person continually in order to know who he or she really is. Such persons internalize and make their own what others say, do, and think about them, because they believe it is necessary, for being human, to live out the expectations of others. These persons conceive of themselves as always interrelated to other persons while occupying a distinct social position both horizontally (with others sharing the same status, moving from center to periphery) and vertically (with others above and below in social rank). Such persons need to test this interrelatedness, with the focus of attention away from ego, on the demands and expectations of others who can grant or withhold reputation. In other words, dyadic personalities are people whose self-perception and self-image are formed in terms of what others perceive and feed back to them.[168]

For these people, the goals of the group take precedence over individual goals. They regard traditions from the ancestors as inviolable and vigorously maintain group values. The self is group-oriented or, as Triandis says, "The self overlaps with a group,

---

166. See above on the nature of the language of alienation in 1 Peter.

167. Bruce J. Malina and Jerome H. Neyrey, *Portraits of Paul: An Archaeology of Ancient Personality* (Louisville: Westminster John Knox, 1996), 16, see esp. 153–201.

168. Mark Roncace, et al., "Dyadic Personality."

such as family or tribe."[169] Indeed, "Allocentrics tend to define themselves with reference to social entities."[170]

The first readers of 1 Peter were people of collectivist communities, so their deviation from the social norms not only shifted their status from friend to enemy but also meant the loss of identity, which was bound tightly with kinship, community, and geographical relations. Peter's response to alienation and identity loss is to reconstruct the identity of the believers around Christ and those who go by the name Christian (4:16). Community building is a central, not secondary, concern in Peter's theology. Peter's goal of establishing stasis and morality in these new Christian communities is tightly bound with this experiment.

The conceptualization of the Christian community in 1 Peter is rich in variety. Peter employs filial language (φιλαδελφίαν [1:22]; ἀδελφότητα [2:17]) and pastoral imagery (2:25; 5:2–3). He calls the believers a chosen race (2:9), a royal household (2:9), a priesthood (2:5, 9), a nation (2:9), and the people of God (2:9–10). He views them as a temple (2:5; 4:17), even a household, and God's children (1:14). Peter embraces the epithet "Christian" as an honorable marker of their corporate identity (4:16). He also builds their identity around the concept of alienation, thus reinforcing their distance from their former collective identity as "Gentiles." They are resident aliens and exiles (1:1, 17; 2:11) in the places where they live and therefore do not draw their fundamental identity from their traditional communities. There is no indication that they were coerced in the process of cultural alienation and new identification.[171]

Despite the polyvalent nature of Peter's ecclesiology, central to his understanding of community is their relationship with Christ and God the Father. They are identified as followers of Christ (4:16), and their identity as the temple is linked with their relationship to the Stone (2:4–7). Throughout the letter, Christ's sufferings and glories are linked with the believers' experience of rejection and their own hope of ultimate

---

169. Harry C. Triandis, "Cross-Cultural Studies of Individualism and Collectivism," in *Nebraska Symposium on Motivation 1989: Cross-Cultural Perspectives*, ed. John J. Berman (Lincoln, NE: University of Nebraska Press, 1990), 78, cited in Malina and Neyrey, *Portraits of Paul*, 154. See also Harry C. Triandis, "Individualism-Collectivism and Personality," *Journal of Personality* 69 (2001) 917, who says, "In many collectivist cultures, morality consists of doing what the in-group expects."

170. Triandis, "Individualism-Collectivism and Personality," 913.

171. A. D. Nock defines conversion this way: "By conversion we mean the reorientation of the soul of an individual, his deliberate turning from indifference or from an earlier form of piety to another, a turning which implies a consciousness that a great change is involved, that the old was wrong and the new is right. It is seen at its fullest in the positive response of a man to the choice set before him by the prophetic religions" (Arthur Darby Nock, *Conversion: The Old and the New in Religion from Alexander the Great to Augustine of Hippo* [Oxford: Oxford University Press, 1933], 7). Conversion, therefore, is not simply about a change in dogma but a reorientation of life that is so radical that the person converted could be alienated from his traditional community and integrated into a new one. Nock points out the uniqueness of biblically-oriented conversion and community: "Judaism and Christianity demanded renunciation and a new start. They demanded not merely acceptance of a rite, but the adhesion of the will to a theology, in a word faith, a new life in a new people" (Nock, *Conversion*, 14). Conversion was disrupting, disconcerting, and dangerous business.

honor (4:13–14). God the Father has taken the initiative in choosing them (1:2), making them his children by new birth (1:3, 14), and constituting them as the people of God (2:9–10). God's choice of these people resulted in their abandonment of the false gods and "lawless idolatry" (4:3), which brought them into a state of alienation in their communities (1:1–2). But they have become clients of the "faithful Creator" (4:19) with all the moral and social obligations that relationship entails. Peter's ecclesiology is not simply sociological but theological.

The People of God

Peter identifies the Christian community with the historic people of God, whose roots can be traced back to the Old Testament. He refrains from exploring the relationship between Israel and the church and does not discuss how the Gentiles may be included alongside ethnic Israel as heirs to God's promises. Peter simply frames his Gentile readers as the people of God who inherit the promises of God. They have entered into God's New Covenant (1 Pet 1:2; cf. Exod 24:1–2) and anticipate receiving their inheritance, which is currently kept secure for them in heaven (1 Pet 1:4; cf. Deut 15:4; Dan 12:13). Peter affirms that they are God's elect (1 Pet 1:1; cf. Deut 4:37; Ps 105:6) and "exiles of the Dispersion" (1 Pet 1:1; Gen 23:4; Lev 25:23). Given their election and entry into the New Covenant, Peter identifies them by using titles ascribed to the people of God in the Old Testament: "A chosen people, a royal household, a priesthood, a holy nation, a people of God's possession" (1 Pet 2:9, author's translation; Exod 19:6; Isa 43:20–21). The apostle calls Christian wives daughters of Sara (1 Pet 3:5–6) and through typology, binds the baptized believers with Noah and his kin, who were saved through the flood (3:20–21). Before coming to Christ, they "were not a people," but now they are "God's people" (2:10; Hos 2:23). God chose them to be his people (1 Pet 1:2), and this new identity brought with it the social stigma as being non-citizens and resident aliens (2:11; 1:1, 17). Gentile inclusion in God's people reaches its pinnacle in 1 Peter as the apostle does not worry over their placement within God's story of salvation. Their place is found within the story of Israel and is not an appendage to it. They are fully the people God has chosen and redeemed.

Elliott contends that these Christians were non-citizens who were then converted,[172] but Peter draws the line between their social status as aliens and their election (1:1; 2:10, 11). They have become the diaspora (1:1), scattered throughout the world (5:9) and separated from their true inheritance now kept in heaven (1:4). Christians have a new social identity as the people of God, which links them with the ancient story of Israel. Their election and conversion to Christ bring them into this story. This was no afterthought or cobbled-together contingency plan. Rather, God designed it before creation (1:20), the prophets of Israel such as Isaiah and Hosea predicted it (1:10), Jesus accomplished it through his sufferings and glories (1:11), and

---

172. See the comments above on the language of alienation.

it was then proclaimed to these (1:12) who have now responded in obedience, faith, and love (1:2, 8–9).

As argued previously, the believers' election and conversion constituted them as proselytes, Gentiles who are now joined to the story of Israel. Some of the "builders" in Israel rejected Christ, but these Gentile have "come to him, the living Stone" (2:7, NIV; cf. 3:18). The language of alienation is proselyte imagery, as Seland has shown. "Aliens and exiles" (παροίκους καὶ παρεπιδήμους, 2:11) are metaphors drawn from the Jewish institution of proselytism. Philo, for example, styles Abraham as a model proselyte and places "alien" and "proselyte" within the same conceptual frame.[173] As Seland notes, 1 Peter's "recipients were not παρεπιδήμοι before they became Christians but entered this state upon their conversion."[174] Although deemed to be aliens in the communities where they once had complete solidarity they are now embraced as members of the people of God. The language of alienation in 1 Peter is integral to his conception of these Gentiles converts as the people of God. "Aliens and exiles" mark out both their separation and belonging.

As the people of God, these believers in the Roman provinces of Asia Minor are called by titles of the elect people of God who were delivered from Egypt in the Exodus. In 2:9 Peter conflates the titles found in Exodus 19:6 and Isaiah 43:20–21. From Exodus 19:6 Peter styles them as "a chosen race, a royal priesthood"(γένος ἐκλεκτόν, βασίλειον ἱεράτευμα, ἔθνος ἅγιον). Elliott comments that "this verse originally formed part of the Covenant Formula Ex. 19:3b-6. Inasmuch as this pericope represents the origin of Israel's proclamation of herself as the elect and chosen nation of God, Ex. 19:3ff. has been described [as] one of the most dominant, central expressions of Israel's theology of faith in the entire OT."[175] They are the "chosen race," or, as Elliott translates, an "elect stock" or 'line of persons descended from a common ancestor—in the case of Israel, the stock of Jacob (Isa 43:1; Exod 19:3) or Abraham (Acts 13:26; cf. Gal 3:7–9).'"[176] The idea is similar to "house" or "family." Their election is the foundation of their new social identity.

Elliott also has argued that "royal" (βασίλειον) should be understood as a "royal residence" or "royal house" (cf. Philo, Sobr. 66).[177] This corporate or familial imagery continues in their identification as a "priesthood" (βασίλειον). As noted above, Elliott seeks to minimize the cultic reference, a position difficult to maintain in light of 1 Peter 2:5. He is correct, however, in affirming the communitarian dimensions of this

---

173. Seland, "πάροικος καὶ παρεπίδημος," 249–56. "Philo describes Abraham as a proselyte.... Philo's conclusion runs thus (Virt. 219): he is the standard of nobility for all proselytes ... who abandoning the ignobility of strange laws and monstrous customs which assigned the divine honors to stocks and stones and soulless things in general, have come to settle in a better land, in a commonwealth full of true life and vitality, with truth as its director and president" ("πάροικος καὶ παρεπίδημος," 255).

174. Seland, "πάροικος καὶ παρεπίδημος," 257.

175. John H. Elliott, *The Elect and the Holy*, 39.

176. John H. Elliott, *1 Peter*, 435.

177. John H. Elliott, *1 Peter*, 435–36; John H. Elliott, *The Elect and the Holy*, 266–67.

priesthood. Peter does not talk about individual priests but only a corporate body of believers who have priestly obligations. The primary emphasis in 2:9 falls upon their corporate identification as a "priestly community." Moreover, Peter's communities are "a holy nation" (ἔθνος ἅγιον). While "holy" may refer to moral character in 1 Peter (1:15-16), in 2:9 the apostle focuses on the believers' separation to God. They are distinct from those who do not believe in that they adhere to Christ, the Stone (2:7-8), and are a separate nation as a diaspora community in the midst of the nations (1:1; 5:9). Elliott argues that "nation" in 2:9 "identifies the believers not as a politically constituted 'nation' or state but rather as a *(holy) people* sharing a common historical, cultural, and religious heritage."[178] As such, it covers similar conceptual space as "race" (γένος) in 2:9a and, together with the previous titles, underscores the believers' common identity. That identity derives from Exodus 19:6, which described Israel's identity as the people of God of the Exodus (Exod 19:1-5).

Peter joins these titles of Israel from Exodus 19:6 with that found in Isaiah 43:21, "God's own people" (λαὸς εἰς περιποίησιν). The title is a variant of the one in its source, Exodus 19:5: "A treasured people" (λαὸς περιούσιος, as God's rich possession, not simply those who belong to him).[179] The focus of the title λαὸς εἰς περιποίησιν in Exodus 43:20 and 1 Peter 2:9b is that the people are God's very own and are protected by him given their value.[180] The title binds these believers to God, underscores their honor, and joins them together in community. Isaiah 43 is an integral part of the prophet's New Exodus theology, a theme not absent from Peter's use of this chapter and Exodus 19. Peter's readers are members of the New Exodus community.

But as his source, Peter not only builds their corporate identity in relation to God but points them out to their surrounding community: "in order that you may proclaim the mighty acts of him who called you out of darkness into his marvelous light" (ὅπως τὰς ἀρετὰς ἐξαγγείλητε τοῦ ἐκ σκότους ὑμᾶς καλέσαντος εἰς τὸ θαυμαστὸν αὐτοῦ φῶς). Peter picks up the idea of proclamation from Isaiah 43:21 as he orients the community outward towards those from whom they are alienated. Their calling is to offer testimony of God's "mighty acts" (τὰς ἀρετὰς, as LXX Ps 9:14; 78:4; 79:13).[181] Peter will add to this verbal testimony about God's mighty acts of salvation the witness of the believers' *praxis* (2:11-12). In the end, proclamation is in both word and deed. The content of the declaration derives from the Exodus and the New Exodus.

---

178. John H. Elliott, *1 Peter*, 438; Goppelt, *A Commentary on 1 Peter*, 152; Achtemeier, *1 Peter*, 165.

179. *TDNT*, 57; *NIDNTT*, 2:838-39. Or *BDAG*, 802-3: "pert. to being of very special status, *chosen, especial*" (Titus 2:14; LXX Deut 7:6; 14:2; 28:16).

180. *TLNT*, 3:100-103. *BDAG*, 804, "that which is acquired, *possessing, possession, property*." *BDAG*, however, misses the interpersonal concept when referencing 1 Peter 2:9, but it does point to LXX Malachi 3:17: "And they shall be mine (ἔσονταί μοι), says the Lord Almighty, in the day when I make them my acquisition (εἰς περιποίησιν), and I will choose them (αἱρετιῶ αὐτοὺς) as a person chooses his son who is subject to him." The title leads into Peter's quotation of Hosea 2:23 in 1 Peter 2:10.

181. Deissmann, *Bible Studies*, 95-96.

Elliott remarks, "The salvation of the Christian believers is depicted here in language reminiscent of the terms with which Isaiah portrayed Israel's deliverance from Egypt's darkness and its captivity in Babylon (Isa 42:16; 58:10); see especially Isa 9:2, 'The people who walked in darkness have seen a great light; those who dwelt in a land of deep darkness, on them light has shined.'"[182] The New Exodus is always close to the surface throughout Peter's theology.

The heart of Peter's affirmation about his readers being member of the people of God is 2:10: "Once you were not a people, but now are you God's people; once you had not received mercy, but now you have received mercy." Peter's quotation from the LXX conflates Hosea 1:6 with 1:9–10 and 2:23 (cf. Rom 9:25–26). He adds "once you were" and "but now" to heighten the contrast between their previous and present existence. Formerly they were in darkness (1 Pet 2:9b), were not a people (2:10a), and had not received mercy (2:10b). But now they live in the light of God (2:9b), are God's people (2:10a), and have received his mercy (2:10b). Peter's description of their former existence is extremely harsh given that God is the Creator of all (Acts 17:24), loves all (John 3:16), Fathers all (Eph 4:6), providentially cares for all (Acts 17:25–28), and that Christ's sacrifice was for all (1 John 2:2). How can Peter affirm that these Gentiles were formerly "not a people," an expression that degrades their cultural identity? The quotation in Hosea referred to Israel, God's very own people, who were called "no people" in the context of the prophet's polemic against idolatry (Hos 4:17; 8:4; 10:5–6; 11:2; 13:2; 14:8). The abandonment of Yahweh through the idolatrous worship of other gods had sullied their identity. They had broken covenant with him. Peter's readers were themselves former idolaters (1 Pet 4:3; 1:18) whose worship was false and linked with immorality. Despite this, they were chosen by God, made his special people, and may now be called "God's people." These Gentiles have received God's mercy and have entered into the promise of God to renew his people (Ezek 11:19–20; 14:10–11; 26:22–28; Jer 24:7; 20:22; 31:31–34; 32:37–40). The prophetic hope offered to Israel now finds fulfillment in these elect communities of those who have turned to Jesus Christ.

The Household and Temple of God

As noted above, God the Father has given Peter's readers new life. They have been reborn (1:3, 23) and are therefore now "newborn infants" (2:2). As the giver of life, the Father has formed "the believing community as God's family or household (2:5; 4:17) and 'brotherhood' (2:17; 5:9)."[183] Peter addresses his readers as "children" (1:14), and they invoke God as Father (1:17), likely a reference to the Lord's prayer (Matt 6:9), which was used or echoed in their invocations. Through their relationship with God, they have new life (2:5, 24). Peter may also understand Christian baptism as the time of

---

182. John H. Elliott, *1 Peter*, 440.
183. John H. Elliott, *1 Peter*, 331.

new birth (3:21). Baptism marks their deliverance, but Peter also reflects on the moral dimension of the ceremony (3:21b). He comments that baptism "now saves you—not as a removal of dirt from the body, but as an appeal to God for a good conscience." We may translate the οὐ . . . ἀλλά ("not . . . but") as a relative contrast ("not only . . . but also"; cf. Matt 10:20; Mark 9:37; John 12:44; Acts 5:4)[184] instead of an absolute contrast (cf. Matt 9:12; Mark 10:45; John 6:38; Rom 4:4, 10). Baptism is repeatedly regarded an act of conversion in which the initiate renounces immoral practices (Acts 2:38; 22:16; Rom 6:2–4; Col 2:11–12). Peter's thought most likely runs along this line. Baptism is the time of regeneration (1:3, 23; cf. John 3:3–8). Peter employs a rich array of imagery to underscore the believers' belonging to a new family under God's care.

The image of the Christian community as a household, a "home for the homeless," is one of the most powerful theological constructions in Peter's epistle. Regardless of whether we accept Elliott's analysis that the audience of 1 Peter were resident aliens who were converted to Christ or hold the view that their alien status was the result of their conversion, Elliott has painted the vivid reality of those deemed to be "other" in their communities. He lays out how resident aliens and transient strangers (πάροικοι καὶ παρεπίδημοι [2:12]; 1:1, 17) were some of the most vulnerable members of ancient Mediterranean society. "Legally," he says, "their status within the empire, according to both local and Roman law, involved restrictions concerning intermarriage and commerce (*connubium et commercium*), succession of property and land tenure, participation in public assembly and voting, taxes and tribute, the founding of associations (*koina, collegia*), and susceptibility to severer forms of civil and criminal punishment." They maintained limited legal rights so their place in society was "far superior to the *xenos* status with no legal protection whatsoever."[185] Elliott further shows the *paroikoi* "were differentiated from the natives among whom they lived in respect to their land of origin, ethnic or familial roots, their different views and opinions, and their language, property and religion. In general, furthermore, such distinctions inevitably involved political, legal, economic and social restrictions and disadvantages for those so identified as 'strangers' and 'foreigners.'"[186] Through the abandonment of the gods and non-participation in the recognized social institutions, the believers lost their place of belonging and were the source of confusion for their contemporaries (4:4–4). As argued previously, their alien status was the result of their conversion.

The dissonance was exacerbated by the fact that they continued to live in their communities, participated in public affairs, and maintained private relationships, yet they acted as those who did not belong. They were questioned publicly (3:15), endured verbal abuse (2:12, 15; 3:16), and were subjected to violence (2:20; 3:6; 4:1). Legal action, economic deprivation, and even curses were likely aspects of the adversity they

---

184. *BDF* §448.
185. John H. Elliott, *A Home for the Homeless*, 37–38.
186. John H. Elliott, *A Home for the Homeless*, 67.

faced,[187] prompting Peter to underscore God's care for them amidst their multiple anxieties (5:7). They could resist the supernatural forces of evil through faith (5:8-9). Those who once lived under the *patria potestas* had stepped out from under that authority (1:18), slaves abandoned the cult of their masters (2:18-20), and women worshiped Christ instead of the gods of their husbands (3:1-2). The communities where they belonged became alien spaces, and they were consequently othered and shamed (4:16). A rupture had occurred that broke them from their traditional households.

Peter's response was to turn them to the households to which they now fully belonged, regardless of gender (3:7) or social class (2:18; cf. 2:17; 3:3). Those who were πάροικοι are built together by God into a "spiritual house" (2:5). As "living stones" they are built together by God into this temple. As a "holy priesthood" they "offer spiritual sacrifices," which would include worship (cf. Heb 13:15), service (cf. Rom 12:1; Heb 13:16), and even suffering (Wis 3:6). Witness is not the primary function of the temple (see 1 Pet 2:9), but, as McKelvey notes, "When we ask where the prophets envisaged Israel prosecuting her missionary task we have an insight into the thought of the text before us. It was the new temple (Isa 2:2-4 etc.)."[188] Indeed, Peter's new temple is the fulfillment of Israel's eschatological hope.[189] The believers' identity as the temple of God is bound up with their association with Christ, the Stone (1 Pet 2:5-8).[190]

Although this imagery is primarily cultic, as noted above, the temple and household imagery intersect in 1 Peter. Those who were the supposed builders (οἱ οἰκοδομοῦντες) of the temple or house had rejected Christ, just as these believers were rejected in their communities (2:7). Achtemeier points up that "house" (οἶκος) may denote a building or those who reside in the building, so the temple and household imagery share conceptual space. The "spiritual house" (2:5) or "house of God" (4:17) is not only the temple but also the community that comprises it. Achtemeier catches this conceptual creation, saying, "Perhaps it would be most accurate to see there the metaphor of God's house pointing to the Christian community where, as in the sanctuary, God is present to human beings."[191]

The household imagery weaves through other passages in the epistle. Household slaves (οἱ οἰκέται) experienced physical abuse by their masters but are identified with Christ in his sufferings (2:18, 21). Those once alienated become household stewards (οἰκονόμοι)[192] who serve one another with the gifts of grace God has entrusted to them (4:10). Indeed, as Elliott has demonstrated, the apostle calls the believers "a royal

---

187. Williams, *Persecution in 1 Peter*, 334.

188. R. J. McKelvey, *The New Temple: The Church in the New Testament* (London: Oxford University Press, 1968), 130.

189. Best, *1 Peter*, 101-2; Gärtner, *The Temple and the Community at Qumran and the New Testament*, 22-44.

190. Nicholas Perrin, *Jesus the Temple* (Grand Rapids: Baker Academic, 2010), 55-57.

191. Achtemeier, *1 Peter*, 155; *LSJ*, 1204-5, showing the use of οἶκος as either a temple, family or even a reigning house. Cf. 1 QS 8.4-10; 4 QFlor 1-10; John 14:2.

192. *TLNT*, 2:568-75.

household" (βασίλειον, 2:9).¹⁹³ Those who became proselytes (πάροικοι) found their home within the Christian community.

The Flock of God

Peter uses pastoral imagery when describing these Christian communities. They are "the flock of God" (5:2–3). Before their conversion to Christ they "were going astray like sheep," but now they have "returned to the shepherd and guardian of your souls" (2:25). Peter charges the elders of these communities with shepherding responsibility "to tend the flock of God that is in your charge" and to "be examples to the flock" (5:2–3). Their pastoral duties follow the model of Christ, the Shepherd. He is the "chief shepherd" who will honor them upon his appearing (5:4). As discussed above, Peter describes his readers as those who were "going astray like sheep." His language draws from the Servant Song in Isaiah 53:6, where Israel is described as having been like lost and scattered sheep (1 Kgs 22:17; 2 Chr 18:16; Jer 50:6; Ezek 34:5–6; Zech 10:2; Matt 15:24). Peter draws in this imagery to describe the Gentile Christians. They are now members of the people of God since turning to Christ, their Shepherd. They have "returned" (ἐπεστράφητε), language commonly used to describe the conversion to God (Luke 1:16; Acts 9:35; 11:21; 14:15; 15:19; 26:20; 2 Cor 3:16; 1 Thess 1:9; Jas 5:30). The pastoral language is salvific. The Shepherd's sacrifice saves them (see 1 Pet 2:22–24). Their "return" implies, however, a previous divine claim upon these Gentiles. They were not turning to an alien god or savior but coming back to the one who claimed them from the beginning of all things. God is the "faithful Creator" (4:19). The pastoral language used to describe the community and their Savior finds its roots in the biblical account of creation, God's election, and the story of God's people.

Christians

Just as the recipients are "living stones" due to their relationship with "the Stone" (2:4–5), so also their association with Christ (1:2, 19; 2:21; 3:15–16, 18; 4:1, 13–14; 5:14) constitutes them as "Christians" (4:16). They find salvation in Christ and have been called by God "to his eternal glory in Christ" (5:10), but they also are "sharing Christ's sufferings" and are "reviled for the name of Christ" (4:13). Therefore, they bear the name "Christian." The title did not originate within the church but was ascribed to believers by their Gentile contemporaries (Acts 11:26; 26:28). It did not become a common self-designation for believers until the second century. The term is pejorative (cf. 3:16) and therefore could be cause for shame (4:16).¹⁹⁴ The *-ianos / -ianus* endings in Greek and Latin "designated a partisan, adherent, or client of the one named," but also "something like 'Christ-lackeys,' shameful sycophants of Christ, a criminal put to

---

193. John H. Elliott, *1 Peter*, 435–37; John H. Elliott, *The Elect and the Holy*, 50–128.
194. *NIDNTT*, 2:342; BDF §24; BDAG, 1090.

ignominious death by the Romans years earlier."[195] We hear it echoed in the writings of various Gentile authors of the era (Tacitus 15.44; Suetonius, *Nero* 16; Pliny the Younger, *Ep.* 10.96–97). Pliny the Younger's letter to the Emperor Trajan (AD 112) shows with clarity the dishonor embedded with the name "Christian":

> Consequently, I do not know the nature or the extent of the punishments usually meted out to them, nor the grounds for starting an investigation and how far it should be pressed. Nor am I at all sure whether any distinction should be made between them on the grounds of age, or if young people and adults should be treated alike; whether a pardon ought to be granted to anyone retracting his beliefs, or if he has once professed Christianity, he shall gain nothing by renouncing it; and whether it is the mere name of Christian which is punishable, even if innocent of crime, or rather the crimes associated with the name.

Tacitus echoes the way residents of Rome maligned the Christians, giving Nero a convenient scapegoat for the conflagration he set ablaze in the city:

> Therefore, to scotch the rumour, Nero substituted as culprits, and punished with the utmost refinements of cruelty, a class of men, loathed for their vices, whom the crowd styled Christians. Christus, the founder of the name, had undergone the death penalty in the reign of Tiberius, by sentence of the procurator Pontius Pilatus, and the pernicious superstition was checked for a moment, only to break out once more, not merely in Judaea, the home of the disease, but in the capital itself, where all things horrible or shameful in the world collect and find a vogue.

Suetonius says that in Nero's day, "Punishment was inflicted on the Christians, a class of men given to a new and mischievous superstition." First Peter reflects the early social burden of the name Christian, which continued in the early centuries of the church. Followers of Christ entered into the reproach of the name among the Gentiles. Peter, however, turns their shame into honor: "Yet if any of you suffers as a Christian, do not consider it a disgrace, but glorify God because you bear his name" (4:16). The name brings us to the heart of Peter's theology of suffering and glory, both for Christ and his followers.

God's Elect and Holy People

The multiple images Peter utilizes to describe the Christian communities in Asia Minor revolve around these believers' identification with Christ in both his shame and honor. They are calculated to give these believers, who were alienated from their communities, an understanding of their new community to which they have been called by God. Peter's ethics of community grow out of this identification with Christ

---

195. John H. Elliott, *1 Peter*, 789–91.

and one another (4:7–11). Since they are people whose cultural roots are within collectivism, the reconstruction of community identity is an essential task for the apostle. Who they are together is the ground of their hope and continuance in the gospel they had received (1:12). Although their primary relationship is with Christ, to whom they have come, and with God, to whom Christ has brought them, Peter affirms that God has cobbled them together as a temple and priesthood, a household and a nation, a race, a flock, and the very people of God continuous with the ancient people of God. While they have endured the agony of becoming aliens within their communities, that very alien existence becomes a bond and a way of life as they, as proselytes, now live out their new allegiances. Peter places community at the very heart of his theology and ethics. His community theology cannot be separated from God's plan centered in Christ's sufferings and glories.

THE HOLY WAY OF LIFE

Peter's moral teaching for the persecuted believers in Asia Minor is not a systematic treatment of Christian ethics. The situation in which his readers find themselves prompts him to trace out these particular theological and ethical lines of teaching. How should Christians live as God's people in relation to the gospel they received and the communities in which they lived? Peter's readers were caught between choosing to conduct themselves according to their inherited way of life (1:17), the social norms of their communities (4:3–4), and their desires (1:14; 4:2) or to live in obedience to God's will (4:2; 1:14) and conform to his holy character (1:15–16). First Peter is an impassioned plea to be oriented to God in their moral life despite the high cost of obedience.

The Former Life

The recipients of the letter formerly lived in harmony with the social norms of their day, which Peter calls ὁ βούλημα τῶν ἐθνῶν ("the will of the Gentiles" [4:3]) and contrasts sharply with the θέλημα θεοῦ ("the will of God" [4:2]). Their former life was governed by many-faceted "human desires" (ἀνθρώπων ἐπιθυμίαις, 4:2; 1:14), which, as Hort said, "Are represented as so many individual impulses having no root beyond themselves, and not forming part of a great and worthy whole."[196] These lusts ruled their lives when they were ignorant of the true God (1:14) and dedicated to "lawless idolatry" (4:2–3). Peter tags that life as "vain" (1:18), perhaps a reference to the way

---

196. Hort, *The First Epistle of St. Peter 1:1–2:17*, 69. "The essential point in ἐπιθυμία is that it is desire as impulse, as a motion of the will. It is, in fact, lust, since the thought of satisfaction gives pleasure and that of non-satisfaction pain. ἐπιθυμία is anxious self-seeking" (*TDNT*, 3:171). Such desires are sinful (2:11; Mark 4:19; Rom 7:7–8; Gal 5:16–17; 1 Thess 4:5; 1 Tim 6:9; Titus 3:3; Josephus, *Ant.* 2.53; T. Josh. 7.8. *BDAG*), while at times desires are identified as sexual (Rom 1:24; Matt 5:28; 1 Thess 4:5; 1 Pet 4:3; Plutarch, *Mor.* 525A-B; Josephus, *Ant.* 4.130). See *BDAG*, 603; *MM*, 473; *TDNT*, 5.926–30; *LSJ*, 1285.

idolatry was the hub of their former life.[197] Generations of inherited tradition canonized their former life and allegiances (ἀναστροφῆς πατροπαραδότου). Gentile desires enjoyed both historic and social sanction (4:2–4). In 4:3 Peter inserts a vice-list that enumerates the desires he has in mind: "Licentiousness, passions, drunkenness, revels, carousing, and lawless idolatry." The predominant sins are sexual immorality and intemperance. Peter follows the common Jewish assessment that these excesses were associated with idolatry (Wis 14:12; Bar 6:43–44; 2 En. 10:4–6)[198] and formed the center of social life as well as the religious cultus of ancient society. To withdraw from them was to separate from the root of ancient vice.[199] Gentile vices extended to their disposition as well as their social activities. Peter calls them to separate themselves from such vices in 2:1: "Rid yourselves, therefore, of all malice, and all guile, insincerity, envy, and all slander." These vices tear apart community by eroding the social bond of love (1:22; 4:8). Other vices are enumerated throughout the letter such as retaliation to regain social honor (2:23; 3:9), material excess (3:3), and lack of understanding and honor towards one's wife (3:7). All these marked their former life.

Turning from Darkness to Light

Repeatedly in this letter, Peter references the decisive change in their way of life as he calls them not to return to the lifestyle they once embraced (1:14). God had chosen them (1:1) and called them (2:9) in order that they might obey him (1:2) and come out of darkness into light (2:9). The transition was effected through Christ's redemption (1:18–19), who then reconciled them to God (3:18). They responded to God's call through the gospel proclamation (1:12) by becoming obedient to the truth of the gospel and were subsequently purified to the core of their being (1:22). The moral transformation was a new birth (1:3, 23; 2:2). They had come to the living Stone (2:4) and returned to him as their Shepherd and Overseer (2:24). As a result they became "the people of God" (2:10).

These new believers were also baptized as a sign of salvation (3:21), an event that Peter may have regarded as the time of their renunciation of evil (2:1), new birth, and

---

197. Eugenio Green, *1 Pedro y 2 Pedro*, 98; LXX Lev 17:7; 2 Chr 11:15; Isa 2:20; Jer 2:5; 8:19; Wis 15:8; Acts 14:15; Eph 4:17.

198. On vice and virtue lists, see B. S. Easton, "New Testament Ethical Lists," *JBL* 51 (1932) 1–12; Anton Vögtle, *Die Tugend-und Lasterkataloge im Neuen Testament: Exegetisch, religions-und formgeschichtlich Untersucht* (Münster: Aschendorff, 1936); S. Wibbing, *Die Tugend-und Lasterkataloge im Neuen Testament und ihre Traditionsgeschichte unter besonderer Berücksichtigung der Qumran-Texte* (Berlin: Töpelmann, 1959); John T. Fitzgerald, "Virtue/Vice Lists," in *The Anchor Bible Dictionary*, ed. David Noel Freedman (New York: Doubleday, 1982), 6:857–59; J. Daryl Charles, *Virtue Amidst Vice: The Catalogue of Virtues in 2 Peter 1* (Sheffield: Sheffield Academic, 1997); J. Daryl Charles, "Vice and Virtue Lists," in *Dictionary of New Testament Background*, ed. Craig A. Evans and Stanley E. Porter (Downers Grove, IL: InterVarsity, 2000), 1252–57; Troels Engberg-Pedersen, "Paul, Virtues and Vices," in *Paul in the Graeco-Roman World: A Handbook*, ed. J. Paul Sampley (Harrisburg, PA: Trinity, 2003), 608–33; Réne A. López, "Vice Lists in Non-Pauline Sources," *BSac* 168 (2011) 178–95.

199. Goppelt, *A Commentary on 1 Peter*, 284–87.

purification (1:3, 22–23).²⁰⁰ Baptism was the time when vices were "put off" and new moral commitments began. In 3:21 he states that baptism is not only the removal of fleshly immorality (οὐ σαρκὸς ἀπόθεσις ῥύπου). "Filth" (ῥύπου) can have either a literal or metaphorical meaning in the LXX (Job 9:31; 11:15; 14:4; Isa 4:4), while in classical Greek confined it to physical dirt. No other NT author uses the term. In Patristic literature it may mean either literal or metaphorical filth (Bar 8:6; Origen, *Commentarii in Jo.* 32.7; Athanasius *C. Gent.* 34). "Flesh" in 1 Peter means transient human existence (1:24; 3:18; 4:1–2, 6). It does not, however, appear to have the Pauline sense of "fallen human nature." But neither does it simply mean "body" in Peter's epistle. "Removal" (ἀπόθεσις) is never used of the act of physical washing.²⁰¹ This verbal noun is related to ἀποτίθημι (to put off), which earlier in 2:1 referred to moral renunciation as also elsewhere in the New Testament (Jas 1:21; Col 3:8; Eph 4:25; Rom 13:12; Heb 12:1). Peter states that baptism is not only a time of moral renunciation but also "the pledge of a clear conscience toward God" (συνειδήσεως ἀγαθῆς ἐπερώτημα εἰς θεόν, 3:21b). It is not an "appeal to God" (NRSV) but rather a "pledge" (ἐπερώτημα). As Elliott notes, "Evidence from contracts preserved on papyrus . . . indicates the use of both the verb and the noun as part of a stipulatory legal formula involving a formal question followed by an acknowledgement of consent." Therefore, "at the occasion of baptism, assent is given to certain behavioral requirements."²⁰² Baptism marked the transition from their former way of life the new way of life lived before God (1:18; 4:2–4).

These believers had undergone a moral transformation. The power behind their transformation was the redemption of Christ's sacrifice (1:18–19), the resurrection of Jesus Christ from the dead (1:3; 3:21), and the proclamation of God's word in the gospel (1:12, 23–25). Peter is no moralist who simply exhorts his readers to live a holy life but recognizes divine agency through their calling and the work of the Holy Spirit (1:1–2). God has saved them, and Christ has brought them to God. Christian ethics in 1 Peter are bound with God's mighty acts.

Peter's readers have turned from darkness to light and have become the people of God (2:9–10). The movement of salvation also transformed their status in society into that of aliens (1:1, 17; 2:11). They still live among the structures of society (2:13—3:7), but they no longer live by its moral norms (2:11–12), which stand under the judgment of God (3:12; 4:5, 17–18). There is both continuity and discontinuity in their social existence, and this is the field where Peter develops his theological ethic.

---

200. I argued above that the οὐ . . . ἀλλά contrast is not absolute in 3:21 ("not . . . but") but rather relative ("not only . . . but also"). See Matt 10:20; Mark 9:37; John 12:44; Acts 5:4; *BDF* §448(6); Gene L. Green, "Theology and Ethics in 1 Peter," 227–35; Eugenio Green, *1 Pedro y 2 Pedro*, 224–25. The thought is similar to Jas 1:21. Baptism was the time when one "put off" the life of immorality (2:1; Col 2:11–12; 3:8; Eph 4:25; Rom 13:12; Heb 12:1; Acts 2:38a).

201. Used only here in the NT and in 2 Pet 1:14, where it appears in the context of death.

202. Eugenio Green, *1 Pedro y 2 Pedro*, 225; Achtemeier, *1 Peter*, 270–71; John H. Elliott, *1 Peter*, 680; Jobes, *1 Peter*, 255.

The discontinuity and the opposition it generates becomes a moral problem for Peter's readers. Peter refers to their persecution as "various trials" whose purpose is "that the genuineness of your faith—being more precious than gold what, though perishable, is tested by fire—may be found to result in praise and glory and honor when Jesus Christ is revealed" (1:6-7). The trials are a test of the genuine character of their faith. "Trials" (πειράσμοι) are a test to examine whether a person or a people will remain faithful to God. Later in the letter Peter calls such trials "the fiery ordeal" (πυρώσει πρὸς πειρασμὸν). The purpose of such trials, according to Peter, is not to bring about moral purification but rather to examine the character of their faith (Prov 17:3; 27:21; Sir 2:5; Wis 3:6).[203] Satanic opposition has the opposite goal of destruction and death (5:9-9). People in the community may fail the test. A warfare goes on in the midst of testing and Peter, therefore, calls them to be well armed for the conflict, with Christ as the moral example (4:1). These believers had suffered to the point of having "finished with sin," that is, the one who had gone so far as to suffer physical abuse for righteousness shows that they had finished with sin as a way of life.[204] Peter clarifies the thought in the following verse: "So as to live for the rest of your earthly life no longer by human desires but by the will of God" (4:2). People may slander them as those who act immorally in society even as they have a demonstrably good way of life (2:12; 4:4).

The New Life in the Will of God

Peter's ethics revolve around the will of God. He explicitly mentions God's will in four passages (2:15; 3:17; 4:2, 19), although only two refer to his will as an ethical directive (3:17 and 4:19 speak of it in relation to the believers' sufferings). In the phrase, "For it is God's will" (ὅτι οὕτως ἐστὶν τὸ θέλημα τοῦ θεοῦ [2:15]), οὕτως has a backwards reference as in 3:5 and as it does elsewhere in the New Testament.[205] In this case the will of God is that they are subordinate to "every human institution" (Ὑποτάγητε πάσῃ ἀνθρωπίνῃ κτίσει διὰ τὸν κύριον). The will of God has to do with how they relate to the various institutions of society. In 4:2 the will of God is the single ethical rule by which the believers orient their lives, being set over against the multiple desires that characterize their contemporaries (cf. 1:14) who engage in sinful actions as directed by their

---

203. *TDNT*, 6:30; Rudolf Schnackenburg, *The Moral Teaching of the New Testament* (London: Burns & Oates, 1975), 296; Kelly, *A Commentary on the Epistles of Peter and Jude*, 185.

204. Wand, *The General Epistles of St. Peter and St. Jude*, 103-4. "Under the conditions of the time he who obeyed the Christian calling was thereby cut off from the bulk of society. This involved persecution and suffering, but it also meant removal from the moral indiscipline of Pagan manners. To this extent was suffering identical with 'ceasing from sin.'" It does not appear that 4:1 refers to Christ but rather the believer who suffers. Christ is the moral example they follow (Eugenio Green, *1 Pedro y 2 Pedro*, 234-36).

205. Hort, *The First Epistle of St. Peter 1:1-2:17*, 143; Edwin Gordon Selwyn, *The First Epistle of Peter*, 173; Kelly, *A Commentary on the Epistles of Peter and Jude*, 110; Beare, *The First Epistle of Peter*, 143; Achtemeier, *1 Peter*, 185.

own will (4:3). God has called them to himself and to do his will (1:1, 15; 2:9; 5:10). He has called them to a certain pattern of life that is marked by holiness (1:1–2, 15), light (2:9), doing good while enduring suffering (2:21), and blessing rather than retaliation (3:9). Living according to God's will means to live in the fear of God, honoring him above all other loyalties (1:17; 2:17–28; 3:2, 16). The fear of God is set over against the fear of people (3:6, 14) and implies a certain course of conduct (3:14–15). To fear God is to live according to his character (4:2–4). Conversely, Peter understands wickedness as disobedience to the will of God as it is expressed in the gospel (4:17; 2:7–8; 3:20). Peter wants his readers to imitate the character of those who lived in obedience to God such as Noah (implied in 3:20), Sarah (3:6), Israel (1:2; cf. Exod 24), and, especially, Jesus Christ (2:22–23).

Peter gives texture to the meaning of living according to God's will in the call to holiness (1:14–15; cf. Lev 11:44–45; 19:2; 20:7, 26). God called Israel to holiness, which meant the separation from the evil in the land of Caanan (Lev 18:3; 20:26). Peter's readers had been similarly redeemed, not from a land but from a way of life (1:18). God's holiness means a separation from all that is creaturely and, by extension, from all that is immoral.[206] The believers are to be separate from the defiling elements of their surrounding society. To live according to the will of God means to adopt a way of life (ἀναστροφή) that is chaste (ἁγνή [3:2, 5]). Holiness should mark all their way of life (αὐτοὶ ἅγιοι ἐν πάσῃ ἀναστροφῇ γενήθητε [1:15]). At all times, and especially under severe questioning by their contemporaries, they should "sanctify Christ as Lord," which means revere or honor Christ as holy (3:15; cf. Matt 6:9; Isa 19:23; Ezek 20:41; Sir 26:4). Honoring him before their adversaries includes adopting his holy way of life. Peter develops the call to a holy way of life throughout the epistle primarily in terms of "doing good" in society, as we will see.

The Imitatio Dei and the Imitatio Christi

Some years ago Ernest Tinsley commented, "If one had to choose a single book from the New Testament to illustrate the Christian conception of the imitation of God, none could be better than the First Epistle of St Peter."[207] While imitation of a deity was current in Greek thought,[208] Peter's source is the holiness code of the Old Testament (1 Pet 1:15–16; Lev 19:2). Jesus introduced the *imitatio Dei* into the church (Matt 5:48; cf. Deut 18:13; Lev 19:2). Peter informs his readers that God has called them to imitate

---

206. TDNT, 1:91–92; Hort, *The First Epistle of St. Peter 1:1–2:17*, 69–70.

207. Ernest John Tinsley, *The Imitation of God in Christ: An Essay on the Biblical Basis of Christian Spirituality* (London: SCM, 1960). See Anselm Schulz, *Nachfolgen und Nachahmen: Studien über das Verhältnis der neutestamentlichen Jüngerschaft zur urchristlichen Vorbildethik* (Munich: Kosel, 1962); Hans Dieter Betz, *Nachfolge und Nachahmung Jesu Christi im Neuen Testament* (Tübingen: Mohr Siebeck, 1967); Israel Abrahams, *Studies in Pharisaism and the Gospels: Second Series* (Eugene, OR: Wipf & Stock, 2004).

208. Goppelt, *A Commentary on 1 Peter*, 203–4.

his holiness (1:15) rather than be ruled by desire. Surprisingly, the call to imitate God's holiness in 1:15-16 is not repeated again in the letter. Rather, Peter develops the *imitatio Dei* with reference to the *imitatio Christi*. As Dodd said:

> The New Testament idea of the imitation of Christ is a way of making explicit what kinds of divine activity should be imitated by men, and how, and why, and in what circumstances.... To follow in His [Christ's] steps is to have before us a truly human example, but it is also to have the divine pattern made comprehensible and imitable. Hence, the imitation of Christ, being the imitation of God Himself so far as God can be a model to His creatures, becomes a mode of absolute ethics.[209]

For Peter and his readers, Christ serves as the model of the holy character of God, which they then can imitate in the midst of the adversities they encountered (1:16, 19; 2:22-24; 3:18). The domestic slaves, and, by extension, the rest of the Christian communities, are called to follow his footprints as they, too, suffer (2:21). Christ's sufferings are redemptive in a way that theirs are not (2:21, 24; 3:18). However, Peter smoothly transitions between that which is imitable to that which is inimitable. They can conduct themselves in the middle of suffering the way that he did by avoiding sin, shunning deceit and retaliation, and committing oneself to God, the Judge (2:21-24). As Christ, they should only suffer for doing good, not evil (3:17-18).

The *imitatio Christi* is the closest Peter comes to the notion of discipleship embedded in Jesus' teaching. Jesus repeatedly called the disciples to follow him (ἀκολουθεῖν, Mark 8:34 and plls.; 10:21, 28, 32, 52; 11:9; 15:41). Such discipleship meant breaking previous social ties in order to share in the ministry and sufferings of the Messiah.[210] Peter develops the idea of following Jesus by calling the slaves and others to "follow in his steps" (ἐπακολουθήσητε τοῖς ἴχνεσιν αὐτοῦ [1 Pet 2:21]). The one who follows the footprints of another "does not emulate a partner, but sets out in the direction indicated, indeed journeyed, by the one followed."[211] So, for example, Peter elaborates the call to follow Christ's footprints (2:21) in the following verses, which includes the example of Christ's refusal to retaliate: "When he was abused, he did not return abuse; when he suffered, he did not threaten" (2:23). Peter repeats the theme in 3:9: "Do not repay evil for evil or abuse for abuse." Peter tells his readers that in his sufferings Christ "entrusted himself to the one who judges justly" (2:23). This example then turns into an imperative in 4:19: "Let those suffering in accordance with God's will entrust themselves to a faithful Creator, while continuing to do good." The *imitatio Christi* extends to sharing his sufferings (4:13), leading a guileless life (2:21; 2:1), and sharing his glory (1:21; 5:1). Christ's example shows the readers how to do the will of God in the midst

---

209. C. H. Dodd, *Gospel and Law: The Relation of Faith and Ethics in Early Christianity* (Cambridge: Cambridge University Press, 1951), 41-42. See Tinsley, *The Imitation of God in Christ*, 166.

210. *TDNT*, 1:213.

211. Goppelt, *A Commentary on 1 Peter*, 204.

of adversity and moral crisis.[212] Christ shows these believers how to imitate God in concrete ways since he suffered humiliation and shame as they do in society.

The Christian Way of Life

Peter links the call to holiness in 1:15–16 with the appeal, "Be holy yourselves in all your conduct" or "way of life" (ἀναστροφῇ), one's ethical behavior.[213] Holiness in 1 Peter is not simply a state of being but a way of life or a way of conducting oneself in society. Elsewhere Peter calls this a "good" (καλή) way of life (2:12), that is, one that is noble and recognized as such (cf. Matt 5:16). As Achtemeier says, "καλός ('good') here links Christian ethics to the best of pagan culture to show that Christians are not a threat by reason of their standard of conduct."[214] In 3:16 Peter describes their conduct as a "good" (ἀγαθή) way of life "in Christ." Achtemeier again notes, "The addition of the phrase ἐν Χριστῷ makes clear that 'good' is here defined not by cultural norms but by the Christian faith."[215] Peter hopes that the "purity" of the Christian wives' conduct (ἁγνὴν ἀναστροφήν),[216] that which demonstrates reverence for God (ἐν φόβῳ), will win their husbands for the gospel (3:1–2; cf. 2:18). Believers are called to conduct themselves in a way that shows reverence and honor to God as they live as resident aliens in society (1:17). Peter hopes that the conduct of the Christians will problematize the false opinions of their contemporaries to the point of bringing shame upon them for their unjust accusations (3:16).

As Peter develops the ethics of the Christian way of life, he changes up the language from being "holy" to "doing good." In 3:16–17 he describes their good conduct as "doing good"(ἀγαθοποιοῦντας), while in 2:12 he identifies it as "good works" (τῶν καλῶν ἔργων). The "will of God" means "doing good" (ἀγαθοποιοῦντας) in society (2:15). The verb "to do good" (ἀγαθοποιέω) appears four times in the letter (2:15, 20; 3:6, 17), while Peter also inserts the cognate expressions "doing good" (ἀγαθοποιΐα, 4:19) and "the one who does good" (ἀγαθοποιῶν [2:14]). Related expressions are salted throughout the letter (ποιησάτω ἀγαθόν, "do good" [3:11]; τοῦ ἀγαθοῦ ζηλωταί, "zealous for good" [3:13]; τὴν ἀγαθὴν ... ἀναστροφήν, "good way of life" [3:16]). Doing good is one of the controlling ethical concepts in 1 Peter, being adapted from Psalm 34:12–16, which is cited in 1 Peter 3:10–12: "Let them turn from evil and do good."

Van Unnik was the earliest to argue that the teaching on good works in 1 Peter had to do with varied forms of social benefaction. He demonstrated that in Greek and Roman thought "good works" was a broad social concept, its object being parents,

---

212. Peter's thought is unlike WWJD, "What Would Jesus Do?" which echoes the thesis in Charles M. Sheldon, *In His Steps: What Would Jesus Do?* (Radford, WA: Wilder, 2008). Peter's question is not "what would Jesus do?" but "what did Jesus do?"

213. Cf. Tob 4:14; 2 Macc 6:23; and the verbal form ἀναστρέφω in Wis 50:28; Sir 38:25.

214. Achtemeier, *1 Peter*, 177; BDAG, 504–5.

215. Achtemeier, *1 Peter*, 236; Beare, *The First Epistle of Peter*, 166.

216. BDAG, 13.

friends, or the state. It was the social virtue of "friendliness and willingness to help towards all men without distinction."[217] On the other hand, the Jewish conception was narrower since good works were understood as works of charity, such as visitation of the sick, hospitality towards strangers, aid to poor brides, assistance in funeral and marriage ceremonies, care for the dead, comforting the distressed, among other good acts done for the poor and afflicted. Subsequently, Winter argued that the primary focus of "good works" in 1 Peter was civic benefaction. In his work on Romans 13:3-4 and 1 Peter 2:14-15 he argues that:

> The picture emerges of a positive rôle being taken by rich Christians for the well-being of the community at large and the appropriateness and importance of due recognition by ruling authorities for their contribution. The Christians in Greek cities in the East were exhorted to undertake the same benefactions as did their secular counterparts. In fact this would have been expected of them by their fellow citizens if they were 'well-to-do'. Conversion to Christianity did not mean that civic benefactors ceased to seek the welfare of their earthly cities in keeping with their Old Testament counterparts in the Exile (Jer 29:7).[218]

Winter is correct in his assessment of 1 Peter 2:14, where the apostle states that the governors' obligation is to "punish those who do evil and praise those who do good" (not "do right" as the NRSV). Peter's language, as that of Paul, echoes the numerous benefactor inscriptions that honored public benefactors.[219] However, not everyone in Peter's communities was in a position to provide public benefaction, and we may conclude with van Unnik that Peter's concept of "doing good" could include public benefaction but was not limited to it. Williams weighs in on the matter with the most comprehensive study on the subject of benefaction in 1 Peter. He underscores the community benefit aspect of the varied forms of "doing good" but focuses sharply on the social situation of the readers. He states, "We concluded that the author's response constituted a form of subaltern accommodation. That is, the readers were instructed to comply with the standards of popular society as a way of preserving the basic safety of the most at-risk readers; yet, in each case, social conformity was balanced by some form of resistance which cautiously challenged existing social structures and quietly asserted the insubordination of the author."[220] As we have seen, Peter places "theological value" on good deeds and these works, while winning praise and even conversion (2:11-17; 3:1-2), could likewise result in further hostility (2:19-20; 3:13-14, 16-17). It would be better to suffer for doing good than doing evil, whatever the outcomes

---

217. W. C. van Unnik, "The Teaching of Good Works in 1 Peter," *NTS* 1 (1955) 96; W. C. van Unnik, "A Classical Parallel to 1 Peter 2:14 and 20," *NTS* 2 (1956) 198-202. See also Danker, *Benefactor*.

218. Bruce W. Winter, *Seek the Welfare of the City: Christians as Benefactors and Citizens* (Grand Rapids: Eerdmans, 1994), 39.

219. Winter, *Seek the Welfare of the City*, 26-29.

220. Williams, *Persecution in 1 Peter*, 277-78.

in their communities. Peter at least hopes that their deeds will silence their accusers (2:15) and bring shame upon them (3:16).

While Williams makes the case that there is a "subversive nature" within the theme of "good works" that is "a means of subverting oppressive powers," it is not the case that such works are "instrumental in attaining God's eschatological salvation."[221] God will indeed honor those who have maintained good deeds in the midst of adversity, thus showing that their faith is genuine (1:7). But "good works" are the outcome of following Christ and the proper response to God's call to holiness. Peter calls his readers to structure their lives according to God's will and character and are urged to imitate Christ's conduct. They may change the opinion of their peers, or they may not, as they live according to the highest norms of society yet maintain a primary allegiance and orientation to Christ. Williams's conclusion is insightful: "By adopting the language of social and political elites and then transforming it for the sake of marginalized communities, the Petrine author provides his readers with a newly constituted and highly esteemed social identity."[222]

Peter also describes the good way of life as "righteousness" (3:13–14, 17–18; 2:19–20, 24). Peter understands righteousness as "the doing of right as acceptable conduct," that is, "the right conduct of a man which follows the will of God and is pleasing to him."[223] Those who suffered for righteousness are blessed (3:14; cf. Matt 5:10). Such people have ceased embracing a sinful way of life (2:24) and have therefore become "the righteous" (3:12; 4:18) as those who emulate Christ's character (3:18; cf. 2:23).

Over against vice lists of behavior the new believers should avoid (as 2:1, 23; 3:9), Peter catalogs virtues that should mark the community. For example, in 3:8 he exhorts them, saying, "Finally, all of you, have unity of spirit, sympathy, love for one another, a tender heart, and a humble mind." To these he adds the blessing of the ones who wrong you (3:9) and, citing Psalm 34, includes "do good" and "seek peace and pursue it" (3:11). "Unity of spirit" (ὁμόφρονες) is a virtue of community harmony, highly prized in the "hostile environment" in which the readers found themselves (cf. Phil 2:2).[224] "Sympathy" (συμπαθεῖς) "does not denote active sympathy with those in distress but understanding and sympathetic participation in the destiny of others in all situations."[225] "Love for one another" (φιλάδελφοι) is the filial love within the new Christian family that is the result of their new birth (1:22). "A tender heart" (εὔσπλαγχνοι) is the compassion (Eph 4:32) that contrasts with harsh attitudes towards those in need.[226] "A humble mind" (ταπεινόφρονες) was not a virtue in Greek ethics, where the lexeme attached to the concept of being mentally servile or inferior. But in

---

221. Williams, *Persecution in 1 Peter*, 278.
222. Williams, *Persecution in 1 Peter*, 279.
223. TDNT, 2:198–99.
224. Kelly, *A Commentary on the Epistles of Peter and Jude*, 135; Achtemeier, *1 Peter*, 222.
225. TDNT, 5:935.
226. BDAG, 413.

Jewish and Christian literature it was turned into a virtue that stood over against pride and arrogance (Prov 29:23; Matt 11:29; 18:4, 23; 1 Pet 5:5).[227] All these virtues build community, as also does the faithful love Peter calls them to demonstrate towards one another (1:22; 4:8).[228]

When it comes to those outside the community, the apostle exhorts them to "bless" (ὐλογοῦντες [3:9a]), which may mean either that they are to speak well of others (Luke 6:28; Rom 12:14; Did. 1:3) or, more likely here, the act of petitioning God to pour his grace on someone (Luke 24:50-51; Heb 7:1, 6; see 1 Pet 3:9b). With regard to outsiders, they are also called to do them good, as discussed above, and "seek peace." "Peace" is not an emotional state; rather, they should seek to have positive relationships even with those who show hostility towards them (Rom 12:18; Heb 12:14; Matt 5:9). Peter understands that within the company of believers, community cohesion is an essential element of community identity. His ethics build around enforcing mutual care, even to the point of forgiving those who have broken faith with others (4:8).[229] In the wider community they should seek to live in harmony as much as possible, and yet Peter fully recognizes that their best efforts may not be successful. Peter orients his ethics around the character of God (1:15-16) and Christ (2:21). He presents an ethic that is out of step with the agonistic culture in which he and his readers found themselves. Virtues held dear among popular and classical ethicists of the day, such as tranquility (ἀτάρακτος) and self-sufficiency (αὐτάρκης), find no parallel in the ethics of our author. At times he flies in the face of popular ethics, such as his emphasis on humility. Peter presents a fully Christian ethic for those who live in a society that shows itself hostile to their faith.

Living Under the Orders of Society

In 2:13—3:7 Peter inserts a domestic code (*Haustafel*) similar to the ones found in the Pauline corpus (e.g., Col 3:18-4:1; Eph 5:22-6:9; Rom 13:1-7). Peter's primarily focuses on those classes of people who find themselves in conflict with the superordinate powers, with husbands being the one exception to this rule (3:7). Parallels exist with non-Christian domestic codes, and these are well documented.[230] Peter

---

227. *BDAG*, 989; *NIDNTT*, 2:259-64.

228. Hort, *The First Epistle of St. Peter 1:1-2:17*, 90-91.

229. 4:8b, "love covers a multitude of sins," comes from Prov 10:12 and appears in NT and Patristic literature (Jas 5:20; 1 Clem 49:5; 2 Clem 16:4). Most likely Peter has in mind that love covers or forgives the faults of others (cf. Ps 32:5; 85:2; Matt 6:12, 14-15; 18:21, 35; Mark 11:25; Luke 6:37; 11:4; 17:3-4; 2 Cor 2:7; Col 3:13). See Eugenio Green, *1 Pedro y 2 Pedro*, 249-50.

230. See, for example, James E. Crouch, *The Origin and Intention of the Colossian Haustafel*; David L. Balch, *Let Wives Be Submissive*; Hans-Josef Klauck, *Hausgemeinde un Hauskirche im frühen Christentum* (Stuttgart: Katholisches Bibelwerk, 1981); David C. Verner, *The Household of God: The Social World of the Pastoral Epistles* (Chico, CA: SBL, 1983); James Hering, *The Colossian and Ephesian Haustafeln in Theological Context: An Analysis of Their Origins, Relationship, and Message* (New York: Lang, 2007).

calls his readers to subordinate themselves to the superordinate powers such as the state (2:13), masters (2:18), husbands (3:1, 5), and elders (5:5), while subverting and relativizing the orders of the surrounding society. Christ has subordinated all powers as the resurrected and exalted Lord (3:22).

The verb "subordinate" (ὑποτάσσω) does not simply mean "accept the authority of," as the NRSV renders the verb in English. Nor does the NIV's translation "submit" draw close to the concept attached to the lexeme. Contrary to contemporary hermeneutical concerns surrounding the use of the term in the reciprocal relationships codified in the *Haustafeln*, the term was commonplace in a world structured vertically with superordinate and subordinate powers. Elliott's lengthy discussion is worth excerpting:

> The verb is a compound of the preposition *hypo-* (*sub-*, "under") and the verb *tassō* ("order," "place," "station"), which in turn is a derivative of the Greek noun for "order" (*taxis*; cf. *tagma*, "that which has been ordered").... The verb *hypotassō* (including the middle *hyupotassomai*, "subordinate oneself to") and its related noun *hypotagē* ("subordination"), like *taxis* and *tagma*, presume a concept and standard of natural and social order prevalent throughout the Greco-Roman world. This cosmic and social order, it was held, generated reciprocal relationships in which one or more parties occupies a superior social position and the other, an inferior position.... Superordination and subordination involved the acting out of statuses and roles determined by one's assigned place in the stratified social order. Focus on subordination is a typical feature of collectivist, group-oriented societies such as those of the ancient Circum-Mediterranean.... At the apex of the Roman social order stood the emperor and his retinue. Below the imperial house was the "order" (Latin, *ordo*) of senators, then the equestrians and lesser nobility, then the order of local provincial decurions. From these elites ... was distinguished the remainder of the population, the lower class, ranked in the descending order of urban and rural free plebians (*eleutheroi*, *liberi*), freed persons (*apeleutheroi*, *liberti*), slaves (*douloi*, *servi*), the destitute (*ptōchoi*), and finally the aliens (*xenoi*, *alieni*) at the very bottom of the pecking order. Within the household, the microcosm of the state, beneath the male heads of the household in their roles of husbands, fathers, and masters/owners, were subordinated the wives, children, and slaves, respectively. The subordination of children to their parents (male and female) and of younger persons to their elders (male and female) rounded out the general picture.[231]

Peter's ethic calls for subordination to the state, masters, husbands, and elders. Christians are to live as those who are "under the orders," recognizing and honoring those deemed to be superordinate powers. His call is not merely to acknowledge or

---

231. John H. Elliott, *1 Peter*, 486–87; Géza Alföldy, *Römische Sozialgeschichte* (Stuttgart: Steiner, 1984), 85–132.

respect those in superordinate positions but to act in ways that are consistent with these vertical relationships. Those under the emperor, the supreme authority, or his delegated governors are to "do good" to win their praise or public honor (2:13–14). Slaves should submit to their masters whether they are good or twisted, and in this relationship they, too, should do good (2:18–20). Wives are to be chaste and obedient (3:1, 5–6). The younger, likewise, should be subordinate to the elders (5:5). Such relationships are not "complementary" but reciprocal with respect to the respective obligations of the subordinate and superordinate powers.[232]

Peter does not counsel social revolution but rather urges the believers to conduct themselves as honorable people within these hierarchical relationships. The hermeneutical question is left open as to whether or not the "orders" of society may be changed. During the Civil War era, some in the United States took this and other texts regarding the subordination of slaves as a sign that slavery was divinely sanctioned. Others approached the issue theologically and viewed the order of master/slave as contrary to God's will, given that he created all and offered redemption to all.[233] Peter's strategy is to show how to live within the orders, but he does not directly set his readers to change the orders. Yet within the code of subordination, the elements that later flourished in social change are already present.

However, the apostle's domestic code is subversive in that it turns to God and Christ as the ultimate power and regards earthly and supernatural powers as subordinate to him. Those under the control of the state are to "honor the emperor" but have a higher allegiance marked in the exhortation to "fear God" (cf. Prov 24:21). Slaves live out their existence with an awareness of God (2:19) and follow the example of Christ (2:21–25). Peter directly addresses these who were at the lowest of orders and offers them the highest moral example. He reminds husbands that their wives are co-heirs of the grace of life and that mistreatment of them will turn their prayers back on their heads (3:7). Peter pulls the thread of the hierarchical social orders of his day. The task he began is still underway. As in his call to "do good" in society, Peter presents his readers with a double strategy of conformity and subversion.

Peter calls his readers to be subordinate to "every human institution" (ἀνθρωπίνῃ κτίσει), not simply because of the social status of those who rule but "for the Lord's sake" (2:13). Many have argued the call serves as a general heading for the whole section ending at 3:7, or even 3:12.[234] Given that the household codes included the

---

232. Mutuality in "subordination" would be an alien concept in this social context. Paul's call to "submit yourselves to one another" (Eph 5:25) does not mean that superordinates should subject themselves to subordinates, as he makes clear in the following instructions (5:22–6:9). Paul calls wives, children, and slaves to be subordinate (5:22; 6:1, 5), whereas he exhorts husbands, fathers, and masters to love, not exasperate, and not treat their slaves in a threatening way (5:25; 6:4, 9). In accordance with ancient usage, Paul and Peter never use the verb *hypotassō* to refer to the responsibility of those in superordinate positions.

233. See Noll, *The Civil War as a Theological Crisis*.

234. *TDNT*, 3:1034; Edwin Gordon Selwyn, *The First Epistle of Peter*, 144; C. E. B. Cranfield, *The*

teaching on the state, which was the larger household, alongside the codes governing the network of household relationships, interpreting 2:13 as a general heading has merit. The call to subordination echoes through the section, tying the whole together. But Peter clarifies the exhortation in 2:13a, saying, "Whether of the emperor . . . or of governors." When speaking of "every human institution," he has leaders of the state particularly in mind.

The expression "human institution" (ἀνθρωπίνῃ κτίσει) has been understood in a variety of ways. The κτίσις means either "the act of creation" (Rom 1:20) or "that which is created" (Rom 8:39; Col 1:15; Heb 4:13). Peter, however, steers his readers away from the notion of divine creation with the adjective "human." The term was also used of a "governance system, authority system," a concept Peter appears to have in mind in this section. The idea of creating or establishing something is not entirely absent here, however, since the term could be used of the founding of a city or a governing body.[235] While governing institutions are "human" according to Peter, Christian obedience to the state is done "for the Lord's sake" (2:13).

Peter addresses the way the governing authority has judicial functions but also rewards those who serve as public benefactors (2:14).[236] He recognizes that the authorities should be honored, but only God is the proper object of their fear or reverence. In 2:17 the exhortation to "fear God. Honor the emperor" (lit. "king") derives from the LXX Proverbs 24:21–22, which says, "My son, fear God and the king, and disobey neither of them, for they will unexpectedly punish the impious, and who shall know their punishments?" Peter changes the language since the "king" or emperor is not God's regent as in Israel but only part of the "human institution" that provides for social order (cf. Rom 13:1–7). Subordination to the orders and subversion of the extant authority structures go hand in hand in this section. Peter's hope is that doing good and being publicly honored will "silence the ignorance of the foolish" (2:15). Those who are "free people" should not use their social status for evil but should show deference to all: "Honor everyone. Love the family of believers" (τὴν ἀδελφότητα).

Peter turns to address the domestic slaves (οἱ οἰκέται) in 2:18–25. Slaves were included in ancient domestic codes but not addressed directly as here and in the Paulines. Slaves were considered chattel with no legal rights and were not the proper objects of moral instruction. Indeed, they were expected to follow the religion of their master (Columela 1.8; Cato, *Agr.* 5). Yet Peter honors them as fellow members of the Christian household. Indeed, he places before them the highest example to follow, Jesus Christ (2:21–25). Slaves are told that if they are going to suffer it should

---

First Epistle of Peter (London: SCM, 1950), 57; Schelkle, *Die Petrusbriefe, Der Judasbrief*, 73; Kelly, *A Commentary on the Epistles of Peter and Jude*, 108; Wolfgang Schrage, *Die "Katholischen" Briefe: Die Briefe des Jakobus, Petrus, Johannes, und Judas* (Göttingen: Vandenhoeck & Ruprecht, 1973), 88; Goppelt, *A Commentary on 1 Peter*, 182.

235. BDAG, 572–73.

236. Winter, *Seek the Welfare of the City*, 25–40, and the discussion above.

be for doing good and not evil (2:19–20), regardless of the character of their master (2:19), since they live being "aware of God" and their credit or reward comes from him (2:19a, 20a). In the case of slaves, "doing good" could include shunning idolatry. Non-participation in the master's sacrifices would have placed these slaves in a precarious position. Peter speaks of such good behavior as that which receives honor through God's "approval" from God (χάρις, used here as in Luke 6:32–33) or "credit" (κλέος).[237] The language points to God's honor given them as they conduct themselves in a good way and follow the example of Christ (2:21–25, as above). Their true master is God.

Just as slaves were to be subject to their masters regardless of their character, Peter exhorts the wives to subordinate themselves to their husbands whether or not they "obey the word" of the gospel (3:1). She is obedient to her husband (3:5–6) in hopes of winning her husband's obedience to the gospel (cf. 1:22). Peter's hope is that their conduct will win their husband for the faith. In an age when the wife was expected to be subordinate to her husband (Plutarch, *Conj. praec.* 142E; Livy 34.1.12; Pseudo-Callisthenes, *Alex.* 1.22.19–20) and follow the religion of her husband (Plutarch, *Conj. praec.* 140D; Cicero, *Leg.* 2.7.19–27; Juvenal, *Sat.* 6), the affirmation of the wives' faith in Christ over against that of her husband is truly remarkable. The wife lives by the standards of the age, yet her highest allegiance is to Christ.

Peter focuses on the wives' "pure" moral character and "reverence" towards God (ἣν ἐν φόβῳ ἁγνὴν ἀναστροφὴν ὑμῶν). These stand as a testimony for her husband to read as he observes her. Her adornment should come from her character and not hair styles, jewelry, or clothing (3:4). She should exhibit a "gentle and quiet spirit." The women, as with the slaves, are to conduct themselves with reference to God. Such character "is very precious in God's sight." Peter also exhorts them not to be afraid. In the Greek world women were exhorted to fear their husbands (Xenophon, *Oecon.* 7.25; pseud-Aristotle, *Oecon.* 3.144.2), yet Peter calls them to follow Sarah, the mother of women proselytes, who was "an example of not fearing" (Philo, *Names* 264–265; *Abr.* 206; *Spec. Leg.* 2.54–55). While conforming to the standards of the day in respect to subordination and fidelity, the Christian wives subvert the institution of marriage by living in the fear of God, following Christ, and rejecting the gods of their husbands.[238]

One of the curious features of contemporary conservative Christianity is the strong adherence to the ethic of subordination, called "submission" or euphemistically described as "complementarianism," while endorsing the changes in social order with regard to the state (2:13–17) and slavery (2:18–25). The church has long recognized that Roman social order for the state and slavery could be changed. Most contemporary societies do not live under the totalitarian regime of a king (2:13, 17) nor do they endorse slavery (2:18). Those orders changed as representative government was established and slavery was abolished. Peter shows Christian wives how to live under the order of marriage as prescribed in his day, but this does not mean that Roman

---

237. See the discussion in John H. Elliott, *1 Peter*, 518–21.
238. See the texts and discussion in Balch, *Let Wives Be Submissive*, 240–60.

structures of marriage need to be preserved. Changes in the marriage institution are underway in 1 Peter just as they are in Peter's ethic regarding the state and slavery.[239]

Peter's call to husbands is more succinct (3:7), most likely because his primary focus is on those in subordinate social positions. He previously suggested that there were indeed Christian husbands among his readers (3:1), so he turns now to address them directly. Most of their wives would have become followers of Christ since, as noted above, it was customary for wives to worship and serve those of her husband. Christian husbands are called to show honor to their wives, recognizing that they are the "weaker vessel" (ἀσθενεστέρῳ σκεύει). "Vessel" here refers to the body (Rom 9:22–23; 2 Cor 4:7; 1 Thess 4:4),[240] and the weakness he has in mind is physical (Matt 26:41; Mark 14:38; 2 Cor 10:10). The ancients did not consider weakness a virtue, so Peter's teaching is extraordinary as a warrant for Christian behavior. Peter orients the husbands around the fact that they are on equal footing with their wives as "co-heirs of the grace of life" (συγκληρονόμοις χάριτος ζωῆς, cf. 1:3–4), most likely a reference to eternal life (Matt 19:29; Mark 10:17). Peter adds the additional motivation for the husbands by warning them that non-compliance will shut their prayers off from God (3:7b).

The code of subordination continues with the younger, who are called to be subordinate to their elders (5:5). The elders may be those who have leadership roles in the churches, as the previous section suggests (5:1–4). But in ancient Mediterranean societies age and leadership were twined. The "young" may be novitiates in ministry who serve under the elders or may simply be those who are young in age. In either case, Peter calls them to subordination, while everyone is to exhibit the character of humility (5:5b).

Peter on the Christian Way of Life

Christian ethics in 1 Peter revolves around the person and work of God through Christ, the conversion and new life of the Gentile readers of the letter, and the hostility that these Christians faced within their social matrices. Peter marks out their pre-conversion existence as sinful and oriented around idolatry. Before coming to Christ they were governed by desire and the social norms of their contemporaries. Peter recalls their conversion from idolatry and their coming to Christ, the Stone, who then leads them to God. They were baptized as a rite of initiation. Baptism marked the time when they put off old vices and pledged themselves to live a holy life before God. Peter reminds them of their call to imitate God in his holiness and Christ in his suffering

---

239. Some seminaries focus almost exclusively on linguistic and exegetical training while neglecting hermeneutics and theology, both carried out with reference to the theological tradition and contemporary social matrices of the interpretive community. The unfortunate outcome is a literalism in biblical interpretation that has no room for wider hermeneutical issues as they relate to theology and *praxis*.

240. *BDAG*, 927–28.

for righteousness. No longer should they live according to the moral constructs established by their society but by the will of God. Living before God and in consciousness of him brought social obligations within the community. The apostle calls believers to do those acts that promote social harmony, loving one another and forgiving one another. But they also had to negotiate the hostility they faced in society. Much of Peter's ethical teaching is devoted to helping them know how to live as Christians within the orders of society. They are to avoid retaliation and live by the highest norms of their communities. Yet, at the same time, Peter problematizes their relationship with extant social structures by counseling behavior governed by higher norms set by God and Christ. Above all, Peter calls the community to live in holiness. He does not abstract this moral concept but offers an ethic in which true holiness is seen in doing good to all in society. Peter holds out hope that such conduct will change the opinion of their contemporaries and, indeed, may even lead to their own conversion. Yet he recognizes that all such efforts may fail. No matter, since God's holiness and Christ's righteousness are their norm. And in the end their social dishonor will turn into honor at the time of Christ's revelation. They anticipate joy in the future but also in the present since they share in the sufferings of Christ.

PETER'S TESTIMONY 1 PETER

Peter addressed his letter to Gentile converts in northern Asia Minor. Because of their conversion to Christ, they passed into a new social status of aliens and were consequently subjected to severe social rejection, which manifested itself in verbal and physical abuse. Although alienated from their societies, Peter shows them their place within the plan of God. They have been caught up into the divine plan, which centered on Christ. The arc of Peter's understanding of God's purposes extends from creation, through the present, and into the future, when Christ will be revealed. Peter frames this plan within the theology of the New Exodus. These Gentiles were chosen by God and have become his people. The story of the restoration of Israel is their story. This is Peter's response to the alienation the believers experienced within their communities.

Peter understands the transcendence of God and his role as the Creator, Father, and Judge. God's character is holy, and he is the one who extends grace to these believers. Jesus Christ is the center of God's plan. Peter touches upon Christ's preexistence but focuses primarily on his sufferings and glories. The apostle regards Christ as the Suffering Servant of Isaiah, the Lord, the Stone, the Lamb of God, and the Shepherd of Israel. His death was vicarious and redemptive since he died as a ransom for sin. God, however, raised Christ from the dead, giving him glory, and Christ ascended to heaven with all powers subjected to him. He is sovereign over all. Christ's resurrection is the power that effects the believers' salvation. Peter anticipates Christ's revelation, a time when his people will have indescribable joy. In the interim between his ascension and revelation Christ is not absent but only veiled. In the present time the Spirit of

God also rests upon the believers. Through the prophets, the Spirit predicted Christ's sufferings and glories and offered testimony along with those who proclaimed the gospel to them. The Spirit is present with the community as God's temple.

Given the social alienation Peter's readers faced, the apostle develops a robust theology of community. They are the people of God, God's household and his flock. Their identity as God's people stems from their divine election and their identification with Christ. He is the Stone, but they are living stones, built into the temple of God. Peter regards them as the very people of God, his special people, and a holy nation. They find their identity in the story of Israel since they are the people of the New Exodus. Not only do they enjoy divine acceptance and grace, but God's grace becomes a call to a life that conforms to the holy character of God and the righteousness of Christ. They live in obedience to God within the structures of society. Peter orients his readers to an ethic geared to cohesion within the Christian community while exhorting them to live by the highest standards of society, always conscious of God's plan and will. They have come out of darkness into light and now live within the orders of society, where they do good as God's holy people.

CHAPTER 9

Vox Petri—Peter's Theological Contribution to the Church

Can we hear Peter's theological testimony within the pages of the New Testament? The argument of the preceding chapters is that we indeed hold the testimony of Peter. The *vox Petri* comes down to us as an interpreted witness to his thought. If we accept that the testimony of Peter has been preserved for us, the question remains whether there are coherent strains throughout these witnesses which constitute an outline of the apostle's theology. While there are indeed commonalities which run through all the witnesses, there are also differences. Since Peter's testimony has come to us as both text and interpretation, we would expect variants to exist. The points of convergence, however, bring us to the heart of early Christian theology as elaborated by Peter, the Rock.

The first conclusion reached in this study was that, according to ancient testimony, the preaching of Peter stood behind Mark's Gospel. Mark was Peter's translator, and from what we know, he followed the apostle's *chreia* closely when he translated and wrote down what he remembered from Peter. As Papias said, Mark "wrote accurately all that he remembered, not, indeed in order of the things said or done by the Lord." With these words, Papias indicates that Mark's Gospel was not a finished literary product and that Mark was relatively faithful in his translation of Peter's *chreia*. He did not substantially alter what came to him, and he was comprehensive and careful "to leave out nothing of what he had heard and to make no false statements in them." In other words, Mark allowed the *vox Petri* to be heard. We may not be able to verify every piece of testimony preserved in Mark, but such is the nature of testimony. This Gospel was likely the foundation for the Synoptic tradition, along with Q. If this is indeed the case, the gospel story as it comes down to us has its roots in the preaching of Peter as translated and transcribed by Mark. What is unusual is that Matthew and Luke would have utilized a piece of literature as their source since it was clearly not a final, finished product. The most likely cause for its use was that it offered the very apostle Peter's witness to Jesus' teaching. Indeed, as Hengel said, "The best explanation of the fact that the Second Gospel lived on in the church, although Matthew had taken over about 90 percent of the material in it, is that the work of Mark was from the beginning bound up with the authority of the name of Peter."[1] The fact that Mark is a translation indicates that the author shaped what he had received from the apostle but, at the same time, held as closely as possible to what was actually spoken. Mark offers us Peter's theological vision of the person, work, and teaching of Jesus. This is the heart of the *vox Petri*.

The other major witness considered is the Petrine speeches in the Acts of the Apostles. The conclusion reached here is that we should not dismiss the speeches in Acts as mere Lukan inventions that only display the author's own theological perspective and rhetorical skill. To the contrary, the author of Acts holds faithfully to his sources, which provided testimony. Yet he molded what was handed down to him and presented his theological understanding of the events and speeches that were the components of early Christian history. Given the rhetorical concerns, we would expect to hear the author's viewpoint and his voice and not the *ipsissima verba* of any the actors on the stage. His rhetorical concern accounts for whatever similarities there are between the Petrine and Pauline speeches in this book. If, however, Luke is a credible historian of his age—as he claims—we may indeed hope to hear within his book the *ipsissima vox* of the ones who speak as he "adhered as closely as possible to the general sense of what was actually said," as did Thucydides (1.22.1). Luke is not like Timaeus, who "shows off his oratorical power but gives no report of what was actually spoken" (Polybius 12.25a.5). We may not be able to ferret out fully the interpretive elements that Luke inserted into the Petrine speeches in Acts. Every sermon presented is an interpretive summary. But we may expect that Luke remained faithful to the apostle's ideas and the setting in which he expressed them. We know that he carefully handled his sources from what we can ascertain from the historical record, as Hemer argued,[2] and we may rightly expect that he did the same in his account of Peter's proclamation and theology.

The historical record testifies that the apostle Peter needed the help of others when proclaiming the gospel. This was also the case upon writing 1 Peter. Whether Silvanus (1 Pet 5:12) was his amanuensis or not matters little since Peter most likely

---

1. Hengel, *Studies in the Gospel of Mark*, 52.

2. Colin J. Hemer, *The Book of Acts in the Setting of Hellenistic History*, ed. Conrad H. Gempf (Winona Lake, IN: Eisenbrauns, 1990).

would have used such services, and this help could well have stretched beyond translation to editing. Early Christian testimony regards this epistle as an authentic work of the apostle, yet we know that he was part of an authorial community that included Mark, Silvanus, and the believers in Rome (5:13). The argument in chapter 2 is that this letter represents the *vox Petri* but not the exact *verba Petri*. As with other works that provide testimony to Peter's thought, the apostle's amanuensis or translator left his stamp upon the document. Given ancient compositional practices, whatever shaping occurred would have been approved by the author before the document was dispatched. Ancient authors would review what was written and attach a final greeting in their own hand (cf. 2 Thess 3:17).[3]

First Peter harkens back to prophetic testimony, now fulfilled and interpreted in light of Christ's sufferings and glories, which were then proclaimed to the believers in Asia Minor (1:10–12). Peter then added his own testimony to God's grace in this letter, indicating that this grace is both a gift and demand (5:12). Peter stands as an eyewitness to Christ's sufferings, and now he bears witness to the grace of God. First Peter, therefore, serves as an essential source for understanding the theology of the prime witness of Christ's suffering and glorification. Moreover, Peter places his testimony regarding Christ alongside that of the prophets. These two serve as the foundation for the faith of the church. In an amazingly Petrine sounding statement, Ephesians 2:19–22 declares, "So then you are no longer strangers and aliens, but you are citizens with the saints and also members of the household of God, built upon the foundation of the apostles and prophets, with Christ Jesus himself as the cornerstone. In him the whole structure is joined together and grows into a holy temple in the Lord; in whom you also are built together spiritually into a dwelling place for God."

The first chapters of this book examined whether or not it is possible to speak about a Petrine theology in the New Testament. Given the sources we possess and the character of testimony that shaped the story therein, the conclusion reached is that we can affirm that the New Testament bears witness to the *vox Petri*. What remains, however, is to draw together some of the various theological threads in the witness contained in Mark, Acts, and 1 Peter. What picture of Peter's theology emerges from these documents?

A THEOLOGY OF PETER

Throughout the New Testament literature associated with the apostle Peter, there are numerous points of commonality, as we might expect if indeed the apostle's voice stands behind these works. Isolating a number of these is the burden of the following pages. But decided differences between the witnesses also exist, such as the prevalence

---

3. E. Randolph Richards, *The Secretary in the Letters of Paul* (Tübingen: Mohr Siebeck, 1991); E. Randolph Richards, *Paul and First-Century Letter Writing: Secretaries, Composition, and Collection* (Downers Grove, IL: InterVarsity, 2004).

of "kingdom" language in Mark and its absence from 1 Peter. Neither do we hear Peter reflecting on the kingdom in the Petrine speeches in Acts. The discontinuities may be entered as evidence against positing the preservation of the *vox Petri* across the witnesses or regarded as further evidence for the way rhetorical concerns have modified Peter's voice. Differences can arise due to the traditional material received, audience and situational awareness, or both. Are these variants of sufficient weight to count as sure evidence against identifying a distinctly Petrine voice in the New Testament, or do they simply show that Peter got by with a little help from his friends? I have attempted to argue the latter point throughout. Peter always stands together with others in both his innovations and failures. He was a recognized leader who was also deeply embedded in community, and that community was involved in the preservation of the *vox Petri*.

Moreover, some themes that we may identify across the Petrine literature also surface in other writings. Although the "Stone" testimonies from Psalms 118:2, Isaiah 8:14 and 28:16 are a centerpiece in Peter's thought (1 Pet 2:6–8; Acts 4:11–12; Mark 12:10–11), Paul likewise refers to Christ as the Stone in Romans 9:32–33 (citing Isa 28:16). Other theological high points in Peter's thought are not always unique to him. Both Peter and Paul appeal to Isaiah 53:12 to show that Christ's death was substitutionary (1 Pet 2:24; Rom 4:25), and both affirm that moral renewal is another outcome of Christ's sacrifice (1 Pet 2:24b; Rom 6:2, 11, 18). Complicating the question further is the fact that Peter, as Paul, likely drew from an extant body of teaching, as suggested by their common utilization of the domestic codes[4] and other didactic forms.[5]

But as the first leader of the early church, we would expect Peter to harmonize with other theological voices in the church. Indeed, those others may well have derived their thought from the apostle given his primacy and theological innovation.

---

4. James P. Hering, *The Colossian and Ephesian Haustafeln in Theological Context: An Analysis of Their Origins, Relationship, and Message* (New York: Lang, 2007).

5. Earlier discussion on this topic included an examination of a possible early Christian catechism (Philip Carrington, *The Primitive Christian Catechism* [Cambridge: Cambridge University Press, 1940]). Selwyn made a case for the form criticism of the epistles (Edwin Gordon Selwyn, *The First Epistle of Peter: The Greek Text with Introduction, Notes and Essays* [London: Macmillan, 1947], 362–466). Collections of OT passages or testimonia may have been a source (J. Rendel Harris, *Testimonies* [Cambridge: Cambridge University Press, 1916–1920]), as also hymnic and creedal materials (Rudolf Bultmann, "Bekenntnis-und Liedfragmente im ersten Petrusbrief," in *Coniectanea Neotestamentica XI: In honorem Antonii Fridrichsen sexagenarii* [Lund: Gleerup, 1947], 1–14; Oscar Cullmann, *The Earliest Christian Confessions* [London: Lutterworth, 1949]; M.-E. Boismard, *Quatre hymnes baptismales dans la première Épître de Pierre* [Paris: Cerf, 1961]; Vernon H. Neufeld, *The Earliest Christian Confessions* [Leiden: Brill, 1963]; Reinhard Deichgräber, *Gotteshymnus und Christushymnus in der frühen Christenheit: Untersuchungen zur Form, Sprache und Stil der frühchristlichen Hymnen* [Göttingen: Vandenhoeck & Ruprecht, 1967]; Jack T. Sanders, *The New Testament Christological Hymns: Their Historical Religious Background* [Cambridge: Cambridge University Press, 1971]). The *Haustafeln* predated the NT writings (James E. Crouch, *The Origin and Intention of the Colossian Haustafel* [Göttingen: Vandenhoeck & Ruprecht, 1972]; David L. Balch, *Let Wives Be Submissive: The Domestic Code in 1 Peter* [Chico, CA: Scholars, 1981]; Hering, *The Colossian and Ephesian Haustafeln in Theological Context*).

Arguably, Peter was the progenitor of some of the substrata of early Christian *didachē*, but this must remain an historical possibility and no more. However, we can affirm with high certainty that embracing the criteria of dissimilarity in order to ferret out a truly "Petrine" theology flies in the face of the evidence we have, which shows Peter as a man of the community, not an isolated and unattached figure. Our purpose here, however, is not to prove that Peter was the sole theological innovator in the church. Indeed, Jesus holds the place of honor when it comes to this "new thing" that God was doing. Paul's contribution as a leader in the church's theological development can hardly be gainsaid. But we should also regard Peter as a key theological voice who contributed to the church's foundational understanding of the meaning of Christ's person and work. Most likely, our understanding of Christ's death as an atonement and the inclusivity of the gospel for all ethnicities find their roots in Peter. Peter stood at the head of the early church after the ascension of Jesus and helped lead the fledgling community in developing their understanding of who Jesus was and what his life meant. He was a theological "Rock" whose contribution oriented the church.

The Plan of God

The fisherman from Galilee is perhaps the last person one might expect to hold a sweeping view of God's overarching plan, yet this is precisely what emerges from the Petrine witnesses. The man whom the Gospels identify as a capable fisherman, who could cast, let down, and care for nets (Mark 1:16–20; Luke 5:1–11), also saw and described the wide vistas of God's plan for humanity. In the midst of the sufferings that he and his communities faced, Peter lifted his eyes beyond the immediate adversities and demonstrated that those rejected and maligned by the surrounding society were not forsaken by God. They had a purposed place within his overall designs.

In Mark and Acts the outline of the divine plan takes the form of a founding epic that frames the facts of history within a unified and universal story. The story is an *aemulatio*, a counter to imperial claims about Roman power and glory in the Augustan age. The question on the ground was, "Who will rule the nations?" Peter responded that the true Son of God, Jesus Christ, is the Sovereign who rules over all. The kingdom of God is the true eternal government, surpassing all claims to empire. With its advent, the new age has dawned. The vision of universal rule is not sullied by the suffering endured by the Son of God; rather, through Christ's work, humanity finds redemption and demonic forces are overcome. Christ even conquers death. A new era has arrived, but it is not Roman imperial. The prophets predicted these events, and they are now brought to pass in the person of Jesus. That divine plan included the cross, which Peter consistently frames within the Stone testimony of Psalm 118:22: "The stone that the builders rejected has become the chief cornerstone." The rejection of Christ and his placement as the cornerstone had significance for Israel, but in 1 Peter the apostle also places that claim as a counter to the surrounding Gentile rejection of Christ and, by extension, his community (1 Pet 1:1; 2:7).

In his first epistle Peter does not utilize "kingdom" to describe this plan of God, although he holds to Christ's sovereignty (3:22), nor is the category of "epic" apropos to the letter genre. Yet even here the apostle frames the situation his readers endured within the large arc of God's plan. He paints the horizon to include God's designs for Christ starting before creation, the prophetic testimony of that plan, which centered on Christ's sufferings and glories, and the consummation of that plan at the time of Christ's revelation. Suffering in no way negates that divine design—a consistent, central tenet in Peter's thought. The end of all things is right at hand in this letter, in the same way that Peter lays out a clear vision of the end in Mark and the speeches in Acts. The plan was predicted, then realized, in the midst of suffering and now anticipates its final consummation with Christ.

The vistas of Peter's theology of the divine plan embrace the inclusion of God's people, who, according to all the witness, are now not only Jews but also Gentiles. Inclusion, and not simply wonder, is characteristic of Peter's understanding of the God's purposes and acts. We see Gentile faith in Mark, the opening of the community to the Gentiles and their full embrace in Acts, and the way Gentiles become the people of God through God's election and their relation with Christ. Indeed, in 1 Peter the apostle constantly points to the way believers are in God's will. Gospel events have transpired for their benefit, "for you" (1:12) as he says.

Peter's vision is large despite the vicissitudes of early Christian existence. Christ, though he suffered, already reigns over all powers, and that universal rule will be fully revealed in his time. His plan includes those who respond to God's initiative but also spells the rejection of all who oppose the divine plan. God's grace is balanced against his judgment, which has begun with the overthrow of the powers and will be consummated when people give an account to the one who judges the living and the dead. Peter unfolds before his readers the fact that God makes no small plans.

The New Exodus

Peter's principle framing of the divine plan finds its roots in Isaiah's vision of the New Exodus (Isa 40–55). The New Exodus is a consistent and prominent theme across the Petrine witnesses. The first Exodus was the founding moment for Israel, and that divine liberation became paradigmatic for Isaiah's vision of a New Exodus. The New Exodus included the restoration of the Davidic kingdom and the renewal of the nation of Israel. But it also anticipated the inclusion of the Gentiles, a fact that Peter was the first to understand. The salvation of God was not limited to the gathering of Israel but also reached out to embrace those who were once "no people." Peter stands as a leader in the New Exodus, as one who opens the gate for the redemption for every nation over which Christ is Lord. He understands that both Jews and Gentiles are redeemed through Christ and become God's holy and elect people.

The Liberator of Peter's New Exodus theology is the one who had suffered and died but was raised from the dead. In the language of 1 Peter, the New Exodus embraced Christ's sufferings and glories as the Servant of the Lord. He was the rejected Stone who was then exalted to the place of honor. In his New Exodus theology, Peter regards Christ's death as substitutionary, a ransom for sin that effects their deliverance. Christ's death is also the means by which they enter into the New Covenant with God.

The New Exodus theology, as that of the first Exodus, meant deliverance. But in Peter's vision this liberation was not from the surrounding society but happened in the midst of the extant social structures. The redemption is from evil and includes moral renewal. At its heart, it includes the call to repentance, washing through baptism, and the reception of the Spirit. It also meant deliverance from demonic powers and idolatry. The New Exodus' anti-idol polemic stands alongside Peter's understanding of Christ's royal enthronement over all powers. He is Lord over all, including the powers of evil. Consistent throughout the Petrine literature is the shout of victory over supernaturally empowered evil.

Christ's enthronement, however, does not mean absence from his people. The New Exodus carries with it the promise of the divine presence, a key feature of Peter's theology. He understands the way that Christ called people to himself and brought them near, whether Jew or Gentile. Salvation in the present time continues to mean coming to him and coming to God through him. But the apostle also sees Christ as active among his people even though he is the exalted Lord.

Across the Petrine literature, the New Exodus included the proclamation of the word of God to both Israel and the Gentiles. That word was proclaimed by Christ and continued to be announced by Peter and then, in turn, by those who were the messengers of the gospel. God's word comes to all, even the Gentiles, as Peter was bold to declare to those gathered with Cornelius (Acts 10:34–43). In 1 Peter the apostle underscores the importance of the word and witness as he recounted how the prophetic message of Christ's sufferings and glories was then proclaimed as the heart of the gospel (1 Pet 1:12). In the New Exodus and its proclamation, the way of the Lord opens and people follow in response to the call. But following also means exile in society. Belonging and alien existence are the obverse and reverse of the coin. The end of that following and exile, however, is the incorruptible inheritance inherent in God's New Exodus promise. Hope and faith dominate in Peter's theology.

The Person and Work of Christ

Central to Peter's theology is the person and work of Jesus Christ. Indeed, Peter's understanding of who Christ is and what he accomplished is foundational for all Christian theology. According to Peter's testimony in Mark, the apostle was the first to realize and testify that Jesus was the Christ: "You are the Messiah" (Mark 8:29b). If indeed Mark was the first Gospel written, which was then used by Matthew and Luke and known by John, then this fundamental understanding of Jesus' person is traceable back to Peter. Matthew's Gospel adds the comment that God had revealed to Peter that Jesus truly was the Messiah (Matt 16:7), a note suggested in Mark by the juxtaposition of the confession with the miracle of regained sight (Mark 8:22–26). From the beginning of the Gospel, Mark focuses on Jesus' sovereignty as the Messiah, heir to the promise given to David (Mark 1:1; 12:35–37). Jesus fully embraced the messianic title, although the "Messianic secret" in Mark alerts us to the caution found in the gospel about misconstrual of his messiahship.

Mark writes for a Roman audience, and therefore he juxtaposes the title with "Son of God." This was a counterpoint to imperial claims to sovereignty (1:1; 15:39) as well as a title that identified Jesus as the heir to the Davidic promise of his descendant's rule (2 Sam 7:14). Moreover, the sovereignty implicit in Jesus' messianic rule is further developed through the Son of Man language in the Gospel. Jesus is the sovereign of Daniel 7:13–14. Son of Man and Messiah share a considerable amount of conceptual information about Jesus' person and work (Mark 8:29, 31).

Both Acts and 1 Peter contain central robust affirmations regarding Jesus, the Messiah. He was foretold by the prophets, and in 1 Peter the apostle adds that the "Spirit of Christ" inspired the prophetic witness (1 Pet 1:11). Peter understood that Jesus was not only the fulfillment of prophetic hopes but also the preexistent one (1:20). As Christ, he stands in the center of God's plan, and in the present time he is the exalted sovereign over all powers. Attendant upon his exaltation and sovereignty in the present is Peter's firm conviction that Christ will be revealed in the future.

Peter did not have a full-orbed understanding of the entailments of Jesus' messianic mission when he first made his confession. When Jesus subsequently announced that he would suffer, die, and subsequently be raised, "Peter took him aside and began to rebuke him" (8:32). However, as seen in all the Petrine testimony, the apostle arrived at the deepest understanding of the divine purpose in the Messiah's sufferings and death. While initially rejecting the idea of the Messiah's suffering and death, Peter subsequently fully embraced this understanding of Jesus' messianic mission. Indeed, Peter became the foundational theologian when it came to the integration of the theology of the Davidic Messiah and the cross. He also offered the first theological understanding of the significance of Christ's death as a ransom for sin. We may trace back to Peter our fundamental understanding of the Messiah's substitutionary death as a means of redemption from sin. He bore witness to the merger of the Davidic messianic promise with Isaiah's Suffering Servant. He recognized that his death was for others and that through his death the New Covenant with God was established. Peter is our first theologian of the cross. Although we remember Peter for his failures, the apostle also turns to become an advocate of the very realities he was unable to grasp at the beginning. The consistent picture is of a theological leader given to failure yet able to turn and advocate for positions he once refused. His is the model leader as well as theologian.

Standing alongside Peter's confession that Jesus is the suffering and exalted Messiah is his declaration that Jesus is the Lord of all. Peter roots this confession principally in Psalm 110:1: "The Lord said to my lord, 'Sit at my right hand until I make your enemies your footstool'" (Mark 12:36; Acts 2:34–35; 1 Pet 3:22). Although Jesus is the son of David, he is also David's Lord. All the Petrine witnesses view Christ's lordship as an indication of his transcendence and, indeed, divinity. "Lord" was the divine name in the LXX and was also understood as a title of deity in the Greco-Roman world. Peter does not hesitate to ascribe the divine title to Jesus (1 Pet 3:15, citing Isa 8:13). The apostle goes beyond seeing Christ as preexistent to testifying to his divinity. He falls short of calling Jesus Christ "God" but fully embraces the notion of Christ's divinity. The epistolary greeting in 1 Peter places the Father, the Spirit, and Jesus Christ together in what may be regarded as an early Trinitarian formula (1:2). Second Peter takes the further step, however, of calling Jesus Christ "God and Savior."[6]

A further distinctive of Peter's Christology is his use of the Stone testimony to describe Jesus' person and work. Citing Psalms 118:22–23, we first hear Jesus' self-understanding as the Rejected Stone in Mark 12:10–11: "Have you not read this scripture: 'The stone that the builders rejected has become the cornerstone; this was the Lord's doing, and it is amazing in our eyes'?" Peter again returns to the Stone testimony in Acts 4:11 as a means of explaining that Jesus' rejection by the Jewish leaders was reversed by God since he has now become the cornerstone. In 1 Peter he framed the leaders' or builders' rejection of Jesus, the Stone, together with the rejection Peter's readers experienced within their communities in Asia Minor. First Peter 2:4–8 draws together a litany of Stone testimonies from Psalm 118:22, Isaiah 28:16, and Isaiah 8:14. In all these texts Peter deals with the problem of Christ's rejection as a fulfillment of God's plan and with them affirms the honor that God gave him as the Rejected Stone. The divine verdict trumps the human. But in each instance the Stone testimony becomes an integral piece of Peter's temple theology set over against other sanctuaries, whether Jewish or Gentile. Jesus is the true cornerstone of God's habitation. He is also the elect Stone, chosen by God, who reverses the rejection Christ suffered at the hands of the leaders and people. Peter holds together Jesus' death, resurrection, and exaltation with the Stone testimonies. Possibly Peter's naming was, in part, the root of this special attention to the title (John 1:42; Matt 16:18), although the Petrine witnesses do not make this connection.

Peter also understands Jesus' suffering and death with his identity as the Lamb. Peter points back to the Passover meal when Jesus identified himself with the blood of the sacrificed Lamb. His shed blood was that which established the New Covenant (Mark 14:12–16, 22–25) and was the effective agent in God's New Exodus. In Mark 10:45 we hear the echo of the Servant Song of Isaiah 53:11–12. Christ came to give

---

6. See the discussion in Green, *Jude and 2 Peter*, 174–75.

his life as a ransom for many. Peter's testimony in Mark lays out the fundamental theology of Christ's death as that of the Servant whose demise was "like a lamb that is led to the slaughter, and like a sheep that before its shearers is silent" (Isa 53:7). Peter picks up the Lamb and redemption imagery in 1 Peter 1:18–19, as well as echoing the Servant Songs in 2:22–24. The apostle regards Jesus' death as that of the Lamb who atones for sin, redeems from the bondages of sin, and effects the New Exodus. The Petrine speeches in Acts do not envision Jesus' person and death as a sacrificial Lamb. However, they show the apostle's particular concern with the New Covenant blessing of the forgiveness of sins and salvation through Jesus.

Another place where Mark and 1 Peter coalesce is the development of the idea that Jesus is the Shepherd. Mark regards him as the Shepherd-Messiah who cares for the flock yet is smitten as the sheep are scattered (Mark 6:34; 14:26–31). The oversight and care that Jesus shows as the Shepherd becomes a focal point in 1 Peter (2:25; 5:4), but the emphasis here is not on the Shepherd's rejection but rather on the protection of his people and the honor he will give to pastoral leaders. Similarly, both Mark and 1 Peter see Jesus in a priestly role as he assumes priestly responsibilities such as declaring the lepers clean and forgiving in Mark, and mediating in 1 Peter. The Petrine speeches in Acts cast Jesus in this priestly role but do not describe him as the Lamb of God.

On the other hand, all three witnesses to Peter's theology underscore his prophetic ministry. He appears with the prophets Moses and Elijah in Mark, yet he is one who, according to the divine call ("Listen to him!"), is greater than they are since he is the Son (9:7), the one predicted by Moses. Peter's Acts speech also casts Jesus as the prophet Moses predicted (3:22–23). Jesus' prophetic ministry rises even further in 1 Peter since the "Spirit of Christ" inspired the prophets who predicted the Christ's sufferings and glories (1:10–11). Jesus is the Prophet whose words are final and authoritative. As Prophet, Jesus is the one who supremely reveals God's will. The three Petrine witnesses also concur that Jesus is the Righteous One, whose suffering cannot be attributed to his own misdeeds but rather who endures suffering and death for the sake of those who are unrighteous. Mark frames Jesus as the Suffering Righteous One of Isaiah while both Acts and 1 Peter directly call him the Righteous One (Acts 3:14; 1 Pet 3:18). Peter regards Jesus as the one who reveals God's will and who suffered for no cause of his own since he was righteous.

While common themes emerge across all or most of the witness to Peter's Christology, other concepts are unique to each of these. Mark, for example, highlights that Jesus was the Teacher who delivered authoritative instruction and interpretation of Scripture and who directed his disciples to teach. The speeches in Acts contain a number of distinctive christological titles such as Author of Life, Leader, and Savior. First Peter is the sole witness that reflects on Christ's proclamation of victory over the powers upon his ascension (3:18–22), although the whole passage resonates with Petrine themes such as Christ's substitutionary death, resurrection, ascension, and his session at the right hand of God. Given that the theological materials associated with Peter are always mediated and modified by those who offered testimony regarding his teaching, we should expect variances among them. Peter's voice does not come to us unmediated as the *verba Petri* but has been handed down as the *vox Petri*. Multiple attestation neither confirms nor negates that a particular current in the theology is genuine. What we do know is that Peter had a surprising theological range for a Galilean fisherman, and he possessed creative and inspired theological insight. His Christology is a prime example of his theological breadth, which is entirely in harmony with the theologies developing in the early church. Indeed, Peter's theology was foundational and not simply derivative or common.

The Agency of the Holy Spirit

While Peter pays particular attention to God's plan and Christ's role within it, he also holds a robust theology of the Holy Spirit, whom he regards as a central actor in the story of salvation. In both Mark and the Petrine speeches in Acts, the apostle points to Jesus' own reception of the Spirit, which enables his ministry of benefaction (Acts 10:38) and identifies him as Isaiah's Servant (Isa 42:1; Mark 1:10–11). Peter links Jesus' reception of the Spirit with John's baptism, and he highlights John's prophetic witness that Jesus would be the one who would baptize with the Holy Spirit. Peter frames the coming of the Holy Spirit as the fulfillment of the prophetic witness in Joel 2, understanding that the exalted Christ was the one who gives the Spirit (Acts 2:33). Peter teaches that the Spirit's advent is a blessing of the New Covenant (Acts 2:38).

Although the prediction of the Spirit's coming was fulfilled at Pentecost, Jesus empowered the disciples before then by granting them authority over the powers (Mark 3:14–15; 6:7; 9:38) and assuring them of the Holy Spirit's witness as they faced persecution (13:9–11). Peter was particularly concerned with testimony through the agency of the Holy Spirit in the life of Jesus and the followers of Christ. Indeed, Peter bears witness at Pentecost through the agency of the Spirit, and he affirms the Spirit's witness alongside the apostolic testimony (Acts 5:32). In the same way, Peter reminds the readers of the Spirit's testimony through those who preached the gospel to them through the Holy Spirit (1 Pet 1:12; Acts 2:17b–18). The Spirit had inspired the prophetic testimony (Mark 12:36; 13:11; Acts 1:16; 1 Pet 1:11), and the same Spirit now speaks through the Christian prophetic witness. The Spirit both leads and empowers Christian mission.

The Spirit testifies with those who offer witness when enduring persecution (Mark 13:11) but also rests upon those who are persecuted, according to 1 Peter 4:14. Peter combines his theology of suffering with a strong affirmation of the Spirit's presence in the most adverse circumstances. Only in Mark does Peter touch the idea of Jesus' being led by the Spirit out to the wilderness where he is tested. The presence of the Spirit with Jesus in the wilderness may be a prelude to Peter's understanding of the testing that comes in the face of social ostracism and persecution (1 Pet 1:6–7).

Peter's theology connects the Spirit's agency and the inclusion of the Gentiles in God's plan. This theme does not appear in Mark but comes to the fore in Acts at Pentecost (Acts 2:38–39), the proclamation to the first Gentile converts in the house of Cornelius (10:19:44–45, 47), and the proclamation through the Spirit to the Gentile recipients of 1 Peter (1:12). The presence of the Spirit among the Gentiles is a sign of God's acceptance of all people without distinction. Peter bears witness to the way the Spirit forms the community of Gentiles into a temple indwelt by the Spirit of God (1 Pet 2:5). God is present among them and gives them honor through the Spirit.

The Salvation of God

Peter presents a robust theology of salvation, which surfaces throughout all the witnesses. As discussed above, Peter regards Jesus' death as substitutionary and a ransom for sin. Christ's death effects the New Exodus and brings people into the New Covenant with God. The Petrine speeches in Acts do not present a theology of ransom or redemption, but Peter indeed introduces the New Covenant and New Exodus concepts in his discourse. According to the apostle, people enter into the New Covenant through obedience, faith, and baptism, all key concepts within Peter's understanding of the process of salvation. Through Christ's redemption within the New Covenant, Peter holds forth the promise of forgiveness of sins.

Peter stands out as the apostle of inclusion in his understanding of the extent of God's salvation. Men and women, young and old, people of all social classes, and Gentiles as well as Jews are recipients of God's saving grace. Peter's theological innovation includes widening the tent of salvation, a lesson hard-learned. Peter's quotation of Joel 2 in his Pentecost sermon marked the opening of his understanding of the way salvation reaches across gender, age, and class, but the apostle was slow to realize that Gentiles were included as recipients of salvation. Although he affirmed at Pentecost that the salvific blessings of the New Covenant were "for all who are far away" (Acts 2:39), not until the encounter with Cornelius did he fully grasp the reality of his earlier statement. Peter stood at the Jerusalem Council as the principle witness for Gentile inclusion in the gospel, above Paul and Barnabas, and James recognized him as the one who was the theological point-man for the universality of salvation's reach. Both Mark and 1 Peter testify to Peter's full embrace of the universal offer of salvation.

Peter became the apostle of grace as he summarizes the fullness of God's saving act with this term (1 Pet 5:12). Understood within the frame of benefaction, Peter viewed salvation as a gift of God's benefaction. Indeed, Peter identified Christ as the Benefactor when he opened the door of salvation to Cornelius and those gathered with him (Acts 10:38). Peter's understanding of salvation as divine benefaction included the dual realities of liberation from demonic powers and divine healing, not only from sin but from sickness and disease. Peter bore witness to Jesus' ministry of healing but also came to understand that healing was part of the salvation made available through the cross. Unlike Paul, however, Peter does not extend this understanding out to include the resurrection from the dead. Peter is decidedly reserved about life after death and the final destiny of those who have died.

The apostle regarded Christ's ascent as the time when he proclaimed victory over the powers and baptism as the entry into the blessing of salvation from those powers. Peter ties his theology of baptism with entry into the New Covenant but also with liberation from the demonic and likely from idolatry. Peter also joins together forgiveness of sins and moral cleansing with baptism, viewing this ceremony as more than an empty rite but a true transition into the benefits of God's grace.

The Christian Community

A vivid thread running through all the witnesses to Peter's theology is the formation of a new community of the people of God. Peter preached and wrote to disciples of Christ who faced serious opposition from their surrounding communities and who had become disenfranchised due to their commitment to follow the way of Christ. The language of separation and alienation found in Peter's theology finds its counterpoint in his concepts of community formation and solidarity.

In the first place, Peter's concept of community wraps around the people's commitment to Christ. Peter does not build his theology of community upon notions such as common humanity or commitment to unique philosophical tenets. Rather, the person of Christ is central both for their salvation and for their union together as those who experience his redemption. They have been called by God, chosen by him, and thus join in Jesus' mission as followers or disciples. The language of following and discipleship appears in Mark and 1 Peter and speaks of following in his footprints, but the commitment to Christ is central throughout the witnesses. Their allegiance to Christ plays out against the backdrop of social alienation and its attendant identity concerns. Following Christ entails enduring rejection as Christ was rejected. Suffering and denial of self are part of following Christ and being a Christian or "Christ lackey." Social shame and identity loss are issues Peter must manage in the collectivist cultures in which he develops his theology of community.

Peter regards the Christian community as the people of God of the New Exodus. Traditional New Exodus theology included the restoration of Israel and the inclusion of the Gentiles. Although Peter touches on Israel's restoration in the Acts speeches, at the core of his theology is the people of God, which now includes both Gentiles and Jews. Peter stands for the inclusion of the Gentiles into the people of God yet does not struggle—as does Paul—with the relationship between Jews and Gentiles in God's plan. For Peter, there is one people of God: those who have come to Christ, the Stone rejected by the builders. This people is continuous with Israel of old and becomes heir to the identity once reserved for the Jewish people (1 Pet 2:9–10). Peter stands at the beginning of the theology of inclusivity in the people of God, not only in preaching and teaching but also in his actions. He opened the door of salvation to the Gentiles (Acts 10) and stood for their undifferentiated inclusion (Acts 15). Peter was a conciliatory figure in the early church. While he employed the language of alienation to describe the people's relationship with the surrounding society, he embraced the idea of proselyte conversion as the entryway into the people of God.

Unlike Paul, Peter does not utilize the concept "church" to describe the people of God. He is more at home with traditional Jewish titles such as those found in 1 Peter 2:9: "But you are a chosen race, a royal priesthood, a holy nation, God's own people." Peter prefers familial and household language to speak of the Christian community, as Elliott has argued. Peter adds to this pastoral imagery by calling the people God's flock, whose Shepherd is Christ. Surprisingly, Peter introduces a redefinition of the temple of God in his view that now God's people are his temple, the habitation of God through the Spirit. The use of temple imagery to describe the people of God is not unique to Paul. The unique contribution Peter brings is to associate the "stones" with Christ, the Stone. They find their identity as the temple of God in relation to Christ.

The language of discipleship in Mark and Acts implies that Peter regards the people of God as a community of learners. As those who are attached to Christ, they suffer as he did but are called to not be ashamed of their master. Community identity with Christ and one another stands as a bulwark against the social ostracism early Christians experienced. Christian community is not a secondary piece in Peter's theology but an essential component of his theology on the road, that place where "life is tensely lived."[7] Peter links his ecclesiology with Christology and a theology of suffering. These Christians are God's elect people who live out the reality of participating in God's plan as the community of the New Exodus.

The Last Things

All the witnesses to Peter's theology have a robust eschatology, although they do not shape the presentation of the last things uniformly. In Mark's telling, eschatology has to do with the advent of the kingdom of God, whereas in Acts the coming of the Spirit on Pentecost is the sign of the presence of the last days. Peter's first epistle marks the present as the time of prophetic fulfillment but also notes that the "last times" have come with the revealing of Christ in the present (1 Pet 1:20). Yet a primary feature throughout them all is that the present time is the fulfillment of prophetic promises, marking this time as the last days. Eschatology in Peter's view is not simply future but also present, and in this he accords with other New Testament witnesses. Peter embeds his eschatology within the theology of the New Exodus. God's promise of renewal and restoration for his people and the inclusion of the Gentiles has already

---

7. John A. Mackay, *A Preface to Christian Theology* (New York: Macmillan, 1941), 30.

begun. The apostle also affirms that the present is also a time of suffering for God's people and that this adversity marks the days up until the final consummation. Peter views Christ's sufferings, and those of his readers, as components of God's plan, which he then binds tightly with the promise of final consummation.

Peter also links ethics with eschatology in Mark and 1 Peter. Morality in the present time is rooted in the character of God and Christ, but Peter also links it with the revelation of Christ. Now is the time to watch and be ready since Christ will soon appear. Peter anticipates the final judgment of God, but his primary emphasis is upon the future revelation of Christ, the time when God's grace will be revealed fully. While Mark speaks about the Son of Man's coming with the clouds of heaven and the Acts speeches tell of Christ's return, 1 Peter emphasizes the unveiling of Christ, who is hidden in the present time but will be revealed. In all three witnesses Peter emphasizes the nearness of the final events. The end is at hand.

First Peter makes unique contributions by speaking of the final events from the resurrection to his unveiling as Christ's glories, the counterpoint to his sufferings. Although his theology in the epistle does not echo the vision of the Son of Man coming with the clouds of heaven as in Mark 13, 1 Peter presents Christ as the universal sovereign over all at the present time. His unveiling will usher in the time of final judgment. Before that final event, however, the gospel will be proclaimed universally according to Mark. Acts shows that proclamation to both Jews and Gentiles, although Peter does not link the universal reach of the gospel with eschatology in those speeches. First Peter, however, views the proclamation of the gospel as the outcome of the fulfillment of the prophetic hope in Christ's sufferings and glories (1 Pet 1:10–12).

Peter's eschatology is replete with themes which became commonplace in the early church. The end has begun with Christ's ministry and sufferings, the rule of God has begun in Christ, the sufferings of Christ and his people are signs of the end and not a negation of God's plan. A New Exodus has begun that includes all people, and what has begun will come to its final consummation upon Christ's final unveiling. That event will be a time of restoration and salvation but also judgment. Christian conduct in the present is lived with a keen consciousness that the end of all things is near at hand. Peter's theology is replete with hope in the present and for the future. God's grace has and will come.

The Honorable Way of Life

The witnesses to Peter's theology all agree that the apostle not only had an overarching vision of the plan of God but also saw his and other Christian's place in that plan. God's person and actions are the roots of Peter's ethical teaching. The apostle finds the ethical imperative buried within the indicative of God's being, Christ's person, and their redemptive activity. Peter holds a theological ethic that does not separate Christian conduct from the great truths of the gospel. For Peter, Christian action means participation in the plan of God. The *imitatio Dei* and *imitatio Christi* hold a central place in Peter's ethical teaching. God's people are those who live according to the will of God, even as Christ did.

Throughout the witnesses, we hear Peter's emphasis on divine calling and the necessity of responding in obedience to God's summons. This movement towards God in obedience carries with it the call to repent and turn from former ways, including idolatry. Baptism is the rite of conversion and initiation whereby one puts away immorality in the turn to do God's will. The apostle holds out the promise of forgiveness and moral renewal. Peter understands that the heart of Christian ethics lies within the redemption of Christ effected through the cross, although he also orients his ethics around eschatology. God's word and his Spirit are agents in Christian moral renewal. Peter is no mere moralist since he views the possibility of a renewed life as dependent upon God's initiative, Christ's work, and the Spirit's agency in sanctification.

Although he calls his readers to eschew vice and embrace virtue in 1 Peter, his principle ethical exhortation is to demonstrate love in relationships and do good to all people as those who follow Christ. Christ was the supreme benefactor, and Peter calls his readers to social benefaction as well. His call to Christian ethics plays out in contexts of adversity and hostility. Central to Peter's ethical teaching is the notion of "heroic discipleship," which maintains an outward directed moral life in the face of persecution. As Christ served others and not himself, so also those who walk in his way are to do good to all people, even those who oppose them.

Mark and 1 Peter are the central loci of Peter's ethical teaching, while the Petrine speeches in Acts contain just the bare outline of his thought on the topic. While Mark and 1 Peter share many common ethical teachings, such as the centrality of love and morality in adversity, each has their own particular ethical contributions given their genres and settings. Mark, for example, frames Jesus' ethical instruction within the advent of the kingdom of God, language which is absent from the other witnesses. First Peter highlights the break from idolatry and the moral corruption centered on the idol cult. He understands "doing good" as central to a life of holiness. The epistle extensively develops what it means to maintain a moral life within the structures of society, doing good while living "under the orders."

Petrine ethics are theological at their core, finding their impetus and orientation in the character and acts of God. For Peter, the divine imperative is inherent in the divine indicative. He refuses to pull apart theology and ethics. The apostle shares much of his ethical instruction with the rest of the New Testament witnesses, although he does not develop the place of the Spirit in moral renewal as extensively as Paul. He understands the intimate link between God's call, Christ's cross, the final consummation, and Christian conduct, themes he develops as does Paul. But Peter also takes the lead in showing how the Christian life develops and is maintained in the midst of hostility, forming part of Christian witness within the structures of society. He lays the foundation for a Christian social ethic that guides the churches of his day and speaks powerfully to those in ours.

PETER AND THE FOUNDATIONS OF CHRISTIAN THEOLOGY

The brief summary of Peter's theology in this chapter only skims the surface of the apostle's thought as it has come down to us in the various Petrine witnesses. Peter was a prime leader in the early church, and as part of his ministry he framed early Christian life within God's plan, Christ's work, and eschatological hope. Peter offered the church its earliest theological understanding of the cross of Christ and located early Christian life within the large arc of God's plan. As members of the Sanhedrin observed, he and John "were uneducated and ordinary men," but they saw they were "companions of Jesus" (Acts 4:13). Peter was the first to tell the story of Jesus as a narrative whole, the first to identify Jesus as the Messiah, and the first to explain the meaning of the cross of Christ. He developed his theology on the road in the face of opposition, offering the church a theology of suffering and glory. He stood at the very beginning of Christian understanding of the inclusive nature of God's saving work through Christ. All people, both Gentiles and Jews, have a place in God's plan. The apostle lifted the church's eyes in hope to the final consummation of all things when God's act of restoration would be complete.

Peter's theology is, in the end, very much the theology of the early church. At various points we encounter unique contributions to early Christian theologizing, such as the apostle's discussion of Christ's proclamation to the spirits in prison (1 Pet 3:18–22) and his affirmation that if Israel repents, "times of refreshing" will arrive "from the presence of the Lord," and then God will "send the Messiah appointed for you, that is, Jesus" (Acts 3:19–20). Yet on the main, Peter's theology looks comfortably familiar, with recognizable avenues and structures which lead us to believe that we have indeed been here before. Peter's theology does not contrast strikingly with that found in other New Testament witnesses. The contours of the Christ story are all here, accompanied by the apostolic interpretation of the life, death, resurrection, authority, and advent of Jesus. The salvation Peter describes centers on Christ and embraces all peoples who, though varied in their ethnicity, are brought together to form one holy and elect people of God. Peter, as others, looks forward to a final consummation of all things which will occur at the advent of Christ. Peter understands the wide scope of God's plan and frames it together with the theology of the New Exodus. The walk through Peter's theology brings us into familiar surroundings, the theological home of the people of God.

Given Peter's central role in the development of Christian theology, we would not expect it to be otherwise. Peter stands as the rock (*petra*) in the center of Christian theology and, indeed, he was a leader and innovator of the first order. Were the contours of Peter's theology surfaced in this study out of sync with the central themes of Christian theology shot throughout the New Testament, we could not reconcile the differences with the consistent presentation of the apostle as the central apostolic leader in the early years of the church. Peter stands at the beginning of Christian theology, a person who, following Jesus, laid the foundations and innovated as new realities arose. Our central confessions regarding the person of Jesus, the cross, salvation, the inclusive nature of people of God, and the end of all things come to us through him. He is indeed the apostle for the whole church, and the whole church resonates with his theology. Perkins gets it right when she says, "Peter is not depicted as the founder of any particular churches. Rather, Peter is the universal 'foundation' for all the churches. The canon itself might be viewed from this Petrine perspective. With the attribution of Mark to Peter's oral tradition and the addition of Peter as the shepherd in John 21:15–17, all four Gospels as well as Acts have some connection to the Petrine tradition. 1 Peter directs exhortation much like that found in Pauline churches in Asia Minor."[8] We may say that New Testament theology, though diverse, harmonizes with Peter's thematic strains. We sing his song, though we may not have looked to the bottom of the page in the hymnbook to see who wrote the words and composed the tune.

Peter stands at the very beginning of Christian theology.[9] May the "lost boy" of Christian theology find his rightful place at the table once again. But if we look closely, we will see that he has been seated at the head of the table all along.

---

8. Perkins, *Peter*, 184. Perkins adds, "2 Peter even brings the Pauline letter collection into the Petrine fold."

9. As Barnett says, "All the evidence points to the leadership of Peter in the first community of the Messiah in Jerusalem, as spokesman and *as the first theologian of Christianity*, though one whose theology is partially hidden in the shadows and has to be inferred" (*Paul in Syria*, 75 [emphasis mine]).

Bibliography

Abrahams, Israel. *Studies in Pharisaism and the Gospels: Second Series*. Eugene, OR: Wipf & Stock, 2004.

Achtemeier, Paul J. *1 Peter: A Commentary on First Peter*. Hermeneia. Minneapolis: Fortress, 1996.

Adcock, F. E. *Thucydides and History*. Cambridge: Cambridge University Press, 1963.

Adler, Eve. *Vergil's Empire: Political Thought in the Aeneid*. Oxford: Rowman & Littlefield, 2003.

Alexander, Loveday. *The Preface to Luke's Gospel: Literary Convention and Social Context in Luke 1:1-4 and Acts 1:1*. SNTSMS 78. Cambridge: Cambridge University Press, 1993.

Alföldy, Géza. *Römische Sozialgeschichte*. Stuttgart: Steiner, 1984.

Allison, Dale C. "The Pauline Epistles and the Synoptic Gospels: The Pattern of the Parallels." *NTS* 28 (1982) 1-32.

Anderson, Bernhard W. "Exodus Typology in Second Isaiah." In *Israel's Prophetic Heritage: Essays in Honor of James Muilenburg*, edited by Bernhard W. Anderson and Walter Harrelson, 176-95. New York: Harper & Brothers, 1962.

Anderson, Robert T., and Terry Giles. *The Keepers: An Introduction to the History and Culture of the Samaritans*. Grand Rapids: Baker Academic, 2001.

Arav, Rami, and Richard A. Freund, eds. *Bethsaida: A City By the North Shore of the Sea of Galilee*. Vol. 1. Kirksville, MO: Thomas Jefferson University Press, 1995.

Arav, Ravi. "Bethsaida." *IEJ* 51 (2001) 239-46.

———. "New Testament Archaeology and the Case of Bethsaida." In *Das Ende der Tage und die Gegenwart des Heils*, edited by Michael Becker and Wolfgang Fenske, 75-99. Leiden: Brill, 1999.

Ashton, Mark. *On My Way to Heaven: Facing Death with Christ*. Chorley, UK: 10Publishing, 2011.

Audi, Robert. "The Place of Testimony in the Fabric of Knowledge and Justification." *American Philosophical Quarterly* 34 (1997) 405-22.

Augustine. *On the Trinity: Books 8-15*. Edited by Gareth B. Matthews. Translated by Stephen McKenna. Cambridge: Cambridge University Press, 2002.

Aune, David E. *The New Testament in Its Literary Environment*. LEC 8. Philadelphia: Westminster, 1987.

Baban, Octavian. *On the Road Encounters in Luke-Acts: Hellenistic Mimesis and Luke's Theology of the Way*. Paternoster Biblical Monographs. Milton Keynes: Paternoster, 2006.

Bacon, B. W. "The Elder John, Papias, Irenæus, Eusebius, and the Syriac Translator." *JBL* 1 (1908) 1–23.

Baker, Coleman A. *Identity, Memory, and Narrative in Early Christianity: Peter, Paul, and Recategorization in the Book of Acts*. Eugene, OR: Pickwick, 2011.

Balch, David L. *Let Wives Be Submissive: The Domestic Code in 1 Peter*. SBLMS 26. Chico, CA: Scholars, 1981.

Barnett, A. E. *Paul Becomes a Literary Influence*. Chicago: University of Chicago Press, 1941.

Barnett, Paul W. *Paul in Syria: The Background to Galatians*. Milton Keynes: Paternoster, 2014.

Barrett, C. K. *A Critical and Exegetical Commentary on the Acts of the Apostles*. 2 vols. ICC. Edinburgh: T. & T. Clark, 1998.

———. "Faith and Eschatology in Acts 3." In *Glaube und Eschatologie: Festschrift für Werner Georg Kümmel zum 80. Geburtstag*, edited by Erich Gräßer and Otto Merk, 1–17. Tübingen: Mohr Siebeck, 1985.

Barton, Stephen C. *Discipleship and Family Ties in Mark and Matthew*. SNTSMS 80. Cambridge: Cambridge University Press, 1994.

Bates, Catherine, ed. *The Cambridge Companion to the Epic*. Cambridge: Cambridge University Press, 2010.

Bauckham, Richard. "For Whom Were Gospels Written?" In *The Gospels for All Christians: Rethinking the Gospel Audiences*, edited by Richard Bauckham, 9–48. Grand Rapids: Eerdmans, 1998.

———, ed. *The Gospels for All Christians: Rethinking the Gospel Audiences*. Grand Rapids: Eerdmans, 1998.

———. "James, Peter, and the Gentiles." In *The Missions of James, Peter, and Paul: Tensions in Early Christianity*, edited by Bruce Chilton and Craig Evans, 91–142. Leiden: Brill, 2005.

———. *Jesus and the Eyewitnesses: The Gospels as Eyewitness Testimony*. Grand Rapids: Eerdmans, 2017.

———. "John for Readers of Mark." In *The Gospels for All Christians: Rethinking the Gospel Audiences*, edited by Richard Bauckham, 147–71. Grand Rapids: Eerdmans, 1998c.

———. *Jude, 2 Peter*. WBC 50. Waco, TX: Word, 1983.

———. "The Martyrdom of Peter in Early Christian Literature." *Aufsteig und Niedergang der römischen Welt* 2.26.1 (1992) 539–95.

———. "Pseudo-Apostolic Letters." *JBL* 107 (1988) 469–94.

Bayer, Hans F. "The Preaching of Peter in Acts." In *Witness to the Gospel: The Theology of Acts*, edited by I. Howard Marshall and David Peterson, 257–74. Grand Rapids: Eerdmans, 1998.

Beare, Francis Wright. *The First Epistle of Peter*. 3rd ed. Oxford: Basil Blackwell, 1970.

Beasley-Murray, G. R. *Baptism in the New Testament*. Grand Rapids: Eerdmans, 1973.

Beavis, Mary Ann. *Mark's Audience: The Literary and Social Setting of Mark 4:11–12*. JSNTSup 33. Sheffield: Sheffield Academic, 1989.

Bede the Venerable. *The Commentary on the Seven Catholic Epistles of Bede the Venerable*. Translated by David Hurst. Kalamazoo, MI: Cistercian, 1985.

Benedict XVI. *Jesus of Nazareth: From the Baptism in the Jordan to the Transfiguration.* Translated by Adrian J. Walker. New York: Doubleday, 2007.

Berkey, Robert F. "*Eggizein, Phthanein*, and Realized Eschatology." *JBL* 82 (1963) 177–87.

Best, Ernest. *1 Peter*. NCB. Grand Rapids: Eerdmans, 1971.

———. "1 Peter 2:4–10—A Reconsideration." *NovT* 11 (1969) 270–93.

———. "1 Peter and the Gospel Tradition." *NTS* 16 (1970) 95–113.

———. *Disciples and Discipleship: Studies in the Gospel According to Mark*. Edinburgh: T. & T. Clark, 1986.

———. *Following Jesus: Discipleship in the Gospel of Mark*. JSNTSup 4. Sheffield: Sheffield Academic, 1981.

Betz, Hans Dieter. *Nachfolge und Nachahmung Jesu Christi im Neuen Testament*. BHT 37. Tübingen: Mohr Siebeck, 1967.

Bigg, Charles. *A Critical and Exegetical Commentary on the Epistles of St. Peter and St. Jude.* ICC. Edinburgh: T. & T. Clark, 1901.

Black, C. Clifton. *The Disciples According to Mark: Markan Redaction in Current Debate.* JSNTSup 27. Sheffield: Sheffield Academic, 1989.

Black, Matthew. *An Aramaic Approach to the Gospels and Acts*. Oxford: Oxford University Press, 1967.

Blackburn, Barry. *Theios Anēr and the Markan Miracle Traditions: A Critique of the Theios Anēr Concept as an Interpretive Background of the Miracle Traditions Used by Mark.* WUNT 2.40. Tübingen: Mohr Siebeck, 1991.

Blevins, J. L. *The Messianic Secret in Markan Research 1901–1976*. Washington: University Press of America, 1981.

Boccaccini, Gabriele, ed. *Enoch and the Messiah Son of Man: Revisiting the Book of Parables.* Grand Rapids: Eerdmans, 2007.

Bock, Darrell L. *Acts*. BECNT. Grand Rapids: Baker Academic, 2007.

———. *Blasphemy and Exaltation in Judaism and the Final Examination of Jesus: A Philological-Historical Study of the Key Jewish Themes Impacting Mark 14:61–64*. WUNT 2.106. Tübingen: Mohr-Siebeck, 1998.

———. *Luke, 1:1–9:50*. Vol. 1 of *Luke*. BECNT. Grand Rapids: Baker, 1994.

———. "The Use of Daniel 7 in Jesus' Trial, with Implications for His Self-Understanding." In *Who is This Son of Man? The Latest Scholarship on a Puzzling Expression of the Historical Jesus*, edited by Larry W. Hurtado and Paul L. Owen, 78–100. LNTS 390. London: T. & T. Clark, 2011.

———. "The Words of Jesus in the Gospels: Live, Jive, or Memorex?" In *Jesus Under Fire: Modern Scholarship Reinvents the Historical Jesus,* edited by Michael J. Wilkins and J. P. Moreland, 73–99. Grand Rapids: Zondervan, 1995.

Bockmuehl, Markus. *The Remembered Peter in Ancient Reception and Modern Debate*. Tübingen: Mohr Siebeck, 2010.

———. *Seeing the Word: Refocusing New Testament Study*. Studies in Theological Interpretation. Grand Rapids: Baker Academic, 2006.

———. *Simon Peter in Scripture and Memory: The New Testament Apostle in the Early Church*. Grand Rapids: Baker Academic, 2012.

Boismard, M.-E. *Quatre hymnes baptismales dans la première Épître de Pierre*. LD 30. Paris: Cerf, 1961.

Bolt, Peter G. *The Cross from a Distance: Atonement in Mark's Gospel*. NSBT 18. Downers Grove, IL: InterVarsity, 2004.

———. *Jesus' Defeat of Death: Persuading Mark's Early Readers*. SNTSMS 125. Cambridge: Cambridge University Press, 2003.

Bond, Helen K. "Was Peter behind Mark's Gospel?" In *Peter in Early Christianity*, edited by Helen K. Bond and Larry W. Hurtado, 46–61. Grand Rapids: Eerdmans, 2015.

Bond, Helen K., and Larry W. Hurtado, eds. *Peter in Early Christianity*. Grand Rapids: Eerdmans, 2015.

Bonz, Marianne Palmer. *The Past as Legacy: Luke-Acts and Ancient Epic*. Minneapolis: Augsburg Fortress, 2000.

Borrell, Agustí. *The Good News of Peter's Denial: A Narrative and Rhetorical Reading of Mark 14:54.66–72*. University of South Florida International Studies in Formative Christianity and Judaism 7. Atlanta: Scholars, 1998.

Borsch, Frederick H. *Power in Weakness: New Hearing for Gospel Stories of Healing and Discipleship*. Philadelphia: Fortress, 1983.

Bovon, François. *Luke 1: A Commentary on the Gospel of Luke 1:1–9:50*. Hermeneia. Minneapolis: Fortress, 2002.

Bowen, Edwin W. "Roman Currency Under the Republic." *CJ* 47 (1951) 92–97.

Brandt, Pierre-Yves. *L'identité de Jésus et l'identité de son disciple: Le récit de la transfiguration comme clef de lecture de l'Évangile de Marc*. NTOA 50. Göttingen: Vandenhoeck & Ruprecht, 2002.

Briones, David. "Mutual Brokers of Grace: A Study in 2 Corinthians 1:3–11." *NTS* 56 (2010) 536–56.

Broadhead, Edwin K. "Christology as Polemic and Apologetic. The Priestly Portrayal of Jesus in the Gospel of Mark." *JSNT* 47 (1992) 21–34.

———. "Jesus and the Priests of Israel." In *Jesus from Judaism to Christianity: Continuum Approaches to the Historical Jesus*, edited by Tom Holmén, 125–44. LNTS 352. London: T. & T. Clark, 2007.

———. *Naming Jesus: Titular Christology in the Gospel of Mark*. JSNTSup 175. Sheffield: Sheffield Academic, 1999.

Brooke, George. *The Bible and Its Interpretation*. Literature of the Dead Sea Scrolls. London: Routledge, 2011.

Brown, Raymond E., and John P. Meier. *Antioch and Rome: New Testament Cradles of Catholic Christianity*. Mahwah, NJ: Paulist, 1983.

Brown, Raymond E., et al., eds. *Peter in the New Testament: A Collaborative Assessment by Protestant and Roman Catholic Scholars*. Minneapolis: Augsburg; New York: Paulist, 1973.

Brox, Norbert. *Der erste Petrusbrief*. EKKNT. Zürich: Benzinger, 1986.

Bruce, F. F. *The Acts of the Apostles: Greek Text with Introduction and Commentary*. Grand Rapids: Eerdmans, 1951.

———. *The Book of the Acts*. NICNT. Grand Rapids: Eerdmans, 1988.

———. *Peter, Stephen, James, and John: Studies in Early Non-Pauline Christianity*. Grand Rapids: Eerdmans, 1980.

———. "The Speeches in Acts–Thirty Years After." In *Reconciliation and Hope: New Testament Essays on Atonement and Eschatology Presented to L. L. Morris on His 60th Birthday*, edited by Robert Banks, 53–68. Carlisle: Paternoster, 1974.

Brunson, Andrew C. *Psalm 118 in the Gospel of John: An Intertextual Study on the New Exodus Pattern in the Theology of John*. WUNT 2.158. Tübingen: Mohr Siebeck, 2003.

Bultmann, Rudolf. "Bekenntnis- und Liedfragmente im ersten Petrusbrief." In *Coniectanea Neotestamentica XI: In honorem Antonii Fridrichsen sexagenarii*, 1–14. ConNT 11. Lund: Gleerup, 1947.

Burkett, Delbert. *Rethinking the Gospel Sources: From Proto-Mark to Mark*. New York: T. & T. Clark: 2004.

———. *The Son of Man Debate: A History and Evaluation*. SNTSMS 107. Cambridge: Cambridge University Press, 1999.

Burridge, Richard A. *What Are the Gospels? A Comparison with Graeco-Roman Biography*. Grand Rapids: Eerdmans, 2004.

Burton, Ernest De Witt. *A Critical and Exegetical Commentary on the Epistle to the Galatians*. ICC 35. Edinburgh: T. & T. Clark, 1920.

Byung-Mu, Ahn. "The Historical Subject in a Perspective of the Gospel of Mark." In *Minjung and Korean Theology*, edited by the Korean National Council of Churches Committee on Theological Study, 177–84. Seoul: Korean Theological Study Institute, 1982.

Cadbury, Henry J. "The Speeches in Acts." In vol. 5 of *The Beginnings of Christianity*, edited by F. J. Foakes Jackson and Kirsopp Lake, 402–27. Grand Rapids: Baker, 1979.

Campbell, Barth L. *Honor, Shame, and the Rhetoric of 1 Peter*. SBLDS 160. Atlanta: Scholars, 1998.

Campbell, R. A. "The Elders of the Jerusalem Church." *JTS* 44 (1993) 511–28.

Čapek, Milič, ed. *The Concepts of Space and Time: Their Structure and Their Development*. Synthese Library 74. Boston Studies in the Philosophy of Science 22. Boston: Reidel, 1976.

Caragounis, Chrys C. *The Son of Man: Vision and Interpretation*. WUNT 38. Tübingen: Mohr, 1986.

Carrington, Philip. *The Primitive Christian Catechism*. Cambridge: Cambridge University Press, 1940.

Casey, Maurice. *Aramaic Sources of Mark's Gospel*. SNTSMS 102. Cambridge: Cambridge University Press, 1998.

Cassese, Giácomo. *Epístolas Universales*. Minneapolis: Augsburg Fortress, 2007.

Casson, Lionel. *Ships and Seamanship in the Ancient World*. 2nd ed. Baltimore: Johns Hopkins University Press, 1995.

———. *Travel in the Ancient World*. 2nd ed. Baltimore: Johns Hopkins University Press, 1994.

Champlin, Edward. *Nero*. Cambridge, MA: Harvard University Press, 2003.

Chancey, Mark A. *Greco-Roman Culture and the Galilee of Jesus*. SNTSMS 134. Cambridge: Cambridge University Press, 2005.

———. *The Myth of a Gentile Galilee*. SNTSMS 118. Cambridge: Cambridge University Press, 2002.

Charles, J. Daryl. "Vice and Virtue Lists." In *Dictionary of New Testament Background*, edited by Craig A. Evans and Stanley E. Porter, 1252–57. Downers Grove, IL: InterVarsity, 2000.

———. *Virtue Amidst Vice: The Catalogue of Virtues in 2 Peter 1*. JSNTSup 150. Sheffield: Sheffield Academic, 1997.

Charles, J. Daryl, and Erland Waltner. *First-Second Peter, Jude*. Scottdale, PA: Herald, 1999.

Chester, Andrew, and Ralph P. Martin. *The Theology of the Letters of James, Peter, and Jude*. New Testament Theology. Cambridge: Cambridge University Press, 1994.

Chilton, Bruce, et al., eds. *A Comparative Handbook to the Gospel of Mark: Comparisons with Pseudepigrapha, the Qumran Scrolls, and Rabbinic Literature*. The New Testament Gospels in Their Judaic Contexts 1. Leiden: Brill, 2010.

Chilton, Bruce, and Craig Evans. *The Missions of James, Peter, and Paul: Tensions in Early Christianity*. Leiden: Brill, 2005.

Clark Wire, Antoinette. *The Case for Mark Composed in Performance*. Eugene, OR: Cascade, 2011.

Coady, C. A. J. *Testimony: A Philosophical Study*. Oxford: Clarendon, 1992.

Cogan, Mark. *The Human Thing: The Speeches and Principles of Thucydides's History*. Chicago: University of Chicago Press, 1981.

Collins, Adela Yarbro. *Mark: A Commentary*. Hermeneia. Minneapolis: Fortress, 2007.

———. "Mark and His Readers: The Son of God Among Greeks and Romans." *HTR* 93 (2000) 85–100.

———. "Mark and His Readers: The Son of God Among Jews." *HTR* 92 (1999) 393–408.

Conlin, Diane Atnally. *The Artists of the Ara Pacis: The Process of Hellenization in Roman Relief Sculpture*. Chapel Hill: University of North Carolina Press, 1997.

Conte, Gian Biagio. *The Rhetoric of Imitation: Genre and Poetic Memory in Virgil and Other Latin Poets*. Edited by Charles Segal. Cornell Studies in Classical Philology 44. Ithaca: Cornell University Press, 1986.

Conzelmann, Hans. *Acts of the Apostles*. Translated by James Limburg, et al. Philadelphia: Fortress, 1987.

———. *Gentiles, Jews, Christians: Polemics and Apologetics in the Greco-Roman Era*. Minneapolis: Augsburg Fortress, 1992.

———. *An Outline of the Theology of the New Testament*. London: SCM, 1969.

Coogan, Jeremiah. "Silvanus as Secretary: 1 Peter 5:12 and the Idiom γράφω διὰ τινὸς." Paper presented at the Annual Meeting of the Midwest Region of the SBL, Olivet Nazarene University, February 9, 2013.

Cook, John Granger. *Crucifixion in the Mediterranean World*. WUNT 327. Tübingen: Mohr Siebeck, 2014.

Cooley, Alison E. *Res Gestae Divi Augusti: Text, Translation and Commentary*. Cambridge: Cambridge University Press, 2009.

Counet, Chatelion. "Pseudepigraphy and the Petrine School: Spirit and Tradition in 1 and 2 Peter and Jude." *HvTSt* 62 (2006) 403–424.

Cranfield, C. E. B. *1 & 2 Peter and Jude: Introduction and Commentary*. TBC. London: SCM, 1960.

———. *The First Epistle of Peter*. London: SCM, 1950.

———. *The Gospel According to Saint Mark*. Cambridge: Cambridge University Press, 1959.

Crouch, James E. *The Origin and Intention of the Colossian Haustafel*. FRLANT 109. Göttingen: Vandenhoeck & Ruprecht, 1972.

Cullmann, Oscar. *The Christology of the New Testament*. Translated by Shirley C. Guthrie and Charles A. M. Hall. Rev. ed. Philadelphia: Westminster, 1963.

———. *The Earliest Christian Confessions*. London: Lutterworth, 1949.

———. *Peter: Disciple-Apostle-Martyr: A Historical and Theological Study*. Translated by Floyd V. Filson. London: SCM, 1953.

———. *Peter: Disciple-Apostle-Martyr: A Historical and Theological Study*. 2nd rev. and exp. ed. Translated by Floyd V. Filson. London: SCM, 1962.

———. *Salvation in History*. London: SCM, 1967.

Dalton, William Joseph. *Christ's Proclamation to the Spirits: A Study of 1 Peter 3:18–4:6.* AnBib 23. Rome: Pontifical Biblical Institute, 1989.

Danker, Frederick W. *Benefactor: Epigraphic Study of a Graeco-Roman and New Testament Semantic Field.* St. Louis: Clayton, 1982.

Davids, Peter H. *The First Epistle of Peter.* NICNT. Grand Rapids: Eerdmans, 1990.

———. *A Theology of James, Peter, and Jude.* Biblical Theology of the New Testament. Grand Rapids: Zondervan, 2015.

Davis, Jud. "Acts 2 and the Old Testament: The Pentecost Event in Light of Sinai, Babel, and the Table of Nations." CTR 7 (2009) 29–48.

Davis, William Stearns, ed. *Rome and the West.* Vol. 2 of *Readings in Ancient History: Illustrative Extracts from the Sources.* Boston: Allyn & Bacon, 1913.

Dawsey, James. *Peter's Last Sermon: Identity and Discipleship in the Gospel of Mark.* Macon, GA: Mercer University Press, 2010.

Deichgräber, Reinhard. *Gotteshymnus und Christushymnus in der frühen Christenheit: Untersuchungen zur Form, Sprache und Stil der frühchristlichen Hymnen.* SUNT 5. Göttingen: Vandenhoeck & Ruprecht, 1967.

Deissmann, Adolf. *Bible Studies.* Translated by A. Grieve. Edinburgh: T. & T. Clark, 1901.

Deloria, Vine, Jr. *God is Red: A Native View of Religion.* Golden, CO: Fulcrum, 2003.

Derrenbacker, R. A., Jr. *Ancient Compositional Practices and the Synoptic Problem.* BETL 186. Leuven: Leuven University Press, 2005.

Derrett, J. Duncan M. "The Stone Which the Builders Rejected." SE 4 (1968) 180–86.

deSilva, David A. *Despising Shame: Honor Discourse and Community Maintenance in the Epistle to the Hebrews.* SBLDS 152. Atlanta: Scholars, 1995.

———. *Honor, Patronage, Kinship and Purity: Unlocking New Testament Culture.* Downers Grove, IL: InterVarsity, 2000.

———. "Honor, Shame, and the Rhetoric of First Peter." ATJ 32 (2000) 129–32.

Deterding, Paul L. "Exodus Motifs in 1 Peter." *Concordia Journal* 7 (1981) 58–65.

Dibelius, Martin. *Studies in the Acts of the Apostles.* Edited by Heinrich Greeven. Translated by Mary Ling. London: SCM, 1956.

Dickson, John P. "Gospel as News: εὐαγγελ—From Aristophanes to the Apostle Paul." NTS 51 (2005) 212–30.

Dillon, Richard J. "The Prophecy of Christ and His Witnesses According to the Discourses in Acts." NTS 32 (1986) 544–56.

Dines, Jennifer M. *The Septuagint.* London; New York: T. & T. Clark, 2004.

Dodd, C. H. *The Apostolic Preaching and Its Developments.* London: Hodder & Stoughton, 1944.

———. *Gospel and Law: The Relation of Faith and Ethics in Early Christianity.* Cambridge: Cambridge University Press, 1951.

———. *The Parables of the Kingdom.* New York: Scribner's Sons, 1961.

Donahue, John R. *The Theology and Setting of Discipleship in the Gospel of Mark.* Milwaukee: Marquette University Press, 1983.

Donahue, John R., and Daniel J. Harrington. *The Gospel of Mark.* SP 2. Collegeville, MN: Liturgical, 2002.

Donaldson, Terence L. *Paul and the Gentiles: Remapping the Apostle's Convictional World.* Minneapolis: Augsburg Fortress, 2006.

Dschulnigg, Peter. *Petrus im Neuen Testament.* Stuttgart: Katholisches Bibelwerk, 1996.

———. *Sprache, Redaktion und Intention des Markus-Evangeliums: Eigentümlichkeiten der Sprache des Markus-Evangeliums und ihre Bedeutung für die Redaktionskritik*. SBB 11. Stuttgart: Katholisches Bibelwerk, 1984.
Dubis, Mark. *Messianic Woes in 1 Peter: Suffering and Eschatology in 1 Peter 4:12–19*. StBibLit 33. New York: Lang, 2002.
Duling, Dennis C. "Solomon, Exorcism, and the Son of David." *HTR* 68 (1975) 235–52.
Dungan, David L. *The Sayings of Jesus in the Churches of Paul: The Use of the Synoptic Tradition in the Regulation of Early Church Life*. Philadelphia: Fortress, 1971.
Dunn, James D. G. *The Acts of the Apostles*. Valley Forge: Trinity, 1996.
———. *Baptism in the Holy Spirit: A Re-Examination of the New Testament on the Gift of the Spirit*. Philadelphia: Westminster John Knox, 1977.
———. *Christology in the Making: An Inquiry Into the Origins of the Doctrine of the Incarnation*. Grand Rapids: Eerdmans, 1996.
———. *Jesus and the Spirit: A Study of the Religious and Charismatic Experience of Jesus and the First Christians as Reflected in the New Testament*. London: SCM, 1975.
———. *Jesus Remembered*. Vol. 1 of *Christianity in the Making*. Grand Rapids: Eerdmans, 2003.
———. "The Messianic Secret in Mark." *TB* 21 (1970) 92–117.
———. "The Relationship Between Paul and Jerusalem According to Galatians 1 and 2." *NTS* 28 (1982) 463–66.
———. *Unity and Diversity in the New Testament: An Inquiry Into the Character of Earliest Christianity*. 2nd ed. Philadelphia: Trinity, 1990.
Easton, B. S. "New Testament Ethical Lists." *JBL* 51 (1932) 1–12.
Edwards, James R. *The Gospel According to Mark*. PNTC. Grand Rapids: Eerdmans, 2002.
———. "Markan Sandwiches. The Significance of Interpolations in Markan Narratives." *NovT* 31 (1989) 193–216.
———. "The Son of God: Its Antecedents in Judaism and Hellenism and Its Use in the Earliest Gosepl." PhD diss., Fuller Theological Seminary, 1978.
Egan, Patrick T. "'This Word Is the Gospel Preached to You': Ecclesiology and the Isaianic Narrative in 1 Peter." PhD diss., University of St. Andrews, 2011.
Ehrman, Bart D. *Peter, Paul, and Mary Magdalene: The Followers of Jesus in History and Legend*. Oxford: Oxford University Press, 2006.
Elgin, Catherine Z. "Take It From Me: The Epistemological Status of Testimony." *Philosophy and Phenomenological Research* 65 (2002) 291–308.
Elliott, John H. *1 Peter: A New Translation with Introduction and Commentary*. AB 37B. New York: Doubleday, 2000.
———. "Disgraced Yet Graced: The Gospel According to 1 Peter in the Key of Honor and Shame." *BTB* 25 (1995) 166–78.
———. *The Elect and the Holy: An Exegetical Examination of 1 Peter 2:4–10 and the Phrase* βασίλειον ἱεράτευμα. NovTSup 12. Leiden: Brill, 1966.
———. *A Home for the Homeless: A Sociological Exegesis of 1 Peter, Its Situation and Strategy*. Philadelphia: Fortress, 1981.
———. "The Rehabilitation of an Exegetical Step-Child: 1 Peter in Recent Research." *Journal of Biblical Literature* 95 (1976) 243–54.
Ellis, E. Earle. "How the New Testament Uses the Old." In *New Testament Interpretation: Essays on Principles and Methods*, edited by I. Howard Marshall, 199–219. Exeter: Paternoster, 1977.

Engberg-Pedersen, Troels. "Paul, Virtues and Vices." In *Paul in the Graeco-Roman World: A Handbook*, edited by J. Paul Sampley, 608-33. Harrisburg, PA: Trinity, 2003.

Epiphanius. *The Panarion of Epiphanius of Salamis*. Translated by Frank Williams. Leiden: Brill, 1994.

Epstein, David F. *Personal Enmity in Roman Politics 218-43 BC*. London: Routledge, 1987.

Eusebius. *Eusebius's Ecclesiastical History*. Translated by C. F. Cruse. Updated ed. Peabody, MA: Hendrickson, 1998.

Evans, C. F. *The Beginning of the Gospel: Four Lectures on St Mark's Gospel*. London: SPCK, 1968.

Evans, C. Stephen. "Critical Historical Judgment and Biblical Faith." In *History and the Christian Historian*, edited by Ronald A. Wells, 41-67. Grand Rapids: Eerdmans, 1998.

———. *The Historical Christ and the Jesus of Faith: The Incarnational Narrative as History*. Oxford: Clarendon, 1996.

Evans, Craig A. *Mark 8:27-16:20*. WBC 34B. Nashville: Thomas Nelson, 2001.

Feagin, Glyndle M., Jr. *Irony and the Kingdom in Mark: A Literary-Critical Study*. Mellen Biblical Press Series 56. Lewiston, NY: Mellen Biblical, 1997.

Feldmeier, Reinhard. "Die Darstellung des Petrus in den synoptischen Evangelien." In *Das Evangelium und die Evangelien. Vorträge vom Tübinger Symposium 1982*, edited by Peter Stuhlmacher, 267-71. Tübingen: Mohr Siebeck, 1983.

Ferguson, Everett. *Backgrounds of Early Christianity*. 3rd ed. Grand Rapids: Eerdmans, 2003.

———. *Baptism in the Early Church: History, Theology, and Liturgy in the First Five Centuries*. Grand Rapids: Eerdmans, 2009.

Filson, F. V. "Partakers with Christ: Suffering in First Peter." *Int* 9 (1959) 400-412.

Finegan, Jack. *Encountering New Testament Manuscripts: A Working Introduction to Textual Criticism*. London: SPCK, 1975.

Fischer, Karl-Martin. *Tendenz un Absicht des Epheserbriefes*: FRLANT 111. Göttingen: Vandenhoeck & Ruprecht, 1973.

Fisher, Joan E. "Corinth Excavations, 1977, Forum Southwest." *Hesperia* 53 (1977) 217-50.

Fitzgerald, John T. "Virtue/Vice Lists." In vol. 6 of *The Anchor Bible Dictionary*, edited by David Noel Freedman, 857-59. New York: Doubleday, 1982.

Fitzmyer, Joseph A. *The Acts of the Apostles*. AB 31. New York: Doubleday, 1998.

———. *The Gospel According to Luke (I-IX)*. AB 28. Garden City, NY: Doubleday, 1981.

Flusser, David. *The Jewish Sages and Their Literature*. Vol. 2 of *Judaism of the Second Temple Period*. Grand Rapids: Eerdmans, 2009.

Foakes-Jackson, F. J. *Peter: Prince of Apostles*. London: Hodder & Stoughton, 1927.

Foakes-Jackson, F. J., and Kirsopp Lake. *The Acts of the Apostles: English Translation and Commentary*. Vol. 4 of *The Beginnings of Christianity*. Grand Rapids: Baker, 1920-33.

Foster, Giraud V., et al. "News and Short Contributions." *JFA* 16 (1989) 245-55.

Foster, Ora Delmer. "The Literary Relations of 'The First Epistle of Peter.'" *Transactions of the Connecticut Academy of Arts and Sciences* 13 (1913) 363-538.

Foster, Paul. "Peter in Noncanonical Traditions." In *Peter in Early Christianity*, edited Helen K. Bond and Larry W. Hurtado, 222-62. Grand Rapids: Eerdmans, 2015.

France, R. T. *Divine Government: God's Kingship in the Gospel of Mark*. Vancouver: Regent College Publishing, 1990.

———. *The Gospel of Mark: A Commentary on the Greek Text*. NIGTC. Grand Rapids: Eerdmans, 2002.

Freedman, H., and Maurice Simon, eds. *Exodus, Leviticus.* Vol. 2 of *The Midrash Rabbah.* London: Soncino, 1939.

French, Roger. "General Series Introduction." In *Ancient Astrology*, by Tamsyn Barton, x-xxiii. London: Routledge, 1994.

Fricker, Elizabeth. "The Epistemology of Testimony." *Proceedings of the Aristotelian Society* Supp. 61 (1987) 57–83.

———. "Telling and Trusting: Reductionism and Anti-Reductionism in the Epistemology of Testimony." *Mind* 104 (1995) 393–411.

Furnish, Victor Paul. *Jesus According to Paul.* Cambridge: Cambridge University Press, 1993.

Gadamer, Hans-Georg. *Truth and Method.* New York: Continuum, 2004.

Gaechter, Paul. *Petrus und seine Zeit.* Innsbruch: Tyrolia, 1958.

Gager, John G. *Curse Tablets and Binding Spells from the Ancient World.* Oxford: Oxford University Press, 1992.

Gamble, Harry Y. *Books and Readers in the Early Church: A History of Early Christian Texts.* New Haven, CT: Yale University Press, 1995.

Garrett, Susan R. "Exodus from Bondage: Luke 9:31 and Acts 12:1–24." *CBQ* 52 (1990) 656–80.

Gärtner, Bertil. *The Temple and the Community at Qumran and the New Testament: A Comparative Study in the Temple Symbolism of the Qumran Texts and the NT.* SNTSMS 1. Cambridge: Cambridge University Press, 1965.

Gathercole, Simon. "The Son of Man in Mark's Gospel." *ExpTim* 115 (2004) 366–72.

Gempf, Conrad. "Public Speaking and Published Accounts." In *The Book of Acts in Its Ancient Literary Setting*, edited by Bruce W. Winter and Andrew D. Clarke, 259–303. Vol. 1 of *The Book of Acts in Its First Century Setting.* Grand Rapids: Eerdmans, 1993.

Gill, David W. *Peter the Rock: Extraordinary Insights from an Ordinary Man.* Downers Grove, IL: InterVarsity, 1986.

Glasson, T. Francis. "The Speeches in Acts and Thucydides." *ExpTim* 76 (1964–65) 165.

Gnilka, Joachim. *Petrus und Rom: Das Petrusbild in den ersten zwei Jahrhunderten.* Freiburg; Basil; Wien: Herder, 2002.

Gold, Barbara K. *Literary Patronage in Greece and Rome.* Chapel Hill: University of North Carolina Press, 1987.

González, Justo. *Acts. The Gospel of the Spirit.* Maryknoll, NY: Orbis, 2001.

———. *Hechos.* Comentario Bíblico Hispanoamericano. Miami: Editorial Caribe, 1992.

Goppelt, Leonhard. *A Commentary on 1 Peter.* Edited by Ferdinand Hahn. Translated and augmented by John E. Alsup. Grand Rapids: Eerdmans, 1993.

Goulder, Michael. *St. Paul Versus St. Peter: A Tale of Two Missions.* Louisville: Westminster John Knox, 1994.

Graf, Fritz. *Magic in the Ancient World.* Cambridge, MA: Harvard University Press, 1997.

Graham, Peter J. "What is Testimony?" *Philosophical Quarterly* 47 (1997) 227–32.

Grant, Michael. *Saint Peter: A Biography.* New York: Scribner, 1994.

Grappe, Christian. *Images de Pierre aux deux premiers siècles: Études d'historie et de philosophie religieuses.* Paris: Presses Universitaires de France, 1995.

Gray, Timothy C. *The Temple in the Gospel of Mark: A Study in Its Narrative Role.* WUNT 2.242. Tübingen: Mohr Siebeck, 2008.

Gréaux, Eric James. "'To the Elect Exiles of the Dispersion . . . from Babylon': The Function of the Old Testament in 1 Peter." PhD diss., Duke University, 2003.

Green, Eugenio. *1 Pedro y 2 Pedro*. Comentario Bíblico Hispanoamericano. Miami: Editorial Caribe, 1993.

Green, Gene L. "'As for Prophecies, They Will Come to an End': 2 Peter, Paul, and Plutarch on 'the Obsolescence of Oracles.'" JSNT 82 (2001) 107–22.

———. "Intertextuality and Sociology in Early Christianity: A Study of 2 Peter and Jude." In *Reading Jude with New Eyes: Methodological Reassessments of the Letter of Jude*, edited by Robert L. Webb and Peter Hugh Davids, 1–25. LNTS 383. London: T. & T. Clark, 2009.

———. *Jude and 2 Peter*. BECNT. Grand Rapids: Baker Academic, 2008.

———. *The Letters to the Thessalonians*. PNTC. Grand Rapids: Eerdmans, 2002.

———. "Lexical Pragmatics and Biblical Interpretation." *JETS* 50 (2007) 799–812.

———. "Lexical Pragmatics and the Lexicon." *BBR* 22 (2012) 315–34.

———. "Relevance Theory and Biblical Interpretation." In *The Linguist as Pedagogue: Trends in the Teaching and Linguistic Analysis of the New Testament*, edited by Stanley E. Porter and Matthew Brook O'Donnell, 217–50. Sheffield: Sheffield Phoenix, 2009.

———. "Theology and Ethics in 1 Peter." PhD diss., University of Aberdeen, 1979.

———. "The Use of the Old Testament for Christian Ethics in 1 Peter." *TynBul* 41 (1990) 276–89.

Green, Joel B. *1 Peter*. THNTC. Grand Rapids: Eerdmans, 2007.

———. *The Gospel of Luke*. NICNT. Grand Rapids: Eerdmans, 1997.

Grindheim, Sigurd. *Christology in the Synoptic Gospels: God or God's Servant*. London: T. & T. Clark, 2012.

Grudem, Wayne. *1 Peter: An Introduction and Commentary*. TNTC 17. Grand Rapids: Eerdmans, 1988.

Gschwind, Karl. *Die Niederfahrt Christi in die Unterwelt: Ein Beitrag zur Exegese des Neuen Testamentes und zur Geschichte des Taufsymbols*. NTAbh 2. Münster: Aschendorff, 1911.

Guelich, Robert A. *Mark 1–8:26*. WBC 34A. Dallas: Word, 1989.

Gundry, Robert H. "Further *Verba* on *Verba Christi* in First Peter." *Bib* 55 (1974) 211–32.

———. *Mark: A Commentary on His Apology for the Cross*. Grand Rapids: Eerdmans, 1993.

———. "*Verba Christi* in 1 Peter: Their Implications Concerning the Authorship of 1 Peter and the Authenticity of the Gospel Tradition." *NTS* 13 (1967) 336–50.

Haenchen, Ernst. *The Acts of the Apostles: A Commentary*. Translated by Bernard Noble, et al. Philadelphia: Westminster, 1971.

Hagedorn, A. C., and Jerome H. Neyrey. "'It Was Out of Envy That They Handed Jesus Over' (Mark 15:10): The Anatomy of Envy and the Gospel of Mark." *JSNT* 69 (1998) 15–56.

Hagner, Donald A. *The Use of the Old and New Testaments in Clement of Rome*. Leiden: Brill, 1973.

Hahneman, Geoffrey Mark. *The Muratorian Fragment and the Development of the Canon*. Oxford: Clarendon, 1992.

Hannah, Darrell D. "The Elect Son of Man of the *Parables of Enoch*." In *Who Is This Son of Man? The Latest Scholarship on a Puzzling Expression of the Historical Jesus*, edited by Larry W Hurtado and Paul L. Owen, 130–58. LNTS 390. London: T. & T. Clark, 2011.

Hare, Douglas R. A. *The Son of Man Tradition*. Minneapolis: Fortress, 1990.

Harmon, William. *A Handbook to Literature*. Upper Saddle River, NJ: Prentice Hall, 2003.

Harris, J. Rendel. *Testimonies*. 2 vols. Cambridge: Cambridge University Press, 1916–20.

Harrison, James R. "The Brothers as the 'Glory of Christ' (2 Cor 8:23) Paul's *Doxa* Terminology in Its Ancient Benefaction Context." *NovT* 52 (2010) 156–88.

Hatina, Thomas R. *In Search of a Context: The Function of Scripture in Mark's Narrative*. JSNTSup 232. London: Sheffield Academic, 2002.

Havelaar, Henriette. "Hellenistic Parallels to Acts 5:1–11 and the Problem of Conflicting Interpretations." *JSNT* 67 (1997) 63–82.

Hays, Christopher M., et al. *When the Son of Man Didn't Come: A Constructive Proposal on the Delay of the Parousia*. Minneapolis: Fortress, 2016.

Hays, Richard B. *The Moral Vision of the New Testament: Community, Cross, New Creation*. San Francisco: HarperSanFrancisco, 1996.

Head, Peter. "A Text-Critical Study of Mark 1:1 'The Beginning of the Gospel of Jesus Christ.'" *NTS* 37 (1991) 621–29.

Heil, John Paul. *The Transfiguration of Jesus: Narrative Meaning and Function of Mark 9:2–8, Matt 17:1–8, and Luke 9:28–36*. AnBib 144. Rome: Editrice Pontifico Istituto Biblico, 2000.

Helyer, Larry R. *The Life and Witness of Peter*. Downers Grove, IL: IVP Academic, 2012.

Hemer, Colin J. "The Address of 1 Peter." *ExpTim* 89 (1978) 239–43.

———. *The Book of Acts in the Setting of Hellenistic History*. Edited by Conrad H. Gempf. Winona Lake, IN: Eisenbrauns, 1990.

———. "Luke the Historian." *BJRL* 60 (1978) 28–51.

Henderson, Suzanne Watts. *Christology and Discipleship in the Gospel of Mark*. SNTSMS 135. Cambridge: Cambridge University Press, 2006.

Hengel, Martin. *Acts and the History of Earliest Christianity*. Translated by John Bowden. Philadelphia: Fortress, 1979.

———. *The Charismatic Leader and His Followers*. New York: Crossroad, 1981.

———. *Crucifixion in the Ancient World and the Folly of the Message of the Cross*. Philadelphia: Fortress, 1977.

———. *Der unterschätzte Petrus: Zwei Studien*. Tübingen: Mohr Siebeck, 2006.

———. *The Four Gospels and the One Gospel of Jesus Christ: An Investigation of the Collection and Origin of the Canonical Gospels*. Harrisburg, PA: Trinity, 2000.

———. *Judaism and Hellenism: Studies in Their Encounter in Palestine During the Early Hellenistic Period*. 2 vols. Philadelphia: Fortress, 1974.

———. *Saint Peter: The Underestimated Apostle*. Grand Rapids: Eerdmans, 2010.

———. *The Septuagint as Christian Scripture: Its Prehistory and the Problem of Its Canon*. Edinburgh: T. & T. Clark, 2002.

———. *Studies in Early Christology*. Edinburgh: T. & T. Clark, 1995.

———. *Studies in the Gospel of Mark*. Philadelphia: Fortress, 1985.

Hering, James P. *The Colossian and Ephesian Haustafeln in Theological Context: An Analysis of Their Origins, Relationship, and Message*. American University Studies VII: Theology and Religion 260. New York: Lang, 2007.

Hilgert, Earle. "Speeches in Acts and Hellenistic Canons of Historiography and Rhetoric." In *Good News in History: Essays in Honor of Bo Reicke*, edited by Ed. L. Miller, 83–109. Atlanta: Scholars, 1993.

Hock, Ronald F., and Edward N. O'Neil, eds. *The Chreia in Ancient Rhetoric: Classroom Exercises*. Writings from the Greco-Roman World 2. Atlanta: SBL, 2002.

———, eds. *The Chreia in Ancient Rhetoric: The Progymnasmata*. Texts and Translations 27. Graeco-Roman Religious Series 9. Atlanta: Scholars, 1986.

Hofius, Otfried. "Gal 1:18: Historesai Kephan." *ZNW* 75 (1984) 73–85.

Hohti, Paavo. *The Interrelation of Speeches and Action in the Histories of Herodotus.* Commentationes humanarum litterarum 57. Helsinki: Societas Scientiarum Fennica, 1976.

Holladay, Carl H. *Theios Aner in Hellenistic-Judaism: A Critique of the Use of This Category in New Testament Christology.* SBLDS 40. Missoula, MT: Scholars, 1977.

Hollander, Harm W. "The Words of Jesus: From Oral Traditions to Written Record in Paul and Q." *NovT* 42 (2000) 340–57.

Holliday, Peter J. "Time, History, and Ritual on the Ara Pacis Augustae." *The Art Bulletin* 72 (1990) 542–57.

Hooker, Morna D. *The Gospel According to Mark.* BNTC. Peabody, MA: Hendrickson, 1991.

———. *The Message of Mark.* London: Epworth, 1983.

———. *The Son of Man in Mark: A Study of the Background of the Term 'Son of Man' and Its Use in St. Mark's Gospel.* London: SPCK, 1967.

———. "'Who Can This Be?' The Christology of Mark's Gospel." In *Contours of Christology in the New Testament*, edited by Richard N. Longenecker, 79–99. McMaster New Testament Studies. Grand Rapids: Eerdmans, 2005.

Horbury, William. "Jewish Messianism and Early Christology." In *Contours of Christology in the New Testament*, edited by Richard N. Longenecker, 3–24. McMaster New Testament Studies. Grand Rapids: Eerdmans, 2005.

Horgan, Maurya P. *Pesharim: Qumran Interpretations of Biblical Books.* Washington: Catholic Biblical Association of America, 1979.

Hornblower, Simon. *A Commentary on Thucydides.* Vol. 1. Oxford: Clarendon, 1991.

Horrell, David G. *Becoming Christian: Essays on 1 Peter and the Making of Christian Identity.* LNTS 394. London: T. & T. Clark, 2013.

———. *The Epistles of Peter and Jude.* Epworth Commentaries. London: Epworth, 1998.

Horsley, G. H. R. "Speeches and Dialogue in Acts." *NTS* 32 (1986) 609–14.

Horsley, Richard A. *Archaeology, History, and Society in Galilee: The Social Context of Jesus and the Rabbis.* Valley Forge, PA: Trinity, 1996.

———. *Galilee: History, Politics, People.* Valley Forge, PA: Trinity, 1995.

———. *Hearing the Whole Story: The Politics of Plot in Mark's Gospel.* Louisville: Westminster John Knox, 2001.

———. *Paul and Empire: Religion and Power in Roman Imperial Society.* Harrisburg, PA: Trinity, 1997.

Hort, F. J. A. *The First Epistle of St. Peter 1:1–2:17.* London: Macmillan, 1898.

Houlden, J. L. *Ethics and the New Testament.* Middlesex: Penguin, 1973.

Hurtado, Larry W. "The Apostle Peter in Protestant Scholarship: Cullman, Hengel, and Bockmuehl." In *Peter in Early Christianity*, edited by Helen K. Bond and Larry W. Hurtado, 1–15. Grand Rapids: Eerdmans, 2015.

———. *Lord Jesus Christ: Devotion to Jesus in Earliest Christianity.* Grand Rapids: Eerdmans, 2003.

———. "Summary and Concluding Observations." In *Who is This Son of Man? The Latest Scholarship on a Puzzling Expression of the Historical Jesus*, edited by Larry W Hurtado and Paul L. Owen, 159–77. LNTS 390. London: T. & T. Clark, 2011.

Hurtado, Larry W., and Paul L. Owen, eds. *Who is This Son of Man? The Latest Scholarship on a Puzzling Expression of the Historical Jesus.* LNTS 390. London: T. & T. Clark, 2011.

Ilan, Tal. *Lexicon of Jewish Names in Late Antiquity I: Palestine 330 BCE–200 CE.* TSAJ 91. Tübingen: Mohr Siebeck, 2002.

———. *Lexicon of Jewish Names in Late Antiquity III: The Western Diaspora 330 BCE–650 CE*. TSAJ 126. Tübingen: Mohr Siebeck, 2008.

Immerwahr, Henry R. "Pathology of Power and the Speeches in Thucydides." In *The Speeches in Thucydides*, edited by Philip A. Stadter, 16–31. Chapel Hill: University of North Carolina Press, 1972.

Incigneri, Brian J. *The Gospel to the Romans: The Setting and Rhetoric of Mark's Gospel*. BibInt 65. Leiden: Brill, 2003.

Instone-Brewer, David. "The Eighteen Benedictions and the *Minim* Before 70 CE." *JTS* 54 (2003) 25–44.

Iverson, Kelly R. *Gentiles in the Gospel of Mark: 'Even the Dogs Under the Table East the Children's Crumbs.'* LNTS 339. London: T. & T. Clark, 2007.

Jennings, Willie James. *Acts*. Belief: A Theological Commentary on the Bible. Louisville: Westminster John Knox, 2017.

Jeremias, Joachim. *The Eucharistic Words of Jesus*. London: SCM, 1966.

———. *Jerusalem in the Time of Jesus*. Minneapolis: Fortress, 1969.

———. *New Testament Theology*. New York: Scribner's Sons, 1971.

Jervell, Jacob. *The Theology of the Acts of the Apostles*. New Testament Theology. Cambridge: Cambridge University Press, 1996.

Jobes, Karen H. *1 Peter*. BECNT. Grand Rapids: Baker Academic, 2005.

Jobes, Karen H., and Moises Silva. *Invitation to the Septuagint*. Grand Rapids: Baker Academic, 2000.

Johansson, Daniel. "*Kyrios* in the Gospel of Mark." *JSNT* 33 (2010) 101–24.

Johnson, Luke Timothy. *The Acts of the Apostles*. SP 5. Collegeville, MN: Liturgical, 1992.

Johnson, Sherman E. "Sabaoth/Sabazios: A Curiosity in Ancient Religion." *LTQ* 13 (1978) 97–103.

Käsemann, Ernst. *Jesus Means Freedom: A Polemical Survey of the New Testament*. London: SCM, 1969.

Keck, Leander E. "The Introduction to Mark's Gospel." *NTS* 12 (1966) 352–70.

Kee, Howard Clark. *The Community of the New Age: Studies in Mark's Gospel*. Philadelphia: Westminster, 1977.

Keener, Craig S. *Acts: An Exegetical Commentary*. 4 vols. Grand Rapids: Baker Academic, 2012–15.

———. *The Historical Jesus of the Gospels*. Grand Rapids: Eerdmans, 2009.

Kelber, Werner H. *The Kingdom in Mark: A New Place and a New Time*. Philadelphia: Fortress, 1974.

Kelly, J. N. D. *A Commentary on the Epistles of Peter and Jude*. BNTC. Grand Rapids: Baker, 1969.

Kennedy, George A. *New Testament Interpretation Through Rhetorical Criticism*. Chapel Hill: University of North Carolina Press, 1984.

———, ed. *Progymnasmata: Greek Textbooks of Prose Composition and Rhetoric*. Translated by George A. Kennedy. Writings from the Greco-Roman World 10. Atlanta: SBL, 2003.

Kessler, William Thomas. *Peter as the First Witness of the Risen Lord: An Historical and Theological Investigation*. TGST 37. Rome: Editrice Pontificia Università Gregoriana, 1998.

Kilgallen, John J. "Peter's Argument in Acts 15." In *"Il Verbo di Dio è vivo": Studi sul Nuovo Testamento in onore del Cardinale Albert Vanhoye, SI*, edited by José Enrique Aguilar Chiu, et al., 233–47. AnBib 165. Rome: Pontifical Biblical Institute, 2007.

———. "'With Many Other Words' (Acts 2:40) Theological Assumptions in Peter's Pentecost Speech." *Bib* 83 (2002) 71–87.

Kilpatrick, George D. "Galatians 1:18: Historēsai Kēphan." In *New Testament Essays: Studies in Memory of Thomas Walter Manson, 1893–1958*, edited by A. J. B. Higgins, 144–49. Manchester: Manchester University Press, 1959.

Kim, Seyoon. "Jesus—The Son of God, the Stone, the Son of Man, and the Servant: The Role of Zechariah in the Self-Identification of Jesus." In *Tradition and Interpretation in the New Testament: Essays in Honor of E. Earle Ellis for His 60th Birthday*, edited by Gerald F. Hawthorne and Otto Betz, 134–48. Grand Rapids: Eerdmans, 1987.

Kim, Tae Hun. "The Anarthrous υἱὸς θεοῦ in Mark 15:39." *Bib* 79 (1998) 221–41.

King, Katherine Callen. *Ancient Epic*. Malden, MA; Oxford: Wiley-Blackwell, 2009.

Kingsbury, Jack Dean. *The Christology of Mark's Gospel*. Philadelphia: Fortress, 1983.

———. *Conflict in Mark: Jesus, Authorities, Disciples*. Minneapolis: Fortress, 1989.

Kinman, Brent. *Jesus' Entry Into Jerusalem in the Context of Lukan Theology and the Politics of His Day*. AGJU 28. Leiden: Brill, 1995.

Klauck, Hans-Josef. *Hausgemeinde un Hauskirche im frühen Christentum*. SBS 103. Stuttgart: Katholisches Bibelwerk, 1981.

———. *The Religious Context of Early Christianity: A Guide to Graeco-Roman Religions*. Minneapolis: Fortress, 2003.

Klawans, Jonathan. *Josephus and the Theologies of Ancient Judaism*. Oxford: Oxford University Press, 2012.

Kloppenborg, John S. *Q, The Earliest Gospel: An Introduction to the Original Stories and Sayings of Jesus*. Philadelphia: Westminster John Knox, 2008.

Kmiecik, Ulrich. *Der Menschensohn im Markusevangelium*. FB 81. Würzburg: Echter, 1997.

Knoppers, Gary N. *Jews and Samaritans: The Origins and History of Their Early Relations*. Oxford: Oxford University Press, 2013.

Körtner, Ulrich H. J. "Markus der Mitarbeiter des Petrus." *ZNW* 71 (1980) 160–73.

Kraus, Thomas J. "'Uneducated,' 'Ignorant,' or Even 'Illiterate'? Aspects and Background for an Understanding of ΑΓΡΑΜΜΑΤΟΙ (and ΙΔΙΩΤΑΙ) in Acts 4:13." *NTS* 45 (1999) 434–49.

Kreitzer, Larry. "Apotheosis of the Roman Emperor." *BA* 53 (1990) 210–17.

Kümmel, Werner Georg. *Promise and Fulfilment: The Eschatological Message of Jesus*. SBT 23. London: SCM, 1957.

Kurz, William. "Promise and Fulfilment in Hellenistic Jewish Narratives and in Luke and Acts." In *Jesus and the Heritage of Israel: Luke's Narrative Claim Upon Israel's Legacy*, edited by David P. Moessner, 147–70. Harrisburg, PA: Trinity, 1999.

Kusch, Martin. *Knowledge by Agreement: The Programme of Communitarian Epistemology*. Oxford: Oxford University Press, 2002.

Kusch, Martin, and Peter Lipton. "Testimony: A Primer." *Studies in History and Philosophy of Science Part A* 33.2 (2002) 209–17.

Lackey, Jennifer. "Introduction." In *The Epistemology of Testimony*, edited by Jennifer Lackey and Ernest Sosa, 1–21. Oxford: Clarendon, 2006.

———. "It Takes Two to Tango: Beyond Reductionism and Non-Reductionism in the Epistemology of Testimony." In *The Epistemology of Testimony*, edited by Jennifer Lackey and Ernest Sosa, 160–89. Oxford: Clarendon, 2006.

———. "Knowing from Testimony." *Philosophy Compass* 1.5 (2006) 432–88.

———. *Learning from Words: Testimony as a Source of Knowledge*. Oxford: Oxford University Press, 2008.

———. "The Nature of Testimony." *Pacific Philosophical Quarterly* 87 (2006) 177–97.

———. "Testimonial Knowledge and Transmission." *Philosophical Quarterly* 49 (1999) 471–90.

Lackey, Jennifer, and Ernest Sosa, eds. *The Epistemology of Testimony*. Oxford: Clarendon, 2006.

Ladd, George Eldon. *New Testament Theology*. Edited by Donald Hagner. Grand Rapids: Eerdmans, 1993.

Lai, Kenny Ke-Chung. "The Holy Spirit in 1 Peter: A Study of Petrine Pneumatology in Light of the Isaianic New Exodus." PhD diss., Dallas Theological Seminary, 2009.

Lane, William L. "The Speeches in the Book of Acts." In *Jerusalem and Athens: Critical Discussions on the Philosophy and Apologetics of Cornelius Van Til*, edited by E. R. Geehan, 260–72. Phillipsburg, NJ: Presbyterian & Reformed, 1971.

Lange, Armin. "Jews in Ancient and Late Ancient Asia Minor Between Acceptance and Rejection." *Journal of Ancient Judaism* 5 (2014) 223–44.

Langer, Gerhard. "Rabbinic References to Asia Minor." *Journal of Ancient Judaism* 5 (2014) 259–69.

Lapham, F. *Peter: The Myth, the Man, and the Writings*. London: T. & T. Clark, 2003.

Lattimore, Richmond. *Themes in Greek and Latin Epitaphs*. Urbana: University of Illinois Press, 1942.

Lee, Simon S. *Jesus' Transfiguration and the Believers' Transformation: A Study of the Transfiguration and Its Development in Early Christian Writings*. WUNT 2.265. Tübingen: Mohr Siebeck, 2009.

Lemcio, Eugene E. "The Unifying Kerygma of the New Testament." *JSNT* 33 (1988) 3–17.

———. "The Unifying Kerygma of the New Testament, Pt. 2." *JSNT* 38 (1990) 3–11.

Levinskaya, Irina. *The Book of Acts in Its Diaspora Setting*. Vol. 5 of *The Book of Acts in Its First Century Setting*. Edited by Bruce W. Winter. Grand Rapids: Eerdmans, 1996.

———. "The Traces of Jewish Life in Asia Minor." In *Neues Testament und hellenistich-jüdische Alltagskultur: Wechselseitige Wahrnehmungen: III. Internationales Symposium zum Corpus Judaeo-Hellenisticum Novi Testamenti, 21.-24. Mai 2009, Leipzig*, edited by Roland Deines, et al., 347–57. WUNT 274. Tübingen: Mohr Siebeck, 2011.

Liebengood, Kelly D. *The Eschatology of 1 Peter: Considering the Influence of Zechariah 9–14*. SNTSMS 157. Cambridge: Cambridge University Press, 2014.

Lipton, Peter. "The Epistemology of Testimony." *Studies in History and Philosophy of Science* 21 (1998) 1–31.

Llewelyn, Stephen. *New Documents Illustrating Early Christianity*. Vols. 1–2. Grand Rapids: Eerdmans, 1997–1998.

Lo, Jonathan W. "Did Peter Really Say That? Revisiting the Petrine Speeches in Acts." In *Peter in Early Christianity*, edited by Helen K. Bond and Larry W. Hurtado, 62–75. Grand Rapids: Eerdmans, 2015.

Longenecker, Richard N. *Biblical Exegesis in the Apostolic Period*. Grand Rapids: Eerdmans, 1975.

———. *The Christology of Early Jewish Christianity*. London: SCM, 1970.

López, Réne A. "Vice Lists in Non-Pauline Sources." *BSac* 168 (2011) 178–95.

Loubser, Johannes A. "Media Criticism and the Myth of Paul, the Creative Genius, and His Forgotten Co-Workers." *Neot* 34 (2000) 329–45.

Love, Julian Price. *The First, Second and Third Letters of John; The Letter of Jude; the Revelation to John*. Richmond: John Knox, 1960.

Luck, Georg. *Ancient Pathways and Hidden Pursuits: Religion, Morals, and Magic in the Ancient World*. Ann Arbor: University of Michigan Press, 2000.

———. *Arcana Mundi: Magic and the Occult in the Greek and Roman Worlds*. Baltimore: Johns Hopkins University Press, 1985.

Maartens, P. J. "The Son of Man as a Composite Metaphor in Mark 14:62." In *A South African Perspective on the New Testament: Essays by South African New Testament Scholars Presented to Bruce Manning Metzger During His Visit to South Africa in 1985*, edited by J. H. Petzer and P. J. Hartin, 76–98. Leiden: Brill, 1986.

MacCarney, Daniel G. "The Atonement in James, Peter and Jude." In *The Glory of the Atonement: Biblical, Historical, and Practical Perspectives*, edited by Charles E. Hill and Frank A. James III, 176–89. Downers Grove, IL: InterVarsity, 2000.

MacDonald, Dennis R. *Does the New Testament Imitate Homer? Four Cases from the Acts of the Apostles*. New Haven, CT: Yale University Press, 2003.

———. *The Gospels and Homer: Imitations of Greek Epic in Mark and Luke-Acts*. London: Rowman & Littlefield, 2015.

———. *The Homeric Epics and the Gospel of Mark*. New Haven, CT: Yale University Press, 2000.

———. *Luke and Virgil: Imitations of Classical Greek Literature in the "Aeneid" and Luke-Acts*. London: Rowman & Littlefield, 2015.

Macey, Samuel L. "The Concept of Time in Ancient Rome." *International Social Science Review* 65 (1990) 72–79.

MacIsaac, John D. "Corinth: Coins, 1925–1926 the Theater District and the Roman Villa." *Hesperia* 56 (1987) 97–157.

MacKay, Ian D. *John's Relationship with Mark: An Analysis of John 6 in the Light of Mark 6–8*. WUNT 2.182. Tübingen: Mohr Siebeck, 2004.

Mackay, John A. *A Preface to Christian Theology*. New York: Macmillan, 1941.

Macleod, Colin W. *Collected Essays*. Oxford: Clarendon, 1983.

Maier, Gerhard. "Jesustradition im 1. Petrusbrief?" In *The Jesus Tradition Outside the Gospels*, edited by David Wenham, 85–128. Sheffield: JSOT, 1984.

Malina, Bruce J., and Jerome H. Neyrey. *Portraits of Paul: An Archaeology of Ancient Personality*. Louisville: Westminster John Knox, 1996.

Maloney, E. C. *Semitic Interference in Marcan Syntax*. SBLDS 51. Chico, CA: Scholars, 1981.

Mánek, Jindrich. "The New Exodus in the Book of Luke." *NovT* 2 (1957) 8–23.

Mann, Jacob. *The Bible as Read and Preached in the Old Synagogue: A Study in the Cycles of the Readings from Torah and Prophets, as Well as from Psalms, and in the Structure of the Midrashic Homilies*. Vol. 1. New York: KTAV, 1971.

Manson, T. W. *Studies in the Gospels and Epistles*. Edited by Matthew Black. Manchester: Manchester University Press, 1962.

Marcus, Joel. "The Beelzebul Controversy and the Eschatologies of Jesus." In *Authenticating the Activities of Jesus*, edited by Bruce Chilton and Craig A. Evans, 247–77. Leiden: Brill, 1999.

———. "Entering Into the Kingly Power of God." *JBL* 107 (1986) 663–75.

———. "The Jewish War and the *Sitz Im Leben* of Mark." *JBL* 111 (1992) 441–62.

———. *Mark 1–8: A New Translation with Introduction and Commentary*. AB 27. New York: Doubleday, 2000.

———. *Mark 8–16: A New Translation with Introduction and Commentary*. AB 27A. New Haven, CT: Yale University Press, 2009.

———. "Mark 14:61: 'Are You the Messiah-Son-of-God?'" *NovT* 31 (1989) 125–41.

———. *The Way of the Lord: Christological Exegesis of the Old Testament in the Gospel of Mark*. Louisville: Westminster John Knox, 1992.

Marshall, I. Howard. *1 Peter*. IVP New Testament Commentary Series. Downers Grove, IL: InterVarsity, 1991.

———. "Acts and the 'Former Treatise.'" In *The Book of Acts in Its Ancient Literary Setting*, edited by Bruce W. Winter and Andrew D. Clarke, 163–82. Vol. 1 of *The Book of Acts in Its First Century Setting*. Edited by Bruce W. Winter. Grand Rapids: Eerdmans, 1993.

———. *The Acts of the Apostles: An Introduction and Commentary*. TNTC 5. Grand Rapids: Eerdmans, 1980.

———. *The Gospel of Luke: A Commentary on the Greek Text*. NIGTC. Grand Rapids: Eerdmans, 1978.

———. *Jesus the Saviour*. London: SPCK, 1990.

———. *Kept by the Power of God*. Minneapolis: Bethany Fellowship, 1969.

———. *Luke: Historian and Theologian*. Downers Grove, IL: InterVarsity, 1988.

———. *New Testament Theology: Many Witnesses, One Gospel*. Downers Grove, IL: InterVarsity, 2004.

———. *The Origins of New Testament Christology*. 2nd ed. Leicester, UK: Apollos, 1990.

Marshall, I. Howard, and David Peterson, eds. *Witness to the Gospel: The Theology of Acts*. Grand Rapids: Eerdmans, 1998.

Martin, Ralph. *Mark: Evangelist and Theologian*. Grand Rapids: Zondervan, 1972.

Martin, Richard P. "Epic as Genre." In *A Companion to Ancient Epic*, edited by John Miles Foley, 9–19. Blackwell Companions to the Ancient World: Literature and Culture. Oxford: Blackwell, 2005.

Martínez, Florentino García. *The Dead Sea Scrolls Translated: The Qumran Texts in English*. Leiden: Brill, 1994.

Marxsen, Willi. *Mark the Evangelist: Studies on the Redaction History of the Gospel*. Nashville: Abingdon, 1969.

Mason, Steve. "Chief Priests, Sadducees, Pharisees and Sanhedrin in Acts." In *The Book of Acts in Its Palestinian Setting*, edited by Richard Bauckham, 115–77. Vol. 4 of *The Book of Acts in Its First Century Setting*. Edited by Bruce W. Winter. Grand Rapids: Eerdmans, 1995.

Matera, Frank J. *The Kingship of Jesus: Composition and Theology in Mark 15*. SBLDS 66. Chico, CA: Scholars, 1982.

———. *New Testament Christology*. Louisville: Westminster John Knox, 1999.

———. *New Testament Ethics: The Legacies of Jesus and Paul*. Louisville: Westminster John Knox, 1996.

———. *New Testament Theology: Exploring Diversity and Unity*. Louisville: Westminster John Knox, 2007.

McConnell, James R., Jr. *The Topos of Divine Testimony in Luke-Acts*. Eugene, OR: Pickwick, 2014.

McDonald, James I. H. *Kerygma and Didache: The Articulation and Structure of the Earliest Christian Message*. SNTSMS 37. Cambridge: Cambridge University Press, 1980.

McDonald, Lee Martin. *The Formation of the Christian Biblical Canon*. Rev. and exp. ed. Peabody, MA: Hendrickson, 1995.

McDonald, Lee Martin, and James A. Sanders, eds. *The Canon Debate*. Peabody, MA: Hendrickson, 2002.

McGill, Scott. *Virgil Recomposed: The Mythological and Secular Centos in Antiquity*. American Classical Studies 48. Oxford: Oxford University Press, 2005.

McKelvey, R. J. "Christ the Cornerstone." *NTS* 8 (1961–62) 352–59.

———. *The New Temple: The Church in the New Testament*. Oxford Theological Monographs. London: Oxford University Press, 1968.

McLay, R. Timothy. *The Use of the Septuagint in New Testament Research*. Grand Rapids: Eerdmans, 2003.

McNeile, Alan Hugh. *New Testament Teaching in Light of St. Paul's*. Cambridge: Cambridge University Press, 1923.

Merritt, Robert L. "Jesus Barabbas and the Paschal Pardon." *JBL* 104 (1985) 57–68.

Metzger, Bruce M. *The Canon of the New Testament: Its Origin, Development, and Significance*. Oxford: Clarendon, 1987.

———. *A Textual Commentary on the Greek New Testament*. 2nd ed. Stuttgart: German Bible Society; New York: United Bible Societies, 1994.

Metzner, Rainer. *Die Rezeption des Matthäusevangeliums im 1. Petrusbrief: Studien zum traditionsgeschichtlichen und theologischen Einfluß des 1. Evangeliums aud fen 1. Petrusbrief*. WUNT 2.74. Tübingen: Mohr Siebeck, 1995.

Meye, Robert P. *Jesus and the Twelve: Discipleship and Revelation in Mark's Gospel*. Grand Rapids: Eerdmans, 1968.

Meyendorff, John, ed. *The Primacy of Peter*. Crestwood, NY: St. Vladimir's Seminary Press, 1992.

Michaels, J. Ramsey. *1 Peter*. WBC 49. Waco, TX: Word, 1988.

Millauer, Helmut. *Leiden als Gnade: Eine traditionsgeschichtliche Untersuchung zur Leidenstheologie des ersten Petrusbriefes*. Europäische Hochschulschriften 23.56. Frankfurt: Lang, 1976.

Mitchell, Margaret M. "Patristic Counter-Evidence to the Claim That 'The Gospels Were Written for All Christians.'" *NTS* 51 (2005) 36–79.

Mitchell, Stephen. *The Celts in Anatolia and the Impact of Roman Rule*. Vol. 1 of *Anatolia: Land, Men, and Gods in Asia Minor*. Oxford: Clarendon, 1993.

Moessner, David P. "'The Christ Must Suffer': New Light on the Jesus—Peter, Stephen, Paul Parallels in Luke-Acts." *NovT* 28 (1986) 220–56.

———. "Luke 9:1–50: Luke's Preview of the Journey of the Prophet Like Moses of Deuteronomy." *JBL* 102 (1983) 575–605.

———. "The 'Script' of Scriptures in Acts: Suffering as God's 'Plan' (Βουλή) for the World and the 'Release of Sins.'" In *History, Literature, and Society in the Book of Acts*, edited by Ben Witherington III, 218–50. Cambridge: Cambridge University Press, 1996.

Moffatt, James. *The General Epistles: James, Peter and Judas*. MNTC. London: Hodder & Stoughton, 1928.

Moo, Douglas J. *Galatians*. BECNT. Grand Rapids: Baker Academic, 2013.

———. *The Old Testament in the Gospel Passion Narratives*. Sheffield: Almond, 1983.

Moore, George F. *Judaism in the First Centuries of the Christian Era*. New York: Schocken, 1971.

Morris, Leon. *The Apostolic Preaching of the Cross*. London: Tyndale, 1965.

Mounce, Robert H. *The Essential Nature of New Testament Preaching*. Grand Rapids: Eerdmans, 1960.

Mournet, Terence C. *Oral Tradition and Literary Dependency: Variability and Stability in the Synoptic Tradition and Q*. WUNT 2.195. Tübingen: Mohr Siebeck, 2005.

Müller, Mogens. *The Expression 'Son of Man' and the Development of Christology: A History of Interpretation*. Copenhagen International Seminar. London: Equinox, 2008.

Munck, Johannes. "Presbyters and Disciples of the Lord in Papias: Exegetic Comments on Eusebius, Ecclesiastical History, III, 39." *HTR* 52 (1959) 223–43.

Mussner, Franz. *Petrus und Paulus—Pole der Einheit: Eine Hilfe für dir Kirchen*. Quaestiones Disputatae 76. Freiburg: Herder, 1976.

Myers, Ched. *Binding the Strong Man: A Political Reading of Mark's Story of Jesus*. Maryknoll, NY: Orbis, 2008.

Neill, Stephen. *The Interpretation of the New Testament, 1861–1961*. Oxford: Oxford University Press, 1964.

Neufeld, Vernon H. *The Earliest Christian Confessions*. NTTS 5. Leiden: Brill, 1963.

Newbigin, Lesslie. *The Open Secret: An Introduction to the Theology of Mission*. London: SPCK, 1995.

Niederwimmer, Kurt. "Johannes Markus und die Frage nach dem Verfasser des zwelten Evangeliums." *ZNW* 58 (1967) 172–88.

Nienhuis, David R. *Not By Paul Alone: The Formation of the Catholic Epistle Collection and the Christian Canon*. Waco, TX: Baylor, 2007.

Nock, Arthur Darby. *Conversion: The Old and the New in Religion from Alexander the Great to Augustine of Hippo*. Oxford: Oxford University Press, 1933.

Noll, Mark A. *The Civil War as a Theological Crisis*. Chapel Hill: University of North Carolina Press, 2006.

Nolland, John. *Luke 1–9:20*. WBC 35A. Dallas: Word, 1989.

O'Brien, Kelli S. *The Use of Scripture in the Markan Passion Narrative*. LNTS 384. London: T. & T. Clark, 2010.

O'Connor, Daniel William. *Peter in Rome: The Literary, Liturgical, and the Archeological Evidence*. New York: Columbia University Press, 1969.

O'Neill, J. C. *The Theology of Acts in Its Historical Setting*. London: SPCK, 1970.

Oropeza, B. J. "The Expectation of Grace: Paul on Benefaction and the Corinthians' Ingratitude (2 Corinthians 6:1)." *BBR* 24 (2014) 207–26.

Padilla, Oswaldo. *The Acts of the Apostles. Interpretation, History and Theology*. Downers Grove, IL: IVP Academic, 2016.

———. "The Speeches in Acts: Historicity, Theology and Genre." In *Issues in Luke-Acts: Selected Essays*, edited by Sean A. Adams and Michael Pahl, 171–93. Piscataway, NJ: Gorgias, 2012.

———. *The Speeches of Outsiders in Acts. Poetics, Theology and Historiography*. SNTSMS 144. Cambridge, UK: Cambridge University Press, 2008.

Padilla, René. "Evangelism and the World." In *Let the Earth Hear His Voice: International Congress on World Evangelization Lausanne, Switzerland*, edited by J. D. Douglas, 116–45. Minneapolis: World Wide, 1975.

———. "Una Visión Bíblica de la Iglesia." *El Blog de Bernabé* (blog), August 7, 2012. https://www.elblogdebernabe.com/2012/08/una-vision-biblica-de-la-iglesia-por-c.html.

Pao, David W. *Acts and the Isaianic New Exodus*. Biblical Studies Library. Grand Rapids: Baker Academic, 2002.

Park, Andrew S. *The Wounded Heart of God: The Asian Concept of Han and the Christian Doctrine of Sin*. Nashville: Abingdon, 1993.

Parsons, Mikeal C., and Richard I. Pervo. *Rethinking the Unity of Luke and Acts*. Minneapolis: Fortress, 1993.

Patte, Daniel. *Early Jewish Hermeneutic in Palestine*. Missoula: Scholars, 1975.

Perkins, Pheme. *Peter: Apostle for the Whole Church*. Edinburgh: T. & T. Clark, 2000.

Perrin, Nicholas. *Jesus the Temple*. Grand Rapids: Baker Academic, 2010.

Person, Raymond F., Jr. "Biblical Historiography as Traditional History." In *Oxford Handbook of Biblical Narrative*, edited by Danna Nolan Fewell, 73–83. New York: Oxford University Press, 2015.

Pervo, Richard I. *Acts: A Commentary*. Hermeneia. Minneapolis: Fortress, 2009.

Pesch, Rudolf. *Simon-Petrus: Geschichte und geschichtliche Bedeutung des ersten Jüngers Jesu Christi*. Päpste und Papsttum 15. Stuttgart: Anton Hiersemann, 1980.

Peterson, David G. *The Acts of the Apostles*. PNTC. Grand Rapids: Eerdmans, 2009.

———. "Kerygma or Kerygmata: Is There Only One Gospel in the New Testament?" In *God's Power to Save: One Gospel for a Complex World?*, edited by Chris Green, 155–84. Leicester: Apollos, 2006.

———. "The Motif of Fulfilment and the Purpose of Luke-Acts." In *The Book of Acts in Its Ancient Literary Setting*, edited by Bruce W. Winter and Andrew D. Clarke, 83–104. Vol. 1 of *The Book of Acts in Its First Century Setting*. Edited by Bruce W. Winter. Grand Rapids: Eerdmans, 1993.

Peterson, Dwight H. *The Origins of Mark: The Markan Community in Current Debate*. BibInt 48. Leiden: Brill, 2000.

Pierce, Chad T. *Spirits and the Proclamation of Christ: 1 Peter 3:18–22 in Light of Sin and Punishment Traditions in Early Jewish and Christian Literature*. WUNT 2.305. Tübingen: Mohr Siebeck, 2011.

Pierce, Charles Anthony. *Conscience in the New Testament*. London: SCM, 1955.

Pitstick, Lyra. *Christ's Descent Into Hell: John Paul II, Joseph Ratzinger, and Hans Urs von Balthasar on the Theology of Holy Saturday*. Grand Rapids: Eerdmans, 2016.

Porter, Stanley E. "Jesus and the Use of Greek in Galilee." In *Studying the Historical Jesus: Evaluations of the State of Current Research*, edited by Bruce Chilton and Craig A. Evans, 123–54. New Testament Tools and Studies 19. Leiden: Brill, 1994.

Powell, Mark Allan. *What Are They Saying About Acts?* Mahwah, NJ: Paulist, 1991.

Price, Robert M. *Deconstructing Jesus*. Amherst, NY: Prometheus, 2000.

Quint, David. "Epic and Empire." *Comparative Literature* 41 (1989) 1–32.

Ray, Stephen K. *Upon This Rock: St. Peter and the Primacy of Rome in Scripture and the Early Church*. San Francisco: Ignatius, 1999.

Reece, Richard. "Roman Coinage in the Western Empire." *Britannia* 4 (1973) 227–51.

Reicke, Bo. *The Disobedient Spirits and Christian Baptism: A Study of 1 Pet. 3:19 and Its Context*. ASNU 13. København: Munksgaard, 1946.

———. *The Epistles of James, Peter, and Jude*. AB 37. Garden City, NY: Doubleday, 1964.

Reynolds, Stephen L. "Testimony, Knowledge, and Epistemic Goals." *Philosophical Studies* 110 (2002) 139–61.

Richards, E. Randolph. *Paul and First-Century Letter Writing: Secretaries, Composition, and Collection*. Downers Grove, IL: InterVarsity, 2004.

———. *The Secretary in the Letters of Paul*. WUNT 2.42. Tübingen: Mohr Siebeck, 1991.

———. "Silvanus Was Not Peter's Secretary: Theological Bias in Interpreting διὰ Σιλουανοῦ . . . ἔγραψα in 1 Peter 5:12." *JETS* 43 (2000) 417–32.

Richards, E. Randolph, and Brandon J. O'Brien. *Misreading Scripture with Western Eyes: Removing Cultural Blinders to Better Understand the Bible*. Downers Grove, IL: InterVarsity, 2012.

Ricoeur, Paul. *Essays on Biblical Interpretation*. Edited by Lewis S. Mudge. Philadelphia: Fortress, 1980.

Ridderbos, Herman N. *The Speeches of Peter in the Acts of the Apostles*. London: Tyndale, 1962.

Robbins, Vernon K. "The Chreia." In *Greco-Roman Literature and the New Testament: Selected Forms and Genres*, edited by David E. Aune, 1–23. Atlanta: Scholars, 1988.

Roberts, Robert C., and W. Jay Wood. *Intellectual Virtues: An Essay in Regulative Epistemology*. Oxford: Oxford University Press, 2007.

Robinson, James M. "The Possibility of a New Quest." In *The Historical Jesus: Critical Concepts in Religious Studies*, edited by Craig A. Evans, 191–210. London: Routledge, 2004.

Roncace, Mark, et al. "Dyadic Personality." *Dictionary of Socio-Rhetorical Terms*. Online. http://www.religion.emory.edu/faculty/robbins/SRI/defns/d_defns.cfm.

Roskam, Hendrika Nicoline. *The Purpose of the Gospel of Mark in Its Historical and Social Context*. NovTSup 114. Leiden: Brill, 2004.

Rowe, Robert D. *God's Kingdom and God's Son: The Background to Mark's Christology from Concepts of Kingship in the Psalms*. AGJU 50. Leiden: Brill, 2002.

Russell, D. A. "De Imitatione." In *Creative Imitation and Latin Literature*, edited by David Alexander West and Tony Woodman, 1–16. Cambridge: Cambridge University Press, 1979.

Russell, Ronald. "Eschatology and Ethics in 1 Peter." *EQ* 47 (1975) 78–84.

Saller, Richard P. *Patriarchy, Property, and Death in the Roman Family*. Cambridge Studies in Population, Economy, and Society in Past Time 25. Cambridge: Cambridge University Press, 1994.

Samkutty, V. J. *The Samaritan Mission in Acts*. LNTS 328. London: T. & T. Clark, 2006.

Samuel, Simon. *A Postcolonial Reading of Mark's Story of Jesus*. LNTS 340. London: T. & T. Clark, 2007.

Samuelsson, Gunnar. *Crucifixion in Antiquity: An Inquiry into the Background of the New Testament Terminology of Crucifixion*. Gothenburg: University of Gothenburg, 2010.

Sanders, E. P. *Judaism: Practice and Belief 63 BC–66 CE*. Philadelphia: Trinity, 1992.

Sanders, Jack T. *The New Testament Christological Hymns: Their Historical Religious Background*. SNTSMS 15. Cambridge: Cambridge University Press, 1971.

Sandnes, Karl Olav. *The Gospel 'According to Homer and Virgil': Cento and Canon*. NovTSup 138. Leiden: Brill, 2011.

Schäfer, Peter. *Judeophobia: Attitudes Toward the Jews in the Ancient World*. Cambridge, MA: Harvard University Press, 1997.

Schelkle, Karl H. *Die Petrusbriefe, Der Judasbrief*. HThKNT 13. Freiburg: Herder, 1961.

Schmahl, Gunter. *Die Zwölf im Markusevangelium*. Trier: Paulinus, 1977.

Schnackenburg, Rudolf. *The Moral Teaching of the New Testament*. London: Burns & Oates, 1975.

Schneck, Richard. *Isaiah in the Gospel of Mark I–VIII*. BIBAL Dissertation Series 1. Vallejo, CA: BIBAL, 1994.

Schnelle, Udo. *Theology of the New Testament*. Translated by M. Eugene Boring. Grand Rapids: Baker Academic, 2009.

Schrage, Wolfgang. *Die "Katholischen" Briefe: Die Briefe des Jakobus, Petrus, Johannes, und Judas.* NTD 10. Göttingen: Vandenhoeck & Ruprecht, 1973.

Schreiner, Thomas R. *1, 2 Peter, Jude.* NAC 37. Nashville: Broadman & Holman, 2003.

Schubert, Paul. "The Final Cycle of Speeches in the Book of Acts." *JBL* 87 (1968) 1–16.

Schulz, Anselm. *Nachfolgen und Nachahmen: Studien über das Verhältnis der neutestamentlichen Jüngerschaft zur urchristlichen Vorbildethik.* SANT 6. Munich: Kosel, 1962.

Schürer, Emil. *The History of the Jewish People in the Age of Jesus Christ (175 BC–AD 135).* Edinburgh: T. & T. Clark, 1979.

Schutter, William L. *Hermeneutic and Composition in 1 Peter.* WUNT 2.30. Tübingen: Mohr, 1989.

Schweizer, Eduard. "Concerning the Speeches in Acts." In *Studies in Luke-Acts*, edited by Leander E. Keck and J. Louis Martyn, 208–16. Nashville: Abingdon, 1966.

Seland, Torrey. "πάροικος καὶ παρεπίδημος: Proselyte Characterizations in 1 Peter?" *BBR* 11 (2001) 239–68.

Selwyn, Edward G. "Eschatology in 1 Peter." In *The Background of the New Testament and Its Eschatology*, edited by W. D. Davies and David Daube, 394–408. Cambridge: Cambridge University Press, 1964.

———. *The First Epistle of Peter: The Greek Text with Introduction, Notes, and Essays.* London: Macmillan, 1947.

———. "The Persecutions in 1 Peter." *BSNTS* 1 (1950) 39–50.

Senior, Donald. *1 and 2 Peter.* NTM 20. Wilmington, DE: Glazier, 1980.

Sevenster, J. N. *Do You Know Greek? How Much Greek Could the First Jewish Christians Have Known?* NovTSup 19. Leiden: Brill, 1968.

———. *The Roots of Pagan Anti-Semitism in the Ancient World.* NovTSup 41. Leiden: Brill, 1975.

Sheldon, Charles M. *In His Steps: What Would Jesus Do?* Radford, WA: Wilder, 2008.

Shepherd, Tom. "The Narrative Function of Markan Intercalation." *NTS* 41 (1995) 522–40.

———. "The Narrative Role of John and Jesus in Mark 1:1–15." In *The Gospel of Mark*, edited by Thomas R. Hatina, 151–68. Vol. 1 of *Biblical Interpretation in Early Christian Gospels*. London: T. & T. Clark, 2006.

Shiner, Whitney Taylor. *Follow Me! Disciples in Markan Rhetoric.* SBLDS 145. Atlanta: Scholars, 1995.

———. *Proclaiming the Gospel: First-Century Performance of Mark.* Harrisburg, PA: Trinity, 2003.

Slomp, Jan. "Are the Words 'Son of God' in Mark 1:1 Original?" *BT* 28 (1977) 143–50.

Small, Jocelyn Penny. *Wax Tablets of the Mind: Cognitive Studies of Memory and Literacy in Classical Antiquity.* London: Routledge, 1997.

Smith, D. Moody. *John Among the Gospels: The Relationship in Twentieth-Century Research.* Columbia, SC: University of South Carolina Press, 2001.

Smith, Terence V. *Petrine Controversies in Early Christianity: Attitudes Towards Peter in Christian Writings of the First Two Centuries.* WUNT 2.15. Tübingen: Mohr Siebeck, 1985.

Snaith, Norman H. *The Distinctive Ideas of the Old Testament.* London: Epworth, 1944.

Soards, Marion L. "1 Peter, 2 Peter, and Jude as Evidence for a Petrine School." *Aufstieg und Niedergang der römishen Welt* 2.25.5 (1988) 3827–49.

———. *The Speeches in Acts: Their Content, Context, and Concerns*. Louisville: Westminster John Knox, 1994.

Sosa, Ernest. *Knowledge in Perspective: Selected Essays in Epistemology*. Cambridge: Cambridge University Press, 1991.

Sperber, Daniel. "Mark 12:42 and Its Metrological Background: A Study in Ancient Syriac Versions." *NovT* 9 (1967) 178–90.

Sperber, Daniel, and Deirdre Wilson. *Relevance: Communication and Cognition*. 2nd ed. Oxford: Blackwell, 1995.

Squires, John T. *The Plan of God in Luke-Acts*. SNTSMS 76. Cambridge: Cambridge University Press, 1993.

Stahl, Hans-Peter. "Speeches and Course of Events in Books Six and Seven of Thucydides." In *The Speeches in Thucydides*, edited by Philip A. Stadter, 60–78. Chapel Hill: University of North Carolina Press, 1972.

Stanley, David Michael. "Pauline Allusions to the Sayings of Jesus." *CBQ* 23 (1961) 26–39.

Starner, Rob. *Kingdom of Power, Power of Kingdom: The Opposing World Views of Mark and Chariton*. Eugene, OR: Pickwick, 2011.

Stein, Robert H. *Luke*. NAC 24. Nashville: Broadman & Holman, 1992.

———. *Mark*. BECNT. Grand Rapids: Baker Academic, 2008.

Stelzenberger, Johannes. *Syneidesis Im Neuen Testament*. Abhandlungen zur Moraltheologie 1. Paderborn: Schöningh, 1961.

Still, Todd D. "Images of Peter in the Apostolic Fathers." In *Peter in Early Christianity*, edited Helen K. Bond and Larry W. Hurtado, 161–67. Grand Rapids: Eerdmans, 2015.

Stowers, Stanley K. *Letter Writing in Greco-Roman Antiquity*. LEC 5. Philadelphia: Westminster, 1986.

Strauss, Mark L. *The Davidic Messiah in Luke-Acts: The Promise and Its Fulfillment in Lukan Christology*. JSNTSup 110. Sheffield: Sheffield Academic, 1995.

Streeter, B. H. *The Four Gospels: A Study of the Origins, Treating of the Manuscript Tradition, Sources, Authorship, and Dates*. London: Macmillan, 1924.

Suh, Joong Suk. *Discipleship and Community: Mark's Gospel in Sociological Perspective*. Nexus Monograph Series. Claremont: Center for Asian-American Ministries, School of Theology at Claremont, 1991.

Swartley, Willard M. "The Structural Function of the Term 'Way' (Hodos) in Mark's Gospel." In *The New Way of Jesus: Essays Presented to Howard Charles*, edited by William Klassen, 73–86. Newton, KS: Faith & Life, 1980.

Talbert, Charles H. *Reading Acts: A Literary and Theological Commentary on The Acts of the Apostles*. New York: Crossroad, 1997.

———. *What Is a Gospel? The Genre of the Canonical Gospels*. Macon, GA: Mercer University Press, 1986.

Talbert, Richard J. A., ed. *Barrington Atlas of the Greek and Roman World*. Princeton: Princeton University Press, 2000.

Tannehill, Robert C. "The Disciples in Mark: The Function of a Narrative Role." *JR* 57 (1977) 386–405.

———. *The Narrative Unity of Luke-Acts: A Literary Interpretation*. 2 vols. Philadelphia: Fortress, 1991–1994.

Tarrant, R. J. "Aspects of Virgil's Reception in Antiquity." In *The Cambridge Companion to Virgil*, edited by Charles Martindale, 56–72. Cambridge: Cambridge University Press, 1997.

Taylor, Vincent. *The Gospel According to Mark*. 2nd ed. Grand Rapids: Baker, 1966.

Telford, William R. *The Barren Temple and the Withered Tree: A Redaction-Critical Analysis of the Cursing of the Fig-Tree Pericope in Mark's Gospel and Its Relation to the Cleansing of the Temple Tradition*. JSNTSup 1. Sheffield: JSOT, 1980.

———. *The Theology of the Gospel of Mark*. New Testament Theology. Cambridge: Cambridge University Press, 1999.

———. *Writing on the Gospel of Mark*. Guides to Advanced Biblical Research 1. Dorset, UK: Deo, 2009.

Theissen, Gerd. *The Gospels in Context: Social and Political History in the Synoptic Tradition*. Minneapolis: Fortress, 1991.

Thiede, Carsten P. *Geheimakte Petrus: Auf den Spuren des Apostels*. Stuttgart: Kreuz, 2000.

———. *Simon Peter: From Galilee to Rome*. Grand Rapids: Zondervan, 1988.

Thompson, Mary R. *The Role of Disbelief in Mark: A New Approach to the Second Gospel*. Mahwah, NJ: Paulist, 1989.

Thurén, Lauri. *Argument and Theology in 1 Peter: The Origins of Christian Paraenesis*. JSNTSup 114. Sheffield: Sheffield Academic, 1995.

———. *The Rhetorical Strategy of 1 Peter*. Åbo: Åbo Akademi University, 1990.

Tinsley, Ernest John. *The Imitation of God in Christ: An Essay on the Biblical Basis of Christian Spirituality*. Library of History and Doctrine. London: SCM, 1960.

Tolbert, Mary Ann. *Sowing the Gospel: Mark's World in Literary-Historical Perspective*. Minneapolis: Fortress, 1989.

Toohey, Peter. "Roman Epic." In *The Cambridge Companion to the Epic*, edited by Catherine Bates, 31–54. Cambridge: Cambridge University Press, 2010.

Townsend, John T. "The Speeches in Acts." *AThR* 42 (1960) 150–59.

Trebilco, Paul R. *Jewish Communities in Asia Minor*. SNTSMS 69. Cambridge: Cambridge University Press, 1991.

Triandis, Harry C. "Cross-Cultural Studies of Individualism and Collectivism." In *Nebraska Symposium on Motivation 1989: Cross-Cultural Perspectives*, edited by John J. Berman, 41–133. Lincoln, NE: University of Nebraska Press, 1990.

———. "Individualism-Collectivism and Personality." *Journal of Personality* 69 (2001) 907–24.

Tuckett, Christopher M. *The Revival of the Griesbach Hypothesis: An Analysis and Appraisal*. SNTSMS 44. Cambridge: Cambridge University Press, 1983.

Turner, C. H. "The Gospel According to St. Mark." In *A New Commentary on Holy Scripture*, edited by Charles Gore, et al., 42–124. London: SPCK, 1937.

———. "Marcan Usage: Notes, Critical and Exegetical, on the Second Gospel." *JTS* 26 (1925) 225–40.

Turner, Max. *Power from on High: The Spirit in Israel's Restoration and Witness in Luke-Acts*. Sheffield: Sheffield Academic, 1996.

Turner, Nigel. *Style*. Vol. 4 of *A Grammar of New Testament Greek*. Edited by James Hope Moulton. Edinburgh: T. & T. Clark, 1976.

Tyson, Joseph. "The Blindness of the Disciples in Mark." *JBL* 80 (1961) 261–68.

Unnik, W. C. van. "A Classical Parallel to 1 Peter 2:14 and 20." *NTS* 2 (1956) 198–202.

———. "Once More St. Luke's Prologue." *Neot* 7 (1973) 7–26.

———. "The Redemption in 1 Peter 1:18–19 and the Problem of the First Epistle of Peter." In *Sparsa Collecta: The Collected Essays of W. C. van Unnik, Part Two: 1 Peter, Canon, Corpus Hellenisticum, Generalia*, 1–82. NovTSup 30. Leiden: Brill, 1973.

———. "The Teaching of Good Works in 1 Peter." *NTS* 1 (1955) 92–110.

VanGemeren, Willem A. "'ABBĀ' in the Old Testament." *JETS* 31 (1988) 385–89.

Vanhoozer, Kevin J. *First Theology: God, Scripture & Hermeneutics*. Downers Grove, IL: InterVarsity, 2002.

Verhey, Allen. *The Great Reversal: Ethics and the New Testament*. Grand Rapids: Eerdmans, 1984.

Verheyden, Joseph. "The Unity of Luke-Acts. What Are We Up To?" In *The Unity of Luke-Acts*, edited by Joseph Verheyden, 3–56. Leuven: Peeters, 1999.

Verner, David C. *The Household of God: The Social World of the Pastoral Epistles*. SBLDS 71. Chico, CA: SBL, 1983.

Via, Dan O., Jr. *The Ethics of Mark's Gospel—In the Middle of Time*. Philadelphia: Fortress, 1985.

Vögtle, Anton. *Die Tugend- und Lasterkataloge im Neuen Testament: Exegetisch, religions- und formgeschichtlich Untersucht*. NTAbh 16. Münster: Aschendorff, 1936.

Walbank, F. W. *Speeches in the Greek Historians*. Oxford: Blackwell, 1965.

Wallace-Hadrill, Andrew. "Patronage in Roman Society: From Republic to Empire." In *Patronage in Ancient Society*, edited by Andrew Wallace-Hadrill, 63–87. London: Routledge, 1989.

Walls, Andrew F. "Introduction." In *The First Epistle General of Peter*, by Alan M. Stibbs, 15–70. Grand Rapids: Eerdmans, 1959.

Walsh, Patrick G. *Livy: His Historical Aims and Methods*. Cambridge: Cambridge University Press, 1961.

Walter, Nikolaus. "Paulus und die urchristliche Jesustradition." *NTS* 31 (1985) 498–522.

Waltner, Erland, and J. Daryl Charles. *1 & 2 Peter, Jude*. Believers Church Bible Commentary. Scottdale, PA: Herald, 1999.

Wand, J. W. C. *The General Epistles of St. Peter and St. Jude*. WC. London: Methuen, 1934.

Wasserman, Tommy. "The 'Son of God' Was in the Beginning (Mark 1:1)." *JTS* 62 (2011) 20–50.

Watts, Rikki E. *Isaiah's New Exodus in Mark*. Grand Rapids: Baker Academic, 1997.

Weeden, Theodore J. "The Heresy That Necessitated Mark's Gospel." *ZNW* 59 (1968) 148–58.

———. *Mark: Traditions in Conflict*. Philadelphia: Fortress, 1971.

Weima, Jeffrey A. D. *Neglected Endings: The Significance of the Pauline Letter Closings*. JSNTSup 101. Sheffield: Sheffield Academic, 1994.

Weiner, Matthew. "Accepting Testimony." *Philosophical Quarterly* 53 (2003) 256–64.

Wenham, David, ed. *The Jesus Tradition Outside the Gospels*. Sheffield: JSOT, 1985.

———. "Paul's Use of the Jesus Tradition: Three Samples." In *The Jesus Tradition Outside the Gospels*, edited by David Wenham, 7–37. Sheffield: JSOT, 1984.

West, David, and Tony Woodman. *Creative Imitation and Latin Literature*. Cambridge: Cambridge University Press, 1986.

White, John L. *Light from Ancient Letters*. Philadelphia: Fortress, 1986.

White, L. Michael. *Scripting Jesus: The Gospels in Rewrite*. New York: Harper One, 2010.

Wiarda, Timothy. *Peter in the Gospels: Pattern, Personality, and Relationship*. WUNT 2.127. Tübingen: Mohr Siebeck, 2000.

Wibbing, S. *Die Tugend- und Lasterkataloge im Neuen Testament und ihre Traditionsgeschichte unter besonderer Berücksichtigung der Qumran-Texte*. BZNW 25. Berlin: Töpelmann, 1959.

Wikgren, Allen. "ΑΡΧΗ ΤΟΥ ΕΥΑΓΓΕΛΙΟΥ." *JBL* 61 (1942) 11–20.

Wilckens, Ulrich. *Die Missionsreden der Apostelgeschichte: Form- und traditionsgeschichtliche Untersuchungen*. Neukirchen-Vluyn: Neukirchener Verlag, 1974.

Williams, Travis B. *Persecution in 1 Peter: Differentiating and Contextualizing Early Christian Suffering*. NovTSup 145. Leiden: Brill, 2012.

Wilson, Andrew P. *Transfigured: A Derridean Rereading of the Markan Transfiguration*. Playing the Texts 13. New York: T. & T. Clark, 2007.

Wilson, Deirdre. "Irony and Metarepresentation." *UCL Working Papers in Linguistics* 21 (2009) 183–226.

Wilson, John. "What Does Thucydides Claim for His Speeches?" *Phoenix* 36 (1982) 95–103.

Winn, Adam. *The Purpose of Mark's Gospel: An Early Christian Response to Roman Imperial Propaganda*. WUNT 2.245. Tübingen: Mohr Siebeck, 2008.

Winter, Bruce W. *Seek the Welfare of the City: Christians as Benefactors and Citizens*. Grand Rapids: Eerdmans, 1994.

Witherington, Ben. *The Acts of the Apostles: A Socio-Rhetorical Commentary*. Grand Rapids: Eerdmans, 1998.

———. *The Christology of Jesus*. Minneapolis: Fortress, 1990.

———. *The Gospel of Mark: A Socio-Rhetorical Commentary*. Grand Rapids: Eerdmans, 2001.

———. *A Socio-Rhetorical Commentary on 1–2 Peter*. Vol. 2 of *Letters and Homilies for Hellenized Christians*. Downers Grove, IL: IVP Academic, 2007.

Woodley, Randy S. *Shalom and the Community of Creation: An Indigenous Vision*. Grand Rapids: Eerdmans, 2012.

Wrede, William. *Das Messiasgeheimnis in den Evangelien: Zugleich ein Beitrag zum Verständnis des Markusevangeliums*. Göttingen: Vandenhoeck & Ruprecht, 1901.

———. *The Messianic Secret*. Translated by J. C. G. Greig. Cambridge: Clarke & Co., 1971.

Wright, N. T. *Jesus and the Victory of God*. Vol. 3 of *Christian Origins and the Question of God*. Minneapolis: Fortress, 1996.

———. *The New Testament and the People of God*. Vol. 1 of *Christian Origins and the Question of God*. Minneapolis: Fortress, 1992.

———. *Paul and the Faithfulness of God*. Vol. 4 of *Christian Origins and the Question of God*. Minneapolis: Fortress, 2013.

Yewangoe, Andreas Anangguru. *Theologia Crucis in Asia: Asian Christian Views on Suffering in the Face of Overwhelming Poverty and Multifaceted Religiosity in Asia*. Amsterdam: Rodopi, 1987.

Zanker, Paul. *The Power of Images in the Age of Augustus*. Ann Arbor: University of Michigan Press, 1988.

Zehnle, Richard F. *Peter's Pentecost Discourse: Tradition and Lukan Reinterpretation in Peter's Speeches of Acts 2 and 3*. SBLMS 15. Nashville: Abingdon, 1971.

Zetzel, James E. G. "Rome and Its Traditions." In *The Cambridge Companion to Virgil*, edited by Charles Martindale, 188–203. Cambridge: Cambridge University Press, 1997.

Zimmerli, Walther, and Joachim Jeremias. *The Servant of God*. SBT 20. London: SCM, 1965.

Author Index

Abrahams, Israel, 388
Achtemeier, Paul J., 72, 74, 75, 76, 78, 79, 81, 82, 85, 86, 90, 91, 95, 304, 312, 313, 317, 319, 324, 332, 333, 334, 339, 341, 342, 351, 355, 356, 360, 361, 362, 367, 368, 371, 372, 373, 378, 381, 386, 387, 390, 392
Adams, Sean A., 3, 67
Adcock, F. E., 54
Adler, Eve, 136, 139, 140, 141
Alexander, Loveday, 61, 62, 245
Alföldy, Géza, 394
Allison, Dale C., 80, 82
Anderson, Bernhard W., 248, 322, 326
Anderson, Robert T., 280
Arav, Rami, 88
Arav, Ravi, 88
Ashton, Mark, 160
Audi, Robert, 21
Aune, David E., 39, 68, 103

Baban, Octavian, 138
Bacon, B. W., 33
Baker, Coleman, 59
Balch, David L., 353, 393, 397, 404
Banks, Robert, 244
Barnett, A. E., 77
Barnett, Paul W., 2, 3, 418
Barrett, C. K., 60, 175, 242, 244, 251
Barton, Tamsyn, 247
Barton, Stephen C., 210
Bates, Catherine, 253, 253
Bauckham, Richard, 1, 7, 27, 28, 29, 32, 34, 35, 37, 39, 41, 42, 43, 45, 73, 82, 97, 101, 105, 109, 114, 115, 116, 117, 118, 121, 122, 236, 237, 238, 265, 275

Bayer, Hans F., 235, 236, 244, 298
Beare, Francis Wright, xv, 72, 73, 77, 84, 85, 316, 327, 333, 334, 337, 339, 346, 348, 350, 355, 361, 387, 390
Beasley-Murray, G. R., 279
Beavis, Mary Ann, 39, 40, 106, 121, 122, 210
Becker, Michael, 88
Benedict XVI. (Pope), 20
Berkey, Robert F., 318
Berman, John J., 375
Best, Ernest, xv, 79, 80, 85, 146, 210, 215, 218, 220, 222, 223, 224, 225, 312, 333, 334, 339, 341, 343, 350, 356, 359, 360, 368, 369, 370, 371, 372, 381
Betz, Otto, 189
Betz, Hans Dieter, 210, 211, 388
Bigg, Charles., 75, 95, 97, 333, 334, 342, 361, 371, 373
Black Matthew, 42, 111
Black, C. Clifton, 210
Blackburn, Barry, 153, 171
Blevins, J. L., 190
Boccaccini, Gabriele, 175
Bock, Darrell L., 176, 237, 241, 242, 257, 270, 290, 291
Bockmuehl, Markus, 1, 3, 4, 10, 15, 16, 17, 28, 98, 241
Boismard, M. E., 404
Bolt, Peter G., 156, 158, 159, 184, 195, 198
Bond, Helen K., 98
Bonz, Marianne Palmer, 136, 137, 138, 141, 252, 253, 254, 285
Borrell, Agustí, 216
Borsch, Frederick H., 210
Bovon, François, 60, 61, 62, 66

AUTHOR INDEX

Bowen, Edwin W., 110
Brandon J. O'Brien, 336
Brandt, Pierre-Yves, 173
Briones, David., 335
Broadhead, Edwin K., 189
Brown, Colin, xx
Brown, Raymond E., xiv, 12, 13, 15, 16, 33, 34, 110, 241
Brox, Norbert., 74, 78
Bruce, F. F., 10, 11, 244, 257, 262, 269, 276, 299
Brunson, Andrew C., 343
Bultmann, Rudolf, 404
Burkett, Delbert, 66, 175, 176
Burridge, Richard, 103, 227
Burton, Ernest De Witt, 301
Byung-Mu, Ahn., 197

Cadbury, Henry J., 47, 48, 49, 50, 51, 68
Campbell, Barth L., 366
Campbell, R. A., 72
Čapek, Milič, 318
Caragounis, Chrys C., 176
Carrington, Philip, 78, 404
Casey, Maurice., 44, 102, 111, 175
Cassese, Giácomo, 372
Casson, Lionel, 115, 156, 306
Champlin, Edward, 133
Chancey, Mark A., 88
Charles, J. Daryl, 88, 97, 103, 278, 281, 385
Chester, Andrew, 316, 327
Chilton, Bruce , 98
Chiu, José Enrique Aguilar , 280
Clarke Andrew D. , 46, 68, 235, 255
Coady, C. A. J., 21, 22, 23, 24, 27
Cogan, Mark., 47, 59
Collins, Adela Yarbro, 170, 207, 220
Conte, Gian Biagio, 132
Conzelmann, Hans, 269, 287
Coogan, Jeremiah, 303
Cook, John Granger, 353
Cooley, Alison E., 132
Counet, Chatelion, 93
Craig, Evans, 88, 98, 125, 153, 198, 239, 385
Cranfield, C. E. B., 34, 111, 121, 334, 361, 395
Crouch, James E., 353, 393, 404
Cullmann, Oscar, xv, 11, 73, 96, 109, 162, 240, 266, 270, 271, 272, 287, 301, 317, 319, 320, 339, 352, 360, 404

Dalton, William Joseph, 332, 338, 356, 360, 361, 362
Daniel J. Harrington, 113
Danker, Frederick W., 134, 262, 334, 391
Daube, David , 316

Davids, Peter Hugh , 3, 73, 81, 95, 97, 316, 327, 339
Davies W. D. , 316
Davis, David Brion, 315
Davis, Jud., 275
Davis, William Stearns, 48
Dawsey, James, 210, 215
Deichgräber, Reinhard, 404
Deines, Roland , 308
Deissmann, Adolf, 302, 357, 378
Deloria, Vine, Jr., 329
Derrenbacker, R. A., Jr., 45, 61, 67, 116, 138, 161
Derrett, J. Duncan M., 187
Deterding, Paul L., 322
Dibelius, Martin, 46, 48, 49, 50, 51, 66, 67, 69, 243
Dickson, John P., 134
Dillon, Richard J., 275
Dines, Jennifer M., 92, 425
Dodd, C. H., 124, 150, 242, 243, 255, 317, 389
Donahue, John R., 113, 121, 149, 182, 198, 210, 211, 219
Donaldson, Terence L., 296
Donfried, Karl P., 15, 16, 33, 241
Douglas J. D. , 185
Dschulnigg, Peter, 17
Dubis, Mark, 341
Duling, Dennis C. , 154
Dungan, David L., 80, 81
Dunn, James D. G., 66, 162, 190, 191, 242, 245, 263, 268, 289, 290, 292, 294

Easton, B. S., 385
Edwards, Dennis R., 3
Edward, N. O'Neil, 39, 40
Edwards, James R., 34, 115, 150, 157, 162, 169, 171, 179, 190, 211, 213
Egan, Patrick T., 322
Ehrman, Bart D., 14
Elgin, Catherine Z., 21, 25, 43, 44
Elliott, John H., xiii, xv, 71, 72, 73, 74, 75, 76, 78, 79, 80, 82, 85, 86, 90, 91, 93, 95, 96, 109, 302, 302, 304, 305, 306, 307, 308, 309, 310, 311, 313, 315, 317, 318, 319, 324, 328, 330, 332, 333, 336, 337, 338, 339, 341, 343, 344, 346, 351, 354, 356, 358, 360, 361, 362, 365, 367, 369, 371, 372, 372, 376, 377, 378, 379, 380, 381, 382, 383, 386, 394, 397
Ellis, E. Earle., 189, 297, 298
Engberg-Pedersen, Troels, 385
Epiphanius, 37, 72, 305
Epstein, David F., 314
Erland, Waltner, 88

Ernest, J. D., xxi
Evans, Craig A., 98
Evans, C. F., 184, 185
Evans, C. Stephen., 20, 27
Evans, Craig A., 88, 98, 125, 133, 134, 153, 167, 178, 180, 190, 197, 198, 202, 204, 206, 207, 223, 239, 385

Feagin, Glyndle M., Jr., 164
Feldmeier, Reinhard, 105
Fenske, Wolfgang, 88
Ferguson, Everett, 159, 277, 279
Fewell, Danna Nolan, 252
Filson, F. V., 313
Finegan, Jack., 68
Fischer, Karl-Martin, 77
Fisher, Joan E., 110
Fitzmyer, Joseph A., 46, 60, 62, 64, 66, 237, 243, 255, 270, 275, 301
Flusser, David., 259
Foakes-Jackson, F. J., 9, 10, 12, 47, 60, 73, 109, 237
Foley, John Miles, 253
Foster, Giraud V, 111
Foster, Ora Delmer, 77
Foster, Paul., 2, 16
France, R. T., 32, 34, 105, 115, 149, 150, 153, 161, 169, 177, 179, 183, 188, 198, 207, 211
Freedman, David Noel, 385
Freedman, H., 146
French, Roger., 247
Fricker, Elizabeth., 21, 24, 25
Furnish, Victor Paul., 80

Gadamer, Hans-Georg, 5
Gaechter, Paul., 12
Gager, John G., 277
Gamble, Harry Y., 68, 106
Garrett, Susan R., 260, 275
Gärtner, Bertil, 187, 188, 371, 381
Gathercole, Simon, 175
Geehan E. R., 244
Gempf, Conrad H., 46, 52, 58, 69, 235, 402
Gill, David W., 10
Glasson, T. Francis, 68
Gnilka, Joachim, 13
Gold, Barbara K., 103, 118, 245
González, Justo, xvi, 281
Gore, Charles, 41
Goulder, Michael, 3, 14, 34, 240, 246
Graf, Fritz, 277, 292
Graham, Peter J., 21
Grant, Michael, 14, 34, 73, 109
Grappe, Christian, 17

Gray, Timothy C., 188, 222, 276
Gréaux, Eric James, 322
Green, Chris, 242
Green, Gene L. (Eugenio), 1, 2, 3, xiii, xiv, xvi, 10, 73, 75, 77, 81, 91, 95, 97, 127, 158, 212, 255, 290, 299, 301, 315, 328, 332, 339, 343–44, 350, 362, 367, 370, 385–87, 393, 409
Green, Joel B., 2, 60, 67, 80, 81, 237, 319
Green, Michael, 97
Grindheim, Sigurd, 271
Grudem, Wayne, 95, 332, 361
Gschwind, Karl, 360
Guelich, Robert A., 42, 120, 154, 161, 169, 177
Gundry, Robert H., 34, 44, 79, 81, 101, 105, 110, 121, 127, 144, 146, 148, 153, 153, 169, 200, 201

Haenchen, Ernst, 48, 243
Hagedorn, A. C., 199
Hagner, Donald, 75
Hahneman, Geoffrey Mark, 76
Hannah, Darrell D., 175
Hare, Douglas R. A., 175
Harmon, William, 253
Harrelson, Walter, 248, 322
Harris, J. Rendel, 404
Harrison, James R., 336
Hatina, Thomas R., 129, 429
Hawthorne, Gerald F., 189
Hays, Christopher M., 318, 340
Hays, Richard B., 174, 226, 227, 229, 230
Head, Peter., 169
Heil, John Paul, 173
Helyer, Larry R., 241
Hemer, Colin J., 306, 402
Henderson, Suzanne Watts, 210, 217, 218, 219
Hengel, Martin, xvi, xvii, 3, 10, 12, 16, 34, 44, 45, 64, 65, 66, 73, 87, 88, 92, 98, 104, 105, 107, 110, 113, 122, 135, 159, 162, 197, 205, 210, 211, 238, 239, 240, 241, 242, 246, 272, 352, 402
Hering, James P., 393, 404
Higgins A. J. B., 263
Hilgert, Earle, 243, 258, 275, 277
Hill Charles E., 350
Hock, Ronald F., 39, 40
Hofius, Otfried, 262
Hohti, Paavo, 59
Holladay, Carl H., 171
Hollander, Harm W., 80, 82
Holliday, Peter J., 132
Hooker, Morna D., 34, 162, 175, 177, 179, 188, 210, 213, 217, 223

Horbury, William, 266
Horgan, Maurya P., 297
Hornblower, Simon., xx, 54
Horrell, David G., 78, 83, 84, 93, 311
Horsley, G. H. R., 68
Horsley, Richard A., 87, 149, 155
Hort, F. J. A., 306, 334, 351, 368, 384, 387, 388, 393
Houlden, J. L., 226, 227
Hurtado, Larry W , 98

Ilan, Tal., 162, 265, 301
Immerwahr, Henry R., 47
Incigneri, Brian J., 106, 110
Instone-Brewer, David, 348
Iverson, Kelly R., 143, 155

Jackson F. J. Foakes , 9, 10, 12, 47, 60, 73, 109, 237
James Frank A. III, 350
Jennings, Willie James, 278, 281
Jeremias, Joachim, 200, 284, 330
Jerome H. Neyrey, 37, 199, 305, 374
Jervell, Jacob, 242
Joachim, Jeremias, 271, 284, 330
Jobes, Karen H., 72, 75, 79, 85, 86, 87, 90, 92, 95, 306, 308, 310, 311, 317, 333, 342, 346, 355, 356, 360, 361, 362, 363, 386
Johansson, Daniel., 181
John P. Meier., 34, 110
Johnson, Luke, 64, 65, 89, 245
Johnson, Sherman E., 308
Helen, K. Bond, 34, 67

Käsemann, Ernst., 155
Keck, Leander E. , 48, 134
Kee, Howard Clark., 112
Keener, Craig S., 227, 256, 257, 258, 259, 262, 264, 266, 269, 270, 274, 275, 276, 277, 278, 280, 282, 283, 284, 286, 289, 292, 295, 296, 298
Kelber, Werner H., 111, 144, 145
Kelly, J. N. D., 85, 95, 320, 332, 337, 338, 340, 350, 352, 355, 356, 360, 364, 369, 371, 387, 392, 395
Kennedy, George A., 39, 52
Kessler, William Thomas, 96, 241
Kilgallen, John J., 265, 266, 268, 280, 282
Kilpatrick, George D., 263
Kim, Seyoon., 189
Kim, Tae Hun., 170, 171
King, Katherine Callen, 252
Kingsbury, Jack Dean, 162, 175, 176, 217
Kinman, Brent, 144

Klassen, William , 145
Klauck, Hans-Josef, 277, 292, 393
Klawans, Jonathan, 259
Kloppenborg, John S., 66
Kmiecik, Ulrich, 175
Körtner, Ulrich H. J., 280
Kraus, Thomas J., 88
Kreitzer, Larry, 144
Kümmel, Werner Georg, 244, 317
Kurz, William, 255
Kusch, Martin, 21

Lackey, Jennifer , 21, 22, 24, 25, 26, 27, 64, 70
Ladd, George Eldon, 124, 271
Lai, Kenny Ke-Chung, 322
Lake, Kirsopp, 47, 60
Lane, William L., 243, 244
Lange, Armin, 308
Langer, Gerhard, 308
Lapham, F., 9, 10, 16, 17, 34, 98, 99
Larry, W. Hurtado, 10, 16, 34, 67, 98, 175, 176, 270
Lattimore, Richmond, 159
Lee, Simon S., 173
Lemcio, Eugene E., 124, 242
Levinskaya, Irina, 120, 162, 297, 307
Liebengood, Kelly D., 307
Lipton, Peter, 21
Llewelyn, Stephen., 277
Lo, Jonathan W., 67
Longenecker, Richard N. , 162, 266, 270, 287, 297
López, Réne A., 385
Loubser, Johannes A., 93, 304
Love, Julian Price, 317
Luck, Georg, 193

Maartens, P. J., 180
MacCarney, Daniel G., 350
MacDonald, Dennis R., 138, 139, 252, 253, 254
Macey, Samuel L., 318
MacIsaac, John D., 110
MacKay, Ian D., 116
Mackay, John A., 414
Macleod, Colin W., 54, 59, 70
Maier, Gerhard, 79
Malina, Bruce J., 374, 375
Maloney, E. C., 110
Mánek, Jindrich, 248
Mann, Jacob, 128
Manson, T. W., 42, 263
Marcus, Joel, 111, 112, 113, 114, 115, 120, 128, 129, 131, 135, 145, 147, 148, 149, 152, 153, 154, 155, 158, 159, 162, 163, 165, 166, 167, 169, 171, 172, 173, 174, 177,

179, 180, 181, 183, 187, 188, 190, 196, 197, 200, 202, 203, 206, 207, 208, 212, 214, 215, 221, 223, 224
Marshall I. Howard, Xv, 2, 5, 62, 63, 66, 67, 68, 182, 212, 235, 237, 242, 246, 270, 271, 280, 282, 285, 288, 289, 298, 314, 332, 360
Martin, Ralph, 184, 185, 190, 316, 327
Martin, Richard P., 253
Martindale, Charles , 137, 442
Martínez, Florentino García., 170
Martyn J. Louis , 48
Marxsen, Willi, 111
Mason, Steve, 275
Matera, Frank J., 162, 177, 179, 182, 220, 228
Matthews, Gareth B. , 419
McConnell, James R., Jr., 255
McDonald, James I. H., 124
McDonald, Lee Martin, 76
McGill, Scott., 137
McKelvey, R. J., 187, 381
McLay, R. Timothy, 92
McNeile, Alan Hugh, 78, 316
Merk, Otto, 244
Merritt, Robert L., 199
Metzger, Bruce M., 201, 207, 340, 346, 355
Metzner, Rainer, 80
Meye, Robert P., 210
Meyendorff, John, 4, 11, 241
Michaels, J. Ramsey, 78, 85, 90, 91, 95, 333, 339, 357, 360
Millauer, Helmut, 313
Miller, Ed. L. , 243
Mitchell, Margaret M., 117
Mitchell, Stephen, 71, 305, 306
Moessner, David P. , 245, 255, 262, 271, 274
Moffatt, James, 78
Moises, Silva, 92
Moo, Douglas J., 97, 202, 239
Moore, George F., 162
Moreland, J. P. , 32
Morris, Leon, 244, 350, 422
Moulton, James Hope, xx, 110
Mounce, Robert H., 124
Mournet, Terence C., 106
Mudge, Lewis S. , 27
Müller, Mogens, 175
Munck, Johannes, 33
Mussner, Franz, 18
Myers, Ched, 111, 155

Neufeld, Vernon H., 404
Newbigin, Lesslie, 191
Niederwimmer, Kurt, 33, 44

Nienhuis, David R., 76
Nock, Arthur Darby, 375
Noll, Mark A., 353, 395
Nolland, John, 62, 66, 237

O'Brien, Brandon J., 336
O'Brien, Kelli S., 195, 198, 202
O'Connor, Daniel William, 73, 109
O'Donnell, Matthew Brook , 127
O'Neill, J. C., 242
Oropeza, B. J., 334

Padilla, Oswaldo, 47, 67
Padilla, René, 185, 210
Pahl, Michael , 67
Pao, David W., 248, 249, 250, 252, 256, 257, 268, 273, 285, 293, 322
Park, Andrew S., 197
Parsons, Mikeal C., 67
Patte, Daniel., 297
Paul, L. Owen, 175, 176
Perkins, Pheme, 3, 4, 14, 15, 16, 17, 34, 71, 73, 83, 109, 238, 240, 241, 418
Perrin, Nicholas., 188, 222, 276, 381
Person, Raymond F., Jr., 252
Pervo, Richard I., 67, 242, 244, 246, 247, 251, 253, 257, 265, 268, 274, 276, 280
Pesch, Rudolf., 9, 13
Peter, Lipton, 21
Peterson, David G., 235, 242, 255, 257
Peterson, Dwight H., 115, 118, 127
Petzer, J. H. , 180
Pierce, Chad T., 360, 361, 362, 364
Pierce, Charles Anthony, 328, 329
Pitstick, Lyra., 361
Porter, Stanley E., 88, 127, 385, 423, 429
Powell, Mark Allan, 8, 245, 246
Price, Robert M., 103

Quint, David., 139, 156

Ray, Stephen K., 11
Reece, Richard, 110
Reicke, Bo., 77, 243, 361, 430
Reumann, John, 12, 15, 16, 33, 241
Richard, A. Freund, 88, 419
Richard, I. Pervo., 242, 438
Richards, E. Randolph, 90, 91, 92, 93, 104, 302, 303, 306, 336, 403, 419
Ricoeur, Paul., 27, 28, 99
Ridderbos, Herman N., 235, 236, 243, 244, 255, 260, 260, 267, 272, 298
Robbins, Vernon K., 39
Roberts, Robert C., 22

Robinson, James M., 124
Roncace, Mark, 374
Roskam, Hendrika Nicoline, 111, 115, 169
Rowe, Robert D. God's, 162
Russell, D. A., 81, 138
Russell, Ronald., 315, 316
Saller, Richard P., 330

Samkutty, V. J., 280
Sampley, J. Paul , 385
Samuel, Simon, 135
Samuelsson, Gunnar, 159
Sanders, E. P., 200
Sanders, Jack T., 404
Sandnes, Karl Olav, 137, 138
Schäfer, Peter, 120
Schelkle, Karl H., 307, 339, 343, 361, 368, 369, 395
Schmahl, Gunter, 210
Schnackenburg, Rudolf, 387
Schneck, Richard, 129
Schnelle, Udo, 280
Schrage, Wolfgang, 77, 395
Schreiner, Thomas R., 72, 85, 87, 95, 97
Schubert, Paul, 236
Schulz, Anselm., 338
Schürer, Emil, 265, 266, 275, 282
Schutter, William L., 86
Schweizer, Eduard, 48, 50
Segal, Charles , 81
Seland, Torrey, 308, 311, 312, 377
Selwyn, Edward G., xv, xvii, 72, 73, 78, 84, 85, 90, 95, 243, 284, 303, 312, 313, 316, 317, 319, 322, 327, 328, 334, 336, 341, 350, 355, 357, 369, 370, 372, 387, 395, 404
Senior, Donald, 82
Sevenster, J. N., 87, 120
Sheldon, Charles M., 390
Shepherd, Tom, 129, 157
Shiner, Whitney Taylor, 106, 107, 211, 217
Simon, Maurice , 146
Slomp, Jan, 169
Small, Jocelyn Penny, 36, 39
Smith, D. Moody., 45
Smith, Terence V., 16, 17, 45, 98
Snaith, Norman H., 336
Soards, Marion L., 46, 48, 69, 93, 242, 256, 266, 290
Sosa, Ernest , 21, 22
Sperber, Daniel, 111, 127
Squires, John T., 255
Stadter Philip A., 59
Stahl, Hans-Peter, 47
Stanley, David Michael, 80

Starner, Rob, 107
Stein, Robert H., 106, 110, 113, 115, 119, 120, 121, 143, 168, 196, 200, 201, 211, 215, 220, 223, 237,
Stelzenberger, Johannes, 364
Still, Todd D., 16
Stowers, Stanley K., 303
Strauss, Mark L., 236, 255, 267, 268, 275, 291
Streeter, B. H., 66
Stuhlmacher, Peter, 105
Suh, Joong Suk., 210
Swartley, Willard M., 145

Talbert, Charles H., 103, 246, 247, 280, 284
Talbert, Richard J. A, 306
Tannehill, Robert C., 67, 210
Tarrant, R. J., 137
Taylor, Vincent, 34, 36, 41, 42, 108, 110, 111, 112
Telford, William R., 122, 123, 142, 162, 163, 174, 184, 188, 190, 217, 218, 276
Terry, Giles, 280
Theissen, Gerd, 112, 113
Thiede, Carsten P., 10, 11, 73, 109
Thurén, Lauri, 86
Tinsley, Ernest John, 388, 389
Tolbert, Mary Ann., 114, 122
Tom, Holmén, 189
Tony, Woodman, 81, 138, 156
Toohey, Peter, 253
Townsend, John T., 50, 69
Trebilco, Paul R., 363
Triandis, Harry C., 374, 375
Tuckett, Christopher M., 66
Turner, C. H., 41, 42
Turner, Max, 268, 275, 280, 289, 290, 291
Turner, Nigel, 110, 111
Tyson, Joseph, 210, 218

Unnik, W. C. van., 62, 66, 350, 390, 391

Verhey, Allen, 227
Verheyden, Joseph , 67
Verner, David C., 393
Via, Dan O., Jr., 226
Vögtle, Anton, 385

Wood, W. Jay , 22
Walbank, F. W., 56, 69
Wallace-Hadrill, Andrew , 336
Walls, Andrew F., 77
Walsh, Patrick G., 58, 59
Walter, Nikolaus, 82
Waltner, Erland, 248
Wand, J. W. C., 371, 387

Wasserman, Tommy, 169
Watts, Rikki E., 128, 129, 130, 131, 142, 146, 148, 151, 152, 153, 163, 183, 187, 217, 247, 248, 322
Webb, Robert L. , 81
Weeden, Theodore J., 210, 217
Weima, Jeffrey A. D., 303
Weiner, Matthew, 21
Wells, Ronald A. , 21
Wenham, David , 79, 80, 82
West, David Alexander , 81, 138
White, John L., 92
White, L. Michael, 107
Wiarda, Timothy., 9, 15
Wibbing, S., 385
Wikgren, Allen., 161
Wilckens, Ulrich., 48
Wilkins, Michael J. , 32
Williams, Travis B., 305, 313, 315, 380, 391, 392

Wilson, Andrew P., 173
Wilson, Deirdre, 127, 164, 442, 445
Wilson, John., 54
Winn, Adam, 116
Winter Bruce W. , 46, 68, 235, 255, 262, 391
Wire, Antoinette Clark, 107
Witherington, Ben III, 51, 52, 69, 72, 89, 91, 97, 110, 113, 120, 121, 135, 176, 203, 242, 245, 247, 262, 269, 307
Woodman Tony , 81, 138
Wrede, William, 190, 191, 193
Wright, N. T., 143, 266, 282

Yewangoe, Andreas Anangguru, 125

Zanker, Paul, 132
Zehnle, Richard F., 242, 243, 274
Zetzel, James E. G., 137, 141
Zimmerli, Walther, 271

Index of Ancient Sources

OLD TESTAMENT

Genesis

1:1	161
5:21–24	362
6:1–4	362
12:3	294
14:18–20	172
18:18	294
18:25	299
22:2	131, 170
22:12	131
22:16	131
22:18	273, 294
23:4	311, 320, 376
50:24–25	333

Exodus

3:6	261
3:9	337
3:13–15	277
3:15	261
3:18	328
4:13	261
5:1	293
6:1	337
6:6	322, 341, 347
7	285
7:4	293
9:16	154
12:1–32	199
12:5	323, 341, 347, 350
12:6	350
12:7–13	347
12:7	350
12:11	323
12:15–20	199
12:21–27	200, 347
12:24	350
12:48–49	311
13:4	131
13:6–7	199
13:8	131
13:17–18	130
13:21	130
14	147
14:1—15:22	154
14:1–31	130
14:2	147
14:8	131
14:9	147
14:12	199
14:22–25	200
14:22	154
14:27	154
14:28–30	154, 157
14:28	154
14:31	154
15:1–18	150
15:1	147
15:2	154
15:4–5	157
15:4	154
15:6	154, 343, 364
15:8	157
15:10	157
15:12	343, 364
15:13	154, 347

455

Exodus (continued)

15:14–15	154
15:16	347
15:17	325
15:19	154, 157
15:21	147
16	147
16:9	365
16:35	130
17:2	285
17:9–10	162
19	147
19:1–5	378
19:3	275
19:4	328
19:5–6	320, 324
19:5	293, 294, 324, 378
19:6	306, 376, 377, 378
20:10	311
20:20	130
21:30	322
22:20	311
22:21	311
23	128
23:9	311
23:12	311
23:20	128, 145, 183
23:20a	128
23:20b	128
23:24	129
24	147, 323, 388
24:1–8	306, 320, 349, 369
24:1–2	376
24:2–8	323
24:6	349
24:7	323, 349
24:8	201, 323, 349
24:15–17	172
24:16–17	336
24:17	173
26:31–35	186
29:4	356
28:8	
29:21	349
30:12–16	322
33:18–23	336
34:5–8	336
40:12	356
40:17	131
43:20	378

Leviticus

1:2	356
3:12	356
4:4	356
4:5	163
4:7	202
4:16	163
4:18	202
4:25	202
4:30	202
4:34	202
5:5–11	355
6:5	163
6:18	355
6:23	355
8:3	349
8:14	356
8:15	202
9:5	365
9:7–8	365
9:9	202
11:1–47	285
11:44–45	333, 334, 369, 388
14:1–7	349
14:2–9	189
14:19	355
16:3	355
16:5	355
16:29–34	189
17:7	307
18:3	334, 388
19:2	333, 369, 388
19:3	331
19:18	230
20:7	388
20:26	334, 388
21:17–18	365
21:21	365
21:23	365
25	322
25:23	311, 320, 376
26:1	223
26:30	223
27	322

Numbers

3:44–51	322
8:9–10	356
11:29	290, 291
14:33–34	147, 352
18:3–4	365
18:22	365

22:15	344
24:16	172
27:17	183, 224
27:18	183
32:13	147

Deuteronomy

2:7	130
3:18	221
3:24	337
4:34	337
4:37	376
5:27	365
6:4–5	230
6:16	285
7:7	324
8:2	130, 147
8:10	183
9:29	325
10:19	311
11:10	131
14:2	294
15:4	320, 376
16:1–8	199
16:3	200
18:13	388
18:15	172, 186, 274
18:15–20	258, 298
18:18–19	172, 186, 274
18:19	258, 294
21:23	263, 352
23:5	131
24:15–17	172
25:5–10	160
26:5–9	200
28:15–24	152
29:17–18	251
32:5	284, 286
32:17	155
32:18	172
32:21b	325

Joshua

2:10	131
3	130
3:12	261
7:1–26	285

Judges

18:31	371

1 Samuel

2:21	333
21:1–7	177

2 Samuel

7	169
7:12–17	163
7:12–16	266
7:12–13	169
7:12	144
7:13	267
7:14	131, 133, 169, 170, 171, 173, 232, 408
7:16	169
12:20	371
22:14	172
22:32	329
22:33–51	329
22:51	169
23:1	169
23:2	370

1 Kings

1:38–40	143
2:19	343, 364
5:5	371
8:10–11	143
19:1–18	165
22:17	346, 382

2 Kings

1:8	130
9:13	143

2 Chronicles

11:15	207
16:14	207
18:16	346, 382

Ezra

3:1	175
6:20	200
7:10	185

Nehemiah

1:10	347

Job

9:31	386
10:12	333
11:15	386
14:4	386
20:29	346
30:21	337

Psalm

2	169, 170
2:1–11	282
2:2	169, 289
2:6	169
2:7	169, 171, 173
3:22–23	298
9:14	378
16:5	320
16:8–11	257, 267, 298
16:8–10	291
16:10	267
17:7	343, 364
20:6	343, 364
21:8	343, 364
22	198
22:1	197
22:4–5	198
22:7	197
22:18	204
22:22–23	221
23:1	345
24:5	287
25:5	287
33:6	344
33:9	342
34	392
34:9	364
34:5	344
34:15	328
39:12	311
41	178
45:9	343, 364
63:8	343, 364
68:18	291
68:5	256
69	178, 256
69:21	256
69:22–23	256
69:25	255
69:4	256
69:9	256
77:20	345
78:4	378
78:8	284, 286
78:18	285
78:37	284
78:71	345
79:9	287
79:13	345, 378
95:9	285
105:6	376
107:17–20	152
107:23–32	157
107:29	157
109	256
109:1	342
109:8	255, 256
110	178
110:1	165, 167, 174, 117, 181, 182, 251, 257, 267, 269, 270, 287, 291, 298, 342, 360, 364
110:1–2	282
113–118	200
118	188, 258, 276
118:2	404
118:15	364
118:10–12	189
118:15	343
118:22–23	181, 187, 188, 198, 206, 223, 343, 409
118:22	143, 179, 188, 251, 258, 275, 276, 298, 323, 324, 343, 344, 409
118:23–28	188
118:25–26	143, 165, 188, 323
118:25	181
118:26a	143
118:26b	143, 323
119:19	311
132:11	267
147:2	307

Proverbs

11:31	331, 332
17:3	387
24:21	313, 395
27:21	387
29:23	393

Isaiah

1:3	293
2:2	298
2:2–4	381
2:18	223
2:20	307
4:4	386
5:1–7	223
6:5	237
6:8–13	237
6:9–10	193
8:13	182, 342, 364, 364, 409
8:14	188, 343, 404, 409
9:2	379
9:6–7	144
9:7	266
10:3	333
10:12	331
11:1	144, 372
12:2	287
13:6	298
13:9	298
14:14	172
17:10	287
19:23	388
22:18	345
23:17	333
25:6–9	183
28:16	188, 323, 343, 358, 404, 409
29:18–19	152
29:23	364
32:1–4	152
32:15	249, 290
35:1–10	152
35:1	147
35:2	147
35:5–6	147
35:6	147
35:8–10	147
35:8	147
40:1–11	249
40:3–5	248
40:3	129, 130, 145, 146, 180, 284
40:3b	129
40:5	272
40:6	326
40:8–9	326
40:8	326, 342
40:9–10	134
40:9	134, 149
40:11	183, 224, 345
40:12–31	251, 325
40:31	183
40–55	129, 248, 406
41:1–10	251, 325
41:8–9	326
41:14	203
42	170
42:1	131, 170, 171, 411
42:4	184, 185
42:6–7	152
42:6	271
42:10–12	251, 325
42:10	272
42:12	272, 324
42:16–17	152
42:16	379
42:21	184
43	378
43:1–7	142, 325
43:1	203, 377
43:9–12	271
43:11	287
43:14	203
43:15–19	147
43:15	164
43:16–17	130
43:16	147
43:19–20	130
43:19	147
43:20–21	306, 320, 376
43:21	324, 357, 378
44:6	164
44:9–20	251, 325
44:22–24	203
44:23	272
45:13	203
45:15	287
45:20–21	287
45:21	287
45:22–23	251, 325
46:1–13	251, 325
49:3	262, 271, 272, 352
49:5	271
49:6–7	203
49:6	249, 251, 271, 273, 325
49:8	271, 273
46:13	163, 343
48:17	184
48:21	130
49:18–21	220
49:24–26	153
50	180
50:4–9	179
50:4	184
50:6	179
51:1–2	326

Isaiah (continued)

51:4–5	152, 251, 325
51:4	184, 185
51:7	184
51:11	203
52–53	180, 351
52:3	203, 348, 351
52:4	293, 351
52:7	134, 149, 150, 164, 282, 289, 326
52:8	143
52:10	203
52:13—53:12	179, 271, 282, 289
52:13	262, 271, 272, 352
52:14–15	203
52:14	215
52:15	203
53	83, 203, 271, 272, 323
53:3	197, 215, 353
53:4–12	323
53:4–6	271, 152
53:4–5	198
53:4	352, 353
53:5	353, 354
53:6	179, 180, 272, 288, 346, 354
53:7–8	347
53:7	204, 341, 348, 351, 410
53:8	198, 215, 293
53:9	352
53:10–12	203, 271
53:10–11	355
53:10	203
53:11–12	160, 202, 262, 409, 352
53:11	204, 271, 273
53:12	152, 179, 180 ,202, 272, 288, 352, 404
54:4–8	142, 325
55:3–4	273
55:5	251, 325
55:12–13	248
56:1–8	325
56:1–5	143
56:7	141, 187, 188, 224, 371
57:17–18	152
57:18	152
57:19	251, 257, 260, 282, 289, 324
58:10	379
58:14	325
59:21	370
60:3	203
60:4	220
60:6	134
61:1	153, 170, 262, 265, 289, 370
61:1–7	164
61:1–3	134
61:1–2	149
61:8	271
62:11	287
62:12	203
63:11—64:1	131
63:11	224
65:3–4	155
65:11	155
65:17	257
66	129
66:1–7	154
66:11	154
66:18	251
66:18–21	143, 325
66:22	257

Jeremiah

2:5	307
2:8	345
3:15	345
6:15	333
7:11	187
8:19	307
10:5	333
10:21	345
13:18	345
20:22	379
23:5–6	266
24:7	379
25:29	331
29:7	391
30:9	144
31:31–34	131, 201, 260, 288, 293, 350, 369, 379
31:34	208
32:37–40	379
50:6	346, 382

Ezekiel

9:6	331
11:19–20	379
13:5	298
14:10–11	379
18:20	352
20:34–35	337
20:41	364, 388
26:22–28	369
30:3	298
34	345

34:5–6	346, 382	2:11	298
34:12	345	2:21–32	298
34:23–24	144	2:28	257, 297
34:23	345	2:28–38a	290
36:25–27	131	2:28–32	256
36:26–27	288, 290	2:31–32	270
36:33–36	131	2:32a	260
37:14	290	2:32b	260
37:24	345	3:14	298
		3:18	298

Daniel

Amos

2:28	298		
2:44	134	5:18	298
3:26	172	5:20	298
5:10–11	153	9:11–12	238
7	176, 178, 179, 180, 192		
7:10	177		

Obadiah

7:13	167, 175, 177
7:13–14	167, 175, 176, 178, 189, 408
7:14	177, 178, 179, 202, 232

15–21	298

Jonah

7:23–25	197		
7:26	177	1:6	156
12:13	320, 325, 376	1:14	156
		3:9	156

Hosea

Micah

1:2	161		
1:6	306, 324, 379	5:1–3	345
1:9–10	379		

Zephaniah

1:9	306, 324		
1:10	207	1:7	298
2:1	324	1:14	298
2:3	324		

Zechariah

2:23	376, 379		
2:25	306, 324	1:14	298
3:5	298	2:11	294
4:17	379	9:9	148
6:1–2	200	9:11	201
6:1	206	10:2	346, 382
6:2	206	10:3	224
8:4	379	13:4	130
9:3	325	13:7–9	331
10:5–6	379	13:7	184, 196, 224
11:2	379	13:7a	184
13:2	379	13:7b	184
14:8	379	14:1–21	298

Joel

1:15	298
2	277
2:1	298

Malachi

1:2	130
2:10	129
2:17—3:5	129
3	128
3:1	128, 130, 145
3:1b	128, 146
3:1–6	331
3:2	128
3:6–12	128
3:11	129
3:22–23	299
4:4–5	173
4:5	130, 298
4:5–6	165

NEW TESTAMENT

Matthew

1–2	161
1:20–23	262
1:21	162
3:3	145
3:7–10	165
4:18	301
5–7	226
5:9	393
5:10–16	80
5:10	80, 392
5:11–12	313
5:16	390
5:16a	80
5:16b	80
5:38–41	314
5:48	388
6:9	330, 364, 379, 388
6:10	196
6:11	221
8:14–17	353
9:12	380
10:2	301
10:19–20	372
10:20	380
10:32–32	215
11:29	393
12:4	371
13:35	329
14:28–31	34
15:24	382, 346
16:7	408
16:16	169
16:17–19	34
16:17	195, 341
16:17b	165
16:18	220, 224, 345, 409
16:22	270
17:1–5	96
17:24–27	34
18:4	393
18:23	393
19:4	329
19:29	398
20:28	203
21:13	371
21:25	371
23:37–39	142
23:29–36	165
25:34	319, 329
26:28	349, 350
26:41	398
26:63	169
27:19	347
27:24	347
28:7	105
28:10	105
28:19	368, 369

Mark

1	207
1:1–15	126
1:1–3	164
1:1–4	270
1:1	126, 133, 134, 160, 161, 163, 169, 180, 195, 209, 340, 408
1:2–14	161
1:2–11	290
1:2–8	165
1:2–3	128, 130, 183
1:3	129, 130, 180
1:3c	130
1:4–8	191
1:4	130, 131, 228
1:5	130
1:6	130
1:7–8	187, 289
1:7	131, 153, 180
1:8	130, 291, 368
1:9–11	262, 289
1:9–10	130
1:9	130, 162, 265
1:10–11	411
1:10	131, 170, 187
1:11	131, 133, 134, 148, 150, 166, 169, 170, 171, 172, 173, 187, 194, 195

1:12–13	130, 147, 148, 153, 154	2:9	231
1:14–20	216	2:10	141, 175, 177, 231, 287
1:14–15	122, 134, 139, 148, 154, 185, 191, 209, 212, 228	2:11	213
		2:13	143, 151, 185, 225
1:14	116, 141, 146, 149, 161, 179, 185	2:13–14	122, 147, 221
		2:14–17	211
1:15	126, 140, 141, 149, 151, 156, 163, 176, 213, 214, 255, 228, 371	2:14	212
		2:15–17	221
		2:15	212
1:15a	150	2:16	119, 123
1:16—14:72	105	2:18	123
1:16—8:21	146	2:23—3:6	186
1:16–21	265	2:23–28	229
1:16–20	122, 147, 209, 214, 225, 221, 228, 230, 405	2:24	123
		2:25–26	177, 182
1:16–18	42, 216	2:26	224, 371
1:16–17	105	2:27	177
1:16	41	2:28	146, 175, 177, 182
1:17–18	212	3:1–6	151, 191
1:17	212	3:4	194
1:18	212	3:6	119, 123, 156, 199
1:20	212	3:7–12	147, 172, 191
1:21—2:12	262	3:7–8	119, 212, 213
1:21–28	151, 153	3:7	325
1:21–26	191	3:8	146
1:21–22	185, 186, 225	3:9	151, 225
1:21	41, 119, 185	3:10	146
1:22	141, 185, 186	3:11–12	151
1:24	153, 154, 162, 208, 265	3:11	141, 169
1:25	151, 194	3:12	151
1:27	141, 165, 185	3:13–19	122, 210
1:29–31	105, 151, 159, 221	3:13–19a	212, 220
1:29	41	3:13	147
1:30	304	3:14–15	210, 411
1:32–34	191	3:14	185
1:34	151	3:15	141
1:35–37	191	3:16	35, 301
1:36	105	3:17	35, 111, 119
1:37–39	192	3:19	123, 179
1:38–39	185	3:19a	220
1:39	141, 151	3:19b–27	222
1:40–45	151, 189, 191, 214	3:20	151
1:43–45	191	3:21	123, 220
1:44	119, 213	3:22–27	153, 154
1:45	185, 192	3:22	123, 141
1:46	162	3:27	153
2:1–12	147, 151, 152, 189, 191, 221, 354	3:28	231
		3:30	123
2:1–11	191	3:31–35	213, 220, 221
2:2	143	3:31	213, 220
2:4	151	3:32	151, 220
2:5	214, 231	4–7	143
2:7–8	123	4:1–34	185
2:7	165, 231, 287	4:1–2	185, 225

463

Mark (continued)

4:1	143, 147, 151, 225
4:2	185
4:3	185
4:5–6	223
4:9	185
4:10–12	191, 193, 220
4:10	212
4:11–12	185, 217
4:11	185, 223, 225
4:12	231, 354
4:13–20	225
4:13	185, 217
4:15–20	122, 210
4:15–16	185
4:16	151
4:17	123, 184
4:18	185
4:20	185
4:23–25	185
4:26–32	150
4:33–34	185, 191
4:34	185, 217
4:35—5:1	147
4:35–41	156, 157, 225
4:36	151
4:37	141
4:38–39	194
4:38	156, 185, 194
4:39	141, 156, 217
4:40–41	217
4:41	141, 156, 165
5:1–20	154
5:1–13	151
5:1	154
5:2–3	159
5:3–4	154, 155
5:5	155
5:6	155
5:7	154, 155, 162, 169, 172
5:9	155
5:11–13	155
5:12–13	141
5:13	154, 155, 157
5:14–20	191
5:15	154, 155
5:16	155
5:17	123, 154
5:18–19	213
5:19	154, 182, 213
5:20	123, 155
5:21–24	157, 206, 283
5:21	143, 151
5:23	158, 194
5:24	151
5:24b–34	212
5:25–34	151, 213
5:26	157, 159
5:27	151
5:28	194
5:29	353
5:30–31	212
5:30	151
5:31	151
5:34	194, 213, 214
5:35–43	157, 191, 206, 221, 283
5:35	158, 185
5:36	214
5:41	111, 157, 158
6:1–13	191
6:1–6	213
6:1	212
6:2	165, 185, 186, 225
6:3	123
6:4	165, 213
6:6	185, 225
6:6b–13	186, 210, 221
6:7–13	122
6:7	141, 151, 210, 411
6:10–11	153
6:11	123
6:12	185
6:13	141, 151
6:14–16	165, 199
6:14	119, 158, 166, 206
6:15	213
6:16	158, 166, 206
6:17–29	123, 165, 199
6:19	180
6:22–23	204
6:24	224
6:27	204
6:30–34	183, 192
6:30–32	191
6:30	122, 143, 185, 186, 210, 225, 226
6:31–34	191
6:31–32	183
6:31	147, 192
6:32	147
6:34	143, 151, 183, 185, 225, 345, 410
6:35–44	157
6:35–37	217
6:35	147, 183
6:37–44	183
6:42	183

6:45–52	147, 157, 225	8:27—10:45	146
6:45–46	191	8:27–33	267
6:45	151	8:27–30	146, 164, 191, 214, 216
6:46	147	8:27	146, 164, 165, 172, 212
6:47–52	156, 219	8:28	164, 165, 166, 172
6:48	141	8:29	162, 163, 164, 165, 173, 176,
6:51–52	217		195, 214, 232, 266, 408
6:51	141	8:29b	408
6:52	218, 225	8:30	166, 167, 195
6:53–56	151, 191	8:31–35	230
6:56	194	8:31–33	166, 167, 172, 173, 192, 214,
6:82	183		216, 225, 257
7:1–23	186, 189, 229	8:31—9:1	123
7:1–8	123	8:31	175, 176, 178, 179, 185, 195,
7:1–4	119		196, 198, 199, 205, 206, 223,
7:1	143		228, 408
7:3–4	106	8:32–33	165, 215
7:3	44	8:32	199, 217, 270, 408
7:6–7	185	8:34—9:1	214, 228, 73, 151
7:9	177	8:34–38	124
7:11	106, 111, 119	8:34	212, 216, 389
7:14–19	217	8:35	141, 149, 194, 195, 215, 230,
7:14–15	123		285
7:14	177	8:38	169, 175, 179, 215, 230, 329,
7:17–23	191, 222, 225		358
7:17	185	9:1–8	198
7:19	106	9:1	173
7:24–30	151, 192, 213, 221	9:2–10	191
7:24–25	191	9:2–9	147
7:24	191	9:2–8	150, 151, 191
7:26	44, 113	9:2–7	96
7:28	180, 181, 182	9:2	165, 172
7:29–30	213	9:3–4	171
7:31–37	147, 151, 191	9:3	172
7:31	147	9:5	172, 173, 185
7:33	191, 192	9:5–6	217
7:34	111, 119	9:5–7	165
7:36–37	191	9:7	147, 150, 166, 169, 171, 172,
7:37	186		173, 186, 187, 194, 195, 410,
8:1–10	191	9:9–10	207, 217
8:1–9	157	9:9	175, 179
8:4	147, 217	9:11–13	173
8:11–13	191	9:12	123, 175, 178, 179, 196,
8:14–21	147, 225		197, 257, 270
8:17–18	164	9:13	165
8:21	164	9:14–29	151, 159
8:17–21	217, 218	9:17	185
8:22—11:1	147	9:22	156, 194
8:22–26	147, 151, 164, 165, 185, 191,	9:23–24	214
	232, 408	9:25	194
8:22	146, 164	9:28–29	191, 222
8:23	164, 191, 192	9:30–50	191
8:24–25	164	9:30–32	192, 225
8:26	146	9:30	191

Mark (*continued*)

9:31-32	217
9:31	123, 175, 178, 179, 185, 199, 206, 223
9:33-37	222, 228
9:33-34	146
9:33	212
9:37-41	277
9:37	380
9:38-41	122, 210
9:38	151, 185, 210, 411
9:41	162
9:42	147, 214
9:43	111, 151
9:45	151, 228
9:47	151, 228
10	80
10:1-12	186
10:1	143, 185, 191, 212, 225
10:2-9	229
10:6	161
10:10-12	222, 225
10:10	212, 213
10:13-16	229
10:13	213
10:15	151
10:17-22	228, 229
10:17	146, 140, 185, 398
10:20	185
10:21	212, 213, 389
10:23-28	221
10:23-27	151, 228
10:23-24	213
10:24	202
10:26	195
10:28-40	123
10:28-31	221
10:28	212, 389
10:29-30	220, 221
10:29	141, 149
10:30	123, 140, 184
10:32-37	217
10:32-33	146
10:32	41, 146, 212, 213, 216, 389
10:33-34	197
10:33	175, 179
10:34	147, 179, 199, 206, 223
10:35-40	228
10:35	185
10:37	140
10:38	353
10:41-45	229
10:42-45	80, 215
10:42-44	202
10:42-43	164
10:42	80
10:44	202
10:45	2, 80, 141, 146, 175, 179, 180, 196, 202, 203, 204, 229, 270, 272, 351, 380
10:46—12:37	112
10:46—11:19	160
10:46-52	146, 147, 151, 166, 185, 191
10:46-48	144
10:46	111, 146, 147, 164
10:47-48	144, 150
10:47	162, 166, 208
10:51	213
10:52	146, 147, 164, 194, 212, 214, 389
11:1—16:8	146
11:1-11	144, 147, 192, 206
11:1-10	163, 166, 191
11:1	146, 212
11:2-7	323
11:2	143, 147, 213
11:3	146, 181, 182
11:7-10	212
11:7	143
11:8-9	212
11:8	143, 164
11:9-11	147
11:9-10	143, 145, 150, 164, 188, 276, 323
11:9	166, 181, 389
11:9a	143
11:10	141
11:10a	143
11:10b	143
11:11	144, 188, 222
11:12-14	147, 157, 186
11:12	41
11:13	141
11:15-19	148, 186, 189, 222
11:15	187
11:17	112, 141, 143, 185, 187, 224, 225
11:18	156, 185, 186, 199
11:20-25	157
11:20-21	147
11:21	185
11:23-24	214
11:25	231
11:27—12:34	222
11:27-33	147, 160, 187, 189, 191, 213, 223
11:27	41, 187, 258, 275

11:28	141, 165	13:5–8	139, 140
11:29	141	13:6	277
11:31	214	13:8	161, 178
11:33	141	13:9–27	123
12:1–12	160, 187, 223, 275	13:9–13	141, 229
12:1–2	198	13:9–11	210, 411
12:1	187	13:10–11	210
12:2–3	187	13:10	122, 141, 143, 149, 185
12:4–5	187	13:11	372, 411
12:5	179, 199	13:12–13	214, 221
12:6–8	187	13:13	195, 277, 285
12:6–7	174	13:14–19	113
12:6	169, 187, 194, 198	13:14	106, 112, 225
12:7–8	179	13:19	161
12:7	187, 199	13:20	182
12:8	199	13:21	162
12:9	156, 180, 181, 187	13:24–37	229
12:10–12	206	13:24–27	139, 140, 151
12:10–11	181, 187, 223, 275, 343, 404, , 409	13:24–25	178
		13:26–27	208, 211, 229
12:10	179, 201, 223, 258, 323	13:26	173, 175, 179, 181, 208
12:12	160, 187, 189	13:27	116, 143
12:13–17	160	13:30–31	140
12:14–17	132	13:31	186
12:14	185, 225	13:32–37	151, 222, 229
12:18–37	186	13:32	169, 329
12:18–27	159, 206	13:35	180, 181
12:18	119	14:1—15:47	123
12:19	185	14:1—15:1	198
12:21	185	14	43
12:27	206	14:1–2	199, 216
12:34	151, 230	14:1	119, 179, 199, 200
12:28–34	160, 230	14:2	196
12:29–30	181	14:3–9	213, 221
12:35–37	144, 150, 160, 166, 173, 177, 267, 269, 360, 408	14:9	122, 141, 210
		14:10–11	179, 216
12:35–44	222	14:12–26	222
12:35	162, 163, 185, 187, 225	14:12–16	409
12:36–37	146, 182	14:12	199
12:36	181, 342, 364, 409, 411	14:14	185, 199
12:37	182	14:16	199
12:38	185	14:17–21	184, 200, 216
12:41–4	213	14:18	179
12:41	187	14:21	175, 178, 179, 196
12:42	110	14:22–25	151, 183, 192, 350, 409
13	112, 116, 135, 140, 175, 415	14:22	200
13:1–37	185, 222, 225	14:24	196, 201, 208, 270
13:1–2	142, 186	14:25	141
13:1	185, 187	14:26–31	183, 216, 410
13:2	223	14:26–28	224
13:3–37	191	14:26	330
13:3–23	178	14:27–31	213
13:3–4	139	14:27	143, 216, 345
13:3	165	14:28	158, 184, 207, 216

467

Mark (continued)

14:30	216
14:31	216
14:32–42	217, 230
14:32	41
14:33–34	165
14:34	203
14:36–39	214
14:36	111, 169, 184, 196, 230, 329
14:38	398
14:41–42	179
14:41	175, 178
14:43–15:37	197
14:43–46	216
14:44	179
14:45	185
14:47	204
14:49	140, 151, 185, 186, 196, 225
14:50	207, 216, 230
14:53—15:39	206
14:53–65	164, 191
14:53–60	167
14:55–59	177
14:61–62	191, 192
14:61a	167
14:61b	167
14:66–72	165, 207, 216, 230
14:63–64	167
14–20	142
14:58	222, 223
14:61	162, 163, 166, 167, 169, 174, 177, 271
14:62	175, 177, 179, 205, 267
14:65	165, 179
14:67	162, 208
14:72	207, 216, 230
15:1–15	204
15:1–10	164
15:1–5	191
15:1	119, 179
15:2	167, 134, 192
15:5	169
15:6–15	199, 273, 274
15:6	199, 204
15:7	230
15:8–9	204
15:9	134, 167
15:10	168, 179, 198
15:11	198
15:12	141, 167, 204
15:11–14	168
15:13–15	204
15:12	134
15:15–25	179
15:15	168, 179
15:16–20	144, 168, 204
15:16	112
15:18	134, 141, 167
15:21	115, 119
15:22	111
15:24	204
15:25–32	230
15:26	134, 141, 164, 167, 192
15:27	271
15:29–30	179, 223
15:29	186, 204, 222
15:30–31	195, 204
15:31–32	167
15:32	134, 141, 162, 163, 163, 164, 166, 167, 204, 214
15:33	171
15:34	111, 197
15:35–36	173
15:36	256
15:37–39	186
15:38	171, 186, 204
15:39	116, 133, 147, 150, 169, 174, 192, 194, 195, 213, 408
15:40–41	43
15:40	119, 207, 213
15:41	212, 389
15:42–47	207
15:42	112, 119
15:43–46	201
15:43	135, 141, 150
15:47—16:1	207
15:47	43, 119, 213
16:1	43, 119, 194
16:4–7	43
16:5–7	208
16:6–7	144, 194, 207
16:6	140, 158, 159, 162, 195, 206
16:7	42, 105, 165, 184, 207, 208, 216, 224
16:8	207, 208
16:9	141
16:15	141
16:16	141
16:17	141
16:19	162, 182
16:20	182

Luke

1–2	161
1:1–4	31, 60, 247
1:1	62, 66

1:2	29, 61, 62	4:9	280
1:3	62, 68, 70	6:5–15	183
1:16	346, 382	6:15	200
1:30–35	262	6:38	380
1:47	287	6:69	153
1:69	285	7:15	89
1:71	285	7:35	307
3:4–6	145	8:32	347
3:7–9	165	10:11	345
4:16–21	153	11:27	169
4:16	106	12:20–21	88
4:18–19	289	12:41	339
4:18	262, 265, 289	12:44	380
4:41	169	14:26	371
5:1–11	405	15:25	256
5:10b	237	15:26–27	95
5:5	237	15:26	370, 371
6:4	371	17:1	357
6:20–49	226	17:5	174
6:28	393	17:24	319, 329
6:32–33	397	20:21	169
7:2	344	20:26–29	338
8:25	237	21:15–17	240, 241, 418
8:40–42	283	21:18–19	96
8:49–56	283	21:19	357
9:23	215	21:25	82
9:26	358		
9:28–35	96		
24:5–9	105	## Acts	
24:26	366	1:1	60, 263
24:37–43	338	1:2	261
24:46–49	371	1:3	70
24:47	254	1:4–5	291, 371
24:48	95	1:5	290, 293, 368
24:50–51	393	1:6–8	291
		1:6	249, 257, 348
## John		1:8	95, 178, 247, 249, 250, 254, 280, 371
1:1–2	339	1:9–11	208, 267
1:1	161	1:10	360
1:14–18	262	1:11–12	239
1:14	174, 339	1:11	268, 271, 298
1:19–28	166	1:12–14	238
1:23	145	1:13–17	263
1:29	347	1:14–16	295
1:33	368	1:14	283
1:36	347	1:15–26	238
1:42	409	1:15–22	46, 234, 250, 264
2:3	296	1:16	250, 255, 256, 263, 264, 267, 291, 295, 370, 411
2:16–17	371	1:17	256
2:17	256	1:18–19	256
2:18	298	1:18	284, 299
3:3–8	359, 380	1:19	263
3:16	379		

Acts (continued)

1:20	255, 260
1:21–22	255, 264
1:21	256, 263, 269, 270, 271
1:22	95, 256, 263, 264, 267, 290
1:24	270, 297
1:25	264
1:27	261
2–5	248
2:1–10	263
2:1–4	256, 285, 291, 292
2:4	297
2:5–13	250
2:9–11	254
2:11	237, 285
2:14	239, 250
2:14–41	238
2:14–40	254
2:14–36	46, 234
2:14–21	250
2:16–21	256
2:16–17	254
2:16	255, 274, 290
2:17	257, 283, 285, 289, 297, 371
2:17–18	257, 283
2:17a	252
2:17b–18	290, 411
2:18	284
2:20–21	270
2:20	257, 269, 270, 286, 298
2:21	252, 257, 260, 269, 270, 277, 282, 284, 285, 286, 289
2:22	263, 265
2:22b	265
2:23–24	263
2:23	259, 260, 263, 266, 319
2:23b	260
2:24	259, 260, 263, 267
2:25	269
2:25–36	250, 298
2:25–31	257
2:25–28	267
2:26–31	264
2:26–28	264
2:29–30	265
2:29	295
2:30	264, 267
2:31	266, 267
2:31–36	291
2:32	95, 238, 257, 263, 264, 267
2:32–36	251
2:32–35	208, 360
2:32–33	337
2:33–35	264
2:33	268, 275, 291, 371, 411
2:34–36	257, 269, 270
2:34–35	257, 267, 276, 287, 342, 409
2:34	364
2:35–35	267
2:36	249, 250, 263, 266, 268, 269, 276, 277
2:37–42	249
2:37	295
2:38–40	46, 234
2:38–39	250, 283, 412
2:38	250, 260, 266, 270, 277, 278, 279, 284, 286, 287, 288, 292, 293, 295, 297, 369, 380, 411
2:39	250, 251, 254, 257, 260, 279, 282, 283, 412
2:40	284, 285, 286
2:41	278, 288, 295
2:42	240, 292
2:47	285
3:1	295, 297
3:6	265, 266, 277, 348
3:7	295
3:11	270
3:1–10	238, 239, 270, 286
3:11–26	46, 234, 238
3:11–12	270
3:13–15	263, 274, 337
3:13	244, 261, 262, 263, 264, 270, 271, 272, 273, 287, 288, 352, 261
3:14	153, 270, 271, 273, 347, 410
3:15	95, 262, 263, 267, 271, 274, 276
3:15	261
3:16	270, 277, 287
3:17–18	266
3:17	263, 288
3:18	197, 257, 263, 266, 268, 269, 271, 273
3:19–21	244
3:19–20	250, 417
3:19	268, 271, 272, 274, 279, 285, 288, 354
3:20–21	268, 264, 273, 298, 299
3:20	257, 258, 262, 266, 268, 274, 288, 298, 341
3:20b–21	261
3:21	256, 257, 271, 273, 298
3:22–26	294
3:22–23	258, 270, 274, 410
3:22	274
3:23	274, 294, 299
3:23b	258

3:24–25	271, 273	5:27	276
3:24	255, 258, 274, 370	5:29–32	46, 234
3:25	252, 271, 273, 274, 294	5:28–29	296
3:26	244, 263, 271, 272, 273, 274, 279, 284, 288, 293	5:30	261, 263, 267, 352
3:28	274	5:31	262, 264, 267, 274, 276, 279, 285, 287
3:36	267	5:31	261
4:1–7	258	5:32	95, 255, 267, 290, 371, 411
4:1–4	239	5:32b	296
4:2	264	5:36–37	64
4:4	295	5:36	132
4:5–17	238	5:41	313
4:5–7	275, 286	6:13–16	237
4:6	258	6:14	265
4:8	290, 293, 297	7:2	295
4:8–12	46, 234	7:35–44	274
4:8–10a	286	7:35	322
4:9–10	287	7:36	130, 147
4:10	263, 265, 266, 267, 275, 276, 293	7:42	347
		7:48	223
4:10–11	206, 263	7:55	372
4:10b–11	286	7:56	174
4:11–12	251, 404	8:4–10	249
4:11	188, 258, 275, 323, 344, 409	8:4–5	291
4:12	256, 258, 276, 277, 285, 286, 287, 296	8:5	363
		8:9–25	238
4:13–22	275	8:10	251
4:13	239, 327, 417	8:14–25	249
4:15	275	8:14–24	239
4:18	277	8:14–17	249, 280
4:19	296	8:14	239
4:19–20	46, 234	8:15	291
4:20	249, 255	8:16	291
4:22	123	8:17	292
4:23–31	297	8:18–19	292
4:23–24	251	8:20	292, 299
4:24–30	251	8:21–23	292
4:25	250, 267	8:21	284
4:26	289	8:22	279, 284, 297
4:27	153, 244, 262, 273	8:23	251, 284
4:30	153, 244	8:25	239, 280
5:1–11	237, 239, 285	8:26–15	271
5:3–9	238	8:28–35	83
5:3	285 287	8:28	106
5:4	285 380	8:32–35	370
5:6–7	237	8:32–33	347
5:7	283	8:45	237
5:8	237	8:49–56	237
5:9	256, 283, 285, 287	9:1–30	239
5:12–16	239	9:16	313
5:15	287	9:20	237, 363
5:17–42	239	9:28–36	237
5:20	274	9:32—11:18	248
5:21b	276	9:34	265, 266, 287

471

Acts (continued)

9:35	346, 382
9:36–43	158
9:40	158, 283, 287
9:42	283
9:43	283
10–11	12
10	178, 257, 273, 295, 414
10:1–48	238
10:1–18	249
10:2	119, 297
10:9–23	254
10:9–16	282, 291, 297
10:9	297
10:14–15	281
10:14	269, 285
10:19–45	412
10:19–20	291
10:22	119
10:23	279, 281
10:24	283, 284
10:27–29	46, 234
10:28	267, 281, 285
10:29	279
10:30	296
10:34–43	46, 234, 243, 407
10:34–35	252
10:34	249, 281
10:35	251, 282, 296
10:36–43	239
10:36–37	263, 289
10:36	251, 266, 268, 270, 279, 281, 282, 288
10:37–39	263
10:37	145, 263, 289, 290
10:38	262, 263, 265, 266, 276, 287, 288, 289, 291, 411, 412
10:38b	261
10:39–43	96, 255
10:39	263, 267, 352
10:40–42	293
10:40–41	264, 267
10:40	262, 263
10:41	263, 267
10:42	299, 331, 366
10:43	277, 283, 287, 288, 291, 296
10:43–48	278
10:44	281
10:44–48	282, 288
10:44–47	292
10:44–46	292
10:45	292
10:47–48	292
10:47	46, 234, 278, 283, 293, 412
10:48	266, 279
11:1	281, 283, 295
11:1–18	238
11:4–17	46, 234
11:5–9	291
11:8–9	281
11:8	269, 285
11:12	252, 279, 281, 291
11:13–14	287
11:13	291
11:14	285
11:15–18	281
11:15–17	288, 290
11:16–17	291
11:16	269, 288, 290, 293, 368
11:17–18	292
11:17	261, 266, 269, 278, 292, 293
11:18	252, 261, 274, 279
11:21	346, 382
11:26	295382
11:29	295
11:50	297
12:1–17	254
12:1–5	239
12:6–19	239
12:11	287
12:12	237
12:17	239, 269, 278, 295
12:36	268
12:41	237
13:14	306, 308
13:15	295
13:16	119, 306
13:21	147
13:23	287
13:26	119, 306, 377
13:29	263
13:43	306
13:46–38	306
13:47	254
13:52	295
14:1	306, 308
14:8–18	251
14:14–18	251
14:15	307, 346, 382
14:22	123
14:23	302
14:27	306
15	76, 79, 254, 414
15:1	280, 285
15:6–11	8, 238, 239, 280
16:6–7	370
15:7–11	46, 234, 294, 295

15:7	238, 261, 278, 279, 282, 295
15:8–9	252, 281, 292
15:8	293
15:9	278, 279, 293
15:10	285, 295
15:11	252, 252, 278, 282, 285, 287
15:13–14	239, 295
15:13	295
15:14–17	238
15:14	252, 277, 279, 282, 294, 295
15:15	251, 252
15:19	346, 382
15:21	106
15:22	74
15:27	74
15:32	74
15:40	74
16:17	172
16:19	74
16:25	74
16:29	74
16:30–31	285
16:37–38	74
17	50
17:2–3	370
17:4	74
17:6	123
17:10	74
17:14	74
17:15	74
17:22–31	251
17:24	379
17:25–28	379
17:26–29	297
17:31	299
18:1–2	310
18:2	123
19:3–4	289
18:5	74
19:8	306, 308
18:26	306
18:28	237
19:10	285
19:11–17	154
19:13	363
20:17	302
20:28	302, 346
20:35	81
21:37	89
21:38	132, 142
23:7–8	159
22:8	237, 265
22:14	261, 347
22:16	380
22:21	260
24	188, 276
26:6–7	256
26:9	265
26:16	261
26:20	346, 382
26:26	199, 289
26:28	382
27	156
28:25	370
28:31	363

Romans

1:3–4	338
1:5	296
1:16	293, 358
1:19–20	297
1:20	396
1:25	329
2:14–16	297
3:24	292
4:3	73, 109
4:4	380
4:10	380
4:25	404
5:1	289
5:2	356
6:1–11	369
6:2–4	380
6:2	353, 404
6:10	355
6:11	404
6:18	404
6:19	369
6:22	369
7:17	353
8:1–27	373
8:1–17	369
8:9	370
8:11	356
8:14–16	370
8:15	330
8:17	366
8:29	260
8:39	396
9–11	294, 320
9:22–23	398
9:25–26	379
9:32–33	404
9:33	188, 276
10:8	363
10:9	182
10:14–15	363

473

Romans (continued)

11	353
11:2	260
11:9–10	256
12:1	381
12:2	78
12:7	78
12:14	393
12:18	393
13:1–7	78, 393, 396
13:3–4	391
13:12	386
15:7	281

1 Corinthians

1:8	298
1:9	329
1:10–12	8
1:23	125
1:30	369
1:31	363
2:4–5	371
3:21–23	8
3:16	372
5:1	308
5:7	347
6:11	369
7:10–11	81
8:5	182
9:5	8, 71, 304, 305
9:14	81
10:4	339
10:13	329
11:23–25	3
11:15	349
11:24	200
11:25	201
12:2	308
12:3	182
14:23	121
15	159, 206, 337, 359
15:3–7	3
15:15	8
15:20	274
15:23	365
15:43	366
16:21	303
16:22	270
10:20–21	155
11:24–25	81
15:1–11	263
15:3–4	83
15:35–41	208
15:35–49	356
15:42–44	338
15:8–9	239

2 Corinthians

1:14	298
1:18	329
1:19	74
3:6	201
3:16	346, 382
3:17–18	370, 372
4:7	398
9:13	296
10:10	398
11:32	365
13:14	368

Galations

1:17–18	239
1:18–20	79
1:18	8, 117, 262
2	6
2:1–14	73, 79, 283
2:1–10	8, 79
2:6	295
2:7–8	293
2:7	283
2:11–21	79
2:11–14	8, 283
2:11	71, 305
2:12	283
2:16	282
3:2	282
3:5	282
3:7–9	377
3:13	263, 352
4:6	330, 370
6:11	303

Ephesians

1:4	319, 329
1:20–21	364
2:6	364
2:18	356
2:19–22	403
2:22	372
3:9	329
3:12	356
4–6	368

4:6	379
4:8	291
4:17	307
4:25	386
4:32	392
5:21—6:8	78
5:21—6:9	78
5:22—6:9	393
6:12	364

Philippians

1:1	346
1:6	298
1:10	298
1:15	363
1:19	370
2:2	392
2:11	182, 270
2:16	298
2:19	344

Colossians

1:15	396
2:11–12	380
2:14	288
3:8	386
3:10	329
3:18—4:1	78, 393
3:18–22	78
4:11	73, 109
4:16	106
4:18	303

1 Thessalonians

1:1	74
1:5	371
1:9	346, 354, 382
2:15	165
2:19	365
3:13	365
4:3–4	369
4:4	398
4:5	308
4:7	369
4:8	292
4:13	158
4:13–18	159, 206, 337, 359
4:15	365
5:2	286, 298
5:15	78
5:24	329
5:27	106

2 Thessalonians

1:1	74
1:6–10	298
2:1	365
2:2	286, 298
2:13	369
3:17	303, 403

1 Timothy

2:15	369
3:2	346
3:16	83, 338, 359
4:1	298, 299
4:8	299
4:13	119
5:17	302

2 Timothy

1:8	358
1:9–10	83
4:1	366
4:11	73, 109

Titus

1:1	
1:5	302
1:7	302, 346
2:14	83, 203

Philemon

19	303
24	73, 109

Hebrews

1:13	364
1:14	325
2:3–4	371
2:4	265
2:6	340
2:10	274
3:7	370
4:3	319, 329

Hebrews (continued)

4:13	396
5:9	296
5:12	161
7:1	393
7:6	393
7:27	355
8:6	360
8:8	201
8:13	201
9:8	370
9:11–14	351
9:12	355
9:15–20	349
9:15	201, 360
9:19–22	350
9:26–28	355
9:26	319, 329
9:28	352
10:6	355
10:8	355
10:15	370
10:18	355
10:21	371
10:26	355
10:29	349
11:13	83
12:1	386
12:2	274, 353, 358
12:14	369, 393
12:24	201, 349, 360
13:15	381
13:16	381
13:20	345

James

1:1	83, 307
1:21	386
4:6–10	83
5:7–8	365
5:14–16	152
5:16	353
5:19–20	354
5:30	346, 382

1 Peter

1:1	83, 94, 124, 301, 304, 309, 311, 319, 320, 325, 375, 376, 378, 380, 385, 386, 388, 406
1:1a	71
1:1b	71
1:1–2	388, 259, 319, 323, 349, 376, 386
1:1–3	340
1:2	260, 287, 302, 306, 316, 320, 323, 324, 326, 327, 328, 329, 330, 334, 335, 339, 350, 367, 368, 369, 376, 377, 382, 385, 388, 409
1:2a–c	369
1:2b	369
1:2–3	321
1:3	208, 216, 270, 312, 316, 318, 321, 325, 327, 328, 329, 329, 330, 335, 337, 338, 339, 342, 349, 357, 358, 359, 366, 376, 379, 380, 385, 386
1:3–12	94
1:3–5	316, 317
1:3–4	398
1:4	320, 325, 327, 345, 366, 376
1:5–6	326
1:5	94, 285, 317, 318, 321, 325, 327, 331, 336, 337, 340, 357, 365, 366, 367
1:6–7	387, 331, 337, 412
1:6	314, 317, 318, 321, 327, 366
1:7	78, 272, 316, 318, 321, 325, 331, 336, 339, 340, 342, 345, 349, 365, 366, 373, 392
1:8–9	209, 377
1:8	95, 317, 318, 321, 326, 336, 340, 358, 359, 364, 365, 373
1:9–10	285
1:9	94, 321, 326, 331, 336, 340, 364, 365
1:10–11	94, 255, 266, 367, 410, 317, 320, 326, 339, 341
1:10–12	95, 96, 259, 272, 317, 320, 321, 357, 403, 415
1:10	96, 197, 287, 321, 334, 335, 357, 376, 322
1:11–12	359, 367
1:11	72, 94, 291, 321, 323, 326, 336, 337, 339, 340, 341, 342, 344, 349, 358, 365, 366, 369, 370, 373, 408, 411
1:12	71, 72, 78, 82, 94, 95, 96, 261, 297, 301, 302, 310, 312, 317, 320, 321, 326, 327, 339, 349, 363, 367, 370, 371, 377, 384, 385, 386, 406, 407, 411, 412
1:13	78, 261, 287, 316, 317, 318, 321, 322, 323, 326, 327, 334,

	335, 339, 340, 342, 345, 348, 359, 365	2:4	198, 320, 340, 344, 358, 364, 385
1:13–16	369	2:5–8	381
1:14–16	369	2:5	312, 320, 321, 330, 340, 342, 344, 356, 359, 365, 367, 371, 372, 375, 377, 379, 381, 412
1:14–15	388		
1:14	78, 308, 312, 314, 323, 375, 376, 379, 384, 385	2:6–8	320, 340, 344, 366, 404
1:15	78, 321, 333, 388, 389	2:6–7	372
1:15b	334	2:6	306, 323, 343, 344, 358, 367
1:15–16	389, 316, 378, 384, 388, 390, 393	2:7–8	378, 388
		2:7	258, 261, 321, 323, 343, 357, 358, 359, 366, 377, 381, 406
1:16	389		
1:17–19	353	2:8	317, 332, 343, 366
1:17	297, 309, 316, 325, 327, 328, 329, 331, 332, 367, 375, 376, 379, 380, 384, 386, 388, 390	2:9	78, 294, 319, 320, 321, 324, 333, 344, 356, 357, 375, 376, 377, 378, 381, 382, 385, 388, 414
1:17a	330		
1:17b	331	2:9a	378, 379
1:18–21	83, 321	2:9b	378, 379
1:18–19	203, 348, 350, 351, 322, 339, 347, 385, 386, 410	2:9–10	294, 306, 375, 376, 386, 414
		2:10	317, 321, 324, 328, 349, 354, 370, 376, 379, 385
1:18	80, 307, 308, 325, 334, 351, 356, 374, 379, 381, 384, 386, 388		
		2:10a	379
		2:10b	379
1:19–20	317, 319	2:11–17	391
1:19	83, 318, 323, 340, 341, 347, 349, 350, 351, 382, 389	2:11–12	378, 386
		2:11	309, 311, 312, 325, 375, 376, 386
1:20	259, 298, 317, 318, 319, 320, 321, 327, 328, 329, 330, 339, 341, 345, 357, 367, 370, 376, 408, 414	2:12	80, 307, 308, 311, 313, 321, 325, 333, 335, 353, 359, 364, 373, 380, 387, 390
1:20a	319, 339	2:13—3:7	78, 386, 393
1:20b	318, 319	2:13–17	78, 312, 313, 397
1:21	272, 316, 318, 321, 327, 336, 337, 338, 339, 340, 341, 349, 357, 358, 359, 360, 365, 370, 373, 389	2:13–14	395
		2:13	342, 394, 395, 396
		2:13a	396
		2:14–15	391
1:22	279, 296, 312, 323, 349, 364, 375, 385, 392, 393, 397	2:14	313, 390, 391, 396
		2:15	314, 321, 353, 374, 380, 387, 390, 392, 396
1:23–25	342, 386	2:16	284
1:22–23	386	2:17–18	297, 388
1:23	316, 327, 327, 330, 359, 379, 380, 385	2:17	304, 312, 313, 330, 375, 379, 381, 396
1:24	320, 326, 356, 386	2:18—3:7	78
1:25	320, 321, 327, 342, 363	2:18—3:6	313
2	302, 369, 403	2:18–25	312, 345, 396, 397
2:1	284, 385, 386, 389, 392	2:18–23	352, 353
2:2	285, 312, 330, 343, 379, 385	2:18–20	374, 381, 395
2:3	340, 342, 364, 368	2:18	284, 286, 313, 381, 390, 394, 397
2:4–10	222, 294		
2:4–8	199, 321, 343, 344, 409	2:19	78, 314, 328, 334, 395, 396
2:4–7	188, 276, 375, 345, 382	2:19–24	355
2:4–5			

477

1 Peter (continued)

2:19–20	321, 331, 353, 355, 391, 392, 396
2:19a	396
2:20	314, 334, 353, 380, 390, 396
2:21	78, 340, 352, 353, 355, 381, 382, 388, 389, 393
2:21–25	83, 321, 323, 358, 395, 396, 397
2:21–24	271, 321, 339, 352, 389
2:22–25	347, 351
2:22–23	331, 346, 355, 356, 382, 388, 389, 410
2:22	347, 352
2:23	314, 328, 352, 353, 355, 367, 385, 389, 392
2:24–25	152, 352, 356
2:24	263, 286, 296, 318, 353, 354, 357, 379, 385, 389, 392, 404
2:24b	404
2:25	345, 346, 354, 370, 375, 382, 410
2:39	324
3:1–6	312, 374
3:1–2	381, 390, 391
3:1	296, 394, 395, 397, 398
3:2	297, 333, 388
3:3	381, 385
3:4	312, 328, 364, 397
3:5	388, 394
3:5–6	320, 376, 395, 397
3:6	314, 342, 380, 388, 390
3:7	274, 287, 325, 328, 334, 335, 381, 385, 393, 395, 398
3:7b	398
3:8	392
3:9	78, 313, 314, 325, 352, 385, 388, 389, 392
3:9a	393
3:9b	393
3:10–12	356
3:10	296, 298, 316
3:11	353, 392
3:12	327, 328, 329, 342, 346, 386, 392
3:13–14	353, 391, 392
3:13	353, 364, 390
3:14–15	343, 388
3:14	80, 296, 314, 331, 374, 388, 392
3:14b	364
3:15–16	313, 321, 340, 364, 382
3:15	182, 270, 339, 342, 364, 366, 368, 373, 380, 388, 409
3:16–17	390, 391
3:16	77, 313, 321, 353, 366, 373, 380, 382, 388, 390, 392
3:16b	364
3:17–18	347, 352, 389, 392
3:17	321, 337, 355, 387, 390
3:18–22	83, 318, 321, 325, 331, 338, 354, 358, 360, 362, 367, 410, 415
3:18–20	360
3:18–19	359
3:18	273, 337, 339, 340, 341, 342, 344, 347, 350, 352, 357, 358, 359, 361, 365, 377, 382, 385, 386, 389, 392, 410
3:18a	338, 355
3:18b	356, 360
3:19–22	362
3:19–20	332, 338
3:19	333, 338, 339, 342, 354, 361, 362
3:20–21	320, 376
3:20	333, 388
3:21	285, 312, 317, 321, 333, 337, 339, 340, 342, 357, 358, 359, 365, 369, 370, 379, 385, 386
3:21b	360, 380, 386
3:22	317, 321, 333, 338, 339, 342, 343, 357, 358, 359, 360, 362, 363, 364, 394, 406, 409
4:1–4	312, 369
4:1–2	386
4:1	314, 321, 340, 341, 356, 358, 380, 382, 387
4:2–4	356, 385, 386, 388
4:2–3	311, 314, 334, 384
4:2	312, 321, 384, 387
4:3–4	313, 325, 374, 384
4:3	307, 308, 325, 350, 353, 354, 366, 376, 379, 384, 385, 388
4:4–6	328
4:4	307, 313, 380, 387
4:5	299, 316, 317, 318, 321, 325, 327, 331, 340, 365, 366, 386
4:6	321, 331, 332, 363, 367, 386
4:7	296, 316, 317, 318, 328, 339, 340, 365, 367
4:7–11	384
4:8	385, 393
4:10–11	291, 312
4:10	78, 287, 328, 334, 335, 381
4:11–12	324
4:11	321, 327, 328, 336, 337, 340, 373
4:12	314, 327, 329, 331, 367

4:12–19	332
4:12–16	84
4:13–14	72, 340, 376, 382
4:13	72, 78, 221, 272, 316, 317, 318, 321, 336, 339, 340, 341, 342, 345, 349, 357, 358, 365, 366, 372, 382, 389
4:14–16	321
4:14	313, 318, 326, 327, 328, 336, 358, 366, 367, 368, 372, 373, 411
4:14a	373
4:15–16	329
4:15	313
4:16	84, 272, 312, 313, 314, 341, 353, 357, 373, 375, 381, 382, 383
4:17–18	321, 325, 331, 332, 333, 386
4:17	317, 318, 328, 330, 331, 337, 340, 371, 375, 379, 381, 388
4:17a	331
4:17b	331
4:18	285, 365, 392
4:18a	332
4:18b	331
4:19	316, 318, 321, 321, 327, 328, 329, 330, 331, 376, 387, 390
4:19a	331
5:1–5	312
5:1–4	345, 398
5:1	72, 73, 95, 272, 301, 302, 316, 318, 321, 336, 339, 340, 341, 342, 345, 349, 357, 359, 366, 369, 370, 373, 389
5:2–3	345, 375, 382
5:2	302, 346
5:3	80, 202, 325
5:4	316, 318, 336, 340, 345, 349, 359, 365, 373, 382, 410
5:5	72, 287, 321, 326, 328, 329, 334, 335, 393, 394, 395, 398
5:5b–9	83
5:5b	398
5:6–7	331
5:6	321, 331
5:7	314, 316, 328, 330, 346, 381
5:8–9	314, 339, 342, 360, 363, 381
5:8b	333
5:9	124, 136, 304, 313, 330, 349, 376, 378, 379, 387
5:10–11	94
5:10	77, 78, 272, 287, 316, 318, 321, 326, 327, 334, 335, 336, 337, 340, 349, 359, 366, 367, 382, 388
5:11	327, 336, 337, 367
5:12–13	304
5:12	74, 90, 91, 95, 96, 287, 302, 303, 304, 314, 322, 327, 328, 329, 334, 367, 369, 402, 403, 412
5:12b	365
5:13	73, 74, 109, 304, 311, 319, 403
5:14	77, 312, 321, 340, 382
5:16	333

2 Peter

1:1	96, 252
1:2	287
1:3	292, 357
1:14	96
1:16	365
1:16–21	96
1:16–18	72
1:17–18	96
1:17	340
1:19	370
1:21	370
2:1–3:13	332
2:1	285
2:9	286, 355
2:13	284
2:15	284
2:20	285
3	75
3:1	8, 73, 75, 97
3:2	285
3:3	298
3:4	365
3:6–7	299
3:7	286
3:10	286
3:1–10	259
3:11	296
3:12	286
3:13	257
3:15–16	97
3:15	285
3:17	260
3:18	285, 287

1 John

2:1	347
2:2	355, 379

479

1 John (continued)

4:8	328
4:10	355
5:6	95

2 John

1	304
13	304

3 John

7	308

Jude

11	284
14	262
20–21	368

Revelation

1:13	340
7:17	345
13:8	319, 329
14:8	73, 109
14:14	340
16:19	73, 109
17:5	73, 109
17:8	319, 329
17:9	73, 109
17:18	73, 109
18:2	73, 109
18:10	73, 109
18:21	73, 109
22:20	270

DEUTEROCANONICAL, APOCRYPHAL BOOKS, AND OTHER ANCIENT SOURCES

1 Esdras

1:1	200
1:6	200
1:19	199

2 Baruch

6:43–44	385

8:6	386
73:1–3	152
29:3	183
29:8	183

4 Ezra 163

12:31–33	282
13:32–38	282
13	175

Judith

5:19	307
8:18	223

Testament of Naphtali

3:5	362
6	224

1 Enoch

1:9	362
10:12–14	362
12:3—13:5	362
12:4—14:8	363
15:3–12	362
15:8–12	363
18:14	362
19:1	362
21:6	362
21:10	362
37–71	175
46:4–6	282
48:10	266
52:4	266
52:4–9	282
106:13–19	362
106:13–15	362

2 Enoch

7:1–5	362
10:4–6	385

Tobit

2:10	159
13:1–6	142, 325
13:17	344

1 Macc

1:47	285
1:62–63	285

2 Macc

1:24	329
2:16–18	142, 325
3:7	261
5:25	329
6:12–17	331
7:23	329
8:33	284
9:9	261
11:5	329
13:14	329
14:21	261

4 Macc

8:19	295

Psalms of Solomon

1–26	154
17–18	163, 192
17	134
17:21–34	266
17:21	144, 265
17:32	163, 265, 269
17:35	347
17:37	265
17:45–47	345

Testament of Solomon

1–26	154
22:6–23:4	188, 276

Wisdom

2:22	284
3:6	381, 387
3:1–4	332
3:7	333
4:15	333
1:6	346
14:12	385

Didache

1:3	393

Odes of Solomon

41:15	319

Midrash Rabbah

12:22	350

4Q

174 1:10–12	170
246 2:1	170
252 5.1–4	265

Abot

6.6	186

Ars Rhetorica (Aristotle)

1.15.14	30, 94, 255
1.15.16	30
1.2.1	29
1.2.2	29, 96, 370
1.2.4	29, 94
1.15.13	29, 94, 255
1.15.15–16	29, 94, 255

Poetics (Aristotle)

24.11–14	253

Iliad (Homer)

2.305–319	254
9	254
24	254

m. Šabb.

23:5	207

Rhetorica ad Herennium

4.8.11	86

INDEX OF ANCIENT SOURCES

History of the Peloponnesian War (Thucydides)

1.20.1	30, 54
1.21.1	30, 49, 54, 57, 68, 71, 234, 402
1.22.1	55, 56, 57, 402
1.22.2–4	55
1.22.2	30
1.22.3	31
1.22.4	31
1.56.10–12	56
12.25a.5	57
12.25b.4	57
12.25e.1	57
12.25e.2—12.25g.4	57
36.1.7	56

On Thucydides (Dionysius of Halicarnassus)

36	57
41	57, 58
42	57
44–46	57
49	57
51	57

Gorgias (Plato)

471e	96, 370

Aeneid (Virgil)

2.199–227	254
8.722–28	254

Ecclesiastical History (Eusebius)

2.14.3—2.15.1	109
2.14.6	117, 148
2.15.1–2	117
2.15	73, 109
2.25.5–8	73, 109
3.1.2	305, 307
3.3.1	75
3.3.4	75
3.4.2	75, 307
3.25.2–3	75
3.39.4	33, 101
3.39.7	33, 101
3.39.8	33, 101
3.39.11–13	33
3.39.13	33
3.39.14–15	73, 74
3.39.15	33, 38, 39, 101, 107
3.39.16	75
4.14.9	75
4.23.11	91
6.14.6–7	36, 106, 109
6.14.6	117
6.25.3–6	73
6.25.5	74, 104
6.25.8	75

Disalogue with Trypho

106.3	35, 38

Memorabilia

1.3.1	35

The Controversies 1 (Seneca the Elder)

Preface 3–4	36

Against Heresies

3.1.1

Attic Nights

Preface 2	39

Progymnasmata

3.96	39, 102

Life of Plotinus

1	42
21–22	42

Histories (Tacitus)

5.1–5	120
15.44	383

INDEX OF ANCIENT SOURCES

Nero (Suetonius)

16	383

The Histories (Polybius)

1.1.1	103
1.20.1	70
4.2.1	70
4.2.3	62
12.25a.3	46, 52, 235
12.25a.5	52, 69, 71, 234, 402
12.25b.1–4	47, 69
12.25b.4	52, 69
12.25c.1	52

How to Write History (Lucian)

26, 29, 32, 40, 42, 47, 48, 58	62
47	68
48	103
58	69

Vita Apollonii (Philostratus)

3:38	154
4:20	154

Philopseudes (Lucian)

16	154
34	154

Roman Antiquities

1.7.1–3	60

Letter to Gnaeus Pompeius

3	61

Adversus Haereses

3.1.3	73, 109
4.9.2	75
5.7.2	75
4.16.5	75
4.32.2	75

Ars Poetica (Horace)

131–34	81

Adversus Marcionem. (Tertullian)

4.5	73

On Literary Composition (Dionysius of Halicarnassus)

6	81

Epistulae Morales ad Lucilium (Seneca)

79.6	81
101.14	197

Letters (Pliny)

1.1	39
10.96–97	383
10.96.2	84
10.92.5	84
64.14–17	361

Rhetorica ad Herennium

4.8.11	86

Commentary in John (Origen)

32.7	386

Sirach

2:5	387
3:1	331
38:24–34	185
39:1–11	185

Contra Gentes (Athanasius)

34	386

De Praescriptione Haereticorum (Tertullian)

36	73, 109

Against Marcion (Tertullian)

4.5	109

On Agriculture (Cato)

5	396

Baba Bathra (Talmud)

21a	89

Scorpiace (Tertullian)

12	75

Quintilian

10.1.101	53
11.2.25	60
1.8.5	137
10.1.46–51	137
10.1.85–86	137

Stromata (Clement of Alexandria)

7.17	89

Cato Maior (Plutarch)

12.4	90

De Legibus (Cicero)

2.7.19–27	397

Epistulae ad Familiares (Cicero)

5.20	92

Topica (Cicero)

1.5	107

De Specialibus Legibus (Philo)

2.54–55	397

On Sobriety (Philo)

66	377

Oeconomicus (Xenophon)

7.25	397

Coniugalia Praecepta (Plutarch)

140D	397
142E	397

Oeconomicus (Pseud-Aristotle)

3.144.2	397

Alexander Romance. (Pseudo-Callisthenes)

1.22.19–20	397

Satires (Juvenal)

3.14	120
6	397
6.155–60	120
6.542–50	120
8.159–62	120
14.96–106	120

Claudius (Suetonius)

4	144
25:4	162

Nero (Suetonius)

16	124, 383
25	144

Life of Julius Caesar (Suetonius)

88	144

Life of Vespasian (Suetonius)

7	152

Lactantius, The Divine Institutes.

4.7.5	162

Apology (Tertullian)

3.5	163

Antiquities of the Jews (Josephus)

8.45–49	154
8.71–72	186
9.291	280
10.277–80	259
11.325–45	144
11.340	280
11.341	280
13.173	259
14.21	199
14.36	167
15.127–46	49
15.373	167
16.311	167
17.130	357
17.213	199
18.240–44	135
18.240–52	168
20.5.1.97–98	64
20.97–99	146
20.167–72	142
20.262–65	87
20.263	87
20.264	87

The Jewish War (Bellum Judaicum) (Josephus)

1.373–79	49
2.164	259
2.181–82	135
2.261–363	142
4.618	134
4.618–21	144
4.656	134
5.212–14	186

Contra Apionem (Josephus)

2.218	257

Vita (The Life of Flavius Josephus)

53	365
240	365

Metamorphoses (Ovid)

15.808–9	259

www.ingramcontent.com/pod-product-compliance
Lightning Source LLC
Chambersburg PA
CBHW060302010526
44108CB00042B/2605